Why Do You Need This New Edition?

If you're wondering why you should buy this new edition of *The Prose Reader*, here are six great reasons!

1 Many exciting selections are new to this edition on such interesting topics as critical thinking, social networking, interracial families, birth order, the pursuit of happiness, health, and our educational system.

2 A new Part I, "Critical Thinking—The Key to Success," focuses on critical thinking as the starting point that directs both reading and writing.

3 A new interactive chapter (Chapter 2) in Part I entitled "What Exactly Is Critical Thinking?" is designed around a guided exercise that helps students understand what critical thinking is and how to internalize the habits connected with this skill.

4 Three professional essays about critical thinking are featured in this new interactive chapter (Chapter 2).

5 A new Part III, "Reading and Writing from Sources," is organized as a useful, tabbed reference handbook with information on
- finding and evaluating sources.
- incorporating sources into written assignments
- avoiding plagiarism
- composing source-based essays.

6 An additional pair of prompts ("Writing from Sources") that moves from synthesis to research is included in each set of chapter writing assignments.

PEARSON

THE PROSE READER

Essays for Thinking, Reading, and Writing

NINTH EDITION

Kim Flachmann

California State University, Bakersfield

Michael Flachmann

California State University, Bakersfield

Prentice Hall

Boston   Columbus   Indianapolis   New York   San Francisco   Upper Saddle River
Amsterdam   Cape Town   Dubai   London   Madrid   Milan   Munich   Paris   Montreal   Toronto
Delhi   Mexico City   Sao Paulo   Sydney   Hong Kong   Seoul   Singapore   Taipei   Tokyo

Editorial Director: Joe Opiela
Senior Acquisitions Editor: Brad Potthoff
Senior Marketing Manager: Sandra McGuire
Editorial Assistant: Nancy Lee
Managing Editor: Linda Mihatov Behrens
Associate Managing Editor: Bayani Mendoza de Leon
Project Manager: Raegan Keida Heerema
Permissions Specialist: Kathleen Karcher
Senior Operations Specialist: Nick Sklitsis
Operations Specialist: Mary Ann Gloriande
Art Director, Cover: Anne Bonanno Nieglos
Cover Illustration/Photo: Franz Marc (1880–1916) German, Mandrill, 1913. Private Collection/
   The Bridgeman Library.
Photo Researcher: Sheila Norman
Image Permission Coordinator: Silvana Attanasio
Project Coordination, Text Design, and Electronic Page Makeup: Laserwords

For permission to use copyrighted material, grateful acknowledgment is made to the copyright holders on pages 629 through 631, which are hereby made part of this copyright page.

Library of Congress Cataloging-in-Publication Data

The prose reader : essays for thinking, reading, and writing / Kim Flachmann, Michael
Flachmann.—9th ed.
   p. cm.
   Includes index.
   ISBN 0-205-70843-9
 1. College readers.   2. English language—Rhetoric—Problems, exercises, etc.   3.
Report writing—Problems, exercises, etc.   I. Flachmann, Kim.   II. Flachmann, Michael.
   PE1417.P847 2010
   808'.0427—dc22

                                                                2009047181

Visit us at www.pearsonhighered.com.

1   2   3   4   5   6   7   8   9   10—CRS—13   12   11   10   09

**Prentice Hall
is an imprint of**

PEARSON

ISBN-13: 978-0-205-70843-7
ISBN-10:   0-205-70843-9

For Carter Christopher Flachmann

RHETORICAL TABLE OF CONTENTS

---

5 Narration: *Telling a Story*   110

7 Process Analysis: *Explaining Step by Step*   201

JAY WALLJASPER   *Our Schedules, Our Selves*   213

Are you bound to your Blackberry, enslaved to your daily routine? Jay Walljasper argues that we've booked ourselves so tightly that "there's no time left for those magic, spontaneous moments that make us feel most alive."

JESSICA MITFORD   *Behind the Formaldehyde Curtain*   220

In this chilling and macabre essay, celebrated "muckraker" Jessica Mitford exposes the greed and hypocrisy of the American mortuary business.

ALICE LESCH KELLY   *Toughen Up!*   231

How resilient would you be in a crisis? Author Alice Kelly asks five crucial questions that help predict the difference between confidence and chaos in our response to adversity.

MALCOLM X   *Learning to Read*   238

Do you remember the day you learned to read? Malcolm X was in prison when he first became enchanted with language and literature.

JULIA BOURLAND   *Getting Out of Debt (and Staying Out)*   249

Credit card bills getting you down? Author Julia Bourland suggests eight easy ways to pay off your balance and stay out of debt.

Chapter Writing Assignments   257

8 Division/Classification: *Finding Categories*   259

TAMALA EDWARDS   *Multi-Colored Families*   270

Mixed-race marriages and transracial adoptions have created special challenges for the parents and children involved, but also a new and important dialogue about America's evolving family traditions.

9 Comparison/Contrast: Discovering Similarities and Differences   318

12 Argument and Persuasion: *Inciting People to Thought or Action*   468

---

13 Thinking, Reading, and Writing in Different Literary Forms:
Combining Rhetorical Modes   537

Part III Reference: Reading and Writing from Sources   561

R-1 Introducing the Documented Essay   562

R-2 Reading a Documented Essay   564

R-9 Revising and Editing a Documented Essay   608

THEMATIC TABLE OF CONTENTS

WRITING

PREFACE
TO THE INSTRUCTOR

The Prose Reader is based on the assumption that lucid writing follows lucid thinking, whereas poor written work is almost inevitably the product of foggy, irrational thought processes. As a result, our primary purpose in this book, as in the first eight editions, is to help students *think* more clearly and logically—both in their minds and on paper.

Furthermore, we believe that college students should be able to think, read, and write on three increasingly difficult levels:

1. *Literal*—characterized by a basic understanding of words and their meanings;
2. *Interpretive*—consisting of a knowledge of linear connections between ideas and an ability to make valid inferences based on those ideas; and
3. *Critical*—the highest level, distinguished by the systematic investigation of complex ideas and by the analysis of their relationship to the world around us.

To demonstrate the vital interrelationship between reader and writer, our text provides students with prose models intended to inspire their own thinking and writing. Rhetorical strategies are introduced as methods of thinking and processing information; they provide a productive means of helping students become better writers. These essays are intended to encourage your students to improve their writing through a partnership with some of the best examples of professional prose available today. Just as musicians and athletes richly benefit from studying the techniques of the foremost people in their fields, your students will grow in spirit and language use from their collaborative work with the excellent writers in this collection.

HOW THE TEXT WORKS

Each chapter of *The Prose Reader* begins with an explanation of a single rhetorical technique as a means of processing information. These explanations are divided into six sections that progress from the effect of this technique on our daily lives to its integral role in the writing process. We also include in each introduction a student paragraph and a student essay featuring each rhetorical strategy under discussion and supported by many other strategies. The student essay is annotated to illustrate how a particular rhetorical mode operates and to help bridge the gap between student writing and the professional selections that follow. After each student essay, the writer has drafted a personal note with some useful advice for other student writers.

The essays that follow each chapter introduction are selected from a wide variety of well-known contemporary authors. Although each essay in this collection focuses on a single rhetorical mode as its primary strategy, other modes are always simultaneously at work. These selections concentrate on one primary technique at a time in much the same way a well-arranged photograph highlights a certain visual detail, though many other elements function in the background to make the picture an organic and effective whole.

Before each reading selection, we offer some material to focus your students' attention on a particular writer and topic before they begin reading the essay. This "prereading" segment begins with biographical information about the author and ends with a number of questions to whet the reader's appetite for the essay that follows, including an Internet exercise with a companion writing assignment after the professional essay. This section is intended to help your students discover interesting relationships among ideas in their reading and then anticipate various ways of analyzing the essay. The prereading questions forecast not only the content of the essay, but also the questions and writing assignments that follow.

The questions after each reading selection are designed as guides for thinking about the essay. These questions are at the heart of the relationship represented in this book among thinking, reading, and writing. They are divided into four interrelated sections that shepherd your students smoothly from a literal understanding of what they have just read, to interpretation, and finally to analysis and critical thinking.

After your students have studied the different techniques at work in a reading selection, specific essay assignments let them practice all these skills in unison and encourage them to discover even more secrets about the intricate and exciting details of effective communication. Four "Ideas for Discussion/Writing" topics (one of which is based on the prereading Internet exercise) are preceded by "prewriting" questions to help your students generate new ideas. Most of these topics specify a purpose and an audience so your students can focus their writing as precisely as possible.

The word *essay* (which comes from the Old French *essai*, meaning a "try" or an "attempt") is an appropriate label for these writing assignments, because they all ask your students to wrestle with an idea or problem and then *attempt* to give shape to their conclusions in some effective manner. Such "exercises" can be equated with the development of athletic ability: The essay itself demonstrates that your students can put together all the various skills they have learned; it proves they can actually play the "sport" of writing.

At the end of every chapter is a collection of essay assignments that ask your students to choose a topic in one of four categories: Practicing a particular rhetorical mode, Exploring Ideas, Writing from Sources, or Analyzing Visual Images. Each of these groups of assignments has a slightly different focus so students can choose the prompts that bring out their own individual strengths.

OUR FAVORITE FEATURES

- Special Inventory of the Reading and Writing Processes
- Interactive Chapter on Critical Thinking
- In-Text Critical Thinking Questions
- Companion Internet Activities
- New Reference Section on Documented Essays
- Twenty-five Photographs

Special Inventory of the Reading and Writing Processes

A highlighted, two-sided page at the end of Part I outlines the reading and writing processes. It serves as an overview of the material the students will study in this text and is designed to be used as a set of checklists for reading and writing throughout the text. These inventories are supplemented by the more specific checklists at the end of each chapter introduction.

Interactive Chapter on Critical Thinking

Part I of this edition is dedicated solely to the concept of critical thinking. It furnishes students with ideas and facts to help them discover their own definition of critical thinking so that they are fully aware of this concept as they work through this text and begin to understand the book's primary objective: to improve their ability to think critically.

In-Text Critical Thinking Questions

This edition offers a set of questions in each reading selection that will help students interact critically with the material they read as they prepare for the assignments after each essay. These questions appear at the bottom of the pages of the essays and are designed to provide a "bridge" between the personal prereading questions and the more broad-based academic questions and assignments that follow each essay. They ask the students to interact with their reading through personal and academic inquiries. Students will understand their reading on a deeper level by filtering the content of each essay through their own experience, moving progressively toward interpretive and critical understanding. The questions are marked both in the essays and at the bottom of the pages by sequential numbers within diamonds.

Companion Internet Exercises

Two Internet exercises are linked to each essay. The prereading material before each essay contains an Internet exercise that asks your students to explore some aspect of the topic on the Internet before reading the essay. These exercises offer the students guidance in finding specific sites. Following the essays, this Internet exercise is then linked to the initial writing assignment.

New Tabbed Reference Section on Documented Essays

Part III of this edition features a tabbed reference guide for writing a documented essay. It demonstrates how to approach a writing assignment based on sources by following a student through the entire process. This Part progresses from reading a documented essay to responding to that reading by writing about a similar topic. It covers finding sources, avoiding plagiarism, staying organized, documenting sources, and writing the paper itself—all from the perspective of our model student. This section tries to clarify some of the mysteries connected with research and documentation and provides longer, more elaborate writing assignments.

Twenty-five Photographs

This edition also offers twenty-five photographs in an attempt to access our students' natural interest in visual stimuli. Since most students have grown up accustomed to television, video games, and the Internet, they have the natural ability to "read" pictures. But they need to learn how to analyze them, just as they analyze words and ideas. As a result, we include one photograph for each chapter introduction in Part II to teach critical thinking in that mode, one photograph for each set of writing assignments at the end of each chapter, and seven color photos as a complete pictorial "essay" in Chapter 12.

VERY SPECIAL FEATURES

- Reading and Writing Checklists for Each Rhetorical Mode
- Engaging Chapter Writing Assignments
- Other Selected Literature
- Glossary of Composition Terms

Reading and Writing Checklists for Each Rhetorical Mode

This edition still includes user-friendly checklists for reading and writing at the end of each chapter introduction. These checklists summarize the information in the chapter introduction and serve as references for the students with their own reading and writing tasks. Students should familiarize themselves with these lists as early in the course as possible.

Engaging Chapter Writing Assignments

This edition offers three sets of writing assignments at the end of each chapter. They provide practice in the following categories: (1) more practice in a specific rhetorical mode, (2) a focus on interesting contemporary themes regardless of rhetorical mode, and (3) an opportunity to analyze and respond to a provocative and interesting photograph. This feature gives students even more opportunities to practice their writing.

Other Selected Literature

Following a request by an overwhelming majority of reviewers and instructors using this book, we have retained the collection of literature in "Thinking, Reading, and Writing in Different Literary Forms" (Chapter 13). This chapter includes two essays, two short stories, and two poems—all on the topics of thinking, reading, or writing. In addition to demonstrating all the rhetorical modes at work, these selections provide a strong conclusion to the theoretical framework of this text by focusing intently on the interrelationships among thinking, reading, and writing.

Glossary of Composition Terms

The book concludes with a glossary of composition terms. The glossary provides not only definitions of composition terms but also examples of these terms from essays in this book, including specific page numbers. This serves as an excellent reference tool for students as they progress through the material in the text.

OUR TRADITIONAL FEATURES

- Logical Organization
- Prereading Material
- Prewriting Prompts
- Four Types of Questions

Logical Organization

The Prose Reader is still organized according to the belief that our mental abilities are logically sequential. In other words, students cannot read or write analytically before they are able to perform well on the literal and interpretive levels. Accordingly, the book progresses from selections that require predominantly literal skills (*Description, Narration,* and *Example*) through readings involving more interpretation (*Process Analysis, Division/Classification, Comparison/Contrast,* and *Definition*) to essays that demand a high degree of analytical thought (*Cause/Effect* and *Argument/Persuasion*). Depending on your curriculum and the caliber and experience of your students, these rhetorical modes can, of course, be studied in any order.

Prereading Material

Each reading selection is preceded by thorough biographical information on the author and provocative prereading questions on the subject of the essay. Because students comprehend what they read most thoroughly when they understand the context surrounding the reading material, the biographies explain the real experiences from which each essay emerged, and the prereading questions ("Preparing to Read") help students focus on the purpose, audience, and subject of the essay. The prereading material also foreshadows the questions and writing assignments that follow each selection. Personalizing this introductory material encourages students to identify with both the author of an essay and its subject matter, thereby engaging the students' attention and energizing their responses to the selections they read.

Prewriting Prompts

The writing assignments ("Ideas for Discussion/Writing") are preceded by Preparing to Write questions. These questions are designed to encourage students to express their feelings, thoughts, observations, and opinions on various topics related to their reading. Questions about their own ideas and experiences help students produce strong convictions that they can then mold into compelling essays.

Four Types of Questions

This edition offers four progressively more sophisticated types of questions at the end of each selection. These questions are designed to help students move sequentially from various literal-level responses to interpretation and analysis; they also help reveal both the form and content of the essays so your students can cultivate a similar balance in their own writing.

1. *Understanding Details*—questions that test the students' literal and interpretive understanding of what they have read;
2. *Thinking Critically*—questions that require students to analyze various aspects of the essay;
3. *Discovering Rhetorical Strategies*—questions that investigate the author's rhetorical strategies in constructing the essay;
4. *Making Connections*—questions that ask students to find thematic and rhetorical connections among essays they have read.

OTHER IMPORTANT FEATURES

- Two Tables of Contents
- Student-Friendly Rhetorical Introductions
- Two Student Writing Samples in Each Chapter
- Wide Range of Essay Topics
- Strong Commitment to Cultural and Gender Diversity
- Expanded Chapter on Argument/Persuasion
- Realistic Writing Assignments

Two Tables of Contents

The Prose Reader **provides two Tables of Contents: Rhetorical and Thematic.** First, the book contains a Rhetorical Table of Contents, which includes a one- or two-sentence synopsis of each selection so you can peruse the list quickly and decide which essays to assign. An alternate Thematic Table of Contents lists selections by academic subject for instructors who prefer to teach essays in thematic clusters. The list of "Related Readings" in the Instructor's Resource Manual also supports a thematic approach to *The Prose Reader*.

Student-Friendly Rhetorical Introductions

The chapter introductions are filled with a variety of useful information about each rhetorical mode. Each of the nine rhetorical divisions in the text is introduced by an explanation of how to think, read, and write in that particular mode. Although each chapter focuses on one rhetorical strategy, students are continually encouraged to examine ways in which other modes help support each essay's primary intention.

Student Writing Samples in Each Chapter

Two separate student writing samples are featured in each rhetorical introduction. The chapter introductions contain a sample student paragraph and a complete student essay that illustrate each rhetorical pattern. Each essay is followed by the student writer's analysis of the most enjoyable, exasperating, or noteworthy aspects of writing that particular essay. We have found that this combination of student essays and commentaries makes the professional selections easier for students to read and even more accessible as models of thinking and writing.

Wide Range of Essay Topics

The essays in *The Prose Reader* continue to represent a wide range of topics. As in the past, the essays in this edition were selected on the basis of five important criteria: (1) high interest level, (2) currency in the field, (3) moderate length, (4) readability, and (5) broad subject variety. Together, they portray the universality of human experience as expressed through the viewpoints of men and women, many different ethnic and racial groups, and a variety of ages and social classes. The essay topics in this volume include such provocative subjects as discrimination, ethnic identity, elementary school memories, job opportunities, social networking, aging, war, DNA testing, women's roles, prison life, multi-colored families, travel, risk-taking, birth order, family values, Internet "friendships," managing our busy lives, facing adversity, immigration, physical handicaps, our obsession with illness, reading, and the writing process itself.

Strong Commitment to Cultural and Gender Diversity

This edition continues its strong commitment to cultural and gender diversity. Although multicultural and women's issues have always been well represented in *The Prose Reader,* this edition includes even more essays by women and ethnic minority authors, among them Linda Hogan, Firoozeh Dumas, Sandra Cisneros, Richard Rodriguez, Joel Stein, Malcolm X, Stephanie Ericsson, Mary Pipher, Lyn Mikel Brown, Meda Chesney-Lind, Kim Severson, and Jessica Blau.

Expanded Chapter on Argument/Persuasion

The Argument/Persuasion chapter (Chapter 12) now includes four essays on an interesting variety of topics, one photo essay, and two sets of opposing-viewpoint essays. These essays in Chapter 12 are particularly useful for helping students refine their critical thinking skills in preparation for longer, more sustained papers on a single topic. The first five essays in this chapter, including the photo essay, encourage students to grapple with provocative issues that make a crucial difference in how we all live, such as graffiti, our obsession with illness, binge drinking, violence and TV, and gay marriage. The two sets of opposing-viewpoint essays will help your students see coherent arguments at work from several different perspectives on a single issue. These final essays cover immigration and postconviction DNA testing.

Realistic Writing Assignments

The writing assignments after each essay seek to involve students in realistic situations. For instructors who like to use role-playing in their teaching, many writing assignments provide a specific purpose and audience in the essay topics. In this manner, student writers are drawn into rhetorical scenarios that carefully focus their responses to a variety of interrelated questions or problems. These assignments are designed for use inside or outside the classroom.

WHAT SUPPLEMENTS ARE AVAILABLE?

Available with *The Prose Reader* is an extensive ***Instructor's Resource Manual*** designed to help make your life in the classroom a little easier. It is a combination of the previous ***Annotated Instructor's Edition*** of *The Prose Reader* and ***The Instructor's Resource Manual with Quiz Book***. This supplement is filled with many different kinds of supplementary material, including instructor comments on teaching the different rhetorical modes, provocative quotations, background information on each essay, definitions of terms that may be unfamiliar to your students, a list of related readings from this text that can be taught together, innovative teaching ideas, detailed answers to the questions that follow each selection, additional essay topics, and various revising strategies.

In addition, we identify and discuss some of the most widely used theoretical approaches to the teaching of composition. We also offer innovative options for organizing your course, specific suggestions for the first day of class, a summary of the advantages and disadvantages of using different teaching strategies, several successful techniques for responding to student writing, and a series of student essays (one for each rhetorical strategy featured in the text) followed by the student writer's comments. This supplement ends with an annotated bibliography of books and articles about thinking, reading, and writing.

New in This Edition: Available on the Pearson Web site (www .pearsonhighered.com) under Instructional Resources is the *The Prose Reader Quiz Book*, which includes two objective quizzes on the vocabulary and content of each selection to help you monitor your students' understanding of the selections in this book. These quizzes are posted for you in Word so you can edit and print them out for use in your classes.

This entire instructional package is intended to help your students discover what they want to say and to assist them in shaping their ideas into a coherent form, thereby encouraging their intelligent involvement in the complex and exciting world around them.

MyCompLab™

MyCompLab empowers student writers and facilitates writing instruction by uniquely integrating a composing space and assessment tools with market-leading instruction, multimedia tutorials, and exercises for writing, grammar, and research.

Students can use MyCompLab on their own, benefiting from self-paced diagnostics and a personal study plan that recommends the instruction and practice each student needs to improve her writing skills. The composing space and its integrated resources, tools, and services (such as online tutoring) are also available to each student as he writes.

MyCompLab is an eminently flexible application that instructors can use in ways that best complement their course and teaching style. They can recommend it to students for self-study, set up courses to track student progress, or leverage the power of administrative features to be more effective and save time. The assignment builder and commenting tools, developed specifically for writing instruction, bring instructors closer to their student writers, make managing assignments and evaluating papers more efficient, and put powerful assessment within reach. Students receive feedback within the context of their own writing, which encourages critical thinking and revision and helps them to develop skills based on their individual needs.

Learn more at www.mycomplab.com.

ACKNOWLEDGMENTS

We are pleased to acknowledge the kind assistance and support of a number of people who have helped us put together this ninth edition of *The Prose Reader*. For creative encouragement and editorial guidance at Pearson, we thank Joe Opiela, Editorial Director; Brad Potthoff, Senior Acquisitions Editor; Nancy Lee, Editorial Assistant; Sandi McGuire, Senior Marketing Manager; Raegan Heerema, Production Liaison; Kathleen Karcher, Permissions Specialist; and Karen Berry, Laserwords Maine, Project Coordinator.

For the insightful reviews directly leading to this ninth edition, we are grateful to Brenda Abbott, Bay Path College; James Brumbaugh, Lord Fairfax Community College; Merry Dennehy, Monterey Peninsula College; John Esperian, College of Southern Nevada; Wade King, North Dakota State College of Science; Pam Lieske, Kent State University; Donna Mungen, Pasadena City College; Diana Nystedt, Palo Alto College; Diana Roberts Gruendler, Penn State University; and Angela Saragusa, Brookdale Community College.

For the many reviews of previous editions whose valuable contributions have guided *The Prose Reader* through many successful editions, we wish to thank Maureen Aitkn, University of Michigan; Martha R. Bachman, Camden County College; Christopher Belcher, Community College of Allegheny County; Martha Bergeron, Vance-Granville Community College; Vermell Blanding, Hostos Community College; Arnold Bradford, Northern Virginia Community College, Loudoun Campus; Mickie R. Braswell, Lenoir Community College; Melissa A. Bruner, Southwestern Oklahoma State University; Terrence Burke, Cuyahoga Community College; Judith Burnham, Tulsa Community College; Mechel Camp, Jackson State Community College; Gena

E. Christopher, Jacksonville State University; Bill Clemente, Peru State College; Charles H. Cole, Carl Albert State College; Carolyn D. Coward, Shelby State Community College; Marie T. Cox, Stark State College; Hal Crimmel, Weber State University; Judith Dan, Boston University; Bill Day, Carl Albert State College; Michael W. Donaghe, Eastern New Mexico University; Ellen Dugan-Barrette, Brescia College; Lewis Emond, Dean Junior College; June Farmer, Southern Union State Community College; Geoffrey C. Goodale, University of Massachusetts at Boston; Nate Gordeon, Kiswaukee College; Lorena Horton, San Jacinto College North; Craig Howard White, University of Houston; Jay Jernigan, Eastern Michigan University; Janice Jones, Kent State University; Steve Katz, State Technical Institute; Paul Kistel, Pierce College; Jan LaFever, Friends University; Amy Lawlor, Pasadena City College; Virginia Leonard, West Liberty State College; Todd Lieber, Simpson College; Bill Marsh, National University; Marlene Martin, Monterey Peninsula College.; Beth Maxfield, Blinn College; Helen F. Maxon, Southwestern Oklahoma State University; Nellie McCrory, Gaston College; Paula Miller, Azusa Pacific University; Lyle W. Morgan II, Pittsburgh State University; Robin Morris Hardin, Cape Fear Community College; Kevin Nebergall, Kirkwood Community College; Diana Nystedt, Palo Alto College; Ollie Oviedo, Eastern New Mexico University; Felicia S. Pattison, Sterling College; Arlie R. Peck, University of Rio Grande; Dianne Peich, Delaware County Community College; Teresa Purvis, Lansing Community College; Melissa Richardson, Central Texas College; M. Susan Schmidt, Carteret Community College; Nelda Sellers, Jackson State Community College; Marcia Shams, Gwinnett Technical College; Stella Shepard, Henderson State University; Leslie Shipp, Clark County Community College; Alice Sink, High Point University; Barbara Smith, Iona College; Donna Smith, Odessa College; Rosie Soy, Hudson County Community College; Matthew Stiffler, Utah State University; William F. Sutlife, Community College of Allegheny County; Melanie Whitebread, Luzerne County Community College; K. Siobhan Wright, Carroll Community College; Nancy G. Wright, Austin Peay State University; Donnie Yeilding, Central Texas College; James Zarzana, Southwest State University; John Ziebell, Community College of Southern Nevada; and Melody Ziff, Northern Virginia Community College–Annandale.

Several writing instructors across the United States have been kind enough to help shape *The Prose Reader* over the course of its development by responding to specific questions about their teaching experiences with the book: Charles Bordogna, Bergen Community College; Mary G. Marshall and Eileen M. Ward, College of DuPage; Michael J. Huntington and Judith C. Kohl, Dutchess Community College; Ted Johnston, El Paso County Community College; Koala C. Hartnett, Rick James Mazza, and William H. Sherman, Fairmont State College; Miriam Dick and Betty Krasne, Mercy College; Elvis Clark, Mineral Area College; Dayna Spencer, Pittsburg State University; James A. Zarzana, Southwest

State University; Susan Reinhart Schneling and Trudy Vanderback, Vincennes University; Carmen Wong, Virginia Commonwealth University; John W. Hattman and Virginia E. Leonard, West Liberty State College; Jonathan Alexander, Widener University; Jo Ann Pevoto, College of the Mainland; Anita Pandey, University of Illinois at Urbana–Champaign; Leaf Seligman, University of New Hampshire; Arminta Baldwin, West Virginia Wesleyan College; Joaquim Mendes, New York Institute of Technology; and Sandra R. Woods, Fairmont State College.

We give special thanks to Professor Virginia K. Freed and her fall 2005 writing classes at Bay Path College in Longmeadow, Massachusetts, for providing some excellent suggestions, including important supplementary information on the Bickerson essay.

For student essays and writing samples, we thank Rosa Marie Augustine, Donel Crow, Dawn Dobie, Gloria Dumler, Jeff Hicks, Julie Anne Judd, Judi Koch, Dawn McKee, Paul Newberry, Joanne Silva-Newberry, JoAnn Slate, Peggy Stuckey, and Jan Titus.

We also want to thank two incredibly talented people for helping us with the composition of this particular edition: Lauren Woods and Annalisa Townsend. We are also very grateful to our colleague Randi Brummett, who revised and combined the *Instructor's Resource Manual* and the *Annotated Instructor's Edition*.

In preparing the text and the *IRM*, we owe special gratitude to the following writing instructors, who have contributed their favorite techniques for teaching various rhetorical strategies: Mary P. Boyles, Pembroke State University; Terrence W. Burke, Cuyahoga Community College; Mary Lou Conlin, Cuyahoga Community College; Ellen Dugan-Barrette, Brescia College; Janet Eber, County College of Morris; Louis Emond, Dean Junior College; Peter Harris, West Virginia Institute of Technology, Montgomery; Jay Jernigan, Eastern Michigan University; Judith C. Kohl, Dutchess Community College; Joanne H. McCarthy, Tacoma Community College; Anthony McCrann, Peru State College; Nellie McCrory, Gaston College; Alan Price, Pennsylvania State University–Hazelton; Patricia A. Ross, Moorpark College; Leslie Shipp, Clark County Community College; Rodney Simard (deceased), California State University, San Bernardino; Elizabeth Wahlquist, Brigham Young University; John White, California State University, Fullerton; and Ted Wise, Porterville College.

This book also benefits from the outstanding insights and consummate teaching of Kathryn Benander (Porterville College, Porterville, CA) and Cheryl Smith (Kingsborough Community College, New York City), who have served as editorial consultants for multiple editions of the book. Their work, opinions, and friendship have been tremendously helpful to us over the years. For this edition, we have been freshly inspired by our new daughter-in-law, Abby Flachmann, who is a natural teacher in everything she does.

Our final and most important debt is to our children, Christopher and Laura, who have motivated us to be good teachers since the day they were born.

Part I

Critical Thinking
The Key to Success

Chapter 1

WHY LEARN HOW TO THINK CRITICALLY?

Have you ever had trouble expressing your thoughts? If so, you're not alone. Many people have this difficulty—especially when they are asked to write down their ideas. The good news is that this "ailment" can be cured. We've learned over the years that the more clearly students think about the world around them, the more easily they can express their thoughts through written and spoken language. So thinking more clearly, logically, and critically about important ideas and issues that exist in our world today will actually help your writing. In fact, to succeed in college you need to reason, read, and write about the world in increasingly complex ways, moving steadily from a simple, literal understanding of topics to interpretation and analysis.

The foundation of all successful reading and writing on the college level is critical thinking. You need to know as much as you can about this skill in order to do your best in all your classes. Inspired by the well-crafted prose models in this text and guided by carefully worded questions, you can actually raise the level of your thinking skills while improving your reading and writing abilities on three progressively more difficult levels:

1. *The literal level* is the foundation of all human understanding; it entails knowing the meanings of words—individually and in relation to one another. In order for someone to comprehend the sentence "You must exercise your brain to reach your full mental potential" on the literal level, for example, that person would have to know the definitions of all the words in the sentence and understand the way those words work together to make meaning.

2. *Interpretation* requires the ability to make associations between details, draw inferences from pieces of information, and reach conclusions about the material you have read. An interpretive understanding of the sample sentence in level 1 might be translated into the following thoughts: "Exercising the brain sounds a bit like exercising the body. I wonder if there's any correlation between the two. If the brain must be exercised, it is probably made up of muscles, much like the body is." None of these particular thoughts is made explicit in the sentence, but each is suggested in one way or another.

3. *Thinking critically,* the most sophisticated reasoning ability, involves a type of mental activity that is crucial for successful academic and professional work. A critical analysis of our sample sentence might proceed in the following way: "This sentence is talking to me. It actually addresses me with the word *you*. I wonder what *my* mental potential is. Will I be able to reach it? Will I know when I attain it? Will I be comfortable with it? I certainly want to reach this potential, whatever it is. Reaching it will undoubtedly help me succeed scholastically and professionally. The brain is obviously an important tool for helping me achieve my goals in life, so I want to take every opportunity I have to develop and maintain this part of my body." Students who can disassemble an issue or idea in this fashion and understand its various components more thoroughly after reassembling them are rewarded intrinsically with a clearer knowledge of life's complexities and the ability to generate creative, useful ideas. They are also rewarded extrinsically with good grades and are more likely to earn responsible jobs with higher pay because they are able to apply this understanding effectively to their professional and personal lives.

Recent psychological studies have shown that thinking and feeling are complementary operations. All of us have feelings that are automatic and instinctive. To feel pride after winning first place at a track meet, for example, or to feel anger at a spiteful friend is not behavior we have to study and master; such emotions come naturally to all of us. Thinking, on the other hand, is much less spontaneous than feeling; research suggests that study and practice are required for sustained mental development.

Thinking critically involves grappling with ideas, issues, and problems that surround you in your immediate environment and in the world at large. It does not necessarily entail finding fault, which you might naturally associate with the word *critical,* but rather suggests continually questioning and analyzing the world around you. Thinking critically is the highest form of mental activity that human beings engage in; it is the source of much success in college and in our professional and personal lives. Fortunately, all of us can learn how to think more critically.

Critical thinking means taking apart an issue, examining its various parts, and reassembling the topic with a more complete understanding of its intricacies. Implied in this explanation is the ability to see the topic from several new perspectives. Using your mind in this way will help you find solutions to difficult problems, design creative plans of action, and ultimately live a life consistent with your opinions on important issues that we all must confront daily.

Since critical or analytical thinking is one of the highest forms of mental activity, it requires a great deal of concentration and practice. Once you have actually felt how your mind processes information at this level, however, re-creating the experience is somewhat like riding a bicycle: You will be able to do it naturally, easily, and skillfully whenever you choose.

Our initial goal, then, is to help you think critically when you are required to do so in school, on the job, or in any other area of your life. If this form of thinking becomes part of your daily routine, you will quite naturally be able to call on it whenever necessary. Because rhetorical strategies are presented in this text as ways of thinking and processing information that you can use in all your academic tasks, working with these traditional modes is an effective way to achieve this goal. With some guidance, each rhetorical pattern can give you a mental workout that prepares you for writing and critical or analytical thinking in the same way that physical exercises warm you up for various sports. Just as in the rest of the body, the more exercise the brain gets, the more flexible it becomes and the higher levels of thought it can attain. Through these various guided thinking exercises, you can systematically strengthen your ability to think analytically. We feature one strategy at a time in each chapter so you can understand how it works before you combine it with other strategies, thus providing you with a systematic means of improving your ability to think critically about the complex world around you.

As you move through the following chapters, we will ask you to isolate each rhetorical mode—much like isolating your abs, thighs, and biceps in a weight-lifting workout—so you can concentrate on these thinking patterns one at a time. Each rhetorical pattern you study will suggest slightly different ways of seeing the world, processing information, and solving problems.

Looking closely at rhetorical modes or specific patterns of thought will also allow you to discover how your mind works in that particular mode. In the same fashion, becoming more intricately aware of your thought patterns will help you improve your thinking skills as well as your reading and writing abilities. Thinking critically enables you to identify fresh insights within old ideas, generate new thoughts, and see connections between related issues. It is an energizing mental activity that puts you in control of your life and your environment rather than leaving you at the mercy of your surroundings.

Each chapter introduction provides three exercises—one of which is based on a photograph—specifically designed to help you focus on a particular pattern of thought in isolation. While you are attempting to learn what each pattern feels like in your head, use your imagination to play with these exercises on as many different levels as possible.

Critical thinking does not necessarily occur after completing these exercises but rather is the result of sustained practice. With this in mind, we "coach" you through the entire reading process as you move from a literal understanding of the author's ideas to a critical approach to your reading. If this partnership is successful, you will be able to apply this level of performance to all your academic tasks in this class and throughout the curriculum.

Your approach to critical thinking in any subject must be built on a solid foundation, which is the reason that each essay in this collection is preceded by a number of questions that introduce you to the author's main ideas before you start reading. Forming some initial opinions and relating some of the ideas to your own experiences is the starting point of all good thinking.

Next, this initial engagement with the essay must be woven in and out of the reading process—without abandoning your original thoughts. To this end, critical thinking questions are furnished at the bottom of the pages you are reading to help you make both personal and intellectual connections with the text. These questions (marked in the text by numbers in diamonds) always start by encouraging you to interact personally with each reading selection before you analyze it. You are asked to filter the reading through your own life experiences, which will help you discover meaning by associating the reading with your own worldview. Once you begin to interact personally with the text, the questions will then take you deeper and deeper into the content of the reading. These critical thinking questions will engage you on many different levels, so the act of reading each selection will ultimately become an act of total immersion in the subject matter. These questions essentially serve as a guide through your reading, or a teacher in your head, when you use this feature productively.

To achieve these goals, the "in-text" critical thinking questions progress very consciously from personal to more academic concerns. In other words, they teach you, through carefully scaffolded prompts, how to ascend to understanding at the critical or analytical level. The questions fall quite naturally into the following progressively more difficult levels of interaction:

Making personal associations: These questions ask you to make connections with your own experiences.

Understanding definitions: These questions check your literal understanding.

Engaging curiosity: These questions stimulate your curiosity and require you to look outside yourself to generate some of your own questions.

Drawing conclusions: These questions prompt you to make some deductions from the material you have read so far.

Making connections: These questions ask you to make connections among ideas.

Finding evidence: These questions encourage you to find examples, statistics, data, and reasons that support your conclusions.

Analyzing your discoveries: These questions require you to step away from the reading selection and study the ideas and connections that have resulted from your reading.

Through this entire process, as we guide you to more advanced levels of reasoning, you must be willing to tolerate ambiguity at every stage of the process. This uncertainty allows you ultimately to bring together exciting ideas and make creative discoveries. This approach to your reading will also keep your mind open to new ideas and unique interpretations as you read.

Finally, these in-text questions will lead you smoothly and seamlessly to the questions following each essay. In essence, the in-text questions build a bridge to the post-reading questions. So if you have reflected and taken notes on the critical thinking questions at the bottom of the pages as you were reading, you will be fully prepared for the post-reading questions to take you to even higher levels of thought after reading the essay. In each case, these questions move from literal understanding of details, definitions, and concepts through interpretation to analysis of this same information. Working systematically with the in-text questions will stimulate your own opinions and thoughts, which will help support your final discoveries and analyses.

The in-text critical thinking questions prepare you for what follows so you will be ready to read, write, and discuss the topic at hand from a number of different perspectives and with various audiences and purposes in mind. These final questions, then, will spark your creativity and enable you to think more deeply about the topic. At the end of this process, your head will be filled with ideas that you will want to use in class discussions, papers, oral reports, or any other assignments you might encounter.

As you practice each of the rhetorical patterns of thought in isolation, you should be aware of building on your previous thinking skills. As the book progresses, the rhetorical modes become more complex and require a higher degree of concentration and effort. You should, therefore, keep in mind that you ultimately want to let these skills develop into a high-powered, well-developed ability to process the world around you—including reading, writing, seeing, and feeling—on the most advanced analytical level you can master.

Chapter 2

WHAT EXACTLY IS CRITICAL THINKING?

In this chapter, we offer three essays, each from a different perspective, to help you define critical thinking for yourself, which will allow you to use this skill more effectively than if we were to provide you with a single, working definition of the term. After reading these selections, you will be asked to generate your own definition of critical thinking.

As you read these essays, consider the following issues that you might address in your own definition:

1. What are the main features of critical thinking?
2. What is the relationship between critical thinking and personal success?
3. What is the role of critical thinking in society?

Also as you read, we will occasionally interrupt your thinking with questions for you to consider. The answers to these questions will help you move smoothly to a definition of critical thinking at the end of your reading. Recording your thoughts in this book or on a separate piece of paper as you read is a productive way to approach this activity.

LINDA ELDER

Looking to the Future with a Critical Eye: A Message for High School Graduates

Graduation from high school is an exciting time. Finally you will be able to live your own life, make your own decisions, do exactly what you want. At last!

So the good news is that you now are free to make your own choices. The bad news is that, in this highly complex world, it is all too easy to make decisions which might lead you in a direction you may regret. With every decision that you make, there are choices you accept and choices you reject. With every one you accept, you consequently turn your back on others. How will you know whether you are making the right choices, or the best ones?

What is the author trying to accomplish in this introduction?

Is this an accurate statement about choices?

The best way to face all problems and decisions in your life is with a critical view. By this I do not mean that you should improve your ability to criticize (most of us know how to do that all too well). Rather I mean that you should think critically about the problems and opportunities that face you. In other words, you will have to make lots and lots of decisions in your life, from deciding whether to pursue a college degree to choosing a spouse and having children (or deciding not to); and you will want to do the best reasoning that you possibly can with respect to those decisions. In other words, you will want to make decisions that result in positive consequences. But to do this, you must understand some very basic things about your mind.

The human mind, without discipline and rigor, is prone to shoddy thinking. Oddly enough, very often it would rather not have to "think." Instead it is frequently impulsive, preferring to go with its first response to a situation or problem rather than probing into the complexities of issues. However, although it is non-reflective by nature, it is fully capable of transforming and improving the way it operates. This fact is a mystery to most people because such thinking involves intellectual discipline; and in our culture disciplined thinking is, for the most part, neither understood nor valued.

But we can learn to take charge of our thinking, to monitor and assess the moves our mind makes if we see the value in doing it and are willing to consistently practice it. Despite the fact that becoming highly skilled at good reasoning involves a long, slow process, the basic intellectual moves that the mind must make to do so are assessible to you. By learning these moves, you can learn to approach any subject in college, any course you take with a critical eye. You can learn to ask important questions and can, in essence, take charge of your thinking so that you are not simply "doing what the teacher says to get the grade," but continually asking yourself how the content of your college classes relates to the issues in your life in a meaningful way. In other words, you can use the information you learn in school to do better reasoning if you learn to approach the content in your classes through good reasoning.

How can thinking critically give you more control over your life?

To illustrate what I mean, while introducing you to some of the most basic moves the mind must make if it is to do good reasoning, I will focus on an everyday problem that you might face in your life. However, to make the most of your education, you should apply the same ideas to and be able to make the same intellectual moves in all of your classes and your studies.

FUNDAMENTAL CRITICAL THINKING MOVES

If I am thinking critically, or reasoning well, about a problem in my life or in my coursework, I will begin by determining the precise question I am trying to answer. To a large extent, the quality of my reasoning about any problem will be determined by how well I am able to frame the question that ultimately drives my thinking. Let's say, for example, I am planning to purchase an automobile. My reasoning will be very different if I begin with the question "What type of car do I want to buy?" than if I begin with the question "Given my limited available finances and my plans to save money for college, what is the best car purchase I can make?" The first question is unclear and thus can be interpreted in a number of ways. It does not help to direct my thinking along a clear path. Furthermore, the way the question is put implies that I can "have" any car I "want." On the other hand, the second question is much more precise, and because it narrows the possibilities (due to my limited finances), it serves as a much better guide for my thinking.

What does asking questions have to do with critical thinking?

The next step in the process of thinking through a problem is to ask, "What is my purpose in answering this question?" My purpose works hand in hand with my question to guide my thinking. Let us say that my purpose is to purchase a car that is dependable, safe, and inexpensive, which I will use primarily to drive to college each day. Now I have a clear question and a clear purpose, together which tell me the type of information I must have to answer the question. Now, obviously I will ultimately have to make a decision between this car or that, so that the process of thinking critically about an issue does not tell me exactly which car to purchase. Rather, it guides me to the best possible choices.

So now I know that I need to gather information about dependability, safety, and cost. Perhaps I should begin by reading consumer reports for information related to all three of these. I will then need to shop around to find the best buy for the money. If I am considering purchasing a used car, I should look at the car's maintenance records to see if it has been well cared for (to help determine potential reliability). If I will have a long distance to drive each day, I should consider purchasing only a car that will be reliable traveling long distances. In that case perhaps I should only consider cars that have very low mileage. I might look at any statistics I can gather from automobile companies about the safety of their vehicles.

Once I have gathered the information I need, I will be aware that there is usually more than one way to interpret it. I want to consider only ACCURATE or LOGICAL interpretations of information. Statistics are often presented in ways that are misleading or result in our interpreting information incorrectly. Automobile companies exist for one reason, and that is to make money. Therefore I will guard against simply believing the information they present (and their interpretation of the information) without wondering if there is possibly some other way to interpret it. If I am told, for example, that a particular car is the safest car in the industry (interpretation), based on the fact that fewer people are known to have accidents in this car than in any other car (information), I will question why the accident rate for this car is so low. Perhaps it is that the average person who purchases this type of car is more likely to be a safer driver (perhaps because she is older and more highly educated) rather than that the car itself is safer than other cars on the market.

> What does interpretation have to do with critical thinking?

Furthermore, when I am gathering information I want to make sure I am only considering information that is RELEVANT to the question I am focused on. Therefore I avoid gathering information about cars that are out of my price range, which I know to be unsafe, and which I am relatively certain are undependable. I determine what information is relevant by keeping my question and purpose in clear view.

To summarize, when making a decision or solving a problem, you should begin with a CLEAR, PRECISE question and purpose which directly relate to the problem. Then you should gather only ACCURATE information, which is RELEVANT to the particular problem you are trying to solve. You should figure out if there are alternate ways to interpret a piece of information, continually questioning the way others interpret information or present "facts."

If you learn to ask these questions as a habit of mind, the decisions you make will be much better and the consequences more positive than if you respond to problems in an undisciplined, non-reflective, impulsive way. If you learn to ask these questions, you will be able to approach the content of your courses through reasoning rather than through memorization. Thus, in class, at any given point, you should be able to ask yourself, "What is the key question right now? What information do I need to address the question? How can I make sure the information is relevant and accurate? Is there another way to interpret the information than the instructor or textbook is presenting? How does this content relate to my life in a significant way?"

If you are really interested in becoming a critical thinker, you should understand that developing your mind involves a deliberate, disciplined, committed process, but that its benefits far outweigh its costs.

In one sentence, summarize Linda Elder's definition of critical thinking.

BRIAN DENIS EGAN

The Role of Critical Thinking in Effective Decision Making

WHAT IS CRITICAL THINKING?

Critical thinking is the art of raising what is subconscious in our reasoning to the level of conscious recognition. It is the art of taking control of our thinking processes so as to understand the pathway and inputs that our thinking employs.

Critical thinkers understand the mechanics of reasoning (thinking). They use this understanding to manage the unconscious influences that contribute to their decision-making processes.

By taking charge of the thinking process, critical thinkers develop an understanding of what they do *not* know about a particular subject and make better decisions as a result.

How are critical thinking and decision making related?

WHO NEEDS CRITICAL THINKING?

The study of critical thinking is the study of reasoning. Implicit in this study is the recognition that if we are to become better thinkers, our thinking skills must be practiced and developed, just like any other skill set.

Advocates of critical thinking believe that critical thinking is a philosophical perspective that can help anyone to become more successful. The logic behind this belief is that everyone can benefit from becoming a better thinker and, as a result, have greater control over their thinking processes.

In the business world, a critical thinking approach to problem solving improves the quality of analysis, resulting in a more balanced, reasoned decision-making process.

PREMISE

To become a critical thinker is to become an effective critic of your own thinking. This involves an analysis of the inputs (information, assumptions, and biases) that form part of your reasoning, as well as the outputs (decisions, assumptions, and biases) that result from your reasoning.

As part of your development as a critical thinker, you learn to gauge and measure the outputs of other people's thinking (which are your inputs) and as a consequence develop improved decision-making skills.

According to Egan, how can you become a "critic of your own thinking"?

ARE YOU A CRITICAL THINKER?

Most people, particularly anyone with higher education, consider themselves to be critical thinkers. Unfortunately, quality thinking does not come naturally to most people (maybe to no one), and our education system does not fill the gap.

Critical thinking is the discipline of making sure that you use the best thinking that you are capable of in every situation. To become a skilled critical thinker, it is necessary to understand thought processes and to use that understanding to structure your analysis of anything and everything in a balanced way.

What are the symptoms of being a critical thinker? The indicator that someone is practicing critical thinking (to some degree) is that they continually question their own and other people's assumptions, reasons, motivations, and outlook. This questioning must not focus on generating mere contradiction but rather on the discovery of context, reasoning, and point of view. Critical thinkers ask questions to answer questions and seek reason and logic as the foundation for understanding.

Why are questions important to critical thinking?

DEVELOPING AS A CRITICAL THINKER

Becoming a skilled thinker requires practice. Everyone "practices" thinking, but the question is whether he or she is practicing good or bad habits. The mere act of thinking does not ensure that one is becoming an increasingly skilled thinker over time.

As with every other set of skills, bad habits are easy to learn and difficult to break. To develop as a critical thinker, you must understand and then practice the necessary thinking skills. To determine whether or not you are improving, you must judge your performance against a meaningful set of quality standards.

Give an example of what you think the author is saying here.

It is much the same as the way one would advance in the development of any set of skills, in any sport or activity. Improvement comes from guided skill set development—instruction, practice, criticism, and more practice.

Imagine trying to learn skills any other way. Would you ever become an excellent soccer player without being told what to practice or how to measure improvement? Would any parent launch a child's soccer career by leaving them in a field without any idea of what the rules of the game were, the nature of the activities, or the level of performance of other players? Of course not, but this is exactly how thinking skills are developed.

You develop as a thinker when you begin to notice the way you are thinking and are able to recognize the strengths and weaknesses in that thinking. As your thinking improves, you build an objective view of your own thinking.

When do you know you are a critical thinker?

HOWARD GABENNESCH

Critical Thinking: What Is It Good for? (In Fact, What Is It?)

Is critical thinking worth the costs? Consider for a moment how costly uncritical thinking can be. Stephen Jay Gould (1997, x, xii) calls attention to two precious human potentials that together constitute "the most powerful joint instrument for good that our planet has ever known":

> Only two possible escapes can save us from the organized mayhem of our dark potentialities—the side of human nature that has given us crusades, witch hunts, enslavements, and holocausts. Moral decency provides one necessary ingredient, but not nearly enough. The second foundation must come from the rational side of our mentality. For, unless we rigorously use human reason, . . . we will lose out to the frightening forces of irrationality, romanticism, uncompromising "true" belief, and the apparent resulting inevitability of mob action . . . Skepticism is the agent of reason against organized irrationalism—and is therefore one of the keys to human social and civic decency.

Explain this quotation.

What is the purpose of starting this essay with a quote?

According to this striking claim, critical thinking is one of the most important resources a society could develop. This is because bad things do not emanate only from bad people. Bad things can also occur because of the mistaken thinking of decent people. Even when a bad idea originates with a psychopath, the real danger occurs when it is accepted by the gullible and condoned by the sincere who have little more than a child's understanding of what intellectual due process entails.

It is likely that an important link exists between critical thinking, broadly defined, and democracy itself. The American jurist Learned Hand (1952, 190) described this connection as follows:

> Liberty lies in the hearts of men and women; when it dies there, no constitution, no law, no court can save it. . . . The spirit of liberty is the spirit which is not too sure that it is right; the spirit of liberty is the spirit which seeks to understand the minds of other men and women; the spirit of liberty is the spirit which weighs their interest alongside its own without bias.

So by cultivating genuine critical thinking, we strengthen the crucial underpinnings of democracy (Kuhn 2003). People who are careful about the truth are less likely to be fooled by the ideologies that justify illiberal practices or promise simple solutions. Moreover, such people are more likely to recognize the value of intellectual and ideological diversity—they understand that the truth comes in pieces and is unlikely to be found all in one place. They are the best counterweight to true believers of all stripes. Ultimately, intellectual due process is no less integral to democracy than is due process of law.

Within a democracy, the social world remains a deceptive place for the sophisticated and the innocent alike. The tendency of leaders and large numbers of citizens to underestimate this fact is a source of enormous human misery.

> What is the relationship between critical thinking and a democratic society?

Here is an example. In his book a few years ago and in the 2003 Oscar-winning documentary by Errol Morris, *The Fog of War*, former defense secretary Robert S. McNamara (1995) identifies the mistakes made by him and others that led to calamity in Vietnam. His account describes confident, mostly decent men who did what they thought was best, but who fell prey to a chilling list of errors that could serve as chapters in a textbook on critical thinking: dualistic thinking, wishful thinking, absence of intellectual humility, underestimating complexity, group-think, childlike credulity, rigid adherence to orthodoxy. These were intelligent, educated men whose logical reasoning skills were far above average. Yet McNamara finds it "incredible" that "[w]e failed to analyze our assumptions critically."

Perhaps the architects of the Vietnam war went wrong because they indulged in what Thomas Sowell (2002) calls "shibboleths" as substitutes for critical thinking. A shibboleth is a belief that serves the purpose of identifying the believer as one of the good guys, prominently planted on the side of the angels. Shibboleths "transform questions about facts, causation, and evidence into questions about personal identity and moral worth":

> Mere facts cannot compete with shibboleths when it comes to making people feel good. Moreover, shibboleths keep off the agenda the painful question of how dangerous it is to have policies which impact millions of human beings without a thorough knowledge of the hard facts needed to understand just what that impact has actually been. . . .

Shibboleths are dangerous, not only because they mobilize political support for policies that most of the supporters have not thought through, but also because these badges of identity make it harder to reverse those policies when they turn out to be disastrous.

What are shibboleths?

How are they related to critical thinking?

Why do they threaten society?

Like many other forms of uncritical thinking, shibboleths derive their power from the fact that humans are designed to be social animals more than truth-seeking ones. For all the societal benefits of critical thinking, at the individual level, uncritical thinking offers social and psychological rewards of its own.

References

Gould, Stephen Jay. 1997. The Positive Power of Skepticism. In Michael Shermer, *Why People Believe Weird Things: Pseudoscience, Superstition, and Other Confusions of Our Time*, ix–xii. New York: W.H. Freeman,

Hand, Learned. 1952 (1944). The Spirit of Liberty. In Irving Dillard, ed., *The Spirit of Liberty: Papers and Addresses of Learned Hand*. New York: Alfred A. Knopf.

Kuhn, Robert. 2003. Science as democratizer. *American Scientist* 91(5):388–390.

McNamara, Robert. 1995. *In Retrospect: The Tragedy and Lessons of Vietnam*. New York: Random House.

Sowell, Thomas. 2002. The high cost of shibboleths. Townhall.com. February 15. (Accessed December 1, 2006.)

We know that good critical thinkers accurately define their terms before moving forward, so use the information in the preceding articles to define the primary focus of this text: critical thinking. Move thoughtfully and carefully through the following questions to arrive at your personal definition.

My Definition of Critical Thinking

1. List three basic components of critical thinking.
2. Explain what is not critical thinking.
3. What can you compare it to?
4. Why is it important?

Now write out your definition as clearly and precisely as you can. Include in your definition the significance of critical thinking in the life of a college student.

With a good, clear understanding of critical thinking, you are now ready to move on to the relationship of critical thinking to reading and writing. Your approach to critical thinking will determine your potential as a reader and a writer. Review your notes in this chapter as necessary as you progress through the text. Continuing to adjust and refine your definition of critical thinking is important to your progress and success as a student.

Chapter 3

What Do I Need to Know about Reading and Writing Critically?

Part of becoming a better writer involves understanding that reading and writing are companion activities that engage people in the creation of thought and meaning—either as readers interpreting a text or as writers constructing one. Clear thinking, then, is the pivotal point that joins together these two efforts. Now that you understand the range and power of critical thinking, you can put it to use on some sample reading and writing material. If you learn to apply your critical thinking skills to your reading, you will naturally be able to write critically. You must process thoughts on this higher level as you read in order to produce essays of your own on this level. In other words, you must "import" your reading critically in order to "export" critical writing. This chapter explains the relationship of critical thinking to reading and writing and also gives annotated examples of the processes of reading and writing at work. It will ultimately lead to an understanding of the Reading and Writing Inventories featured at the end of this chapter.

READING CRITICALLY

Reading critically begins with developing a natural curiosity about an essay's subject and then nurturing that curiosity throughout the reading process. To learn as much as you can from an essay, you should first study any preliminary material you can find, then read the essay to get a general overview of its main ideas, and finally read the selection again to achieve a deeper understanding of its content. These three phases of the reading process—preparing to read, reading, and rereading—will help you develop this natural curiosity so you can approach any reading assignment with an active, inquiring mind. The Reading Inventory at the end of this chapter will also guide you through this process.

Preparing to Read

Focusing your attention is an important first stage in both the reading and writing processes. In fact, learning as much as you can about an essay and its context (the circumstances surrounding its development) before you begin reading can help you move through the essay with an energetic, active mind and then reach some degree of analysis before writing on the assigned topics. In particular, knowing where an essay was first published, studying the writer's background, and doing some preliminary thinking about the subject of a reading selection will help you understand the writer's ideas and encourage you to form some valid opinions of your own on the topic.

As you approach any essay, you should concentrate on four specific areas that will begin to give you an overview of the material you are about to read. We will use an essay by Lewis Thomas to demonstrate these techniques.

1. *Title.* A close look at the title will usually provide important clues about the author's attitude toward the topic, his or her stand on an issue, or the mood of the essay. It can also furnish you with a sense of audience and purpose.

To Err Is Human

From this title, for example, we might infer that the author will discuss errors, human nature, and the extent to which mistakes influence human behavior. The title is half of a well-known proverbial quotation written by Alexander Pope ("To err is human, to forgive, divine"), so we might speculate further that the author has written an essay intended for a well-read audience interested in the relationship between errors and humanity. After reading only four words of the essay—its title—you already have a good deal of information about the subject, its audience, and the author's attitude toward both.

2. *Synopsis.* The Rhetorical Table of Contents in this text contains a synopsis of each essay, very much like the following, so you can discover more specific details about its contents before you begin reading.

> Physician Lewis Thomas explains how we can profit from our mistakes—especially if we trust human nature. Perhaps someday, he says, we can apply this same principle to the computer and magnify the advantages of these errors.

From this synopsis, we learn that Thomas's essay will be an analysis of human errors and of the way we can benefit from those errors. The synopsis also tells us the computer has the potential to magnify the value of our own innate errors.

3. *Biography.* Learning as much as you can about the author of an essay will generally stimulate your interest in the material and help you achieve a deeper understanding of the issues to be discussed. It also provides a context for your reading. From the biographies in this book, you can learn, for example, whether a writer is young or old, conservative or liberal, open- or close-minded. You might also discover if the essay was written at the beginning, middle, or end of the author's career or how well versed the writer is on the topic. Such information will invariably help you reach a more thorough understanding of a selection's ideas, audience, and logical structure.

LEWIS THOMAS   (1913–1993)

Lewis Thomas was a physician who, until his death in 1993, was President Emeritus of the Sloan-Kettering Cancer Center and Scholar-in-Residence at the Cornell University Medical Center in New York City. A graduate of Princeton University and Harvard Medical School, he was previously Head of Pathology and Dean of the New York University–Bellevue Medical Center and Dean of the Yale Medical School. In addition to having written over two hundred scientific papers on virology and immunology, he authored many popular scientific essays, some of which have been collected in *Lives of a Cell* (1974), *The Medusa and the Snail* (1979), *Late Night Thoughts on Listening to Mahler's Ninth Symphony* (1983), *Etcetera, Etcetera* (1990), and *The Fragile Species* (1992). The memoirs of his distinguished career have been published in *The Youngest Science: Notes of a Medicine Watcher* (1983). Thomas liked to refer to his essays as "experiments in thought": "Although I usually think I know what I'm going to be writing about, what I'm going to say, most of the time it doesn't happen that way at all. At some point, I get misled down a garden path. I get surprised by an idea that I hadn't anticipated getting, which is a little bit like being in a laboratory."

As this information indicates, Thomas was a prominent physician who published widely on scientific topics. We know that he considered his essays "experiments in thought," which makes us expect a relaxed, spontaneous treatment of his subjects. From this biography, we can also infer that he was a leader in the medical world and that, because of the positions he has held, he was well respected in his professional life. Last, we can speculate that he had a clear sense of his audience because he was able to present difficult concepts in clear, everyday language.

4. *Prereading Questions.* One other type of preliminary material will broaden your overview of the topic and enable you to approach the essay with an active, inquiring mind. The "Preparing to Read" questions following the biographies are intended to focus your attention and stimulate your curiosity before you begin the essay. They will also prepare you to form your own opinions on the essay and its topic as you read. Keeping a journal to respond to these questions is an excellent idea, because you will then have a record of your thoughts on various subjects related to the reading selection that follows.

Preparing to Read

The following essay, which originally appeared in the *New England Journal of Medicine* (January 1976), illustrates the clarity and ease with which Thomas explains complex scientific topics.

Exploring Experience: As you prepare to read this essay, take a few moments to think about the role mistakes play in our lives: What are some memorable mistakes you have made? Did you learn anything important from these errors? Do you make more or fewer mistakes than other people you know? Do you see any advantages to making mistakes? Any disadvantages?

Learning Online: Most computers have games included in their operating systems. Find a game on your computer, and play it for a while. Who won? What types of mistakes did the computer make? What types of mistakes did you make? Consider your experience while reading Thomas's essay.

Learning where, why, and how an essay was first written will provide you with a context for the material you are about to read: Why did the author write this selection? Where was it first published? Who was the author's original audience? This type of information enables you to understand the circumstances surrounding the development of the selection and to identify any topical or historical references the author makes. All the selections in this textbook were published elsewhere first—in another book, a journal, or a magazine. The author's original audience, therefore, consisted of the readers of that particular publication.

Next, two types of questions focus the readers' attention for the first reading. The first type (Exploring Experience) asks you to begin drawing on your prior knowledge in reference to this particular topic; they ask pointed questions about your previous life experiences in preparation for this reading assignment. The second set guides you to an Internet activity that will prepare you for your reading; this activity is then linked to the first writing assignment at the end of the essay.

From the sample "Preparing to Read" material, we learn that Thomas's essay "To Err Is Human" was originally published in the *New England Journal of Medicine,* a prestigious periodical read principally by members of the scientific community. Written in 1976, the article plays on its audience's growing fascination with computers and with the limits of artificial intelligence— subjects just as timely today as they were in the mid-1970s.

The Exploring Experience questions here prompt you to consider your own ideas, opinions, or actions in order to help you generate thoughts on the topic of errors in our lives. The Internet exercise is designed to stimulate your thinking and expand your knowledge on this and related subjects. These queries are, ideally, the last step in preparing yourself for the active role you should play as a reader.

Reading

People read essays in books, newspapers, magazines, and journals for a great variety of reasons. One reader may want to be stimulated intellectually, whereas another seeks relaxation; one person reads to keep up with the latest developments in his or her profession, whereas the next wants to learn why a certain event happened or how something can be done; finally, some people read in order to be challenged by new ideas, whereas others find comfort principally in printed material that supports their own moral, social, or political opinions. The essays in this textbook fulfill all these expectations in different ways. They have been chosen, however, not only for these reasons but for an additional, broader purpose: Reading them can help make you a better writer.

Every time you read an essay in this book, you will also be preparing to write your own essay based on the same rhetorical pattern. For this reason, as you read you should pay careful attention to both the content (subject matter) and the form (language, sentence structure, organization, and development of ideas) of each essay. You will also see how effectively experienced writers use particular rhetorical modes or patterns of thought to organize and communicate their ideas. Each essay in this collection features one dominant pattern that is generally supported by several others. The more aware you are of each author's writing techniques, the more skillfully you will be able to apply these strategies to your own writing.

The questions before and after each essay teach you a way of reading that can help you discover the relationships of a writer's ideas to one another as well as to your own thoughts. These questions can also help clarify for you the connections among the writer's topic, his or her style or manner of expression, and your own composing process. In other words, the questions are designed to help you understand and generate ideas, then discover various choices the writers made in composing their essays, and finally realize the freedom you have to make related choices in your own writing. Such an approach to the process of reading takes some of the mystery out of reading and writing and makes them manageable tasks at which anyone can become proficient.

Within each essay, at the bottom of the pages, are questions designed specifically to raise your level of thinking as you read. They provide a "bridge" between the personal prereading questions and the more broad-based academic questions and assignments that follow each essay. In other words, the questions within each essay prepare you for the thinking and processing you will be asked to do at the end of a reading assignment. These "bridge" questions actually teach you how to interact critically with your reading material, guiding you through the text as you become partners with the essay in the creation of meaning. As you move further into *The Prose Reader,* these questions help you understand each essay on a deeper level by filtering the context through your own experience. They invite you to engage fully with your reading and bring it into your life so you will understand it both instinctively and intellectually. If you take the time to produce a written response to these questions, you will quite naturally form your own opinions and arguments in preparation for the assignments that follow each essay.

To understand your reading material on the critical level, you should be prepared to read each essay at least three times. The first reading is an overview, during which you want to get a general sense of the essay in relation to its title, purpose, audience, and publication information. You should annotate the essay with your personal reactions and make sure you understand all the author's vocabulary. You should also read the questions at the bottom of the pages, but don't answer them until your second reading.

To illustrate this process, on the following pages Lewis Thomas's essay is printed with a student's comments in the margins, showing how she interacted with the essay while reading it for the first time. The student also circled words she didn't know and put their definitions in the margins.

LEWIS THOMAS   (1913–1993)

To Err Is Human

Boy is this true

Everyone must have had at least one personal ex- 1
perience with a computer error by this time. Bank
balances are suddenly reported to have jumped from
$379 into the millions, appeals for charitable contri-
butions are mailed over and over to people with crazy
sounding names at your address, <u>department stores</u>   *Last spring*
<u>send the wrong bills</u>, utility companies write that   *this happened*
they're turning everything off, that sort of thing. If   *to me*
you manage to get in touch with someone and complain, you then get instantaneously typed, guilty letters from the same computer, saying, "Our computer

exactly

was in error, and an adjustment is being made in your
account."

These are supposed to be the sheerest, blindest 2
accidents. Mistakes are not believed to be part of
the normal behavior of a good machine. If things

*How can
this be?*

go wrong, it must be a personal, human error, the result of fingering, tampering, a button getting stuck,
someone hitting the wrong key. The computer, at its
normal best, is (infallible).   (*perfect*)

I wonder whether this can be true. After all, the 3
whole point of computers is that they represent an
extension of the human brain, vastly improved upon
but nonetheless human, <u>superhuman</u> maybe.[1] A good   *In what*
computer can think clearly and quickly enough to   *way?*
beat you at chess, and some of them have even been

*I expected
this essay to
be so much
more stuffy
than it is. I
can even
understand it.*

programmed to write obscure verse. They can do any-   *Can this be*
thing we can do, and more besides.   *proven?*

It is not yet known whether a computer has its own 4
consciousness, and it would be hard to find out about
this. When you walk into one of those great halls now
built for the huge machines, and stand listening, it is
easy to imagine that the faint, distant noises are the

Thinking Critically

[1] To what extent do you feel computers "extend" the human brain? Can humans do anything that computers can't do? If so, what?

sound of thinking, and the turning of the spools gives them the look of wild creatures rolling their eyes in the effort to concentrate, choking with information. <u>But real thinking, and dreaming, are other matters</u>.

In what way?

good, clear comparison for the general reader

On the other hand, the evidences of something like an unconscious, equivalent to ours, are all around, in every mail. As extensions of the human brain, they have been constructed with the same property of error, spontaneous, uncontrolled, and rich in possibilities.[2]   5

so true

<u>Mistakes are at the very base of human thought</u>, embedded there, feeding the structure like <u>root nod-</u>   6
ules. If we were not provided with the knack of being wrong, we could never get anything useful done. We think our way along by choosing between right and wrong alternatives, and the wrong choices have to be made as frequently as the right ones. We get along in life this way. We are built to make mistakes, coded for error.[3]

great image

I don't understand this??

I agree! This is how we learn

We learn, as we say, <u>by "trial and error."</u> Why do we always say that? Why not "trial and rightness" or "trial and triumph"? The old phrase puts it that way because that is, in real life, the way it is done.   7

Another effective comparison for the general reader

A good laboratory, like a good bank or a corpora-   8
tion or government, has to run like a computer. Almost everything is done flawlessly, by the book, and all the numbers add up to the predicted sums. The days go by. And then, if it is a <u>lucky</u> day, and a <u>lucky</u> laboratory, somebody makes a mistake: the wrong (buffer) something in one of the blanks, a decimal misplaced in reading counts, the warm room off by a degree and a half, a mouse out of his box, or just a misreading of the day's (protocol) Whatever, when the results come in, something is obviously screwed up, and <u>then the action can begin</u>.

Isn't this a contradiction? storage area for data being transferred

(plan)

What?

aha!

The misreading is not the important error; <u>it opens the way</u>. The next step is the crucial one. If the investigator can bring himself to say, "But even so, look at that!" then the new finding, whatever it is, is ready for   9

Thinking Critically

[2] How could computer errors be "rich in possibilities"?

[3] Have you ever made an error that turned out to be beneficial? What happened?

snatching. What is needed, for progress to be made, is <u>the move based on error.</u>

Whenever new kinds of thinking are about to be accomplished, or new varieties of music, there has to be an argument beforehand. With two sides debating in the same mind, (haranguing,) there is an amiable understanding that one is right and the other wrong. Sooner or later the thing is settled, but there can be no action at all if there are not the two sides and the argument. <u>The hope is in the faculty of wrongness</u>, the tendency toward error. The capacity to leap across mountains of information and land lightly on the wrong side represents the highest of human endowments. 〔10〕

arguing

interesting idea

I believe Thomas here because of his background

It may be that this is a uniquely human gift, perhaps even stipulated in our genetic instructions.[4] Other creatures do not seem to have DNA sequences for making mistakes as a routine part of daily living, certainly not for programmed error as a guide for action. 〔11〕

Could this be related to the human ability to think critically?

We are at our human finest, <u>dancing with our minds</u>, when there are more choices than two. Sometimes there are ten, even twenty different ways to go, all but one bound to be wrong, and the richness of selection in such situations can lift us onto totally new ground. This process is called exploration and is based on human (fallibility.) If we had only a single center in our brains, capable of responding only when a correct decision was to be made, instead of the jumble of different, (credulous,) easily (conned) clusters of neurons that provide for being flung off into blind alleys, up trees, down dead ends, out into blue sky, along wrong turnings, around bends, we could only stay the way we are today, stuck fast. 〔12〕

Yes, but this is so frustrating

nice mental image

imperfection

gullible

fooled

This is a great sentence— it has a lot of feeling

<u>The lower animals do not have this splendid freedom.</u> They are limited, most of them, to absolute (infallibility.) Cats, for all their good side, never make mistakes. <u>I have never seen a (maladroit, clumsy, or blundering cat.</u> Dogs are sometimes fallible, occasionally able to make charming minor mistakes, but they 〔13〕

I love the phrase "splendid freedom"

perfection

See ¶11

look up "maladroit"

awkward

Thinking Critically

[4] Do you agree with Thomas that we are genetically programmed to make mistakes in our lives? Explain your answer.

I like this idea

get this way by trying to mimic their masters. <u>Fish are flawless in everything they do</u>. Individual cells in a tissue are mindless machines, perfect in their performance, as absolutely inhuman as bees.

I never thought of mistakes this way

14

Thomas makes our technology sound really exciting

We should have this in mind as we become dependent on more complex computers for the arrangement of our affairs. Give the computers their heads, I say; let them go their way. If we can learn to do this, turning our heads to one side and wincing while the work proceeds, the possibilities for the future of mankind, and computerkind, are limitless. <u>Your average good computer can make calculations in an instant which would take a lifetime of slide rules for any of us.</u> Think of what we could gain from the near infinity of precise, <u>machine-made (miscomputation)</u> which is now so easily within our grasp. We would begin the solving of some of our hardest problems. How, for instance, should we go about organizing ourselves for social living on a planetary scale, now that we have become, as a plain fact of life, a single community? We can assume, as a working hypothesis, that all the right ways of doing this are unworkable. What we need, then, for moving ahead, is a set of wrong alternatives much longer and more interesting than the short list of mistaken courses that any of us can think up right now. We need, in fact, an infinite list, and when it is printed out we need the computer to turn itself on and select, at random, the next way to go. If it is a big enough mistake, we could find ourselves on a new level, stunned, out in the clear, ready to move again.[5,6]

so true

error or mistake

yes

We need to program computers to make deliberate mistakes so they can help our natural human tendency to learn thru error

So mistakes have value!

Not a contradiction after all

After you have read the essay for the first time, summarize its main ideas in some fashion. The form of this task might be anything from a drawing of the main ideas as they connect with one another to a succinct written summary. You could draw a graph or map of the topics in the essay (in much the same way that a person would draw a map of an area for someone unfamiliar with a particular route); outline the ideas to get an overview of the piece; or summarize the ideas to check your understanding of the main points of the

---

Thinking Critically

5 What do the author's final words mean to you: "stunned, out in the clear, ready to move again"?

6 Why do you think Thomas ends his essay this way?

selection. Any of these tasks can be completed from your original notes and underlining. Each will give you a slightly more thorough understanding of what you have read.

Finally, read the questions and assignments following the essay to help focus your thinking for the second reading. Don't answer the questions at this time; just read them to make sure you are picking up the main ideas from the selection and thinking about relevant connections among those ideas.

Rereading

The second and third readings will dramatically increase your understanding of each essay in this book. The temptation to skip these two stages of the reading process is often powerful, but these readings are crucial to your development as a critical reader in all of your courses. Rereading can be compared to seeing a good movie for the second or third time: The first viewing provides you with a general understanding of the plot, the characters, the setting, and the overall artistic accomplishment of the director; during the second viewing, however, you would undoubtedly notice many more details and see their specific contributions to the artistic whole. Similarly, the second and third readings of an essay provide for a much deeper understanding of the essay and prepare you to analyze the writer's ideas.

Your second reading is a time to develop a deeper understanding of the author's argument or main ideas. Concentrate on reading "with the grain," as the rhetorician John Bean calls it, meaning you are essentially trying to adopt the author's reasoning in an attempt to learn how he or she thinks and came to certain conclusions. This reading will expand your reasoning capacity and stimulate new ideas.

Also during this reading, you should answer the questions at the bottom of the pages of the essay (the "bridge" questions). These questions are marked throughout the text both in the essay and at the bottom of the pages by numbers within diamonds. Then, you might ask some additional questions of your own. You will get the most out of this process if you respond in writing. Keeping a journal to collect these responses is especially effective as you work to make this essay your own. Here are some sample student responses to the bridge questions accompanying the Thomas essay.

1. Sample response: Computers can supply us with more memory than we could ever have. Perhaps we even rely on them too much for this service. On the other hand, I think we can reason on more complex levels than the computer can.

2. Sample response: Errors on the computer, like errors made by humans, might lead to new discoveries or new insights into old theories and observations.

3. Sample response: I have made several mistakes that turned out to be beneficial: I dated a guy who turned out to be a negative force in my life, which helped me understand what it means to be happy; I followed a lead on the Internet that taught me an important lesson; and I learned a lot about myself when I discovered a mistake I made on a math test.

4. Sample response: Compared to cats and dogs, we are definitely programmed to make mistakes. We are not meant to do everything perfectly, and we learn from our mistakes—in both positive and negative ways.

5. Sample response: My guess is that Thomas means we will be stunned by our new discoveries and ready to break into the clear—like a football player running freely with the ball.

6. Sample response: This ending sounds like a new beginning ("stunned," "into the clear"), which is an effective way to end his essay and get his point across.

Then, during your third reading, you should consciously read "against the grain," actively doubting and challenging what the author is saying. Do some detective work and look closely at the assumptions on which the essay is based: For example, how does the writer move from idea to idea? What hidden assertions lie behind these ideas? Do you agree or disagree with these assertions? Your assessment of these unspoken assumptions will often play a major role in your critical response to an essay. In the case of Thomas's essay, do you accept the unspoken connection he makes between the workings of the human brain and the computer? What parts of the essay hinge on your acceptance of this connection? What other assumptions are fundamental to Thomas's reasoning? If you accept his thinking along the way, you are more likely to agree with the general flow of Thomas's essay. If you discover a flaw in his premises or assumptions, your acceptance of his argument will start to break down.

Next, answer the questions that follow the essay. The "Understanding Details" questions will help you understand and remember what you have read on both the literal and the interpretive levels. Some of the questions (the literal questions) ask you to restate various important points the author makes; others (the interpretive questions) help you see relationships among the different ideas presented.

UNDERSTANDING DETAILS

Literal	1. According to Thomas, in what ways are computers and humans similar? How are they different?
Literal/ Interpretive	2. How do we learn by "trial and error"? Why is this a useful way to learn?
Interpretive	3. What does Thomas mean by the statement, "If we were not provided with the knack of being wrong, we could never get anything useful done" (paragraph 6)?
Interpretive	4. According to Thomas, in what important ways do humans and "lower" animals differ? What does this comparison have to do with Thomas's main line of reasoning?

The "Reading Critically" questions require you to analyze and evaluate some of the writer's ideas in order to form valid opinions of your own. These questions demand a higher level of thought than the previous set and help you prepare more specifically for the discussion/writing assignments that follow the questions.

READING CRITICALLY

Analytical	1. What is Thomas's main point in this essay? How do the references to computers help make his case?
Analytical	2. In paragraph 10, Thomas explains that an argument must precede the beginning of something new and different. Do you think this is an accurate observation? Explain your answer.
Analytical	3. Why does Thomas perceive human error as such a positive quality? What does "exploration" have to do with this quality (paragraph 12)?
Analytical	4. What could we gain from "the near infinity of precise, machine-made miscomputation" (paragraph 14)? In what ways would our civilization advance?

The "Discovering Rhetorical Strategies" questions ask you to look closely at what strategies the writer uses to develop his or her thesis and how those strategies work. The questions address important features of the writer's composing process, such as word choice, use of detail, transitions, statement of purpose, organization of ideas, sentence structure, and paragraph development. The intent of these questions is to raise various elements of the composing process to the conscious level so you can use them later in your own essays. If you are able to understand and describe what choices a writer makes to create certain effects in his or her prose, you are more likely to be able to discover the range of choices available to you as you write, and you will also become more aware of your ability to control your readers' thoughts and feelings.

DISCOVERING RHETORICAL STRATEGIES

1. Thomas begins his essay with a list of experiences most of us have had at one time or another. Do you find this an effective beginning? Why or why not?

2. Which main points in his essay does Thomas develop in most detail? Why do you think he chooses to develop these points so thoroughly?

3. Explain the simile Thomas uses in paragraph 6: "Mistakes are at the very base of human thought, embedded there, feeding the structure like root nodules." Is this comparison between mistakes and root nodules useful in this context? Why or why not? Find another simile or metaphor in this essay, and explain how it works.

4. What principal rhetorical strategies does Thomas use to make his point? Give examples of each from the essay.

A final set of questions, "Making Connections," asks you to consider the essay you have just read in reference to other essays in this book. The questions are written so you can focus in your responses only on the essays you have read. The questions may have you compare the writers' treatment of an idea, the authors' style of writing, the differences in their opinions, or the similarities between their views of the world. Such questions will help you see connections in your own life—not only in your reading and your immediate environment, but also in the larger world around you. These questions, in particular, encourage you to move from specific references in the selections to a broader range of issues and circumstances that affect your daily life.

MAKING CONNECTIONS

1. Kimberly Wozencraft ("Notes from the Country Club") and Judith Wallerstein and Sandra Blakeslee ("Second Chances for Children of Divorce") refer both directly and indirectly to learning from mistakes. Would Lewis Thomas agree with either of their approaches to this topic? In what ways do these authors agree about the benefits of making errors? In what ways do they differ on the topic? Explain your answer.

2. Lewis Thomas, Jessica Mitford ("Behind the Formaldehyde Curtain"), and Michael Dorris ("The Broken Cord") all write about the intersection of science and humanity. Which of these authors, from what you have read, is most intrigued by the human aspect of this equation? Explain your answer.

3. According to Thomas, humans are complex organisms with a great deal of untapped potential. Maya Angelou ("New Directions") and Barbara Ehrenreich ("The Ecstasy of War") also comment on the uniqueness of human beings. In what ways do these three writers agree or disagree with each other on the intelligence and resourcefulness of humans? To what extent would each author argue that we use our mental capacities wisely and completely? Explain your answer.

WRITING CRITICALLY

The last stage of responding to the reading selections in this text offers you various "Ideas for Discussion/Writing" that will allow you to demonstrate the different skills you have learned in each chapter. This material includes questions to consider before you write followed by the writing topics themselves. You will be most successful if you envision each writing experience as an organic process that follows a natural, recursive cycle of prewriting, writing, and rewriting. The Writing Inventory at the end of this chapter will also guide you through this process.

IDEAS FOR DISCUSSION/WRITING

Preparing to Write

Write freely about an important mistake you have made: How did the mistake make you feel? What (if anything) did you learn from this mistake? What did you fail to learn that you should have learned? Did this mistake have any positive impact on your life? What were its negative consequences? How crucial are mistakes in our lives?

Choosing a Topic

1. *Learning Online:* Return to the game you played in "Preparing to Read." If you could change a mistake you made in this game, what mistake would you fix? Why would you rethink this play? Write an analysis in which you reflect on this mistake and offer an explanation of its consequences and outcomes. Then, relate the lesson you learned to a similar life experience.

2. You have decided to write an editorial for your local newspaper concerning the impact of computers on our lives. Cite specific experiences you have had with computers to help make your main point.

3. You have been invited back to your high school to make a speech to a senior English class about how people can learn from their mistakes. Write your speech in the form of an essay explaining what you learned from a crucial mistake you have made. Use examples to show these students that mistakes can be positive factors in their lives.
4. In an essay for your writing class, explain one specific human quality. Use Thomas's essay as a model. Cite examples to support your explanation.

Preparing to Write

The prewriting phase involves choosing a subject, generating ideas, selecting and narrowing a topic, analyzing an audience, and developing a purpose. Preceding the writing assignments are "Preparing to Write" questions you should respond to before trying to structure your thoughts into a coherent essay. These questions will assist you in generating new thoughts on the topics that follow and may even stimulate new approaches to old ideas. Keeping a journal in response to these questions is an excellent technique because you will then have a record of your opinions on various subjects related to the writing assignments. No matter what format you use to answer these questions, the activity of prewriting generally continues in various forms throughout the writing process.

Responses to the prewriting questions can be prompted by a number of different "invention" techniques and carried out by individuals, in pairs, in small groups, or as a class project. Invention strategies can help you generate responses to these questions and discover related ideas through the various stages of writing your papers. Because you will undoubtedly vary your approach to different assignments, you should be familiar with all the following choices available to you.

Brainstorming.   The basis of brainstorming is free association. Ideally, you should get a group of students together and bounce ideas, words, and thoughts off one another until they begin to cluster around related topics. If you don't have a group of students handy, brainstorm by yourself or with a friend. The exchange of thoughts usually starts orally but should transfer to paper when your ideas begin to settle into related categories. The act of recording your ideas becomes a catalyst for other thoughts; you are essentially setting up a dialogue with yourself or with others on paper. Then, keep writing down words and phrases that occur to you until they begin to fall into logical subdivisions or until your new ideas come to an end.

Freewriting. Freewriting means writing to discover what you want to say. Set a time limit of about ten minutes, and write by free association. Write about what you are seeing, feeling, touching, thinking; write about having nothing to say; recopy the sentence you just wrote—anything. Just keep writing on paper or on a computer. After you have generated some material, locate an idea that is central to your writing assignment, put it at the top of another page, and start freewriting again, letting your thoughts take shape around this central idea. This second type of preparation is called *focused freewriting* and is especially valuable when you already have a specific topic.

Journal Entries. Journal entries are much like freewriting, except you have some sense of an audience—probably either your instructor or yourself. In a journal, anything goes. You can respond to the "Preparing to Write" questions, jot down thoughts, paste up articles that spark your interest, write snippets of dialogue, draft letters (the kind you never send), record dreams, or make lists. The possibilities are endless. An excellent way of practicing writing, keeping a journal is also a wonderful means of stimulating new ideas—a way of fixing them in your mind and making them yours.

Direct Questions. This technique involves asking a series of questions useful in any writing situation to generate ideas, arrange thoughts, or revise prose. One example of this strategy is to use the inquiries journalists rely on to develop their articles:

Who:	*Who played the game?*
	Who won the game?
What:	*What kind of game was it?*
	What happened in the game?
Why:	*Why was the game played?*
Where:	*Where was the game played?*
When:	*When was the game played?*
How:	*How was the game played?*

If you ask yourself questions of this type on a specific topic, you will begin to produce thoughts and details that will undoubtedly be useful to you in the writing assignments that follow.

Clustering. Clustering is a method of drawing or mapping your ideas as fast as they come into your mind. Put a word, phrase, or sentence in a circle in the center of a blank page. Then put every new idea that comes to you in its own circle and show its relationship to a previous thought by drawing a line to the circle containing the original thought. You will probably reach a natural stopping point for this exercise in two to three minutes.

Although you can generate ideas in a number of different ways, the main principle behind the "Preparing to Write" questions in this text is to encourage you to do what is called *expressive writing* before you tackle any writing assignment. This is writing based on your feelings, thoughts, experiences, observations, and opinions. The process of answering questions about your own ideas and experiences makes you "think on paper," thereby enabling you to surround yourself with your own thoughts and opinions. From this reservoir, you can then choose the ideas you want to develop into an essay and begin writing about them one at a time.

As you use various prewriting techniques to generate responses to the "Preparing to Write" questions, you should know that these responses can (and probably will) appear in many different forms. You can express yourself in lists, outlines, random notes, sentences, paragraphs, charts, graphs, or pictures—whatever keeps the thoughts flowing smoothly and productively. One of our students used a combination of brainstorming and clustering to generate the following thoughts in response to the prewriting exercise for the Thomas essay:

Brainstorming

Mistakes:

happen when I'm in a hurry	*getting back on track*
make me feel stupid	*parents*
love	*corrections*
relationships	*learning from mistakes*
trip back East	*I am a better person*
pride	*my values are clear*
going in circles	*mistakes help us change*
Bob	*painful*
learned a lot about people	*helpful*
people aren't what they seem	*valuable*

Clustering

From the free-flowing thoughts you generate, you need to decide what to write about and how to limit your subject to a manageable length. Our student writer chose topic 2 from the "Choosing a Topic" list after the essay (see pages 35–36). Her initial responses to the prewriting questions helped her decide to write on "A Time I Got Lost." She then generated more focused ideas and opinions in the form of a journal entry. It is printed here just as she wrote it, errors and all.

Journal Entry

The craziest mistake I think I ever made was on a trip I took recently—I was heading to the east coast from California and reached Durham, North Carolina. I was so excited because I was going to get to see the Atlantic Ocean for the first time in my life and Durham was one of my last landmarks before I reached the sea. In Durham I was going to have to change from a northeast direction to due east.

When I got there the highway was under construction. I took the detour, but got all skrewed up till I realized that I had gone the wrong direction. By this time I was lost somewhere in downtown Durham and didn't know which way was east. I stoped and asked a guy at a gas station and he explained how to get back on the east-bound high-way. The way was through the middle of town. By the time I got to where I was supposed to turn right I could only turn left. So I started left and then realized I couldn't turn back the other way! I made a couple of other stops after that, and one jerk told me I "just couldn't get there from here." Eventually I found a truck driver heading toward the same eastbound highway, and he told me to follow him. An hour and forty minutes after reaching Durham's city limits I finally managed to leave going east. I felt as if I had spent an entire month there!

The thing I learned from this was just how egocentric I am. I would not have made this error if I had not been so damn cocky about my sense of direction. My mistake was made worse because I got flustered and didn't listen to the directions clearly. I find that the reason I most often make a mistake is because I don't listen carefully to instructions. This has been a problem all my life.

After I got over feeling really dum I decided this kind of thing was not going to happen again. It was too much a waste of time and gas, so I was going to be more careful of road signs and directions.

This all turned out to be a positive experience though. I learned that there are lots of friendly, helpful people. It was kind of reassuring to know that other folks would help you if you just asked.

I feel this and other mistakes are crucial not only to my life but to my personal growth in general. It is the making of mistakes that helps people learn where they are misdirecting their energies. I think mistakes can help all of us learn to be more careful about some part of our lives. This is why mistakes are crucial. Otherwise, we would continue in the same old rut and never improve.

This entry served as the foundation upon which the student built her essay. Her next step was to consider *audience* and *purpose* (which are often written into the writing assignments in this text). The first of these features identifies the person or group of people you will address in your essay. The second is a declaration of your principal reason for writing the essay, which usually takes the form of a thesis statement (the statement of purpose or the controlling idea of an essay). Together these pieces of information consciously or subconsciously help you make most of the decisions you are faced with as you write: what words to choose, what sentence structures to use, what order to present ideas in, which topics to develop, and which to summarize. Without a doubt, the more you know about your audience (for example, age, educational background, likes, dislikes, biases, political persuasion, and social status) and your purpose (to inform, persuade, and/or entertain), the easier the writing task will be. In the rough draft and final draft of the essay in the section that follows, the student knew she was writing to a senior English class at her old high school in order to convince them that mistakes can be positive factors in their lives. This clear sense of audience and purpose helped her realize she should use fairly advanced vocabulary, call upon a variety of sentence structures, and organize her ideas chronologically to make her point most effectively to her intended audience.

At this stage of the writing process, some people benefit from assembling their ideas in the form of an outline. Others use an outline to double-check their logic and organization after they write their first draft. Whether your outlines are informal (a simple list) or more structured, they can help you visualize the logical relationship of your ideas to each other. We recommend using a rough outline throughout the prewriting and writing stages to ensure that your work is carefully and tightly organized. Your outline, however, should be adjusted to your draft as it develops.

Writing

The writing stage asks you to draft an essay based on the prewriting material you have assembled. Because you have already made the important preliminary decisions regarding your topic, your audience, and your purpose, the task of actually writing the essay should follow naturally. (Notice we did not say this task should necessarily be easy—just natural.) At this stage, you ought to look upon your essay as a way of solving a problem or answering a question: The problem/question is posed in your writing assignment, and the solution/answer is your essay.

The four "Choosing a Topic" assignments that follow the prewriting questions throughout the text invite you to consider issues related to the essay you just read. Although they typically ask you to focus on one particular rhetorical pattern, they draw on many rhetorical strategies (as do all writing assignments in the text) and require you to support your statements with concrete examples. The assignments for the Lewis Thomas essay (Choosing a Topic, pp. 35–36) emphasize the use of example, his dominant rhetorical strategy.

The following essay is our student's first-draft response to topic 2. After writing her journal entry, the student drafted a tentative thesis statement: "I know there are positive changes that can come from making a mistake because I recently had an opportunity to learn some valuable lessons from one of my errors." This statement helped the student writer further develop and organize her ideas as she focused finally on one well-chosen example to illustrate her thesis. At this point, the thesis is simply the controlling idea around which the other topics take shape; it is often revised several times before the final draft.

First Draft: A Time I Got Lost

Parents and teachers frequently pressure us to avoid committing errors. Meanwhile, our friends laugh at us when we make mistakes. With all these different messages, it is hard for us to think of mistakes as positive events. But if any of you take the time to think about what you have learned from mistakes, I bet you will realize all the good things that have come from these events. I know there are positive changes that can come from making a mistake because I recently had an opportunity to learn some valuable lessons in this way.

While traveling back east this last summer, I made the mistake of turning west on an interstate detour in order to reach the Atlantic Ocean. The adventure took me into the heart of Durham, North Carolina, where I got totally lost. I had to get directions several times until two hours later I was going in the right direction. As I was driving out of town, I realized that although I had made a dumb mistake, I had learned a great deal. Overall, the detour was actually a positive experience.

The first thing I remember thinking after I had gotten my wits together was that I had definitely learned something from making the mistake. I had the opportunity to see a new city, filled with new people—3,000 miles from my own hometown, but very much like it. I also became aware that the beach is not always toward the west, as it is in California. The entire experience was like getting a geography lesson firsthand.

As this pleasant feeling began to grow, I came to another realization. I was aware of how important other people can be in making a mistake into a positive experience. My first reaction was "Oh no, someone is going to know I made a mistake!" But the amazing part about this mistake was how supportive everyone was. The townspeople had been entirely willing to help someone they did not know. This mistake helped me learn that people tend to be nicer than I had imagined.

The final lesson I learned from getting lost in Durham was how to be more cautious about my actions so as not to repeat the same mistake. It was this internalization of all the information I gleaned from making the mistake that I see as the most positive part of the experience. I realized that in order to avoid such situations in the future I would have to be less egocentric in my decisions and more willing to listen to directions from other people. I needed to learn that my set way of doing things was not always the best way. If I had not made the mistake, I would not have been aware of my other options.

By making this mistake I learned that there is a more comprehensive manner of looking at the world. In the future, if we could all stop after making a mistake and ask ourselves, "What can I learn from this?" we would be less critical of ourselves and have a great many more positive experiences. If I were not able to make mistakes, I would probably not be able to expand my knowledge of my environment, my sense of others, and my understanding of myself.

Rewriting

The rewriting stage includes (1) revising, (2) editing, and (3) proofreading. The first of these activities, *revising*, actually starts as you are writing a draft when you change words, recast sentences, and move whole paragraphs from one place to another. Making these linguistic and organizational choices means you will also be constantly adjusting your content to your purpose (what you want to accomplish) and your audience (the readers) in much the same way you alter your speech to communicate more effectively in response to the gestures, eye movements, or facial expressions of your listeners. Revising is literally the act of "re-seeing" your essay, looking at it through your readers' eyes to determine whether or not it achieves its purpose. As you revise, you should consider matters of both content and form on the checklists attached to this book's cover.

Revising the Content
√ Does my essay have a clear, interesting title?
√ Will my statement of purpose or thesis be clear to my audience?
√ Will the introduction make my audience want to read the rest of my essay?
√ Have I included enough details to prove my main points?
√ Does my conclusion sum up my central points?
√ Will I accomplish my purpose with my audience?

Revising the Form
√ Have I organized my ideas as effectively as possible for this specific audience?
√ Do I use appropriate rhetorical strategies to support my main points?
√ Is my sentence structure varied and interesting?
√ Is my vocabulary appropriate for my topic, purpose, and audience?

If you compose on a computer, you will certainly reap the benefits as you revise. Computers remove much of the drudgery of rewriting your drafts since they allow you to move paragraphs or whole sections of your paper from one position to another by pressing a few keys. As a result, you can immediately see if the new organization will improve the logic and coherence of your paper. You may then remove repetitions or insert words and sentences that will serve as the transitions between sections. If you write out your drafts, you may not make as many major revisions as necessary because of the length of time needed to rewrite the material.

You should also consider the value of the graphic design options available in computer software because the way you present your papers generally affects how your instructor evaluates them. If they are clearly laid out without coffee stains or paw prints from your dog, you have a better chance of being taken seriously than if they are sloppily done. A computer can help in this regard, giving you access to boldface type, italics, boxes, bullets, and graphs of all sorts and letting you make a new copy if you do have an unexpected encounter with a coffee cup or a frisky dog.

Editing entails correcting mistakes in your writing so that your final draft conforms to the conventions of standard written English. Correct punctuation, spelling, and mechanics will help you make your points and will encourage your readers to move smoothly through your essay from topic to topic. At this stage, you should be concerned about such matters as whether your sentences are complete, whether your punctuation is correct and effective, whether you have followed conventional rules for using mechanics, and whether the words in your essay are spelled correctly. Refer to the checklist in the front of this book for specific editing questions.

Proofreading involves reading over your entire essay, slowly and carefully, to make certain you have not allowed any errors to slip into your final draft because most college instructors don't look upon errors as kindly as Thomas does. In general, good writers try to let some time elapse between writing the final draft and proofreading it (at least a few hours, or even a day or so). Otherwise, they find themselves proofreading their thoughts rather than their words. Some writers even profit from proofreading their papers backward— a technique that allows them to focus on individual words and phrases rather than on entire sentences. Use the checklist at the front of this book to guide your proofreading.

Following is the student's revised draft of her essay on making mistakes in life. The final draft of this typical freshman essay (written to high school seniors, as the assignment specifies) represents the entire writing process at work. We have made notes in the margin to highlight various effective elements in her essay, some of which we have underlined for emphasis. The various rhetorical modes she draws on are listed in the margins in brackets.

Mistakes and Maturity

Catchy title; good change from first draft

Parents and teachers frequently harp on us to cor– rect our errors. Meanwhile, our friends laugh at us when we make mistakes. With all these negative mes– sages, most of us have a hard time believing that prob– lems can be positive experiences. But if we take the time to think about what we have learned from vari– ous blunders, we will realize all the good that has come from these events. <u>I know that making mistakes can have positive results because I recently learned several valuable lessons from one unforgettable experience.</u>

Rapport with audience and point of view established

Clear, stimulating introduction for high school seniors

Revised thesis statement

Good, brief summary of complex experience (see journal entry from Preparing to Write)

<u>While I was traveling on the East Coast last sum– mer,</u> I made the mistake of turning west on an inter– state detour in an attempt to reach the Atlantic Ocean. This adventure took me into the center of Durham, North Carolina, where I became totally lost, bewil– dered, and angry at myself. I had to ask for directions several times until two hours later, when I finally found the correct highway toward the ocean. As I was

Background information

Good details

driving out of town, I realized that although I had [Narration] made a "dumb" mistake, I had actually learned a great deal. Overall, my adventure had been quite positive.

First topic (topics are in chronological order)

Adequate number of examples

    The first insight I remember having after my wits returned was that <u>I had definitely learned more about United States geography from making this mistake</u>. I had become intimately acquainted with a town 3,000 miles from home that greatly resembled my own city, [Examples] and I had become aware that the beach is not always toward the west, as it is in California. I had also met some pleasant strangers. <u>Looking at my confusion as</u> Nice close <u>a learning experience encouraged me to have posi-</u> to this <u>tive feelings about the mistake.</u> paragraph

[Cause/Effect]

Clear explanation with details

[Description]

    As I relaxed and let this happy feeling grow, I came to another realization. <u>I became aware of how im-</u> Second <u>portant other people can be in turning a mistake into</u> topic <u>a positive event.</u> Although my first reaction had been "Oh, no! Someone is going to know I'm lost," I was amazed by how supportive other people were during my panic and embarrassment. From an old man swinging on his front porch to an elementary school [Examples] boy crossing the street with his bright blue backpack, I found that the townspeople of Durham were entirely willing to help someone they did not even know. <u>I realized that people in general are nicer than</u> Good <u>I had previously thought.</u> summary statement

Third topic

[Process Analysis]

    The final lesson I learned from making this mistake was <u>how to be more cautious about my future decisions.</u> This insight was, in fact, the most positive part Specific of the entire experience. What I realized I must do to details prevent similar errors in the future was to relax, not be [Cause/so bullheaded in my decisions, and be more willing to Effect] listen to directions from other people. <u>I might never</u> Good <u>have had these positive realizations if I had not made</u> summary <u>this mistake.</u> statement

Clear transition statement

[Cause/Effect]

    Thus, <u>by driving in circles for two hours, I devel-</u> <u>oped a more comprehensive way of looking at the</u> Good <u>world.</u> If I were unable to make mistakes, I probably summary of would not have had this chance to <u>learn about my</u> three topics <u>environment, improve my impressions of strangers,</u> without and <u>reconsider the egocentric way in which I act in</u> being <u>certain situations.</u> Perhaps there's a lesson here for all repetitive

[Process Analysis] of us. Instead of criticizing ourselves unduly, if each one of us could pause after we make an error and ask, "How can I profit from this?" <u>we would realize that mistakes can often be turned into positive events that will help us become more confident and mature.</u>

Nicely focused concluding remark

Concluding statement applicable to all readers

As these various drafts of the student paper indicate, the essay assignments in this book encourage you to transfer to your own writing an understanding of how form and content work together. If you use the short-answer questions after each reading selection as a guide, the writing assignments will help you learn how to give shape to your own ideas and how to gain control of your readers' thoughts and feelings. In essence, they help you recognize the power you have through language over your life and your environment.

READING AND WRITING INVENTORIES

Because checklists can provide a helpful method of reviewing important information, we offer a series of questions on the next two pages that represent the reading and writing processes. All these guidelines can be summarized in a checklist for reading and writing academic assignments in any discipline. We recommend that you use these guidelines as you read each essay and then write a response to it. Keeping a continuous journal of your responses to your readings and your ideas for writing assignments is an excellent way to improve your reading and writing.

SOME FINAL THOUGHTS

As you approach the essays in this text, remember that both reading and writing function most efficiently as processes of discovery. Through these skills, you can educate and expand your own mind and the minds of your readers. They can provide a powerful means of discovering new information or clarifying what you already know. Reading and writing lead to understanding. And just as you can discover how to read through writing, so too can you become more aware of the details of the writing process through reading. But always keep in mind that the generating force that fuels these two skills is critical thinking. We hope your time spent with this book is both pleasant and profitable as you refine your ability to discover and express effectively the good ideas within yourself.

THE READING AND WRITING PROCESSES

Using these checklists to respond to and prepare for every reading and writing assignment will help you generate a number of useful ideas and plans throughout your writing course.

READING INVENTORY

Preparing to Read

Title
√ What can I infer from the title of the essay?
√ Who do I think is the author's audience? What is the principal purpose of the essay?

Synopsis
√ What is the general subject of the essay?
√ What is the author's approach to the subject?

Biography
√ What do I know about the author's age, political stance, general beliefs?
√ How qualified is the author to write on this subject?
√ When did the author write the essay? Under what conditions? In what context?

Prereading Questions
√ Where was the essay first published?
√ What would I like to learn about this topic?
√ What are some of my opinions on this subject?

Reading
√ What are the essay's main ideas?
√ What words do I need to look up?
√ What are my initial reactions to the ideas in this essay?

Rereading
√ What do I agree with in this essay? What do I disagree with?
√ What assumptions underlie the author's reasoning?
√ Do I have a solid interpretive understanding of this essay? Do I understand the relationship among ideas? What conclusions can I draw from this essay?
√ Do I have an accurate analytical understanding of this essay? Which ideas can I take apart, examine, and put back together again? What is my evaluation of this material?
√ Do I understand the rhetorical strategies the writer uses and the way they work? What are the effects of these strategies?
√ How does the author achieve his or her purpose in this essay?

WRITING INVENTORY

Preparing to Write
√ Do I understand my assignment?
√ Have I narrowed my topic adequately?
√ Who is my audience (What are their likes/dislikes? What is their educational level? Their knowledge of the subject?)
√ What is my purpose?

Writing
√ Can I express my thesis as a problem or question?
√ Is my essay a solution or an answer to that problem or question?

Rewriting
Revising the Content
√ Does my essay have a clear, interesting title?
√ Will my statement of purpose or thesis be clear to my audience?
√ Will the introduction make my audience want to read the rest of my essay?
√ Have I included enough details to prove my main points?
√ Does my conclusion sum up my central points?
√ Will I accomplish my purpose with my audience?

Revising the Form
√ Have I organized my ideas as effectively as possible for this specific audience?
√ Do I use appropriate rhetorical strategies to support my main points?
√ Is my sentence structure varied and interesting?
√ Is my vocabulary appropriate for my topic, purpose, and audience?

Editing and Proofreading
√ Have I written complete sentences throughout the essay?
√ Have I used punctuation correctly and effectively (check especially the use of commas, apostrophes, colons, and semicolons)?
√ Have I followed conventional rules for mechanics (capitalization, underlining or italics, abbreviations, and numbers)?
√ Are all the words in my essay spelled correctly? (Use a dictionary or a spell-checker when in doubt.)

Part II

Reading and Writing Critically

Chapter 4

DESCRIPTION
Exploring through the Senses

All of us use description in our daily lives. We might, for example, try to convey the horrors of a recent history exam to our parents, help a friend visualize someone we met on vacation, or describe the cars in an accident for a police report. Whatever our specific purpose, description is a fundamental part of communication: We give and receive descriptions constantly, and our lives are continually affected by this simple yet important rhetorical technique.

DEFINING DESCRIPTION

Description may be defined as the act of capturing people, places, events, objects, and feelings in words so that a reader (or listener) can visualize and respond to them. Unlike narration, which traditionally presents events in a clear time sequence, description essentially suspends its objects in time, making them exempt from the limits of chronology. Narration tells a story, while pure description contains no action or time. Description is one of our primary forms of self-expression; it paints a verbal picture that helps the reader understand or share a sensory experience through the process of *showing* rather than *telling*. *Telling* your friends, for example, that "the campgrounds were filled with friendly, happy activities" is not as engaging as *showing* them by saying, "The campgrounds were alive with the smell of spicy baked beans, the sound of high-pitched laughter, and the sight of happy families sharing the warmth of a fire." Showing your readers helps them understand your experience through as many senses as possible.

Descriptions fall somewhere between two extremes: (1) totally objective reports (with no trace of opinions or feelings), such as we might find in a dictionary or an encyclopedia; and (2) very subjective accounts, which focus almost exclusively on personal impressions. The same horse, for instance, might be described by one writer as "a large, solid-hoofed herbivorous mammal having a long mane and a tail" (objective) and by another as "a magnificent and spirited beast flaring its nostrils in search of adventure" (subjective). Most descriptive writing, however, falls somewhere between these two extremes: "a large, four-legged beast in search of adventure."

Objective description is principally characterized by its impartial, precise, and emotionless tone. Found most prominently in technical and scientific writing, such accounts might include a description of equipment to be used in a chemistry experiment, the results of a market survey for a particular consumer product, or a medical appraisal of a heart patient's physical symptoms. In situations like these, accurate, unbiased, and easily understandable accounts are of the utmost importance.

Subjective description, in contrast, is intentionally created to produce a particular response in the reader or listener. Focusing on feelings rather than on raw data, it tries to activate as many senses as possible, thereby leading the audience to a specific conclusion or state of mind. Examples of subjective descriptions are a parent's disapproving comments about one of your friends, a professor's glowing analysis of your most recent "A" paper, or a basketball coach's critique of the team's losing effort in last night's big game.

In most situations, the degree of subjectivity or objectivity in a descriptive passage depends to a large extent on the writer's purpose and intended audience. In the case of the heart patient mentioned above, the person's physician might present the case in a formal, scientific way to a group of medical colleagues; in a personal, sympathetic way to the invalid's spouse; and in financial terms to a number of potential contributors in order to solicit funds for heart disease research.

The following paragraph describes one student's fond memories of visiting a farm. As you read it, notice the writer's use of subjective description to communicate to her readers the multitude of contradictory feelings she connects with this rural retreat.

> *The shrill scream of the alarm shatters a dream. This is the last day of my visit to the place I call "the farm," an old ramshackle house in the country owned by one of my aunts. I want to go out once more in the peace of the early morning,*

walk in the crisp and chilly fields, and breathe the sweet air. My body feels jarred as my feet hit the hard-packed clay dirt. I tune out my stiff muscles and cold arms and legs and instead focus on two herons playing hopscotch on the canal bank: Every few yards I walk toward them, they fly one over the other an almost equal distance away from me. A killdeer with its piercing crystalline cry dips its body as it flies low over the water, the tip of its wing leaving a ring to reverberate outward. The damp earth has a strong, rich, musky scent. To the east, dust rises, and for the first time I hear the clanking and straining of a tractor as it harrows smooth the soil before planting. A crop duster rises close by just as it cuts off its release of spray, the acrid taste of chemicals filtering down through the air. As the birds chatter and peck at the fields, I reluctantly return to my life in the city.

THINKING CRITICALLY THROUGH DESCRIPTION

Each rhetorical mode in this book gives us new insights into the process of thinking by providing different options for arranging our thoughts and our experiences. The more we know about these options, the more conscious we become of how our minds operate and the better chance we have to improve and refine our communication skills.

As you examine description as a way of thinking, consider it in isolation for a moment—away from the other rhetorical modes. Think of it as a muscle you can isolate and strengthen on its own in a weight-training program before you ask it to perform together with other muscles. By isolating description, you will learn more readily what it entails and how it functions as a critical-thinking tool. In the process, you will also strengthen your knowledge of how to recognize and use description more effectively in your reading, in your writing, and in your daily life.

Just as you exercise to strengthen muscles, so too will you benefit from doing exercises to improve your skill in using descriptive techniques. As you have learned, description depends to a great extent on the keenness of your senses. So as you prepare to read and write descriptive essays, do the following tasks so that you can first learn what the process of description feels like in your own head. Really use your imagination to play with these exercises on as many different levels as possible. Also write when you are asked to do so. The combination of thinking and writing is often especially useful when you practice your thinking skills.

1. Imagine what you might smell, taste, hear, feel, or see in the photograph taken by Gerry Gavigan (on page 54). Then, using words that will create these sensory details, write a few sentences that might accompany this photograph if it were published in a newspaper or travel magazine.
2. Make a list of five descriptive words you would use to trigger each of the following senses: taste, sight, hearing, touch, and smell.

© Gerry Gavigan/Growbag

3. Choose an unusual object and brainstorm about its physical characteristics. Then brainstorm about the emotions this object evokes. Why is this object so unusual or special? Compare your two brainstorming results, and draw some conclusions about their differences.

READING AND WRITING DESCRIPTIVE ESSAYS

All good descriptions share four fundamental qualities: (1) an accurate sense of audience (who the readers are) and purpose (why the essay was written), (2) a clear vision of the object being described, (3) a careful selection of details that help communicate the author's vision, and (4) a consistent point of view or perspective from which a writer composes. The dominant impression or main effect the writer wishes to leave with a specific audience dictates virtually all of the verbal choices in a descriptive essay. Although description is featured in this chapter, you should also pay close attention to how other rhetorical strategies (such as example, division/classification, and cause/effect) can best support an essay's dominant impression.

Reading Descriptive Essays

- What is the essay's dominant impression?
- Is the essay mainly objective or subjective?
- What senses does the author engage?

Preparing to Read.   As you approach the reading selections in this chapter, you should focus first on the author's title and try to make some initial assumptions about the essay that follows: Does Ray Bradbury reveal his attitude toward his subject in the title "Summer Rituals"? Can you guess what the general mood of Kimberly Wozencraft's "Notes from the Country Club" will be? Then scan the essay to discover its audience and purpose: Why does Linda Hogan write an essay about "dwellings"? Whom is Malcolm Cowley addressing in "The View from 80"? What do you think John McPhee's purpose is in "The Pines"? You should also read the synopsis of each essay in the Rhetorical Table of Contents (on pages vii–xvii); these brief summaries will provide you with helpful information at this point in the reading process.

Next, learn as much as you can about the author and the conditions under which the essay was composed; this information is provided in the biographical statement before each essay. For a descriptive essay, the conditions under which the author wrote the essay, coupled with his or her purpose, can be very revealing: When and under what conditions did Kimberly Wozencraft write "Notes from the Country Club"? What was her intention in writing the essay? Can you determine when Malcolm Cowley's piece was written? Does it describe the author's life now or in the past? Learning where the essay was first published will also give you valuable information about its audience.

Last, before you begin to read, try to do some brainstorming on the essay's title. In this chapter, respond to the Preparing to Read questions before each essay, which ask you to begin thinking and writing about the topic under consideration. At the same time, take advantage of the Internet prompt to help you find more information on the topic you are about to consider. Then pose your own questions: What are some of the most important rituals in your life (Bradbury)? What is one of your favorite places (Hogan)? What would you like to learn from Cowley about the joys and frustrations of being eighty years old?

Reading.   As you read each essay for the first time, jot down your initial reactions to it, and try to make connections and see relationships among the author's biography; the essay's title, purpose, and audience; and the synopsis. In this way, you will create a context or framework for your reading. See if you can figure out, for example, what Bradbury is implying about rituals in general in his essay "Summer Rituals" or why Wozencraft wrote an essay about her experiences in prison. Try to discover what the relationships are among purpose, audience, and publication information in Cowley's essay.

Also, determine at this point if the author's treatment of his or her subject is predominantly objective (generally free of emotion) or subjective (heavily charged with emotion). Or perhaps the essay falls somewhere between these two extremes.

In addition, make sure you have a general sense of the dominant impression each author is trying to convey. Such an initial approach to reading these descriptive selections will give you a foundation upon which to analyze the material during your second, more in-depth reading.

To help you develop the ability to read critically, a set of questions at the bottom of the essays' pages will prompt you to make connections between ideas, apply the material to your own experiences, and draw analytical conclusions that prepare you to answer the questions after each essay and ultimately write an essay on a related topic. These questions extend the mental exercises you complete before you read each essay to the deeper thinking you must do in the activities at the end of the essays. Responding to these questions in writing is the best way to discover new, innovative ideas about your reading on any subject.

Finally, at the end of your first reading, take a look at the questions after each essay to make certain you can answer them. This material will guide your rereading.

Rereading.   As you reread these descriptive essays, notice each author's careful selection of details that support his or her dominant impression. Also try to determine how certain details add to and detract from that dominant impression and how the writer's point of view affects it. Finally, get a sense of which senses the author is engaging to create this impression: How does Hogan create a sense of wonder in "Dwellings"? How does Cowley enable us to identify with his experiences if we have never been eighty years old?

During this reading, try to find other rhetorical modes that support the description. Although the essays in this chapter describe various persons, places, or objects, all of the authors call upon other rhetorical strategies (especially example and comparison/contrast) to communicate their descriptions. How do these various rhetorical strategies work together in each essay to create a coherent whole? In addition, all the authors attempt to get you to see their view of the world.

Finally, answering the questions after each essay will check your understanding of the author's main points and help you think critically about the essay in preparing for the discussion/writing assignments that follow.

For an inventory of the reading process, you may want to review the checklists at the end of Part I.

Writing Descriptive Essays

- Choose a dominant impression as your thesis.
- Find details that support your thesis.
- Engage all five senses.
- Choose a point of view.
- *Show* rather than *tell.*

Preparing to Write.   Before you choose a writing assignment, use the prewriting questions that follow each essay to help you discover your own ideas and opinions about the general topic of the essay. Next, choose an assignment or read the one assigned to you. Then, just as you do when you read an essay, you should determine the audience and purpose for your description (if these are not specified for you in the assignment). To whom are you writing? Why? Will an impartial, objective report be appropriate, or should you present a more emotional, subjective account to accomplish your task? In assessing your audience, you need to determine what they do and do not know about your topic. This information will help you make decisions about what you are going to say and how you will say it. Your purpose will be defined by what you intend your audience to know, think, or believe after they have read your descriptive essay. Do you want them to make up their own minds about summer rituals or old age, for example, based on an objective presentation of data, or do you hope to sway their opinions through a more subjective display of information? Or perhaps you will decide to blend the two techniques, combining facts and opinions in order to achieve the impression of personal certainty based on objective evidence. What dominant impression do you want to leave with your audience? As you might suspect, decisions regarding audience and purpose are as important to writing descriptions as they are to reading descriptions and will shape your descriptive essay from start to finish.

The second quality of good description concerns the object of your analysis and the clarity with which you present it to the reader. Whenever possible, you should thoroughly investigate the person, place, moment, or feeling you wish to describe, paying particular attention to its effect on each of your five senses. What can you see, smell, hear, taste, and touch as you examine it? If you want to describe your house, for example, begin by asking yourself a series of pertinent questions: How big is the house? What color is it? How many exterior doors does the house have? How many interior doors? Are any of the rooms wallpapered? If so, what are the colors and textures of that wallpaper? How many different shades of paint cover the walls? Which rooms have constant noises (for example, from clocks and other mechanical devices)? Are the kitchen appliances hot or cold to the touch? What is the quietest room in the house? The noisiest? What smells do you notice in the laundry? In the kitchen? In the basement? Most important, do any of these sensory questions trigger particular childhood memories? Although you will probably not use all of these details in your descriptive essay, the process of generating and answering such detailed questions will help reacquaint you with the object of your description as it also assists you in designing and focusing your paper.

To help you generate some of these ideas, you may want to review the prewriting techniques introduced on pages 36–38.

Writing.   As you write, you must select details for your description with great care and precision so that you leave your reader with a specific impression. Pay special attention to the way you engage all five senses in your description. If, for instance, you want your audience to feel the warmth and comfort of your home, you might concentrate on describing the plush carpets, the big upholstered chairs, the inviting scent of hot apple cider, and the crackling fire. If, on the other hand, you want to gain your audience's sympathy, you might prefer to focus on the sparse austerity of your home environment: the bare walls, the quietness, the lack of color and decoration, the dim lighting, and the frigid temperature. You also want to make sure you omit unrelated ideas, such as a conversation between your parents you accidentally overheard. Your careful choice of details will help control your audience's reaction.

The next important quality of an effective descriptive essay is point of view, your physical perspective on your subject. Because the organization of your essay depends on your point of view, you need to choose a specific angle from which to approach your description. If you verbally jump around your home, referring first to a picture on the wall in your bedroom, next to the microwave in the kitchen, and then to the quilt on your bed, no reasonable audience will be able to follow your description. Nor will they want to. If, however, you move from room to room in some logical, sequential way, always focusing on the details you want your readers to know, you will be helping your audience form a clear, memorable impression of your home. Your vision will become their vision. In other words, your point of view plays a part in determining the organization of your description. Working spatially, you could move from side to side (from one wall to another in the rooms we have discussed), from top to bottom (from ceiling to floor), or from far to near (from the farthest to the closest point in a room), or you might progress from large to small objects, from uninteresting to interesting, or from funny to serious. Whatever plan you choose should help you accomplish your purpose with your particular audience.

To make your impression even more vivid, you might use figurative language to fill out your descriptions. Using words figuratively means using them imaginatively rather than literally. The two most popular forms of figurative language are *simile* and *metaphor*. A *simile* is a comparison between two dissimilar objects or ideas introduced by *like* or *as*: "The rocking chairs sounded like crickets" (Bradbury). A *metaphor* is an implied comparison between two dissimilar objects or ideas and is not introduced by *like* or *as*: "Life for younger persons is still a battle royal of each against each" (Cowley). Besides enlivening your writing, figurative language helps your readers understand objects, feelings, and ideas that are complex or obscure by comparing them to those that are more familiar.

Rewriting.   As you reread each of your descriptive essays, play the role of your audience, and try to determine what dominant impression they will receive by the end of your reading.

- Do I create the dominant impression I want to convey?
- Do my details support this dominant impression?
- Which senses do I stimulate?
- Do I have a clear, consistent point of view toward my subject?
- Am I showing rather than telling in my description?
- Do I use similes or metaphors when appropriate?

For additional suggestions on the writing process, you may want to consult the Writing Inventory at the end of Part I.

STUDENT ESSAY: DESCRIPTION AT WORK

In the following essay, a student relives some of her childhood memories through a subjective description of her grandmother's house. As you read it, pay particular attention to the different types of sensual details the student writer chooses to communicate her dominant impression of her grandmother's home. Notice also her use of carefully chosen details to *show* rather than *tell* us about her childhood reminiscences, especially her comparisons, which make the memory as vivid for the reader as it is for the writer.

Grandma's House

Writer's point of view or perspective

Dominant impression

My most vivid childhood memories are set in my Grandma Goodlink's house, a curious blend of familiar and mysterious treasures. Grandma lived at the end of a dead-end street, in the same house she had lived in since the first day of her marriage. That was half a century and thirteen children ago. A set of crumbly steps made of concrete mixed with gravel led up to her front door. I remember a big gap between the house

and the steps, <u>as if someone had not pushed them up</u> Comparison (simile)
<u>close enough to the house</u>. Anyone who looked into
the gap <u>could see old toys and books</u> that had fallen
into the crack behind the steps and had remained
there, forever irretrievable.

   Only a hook-type lock on the front door protected Grandma's many beautiful antiques. Her liv-
ing room was set up <u>like a church or schoolroom</u>, Comparison (simile)
with an <u>old purple velvet couch</u> against the far wall
and two chairs immediately in front of the couch
facing the same direction. <u>One-half of the couch</u>
<u>was always buried in old clothes, magazines, and</u>
<u>newspapers, and a lone shoe sat on top of the pile,</u> Comparison (metaphor)
<u>a finishing touch to some bizarre modern sculpture</u>.
To one side was an aged and <u>tuneless</u> upright piano
with <u>yellowed keys</u>. The ivory overlay was missing so Sight
that <u>the wood underneath showed through</u>, and Sight
many of the keys made only a <u>muffled and frustrat-</u>
<u>ing thump</u>, no matter how hard I pressed them. On
the wall facing the piano was the room's only window, draped with <u>yellowed lace curtains</u>. Grandma Sight
always left that window open. I remember sitting
near it, <u>smelling the rain</u> while the curtains <u>tickled</u> Touch
<u>my face</u>.

   For no apparent reason, <u>an old curtain</u> hung in the Sight
door between the kitchen and the living room. In the
kitchen, a large Formica-topped table always held at
least a half-dozen varieties of <u>homemade jelly, as well</u> Taste
<u>as a loaf of bread, gooseberry pies or cherry pies with</u>
<u>the pits left in, boxes of cereal</u>, and anything else not
requiring refrigeration, <u>as if the table served as a small,</u> Comparison (simile)
<u>portable pantry</u>. Grandma's kitchen always <u>smelled of</u>
<u>toast</u>, and I often wondered—and still do—if she lived
entirely on toast. <u>A hole had eaten through the kitchen</u> Sight
<u>floor</u>, not just the warped yellow linoleum, but all the
way through the floor itself. My sisters and I never
wanted to take a bath at Grandma's house, because we
discovered that anyone who lay on the floor face down
and put one eye to the hole <u>could see the bathtub</u>, Sight
which was kept in the <u>musty</u> basement because the Smell
upstairs bathroom was too small.

Marginal sense labels (left): Sight, Sight, Sight, Sound, Sound, Smell, Smell

The back bedroom was near the kitchen and adjacent to the basement stairs. I once heard one of my aunts call that room a firetrap, and indeed it was. The room was <u>wallpapered with the old newspapers</u>   Sight Grandma liked to collect, and the bed was stacked Sight   high with <u>my mother's and aunts' old clothes.</u> There was no space between the furniture in that room, only a narrow path against one wall leading to the bed. A sideboard was shoved against the opposite wall; a sewing table was pushed up against the side-board; a short chest of drawers lay against the sewing table; and so on. But no one could identify these } Sight pieces of forgotten furniture without digging through the sewing patterns, half-made dresses, dishes, and books. Any outsider would just think this was a part of the room where the floor had been raised to about waist level, so thoroughly was the mass of furniture hidden.

Comparison   Stepping off Grandma's sloping back porch was (simile)   <u>like stepping into an enchanted forest.</u> The grass and weeds were hip level, with a tiny dirt path leading to Comparison   nowhere, <u>as if it had lost its way in the jungle.</u> <u>A fancy</u>   Sight (simile)   <u>white fence,</u> courtesy of the neighbors, bordered the yard in back and vainly attempted to hold in the Sight   <u>gooseberries, raspberries, and blackberries</u> that grew wildly along the side of Grandma's yard. Huge Sight   <u>crabapple, cherry, and walnut trees</u> shaded the house and hid the sky. I used to stand under them and look up, pretending to be deep in a magic forest. The ground was <u>cool and damp</u> under my bare feet, even   Touch in the middle of the day, and my head would fill with Smell   the <u>sweet fragrance of mixed spring flowers</u> and <u>the</u> Sound   <u>throaty cooing of doves</u> I could never find but could always hear. But, before long, the wind would shift, and the <u>musty aroma of petroleum</u> from a nearby   Smell refinery would jerk me back to reality.

Grandma's house is indeed a place of wonderful memories. Just as her decaying concrete steps store the treasures of many lost childhoods, <u>her house still</u>   Dominant <u>stands, guarding the memories of generations of</u>   impression <u>children and grandchildren.</u>   rephrased

Student Writer's Comments

Writing this descriptive essay was easy and enjoyable for me—once I got started. I decided to write about my grandmother's house because I knew it so well, but I had trouble coming up with the impression I wanted to convey to my readers. I have so many recollections of this place I didn't know which set of memories would be most interesting to others. So I began by brainstorming, forcing myself to think of images from all five senses.

After I had accumulated plenty of images, which triggered other memories I had completely forgotten, I began to write. I organized my essay spatially as if I were walking through Grandma's house room by room. But I let my senses lead the way. Before I started writing, I had no idea how many paragraphs I would have, but as I meandered through the house recording my memories of sights, smells, sounds, tastes, and textures, I ended up writing one paragraph on each room, plus one for the yard. For this assignment, I wrote the three paragraphs about the inside of the house first; then, the introduction started to take shape in my head, so I got it down; and last, I wrote the paragraph on the backyard and my conclusion. Finally, my "dominant impression" came to me: This is a house that guards the memories of many generations. My grandmother has always lived in this house, and my mother has her own set of memories associated with this place too.

This focus for my paper made the revising process fairly easy, as I worked on the entire essay with a specific purpose in mind. Previously, my biggest problem had been that I had too many scattered memories and realized I had to be more selective. Once I had my dominant impression, I knew which images to keep and which to drop from my draft. Also, as I reworked my essay, I looked for ways to make my description more exciting and vivid for the reader—as if he or she were right there with me. To accomplish this, I explained some special features of my grandma's house by comparing them with items the reader would most likely be familiar with. I also worked, at this point, on making one paragraph flow into another by adding transitions that would move the reader smoothly from one group of ideas to the next. "Only a hook-type lock on the front door" got my readers into the living room. The old curtain between the kitchen and the living room moved my essay out of the living room and into the kitchen. I started my third paragraph about the indoors by saying "The back bedroom was near the kitchen and adjacent to the basement stairs" so my readers could get their bearings in relation to other parts of the house they had already been introduced to. Finally, I was satisfied that my essay was a clear, accurate description of my view of my grandma's house. My brother might have a completely different set of memories, but this was my version of a single generation of impressions organized, finally, into one coherent essay.

SOME FINAL THOUGHTS ON DESCRIPTION

Because description is one of the most basic forms of verbal communication, you will find descriptive passages in most of the reading selections throughout this textbook. Description provides you with the means to capture your audience's attention and clarify certain points in all of your writing. The examples chosen for the following section, however, are predominantly descriptive—the main purpose in each being to involve the readers' senses as vividly as possible. As you read through each of these essays, try to determine its intended audience and purpose, the object of the description, the extent to which details are included or excluded, and the author's point of view. Equipped with these four areas of reference, you can become an increasingly sophisticated reader and writer of descriptive prose.

DESCRIPTION IN REVIEW

Reading Descriptive Essays

Preparing to Read

√ What assumptions can I make from the essay's title?
√ What do I think the general mood of the essay will be?
√ What is the essay's purpose and audience?
√ What does the synopsis tell me about the essay?
√ What can I learn from the author's biography?
√ Can I predict the author's point of view toward the subject?

Reading

√ What is the essay's dominant impression?
√ Is the essay predominantly objective or subjective?
√ What senses does the author engage?

Rereading

√ What details support the essay's dominant impression?
√ What other rhetorical modes does the author use?

Writing Descriptive Essays

Preparing to Write

√ What is my purpose?
√ Will I be primarily objective or subjective?
√ Who is my audience?
√ What is the dominant impression I want to convey?

Writing

√ Do I have a dominant impression for my thesis?
√ Did I select details that support my dominant impression?
√ Did I engage all five senses?
√ What is my point of view toward my subject (objective or subjective)?
√ Do I *show* rather than *tell* my narrative?

Rewriting

√ Do I create the dominant impression I want to convey?
√ Do my details support this dominant impression?
√ Which senses do I stimulate?
√ Do I have a clear, consistent point of view toward my subject?
√ Am I showing rather than telling in my description?
√ Do I use similes or metaphors when appropriate?

RAY BRADBURY   (1920–   )

Summer Rituals

Ray Bradbury is one of America's best-known and most loved writers of science fiction. His extensive publications include such popular novels as *The Martian Chronicles* (1950), *The Illustrated Man* (1951), *Fahrenheit 451* (1953), *Dandelion Wine* (1957), and *Something Wicked This Way Comes* (1962). He has also written dozens of short stories, poems, essays, plays, and radio and movie scripts (including the screenplay of John Huston's film version of *Moby Dick*). As a child, he escaped his strict Baptist upbringing through a steady diet of Jules Verne, H. G. Wells, and Edgar Rice Burroughs, along with Buck Rogers and Prince Valiant comic books: "I was a sucker for lies, beautiful, fabulous lies, which instruct us to better our lives as a result, but which don't tell the truth." A frequent theme in his many novels is the impact of science on humanity: "My stories are intended," he claims, "as much to forecast how to prevent dooms, as to predict them." Bradbury's more recent publications include *The Last Circus* (1981), *The Complete Poems of Ray Bradbury* (1982), *The Love Affair* (1983), *Dinosaur Tales* (1983), *A Memory for Murder* (1984), *Forever and the Earth* (1984), *Death Is a Lonely Business* (1985), *The Toynbee Convector* (1989), *A Day in the Life of Hollywood* (1992), *Quicker Than the Eye* (1996), *Driving Blind* (1998), *From the Dust Returned* (2000), *Let's All Kill Constance* (2003), and *Bradbury Speaks: Too Soon from the Cave, Too Far from the Stars* (2005). The author lives in Cheviot Hills, California, where he enjoys painting and making ceramics. His advice to student writers is to "look for obvious answers to impossible futures."

Preparing to Read

"Summer Rituals," an excerpt from *Dandelion Wine*, describes the comfortable ceremony of putting up a front-porch swing in early summer. Focusing on the perceptions of Douglas, a young boy, the essay clearly sets forth the familiar yet deeply significant rhythms of life in a small town.

Exploring Experience: Before you read this selection, take a few moments to consider the value of ritual in your own life: Can you think of any activities that you and your family have elevated to the level of ceremonial importance? What about holidays? Birthdays? Sporting events? Spring cleaning? When do these activities take place? Do the same people participate in them every year? Why do you repeat these rituals? What purpose do they have for you? For others whom you know? For society in general?

Learning Online: Go to www.naturephotographs.com, and look at pictures in the "Summer" section. Find a picture that represents summer to you. Study the picture, and think about how you would describe the location or moment in time.

Yes, summer was rituals, each with its natural time and place. The rit-   1
ual of lemonade or ice-tea making, the ritual of wine, shoes, or no
shoes, and at last, swiftly following the others, with quiet dignity, the
ritual of the front-porch swing. ❶

On the third day of summer in the late afternoon Grandfather reappeared   2
from the front door to gaze serenely at the two empty eye rings in the ceiling
of the porch. Moving to the geranium-pot-lined rail like Ahab surveying the
mild day and the mild-looking sky, he wet his finger to test the wind, and
shucked his coat to see how shirt sleeves felt in the westering hours. He acknowledged the salutes of other captains on yet other flowered porches, out themselves
to discern the gentle ground swell of weather, oblivious to their wives chirp-
ing or snapping like fuzzball hand dogs hidden behind black porch screens.

"All right, Douglas, let's set it up."   3

In the garage they found, dusted, and carried forth the howdah, as it were,   4
for the quiet summer-night festivals, the swing chair, which Grandpa chained
to the porch-ceiling eyelets.

Douglas, being lighter, was first to sit in the swing. Then, after a moment,   5
Grandfather gingerly settled his pontifical weight beside the boy. Thus they
sat, smiling at each other, nodding, as they swung silently back and forth, back
and forth.

Ten minutes later Grandma appeared with water buckets and brooms to   6
wash down and sweep off the porch. Other chairs, rockers and straight-backs,
were summoned from the house.

"Always like to start sitting early in the season," said Grandpa, "before the   7
mosquitoes thicken."

About seven o'clock you could hear the chairs scraping back from the   8
tables, someone experimenting with a yellow-toothed piano, if you stood
outside the dining-room window and listened. Matches being struck, the
first dishes bubbling in the suds and tinkling on the wall racks, somewhere,
faintly, a phonograph playing. And then as the evening changed the hour, at
house after house on the twilight streets, under the immense oaks and elms,
on shady porches, people would begin to appear, like those figures who tell
good or bad weather in rain-or-shine clocks. ❷

Uncle Bert, perhaps Grandfather, then Father, and some of the cousins;   9
the men all coming out first into the syrupy evening, blowing smoke, leaving the women's voices behind in the cooling-warm kitchen to set their
universe aright. Then the first male voices under the porch brim, the feet up,

---

Thinking Critically

❶ How can rituals bring dignity to our lives?

❷ How does Bradbury speed up and slow down time? Mark all the time references you can
find, and examine them after you finish the essay.

the boys fringed on the worn steps or wooden rails where sometime during the evening something, a boy or a geranium pot, would fall off.

At last, like ghosts hovering momentarily behind the door screen, Grandma,   10
Great-grandma, and Mother would appear, and the men would shift, move, and offer seats. The women carried varieties of fans with them, folded newspapers, bamboo whisks, or perfumed kerchiefs, to start the air moving about their faces as they talked.

What they talked of all evening long, no one remembered next day. It   11
wasn't important to anyone what the adults talked about; it was only important that the sounds came and went over the delicate ferns that bordered the porch on three sides; it was only important that the darkness filled the town like black water being poured over the houses and that the cigars glowed and that the conversations went on and on. The female gossip moved out, disturbing the first mosquitoes so they danced in frenzies on the air. The male voices invaded the old house timbers; if you closed your eyes and put your head down against the floor boards you could hear the men's voices rumbling like a distant, political earthquake, constant, unceasing, rising or falling a pitch. ③

Douglas sprawled back on the dry porch planks, completely contented and   12
reassured by these voices, which would speak on through eternity, flow in a stream of murmurings over his body, over his closed eyelids, into his drowsy ears, for all time. The rocking chairs sounded like crickets, the crickets sounded like rocking chairs, and the moss-covered rain barrel by the dining-room window produced another generation of mosquitoes to provide a topic of conversation through endless summers ahead.

Sitting on the summer-night porch was so good, so easy and so reassur-   13
ing that it could never be done away with. These were rituals that were right and lasting; the lighting of pipes, the pale hands that moved knitting needles in the dimness, the eating of foil-wrapped, chill Eskimo Pies, the coming and going of all the people. For at some time or other during the evening, everyone visited here; the neighbors down the way, the people across the street; Miss Fern and Miss Roberta humming by in their electric runabout, giving Tom or Douglas a ride around the block and then coming up to sit down and fan away the fever in their cheeks; or Mr. Jonas, the junkman, having left his horse and wagon hidden in the alley, and ripe to bursting with words, would come up the steps looking as fresh as if his talk had never been said before, and somehow it never had. And last of all, the children, who had been off squinting their way through a last hide-and-seek or kick-the-can, panting, glowing, would sickle quietly back like boomerangs along the soundless lawn, to sink beneath the talking talking talking of the porch voices which would weigh and gentle them down. . . . ④

Thinking Critically

③ How many different sound images can you find in the essay? How do these images help characterize Douglas, the young narrator? Which specific sounds are most memorable for him?

④ What is the relationship between the children's games and the adult rituals mentioned by Bradbury? In what way can children's games be called "rituals"?

Oh, the luxury of lying in the fern night and the grass night and the   14
night of susurrant, slumbrous voices weaving the dark together. The
grownups had forgotten he was there, so still, so quiet Douglas lay, noting
the plans they were making for his and their own futures. And the voices
chanted, drifted, in moonlit clouds of cigarette smoke while the moths, like
late appleblossoms come alive, tapped faintly about the far street lights,
and the voices moved on into the coming years. . . .

UNDERSTANDING DETAILS

1. What are the main similarities and differences between Douglas and Grandfather in this essay? How are their views of the world the same? How are their
   views different?
2. From the scattered details you have read in this essay, describe Douglas's
   house. How large do you think the front porch is? What color is the house?
   How many trees and shrubs surround it? What part of your description is
   based on facts in the essay? What part comes from inferences you have made
   on your own?
3. How do the men differ from the women in this excerpt? Divide a piece of
   paper into two columns; then list as many qualities of each gender as you can
   find. (For example, the narrator hears the men's voices "rumbling" like an
   "earthquake"; in contrast, the women move like "ghosts," their gossip "disturbing the . . . mosquitoes.") What other descriptive differences can you find
   between the men and women? What conclusions can you draw from these
   differences?
4. How did the conversation blend with the surroundings in Bradbury's
   description?

READING CRITICALLY

5. A "ritual" may be briefly defined as "a customarily repeated act that expresses
   a system of values." Using this definition, explain why the ritual of the front-
   porch swing is important to Douglas's family. What feelings or implicit values
   lie behind this particular ritual?
6. What other rituals are mentioned in this essay? How are they related to the
   front-porch swing? To summer? To Douglas and his family?
7. Bradbury helps us feel the comfort, warmth, and familiarity of the scene depicted
   in this essay through the use of a number of original descriptive details: for
   example, "summer-night festivals," "yellow-toothed piano," "rain-or-shine
   clocks," "syrupy evening," and "foil-wrapped, chill Eskimo Pies." Find at least
   five other descriptive words or phrases, and explain how each enables us to
   identify with the characters and situations in this story. Which of the five senses
   does each of these details arouse in the reader?
8. In what ways do you think Douglas was "completely contented and reassured"
   (paragraph 12) by the voices around him? Why did Douglas feel this contentment would last "for all time" (paragraph 12)?

DISCOVERING RHETORICAL STRATEGIES

9. Some of the author's sentences are very long and involved, whereas others are quite short. What effects do these changes in sentence length have on you as a reader? Give a specific example of a shift in length from one sentence to another and explain its effect.

10. This descriptive essay is filled with many interesting similes (comparisons using the words *like* or *as*) and metaphors (comparisons without *like* or *as*). For example, Grandfather standing on the front porch looks *like* Ahab, the possessed sea captain from Herman Melville's epic novel *Moby Dick* (paragraph 2). Later, Bradbury uses a metaphor to focus his readers on "the night of susurrant, slumbrous voices weaving the dark together" (paragraph 14). Find at least one other comparison, either a simile or a metaphor, and explain how it works within the context of its sentence or paragraph. What type of comparison is being made (a simile or a metaphor)? What do we learn about the object being described (for example, Grandfather or the night) through its association with the other reference (in this case, Ahab or "voices weaving the dark together")?

11. What is the point of view of the author in this selection? Would the essay be more effective if it were reported from the standpoint of Douglas? Of Grandfather? Of the women? Why or why not? How does the author's point of view help Bradbury organize his description? Should the fact that Bradbury's middle name is Douglas have any bearing on our interpretation of this story?

12. Although Bradbury draws mainly on description to write this essay, what other rhetorical strategies work together to help the reader grasp the full effect of "Summer Rituals"? Give examples of each strategy.

MAKING CONNECTIONS

13. For Douglas, hanging the porch swing was an important yearly ritual. What rituals can you find in the family backgrounds of Firoozeh Dumas ("Leffingwell Elementary School"), Russell Baker ("The Saturday Evening Post"), and/or Michael Dorris ("The Broken Cord")? What specific meanings did these rituals have within each author's family?

14. Compare and contrast Bradbury's neighborhood with that of Robert Ramirez ("The Barrio"). Which neighborhood would you feel more comfortable in? Why would you feel comfortable there?

15. Which author's relationship with his or her parents is most like your own: Ray Bradbury's, Russell Baker's ("The Saturday Evening Post"), or Sandra Cisneros's ("Only daughter")? How did each of these children relate differently to his or her parents?

IDEAS FOR DISCUSSION/WRITING

Preparing to Write

List some of the most important rituals in your life: How many times a year do these rituals occur? What purpose do they serve? How do rituals help create a strong social framework in your life? In your friends' lives? In society in general?

Choosing a Topic

1. *Learning Online:* Using either a photo that has special meaning for you or an image you found on the Internet in Preparing to Read, write an essay describing a moment or place suspended in time. Following Bradbury's approach to his topic, develop your narrative through concrete and consistent details.
2. Write a descriptive essay about a ritual that is significant in your life, addressing it to someone who has never experienced that particular activity. Include the people involved and the setting. Try to use all five senses in your description.
3. Choose a ritual that is part of your family life, and write an essay describing your feelings about this ceremonial event. Address it to someone outside your family. Use similes and metaphors to make your description as vivid as possible.
4. Explain to someone visiting the United States for the first time the value of a particular tradition in American society. Then help this person understand the importance of that tradition in your life.

Before beginning your essay, you might want to consult the checklists on page 64.

KIMBERLY WOZENCRAFT   (1954–   )

Notes from the Country Club

Kimberly Wozencraft grew up in Dallas, Texas, and dropped out of college when she was twenty-one to become a police officer. Her first assignment after training at the police academy was a street-level undercover narcotics investigation. Like many narcotics agents, Wozencraft became addicted to drugs, which impaired her judgment and resulted in a 1981 conviction for violating the civil rights of a reputed child pornographer. After serving an eighteen-month sentence in the Federal Correctional Institution at Lexington, Kentucky, she moved to New York City, where she now lives with her three children. She holds a Master of Fine Arts degree from Columbia University, and her essays, poems, and short stories have appeared in a variety of publications, including *Northwest Review, Quarto, Big Wednesday, Witness, Texas Monthly, New York Newsday,* and the *Los Angeles Times.* Her first novel, *Rush,* was made into a movie in 1991 starring Jennifer Jason Leigh. In 1998, she completed two more books, *The Catch* and *Slam* (with Richard Stratton), followed by *Wanted* in 2004. Her most recent novel, *The Devil's Backbone,* was published in 2006. Her advice to college writers is to read as much as possible. She confesses, "I used to read books late at night under the covers when I was a child."

Preparing to Read

Originally published in *Witness,* "Notes from the Country Club" was selected for inclusion in *The Best American Essays of 1988,* edited by Annie Dillard. Through carefully constructed prose, the author describes her prison environment and the anxiety caused by living for more than a year in such an alien, difficult place.

Exploring Experience: As you prepare to read this essay, take a moment to think about your own behavior in difficult situations: What kind of person do you become? How do you act toward other people? How is this behavior different from the way you usually act? How do you know when you're in a difficult situation? What do you generally do to relieve the tension? How successful are your solutions?

Learning Online: Wozencraft's description of her experience as an undercover narcotics agent was made into a movie entitled *Rush.* To better understand her experience, go to www.mgm.com. Conduct a keyword search for "Rush." Click on the "All Media" link to view photos and clips from the film.

They had the Haitians up the hill, in the "camp" section where they used to keep the minimum security cases. ◆ The authorities were concerned that some of the Haitians might be diseased, so they kept them isolated from the main coed prison population by lodging them in the big square brick building surrounded by eight-foot chain-link with concertina wire on top. We were not yet familiar with the acronym AIDS.

One or two of the Haitians had drums, and in the evenings when the rest of us were in the Big Yard, the drum rhythms carried over the bluegrass to where we were playing gin or tennis or softball or just hanging out waiting for dark. When they really got going some of them would dance and sing. Their music was rhythmic and beautiful, and it made me think of freedom.

There were Cubans loose in the population, spattering their guttural Spanish in streams around the rectangular courtyard, called Central Park, at the center of the prison compound. These were Castro's Boat People, guilty of no crime in this country, but requiring sponsors before they could walk the streets as free people.

Walking around the perimeter of Central Park was like taking a trip in microcosm across the United States. Moving leftward from the main entrance, strolling along under the archway that covers the wide sidewalk, you passed the doorway to the Women's Unit, where I lived, and it was how I imagined Harlem to be. There was a white face here and there, but by far most of them were black. Ghetto blasters thunked out rhythms in the sticky evening air, and folks leaned against the window sills, smoking, drinking Cokes, slinking, and nodding. Every once in a while a joint was passed around, and always there was somebody pinning, checking for hacks on patrol.

Past Women's Unit was the metal door to the Big Yard, the main recreation area of three or four acres, two sides blocked by the building, two sides fenced in the usual way—chain-link and concertina wire. ❷

Past the Big Yard you entered the Blue Ridge Mountains, a sloping grassy area on the edge of Central Park, where the locals, people from Kentucky, Tennessee, and the surrounding environs, sat around playing guitars and singing, and every once in a while passing around a quart of hooch. They make it from grapefruit juice and a bit of yeast smuggled out of the kitchen. Some of the inmates who worked in Cable would bring out pieces of a black foam rubber substance and wrap it around empty Cremora jars to make thermos jugs of sorts. They would mix the grapefruit juice and yeast in the containers and stash them in some out-of-the-way spot for a few

---

Thinking Critically

❶ Does the first sentence catch your attention? Why or why not? How soon do you know what kind of place the author is describing?

❷ Why do you think the prison has two different types of fences?

weeks until presto! you had hooch, bitter and tart and sweet all at once, only mildly alcoholic, but entirely suitable for evening cocktails in Central Park.

Next, at the corner, was the Commissary, a tiny store tucked inside the entrance to Veritas, the second women's unit. It wasn't much more than a few shelves behind a wall of Plexiglas, with a constant line of inmates spilling out of the doorway. They sold packaged chips, cookies, pens and writing paper, toiletries, some fresh fruit, and the ever-popular ice cream, sold only in pints. You had to eat the entire pint as soon as you bought it, or else watch it melt, because there weren't any refrigerators. Inmates were assigned one shopping night per week, allowed to buy no more than seventy-five dollars' worth of goods per month, and were permitted to pick up a ten-dollar roll of quarters if they had enough money in their prison account. Quarters were the basic spending unit in the prison; possession of paper money was a shippable offense. [3] There were vending machines stocked with junk food and soda, and they were supposedly what the quarters were to be used for. But we gambled, we bought salami or fried chicken sneaked out by the food service workers, and of course people sold booze and drugs. The beggars stood just outside the Commissary door. Mostly they were Cubans, saying, "Oyez! Mira! Mira! Hey, Poppy, one quarter for me. One cigarette for me, Poppy?"

There was one Cuban whom I was specially fond of. His name was Shorty. 8 The name said it. He was only about five-two, and he looked just like Mick Jagger. I met him in Segregation, an isolated section of tiny cells where prisoners were locked up for having violated some institutional rule or another. They tossed me in there the day I arrived; again the authorities were concerned, supposedly for my safety. I was a police woman before I became a convict, and they weren't too sure that the other inmates would like that. Shorty saved me a lot of grief when I went into Seg. It didn't matter if you were male or female there, you got stripped and handed a tee shirt, a pair of boxer shorts and a set of Peter Pans—green canvas shoes with thin rubber soles designed to prevent you from running away. As if you could get past three steel doors and a couple of hacks just to start with. When I was marched down the hall between the cells, the guys started whistling and hooting, and they didn't shut up even after I was locked down. They kept right on screaming until finally I yelled out, "Yo no comprendo!" and they all moaned and said, "Another . . . Cuban," and finally got quiet. Shorty was directly across from me, I could see his eyes through the rectangular slot in my cell door. He rattled off a paragraph or two of Spanish, all of which was lost on me,

---

Thinking Critically

[3] How do you feel about these prison rules? Are they appropriate for the situation, or are they too restrictive? Explain your reasoning.

and I said quietly, "Yo no comprendo bien español. Yo soy de Texas, yo hablo inglés?" I could tell he was smiling by the squint of his eyes, and he just said, "Bueno." When the hacks came around to take us out for our mandatory hour of recreation, which consisted of standing around in the Rec area while two guys shot a game of pool on the balcony above the gym, Shorty slipped his hand into mine and smiled up at me until the hack told him to cut it out. He knew enough English to tell the others in Seg [4] that I was not really Spanish, but he kept quiet about it, and they left me alone.

Beyond the Commissary, near the door to the dining hall, was East St. Louis. 9
The prison had a big portable stereo system, which they rolled out a few times a week so that an inmate could play at being a disc jockey. They had a good-sized collection of albums, and there was usually some decent jazz blasting out of there. Sometimes people danced, unless there were uptight hacks on duty to tell them not to. [5]

California was next. It was a laid back kind of corner near the doors to 10
two of the men's units. People stood around and smoked hash or grass or did whatever drugs happened to be available and there was sometimes a sort of slow-motion game of handball going on. If you wanted drugs, this was the place to come.

If you kept walking, you would arrive at the Power Station, the other 11
southern corner where the politicos-gone-wrong congregated. It might seem odd at first to see these middle-aged government mavens standing around in their Lacoste sport shirts and Sans-a-belt slacks, smoking pipes or cigars and waving their arms to emphasize some point or other. They kept pretty much to themselves and ate together at the big round tables in the cafeteria, sipping cherry Kool-Aid and pretending it was Cabernet Sauvignon.

That's something else you had to deal with—the food. It was worse than 12
elementary school steam table fare. By the time they finished cooking it, it was tasteless, colorless, and nutritionless. The first meal I took in the dining room was lunch. As I walked toward the entry, a tubby fellow was walking out, staggering really, rolling his eyes as though he were dizzy. He stopped and leaned over, and I heard someone yell, "Watch out, he's gonna puke!" I ducked inside so as to miss the spectacle. They were serving some rubbery, faint pink slabs that were supposed to be ham, but I didn't even bother to taste mine. I just slapped at it a few times to watch the fork bounce off and then ate my potatoes and went back to the unit.

Shortly after that I claimed that I was Jewish, having gotten the word 13
from a friendly New York lawyer who was in for faking some of his clients'

Thinking Critically

[4] What does the word "Seg" mean? What other prison slang can you find in the essay?
[5] To what extent does each location in the prison have its own ethnic identity?

immigration papers. The kosher line was the only way to get a decent meal in there. In fact, for a long time they had a Jewish baker from Philadelphia locked up, and he made some truly delicious cream puffs for dessert. They sold for seventy-five cents on the black market, but once I had established myself in the Jewish community, I got them as part of my regular fare. They fed us a great deal of peanut butter on the kosher line; every time the "goyim" got meat, we got peanut butter, but that was all right with me. Eventually I was asked to light the candles at the Friday evening services, since none of the real Jewish women bothered to attend. I have to admit that most of the members of our little prison congregation were *genuine alter kokers,* but some of them were amusing. And I enjoyed learning first hand about Judaism. The services were usually very quiet, and the music, the ancient intoning songs, fortified me against the screeching pop-rock vocal assaults that were a constant in the Women's Unit. I learned to think of myself as the *shabot shiksa,* [6] and before my time was up, even the rabbi seemed to accept me.

I suppose it was quite natural that the Italians assembled just "down the 14 street" from the offending ex-senators, judges, and power brokers. Just to the left of the main entrance. The first night I made the tour, a guy came out of the shadows near the building and whispered to me. "What do you need, sweetheart? What do you want, I can get it. My friend Ahmad over there, he's very rich, and he wants to buy you things. What'll it be, you want some smoke, a few ludes, vodka, cigarettes, maybe some kosher salami fresh from the kitchen? What would you like?" I just stared at him. The only thing I wanted at that moment was out, and even Ahmad's millions, if they existed at all, couldn't do that. The truth is, every guy I met in there claimed to be wealthy, to have been locked up for some major financial crime. Had I taken all of them up on their offers of limousines to pick me up at the front gate when I was released and take me to the airport for a ride home in a private Lear jet, I would have needed my own personal cop out front just to direct traffic.

Ahmad's Italian promoter eventually got popped for zinging the cooking 15 teacher one afternoon on the counter in the home economics classroom, right next to the new Cuisinart. The assistant warden walked in on the young lovebirds, and before the week was up, even the Cubans were walking around singing about it. They had a whole song down, to the tune of "Borracho Me Acosté a Noche."

At the end of the tour, you would find the jaded New Yorkers, [7] sitting 16 at a picnic table or two in the middle of the park, playing gin or poker and

---

Thinking Critically

[6] How does the use of foreign language here and elsewhere contribute to the tone of the essay?
[7] Why do you think the New Yorkers are "jaded"?

bragging about their days on Madison Avenue and Wall Street, lamenting the scarcity of good deli, even on the kosher line, and planning where they would take their first real meal upon release.

If you think federal correctional institutions are about the business of re-   17
habilitation, drop by for an orientation session one day. There at the front of the classroom, confronting rows of mostly black faces, will be the warden, or the assistant warden, or the prison shrink, pacing back and forth in front of the blackboard and asking the class, "Why do you think you're here?" This gets a general grumble, a few short, choked laughs. Some wellmeaning soul always says it—rehabilitation.

"Nonsense!" the lecturer will say. "There are several reasons for locking   18
people up. Number one is incapacitation. If you're in here, you can't be out there doing crime. Secondly, there is deterrence. Other people who are thinking about doing crime see that we lock people up for it and maybe they think twice. But the real reason you are here is to be punished. Plain and simple. You done wrong, now you got to pay for it. Rehabilitation ain't even part of the picture. **❽** So don't be looking to us to rehabilitate you. Only person can rehabilitate you is you. If you feel like it, go for it, but leave us out. We don't want to play that game."

So that's it. You're there to do time. I have no misgivings about why I   19
went to prison. I deserved it. I was a cop; I got strung out on cocaine; I violated the rights of a pornographer. My own drug use as an undercover narcotics agent was a significant factor in my crime. But I did it, and I deserved to be punished. Most of the people I met in Lexington, though, were in for drugs, and the majority of them hadn't done anything more than sell an ounce of cocaine or a pound of pot to some apostle of the law.

It seems lately that almost every time I look at the *New York Times* op-ed   20
page, there is something about the drug problem. I have arrested people for drugs, and I have had a drug problem myself. I have seen how at least one federal correctional institution functions. It does not appear that the practice of locking people up for possession or distribution of an insignificant quantity of a controlled substance makes any difference at all in the amount of drug use that occurs in the United States. The drug laws are merely another convenient source of political rhetoric for aspiring officeholders. Politicians know that an antidrug stance is an easy way to get votes from parents who are terrified that their children might wind up as addicts. I do not advocate drug use. Yet, having seen the criminal justice system from several angles, as a police officer, a court bailiff, a defendant, and a prisoner, I am convinced that prison is not the answer to the drug problem, or for that

---

Thinking Critically

❽ Do you believe prison can rehabilitate its inmates? Why or why not?

matter to many other white-collar crimes. If the taxpayers knew how their dollars were being spent inside some prisons, they might actually scream out loud. [9]

There were roughly 1,800 men and women locked up in Lex, at a ratio   21 of approximately three men to every woman, and it did get warm in the summertime. To keep us tranquil they devised some rather peculiar little amusements. One evening I heard a commotion on the steps at the edge of Central Park and looked over to see a rec specialist with three big cardboard boxes set up on the plaza, marked 1, 2, and 3. There were a couple of hundred inmates sitting at the bottom of the steps. Dennis, the rec specialist, was conducting his own version of the television game show *Let's Make a Deal!* Under one of the boxes was a case of soda, under another was a racquetball glove, and under the third was a fly swatter. The captive contestant picked door number 2, which turned out to contain the fly swatter, to my way of thinking the best prize there. Fly swatters were virtually impossible to get through approved channels, and therefore cost as much as two packs of cigarettes on the black market.

Then there was the Annual Fashion Show, where ten or twenty inmates   22 had special packages of clothing sent in, only for the one evening, and modeled them on stage while the baddest drag queen in the compound moderated and everyone else ooohed and aahhed. They looked good up there on stage in Christian Dior and Ralph Lauren instead of the usual fatigue pants and white tee shirts. And if such activities did little to prepare inmates for a productive return to society, well, at least they contributed to the fantasyland aura that made Lexington such an unusual place.

I worked in Landscape, exiting the rear gate of the compound each week-   23 day morning at about nine after getting a half-hearted frisk from one of the hacks on duty. I would climb on my tractor to drive to the staff apartment complex and pull weeds or mow the lawn. Landscape had its prerogatives. [10] We raided the gardens regularly and at least got to taste fresh vegetables from time to time. I had never eaten raw corn before, but it could not have tasted better. We also brought in a goodly supply of real vodka, and a bit of hash now and then, for parties in our rooms after lights out. One guy strapped a six-pack of Budweiser to his arms with masking tape and then put on his prison–issue Army field jacket. When he got to the rear gate, he raised his arms straight out at shoulder level, per instructions, and the hack patted down his torso and legs, never bothering to check his arms. The inmate had been

---

Thinking Critically

[9] Do you think Wozencraft's opinions about the penalties for drug abuse have anything to do with the fact that she was a former drug addict?

[10] Why did most prisoners like Landscape duty?

counting on that. He smiled at the hack and walked back to his room, a six-pack richer.

I was fortunate to be working Landscape at the same time as Horace, a   24
fellow who had actually lived in the city of Lexington before he was locked up. His friends made regular deliveries of assorted contraband, which they would stash near a huge elm tree near the outer stone fence of the reservation. Horace would drive his tractor over, make the pickup, and the rest of us would carry it, concealed, through the back gate when we went back inside for lunch or at the end of the day. "Contraband" included everything from drugs to blue eye shadow. The assistant warden believed that female inmates should wear no cosmetics other than what she herself used—a bit of mascara and a light shade of lipstick. I have never been a plaything of Fashion, but I did what I could to help the other women prisoners in their never-ending quest for that Cover Girl look.

You could depend on the fact that most of the hacks would rather have   25
been somewhere else, and most of them really didn't care *what* the inmates did, as long as it didn't cause any commotion. Of course, there were a few you had to look out for. The captain in charge of security was one of them. We tried a little experiment once, after having observed that any time he saw someone laughing, he took immediate steps to make the inmate and everyone around him acutely miserable. Whenever we saw him in the area, we immediately assumed expressions of intense unhappiness, even of despair. Seeing no chance to make anyone more miserable than they already appeared to be, the captain left us alone.

Almost all of the female hacks, and a good number of the males, had out-   26
rageously large derrières, a condition we inmates referred to as "the federal ass." [1] This condition may have resulted from the fact that most of them appeared, as one inmate succinctly described it, simply to be "putting in their forty a week to stay on the government teat." Employment was not an easy thing to find in Kentucky.

Despite the fact that Lexington is known as a "country club" prison, I   27
must admit that I counted days. From the first moment that I was in, I kept track of how many more times I would have to watch the sun sink behind eight feet of chain-link, of how many more days I would have to spend eating, working, playing, and sleeping according to the dictates of a "higher authority." I don't think I can claim that I was rehabilitated. If anything I underwent a process of dehabilitation. What I learned was what Jessica Mitford tried to tell people many years ago in her book *Kind and Usual Punishment*.

Thinking Critically

[1] What does the author mean by the term "the federal ass"?

Prison is a business,[12] no different from manufacturing tires or selling real estate. It keeps people employed, and it provides cheap labor for NASA, the U.S. Postal Service, and other governmental or quasi-governmental agencies. For a short time, before I was employed in Landscape, I worked as a finisher of canvas mailbags, lacing white rope through metal eyelets around the top of the bags and attaching clamps to the ropes. I made one dollar and fourteen cents for every one hundred that I did. If I worked very hard, I could do almost two hundred a day.

It's not about justice. If you think it's about justice, look at the newspapers and notice who walks. Not the little guys, the guys doing a tiny bit of dealing or sniggling a little on their income tax, or the woman who pulls a stunt with welfare checks because her husband has skipped out and she has no other way to feed her kids. I do not say that these things are right. But the process of selective prosecution, the "making" of cases by D.A.s and police departments, and the presence of some largely unenforceable statutes currently on the books (it is the reality of "compliance": no law can be forced on a public which chooses to ignore it; hence, selective prosecution) make for a criminal justice system which cannot realistically function in a fair and equitable manner. Criminal justice—I cannot decide if it is the ultimate oxymoron or a truly accurate description of the law enforcement process in America. ₂₈

In my police undercover capacity, I have sat across the table from an armed robber who said, "My philosophy of life is slit thy neighbor's throat and pimp his kids." I believe that the human animals who maim and kill people should be dealt with, as they say, swiftly and surely. But this business of locking people up, at enormous cost, for minor, nonviolent offenses does not truly or effectively serve the interest of the people. It serves only to promote the wasteful aspects of the federal prison system, a system that gulps down tax dollars and spews up *Let's Make a Deal!* ₂₉

I think about Lexington almost daily. I will be walking up Broadway to shop for groceries, or maybe riding my bike in the original Central Park, and suddenly I'm wondering who's in there now, at this very moment, and for what inane violations, and what they are doing. Is it chow time, is the Big Yard open, is some inmate on stage in the auditorium singing "As Time Goes By" in a talent show? It is not a fond reminiscence or a desire to be back in the Land of No Decisions.[13] It is an awareness of the waste. The waste of tax dollars, yes, but taxpayers are used to that. It is the unnecessary trashing of lives that leaves me uneasy. The splitting of families, the enforced ₃₀

Thinking Critically

[12] In what way is prison a "business"?
[13] Why does the author refer to prison as "the Land of No Decisions"?

monotony, the programs which purport to prepare an inmate for re-entry into society but which actually succeed only in occupying a few more hours of the inmate's time behind the walls. The nonviolent offenders, such as small-time drug dealers and the economically deprived who were driven to crime out of desperation, could remain in society under less costly supervision, still undergoing "punishment" for their crime, but at least contributing to rather than draining the resources of society.

Horace, who was not a subtle sort of fellow, had some tee shirts made up.   31 They were delivered by our usual supplier out in Landscape, and we wore them back in over our regular clothes. The hacks tilted their heads when they noticed, but said nothing. On the front of each shirt was an outline of the state of Kentucky, and above the northwest corner of the state were the words "Visit Beautiful Kentucky!" Inside the state boundary were

- Free Accommodations
- Complimentary Meals
- Management Holds Calls
- Recreational Exercise

In small letters just outside the southwest corner of the state was: "Length of Stay Requirement." ⁴ And in big letters across the bottom:

Take Time to Do Time
F.C.I. Lexington

I gave mine away on the day I finished my sentence. It is a time-honored tradition to leave some of your belongings to friends who have to stay behind when you are released. But you must never leave shoes. Legend has it that if you do, you will come back to wear them again.

UNDERSTANDING DETAILS

1. Draw Lexington prison, and put the names on the sections of the facility. Then describe each section in your own words.
2. Why was walking around the outside of Central Park "like taking a trip in microcosm across the United States" (paragraph 4)? Give examples to explain your answer.
3. Why was Wozencraft especially fond of Shorty? What secret did they share at the beginning of the author's prison term?
4. Does the author feel she had been unfairly punished by being sent to prison? What had she done wrong?

Thinking Critically

⁴ In what ways do you think a sense of humor would be helpful to inmates doing time in prison?

READING CRITICALLY

5. What was Wozencraft's attitude toward other people in Lexington prison? Why do you think she felt this way? What types of relationships did she have with inmates and staff members?

6. Why does the author say, "If the taxpayers knew how their dollars were being spent inside some prisons, they might actually scream out loud" (paragraph 20)? What exactly is she referring to? What is she implying? Give some examples.

7. Why do you think Lexington is known as a "country club" prison? What features of the prison might have brought about its nickname?

8. Wozencraft feels strongly that people who perform minor, nonviolent crimes should not be put in prison. Why does she feel this way? Who should be locked up, according to the author? From her point of view, how does rehabilitation take place?

DISCOVERING RHETORICAL STRATEGIES

9. This essay is organized predominantly as a clockwise tour of Lexington prison. How and when does Wozencraft introduce the facts about her own imprisonment and her opinions about the current American system of justice? Explain in as much detail as you can the effect of integrating the guided tour and the related facts and opinions.

10. Wozencraft uses specific prison jargon throughout this essay. In what way does this jargon add to or detract from the essay? What effect would the essay have without this jargon?

11. Wozencraft ends her essay with an explanation of "a time-honored tradition." Is this an effective ending for the piece? Why or why not?

12. Though spatial description is the dominant rhetorical strategy the author uses in this essay to accomplish her purpose, what other strategies help make the essay effective? Give examples of these strategies.

MAKING CONNECTIONS

13. If Kimberly Wozencraft, Tamala Edwards ("Multi-Colored Families"), Scott Russell Sanders ("Homeplace"), Robert Ramirez ("The Barrio"), and Mary Pipher ("Beliefs About Families") were discussing the importance of belonging to a "community," which of the authors you read would argue most strongly that community is a positive force in our lives? Explain your answer.

14. Malcolm Cowley ("The View from 80"), Harold Krents ("Darkness at Noon"), Jay Walljasper ("Our Schedules, Our Selves"), and Malcolm X ("Learning to Read") have all felt imprisoned in much the same way Wozencraft does in her essay. In what way is each of these authors "confined"? Have you ever felt imprisoned for any reason? Why? How did you escape?

15. What would Wozencraft, Joel Stein ("You Are Not My Friend"), William Ouchi ("Japanese and American Workers: Two Casts of Mind"), and/or Robert Ramirez ("The Barrio") have to say about the importance of relying on other people to help endure difficult or challenging situations? How much do you rely on friends and relatives in your own life? How comfortable are you with these relationships?

IDEAS FOR DISCUSSION/WRITING

Preparing to Write

Write freely about your memories of a recent difficult or awkward situation in your life: What were the circumstances? What did you do? What did others do? How did you relate to others in this situation? Why was the situation so difficult? How did you get out of it?

Choosing a Topic

1. *Learning Online:* In this essay, Wozencraft develops a descriptive narrative from personal experience. As in the movie version you viewed on the Internet in Preparing to Read, she "shows" rather than "tells" her readers about Lexington prison's attitude toward rehabilitation. Compose either an email to a friend not attending college or a brief script for a movie that describes your current educational experience. Try to show rather than tell your observations, achievements, frustrations, and unique experiences. Remember to organize your descriptions to convey a clear and consistent message.

2. Write an essay describing for your peers a difficult or awkward situation you have been in recently. Why was it awkward? Explain the specific circumstances so that your classmates can clearly imagine the setting and the difficulty or problem. Then discuss your reaction to the situation.

3. A friend of yours has just been sentenced to prison for one year. Write a letter to this person describing what you think his or her biggest adjustments will be.

4. Wozencraft describes many problems within the prison system. With these problems in mind, write a letter to the editor of your local newspaper discussing whether prisons actually rehabilitate criminals. Use examples from Wozencraft's essay to help make your point.

Before beginning your essay, you might want to consult the checklists on page 64.

LINDA HOGAN   (1947–   )

Dwellings

Born in Denver, Linda Hogan is a Chickasaw Indian poet, novelist, essay-ist, and playwright whose many publications center on the theme that all of life is interconnected. Her father was in the army while she was growing up, so she and her family were transferred to many different locations. She has always considered Oklahoma her home, however, because her father grew up there. Her first volume of poetry, *Calling Myself Home* (1978), celebrates the rich oral traditions of her Chickasaw language and heritage in this area of the country. This book of poems was soon followed by many others, including *A Piece of Moon* (1981), *Daughters, I Love You* (1981), *Seeing Through the Sun* (1985), and *Savings* (1988). Hogan next turned to fiction with her first novel, *Mean Spirit* (1990), which was an "ethnohistory" of the Osage oil boom in 1920s Oklahoma. Two other novels, *Solar Storm* (1995) and *Power* (1998), followed, along with another volume of poetry, *Book of Medicines* (1993), and a collec-tion of essays entitled *Dwellings* (1995). Her most recent books are *The Sweet Breathing of Plants: Women and the Green World* (2000), *The Woman Who Watches Over the World: A Native Memoir* (2001), and *Sightings: The Gray Whales' Myste-rious Journey* (2002). Currently a professor at the University of Colorado at Boulder, Hogan has explained that she has a natural calling to write: "Some-thing about the process of doing that writing tapped into my own life in a way I wouldn't have done without the writing."

Preparing to Read

This essay was originally published in 1995 in Hogan's book of nonfiction entitled *Dwellings: A Spiritual History of the Living World.* In it, she considers how we reflect the natural world around us based on the places we choose to "dwell."

Exploring Experience: Nature is a place of peace and solitude for many of us, a retreat from our daily routine: How do you escape from the pressures of everyday life? Do you have ways of getting away both physically and mentally? How are these forms of escape different from each other?

Learning Online: Locate the photo album of Tiger Woods's house on the Hooked on Golf blog (www.hookedongolfblog.com/gallery2/v/TigerWoods/ TigerWoodsHome_16.jpg.html), and view the pictures of his beautiful beachfront house. It has the style and atmosphere we associate with the rich and famous. Keep these images in mind as you read Linda Hogan's essay about dwellings.

Not far from where I live is a hill that was cut into by the moving   1
water of a creek. Eroded this way, all that's left of it is a broken wall
of earth that contains old roots and pebbles woven together and exposed. Seen from a distance, it is only a rise of raw earth. But up close it is
something wonderful, a small cliff dwelling that looks almost as intricate and
well made as those the Anasazi left behind when they vanished mysteriously
centuries ago. This hill is a place that could be the starry skies at night turned
inward into the thousand round holes where solitary bees have lived and
died. It is a hill of tunneling rooms. At the mouths of some of the excava-
tions, half-circles of clay beetle out like awnings shading a doorway. It is
earth that was turned to clay in the mouths of the bees and spit out as they
mined deeper into their dwelling places.

This place is where the bees reside at an angle safe from rain. It faces the   2
southern sun. It is a warm and intelligent architecture of memory[1] learned
by whatever memory lives in the blood. Many of the holes still contain gold
husks of dead bees, their faces dry and gone, their flat eyes gazing out from
death's land toward the other uninhabited half of the hill that is across the
creek from the catacombs.

The first time I found the residence of the bees, it was dusty summer.   3
The sun was hot, and land was the dry color of rust. Now and then a car rum-
bled along the dirt road and dust rose up behind it before settling back down
on older dust. In the silence, the bees made a soft droning hum. They were
alive then, and working the hill, going out and returning with pollen, in and
out through the holes, back and forth between daylight and the cooler, darker
regions of the inner earth. They were flying an invisible map through air, a
map charted by landmarks, the slant of light, and a circling story they told
one another about the direction of food held inside the center of yellow
flowers.

Sitting in the hot sun, watching the small bees fly in and out around the   4
hill, hearing the summer birds, the light breeze, I felt right in the world. I belonged there. I thought of my own dwelling places, those real and those
imagined.[2] Once I lived in a town called Manitou, which means "Great
Spirit," and where hot mineral spring water gurgled beneath the streets and
rose into open wells. I felt safe there. With the underground movement of
water and heat a constant reminder of other life, of what lives beneath us, it
seemed to be the center of the world.

Thinking Critically

[1] What do you think Hogan means by the phrase "a warm and intelligent architecture of memory"?

[2] How does the residence of the bees remind the author of her own dwelling places?

A few years after that, I wanted silence. My daydreams were full of places   5
I longed to be, shelters and solitudes. I wanted a room apart from others, a
hidden cabin to rest in. I wanted to be in a redwood forest with trees so tall
the owls called out in the daytime. I daydreamed of living in a vapor cave a
few hours away from here. Underground, warm, and moist, I thought it
would be the perfect world for staying out of cold winter, for escaping the
noise of living.

And how often I've wanted to escape to a wilderness where a human   6
hand has not been in everything. But those were only dreams of peace, of
comfort, of a nest inside stone or woods, a sanctuary where a dream or life
wouldn't be invaded.

Years ago, in the next canyon west of here, there was a man who followed   7
one of those dreams and moved into a cave that could only be reached by
climbing down a rope. For years he lived there in comfort, like a troglodite.
The inner weather was stable, never too hot, too cold, too wet, or too dry. But
then he felt lonely. His utopia needed a woman. He went to town until he
found a wife. For a while after the marriage, his wife climbed down the rope
along with him, but before long she didn't want the mice scurrying about in
the cave, or the untidy bats that wanted to hang from the stones of the ceiling. So they built a door. Because of the closed entryway, the temperature
changed. They had to put in heat. Then the inner moisture of earth warped
the door, so they had to have air-conditioning, and after that the earth wanted
to go about life in its own way, and it didn't give in to the people. ◆3

In other days and places, people paid more attention to the strong-headed   8
will of earth. Once homes were built of wood that had been felled from a
single region in a forest. That way, it was thought, the house would hold together more harmoniously, and the family of walls would not fall or lend
themselves to the unhappiness or arguments of the inhabitants.

An Italian immigrant to Chicago, Aldo Piacenzi, built birdhouses that   9
were dwellings of harmony and peace. They were the incredible spired shapes
of cathedrals in Italy. They housed not only the birds, but also his memories,
his own past. He painted them the watery blue of his Mediterranean, the wild
rose of flowers in a summer field. Inside them were straw and the droppings
of lives that layed eggs, fledglings who grew there. What places to inhabit, the
bright and sunny birdhouses in dreary alleyways of the city.

Thinking Critically

◆3 What does Hogan mean by "the earth wanted to go about life in its own way"? Can you
find any other places where the author personifies inanimate objects?

One beautiful afternoon, cool and moist, with the kind of yellow light that   10
falls on earth in these arid regions, I waited for barn swallows to return from
their daily work of food gathering. Inside the tunnel where they live, hundreds
of swallows had mixed their saliva with mud and clay, much like the solitary bees,
and formed nests that were perfect as a potter's bowl. At five in the evening, they
returned all at once, a dark, flying shadow. Despite their enormous numbers
and the crowding together of nests, they didn't pause for even a moment before entering the nests, nor did they crowd one another. Instantly they vanished into the nests. The tunnel went silent. It held no outward signs of life.

But I knew they were there, filled with the fire of living. And what a mar-   11
riage of elements was in those nests. Not only mud's earth and water, the fire
of sun and dry air, but even the elements contained one another. The bodies of prophets and crazy men were broken down in that soil.

I've noticed often how when a house is abandoned, it begins to sag. With-   12
out a tenant, it has no need to go on. If it were a person, we'd say it is depressed
or lonely. The roof settles in, the paint cracks, the walls and floorboards warp
and slope downward in their own natural ways, telling us that life must stay
in everything as the world whirls and tills and moves through boundless space.

One summer day, cleaning up after long-eared owls where I work at a re-   13
habilitation facility for birds of prey, I was raking the gravel floor of a flight
cage. Down on the ground, something looked like it was moving. I bent
over to look into the pile of bones and pellets I'd just raked together. There,
close to the ground, were two fetal mice. They were new to the planet, pink
and hairless. They were so tenderly young. Their faces had swollen blue-
veined eyes. They were nestled in a mound of feathers, soft as velvet, each one
curled up smaller than an infant's ear, listening to the first sounds of earth.
But the ants were biting them. They turned in agony, unable to pull away,
not yet having the arms or legs to move, but feeling, twisting away from, the
pain of the bites. I was horrified to see them bitten out of life that way. I
dipped them in water, as if to take away the sting, and let the ants fall in the
bucket. Then I held the tiny mice in the palm of my hand. Some of the ants
were drowning in the water. I was trading one life for another, exchanging
the lives of the ants for those of mice, but I hated their suffering, and hated
even more that they had not yet grown to a life, and already they inhabited
the miserable world of pain. Death and life feed each other. I know that. ❹

Inside these rooms where birds are healed, there are other lives besides   14
those of mice. There are fine gray globes the wasps have woven together, the

---

Thinking Critically

❹ How do "death and life feed each other"?

white cocoons of spiders in a corner, the downward tunneling anthills. All these dwellings are inside one small walled space, but I think most about the mice. Sometimes the downy nests fall out of the walls where their mothers have placed them out of the way of their enemies. When one of the nests falls, they are so well made and soft, woven mostly from the chest feathers of birds. Sometimes the leg of a small quail holds the nest together like a slender cornerstone with dry, bent claws. The mice have adapted to life in the presence of their enemies, adapted to living in the thin wall between beak and beak, claw and claw. They move their nests often, as if a new rafter or wall will protect them from the inevitable fate of all our returns home to the deeper, wider nests of earth that houses us all.

One August at Zia Pueblo during the corn dance, I noticed tourists picking up shards of all the old pottery that had been made and broken there. The residents of Zia know not to take the bowls and pots left behind by the older ones. They know that the fragments of those earlier lives need to be smoothed back to earth, but younger nations, travelers from continents across the world who have come to inhabit this land, have little of their own to grow on. The pieces of earth that were formed into bowls, even on their way home to dust, provide the new people a lifeline to an unknown land, help them remember that they live in the old nest of earth. 15

It was in early February, during the mating season of the great horned owl. It was dusk, and I hiked up the back of a mountain to where I'd heard the owls a year before. I wanted to hear them again, the voices so tender, so deep, like a memory of comfort. I was halfway up the trail when I found a soft, round nest. It had fallen from one of the bare-branched trees. It was a delicate nest, woven together of feathers, sage, and strands of wild grass. Holding it in my hand in the rosy twilight, I noticed that a blue thread was entwined with the other gatherings there. I pulled at the thread a little, and then I recognized it. It was a thread from one of my skirts. It was blue cotton. It was the unmistakable color and shape of a pattern I knew. I liked it, that a thread of my life was in an abandoned nest, one that had held eggs and new life. ⑤ I took the nest home. At home, I held it to the light and looked more closely. There, to my surprise, nestled into the gray-green sage, was a gnarl of black hair. It was also unmistakable. It was my daughter's hair, cleaned from a brush and picked up out in the sun beneath the maple tree, or the pit cherry where the birds eat from the overladen, fertile branches until only the seeds remain on the trees. 16

Thinking Critically

⑤ How does the author feel about finding the blue thread from one of her skirts embedded in a bird's nest? What clues from the text let you know her feelings?

I didn't know what kind of nest it was, or who had lived there. It didn't   17
matter. I thought of the remnants of our lives carried up the hill that way and
turned into shelter. That night, resting inside the walls of our home, the
world outside weighed so heavily against the thin wood of the house. The
sloped roof was the only thing between us and the universe. Everything outside of our wooden boundaries seemed so large. Filled with the night's citizens, it all came alive. The world opened in the thickets of the dark. The wild
grapes would soon ripen on the vines. The burrowing ones were emerging.
Horned owls sat in treetops. Mice scurried here and there. Skunks, fox, the
slow and holy porcupine, all were passing by this way. The young of the solitary bees were feeding on the pollen in the dark. The whole world was a nest
on its humble tilt, in the maze of the universe, holding us. ◈

UNDERSTANDING DETAILS

1. What does the "broken wall of earth" (paragraph 1) consist of? Why is it fascinating to Hogan?
2. What is the "marriage of elements" Hogan refers to in paragraph 11?
3. To what does "the strong-headed will of earth" (paragraph 8) refer? How can
   the earth be "strong-headed"?
4. In what ways were the voices of the owls comforting to Hogan (paragraph 16)?

READING CRITICALLY

5. Why did the town of Manitou seem to be "the center of the world" (paragraph 4)
   to Hogan?
6. Why do the barn swallows (paragraph 10) interest Hogan? What do they
   represent?
7. How do our dwellings represent us and our view of the world?
8. In what ways are humans like the bees that Hogan describes at the beginning
   of this essay?

DISCOVERING RHETORICAL STRATEGIES

9. Why does Hogan include the story about the man in a cave (paragraph 7)?
   What does it add to the essay?
10. In paragraph 16, what is the significance of the thread from Hogan's skirt and
    the "gnarl of hair" from her daughter?
11. This essay is divided by spaces into nine sections. What does each section rep-
    resent? What effect do these divisions have in the essay?

Thinking Critically

◈ Explain the author's concluding sentence, in which she compares the whole earth to a
"nest" holding us all?

12. What is the significance of the "remnants of our lives" (paragraph 17) that Hogan found in the abandoned nest she discovered? In what way does the scene capture the main theme of the entire essay?

MAKING CONNECTIONS

13. Compare and contrast Linda Hogan's sense of place with that described by Kimberly Wozencraft ("Notes from the Country Club"), Firoozeh Dumas ("Leffingwell Elementary School"), and/or Robert Ramirez ("The Barrio"). In which essay is the devotion to a particular place most vivid and compelling? Why?

14. Hogan's reverence for nature is echoed in John McPhee's "The Pines" and Scott Russell Sanders's "Homeplace." Which essay attaches the most religious significance to its natural world? Why do you think this is so?

15. How are the various "dwellings" described by Hogan different from those mentioned in Ray Bradbury's "Summer Rituals," Kimberly Wozencraft's "Notes from the Country Club," Sandra Cisneros's "Only daughter," and/or Richard Rodriguez's "Public and Private Language"?

IDEAS FOR DISCUSSION/WRITING

Preparing to Write

Write freely about the importance of escape in contemporary society: Why do people feel the need to escape or retreat? What are they escaping from? What pressures cause us to look for methods of escape? What are these methods? How are they different from one another? In what ways do these strategies bring relief?

Choosing a Topic

1. *Learning Online:* Picture the "dream" home where you want to retire and grow old. What are the similarities and differences between your "dream home" and the home from the Hooked on Golf website mentioned in Preparing to Read? Is your home luxurious or casual? Large or small? Modern or rustic? Considering the images you have in your mind, write an essay describing your ideal retirement home.

2. You have been asked to write an article for your high school newspaper on safe, healthy methods of escape from the pressures that confront teens today. Explore your thoughts on this topic; then write an essay that will appeal to the values and concerns of today's high school students.

3. Why do we need various forms of escape? Is this need a positive or negative force? Analyze our need to escape, including both the reasons for it and its consequences.

4. Hogan indirectly compares some inhabitants in the wild with humans. Think of another comparison with humans that teaches us important truths about ourselves, and, using Hogan's essay as a model, write an essay that explores this comparison and leads us to new insights about the human race.

Before beginning your essay, you might want to consult the checklists on page 64.

MALCOLM COWLEY   (1898–1989)

The View from 80

Malcolm Cowley had a long and distinguished career as a literary historian, critic, editor, and poet. After receiving his bachelor's degree at Harvard, he served in the American Ambulance Corps during World War I and then pursued graduate studies in literature at the University of Montpellier in France. In 1929, he became Associate Editor of *The New Republic,* presiding over the magazine's literary department for the next fifteen years. Perhaps his most important book of literary criticism is *Exile's Return* (1934), a study of the "lost generation" of expatriate Americans living in Paris in the 1920s, which included Ernest Hemingway, Ezra Pound, F. Scott Fitzgerald, and Hart Crane. Cowley returned to the same topic in 1973 with *A Second Flowering: Works and Days of the Lost Generation.* He also published editions of such authors as Hemingway, William Faulkner, Nathaniel Hawthorne, Walt Whitman, and Fitzgerald; two collections of his own poetry, *Blue Juniata* (1929) and *The Dry Season* (1941); and numerous other translations, editions, and books of criticism. His most recent publications include *The Flower and the Leaf: A Contemporary Record of American Writing Since 1941* (1985) and *Conversations with Malcolm Cowley* (1986). When asked about the secret of his amazing productivity, Cowley replied: "Writers often speak of 'saving their energy,' as if each man were given a nickel's worth of it, which he is at liberty to spend. To me, the mind of the poet resembles Fortunatus's purse: The more spent, the more it supplies."

Preparing to Read

The following essay was originally commissioned by *Life* magazine (1978) for inclusion in a series of articles on aging. Cowley later converted the piece into the first chapter of a book with the same title: *The View from 80* (1980). Through a combination of vivid personal experience and research, the author crafted an essay that helps us experience what life is like for an eighty-year-old.

Exploring Experience: As you prepare to read Cowley's description of "the country of age," take some time to think about age in general: How many people over the age of sixty do you know? Over the age of seventy? How do they behave? Do you think these older people see themselves in the same way you see them? Do you think they consider themselves "old"? What clues remind them of their advancing age? What events and attitudes remind you of your age? In what ways will you be different than you are now when you reach the age of eighty?

Learning Online: Visit the website of the American Association of Retired Persons (www.aarp.org), and read about some of the issues affecting the elderly. Keep these in mind while reading Cowley's observations about aging.

They gave me a party on my 80th birthday in August 1978. First there   1
were cards, letters, telegrams, even a cable of congratulation or con-
dolence; then there were gifts, mostly bottles; there was catered food
and finally a big cake with, for some reason, two candles (had I gone back
to very early childhood?). I blew the candles out a little unsteadily. Amid the
applause and clatter I thought about a former custom of the Northern Ojibwas when they lived on the shores of Lake Winnipeg. They were kind to their
old people, who remembered and enforced the ancient customs of the tribe,
but when an old person became decrepit, it was time for him to go. Sometimes he was simply abandoned, with a little food, on an island in the lake.
If he deserved special honor, they held a tribal feast for him. The old man sang
a death song and danced, if he could. While he was still singing, his son came
from behind and brained him with a tomahawk. [1]

That was quick, it was dignified, and I wonder whether it was any more   2
cruel, essentially, than some of our civilized customs or inadvertencies in disposing
of the aged. I believe in rites and ceremonies. I believe in big parties for special
occasions such as an 80th birthday. It is a sort of belated bar mitzvah, since the
80-year-old, like a Jewish adolescent, is entering a new stage of life; let him (or
her) undergo a *rite de passage,* with toasts and a cantor. Seventy-year-olds, or sep-
tuas, have the illusion of being middle-aged, even if they have been pushed back
on a shelf. The 80-year-old, the octo, looks at the double-dumpling figure and
admits that he is old. The last act has begun, and it will be the test of the play.

To enter the country of age is a new experience, different from what you   3
supposed it to be. Nobody, man or woman, knows the country until he has
lived in it and has taken out his citizenship papers. Here is my own report,
submitted as a road map and guide to some of the principal monuments.

The new octogenarian feels as strong as ever when he is sitting back in a   4
comfortable chair. He ruminates, he dreams, he remembers. He doesn't want
to be disturbed by others. It seems to him that old age is only a costume assumed for those others; the true, the essential self is ageless. In a moment he
will rise and go for a ramble in the woods, taking a gun along, or a fishing
rod, if it is spring. Then he creaks to his feet, bending forward to keep his balance, and realizes that he will do nothing of the sort. The body and its surroundings have their messages for him, or only one message: "You are old."
Here are some of the occasions on which he receives the message:

• when it becomes an achievement to do thoughtfully, step by step, what
  he once did instinctively
• when his bones ache

Thinking Critically

[1] What do you think about the Ojibwa custom described by Cowley? Do you agree or disagree with the author that it conferred a "quick" and "dignified" death on decrepit older
members of the tribe?

- when there are more and more little bottles in the medicine cabinet, with instructions for taking four times a day
- when he fumbles and drops his toothbrush (butterfingers)
- when his face has bumps and wrinkles, so that he cuts himself while shaving (blood on the towel)
- when year by year his feet seem farther from his hands
- when he can't stand on one leg and has trouble pulling on his pants
- when he hesitates on the landing before walking down a flight of stairs
- when he spends more time looking for things misplaced than he spends using them after he (or more often his wife) has found them
- when he falls asleep in the afternoon
- when it becomes harder to bear in mind two things at once
- when a pretty girl passes him in the street and he doesn't turn his head
- when he forgets names, even of people he saw last month ("Now I'm beginning to forget nouns," the poet Conrad Aiken said at 80)
- when he listens hard to jokes and catches everything but the snapper
- when he decides not to drive at night anymore
- when everything takes longer to do—bathing, shaving, getting dressed or undressed—but when time passes quickly, as if he were gathering speed while coasting downhill. The year from 79 to 80 is like a week when he was a boy. ❷

Those are some of the intimate messages. "Put cotton in your ears and pebbles in your shoes," said a gerontologist, a member of that new profession dedicated to alleviating all maladies of old people except the passage of years. "Pull on rubber gloves. Smear Vaseline over your glasses, and there you have it: instant aging." Not quite. His formula omits the messages from the social world, which are louder, in most cases, than those from within. We start by growing old in other people's eyes, then slowly we come to share their judgment.

I remember a morning many years ago when I was backing out of the parking lot near the railroad station in Brewster, New York. There was a near collision. The driver of the other car jumped out and started to abuse me; he had his fists ready. Then he looked hard at me and said, "Why, you're an old man." He got back into his car, slammed the door, and drove away, while I stood there fuming. "I'm only 65," I thought. "He wasn't driving carefully. I can still take care of myself in a car, or in a fight, for that matter."

My hair was whiter—it may have been in 1974—when a young woman rose and offered me her seat in a Madison Avenue bus. That message was kind and also devastating. "Can't I even stand up?" I thought as I thanked her and declined the seat. But the same thing happened twice the following year,

---

Thinking Critically

❷ List five ways you know how old you are.

and the second time I gratefully accepted the offer, though with a sense of having diminished myself. ❸ "People are right about me," I thought while wondering why all those kind gestures were made by women. Do men now regard themselves as the weaker sex, not called upon to show consideration? All the same it was a relief to sit down and relax.

A few days later I wrote a poem, "The Red Wagon," that belongs in the   8
record of aging:

> For his birthday they gave him a red express wagon
> with a driver's high seat and a handle that steered.
> His mother pulled him around the yard.
> "Giddyap," he said, but she laughed and went off
> to wash the breakfast dishes.
>
> "I wanta ride too," his sister said,
> and he pulled her to the edge of a hill.
> "Now, sister, go home and wait for me,
> but first give a push to the wagon."
> He climbed again to the high seat,
> this time grasping that handle-that-steered.
>
> The red wagon rolled slowly down the slope,
> then faster as it passed the schoolhouse
> and faster as it passed the store,
> the road still dropping away.
> Oh, it was fun.
> But would it ever stop?
> Would the road always go downhill?
> The red wagon rolled faster.
> Now it was in strange country.
> It passed a white house he must have dreamed about,
> deep woods he had never seen,
> a graveyard where, something told him, his sister
> was buried.
>
> Far below
> the sun was sinking into a broad plain.
>
> The red wagon rolled faster.
> Now he was clutching the seat, not even trying to steer.
> Sweat clouded his heavy spectacles.
> His white hair streamed in the wind.

Even before he or she is 80, the aging person may undergo another iden-   9
tity crisis like that of adolescence. ❹ Perhaps there had also been a middle-aged crisis, the male or the female menopause, but the rest of adult life he

---

Thinking Critically

❸ Why do you think the author felt "diminished" by accepting someone else's seat on the bus?

❹ What does Cowley mean by the "identity crisis" of old age?

had taken himself for granted, with his capabilities and failings. Now, when he looks in the mirror, he asks himself, "Is this really me?"—or he avoids the mirror out of distress at what it reveals, those bags and wrinkles. In his new makeup he is called upon to play a new role in a play that must be improvised. André Gide, that long-lived man of letters, wrote in his journal, "My heart has remained so young that I have the continual feeling of playing a part, the part of the 70-year-old that I certainly am; and the infirmities and weaknesses that remind me of my age act like a prompter, reminding me of my lines when I tend to stray. Then, like the good actor I want to be, I go back into my role, and I pride myself on playing it well."

In his new role the old person will find that he is tempted by new vices, that he receives new compensations (not so widely known), and that he may possibly achieve new virtues. Chief among these is the heroic or merely obstinate refusal to surrender in the face of time. One admires the ships that go down with all flags flying and the captain on the bridge.   10

Among the vices of age⁵ are avarice, untidiness, and vanity, which last takes the form of a craving to be loved or simply admired. Avarice is the worst of those three. Why do so many old persons, men and women alike, insist on hoarding money when they have no prospect of using it and even when they have no heirs? They eat the cheapest food, buy no clothes, and live in a single room when they could afford better lodging. It may be that they regard money as a form of power; there is a comfort in watching it accumulate while other powers are dwindling away. How often we read of an old person found dead in a hovel, on a mattress partly stuffed with bankbooks and stock certificates! The bankbook syndrome, we call it in our family, which has never succumbed.   11

Untidiness we call the Langley Collyer syndrome. To explain, Langley Collyer was a former concert pianist who lived alone with his 70-year-old brother in a brownstone house on upper Fifth Avenue. The once fashionable neighborhood had become part of Harlem. Homer, the brother, had been an admiralty lawyer, but was now blind and partly paralyzed; Langley played for him and fed him on buns and oranges, which he thought would restore Homer's sight. He never threw away a daily paper because Homer, he said, might want to read them all. He saved other things as well and the house became filled with rubbish from roof to basement. The halls were lined on both sides with bundled newspapers, leaving narrow passageways in which Langley had devised booby traps to catch intruders.   12

On March 21, 1947, some unnamed person telephoned the police to report that there was a dead body in the Collyer house. The police broke down   13

Thinking Critically

⑤ What do you think are the worst "vices" of people who are twenty years old? Forty years old?

the front door and found the hall impassable; then they hoisted a ladder to a second-story window. Behind it Homer was lying on the floor in a bathrobe; he had starved to death. Langley had disappeared. After some delay, the police broke into the basement, chopped a hole in the roof, and began throwing junk out of the house, top and bottom. It was 18 days before they found Langley's body, gnawed by rats. Caught in one of his own booby traps, he had died in a hallway just outside Homer's door. By that time the police had collected, and the Department of Sanitation had hauled away, 120 tons of rubbish, including, besides the newspapers, 14 grand pianos and the parts of a dismantled Model T Ford. [6]

Why do so many old people accumulate junk, not on the scale of Langley Collyer, but still in a dismaying fashion? Their tables are piled high with it, their bureau drawers are stuffed with it, their closet rods bend with the weight of clothes not worn for years. I suppose that the piling up is partly from lethargy and partly from feeling that everything once useful, including their own bodies, should be preserved. Others, though not so many, have such a fear of becoming Langley Collyers that they strive to be painfully neat. Every tool they own is in its place, though it will never be used again; every scrap of paper is filed away in alphabetical order. At last their immoderate neatness becomes another vice of age, if a milder one.   14

The vanity of older people is an easier weakness to explain and to condone. [7] With less to look forward to, they yearn for recognition of what they have been: the reigning beauty, the athlete, the soldier, the scholar. It is the beauties who have the hardest time. A portrait of themselves at twenty hangs on the wall, and they try to resemble it by making an extravagant use of creams, powder, and dyes. Being young at heart, they think they are merely revealing their essential persons. The athletes find shelves for their silver trophies, which are polished once a year. Perhaps a letter sweater lies wrapped in a bureau drawer. I remember one evening when a no-longer athlete had guests for dinner and tried to find his sweater. "Oh, that old thing," his wife said. "The moths got into it, and I threw it away." The athlete sulked, and his guests went home early.   15

But there are also pleasures of the body, or the mind, that are enjoyed by a greater number of older persons. Those pleasures include some that younger people find hard to appreciate. One of them is simply sitting still, like a snake on a sunwarmed stone, with a delicious feeling of indolence that was seldom   16

Thinking Critically

[6] Why do you think some people accumulate junk? Do you feel that older folks collect it more often than younger ones? If so, why?

[7] What kinds of "vanity" do older people have? In what ways do people your age display vanity? How are these two types of vanity different?

attained in earlier years. A leaf flutters down; a cloud moves by inches across the horizon. At such moments the older person, completely relaxed, has become a part of nature—and a living part, with blood coursing through his veins. The future does not exist for him. He thinks, if he thinks at all, that life for younger persons is still a battle royal of each against each, but that now he has nothing more to win or lose. He is not so much above as outside the battle, as if he had assumed the uniform of some small neutral country, perhaps Liechtenstein or Andorra. From a distance he notes that some of the combatants, men or women, are jostling ahead—but why do they fight so hard when the most they can hope for is a longer obituary? He can watch the scrounging and gouging, he can hear the shouts of exultation, the moans of the gravely wounded, and meanwhile he feels secure; nobody will attack him from ambush.

Age has other physical compensations besides the nirvana of dozing in the sun. A few of the simplest needs become a pleasure to satisfy. When an old woman in a nursing home was asked what she really liked to do she answered in one word: "Eat." She might have been speaking for many of her fellows. Meals in a nursing home, however badly cooked, serve as climactic moments of the day. The physical essence of the pensioners is being renewed at an appointed hour; [8] now they can go back to meditating or to watching TV while looking forward to the next meal. They can also look forward to sleep, which has become a definite pleasure, not the mere interruption it once had been.   17

Here I am thinking of old persons under nursing care. Others ferociously guard their independence, and some of them suffer less than one might expect from being lonely and impoverished. They can be rejoiced by visits and meetings, but they also have company inside their heads. Some of them are busiest when their hands are still. What passes through the minds of many is a stream of persons, images, phrases, and familiar tunes. For some that stream has continued since childhood, but now it is deeper; it is their present and their past combined. At times they conduct silent dialogues with a vanished friend, and these are less tiring—often more rewarding—than spoken conversations. If inner resources are lacking, old persons living alone may seek comfort and a kind of companionship in the bottle. I should judge from the gossip of various neighborhoods that the outer suburbs from Boston to San Diego are full of secretly alcoholic widows. One of those widows, an old friend, was moved from her apartment into a retirement home. She left behind her a closet in which the floor was covered wall to wall with whiskey bottles. "Oh, those empty bottles!" she explained. "They were left by a former tenant."   18

Thinking Critically

[8] How is "the physical essence of pensioners . . . renewed" during mealtime in retirement homes? What is the significance of this activity?

Not whiskey or cooking sherry but simply giving up is the greatest temp- 19 tation of age. It is something different from a stoical acceptance of infirmities, which is something to be admired.

The givers–up see no reason for working. Sometimes they lie in bed all 20 day when moving about would still be possible, if difficult. I had a friend, a distinguished poet, who surrendered in that fashion. The doctors tried to stir him to action, but he refused to leave his room. Another friend, once a successful artist, stopped painting when his eyes began to fail. His doctor made the mistake of telling him that he suffered from a fatal disease. He then lost interest in everything except the splendid Rolls-Royce, acquired in his prosperous days, that stood in the garage. Daily he wiped the dust from its hood. He couldn't drive it on the road any longer, but he used to sit in the driver's seat, start the motor, then back the Rolls out of the garage and drive it in again, back twenty feet and forward twenty feet; that was his only distraction. [9]

I haven't the right to blame those who surrender, not being able to put 21 myself inside their minds or bodies. [10] Often they must have compelling reasons, physical or moral. Not only do they suffer from a variety of ailments, but also they are made to feel that they no longer have a function in the community. Their families and neighbors don't ask them for advice, don't really listen when they speak, don't call on them for efforts. One notes that there are not a few recoveries from apparent senility when that situation changes. If it doesn't change, old persons may decide that efforts are useless. I sympathize with their problems, but the men and women I envy are those who accept old age as a series of challenges.

For such persons, every new infirmity is an enemy to be outwitted, an ob- 22 stacle to be overcome by force of will. [11] They enjoy each little victory over themselves, and sometimes they win a major success. Renoir was one of them. He continued painting, and magnificently, for years after he was crippled by arthritis; the brush had to be strapped to his arm. "You don't need your hand to paint," he said. Goya was another of the unvanquished. At 72 he retired as an official painter of the Spanish court and decided to work only for himself. His later years were those of the famous "black paintings" in which he let his imagination run (and also of the lithographs, then a new technique). At 78 he escaped a reign of terror in Spain by fleeing to Bordeaux.

Thinking Critically

[9] The image of Cowley's friend who drove his Rolls Royce in and out of the garage every day is a metaphor for what? Find two other metaphors in this essay.

[10] Why does Cowley use the word "surrender" in this context?

[11] What does Cowley mean when he says "Every infirmity is an enemy to be outwitted"? According to Cowley, what are some other "enemies" of age?

He was deaf, and his eyes were failing; in order to work he had to wear several pairs of spectacles, one over another, and then use a magnifying glass; but he was producing splendid work in a totally new style. At 80 he drew an ancient man propped on two sticks, with a mass of white hair and beard hiding his face and with the inscription "I am still learning."

"Eighty years old!" the great Catholic poet Paul Claudel wrote in his   23 journal. "No eyes left, no ears, no teeth, no legs, no wind! And when all is said and done, how astonishingly well one does without them!"

UNDERSTANDING DETAILS

1. Name five ways, according to Cowley, that people begin to realize they are "old." How did Cowley himself learn that he was old?
2. List three vices of old age, and explain them as Cowley sees them.
3. What are three compensations of advancing age? In what ways are these activities pleasurable?
4. What does Cowley mean in paragraph 15 by "the vanity of older people"? How do older people manifest this vanity?

READING CRITICALLY

5. What does the wagon symbolize in the author's poem about aging (paragraph 8)? What purpose does this poem serve in the essay?
6. For older people, what is the value of the conversations, images, friends, relatives, and melodies that pass through their minds? How might the elderly use these distractions constructively?
7. According to this essay, what qualities characterize those people who "surrender" (paragraph 21) to old age and those who "accept old age as a series of challenges" (paragraph 21)? Why do you think Cowley has more respect for the latter group?
8. What is Cowley's general attitude toward "the country of age" (paragraph 3)? Why does he feel that way about this stage of life?

DISCOVERING RHETORICAL STRATEGIES

9. After reading this essay, try to summarize in a single word or phrase Cowley's impressions of old age. How does this dominant impression help the author organize the many different details presented in his essay?
10. Why did Cowley include the reference to the Ojibwas at the end of the first paragraph? What effect does that anecdote have on our sympathies as readers?
11. Cowley uses a number of distinct metaphors in describing old age. He equates being old, for example, with acting out a certain "role" in life. He also portrays aging as a "rite of passage," a "challenge," and an "unfamiliar country" through which we must travel. In what sense is each of these metaphors appropriate? How does each help us understand the process of growing old?

12. Cowley uses language to describe a state of being that most of us are not familiar with yet. What other rhetorical strategies does he call upon to make his descriptive essay effective? Give examples of each.

MAKING CONNECTIONS

13. What are the primary differences among the "ageism" recounted by Malcolm Cowley, the racism explained by Lewis Sawaquat ("For My Indian Daughter"), and/or the sexism described by Sandra Cisneros ("Only daughter")? Is one of these "isms" more dangerous than the others? Have you ever experienced any of these types of prejudice?

14. Compare and contrast the weaknesses of old age depicted in Cowley's essay with those portrayed by the grandfather in Ray Bradbury's "Summer Rituals," by Fred Brown in John McPhee's "The Pines," and/or by Frank Furedi in "Our Unhealthy Obsession with Sickness." Do you know anyone in his or her eighties? How does that person act? How do you think you will behave when you are that old?

15. How is Cowley's description of the "identity crisis" many older people go through similar to the identity crisis Lewis Sawaquat ("For My Indian Daughter") suffered when he discovered his Native American heritage and/or Malcolm X ("Learning to Read") discovered when he became more aware of his ethnic and racial heritage? Have you ever gone through an identity crisis? How did you resolve it? Was your crisis in any way like those described by Cowley, Sawaquat, or Malcolm X?

IDEAS FOR DISCUSSION/WRITING

Preparing to Write

Write freely about your impressions of one or more older people in your life: Who are they? What characteristics do they share? How are they different from each other? Different from you? Similar to you? How do you know they are "old"?

Choosing a Topic

1. *Learning Online:* In this essay, Cowley details many of the surprises and realities of aging. What "surprises and realities" have you encountered at your current age? Write an email to your future retired self, entitled "The View from _____ [insert your age]," describing these observations and experiences. Revisit www .aarp.org (see Preparing to Read) for ideas.

2. Cowley explains at the outset of his essay that "the country of age is a new experience, different from what you supposed it to be. Nobody, man or woman, knows the country until he has lived in it and has taken out his citizenship papers" (paragraph 3). Interview an older person to discover his or her view of "the country of age." Then write an essay for your peers describing that person's opinions.

3. In his essay, Cowley describes the signals he receives from his body and his environment that tell him he is "old." What messages did you receive when you were young that indicated you were a "child"? What messages do you receive now that remind you of your present age? How are these messages different from those you received when you were a child? Describe these signals in a well-developed essay addressed to your classmates.

4. Do you think that Americans treat their aged with enough respect? Explain your answer in detail to an older person. Describe various situations that support your opinion.

Before beginning your essay, you might want to consult the checklists on page 64.

The Pines

The range of subjects investigated by author John McPhee is quite astounding. In his twenty books and numerous articles, he has written about sports, food, art, geology, geography, science, history, education, and a variety of other topics. One of the most famous of these "non-fictional, book-length narratives," as he calls them, is *A Sense of Where You Are* (1965), a study of former basketball great Bill Bradley; another is *Levels of the Game* (1969), a chronicle of the epic 1968 U.S. Open semifinal tennis match between Arthur Ashe and Clark Graebner. Most of McPhee's essays have appeared first in the *New Yorker,* a prestigious literary magazine for which he has been a staff writer since 1965. His more recent publications include *The Ransom of Russian Art* (1994), *The Second John McPhee Reader* (1996), *Irons in the Fire* (1997), *Annals of the Former World* (1998) (which was awarded the Pulitzer Prize in 1999), and *The Founding Fish* (2002). McPhee lives in New Jersey near Princeton University, where he teaches a seminar entitled The Literature of Fact. His hobbies include going on long bike rides, fishing for shad and pickerel, and skiing. "Try your best," he advises students, "to write about real people and real places. Essays are just milieus in which to sketch people and places."

Preparing to Read

The following essay, "The Pines," is a small section from a longer piece called *The Pine Barrens* (1968), which describes a remote wilderness in southern New Jersey. Like many of McPhee's narrative essays, "The Pines" is structured around colorful characters—in this case, Fred Brown and Bill Wasovwich, who worry openly in this essay about the encroaching civilization that threatens their unique way of life.

Exploring Experience: As you prepare to read this essay, think for a moment about the different types of people you know: Do you have talkative friends? Quiet friends? Which type of person is most appealing to you? Which type are you? Have you ever lived in the woods? What are the advantages of living in a rural environment instead of a big city? What are the disadvantages?

Learning Online: Using Google's search engine (www.google.com), click on the "Images" tab to conduct a picture search for the term "cranberry bog." Take a few minutes to consider how you would describe this particular area. What is unique about this place, and what seems familiar?

Fred Brown's house is on an unpaved road that curves along the edge 1
of a wide cranberry bog. What attracted me to it was the pump that
stands in his yard. It was something of a wonder that I noticed the
pump, because there were, among other things, eight automobiles in the
yard, two of them on their sides and one of them upside down, all ten years
old or older. Around the cars were old refrigerators, vacuum cleaners, partly
dismantled radios, cathode-ray tubes, a short wooden ski, a large wooden
mallet, dozens of cranberry picker's boxes, many tires, an orange crate dated
1946, a cord or so of firewood, mandolins, engine heads, and maybe a thousand other things. The house itself, two stories high, was covered with tarpa-
per that was peeling away in some places, revealing its original shingles, made
of Atlantic white cedar from the stream courses of the surrounding forest. ❶
I called out to ask if anyone was home, and a voice inside called back, "Come
in. Come in. Come on the hell in."

I walked through a vestibule that had a dirt floor, stepped up into a kitchen, 2
and went on into another room that had several overstuffed chairs in it and
a porcelain-topped table, where Fred Brown was seated, eating a pork chop.
He was dressed in a white sleeveless shirt, ankle-top shoes, and undershorts.
He gave me a cheerful greeting and, without asking why I had come or
what I wanted, picked up a pair of khaki trousers that had been tossed onto
one of the overstuffed chairs and asked me to sit down. He set the trousers
on another chair, and he apologized for being in the middle of his breakfast,
explaining that he seldom drank much but the night before he had had a few
drinks and this had caused his day to start slowly. "I don't know what's the
matter with me, but there's got to be something the matter with me, because drink don't agree with me anymore," he said. He had a raw onion in
one hand, and while he talked he shaved slices from the onion and ate them
between bites of the chop. He was a muscular and well-built man, with short,
bristly white hair, and he had bright, fast-moving eyes in a wide-open face.
His legs were trim and strong, with large muscles in the calves. I guessed
that he was about sixty, and for a man of sixty he seemed to be in remark-
ably good shape. He was actually seventy-nine. "My rule is, Never eat except
when you're hungry," he said, and he ate another slice of the onion. ❷

In a straight-backed chair near the doorway to the kitchen sat a young man 3
with long black hair, who wore a visored red leather cap that had darkened
with age. His shirt was coarse-woven and had eyelets down a V neck that was
laced with a thong. His trousers were made of canvas, and he was wearing

---

Thinking Critically

❶ What do the descriptive details in the first paragraph imply about the trustworthiness of
the author?

❷ Do you think this is a sensible rule for good health? Why or why not?

gum boots. His arms were folded, his legs were stretched out, he had one ankle over the other, and as he sat there he appeared to be sighting carefully past his feet, as if his toes were the outer frame of a gunsight and he could see some sort of target in the floor. When I had entered, I had said hello to him, and he had nodded without looking up. He had a long, straight nose and high cheekbones, in a deeply tanned face that was, somehow, gaunt. I had no idea whether he was shy or hostile. Eventually, when I came to know him, I found him to be as shy a person as I have ever had a chance to know. His name is Bill Wasovwich, and he lives alone in a cabin about half a mile from Fred. First his father, then his mother left him when he was a young boy, and he grew up depending on the help of various people in the pines. One of them, a cranberry grower, employs him and has given him some acreage, in which Bill is building a small cranberry bog of his own, "turfing it out" by hand. When he is not working in the bogs, he goes roaming, as he puts it, setting out cross-country on long, looping journeys, hiking about thirty miles in a typical day, in search of what he calls "events"—surprising a buck, or a gray fox, or perhaps a poacher or a man with a still. Almost no one who is not native to the pines could do this, for the woods have an undulating sameness, and the understory—huckleberries, sheep laurel, sweet fern, high-bush blueberry—is often so dense that a wanderer can walk in a fairly tight circle and think that he is moving in a straight line. State forest rangers spend a good part of their time finding hikers and hunters, some of whom have vanished for days. In his long, pathless journeys, Bill always emerges from the woods near his cabin—and about when he plans to. [3] In the fall, when thousands of hunters come into the pines, he sometimes works as a guide. In the evenings, or in the daytime when he is not working or roaming, he goes to Fred Brown's house and sits there for hours. The old man is a widower whose seven children are long since gone from Hog Wallow, and he is as expansively talkative and worldly as the young one is withdrawn and wild. Although there are fifty-three years between their ages, it is obviously fortunate for each of them to be the other's neighbor.

That first morning, while Bill went on looking at his outstretched toes, [4] Fred got up from the table, put on his pants, and said he was going to cook me a pork chop, because I looked hungry and ought to eat something. It was about noon, and I was even hungrier than I may have looked, so I gratefully accepted his offer, which was a considerable one. There are two or three small general stores in the pines, but for anything as fragile as a fresh pork chop it is necessary to make a round trip from Fred's place of about fifty miles.

Thinking Critically

[3] What does Bill's impeccable sense of direction suggest about his moral and ethical "compass" in life?

Fred went into the kitchen and dropped a chop into a frying pan that was crackling with hot grease. He has a fairly new four-burner stove that uses bottled gas. He keeps water in a large bowl on a table in the kitchen and ladles some when he wants it. While he cooked the meat, he looked out a window through a stand of pitch pines and into the cranberry bog. "I saw a big buck out here last night with velvet on his horns," he said. "Them horns is soft when they're in velvet." On a nail high on one wall of the room that Bill and I were sitting in was a large meat cleaver. Next to it was a billy club. The wall itself was papered in a flower pattern, and the wallpaper continued out across the ceiling and down the three other walls, lending the room something of the appearance of the inside of a gift box. ◆ In some parts of the ceiling, the paper had come loose. "I didn't paper this year," Fred said. "For the last couple months, I've had sinus." The floor was covered with old rugs. They had been put down in random pieces, and in some places as many as six layers were stacked up. In winter, when the temperature approaches zero, the worst cold comes through the floor. The only source of heat in the house is a wood-burning stove in the main room. There were seven calendars on the walls, all current and none with pictures of nudes. Fading into pastel on one wall was a rotogravure photograph of President and Mrs. Eisenhower. A framed poem read:

God hath not promised
Sun without rain
Joy without sorrow
Peace without pain. ◆ 5

Noticing my interest in all this, Fred reached into a drawer and showed   5
me what appeared to be a postcard. On it was a photograph of a woman, and Fred said with a straight face that she was his present girl, adding that he meets her regularly under a juniper tree on a road farther south in the pines. The woman, whose appearance suggested strongly that she had never been within a great many miles of the Pine Barrens, was wearing nothing at all.

I asked Fred what all those cars were doing in his yard, and he said that   6
one of them was in running condition and the rest were its predecessors. The working vehicle was a 1956 Mercury. Each of the seven others had at one time or another been his best car, and each, in turn, had lain down like a sick animal and had died right there in the yard, unless it had been towed home after a mishap elsewhere in the pines. Fred recited, with affection, the history of each car. Of one old Ford, for example, he said, "I upset that up to

---

Thinking Critically

◆ How is meeting Fred a "gift" for the narrator and for the readers of his essay?
◆ In what ways does this short poem help us understand the essay?

Speedwell in the creek." And of an even older car, a station wagon, he said, "I busted that one up in the snow. I met a car on a little hill, and hit the brake, and hit a tree." One of the cars had met its end at a narrow bridge about four miles from Hog Wallow, where Fred had hit a state trooper, head on.

The pork was delicious and almost crisp. Fred gave me a potato with it   7 and a pitcher of melted grease from the frying pan to pour over the potato. He also handed me a loaf of bread and a dish of margarine, saying, "Here's your bread. You can have one piece or two. Whatever you want."

Fred apologized for not having a phone, after I asked where I would have   8 to go to make a call, later on. He said, "I don't have no phone because I don't have no electric. If I had electric, I would have had a phone in here a long time ago." He uses a kerosene lamp, a propane lamp, and two flashlights.

He asked where I was going, and I said that I had no particular destina-   9 tion, explaining that I was in the pines because I found it hard to believe that so much unbroken forest could still exist so near the big Eastern cities, and I wanted to see it while it was still there. "Is that so?" he said, three times. Like many people in the pines, he often says things three times. "Is that so? Is that so?"

I asked him what he thought of a plan that has been developed by Burling-   10 ton and Ocean Counties to create a supersonic jetport in the pines, connected by a spur of the Garden State Parkway to a new city of two hundred and fifty thousand people, also in the pines.

"They've been talking about that for three years, and they've never given   11 up," Fred said.

"It'd be the end of these woods," Bill said. This was the first time I heard   12 Bill speak. I had been there for an hour, and he had not said a word. Without looking up, he said again, "It'd be the end of these woods, I can tell you that." ❻

Fred said, "They could build ten jetports around me. I wouldn't give a   13 damn."

"You ain't going to be around very long," Bill said to him. "It would be   14 the end of these woods."

Fred took that as a fact, and not as an insult. "Yes, it would be the end of   15 these woods," he said. "But there'd be people here you could do business with."

Bill said, "There ain't no place like this left in the country, I don't believe—   16 and I traveled around a little bit, too."

Thinking Critically

❻ Why does Bill finally speak about this conflict between nature and civilization?

Eventually, I made the request I had intended to make when I walked in   17
the door. "Could I have some water?" I said to Fred. "I have a jerry can, and
I'd like to fill it at the pump."

"Hell, yes," he said. "That isn't my water. That's God's water. That right,   18
Bill?"

"I *guess* so," Bill said, without looking up. "It's good water, I can tell you   19
that."

"That's God's water," Fred said again. "Take all you want."   20

UNDERSTANDING DETAILS

1. What attracted McPhee to Fred Brown's house? In what ways is this object representative of Fred's yard? Of Fred's life?
2. What other things are in Fred's front yard? What does this collection of junk say about Fred and his lifestyle?
3. In paragraph 3, McPhee comments that, despite the wide difference in age between Fred and Bill, "it is obviously fortunate for each of them to be the other's neighbor." In what ways do the two characters need each other?
4. Describe in your own words the inside of Fred's house. Which details does McPhee stress in his description? Why does he focus on these and not on others?

READING CRITICALLY

5. Why is McPhee visiting "the pines"? What do you think his opinion of "the pines" is? What specific references reveal his opinions?
6. Why does Bill go "roaming"? What do you think the purpose of these journeys is?
7. Why does Bill believe a jetport would be "the end of these woods" (paragraph 12)? Why do you think these were the first words Bill had spoken since the author arrived? Explain your answer.
8. Why do you think McPhee ends this piece with several references to God? How does the dialogue about "God's water" help us understand Fred and Bill even more specifically?

DISCOVERING RHETORICAL STRATEGIES

9. Which senses does McPhee concentrate on most in this description? Choose one paragraph to analyze. In one column, write down all the senses the description arouses; in another, record the words and phrases that activate these senses.
10. What "tone" or "mood" is McPhee trying to create in this excerpt? Is he successful? Explain your answer.
11. What is the author's point of view in this essay? How would the method of description change if the story were told from Fred's vantage point? From Bill's? How does this particular point of view help the author organize his description?
12. McPhee relies heavily on description to make his point. What other rhetorical modes support this narrative essay? Give examples of each of these modes from the essay.

MAKING CONNECTIONS

13. How does the friendship between Fred and Bill described in McPhee's essay differ from friendships in Kimberly Wozencraft's "Notes from the Country Club," Joel Stein's "You Are Not My Friend," and/or Robert Ramirez's "The Barrio"? Which friendships are stronger in your opinion? Explain your answer.

14. Compare and contrast McPhee's concern about preserving the environment with comparable feelings by Linda Hogan ("Dwellings"). How are they similar? How are they different?

15. In McPhee's essay, how does Fred Brown feel about the uses and abuses of technology? Would Jay Walljasper ("Our Schedules, Our Selves"), Jessica Mitford ("Behind the Formaldehyde Curtain"), and/or Dave Grossman ("We Are Training Our Kids to Kill") agree with him? Explain your answer.

IDEAS FOR DISCUSSION/WRITING

Preparing to Write

Write freely about someone you know who represents a specific personality "type": What distinguishes this type from other types you know? What do people of this type have in common? What are their looks, values, needs, desires, living conditions, and so on? What do you have in common with the type of person you have just described? How are you different?

Choosing a Topic

1. *Learning Online:* Using McPhee's example, explain a unique memory to your reader. Use description to convey the significance of this memory. If you need inspiration, go back to the "Images" on Google mentioned in the Preparing to Read exercise.

2. Give a name (either real or fictitious) to the person you have just described in the prewriting exercise, and write an essay depicting the house, apartment, or room in which this person lives. Try to make your description as vivid and as well organized as McPhee's portrait of Fred Brown. Imagine that the audience for your description is someone who has never met this person and has never seen where the person lives.

3. Write an essay describing for your classmates some of the "junk" you have collected over the years. Why are certain items junk to some people and treasures to others? What makes the things you are describing special to you?

4. Describe the inside of your house, apartment, or room, explaining to your class what the decorations say about you as a person. If someone in your class were to see where you live, could he or she make any accurate deductions about your political, social, or moral values based on the contents and arrangement of the place you call "home"?

Before beginning your essay, you might want to consult the checklists on page 64.

Chapter Writing Assignments

Practicing Description

1. Write a spatial description of your home by exploring its basic sections or rooms. What does your home reveal about you as a person? About your family?

2. Think about the extent to which influences such as family, education, and community have contributed to the person you are today. Describe the kind of person you are and the sources of a few of your most important qualities.

3. Consider the health of the environment in your immediate community (air quality, noise, landscape). Describe an environmental problem you have observed. Be sure to provide examples of the problem you are describing.

Exploring Ideas

4. Discuss a cultural icon (such as a rock star or a prominent building) and what it represents about the culture you are describing. How did this person or object become an icon in its culture? What biases or ideals does it express? How do people outside this culture view it?

5. Think about the ways people's physical surroundings (office, weather, house, apartment) affect them. Discuss one important way these surroundings have influenced someone's behavior. Provide examples in your discussion that explore the relationship between various features in your surroundings and the manner in which people react to them.

6. In your opinion, how well are elderly people treated in America? Write an essay describing the level of respect older people get in American society. Use examples of people you know to support your ideas.

Writing from Sources

For detailed information on writing from sources, see Part III.

7. Consider the different security levels of imprisonment in the United States. What qualifies an individual for each level? What are the housing facilities and environment for each level? Research this topic, and write an essay that provides a detailed description of each type of prison.

8. How does attitude affect the aging process? Research the connection between psychological and physical health in the elderly. Then, citing evidence from your research, explain this relationship in a documented essay.

Analyzing Visual Images

© Dave Beckerman Photography

9. Look at the detail in this picture, and try to imagine what smells, tastes, sounds, textures, and sights you might experience while standing in this setting. Write a description of this scene for someone who has never been here, including all the senses that this scene evokes.
10. Look at the photograph by Gerry Gavigan on page 54 at the beginning of this chapter. Choose a sense besides sight (smell, hear, taste, or feel), and explain why this sense is dominant in this picture.

Chapter 5

NARRATION
Telling a Story

A good story is a powerful method of getting someone's attention. The excitement that accompanies a suspenseful ghost story, a lively anecdote, or a vivid joke easily attests to this fact. In reality, narration is one of the earliest verbal skills we all learn as children, providing us with a convenient, logical, and easily understood means of sharing our thoughts with other people. Storytelling is powerful because it offers us a way of dramatizing our ideas so that others can identify with them.

DEFINING NARRATION

Narration involves telling a story that is often based on personal experience. Stories can be oral or written, real or imaginary, short or long. A good story, however, always has a point or purpose. Narration can be the dominant mode (as in a novel or short story) supported by other rhetorical strategies, or it can serve the purpose of another rhetorical mode (as in a persuasive essay, a historical survey, or a scientific report).

In its subordinate role, narration can provide examples or explain ideas. If asked why you are attending college, for instance, you might turn to narration to make your answer clear, beginning with a story about your family's hardships in the past. The purpose of telling such a story would be to show your listeners how important higher education is to you by encouraging them to understand and identify with your family history.

Unlike description, which generally portrays people, places, and objects in *space,* narration asks the reader to follow a series of actions through a particular *time* sequence. Description, however, often complements the movement of narration. People must be depicted, for instance, along with their relationships to one another before their actions can have any real meaning for us; similarly, places must be described so that we can picture the setting and understand the activities in a specific scene. The organization of the action and the time spent on each episode in a story should be based principally on a writer's analysis of the interests and needs of his or her audience.

To be most effective, narration should prolong the exciting parts of a story and shorten the routine facts that simply move the reader from one episode to another. If you were robbed on your way to work, for example, a good narrative describing the incident would concentrate on the traumatic event itself rather than on such mundane and boring details as what you had for breakfast and what chores you did prior to the attack. Finally, just like description, narration *shows* rather than *tells* its purpose to the audience. The factual statement "I was robbed this morning" could be made much more vivid and dramatic through the addition of some simple narration: "As I was walking to work at 7:30 A.M., a huge and angry-looking man ran up to me, thrust a gun into the middle of my stomach, and took my money, my new wristwatch, all my credit cards, and my pants—leaving me penniless and embarrassed."

The following paragraph written by a student recounts a recent parachuting experience. As you read this narrative, notice especially the writer's use of vivid detail to *show* rather than *tell* her message to the readers.

> *I have always needed occasional "fixes" of excitement in my life, so when I realized one spring day that I was more than ordinarily bored, I made up my mind to take more than ordinary steps to relieve that boredom. I decided to go parachuting. The next thing I knew, I was stuffed into a claustrophobically small plane with five other terrified people, rolling down a bumpy, rural runway, droning my way to 3,500 feet and an exhilarating experience. Once over the jump area, I waited my turn, stepped onto the strut, held my breath, and then kicked off into the cold, rushing air as my heart pounded heavily. All I could think was, "I hope this damn parachute opens!" The sensation of falling backward through space was unfamiliar and disconcerting till my chute opened with a loud "pop," momentarily pulling me upward toward the distant sky. After several minutes of floating downward, I landed rudely on the hard ground. Life, I remembered happily, could be awfully exciting, and a month later, when my tailbone had stopped throbbing, I still felt that way.*

THINKING CRITICALLY THROUGH NARRATION

Rhetorical modes offer us different ways of perceiving reality. Narration is an especially useful tool for sequencing or putting details and information in some kind of logical order, usually chronological. Practicing exercises in narrative techniques can help you see clear patterns in topics you are writing about.

Although narration is usually used in conjunction with other rhetorical modes, we are going to isolate it here so you can appreciate its specific mechanics separate from other mental activities. If you feel the process of narration in your head, you are more likely to understand exactly what it entails and therefore use it more effectively in reading essays and in organizing and writing your own essays.

For the best results, we will once again do some warm-up exercises to make your sequencing perceptions as accurate and successful as possible. In this way, you will actually learn to feel how your mind works in this particular mode and then be more aware of the thinking strategies available to you in your own reading and writing. As you become more conscious of the mechanics of the individual rhetorical modes, you will naturally become more adept at combining them to accomplish the specific purpose and the related effect you want to create.

© Scott Alberts

The following exercises, which require a combination of thinking and writing skills, will help you practice this particular strategy in isolation. Just as in a physical workout, we will warm up your mental capabilities one by one as if they were muscles that can be developed individually before being used together in harmony.

1. Write or tell the story that goes with the Scott Alberts photo on page 112. Make this scene the beginning of your story, and then create the remainder of the plot.
2. Make a chronological list of the different activities you did yesterday, from waking in the morning to sleeping at night. Randomly pick two events from your day, and treat them as the highlights of your day. Now write freely for five minutes, explaining the story of your day and emphasizing the importance of these two highlights.
3. Recall an important event that happened to you between the ages of five and ten. Brainstorm about how this event made you feel at the time it happened. Then brainstorm about how this event makes you feel now. What changes have you discovered in your view of this event?

READING AND WRITING NARRATIVE ESSAYS

Making meaning in reading and writing is a fairly straightforward process with the narrative mode. To read a narrative essay most effectively, you should spend your time concentrating on the writer's main story line and use of details. Together, these tasks will help you make meaning as you read. To create an effective story, you have some important decisions to make before you write and certain variables to control as you actually draft your narrative. During the prewriting stage, you need to generate ideas and choose a point of view through which your story will be presented. Then, as you write, the preliminary decisions you have made regarding the selection and arrangement of your details (especially important in a narrative) will allow your story to flow more easily. Carefully controlled organization, along with appropriate timing and pacing, can influence your audience's reactions in very powerful ways.

Reading Narrative Essays

- What is the story's context?
- What is the essay's story line?
- What is the author's purpose?

Preparing to Read.   As you prepare to read the narratives in this chapter, try to guess what each title tells you about its essay's topic and about the author's attitude toward that topic: Can you guess, for example, how

Lewis Sawaquat feels about his daughter from his title "For My Indian Daughter" or what Maya Angelou's attitude is toward the events described in "New Directions"? Also, scan the essay and read its synopsis in the Rhetorical Table of Contents to help you anticipate as much as you can about the author's purpose and audience.

Next, the more you learn from the biography about the author and the circumstances surrounding the composition of a particular essay, the better prepared you will be to read the essay. For a narrative essay, the writer's point of view or perspective toward the story and its characters is especially significant. From the biographies, can you determine Maya Angelou's attitude toward Annie Johnson's energy and determination in "New Directions" or Sandra Cisneros's reason for writing "Only daughter"? Also, what is Russell Baker's opinion of his mother in "The Saturday Evening Post"?

Last, before you begin to read, answer the Preparing to Read questions, and then try to generate some of your own inquiries on the general subject of the essay: What do you want to know about being a Native American (Sawaquat)? What do you think of children in general (Cisneros)? What childhood experience greatly affected your life (Baker)?

Reading.   As you read a narrative essay for the first time, simply follow the story line, and try to get a general sense of the narrative and of the author's general purpose. Is Baker trying to encourage us all to be writers or simply to help us understand why he writes? Record your initial reactions to each essay as they occur to you. Is Dumas's purpose to make us feel sympathetic or antagonistic toward her childhood memories?

At the bottom of the pages of these essays are questions that will help you think analytically about the topic of the essay and related subjects. They are designed to provide a "bridge" between the questions at the beginning of the essay and the more complex questions at the end. Thinking critically is a skill that can be learned if you practice it, which is what these prompts intend to help you do. If you take time to consider and respond to each inquiry, you will be ready to write in depth on the questions and writing assignments that follow each essay.

Based on the biographical information preceding the essay and on the essay's tone, purpose, and audience, try to create a context for the narrative as you read. How do such details help you understand your reading material more thoroughly? A first reading of this sort, along with a survey of the questions that follow the essay, will help prepare you for a critical understanding of the material when you read it for the second time.

Rereading.   As you reread these narrative essays, notice the author's selection and arrangement of details. Why does Angelou organize her story one way and Cisneros another? What effect does their organization create?

Also, pay attention to the timing and the pacing of the story line. What do the long descriptions of Annie's plans add to Angelou's "New Directions"? What does the quick pace of Dumas's narrative communicate?

In addition, consider at this point what other rhetorical strategies the authors use to support their narratives. Which writers use examples to supplement their stories? Which use definitions? Which use comparisons? Why do they use these strategies?

Finally, when you answer the questions after each essay, you can check your understanding of the material on different levels before you tackle the discussion/writing topics that follow.

For a general checklist of reading guidelines, please see the Reading Inventory at the end of Part I.

Writing Narrative Essays

- Decide on your thesis.
- Choose details to support your thesis.
- Arrange your details for a specific effect.
- Follow a time sequence.
- *Show* rather than *tell*.

Preparing to Write.   First, you should answer the prewriting questions to help you generate thoughts on the subject at hand. Next, as in all writing, you should explore your subject matter and discover as many specific details as possible. (See Chapter 3 for a discussion of prewriting techniques.) Some writers rely on the familiar journalistic checklist of *who, what, when, where, why,* and *how* to make sure they cover all aspects of their narrative. If you were using the story of a basketball game at your college to demonstrate the team spirit of your school, for example, you might want to consider telling your readers *who* played in the game and/or *who* attended; *what* happened before, during, and after the game; *when* and *where* it took place; *why* it was being played (or *why* these particular teams were playing each other or *why* the game was especially important); and *how* the winning basket was shot. Freewriting or a combination of freewriting and the journalistic questions is another effective way of getting ideas and story details on paper for use in a first draft.

Once you have generated these ideas, you should always let your purpose and audience ultimately guide your selection of details, but the process of gathering such journalistic information gives you some material from which to choose. You will also need to decide whether to include dialogue in your narrative. Again, the difference here is between *showing* and *telling:* Will your audience benefit from reading what was actually said, word for word, during a discussion, or will a brief description of the conversation be sufficiently effective? In fact, all the choices you make at this stage of the composing process will give you material with which to create emphasis, suspense, conflict, and interest in your subject.

Next, you must decide on the point of view that will most readily help you achieve your purpose with your specific audience. Point of view includes the (1) person, (2) vantage point, and (3) attitude of your narrator. *Person* refers to who will tell the story: an uninvolved observer, a character in the narrative, or an omniscient (all-seeing) narrator. This initial decision will guide your thoughts on *vantage point,* which is the frame of reference of the narrator: close to the action, far from the action, looking back on the past, or reporting on the present. Finally, your narrator will naturally have an *attitude,* or *personal feeling,* about the subject: accepting, hostile, sarcastic, indifferent, angry, pleased, or any number of similar emotions. Once you adopt a certain perspective in a story, you should follow it for the duration of the narrative. This consistency will bring focus and coherence to your essay.

Writing.   After you have explored your topic and adopted a particular point of view, you need to write a thesis statement and to select and arrange the details of your story coherently so that the narrative has a clear beginning, middle, and end. The most natural way to organize the events of a narrative, of course, is chronologically. In your story about the school basketball game, you would probably narrate the relevant details in the order they occurred (i.e., sequentially, from the beginning of the game to its conclusion). More experienced writers may elect to use flashbacks: An athlete might recall a significant event that happened during the game, or a coach might recollect the contest's turning point. Your most important consideration is that the elements of a narrative essay follow some sort of time sequence, aided by the use of clear and logical transitions (e.g., *then, next, at this point, suddenly*) that help the reader move smoothly from one event to the next.

In addition to organization, the development of your essay with enough details is important. In this way, the details that you choose should *show* rather than *tell* your story. This approach will help your essay become interesting and believable to your readers. Furthermore, the point of view of your narrator should remain consistent throughout your essay, which will give the essay a high degree of credibility.

Rewriting.   As you reread the narrative you have written, pretend you are a reader (instead of the writer) and make sure you have told the story from the most effective point of view, considering both your purpose and your audience:

- Is my purpose (or thesis) clearly stated?
- Does my narrator help me achieve my purpose?

Further, as you reread, make certain you can follow the events of the story as they are related:

- Does one event lead naturally to the next?
- Are all the details relevant to my purpose?
- Do I *show* rather than *tell* my message?

For more advice on writing and editing, see the Writing Inventory on page 48.

STUDENT ESSAY: NARRATION AT WORK

The following student essay characterizes the writer's mother by telling a story about an unusual family vacation. As you read it, notice that the student writer states her purpose clearly and succinctly in the first paragraph. She then becomes an integral part of her story as she carefully selects examples and details that help convey her thesis.

A Vacation with My Mother

First-person narrator | I had an interesting childhood—not because of where I grew up and not because I ever did anything particularly adventuresome or thrilling. In fact, I don't think my life seemed especially interesting to me at the time. But now, telling friends about my supposedly ordinary childhood, I notice an array of responses ranging from astonishment to hilarity. The source of their surprise and amusement is my mother— gracious, charming, sweet, and totally out of synchronization with the rest of the world. One strange family trip we took when I was eleven captures the essence of her zaniness. | General subject

Specific subject

Thesis statement

Narrator's attitude | My two sets of grandparents lived in Colorado and North Dakota, and my parents decided we would spend a few weeks driving to those states and seeing all the sights along the relaxed and rambling way. My eight-year-old brother, David, and I had some serious reservations. If Dad had ever had Mom drive him to school, we reasoned, he'd never even consider letting her help drive us anywhere out of town, let alone out of California. If we weren't paying attention, we were as likely to end up at her office or the golf course as we were to arrive at school. Sometimes she'd drop us off at a friend's house to play and then forget where | Examples she'd left us. The notion of going on a long trip with her was really unnerving.

Transition   How can I explain my mother to a stranger? Have you ever watched reruns of the old *I Love Lucy* with Lucille Ball? I did as a child, and I thought Lucy Ricardo was normal. I lived with somebody a lot like her. Now, Mom wasn't a redhead (not usually, anyway), and Dad wasn't a Cuban nightclub owner, but at home we had the same situation of a loving but be-

Narrator's vantage point   mused husband trying to deal with the off-the-wall logic and enthusiasm of a frequently exasperating wife. We all adored her, but we had to admit it: Mom was a flaky, absent-minded, genuine eccentric.

As the first day of our trip approached, David and *Transition* I reluctantly said good-bye to all of our friends. Who knew if we'd ever see any of them again? Finally, the

Careful selection of details   moment of our departure arrived, and we loaded suitcases, books, games, camping gear, and a tent into the car and bravely drove off. We bravely drove off again two hours later after we'd returned home to get the purse and traveler's checks that Mom had forgotten.

David and I were always a little nervous when using gas station bathrooms if Mom was driving while Dad napped: "You stand outside the door and play lookout *Use of dialogue* while I go, and I'll stand outside the door and play lookout while you go." I had terrible visions: "Honey, where are the kids?" "What?! Oh, gosh . . . I thought *Examples* they were being awfully quiet. Uh . . . Idaho?" We were never actually abandoned in a strange city, but we weren't about to take any chances.

Transition   On the fourth or fifth night of the trip, we had trou- *Passage of time* ble finding a motel with a vacancy. After driving futilely for an hour, Mom suddenly had a great idea: Why didn't we find a house with a likely-looking backyard *Example* and ask if we could pitch our tent there? To her, the scheme was eminently reasonable. Vowing quietly to each other to hide in the back seat if she did it, David and I groaned in anticipated mortification. To our profound relief, Dad vetoed the idea. Mom never could understand our objections. If a strange family showed up on her front doorstep, Mom would have been delighted. She thinks everyone in the world is as nice as she is. We finally found a vacancy in the next town. David and I were thrilled—the place featured bungalows in the shape of Native-American tepees.

Transition   <u>The Native-American motif must have reminded my parents that we had not yet used the brand-new tent, Coleman stove, portable mattress, and other camping gear we had brought.</u> We headed to a national park the next day and found a campsite by a lake. It took hours to figure out how to set up

Careful selection of details   the tent: It was one of those deluxe models with mosquito-net windows, canvas floors, and enough room for three large families to sleep in. It was after dark before we finally got it erected, and the night had turned quite cold. We fixed a hurried campfire dinner (chicken burned on the outside and raw in the middle) and prepared to go to sleep. That was when we realized that Mom had forgotten to bring along some important pieces of equipment—our sleeping bags. The four of us huddled together on our thin mattresses borrowed from our station-wagon floor. That ended our camping days. Give me a stucco tepee any time.   Chronological order

Examples (spatial order)   We drove through several states and saw lots of great sights along the way: the Grand Canyon, Carlsbad Caverns, caves, mountains, waterfalls, and even a haunted house. David and I were excited and amazed at all the wonders we found, and Mom was just as enthralled as we were. Her constant pleasure and sense of the world as a beautiful, magical place was infectious. I never realized until I grew up how really childlike—in the best sense of the word—my mother actually is. She is innocent, optimistic, and always ready to be entertained.

Transition   <u>Looking back on that long-past family vacation, I now realize that my childhood was more special because I grew up with a mother who wasn't afraid to try anything and who taught me to look at the world as a series of marvelous opportunities to be explored.</u> What did it matter that she thought England was bordered by Germany? We were never going to try to drive there. So what if she was always leaving her car keys in the refrigerator or some other equally inexplicable place? <u>In the end, we always got where we were going—and we</u>   Narrator's attitude

Concluding remark   <u>generally had a grand time along the way.</u>   Examples

Student Writer's Comments

I enjoyed writing about this childhood vacation because of all the memories it brought back. I knew I wanted to write a narrative to explain my mother, and the word *zany* immediately popped into my mind. So I knew what my focus was going to be from the outset. My prewriting started spontaneously as soon as I found this angle. So many thoughts and memories rushed into my head that I couldn't even get to a piece of paper to write them down before I lost some of them. But there were way too many to put into one essay. The hardest part of writing this narrative was trying to decide what material to use and what to leave out. Spending a little more time before writing my first draft proved to be a good investment in this case. I got a clean piece of paper and began freewriting, trying to mold some of my scattered ideas from brainstorming into a coherent, readable form. During this second stage of prewriting, I remembered one special vacation we took that I thought might capture the essence of my mother—and also of my family.

My first draft was about three times the length of this one. My point of view was the innocent participant/observer who came to know and love her mother or her absent-mindedness. I had really developed my thesis from the time I got this writing assignment. And I told my story chronologically except for looking back in the last paragraph when I attempted to analyze the entire experience. I had no trouble *showing* rather than *telling* because all of the details were so vivid to me—as if they had happened yesterday. But that was my downfall. I soon realized that I could not possibly include everything that was on the pages of my first draft.

The process of cranking out my rough draft made my point of view toward life with my mother very clear to me and helped me face the cutting that was ahead of me. I took the raw material of a very lengthy first draft and forced myself to choose the details and examples that best characterized my mother and what life was like growing up under the care of such a lovely but daffy individual. The sense of her being both "lovely" and "daffy" was the insight that helped me the most in revising the content of my essay. I made myself ruthlessly eliminate anything that interfered with the overall effect I was trying to create—from extraneous images and details to words and phrases that didn't contribute to this specific view of my mom.

The final result, according to my classmates, communicated my message clearly and efficiently. The main criticism I got from my class was that I might have cut too much from my first draft. But I think this focused picture with a few highlights conveys my meaning in the best possible way. I offered enough details to *show* rather than *tell* my readers what living with my mother was like, but not too many to bore them. I was also able to take the time in my essay to be humorous now and then ("David and I reluctantly said good-bye to all of our friends. Who knew if we'd ever see any of them again?" and "Give me a stucco tepee any time."), as well as pensive and serious ("I now realize that my childhood was more special because I grew up with a mother who wasn't afraid to try anything and who taught me to look at the world as a series of marvelous opportunities to be explored."). Even though in looking at the essay now I would tamper with a few things, I am generally happy with the final draft. It captures the essence of my mother from my point of view, and it also gave my class a few laughs. Aren't the readers' reactions the ultimate test of a good story?

SOME FINAL THOUGHTS ON NARRATION

Just as with other modes of writing, all decisions regarding narration should be made with a specific purpose and an intended audience constantly in mind. As you will see, each narrative in this section is directed at a clearly defined audience. Notice, as you read, how each writer manipulates the various features of narration so that the readers are simultaneously caught up in the plot and deeply moved to feel, think, believe, and even act on the writer's personal opinions.

NARRATION IN REVIEW

Reading Narrative Essays

Preparing to Read
√ What assumptions can I make from the essay's title?
√ What do I think the general mood of the essay will be?
√ What is the essay's purpose and audience?
√ What does the synopsis tell me about the essay?
√ What can I learn from the author's biography?
√ Can I predict the author's point of view toward the subject?

Reading
√ What is the story's context?
√ What is the essay's story line?
√ What is the author's purpose?

Rereading
√ What details did the author choose, and how are they arranged?
√ How does the author control the pace of the story?
√ What other rhetorical modes does the author use?

Writing Narrative Essays

Preparing to Write
√ What is my purpose?
√ Who is my audience?
√ What is my narrator's point of view—including person, vantage point, and attitude toward the subject?

Writing
√ What is my thesis?
√ What details will best support this thesis?
√ How can I arrange these details to create a certain effect?
√ Does my narrative essay follow a well-paced time sequence?
√ Do I *show* rather than *tell* my story?

Rewriting
√ Is my purpose (or thesis) clearly stated?
√ Does my narrator help me achieve my purpose?
√ Does one event lead naturally to the next?
√ Are all the details relevant to my purpose?
√ Do I *show* rather than *tell* my message?

LEWIS SAWAQUAT   (1935–   )

For My Indian Daughter

Lewis Sawaquat is a Native American who is now retired from his thirty-year job as a surveyor for the Soil Conservation Service of the U.S. Department of Agriculture. He was born in Harbor Springs, Michigan, where his great-great-grandfather was the last official "chief" of the region. After finishing high school, Sawaquat entered the army, graduated from Army Survey School, and then completed a tour of duty in Korea. Upon returning to America, he enrolled in the Art Institute of Chicago to study commercial art. Sawaquat now lives on a reservation in Peshawbestown, Michigan, where his hobbies include gardening, swimming, walking in the woods, reading, and playing with his cat. He serves as a pipe carrier and cultural/spiritual adviser to his Ottawa tribe. Recently, he started a consulting firm and travels around the country speaking on Native-American issues. He also hopes to write a book entitled *Dreams: The Universal Language,* which will investigate the Native-American approach to dream interpretation. His daughter, Gaia, who is described in the following essay, recently graduated from Yale University. His advice to students using *The Prose Reader* is to "pay attention to life; there's nothing more important to becoming a writer."

Preparing to Read

"For My Indian Daughter" originally appeared in the "My Turn" column of *Newsweek* magazine (September 5, 1983) under the author's former name, Lewis Johnson. In his article, the author speaks eloquently about prejudice, ethnic pride, and growing cultural awareness, which are timely topics for all of us.

Exploring Experience: Before reading this selection, think for a few minutes about your own heritage: What is your ethnic identity? Are you content with this background? Have you ever gone through an identity crisis? Do you anticipate facing any problems because of your ancestry? If so, what do you think these problems will be? How will you handle them when they occur?

Learning Online: To understand the context in which Sawaquat is writing, visit the Smithsonian Web site (www.si.edu), and type "American Indian Art and Design" into the search field. View the online exhibitions of Native-American culture, past and present.

My little girl is singing herself to sleep upstairs, her voice mingling with the sounds of the birds outside in the old maple trees. She is two, and I am nearly 50, and I am very taken with her. She came along late in my life, unexpected and unbidden, a startling gift.

Today at the beach my chubby-legged, brown-skinned daughter ran laughing into the water as fast as she could. My wife and I laughed watching her, until we heard behind us a low guttural curse and then an unpleasant voice raised in an imitation war whoop.

I turned to see a fat man in a bathing suit, white and soft as a grub, ◆ as he covered his mouth and prepared to make the Indian war cry again. He was middle-aged, younger than I, and had three little children lined up next to him, grinning foolishly. My wife suggested we leave the beach, and I agreed.

I knew the man was not unusual in his feelings against Indians. His beach behavior might have been socially unacceptable to more civilized whites, but his basic view of Indians is expressed daily in our small town, frequently on the editorial pages of the county newspaper, as white people speak out against Indian fishing rights and land rights, saying in essence, "Those Indians are taking our fish, our land." It doesn't matter to them that we were here first, that the U.S. Supreme Court has ruled in our favor. It matters to them that we have something they want, and they hate us for it. Backlash is the common explanation of the attacks on Indians, the bumper stickers that say, "Spear an Indian, Save a Fish," but I know better. The hatred of Indians goes back to the beginning when white people came to this country. For me it goes back to my childhood in Harbor Springs, Mich.

Theft

Harbor Springs is now a summer resort for the very affluent, but a hundred years ago it was the Indian village of my Ottawa ancestors. My grandmother, Anna Showanessy, and other Indians like her, had their land there taken by treaty, by fraud, by violence, by theft. They remembered how whites had burned down the village at Burt Lake in 1900 and pushed the Indians out. These were the stories in my family.

When I was a boy, my mother told me to walk down the alleys in Harbor Springs and not to wear my orange football sweater out of the house. This way I would not stand out, not be noticed, and not be a target.

I wore my orange sweater anyway and deliberately avoided the alleys. I was the biggest person I knew and wasn't really afraid. But I met my comeuppance

---

Thinking Critically

◆ How does Sawaquat's description of the "fat man" who was "soft as a grub" betray the author's feelings about the confrontation on the beach? What other words reveal the author's biases in this essay?

when I enlisted in the U.S. Army. One night all the men in my barracks gathered together and, gang-fashion, pulled me into the shower and scrubbed me down with rough brushes used for floors, saying, "We won't have any dirty Indians in our outfit." It is a point of irony that I was cleaner than any of them. Later in Korea I learned how to kill, how to bully, how to hate Koreans. I came out of the war tougher than ever and, strangely, white. [2]

I went to college, got married, lived in La Porte, Ind., worked as a surveyor   8
and raised three boys. I headed Boy Scout groups, never thinking it odd when the Scouts did imitation Indian dances, imitation Indian lore.

One day when I was 35 or thereabouts I heard about an Indian powwow.   9
My father used to attend them and so with great curiosity and a strange joy at discovering a part of my heritage, I decided the thing to do to get ready for this big event was to have my friend make me a spear in his forge. The steel was fine and blue and iridescent. The feathers on the shaft were bright and proud.

In a dusty state fairground in southern Indiana, I found white people   10
dressed as Indians. I learned they were "hobbyists," that is, it was their hobby and leisure pastime to masquerade as Indians on weekends. I felt ridiculous with my spear, and I left.

It was years before I could tell anyone of the embarrassment of this week-   11
end and see any humor in it. But in a way it was that weekend, for all its silliness, that was my awakening. I realized I didn't know who I was. I didn't have an Indian name. I didn't speak the Indian language. I didn't know the Indian customs. Dimly I remembered the Ottawa word for dog, but it was a baby word, *kahgee,* not the full word, *muhkahgee,* which I was later to learn. Even more hazily I remembered a naming ceremony (my own). I remembered legs dancing around me, dust. Where had that been? Who had I been? "Sawaquat," my mother told me when I asked, "where the tree begins to grow." [3]

That was 1968, and I was not the only Indian in the country who was feel-   12
ing the need to remember who he or she was. There were others. They had powwows, real ones, and eventually I found them. Together we researched our past, a search that for me culminated in the Longest Walk, a march on Washington in 1978. Maybe because I now know what it means to be Indian, it surprises me that others don't. Of course there aren't very many of us left. The chances of an average person knowing an average Indian in an average lifetime are pretty slim.

Thinking Critically

[2] How and when did the author first acquire prejudice?

[3] What is the meaning of the Indian word "sawaquat," and how does it help characterize the author's increasing familiarity with his ethnic heritage and personal identity?

Circle

Still, I was amused one day when my small, four-year-old neighbor looked   13
at me as I was hoeing in my garden and said, "You aren't a real Indian, are
you?" Scotty is little, talkative, likable. Finally I said, "I'm a real Indian." He
looked at me for a moment and then said, squinting into the sun, "Then
where's your horse and feathers?" The child was simply a smaller, whiter
version of my own ignorant self years before. ◆ We'd both seen too much
TV, that's all. He was not to be blamed. And so, in a way, the moronic man
on the beach today is blameless. We come full circle to realize other people
are like ourselves, as discomfiting as that may be sometimes.

As I sit in my old chair on my porch, in a light that is fading so the leaves   14
are barely distinguishable against the sky, I can picture my girl asleep upstairs.
I would like to prepare her for what's to come, take her each step of the way
saying, there's a place to avoid, here's what I know about this, but much of
what's before her she must go through alone. She must pass through pain and
joy and solitude and community to discover her own inner self that is unlike
any other and come through that passage to the place where she sees all people are one, and in so seeing may live her life in a brighter future.

UNDERSTANDING DETAILS

1. What is the principal point of this essay by Sawaquat? How many different stories does the author tell to make this point?
2. What does Sawaquat see as the origin of the hatred of Native Americans in the
   United States?
3. What does Sawaquat learn from his first powwow (paragraphs 9 and 10)?
4. How does Sawaquat discover his original identity? In what way does this knowledge change him?

READING CRITICALLY

5. Why does Sawaquat begin this essay with the story about his daughter on the
   beach? How does the story make you feel?
6. Why do thoughts about his daughter prompt Sawaquat's memories of his own
   identity crisis? What does the author's identity have to do with his daughter?
7. The author calls paragraphs 5–12 "Theft" and paragraphs 13–14 "Circle." Explain
   these two subtitles from the author's point of view.
8. Why do you think Sawaquat says that his daughter "must pass through pain
   and joy and solitude and community to discover her own inner self" (paragraph 14)? To what extent do we all need to do this in our lives?

Thinking Critically

◆ What important truths did the author learn about himself during this major transition in
his life?

DISCOVERING RHETORICAL STRATEGIES

9. Sawaquat occasionally uses dialogue to help make his points. What does the dialogue add to the various narratives he cites here?

10. Describe as thoroughly as possible the point of view of Sawaquat's narrator. Include in your answer a discussion of person, vantage point, and attitude.

11. Why do you think Sawaquat divides his essay into three sections? Why do you think he spends most of his time on the second section?

12. Although Sawaquat uses primarily narration to advance his point of view, which other rhetorical strategies help support his essay? Give examples of each.

MAKING CONNECTIONS

13. Compare the concern Lewis Sawaquat has for his daughter with that displayed between parent and child in "Leffingwell Elementary School" (Firoozeh Dumas), "The Saturday Evening Post" (Russell Baker), and/or "Mother Tongue" (Amy Tan). Which parent do you think loves his or her child most? On what do you base this conclusion?

14. How strong is Sawaquat's attachment to his Native-American culture? Contrast the passion of his ethnic identity with that demonstrated by Malcolm X ("Learning to Read"), Sandra Cisneros ("Only daughter"), Robert Ramirez ("The Barrio"), and/or Alice Walker ("Beauty: When the Other Dancer Is the Self").

15. What responsibilities, according to Sawaquat, should parents accept regarding the eventual happiness of their children? Would Bill Cosby ("The Baffling Question"), Ben Dattner ("Is Your Workplace Personality Out of [Birth] Order?"), and/or Michael Dorris ("The Broken Cord") agree with him? Why or why not? To what extent do you agree with Sawaquat?

IDEAS FOR DISCUSSION/WRITING

Preparing to Write

Write freely about your own identity: What is your cultural heritage? How do you fit into your immediate environment? Has your attitude about yourself and your identity changed over the years? Do you know your own inner self? How do you plan to continue learning about yourself?

Choosing a Topic

1. *Learning Online:* If you had a blog that was a forum for your ideas, what topics would you want to write about and publish? Write a narrative for your blog in which you share some personal experiences in a public arena. Using Sawaquat's essay as a model, describe specific incidents and the way they affected you. If possible, to support your story, add artwork similar to that on the Smithsonian website from Preparing to Read.

2. Write a narrative essay that uses one or more stories from your past in order to describe to a group of friends the main features of your identity.

3. Explain to your children (whether real or imaginary) in narrative form some simple but important truths about your heritage. Take care to select your details well, choose an appropriate point of view, and arrange your essay logically so that you keep your readers' interest throughout the essay.

4. Have you recently experienced any social traumas in your life that you would like to prepare someone else for? Write a letter to the person you would like to warn. Use narration to explain the situation, and suggest ways to avoid the negative aspects you encountered.

Before beginning your essay, you might want to consult the checklists on page 122.

MAYA ANGELOU   (1928–   )

New Directions

Maya Angelou was born Marguerite Johnson on April 4, 1928, in St. Louis, Missouri. Nicknamed "Maya" by her brother, she moved with her family to California; then, at age three, she was sent to live with her grandmother in Stamps, Arkansas, where she spent the childhood years later recorded in her autobiographical novel *I Know Why the Caged Bird Sings* (1970). After a brief marriage, she embarked on an amazingly prolific career in dance, drama, and writing. During the past forty years, Angelou has been at various times a night-club performer specializing in calypso songs and dances, an actress, a play-wright, a civil-rights activist, a newspaper editor, a television writer and producer, a poet, and a screenwriter. She has also written several television specials, including *Three Way Choice* (a five-part miniseries) and *Afro-Americans in the Arts,* both for PBS. Her most recent work includes five novels: *I Shall Not Be Moved* (1990), *Lessons in Living* (1993), *Wouldn't Take Nothing for My Journey Now* (1993), *A Brave and Startling Truth* (1995), and *Phenomenal Woman* (2000). In addition, she published *A Song Flung Up to Heaven* (2002) and *Hallelujah! The Welcome Table* (2004), and was given a Grammy Award in 2003 for her recorded reading of *A Song Flung Up to Heaven.* A tall, graceful, and imposing woman, Angelou was once described as conveying "pride without arrogance, self-esteem without smugness." Her advice to writers is "to write so that what you say slides through the brain and goes straight to the heart."

Preparing to Read

Taken from Angelou's book *Wouldn't Take Nothing for My Journey Now,* the following essay describes how Annie Johnson, a strong and determined woman, found "a new path" in her life.

Exploring Experience: Before you read this essay, take a moment to think about a time you changed directions: What were the circumstances surrounding this change? Why did you make the change? What did you learn from the experience? What alterations would you make if you followed this path again?

Learning Online: Maya Angelou has some strong opinions on the topic of courage. To get a sense of Angelou's thoughts on this subject, go to www.oprah.com/magazine/omagazine, and type "Oprah's Cut with Maya Angelou" into the search field. Select the link entitled "Oprah's Cut with Maya Angelou." Read Oprah's summary of the interview and then the interview itself. As you read the essay that follows, consider how her attitudes toward courage and self-identity are evident in Annie Johnson's character.

In 1903 the late Mrs. Annie Johnson of Arkansas found herself with two 1
toddling sons, very little money, a slight ability to read and add simple
numbers. To this picture add a disastrous marriage and the burdensome
fact that Mrs. Johnson was a Negro. **1**

When she told her husband, Mr. William Johnson, of her dissatisfaction 2
with their marriage, he conceded that he too found it to be less than he
expected and had been secretly hoping to leave and study religion. He added
that he thought God was calling him not only to preach but to do so in
Enid, Oklahoma. He did not tell her that he knew a minister in Enid with
whom he could study and who had a friendly, unmarried daughter. They
parted amicably, Annie keeping the one-room house and William taking
most of the cash to carry himself to Oklahoma.

Annie, over six feet tall, big-boned, decided that she would not go to 3
work as a domestic and leave her "precious babes" to anyone else's care.
There was no possibility of being hired at the town's cotton gin or lumber
mill, but maybe there was a way to make the two factories work for her. In
her words, "I looked up the road I was going and back the way I come, and
since I wasn't satisfied, I decided to step off the road and cut me a new path."
She told herself that she wasn't a fancy cook but that she could "mix groceries well enough to scare hunger away from a starving man."

She made her plans meticulously and in secret. One early evening to see 4
if she was ready, she placed stones in two five-gallon pails and carried them
three miles to the cotton gin. She rested a little, and then, discarding some
rocks, she walked in the darkness to the saw mill five miles farther along the
dirt road. On her way back to her little house and her babies, she dumped
the remaining rocks along the path.

That same night she worked into the early hours boiling chicken and fry- 5
ing ham. She made dough and filled the rolled-out pastry with meat. At last
she went to sleep. **2**

The next morning she left her house carrying the meat pies, lard, an iron 6
brazier, and coals for a fire. Just before lunch she appeared in an empty lot
behind the cotton gin. As the dinner noon bell rang, she dropped the savors
into boiling fat, and the aroma rose and floated over to the workers who
spilled out of the gin, covered with white lint, looking like specters. **3**

Most workers had brought their lunches of pinto beans and biscuits or 7
crackers, onions and cans of sardines, but they were tempted by the hot meat

---

Thinking Critically

1 Why does Angelou describe Annie Johnson's ethnicity as "burdensome"?

2 What specific details does the author include to indicate how hard Annie worked for success?

3 How do these particular details affect Angelou's essay?

pies which Annie ladled out of the fat. She wrapped them in newspapers, which soaked up the grease, and offered them for sale at a nickel each. Although business was slow, those first days Annie was determined. She balanced her appearances between the two hours of activity.

So, on Monday if she offered hot fresh pies at the cotton gin and sold the remaining cooled-down pies at the lumber mill for three cents, then on Tuesday she went first to the lumber mill presenting fresh, just-cooked pies as the lumbermen covered in sawdust emerged from the mill.   8

For the next few years, on balmy spring days, blistering summer noons, and cold, wet, and wintry middays, Annie never disappointed her customers, who could count on seeing the tall, brown-skin woman bent over her brazier, carefully turning the meat pies. When she felt certain that the workers had become dependent on her, she built a stall between the two hives of industry and let the men run to her for their lunchtime provisions.   9

She had indeed stepped from the road which seemed to have been chosen for her and cut herself a brand-new path. In years that stall became a store where customers could buy cheese, meal, syrup, cookies, candy, writing tablets, pickles, canned goods, fresh fruit, soft drinks, coal, oil, and leather soles for worn-out shoes.   10

Each of us has the right and the responsibility to assess the roads which lie ahead, and those over which we have traveled, and if the future road looms ominous or unpromising, and the roads back uninviting, then we need to gather our resolve and, carrying only the necessary baggage, step off that road into another direction. ◆ If the new choice is also unpalatable, without embarrassment, we must be ready to change that as well.   11

UNDERSTANDING DETAILS

1. What path is Annie Johnson following that she dislikes? How does she change this path?
2. Describe Annie physically and mentally in your own words. Use as much detail as possible.
3. Why does Annie carry stones in two five-gallon pails for three miles? What is she trying to accomplish?
4. In what ways does Annie's business grow? How does Annie's personality make this growth possible?

Thinking Critically

◆ Have you ever "changed direction" in your life? How did it compare to Angelou's change? Was the change good for you? Why or why not?

READING CRITICALLY

5. Why do you think Annie succeeds in her business? What are the main ingredients of her success?

6. In what ways are the details at the beginning of this narrative essay typical of the year 1903?

7. What does Angelou mean when she says, "Each of us has the right and the responsibility to assess the roads which lie ahead, and those over which we have traveled" (paragraph 11)? In what way is this message basic to an understanding of the essay?

8. Explain the title of the essay. Cite specific details from the essay in your explanation.

DISCOVERING RHETORICAL STRATEGIES

9. Angelou writes this narrative essay in a fairly formal style, using multisyllable words (*concede* rather than *yield* or *let*) and the characters' titles with their names (Mrs. Annie Johnson instead of Annie Johnson). Why do you think Angelou presents her essay in this way? Describe the tone she maintains throughout the essay.

10. The author uses the metaphor of taking a "new road" to describe Annie Johnson's decision. Is this metaphor effective in your opinion? Why or why not?

11. Over what period of time do you think this story took place? How does the author show her readers that time is passing in this narrative essay?

12. Angelou often ends her essays with lessons that she wants the readers to understand. How does her lesson in the last paragraph of this narrative essay affect the story? Does the story itself go with the lesson? How did you respond to having the author tell you what to think at the end of the story?

MAKING CONNECTIONS

13. In Angelou's essay, Annie Johnson cuts "a new path" for herself by selling food to factory workers. Contrast this sudden change in the direction of her life with similar "new paths" taken by Bill Cosby in "The Baffling Question," by Brent Staples in "A Brother's Murder," and/or by female weightlifters in Gloria Steinem's "The Politics of Muscle." Who do you think had the most difficult transition to make? Explain your answer.

14. If Angelou, Sandra Cisneros ("Only Daughter"), Russell Baker ("The Saturday Evening Post"), Harold Krents ("Darkness at Noon"), and/or Ben Dattner ("Is Your Workplace Personality Out of [Birth] Order?") were discussing the value of persistence and determination in life, which author would argue most strongly for the importance of that quality? Why? Would you agree?

15. Food is an important ingredient not only in Angelou's essay, but also in those written by Ray Bradbury ("Summer Rituals"), Kimberly Wozencraft ("Notes from the Country Club"), and John McPhee ("The Pines"). Which of these most involves the topic of food? Which the least? Which authors use food as a structuring device in their essays?

IDEAS FOR DISCUSSION/WRITING

Preparing to Write

Write freely about all the major changes you have made in your life: Were most of these changes for the best? How did they benefit you? How did they benefit others? Did they hurt anyone? Do you think most people have trouble changing directions in their lives? Why or why not? How might we all improve our attitudes about change?

Choosing a Topic

1. *Learning Online:* Go online and find an entrepreneur who inspires you. Possible examples include Shawn Fanning (Napster), Ben Cohen and Jerry Greenfield (Ben & Jerry's Ice Cream), Masaru Ibuka and Akio Morita (Sony), Walt Disney (Disneyland, Walt Disney Pictures), Anita Roddick (The Body Shop), Bill Gates (Microsoft), Oprah Winfrey (*Oprah, O, HARPO*), Ted Turner (Cable News Network, Turner Network Television), or Martha Stewart (Martha Stewart Omnimedia). All of these people had to have courage to accomplish what they have. Gather enough details about this person's life to write a narrative with a clear focus. Using Angelou's essay as a model, organize your story around a central theme or message.

2. The editor of your school newspaper has asked you to write a narrative essay about an important change you made in your life. The newspaper is running a series of essays about changing directions in life, and the staff has heard that you have a story to tell. Tell your story in essay form to be printed in the school newspaper.

3. Why are major changes so difficult for us to make? Write a narrative essay for your peers to respond to this question. Use characters to dramatize your answer.

4. Decide on an important truth about life, and then write a narrative essay to support that truth. Make the details as vivid as possible.

Before beginning your essay, you might want to consult the checklists on page 122.

Leffingwell Elementary School

Born in Abadan, Iran, Firoozeh Jazayeri ricocheted back and forth between the Middle East and the United States with her family before settling in Newport Beach, California. After earning a B.A. at Berkeley, she married a fellow student named Francois Dumas, began a family, and settled into a comfortable middle-class life in northern California. With no prior literary experience, she decided to try to write down some of her many childhood experiences for her children. The result was *Funny in Farsi* (2003), which soon landed on the *San Francisco Chronicle* and *Los Angeles Times* bestseller lists and was a finalist for a number of prestigious awards. Through wit and humor, the book describes Dumas's pride in her Iranian heritage, her struggles with prejudice and racism, and her enduring love of family. She later published *Laughing Without an Accent* (2008), a series of autobiographical essays about her own childhood and adventures as an adult. Through her books, speaking tours, and articles in the *New York Times,* the *Wall Street Journal, Good Housekeeping,* and many other popular magazines and newspapers, Dumas reveals a world in which the similarities and shared humanity among people from different cultures far outweigh their minor differences. Dumas advises student writers to "find a special spot in which to write." "I've just always tried to make sure," she admits, "that the table was clean before I put down my laptop."

Preparing to Read

The following essay, originally published in *Funny in Farsi,* is a masterful demonstration of how to write a narrative essay. In an attempt to record some of her earliest experiences in America, Dumas captures some humorous memories about starting school in a foreign country.

Exploring Experience: As you prepare to read this selection, take a few minutes to think about various experiences from your childhood (with your family, in your house, at school, at a friend's) that have special meaning to you: What are these experiences? Why is each of them significant? How do other people relate to these experiences? In what ways do your surroundings tell different stories about you? What items in your life bring complete stories to your mind? What are some of these stories?

Learning Online: Visit an immigration support Web site (www .immigrationsupport.org/), and notice how many different and complicated forms immigrants must complete. Imagine being new to the United States and having to navigate through a site like this. While reading "Leffingwell Elementary School," keep in mind these details about the immigration process.

When I was seven, my parents, my fourteen-year-old brother, 1
Farshid, and I moved from Abadan, Iran, to Whittier, California.
Farid, the older of my two brothers, had been sent to Philadelphia the year before to attend high school. Like most Iranian youths, he had always dreamed of attending college abroad and, despite my mother's tears, had left us to live with my uncle and his American wife. I, too, had been sad at Farid's departure, but my sorrow soon faded—not coincidentally, with the receipt of a package from him. Suddenly, having my brother on a different continent seemed like a small price to pay for owning a Barbie complete with a carrying case and four outfits, including the rain gear and mini umbrella.

Our move to Whittier was temporary. My father, Kazem, an engineer 2
with the National Iranian Oil Company, had been assigned to consult for an American firm for about two years. Having spent several years in Texas and California as a graduate student, my father often spoke about America with the eloquence and wonder normally reserved for a first love. ◆ To him, America was a place where anyone, no matter how humble his background, could become an important person. It was a kind and orderly nation full of clean bathrooms, a land where traffic laws were obeyed and where whales jumped through hoops. It was the Promised Land. For me, it was where I could buy more outfits for Barbie.

We arrived in Whittier shortly after the start of second grade; my father 3
enrolled me in Leffingwell Elementary School. To facilitate my adjustment, the principal arranged for us to meet my new teacher, Mrs. Sandberg, a few days before I started school. Since my mother and I did not speak English, the meeting consisted of a dialogue between my father and Mrs. Sandberg. My father carefully explained that I had attended a prestigious kindergarten where all the children were taught English. Eager to impress Mrs. Sandberg, he asked me to demonstrate my knowledge of the English language. I stood up straight and proudly recited all that I knew: "White, yellow, orange, red, purple, blue, green."

The following Monday, my father drove my mother and me to school. 4
He had decided that it would be a good idea for my mother to attend school with me for a few weeks. I could not understand why two people not speaking English would be better than one, but I was seven, and my opinion didn't matter much.

Until my first day at Leffingwell Elementary School, I had never thought 5
of my mother as an embarrassment, but the sight of all the kids in the school

---

Thinking Critically

◆ Which three qualities do you love the most about America? Are there any qualities that you dislike? Why?

staring at us before the bell rang was enough to make me pretend I didn't know her. The bell finally rang and Mrs. Sandberg came and escorted us to class. Fortunately, she had figured out that we were precisely the kind of people who would need help finding the right classroom.

My mother and I sat in the back while all the children took their assigned   6
seats. Everyone continued to stare at us. Mrs. Sandberg wrote my name on the board: F-I-R-O-O-Z-E-H. Under my name, she wrote "I-R-A-N." She then pulled down a map of the world and said something to my mom. My mom looked at me and asked me what she had said. I told her that the teacher probably wanted her to find Iran on the map.

The problem was that my mother, like most women of her generation,   7
had been only briefly educated. In her era, a girl's sole purpose in life was to find a husband. ❷Having an education ranked far below more desirable attributes such as the ability to serve tea or prepare baklava. Before her marriage, my mother, Nazireh, had dreamed of becoming a midwife. Her father, a fairly progressive man, had even refused the two earlier suitors who had come for her so that his daughter could pursue her dream. My mother planned to obtain her diploma, then go to Tabriz to learn midwifery from a teacher whom my grandfather knew. Sadly, the teacher died unexpectedly, and my mother's dreams had to be buried as well.

Bachelor No. 3 was my father. Like the other suitors, he had never spo-   8
ken to my mother, but one of his cousins knew someone who knew my mother's sister, so that was enough. More important, my mother fit my father's physical requirements for a wife. Like most Iranians, my father preferred a fair-skinned woman with straight, light-colored hair. Having spent a year in America as a Fulbright scholar, he had returned with a photo of a woman he found attractive and asked his older sister, Sedigeh, to find someone who resembled her. Sedigeh had asked around, and that is how at age seventeen my mother officially gave up her dreams, married my father, and had a child by the end of the year.

As the students continued staring at us, Mrs. Sandberg gestured to my   9
mother to come up to the board. My mother reluctantly obeyed. I cringed. Mrs. Sandberg, using a combination of hand gestures, started pointing to the map and saying, "Iran? Iran? Iran?" Clearly, Mrs. Sandberg had planned on incorporating us into the day's lesson. I only wished she had told us that earlier so we could have stayed home.

Thinking Critically

❷ How do you feel about this old-fashioned Iranian custom? Ask your grandparents or parents if girls in America ever had a "sole purpose"? If so, what was it?

After a few awkward attempts by my mother to find Iran on the map,   10
Mrs. Sandberg finally understood that it wasn't my mother's lack of English
that was causing a problem, but rather her lack of world geography. Smiling
graciously, she pointed my mother back to her seat. Mrs. Sandberg then
showed everyone, including my mother and me, where Iran was on the map.
My mother nodded her head, acting as if she had known the location all
along but had preferred to keep it a secret. Now all the students stared at us,
not just because I had come to school with my mother, not because we
couldn't speak their language, but because we were stupid. I was especially
mad at my mother, because she had negated the positive impression I had
made previously by reciting the color wheel. I decided that starting the next
day, *she* would have to stay home.

The bell finally rang, and it was time for us to leave. Leffingwell Elemen-   11
tary was just a few blocks from our house, and my father, grossly underestimating our ability to get lost, had assumed that my mother and I would be
able to find our way home. She and I wandered aimlessly, perhaps hoping for
a shooting star or a talking animal to help guide us back. ❸ None of the
streets or houses looked familiar. As we stood pondering our predicament,
an enthusiastic young girl came leaping out of her house and said something. Unable to understand her, we did what we had done all day: we
smiled. ❹ The girl's mother joined us, then gestured for us to follow her
inside. I assumed that the girl, who appeared to be the same age as I, was a
student at Leffingwell Elementary; having us inside her house was probably
akin to having the circus make a personal visit.

Her mother handed us a telephone, and my mother, who had, thankfully,   12
memorized my father's work number, called him and explained our situation. My father then spoke to the American woman and gave her our address.
This kind stranger agreed to take us back to our house.

Perhaps fearing that we might show up at their doorstep again, the woman   13
and her daughter walked us all the way to our front porch and even helped
my mother unlock the unfamiliar door. After making one last futile attempt
at communication, they waved good-bye. Unable to thank them in words,
we smiled even more broadly.

After spending an entire day in America, surrounded by Americans, I real-   14
ized that my father's description of America had been correct. The bathrooms
were clean, and the people were very, very kind.

Thinking Critically

❸ How would you characterize the author's sense of humor here and throughout the essay?

❹ Have you ever been in a situation where everyone around you spoke a different language
than you did? How did it make you feel? Why do you think you felt that way?

UNDERSTANDING DETAILS

1. Where does this narrative essay take place? Describe this particular place in detail. What one word might characterize this setting?
2. What grade was Dumas in when her family and she moved to the United States?
3. What gift from her brother studying in Philadelphia made their separation less painful for Dumas?
4. What did Dumas's father do for a living? When did he learn English?

READING CRITICALLY

5. What is the significance of Firoozeh and her mother not speaking English?
6. This essay is the first in a collection of essays that together tell the story of Dumas's childhood. How does she start to establish her character in this narrative? What one word would you use to describe her personality as revealed in this selection?
7. In paragraph 8, Dumas refers to her father as "Bachelor No. 3." What reference is she drawing on? Is it a humorous reference?
8. Why does Dumas comment at the end of her narrative that in America "the bathrooms were clean and the people were very, very kind" (paragraph 14)? What is she actually referring to?

DISCOVERING RHETORICAL STRATEGIES

9. Dumas is a master at timing her narrative to create humor. Find an example of her effective timing of introducing certain information, and explain its effect on you.
10. What comparison does Dumas use to explain how her classmates might feel having Dumas and her mother in her house (paragraph 11)? How effective is this explanation?
11. What does this particular day in school symbolize for Dumas? Explain your answer in detail.
12. How appropriate is the title of this narrative? What are some other possible titles?

MAKING CONNECTIONS

13. Compare and contrast the parent–child relationship depicted in this essay with that described in Lewis Sawaquat's "For My Indian Daughter," Amy Tan's "Mother Tongue," and/or Michael Dorris's "The Broken Cord."
14. If Dumas were having a round-table discussion with Maya Angelou ("New Directions"), Claudia Wallis and Sonia Steptoe ("How to Bring Our Schools Out of the 20th Century"), Lyn Mikel Brown and Meda Chesney-Lind ("Bad Girls, Bad Girls, Whatcha Gonna Do?"), and/or Sherman Alexie ("The Joy of Reading and Writing: Superman and Me"), which author would speak most passionately about the value of getting a good education in life? Why?

15. Throughout her essay, Dumas mentions a number of details that will strike most readers as funny. How is Dumas's use of humor different from that of Bill Cosby ("The Baffling Question"), Jessica Mitford ("Behind the Formaldehyde Curtain"), Marc Gellman ("Worry. Don't Be Happy"), and/or Mary Roach ("Meet the Bickersons")? Which of these essays do you find most entertaining? Explain your answer.

IDEAS FOR DISCUSSION/WRITING

Preparing to Write

Write freely about various personal memories in your life or your family's life: What are these memories? What do they represent? Which of these memories are embarrassing? Which are uplifting? Which of these memories are positive? Which are negative? Which remind you of important stories about yourself or other family members? Why are these stories important? What makes specific family memories so important?

Choosing a Topic

1. *Learning Online:* Recall how difficult some aspects of immigration are by revisiting www.immigrationsupport.org/. Choose a time in your life when you had to overcome a hardship to reach a goal. It can be a short-term goal that took place in a day, like passing a driver's license test, or a long-term goal, like immigrating to the United States. Imagine that you have a friend who is about to attempt the same feat. Write a letter to your friend detailing your experience. Be sure to be specific so your friend will know what to expect and how to be successful.

2. Write a narrative essay introducing yourself to your English class through a special experience in your life. To explain and define your identity, include your relationship to others in your essay.

3. Write a narrative essay that explains how your parents met. What were the highlights of this meeting? Where did it lead? What is their relationship like now?

4. Your school newspaper is running a series of articles on symbols in our lives. You have been asked to submit a narrative essay on the item that best represents you as a student in college. What is this item? How does it represent you? Shape your answers to these questions into a narrative essay.

Before beginning your essay, you might want to consult the checklists on page 122.

SANDRA CISNEROS   (1954–   )

Only daughter

Born in Chicago, Sandra Cisneros was the only daughter raised in a family with six brothers. She moved frequently during her childhood, eventually earning a B.A. in English from Loyola University and an M.F.A. in Creative Writing from the University of Iowa, where she developed her unique voice of a strong and independent working-class, Mexican-American woman. Her first book, *The House on Mango Street* (1984), is a loosely structured series of vignettes focusing on the isolation and cultural conflicts endured by Latina women in America. Later publications include *My Wicked, Wicked Ways* (1987), *Woman Hollering Creek* (1991), *The Future Is Mestizo: Life Where Cultures Meet* (2000), and *Caramelo* (2002). Critics have described her works of fiction as "poetic": "nearly every sentence contains an explosive sensory image. She gives us unforgettable characters that we want to lift off the page and hang out with for a while." Asked to analyze her writing style, Cisneros explains, "I am a woman, and I am a Latina. Those are the things that make my writing distinctive. Those are the things that give my writing power. They are the things that give it *sabor* (flavor), that give it *picante* (spice)." She currently lives in a bright purple house in San Antonio with five cats, three dogs, and two parrots.

Preparing to Read

"Only daughter," an essay first published in *Glamour,* chronicles one of the author's most memorable experiences on a visit to her parents' home in Chicago. Full of family history, the story uses the reunion as a focus for Cisneros's memories and observations about life in a Mexican family.

Exploring Experience: As you prepare to read this essay, take a few moments to consider the many social and cultural influences that shape your life: What is your family like? What activities do you enjoy? Have you ever felt that your family didn't accept these activities? Have you ever been angry at the extent to which social or cultural pressures have governed your life? How did you react to these forces? Can you think of a specific situation in which you overcame social or cultural differences? What were the circumstances? What was the result?

Learning Online: Explore the PBS "American Family" Web site (www .pbs.org/americanfamily) for a dynamic look into the Latino culture. While reading Cisneros's narrative, consider how her experience relates to the accounts on the Web site.

Once, several years ago, when I was just starting out my writing 1
career, I was asked to write my own contributor's note for an
anthology. I wrote: "I am the only daughter in a family of six sons.
That explains everything."

Well, I've thought that ever since, and yes, it explains a lot to me, but for 2
the reader's sake I should have written: "I am the only daughter in a *Mexican*
family of six sons." Or even: "I am the only daughter of a Mexican father and
a Mexican-American mother." Or: "I am the only daughter of a working-
class family of nine." All of these had everything to do with who I am today.

I was/am the only daughter and *only* a daughter. Being an only daughter 3
in a family of six sons forced me by circumstance to spend a lot of time by
myself because my brothers felt it beneath them to play with a *girl* in public. But that aloneness, that loneliness, was good for a would-be writer—it
allowed me time to think and think, to imagine, to read and prepare myself.

Being only a daughter for my father meant my destiny would lead me to 4
become someone's wife. That's what he believed. But when I was in the fifth
grade and shared my plans for college with him, I was sure he understood.
I remember my father saying, "*Que bueno, mi'ja,* that's good." That meant a
lot to me, especially since my brothers thought the idea hilarious. What I
didn't realize was that my father thought college was good for girls—good
for finding a husband. After four years in college and two more in graduate
school, and still no husband, my father shakes his head even now and says I
wasted all that education. ◆

In retrospect, I'm lucky my father believed daughters were meant for hus- 5
bands. It meant it didn't matter if I majored in something silly like English.
After all, I'd find a nice professional eventually, right? This allowed me the liberty to putter about embroidering my little poems and stories without my
father interrupting with so much as a "What's that you're writing?"

But the truth is, I wanted him to interrupt. I wanted my father to under- 6
stand what it was I was scribbling, to introduce me as "My only daughter,
the writer." Not as "This is my only daughter. She teaches." *Es maestra*—
teacher. Not even *profesora.*

In a sense, everything I have ever written has been for him, to win his 7
approval even though I know my father can't read English words, even
though my father's only reading includes the brown-ink *Esto* sports magazines from Mexico City and the bloody *¡Alarma!* magazines that feature yet
another sighting of *La Virgen de Guadalupe* on a tortilla or a wife's revenge

---

Thinking Critically

◆ Which type of discrimination is worst: gender, ethnic, or religious? Why do you think so?

on her philandering husband by bashing his skull in with a *molcajete* (a kitchen mortar made of volcanic rock). Or the *fotonovelas,* the little picture paperbacks with tragedy and trauma erupting from the characters' mouths in bubbles.

A father represents, then, the public majority. A public who is disinterested in reading, and yet one whom I am writing about and for, and privately trying to woo.   8

When we were growing up in Chicago, we moved a lot because of my father. He suffered bouts of nostalgia. Then we'd have to let go of our flat, store the furniture with mother's relatives, load the station wagon with baggage and bologna sandwiches and head south. To Mexico City.   9

We came back, of course. To yet another Chicago flat, another Chicago neighborhood, another Catholic school. Each time, my father would seek out the parish priest in order to get a tuition break, and complain or boast: "I have seven sons." ❷   10

He meant *siete hijos,* seven children, but he translated it as "sons." "I have seven sons." To anyone who would listen. The Sears Roebuck employee who sold us the washing machine. The short-order cook where my father ate his ham-and-eggs breakfasts. "I have seven sons." As if he deserved a medal from the state.   11

My papa. He didn't mean anything by the mistranslation, I'm sure. But somehow I could feel myself being erased. I'd tug my father's sleeve and whisper: "Not seven sons. Six! and one *daughter.*"   12

When my oldest brother graduated from medical school, he fulfilled my father's dream that we study hard and use this—our heads, instead of this—our hands. Even now my father's hands are thick and yellow, stubbed by a history of hammer and nails and twine and coils and springs. "Use this," my father said, tapping his head, "and not this," showing us those hands. He always looked tired when he said it.   13

Wasn't college an investment? And hadn't I spent all those years in college? And if I didn't marry, what was it all for? Why would anyone go to college and then choose to be poor? ❸ Especially someone who has always been poor.   14

Last year, after ten years of writing professionally, the financial rewards started to trickle in. My second National Endowment for the Arts Fellowship. A guest professorship at the University of California, Berkeley. My book, which sold to a major New York publishing house.   15

Thinking Critically

❷ What are the principal differences between Cisneros and her father? How does her status as the "only daughter" affect their love for each other?

❸ What do you believe is the relationship between attending college and the salary you will earn after graduation?

At Christmas, I flew home to Chicago. The house was throbbing, same as always; hot *tamales* and sweet *tamales* hissing in my mother's pressure cooker, and everybody—my mother, six brothers, wives, babies, aunts, cousins—talking too loud and at the same time, like in a Fellini film, because that's just how we are.

I went upstairs to my father's room. One of my stories had just been translated into Spanish and published in an anthology of Chicano writing, and I wanted to show it to him. Ever since he recovered from a stroke two years ago, my father likes to spend his leisure hours horizontally. And that's how I found him, watching a Pedro Infante movie on Galavision and eating rice pudding.

There was a glass filmed with milk on the bedside table. There were several vials of pills and balled Kleenex. And on the floor, one black sock and a plastic urinal that I didn't want to look at but looked at anyway. Pedro Infante was about to burst into song, and my father was laughing. ◆

I'm not sure if it was because my story was translated into Spanish, or because it was published in Mexico, or perhaps because the story dealt with Tepeyac, the *colonia* my father was raised in and the house he grew up in, but at any rate, my father punched the mute button on his remote control and read my story.

I sat on the bed next to my father and waited. He read it very slowly. As if he were reading each line over and over. He laughed at all the right places and read lines he liked out loud. He pointed and asked questions: "Is this So-and-so?" "Yes," I said. He kept reading.

When he was finally finished, after what seemed like hours, my father looked up and asked: "Where can we get more copies of this for the relatives?"

Of all the wonderful things that happened to me last year, that was the most wonderful.

UNDERSTANDING DETAILS

1. How many children are in Cisneros's family? How many are boys?
2. Why does Cisneros's father always say he has seven sons? Why is this detail significant?
3. Why did Cisneros's father let her go to college? Explain your answer.
4. What are the differences in the way the author's father views his sons and his daughter?

Thinking Critically

◆ What do TV viewing habits tell us about someone?

READING CRITICALLY

5. What does Cisneros mean when she says, "I am the only daughter and *only* a daughter" (paragraph 3)?
6. What does her cultural heritage have to do with the fact that she is the only daughter?
7. Why does Cisneros write for her father even though he can't read English?
8. Why was her father's reaction to her story published in Spanish "the most wonderful" (paragraph 22) thing that happened to her last year? Why is her father's opinion so important to her?

DISCOVERING RHETORICAL STRATEGIES

9. From what point of view does Cisneros write this narrative essay? How does this particular point of view help us understand her attitude toward the experience?
10. In writing this essay, Cisneros is making a comment about families in general and Mexican families in particular. What is her ultimate message? What details help you understand this message? Does the fact that she doesn't capitalize "daughter" in her title have anything to do with this message?
11. How does Cisneros organize the details of this narrative? Is this the most effective order for what she is trying to say?
12. Although Cisneros's essay is primarily narrative, what other rhetorical strategies does she use to make her point? Give examples of each.

MAKING CONNECTIONS

13. In "Only daughter," Sandra Cisneros describes the importance of her father's support of and appreciation for her writing career. Compare and contrast the theme of family support described by Sandra Cisneros, Russell Baker ("The Saturday Evening Post"), Tamala Edwards ("Multi-Colored Families"), and/or Mary Pipher ("Beliefs About Families"). Which author would argue that support from one's family is most crucial to our development as a person? Why?
14. Both Sandra Cisneros and Amy Tan ("Mother Tongue") became extremely successful writers in English although they spoke another language at home as they grew up. Can you find any other common denominators in the experiences of these two authors that account for their current skill in using the English language?
15. Compare and contrast the use of examples in the essays by Sandra Cisneros, Harold Krents ("Darkness at Noon"), Brent Staples ("A Brother's Murder"), and/or Frank Furedi ("Our Unhealthy Obsession with Sickness"). Which essay is most densely packed with examples? Which uses example most effectively? Which least effectively? Why?

IDEAS FOR DISCUSSION/WRITING

Preparing to Write

Write freely about a time in your life when you did not fit in with your own family: What were the circumstances? How did you feel? What were your alternatives? Did you take any action? What were the motivating forces for this action? Were you satisfied with the outcome? How do you feel about this experience now?

Choosing a Topic

1. *Learning Online:* Revisit the PBS "American Family" website, and consider a time when you attempted to receive recognition from a family member. Using Cisneros's narrative as a model, write an essay describing your experience for PBS's "American Family" online collection.

2. Write a narrative essay telling your classmates about a time you did not fit in. Make a special effort to communicate your feelings regarding this experience. Remember to choose your details and point of view with an overall purpose in mind.

3. What is America's system of social classes? Where do you fit into the structure? Does our system allow for much mobility between classes? Write a narrative essay for your classmates explaining your understanding of the American class system. Use yourself and/or a friend as an example.

4. Explain in a coherent essay written for the general public why you think we are all sometimes motivated by cultural or personal influences beyond our control. Refer to Cisneros's essay or to experiences of your own to support your explanation.

Before beginning your essay, you might want to consult the checklists on page 122.

The Saturday Evening Post

Russell Baker is one of America's foremost satirists and humorists. Born in Virginia, he grew up in New Jersey and Maryland, graduated from Johns Hopkins University, and then served for two years as a pilot in the U.S. Navy. Following the service, he became a newspaper reporter for the *Baltimore Sun,* which sent him to England as its London correspondent. He subsequently joined the staff of the *New York Times* as a member of its Washington bureau. From 1962 to 1998, he wrote his widely syndicated Observer column in the *Times,* which blended wry humor, a keen interest in language, and biting social commentary about the Washington scene. His books include *An American in Washington* (1961), *No Cause for Panic* (1964), and *Poor Russell's Almanac* (1972), plus two collections of early essays, *So This Is Depravity* (1980) and *The Rescue of Miss Yaskell and Other Pipe Dreams* (1983). *Growing Up* (1982), a best seller vividly recounting his own childhood, earned him the 1983 Pulitzer Prize for biography. His more recent publications include *The Good Times* (1989), which continues his life story from approximately age twenty until he began working for the *New York Times* in the early 1960s; *There's a Country in My Cellar: The Best of Russell Baker* (1990), a collection of his newspaper columns; *Inventing the Truth: The Art and Craft of Memoir* (1995, with William Zinsser), and *Looking Back,* a compilation of some of his articles written for the *New York Review of Books* (2002). His advice to student writers is to "turn off the TV and pick up a book. It will ease your blood pressure. It may even wake up your mind."

Preparing to Read

The following skillfully written essay is an excerpt from Baker's autobiography, *Growing Up.* In it, the author recalls enduring memories from his youth that clearly project the experiences and emotions of his coming of age in 1920s rural Virginia.

Exploring Experience: As you prepare to read this selection, think for a moment about some of your own childhood memories: What were your strengths as a child? Your weaknesses? Have these character traits changed as you've matured? How are you like or unlike various members of your family? How do you react to these similarities and/or differences? What are your main goals in life? How do your character traits affect these goals?

Learning Online: Explore the Norman Rockwell Museum Web site (www .nrm.org) by clicking "Exhibitions" to see online pictures of *Saturday Evening Post* covers and other artistic representations of the 1930s and 1940s. These images represent the time period that Russell Baker describes. How do these pictures differ from your childhood images?

I began working in journalism when I was eight years old. It was my 1
mother's idea. She wanted me to "make something" of myself and, after
a levelheaded appraisal of my strengths, decided I had better start young
if I was to have any chance of keeping up with the competition. **1**

The flaw in my character which she had already spotted was lack of 2
"gumption." My idea of a perfect afternoon was lying in front of the radio
rereading my favorite Big Little Book, *Dick Tracy Meets Stooge Viller.* My
mother despised inactivity. Seeing me having a good time in repose, she
was powerless to hide her disgust. "You've got no more gumption than a
bump on a log," she said. "Get out in the kitchen and help Doris do those
dirty dishes."

My sister Doris, though two years younger than I, had enough gump- 3
tion for a dozen people. **2** She positively enjoyed washing dishes, making
beds, and cleaning the house. When she was only seven, she could carry a
piece of short-weighted cheese back to the A&P, threaten the manager
with legal action, and come back triumphantly with the full quarter-pound
we'd paid for and a few ounces extra thrown in for forgiveness. Doris could
have made something of herself if she hadn't been a girl. Because of this
defect, however, the best she could hope for was a career as a nurse or
schoolteacher, the only work that capable females were considered up to
in those days.

This must have saddened my mother, this twist of fate that had allocated 4
all the gumption to the daughter and left her with a son who was content
with Dick Tracy and Stooge Viller. If disappointed, though, she wasted no
energy on self-pity. She would make me make something of myself whether
I wanted to or not. "The Lord helps those who help themselves," she said.
That was the way her mind worked.

She was realistic about the difficulty. Having sized up the material the 5
Lord had given her to mold, she didn't overestimate what she could do with
it. She didn't insist that I grow up to be President of the United States.

Fifty years ago parents still asked boys if they wanted to grow up to be 6
President, and asked it not jokingly but seriously. Many parents who were
hardly more than paupers still believed their sons could do it. Abraham Lincoln had done it. We were only sixty-five years from Lincoln. Many a grandfather who walked among us could remember Lincoln's time. Men of
grandfatherly age were the worst for asking if you wanted to grow up to be
President. A surprising number of little boys said yes and meant it.

Thinking Critically

1 What does the first paragraph of the essay imply about Baker's opinion of his mother? How
are their personalities different?

2 What proof does the author offer that his sister Doris had "gumption"?

I was asked many times myself. No, I would say, I didn't want to grow up   7
to be President. My mother was present during one of these interrogations.
An elderly uncle, having posed the usual question and exposed my lack of
interest in the Presidency, asked, "Well, what *do* you want to be when you
grow up?"

I loved to pick through trash piles and collect empty bottles, tin cans with   8
pretty labels, and discarded magazines. The most desirable job on earth sprang
instantly to mind. "I want to be a garbage man," I said.

My uncle smiled, but my mother had seen the first distressing evidence   9
of a bump budding on a log. "Have a little gumption, Russell," she said. Her
calling me Russell was a signal of unhappiness. When she approved of me, I
was always "Buddy."

When I turned eight years old she decided that the job of starting me on   10
the road toward making something of myself could no longer be safely
delayed. "Buddy," she said one day, "I want you to come home right after
school this afternoon. Somebody's coming, and I want you to meet him."

When I burst in that afternoon, she was in conference in the parlor with   11
an executive ❸ of the Curtis Publishing Company. She introduced me. He
bent low from the waist and shook my hand. Was it true as my mother had
told him, he asked, that I longed for the opportunity to conquer the world
of business?

My mother replied that I was blessed with a rare determination to make   12
something of myself.

"That's right," I whispered.   13

"But have you got the grit, the character, the never-say-quit spirit it takes   14
to succeed in business?"

My mother said I certainly did.   15

"That's right," I said.   16

He eyed me silently for a long pause, as though weighing whether I could   17
be trusted to keep his confidence, then spoke man-to-man. Before taking a
crucial step, he said, he wanted to advise me that working for the Curtis
Publishing Company placed enormous responsibility on a young man. It
was one of the great companies of America. Perhaps the greatest publishing
house in the world. I had heard, no doubt, of the *Saturday Evening Post?*

Heard of it? My mother said that everyone in our house had heard of the   18
Saturday Post and that I, in fact, read it with religious devotion. ❹

Thinking Critically

❸ Do you think the man introduced to Russell is really an "executive" of the Curtis Publishing Company? How does this word betray his mother's manipulative nature?

❹ What does Baker's mother mean when she claims that her son reads the *Saturday Evening
Post* "with religious devotion"?

Then doubtless, he said, we were also familiar with those two monthly pil-   19
lars of the magazine world, the *Ladies Home Journal* and the *Country Gentleman*.

Indeed we were familiar with them, said my mother.   20

Representing the *Saturday Evening Post* was one of the weightiest honors   21
that could be bestowed in the world of business, he said. He was personally
proud of being a part of the great corporation.

My mother said he had every right to be.   22

Again he studied me as though debating whether I was worthy of a   23
knighthood. Finally: "Are you trustworthy?"

My mother said I was the soul of honesty.   24

"That's right," I said.   25

The caller smiled for the first time. He told me I was a lucky young man.   26
He admired my spunk. Too many young men thought life was all play. Those
young men would not go far in this world. Only a young man willing to
work and save and keep his face washed and his hair neatly combed could
hope to come out on top in a world such as ours. **5** Did I truly and sin-
cerely believe that I was such a young man?

"He certainly does," said my mother.   27

"That's right," I said.   28

He said he had been so impressed by what he had seen of me that he was   29
going to make me a representative of the Curtis Publishing Company. On
the following Tuesday, he said, thirty freshly printed copies of the *Saturday
Evening Post* would be delivered at our door. I would place these magazines,
still damp with the ink of the presses, in a handsome canvas bag, sling it over
my shoulder, and set forth through the streets to bring the best in journalism, fiction, and cartoons to the American public.

He had brought the canvas bag with him. He presented it with reverence   30
fit for a chasuble. He showed me how to drape the sling over my left shoulder and across the chest so that the pouch lay easily accessible to my right
hand, allowing the best in journalism, fiction, and cartoons to be swiftly
extracted and sold to a citizenry whose happiness and security depended
upon us soldiers of the free press.

The following Tuesday I raced home from school, put the canvas bag over   31
my shoulder, dumped the magazines in, and, tilting to the left to balance
their weight on my right hip, embarked on the highway of journalism.

We lived in Belleville, New Jersey, a commuter town at the northern fringe   32
of Newark. It was 1932, the bleakest year of the Depression. **6** My father
had died two years before, leaving us with a few pieces of Sears, Roebuck

---

Thinking Critically

5 Is this still good advice today? What is your advice for success?

6 What signs of the depression can you find in this essay?

furniture and not much else, and my mother had taken Doris and me to live with one of her younger brothers. This was my Uncle Allen. Uncle Allen had made something of himself by 1932. As salesman for a soft-drink bottler in Newark, he had an income of $30 a week; wore pearl-gray spats, detachable collars, and a three-piece suit; was happily married; and took in threadbare relatives.

With my load of magazines I headed toward Belleville Avenue. That's where   33
the people were. There were two filling stations at the intersection with Union Avenue, as well as an A&P, a fruit stand, a bakery, a barber shop, Zuccarelli's drugstore, and a diner shaped like a railroad car. For several hours I made myself highly visible, shifting position now and then from corner to corner, from shop window to shop window, to make sure everyone could see the heavy black lettering on the canvas bag that said THE SATURDAY EVENING POST. When the angle of the light indicated it was suppertime, I walked back to the house.

"How many did you sell, Buddy?" my mother asked.   34

"None."   35

"Where did you go?"   36

"The corner of Belleville and Union Avenues."   37

"What did you do?"   38

"Stood on the corner waiting for somebody to buy a *Saturday Evening Post*."   39

"You just stood there?"   40

"Didn't sell a single one."   41

"For God's sake, Russell!"   42

Uncle Allen intervened. "I've been thinking about it for some time," he   43
said, "and I've about decided to take the *Post* regularly. Put me down as a regular customer." I handed him a magazine, and he paid me a nickel. It was the first nickel I earned.

Afterwards my mother instructed me in salesmanship. I would have to   44
ring doorbells, address adults with charming self-confidence, and break down resistance with a sales talk pointing out that no one, no matter how poor, could afford to be without the *Saturday Evening Post* in the home.

I told my mother I'd changed my mind about wanting to succeed in the   45
magazine business.

"If you think I'm going to raise a good-for-nothing," she replied, "you've   46
got another think coming." She told me to hit the streets with the canvas bag and start ringing doorbells the instant school was out next day. When I objected that I didn't feel any aptitude for salesmanship, she asked how I'd like to lend her my leather belt so she could whack some sense into me. I bowed to superior will [7] and entered journalism with a heavy heart.

Thinking Critically

[7] When Baker admits that he "bowed to superior will," he is being ironic since his mother has threatened to whack him with a belt if he doesn't begin selling the magazine. What other examples of irony can you find in the essay?

My mother and I had fought this battle almost as long as I could remem- 47
ber. It probably started even before memory began, when I was a country
child in northern Virginia and my mother, dissatisfied with my father's plain
workman's life, determined that I would not grow up like him and his people, with calluses on their hands, overalls on their backs, and fourth-grade educations in their heads. She had fancier ideas of life's possibilities. Introducing
me to the *Saturday Evening Post,* she was trying to wean me as early as possible from my father's world where men left with their lunch pails at sunup,
worked with their hands until the grime ate into the pores, and died with a
few sticks of mail-order furniture as their legacy. In my mother's vision of the
better life there were desks and white collars, well-pressed suits, evenings of
reading and lively talk, and perhaps—if a man were very, very lucky and hit
the jackpot, really made something important of himself—perhaps there
might be a fantastic salary of $5,000 a year to support a big house and a
Buick with a rumble seat and a vacation in Atlantic City.

And so I set forth with my sack of magazines. I was afraid of the dogs that 48
snarled behind the doors of potential buyers. I was timid about ringing the
doorbells of strangers, relieved when no one came to the door, and scared
when someone did. Despite my mother's instructions, I could not deliver an
engaging sales pitch. When a door opened I simply asked, "Want to buy a
Saturday Evening Post?" In Belleville few persons did. It was a town of 30,000
people, and most weeks I rang a fair majority of its doorbells. But I rarely sold
my thirty copies. Some weeks I canvassed the entire town for six days and
still had four or five unsold magazines on Monday evening; then I dreaded
the coming of Tuesday morning, when a batch of thirty fresh *Saturday Evening
Posts* was due at the front door. ⑧

"Better get out there and sell the rest of those magazines tonight," my 49
mother would say.

I usually posted myself then at a busy intersection where a traffic light 50
controlled commuter flow from Newark. When the light turned red, I stood
on the curb and shouted my sales pitch at the motorists.

"Want to buy a *Saturday Evening Post?*" 51

One rainy night when car windows were sealed against me, I came back 52
soaked and with not a single sale to report. My mother beckoned to Doris.

"Go back down there with Buddy and show him how to sell these mag- 53
azines," she said.

Brimming with zest, Doris, who was then seven years old, returned with 54
me to the corner. She took a magazine from the bag, and when the light
turned red, she strode to the nearest car and banged her small fist against the

---

Thinking Critically

⑧ In what ways do you think selling is like writing?

closed window. The driver, probably startled at what he took to be a midget assaulting his car, [9] lowered the window to stare, and Doris thrust a *Saturday Evening Post* at him.

"You need this magazine," she piped, "and it only costs a nickel."   55

Her salesmanship was irresistible. Before the light changed half a dozen   56
times, she disposed of the entire batch. I didn't feel humiliated. To the contrary. I was so happy I decided to give her a treat. Leading her to the veg-
etable store on Belleville Avenue, I bought three apples, which cost a nickel,
and gave her one.

"You shouldn't waste money," she said.   57

"Eat your apple." I bit into mine.   58

"You shouldn't eat before supper," she said. "It'll spoil your appetite." [10]   59

Back at the house that evening, she dutifully reported me for wasting a   60
nickel. Instead of a scolding, I was rewarded with a pat on the back for having the good sense to buy fruit instead of candy. My mother reached into her
bottomless supply of maxims and told Doris, "An apple a day keeps the doctor away."

By the time I was ten I had learned all my mother's maxims by heart.   61
Asking to stay up past normal bedtime, I knew that a refusal would be
explained with, "Early to bed and early to rise, makes a man healthy, wealthy,
and wise." If I whimpered about having to get up early in the morning, I
could depend on her to say, "The early bird gets the worm."

The one I most despised was, "If at first you don't succeed, try, try again."   62
This was the battle cry with which she constantly sent me back into the
hopeless struggle whenever I moaned that I had rung every doorbell in town
and knew there wasn't a single potential buyer left in Belleville that week.
After listening to my explanation, she handed me the canvas bag and said,
"If at first you don't succeed . . ."

Three years in that job, which I would gladly have quit after the first day   63
except for her insistence, produced at least one valuable result. My mother
finally concluded that I would never make something of myself by pursuing a life in business and started considering careers that demanded less competitive zeal.

One evening when I was eleven, I brought home a short "composition"   64
on my summer vacation which the teacher had graded with an A. Reading
it with her own schoolteacher's eye, my mother agreed that it was top-drawer
seventh grade prose and complimented me. Nothing more was said about it

---

Thinking Critically

[9] The description of Doris assaulting the car like a "midget" is one among many examples
of humor in this essay. Can you find two other humorous images?

[10] What examples can you find of Doris growing up to be a carbon copy of her mother?

immediately, but a new idea had taken life in her mind. Halfway through supper she suddenly interrupted the conversation.

"Buddy," she said, "maybe you could be a writer."   65

I clasped the idea to my heart. I had never met a writer, had shown no pre-   66
vious urge to write, and hadn't a notion how to become a writer, but I loved stories and thought that making up stories must surely be almost as much fun as reading them. Best of all, though, and what really gladdened my heart, was the ease of the writer's life. ⑪ Writers did not have to trudge through the town peddling from canvas bags, defending themselves against angry dogs, being rejected by surly strangers. Writers did not have to ring doorbells. So far as I could make out, what writers did couldn't even be classified as work.

I was enchanted. Writers didn't have to have any gumption at all. I did not   67
dare tell anybody for fear of being laughed at in the schoolyard, but secretly I decided that what I'd like to be when I grew up was a writer.

UNDERSTANDING DETAILS

1. How does Baker's ideal day differ from that of his sister?
2. According to the author's mother, what is the main flaw in his character? How does this flaw eventually affect his choice of a career?
3. Why does Baker feel he has no "aptitude for salesmanship" (paragraph 46)? What has led him to this conclusion?
4. Which of his mother's maxims does the author dislike the most? Explain his reaction.

READING CRITICALLY

5. Why does Baker begin this selection with a comparison of his personality and his sister's? What does this comparison have to do with the rest of the essay?
6. Why does the author's mother insist that he work for the *Saturday Evening Post?* What does she think he will gain from the experience? What does he actually learn?
7. What "battle" (paragraph 47) have the author and his mother been fighting for as long as he can remember? Who finally wins this battle?
8. Why is Baker so delighted with the idea of becoming a writer when he grows up? How is this notion compatible with his personality?

DISCOVERING RHETORICAL STRATEGIES

9. How does Baker arrange the details in this excerpt? Why do you think he organizes them in this way? How would a different arrangement have changed the essay?
10. Who do you think is Baker's intended audience? Describe them in detail. How did you come to this conclusion?

Thinking Critically

⑪ Do you think a writer's life is "easy"? Why or why not?

11. What is the climax of Baker's narrative? How does he lead up to and develop this climactic moment? What stylistic traits tell us that this is the most exciting point in the story?

12. Besides narration, what other rhetorical strategies does Baker draw on to develop his thesis? Give examples of each of these strategies.

MAKING CONNECTIONS

13. Baker insists on the importance of dedicating oneself to a career. Compare and contrast his feelings on this subject with similar sentiments found in essays by Sandra Cisneros ("Only daughter"), William Ouchi ("Japanese and American Workers: Two Casts of Mind"), and/or Gloria Steinem ("The Politics of Muscle"). How dedicated do you intend to be to your own future career?

14. How is young Russell Baker's naive conception of a writer's "easy" life different from the views on writing expressed by Sandra Cisneros ("Only daughter"), Amy Tan ("Mother Tongue"), and/or Sherman Alexie ("The Joy of Reading and Writing: Superman and Me")? Which of these authors would argue most fervently that writing is "hard" work? How do you feel about the process of writing? Is it easy or difficult for you? Explain your answer.

15. Russell Baker's mother had a strong influence over him as he grew up. Imagine a conversation among Baker, Bill Cosby ("The Baffling Question"), Judith Wallerstein and Sandra Blakeslee ("Second Chances for Children of Divorce"), and/or Mary Pipher ("Beliefs About Families") concerning the importance of proper parental guidance as a child matures. Which author would be most adamant about the importance of the role of parents in a child's upbringing? Explain your answer.

IDEAS FOR DISCUSSION/WRITING

Preparing to Write

Write freely about yourself in relation to your aspirations: What type of person are you? What do you think about? What are your ideals? Your hopes? Your dreams? Your fears? What do you enjoy doing in your spare time? How are you different from other members of your family? Is anyone in your family a model for you? How have members of your immediate family affected your daily life—past and present? Your career goals? How do you anticipate your family will affect your future?

Choosing a Topic

1. *Learning Online:* Reflect on your worst memory of working at a particular job or chore. Write an email to Baker in which you explain how an experience that seemed horrible at the time actually had positive results. Following Baker's example, establish a strong sense of time and place in your narrative. Add a photo or drawing to your narrative that, like those on the Normal Rockwell Museum Web site, captures the memory and the time period.

2. Write a narrative essay introducing yourself to your English class. To explain and define your identity, include descriptions of family members whenever appropriate.

3. Write a narrative that helps explain to a friend how you got involved in a current interest. To expand on your narrative, refer whenever possible to your long-term goals and aspirations.

4. Ten years from now, your local newspaper decides to devote an entire section to people getting started in careers. You are asked to submit the story of how you got involved in your profession (whatever it may be). Write a narrative that might appear in your hometown newspaper ten years from now; be sure to give the article a catchy headline.

Before beginning your essay, you might want to consult the checklists on page 122.

Chapter Writing Assignments

Practicing Narration

1. Think of a story that is often repeated by your family members because of its special significance or its humor. Retell the story to an audience who does not know your family, and explain to your readers the story's significance.

2. What has been the most challenging and life-changing event in your life? Remember this event as clearly as you can by noting special details on scratch paper. Write an essay that describes what led up to this event, what happened, and how you reacted to the event. Explain why this experience was so challenging and/or life-changing.

3. Think of a time when you received a very special gift. Tell the story of how you received this gift, who gave it to you, and why it was memorable. For a more sophisticated approach, try to think of gifts that are not material or tangible objects but rather intangible qualities or concepts (such as love, life, and happiness).

Exploring Ideas

4. Write an essay that identifies the most important qualities in a friend. Explain how each quality is important to a meaningful and fulfilling friendship.

5. Cut an advertisement out of a magazine or newspaper. Examine its "story" and the way the advertiser is selling the product. Write an essay that discusses the effect of advertising on individuals and on American society. How honest or believable should advertising be? What are our expectations for advertising?

6. Describe a time when you quit a job or hobby that others thought you should continue. Discuss the principal features of this activity, your frustration with them, and the main aspects of the job or hobby that others valued. In retrospect, do you think you made a wise decision?

Writing from Sources

For detailed information on writing from sources, see Part III.

7. Many Americans can trace their ancestry to a relative who immigrated to this country. Research one ethnic group—either your own or another that interests you—known for their immigration to the United States. Then, narrate a historical account, including factual information, from the perspective of an individual in that group.

8. Laws have become much more stringent regarding child labor in the United States, but are children across the world protected? What is your position on this issue? What are the causes leading to international abuse of child labor? What are some possible solutions? Research this issue, and write a documented essay comparing the systems and practices of child labor in two different cultures.

Analyzing Visual Images

© www.danheller.com/Dan Heller Photography

9. Think of a time when you went to the beach. Tell a story based on your trip. What was most memorable? What simple pleasures pleased you most? Why was this particular trip to the beach important or noteworthy?
10. Reflect on the picture on page 112 at the beginning of this chapter. Develop the story that might lead up to this picture as its conclusion.

Chapter 6

EXAMPLE
Illustrating Ideas

Citing an example to help make a point is one of the most instinctive techniques we use in communication. If, for instance, you state that being an internationally ranked tennis player requires constant practice, a friend might challenge that assertion and ask what you mean by "constant practice." When you respond "at least three hours a day," your friend might ask for more specific proof. At this stage in the discussion, you could offer the following illustrations to support your statement: When not on tour, Andy Roddick practices three hours per day; Maria Sharapova, four hours; and Roger Federer, five hours. Your friend's doubt will have been answered through your use of examples.

DEFINING EXAMPLES

Well-chosen examples and illustrations are an essay's building blocks. They are drawn from your experience, your observations, and your reading. They help you *show* rather than *tell* what you mean, usually by supplying concrete details (references to what we can see, smell, taste, hear, or touch) to support abstract ideas (such as faith, hope, understanding, and love), by providing specifics ("I like chocolate") to explain generalizations ("I like sweets"), and by giving definite references ("Turn left at the second stoplight") to clarify

Example   159

vague statements ("Turn in a few blocks"). Though illustrations take many forms, writers often find themselves indebted to description or narration (or some combination of the two) in order to supply enough relevant examples to achieve their rhetorical intent.

As you might suspect, examples are important ingredients in producing exciting, vivid prose. Just as crucial is the fact that carefully chosen examples often encourage your readers to feel one way or another about an issue being discussed. If you tell your parents, for instance, that living in a college dormitory is not conducive to academic success, they may doubt your word, perhaps thinking that you are simply attempting to coerce money out of them for an apartment. You can help dispel this notion, however, by giving them specific examples of the chaotic nature of dorm life: the party down the hall that broke up at 2:00 A.M. when you had a chemistry exam that same morning at 8:00; the stereo next door that seems to be stuck on its highest decibel level at all hours of the day and night; and the new "friend" you recently acquired who thinks you are the best listener in the world—especially when everyone else has the good sense to be asleep. After such a detailed and well-documented explanation, your parents could hardly deny the strain of this difficult environment on your studies. Examples can be very persuasive.

The following paragraphs written by a student use examples to explain how the writer reacts to boredom in his life. As you read this excerpt, notice how the writer shows rather than tells the readers how he copes with boredom by providing exciting details that are concrete, specific, and definite.

> We all deal with boredom in our own ways. Unfortunately, most of us have to deal with it far too often. Some people actually seek boredom. Being bored means that they are not required to do anything; being boring means that no one wants anything from them. In short, these people equate boredom with peace and relaxation. But for the rest of us, boredom is not peaceful. It produces anxiety.
>
> Most people deal with boredom by trying to distract themselves from boring circumstances. Myself, I'm a reader. At the breakfast table over a boring bowl of cereal, I read the cereal box, the milk carton, the wrapper on the bread. (Have you ever noticed how many of those ingredients are unpronounceable?) Waiting in a doctor's office, I will gladly read weekly news magazines of three years ago, a book for five-year-olds, advertisements for drugs, and even the physician's odd-looking diplomas on the walls. Have you ever been so bored you were reduced to reading through all the business cards in your wallet? Searching for names similar to yours in the phone book? Browsing through the National Enquirer while waiting in the grocery line? At any rate, that's my recipe for beating boredom. What's yours?

THINKING CRITICALLY THROUGH EXAMPLES

Working with examples gives you yet another powerful way of processing your immediate environment and the larger world around you. It involves a manner of thinking that is completely different from description and narration. Using examples to think critically means seeing a definite order in a series of specific, concrete illustrations related in some way that may or may not be immediately obvious to your readers.

Isolating this rhetorical mode involves playing with related details in such a way that they create various patterns that relay different messages to the reader. Often, the simple act of arranging examples helps both the reader and the writer make sense of an experience or idea. In fact, ordering examples and illustrations in a certain way may give one distinct impression, while ordering them in another way may send a completely different message. Each pattern creates a different meaning and, as a result, an entirely new effect.

With examples, more than with description and narration, patterns need to be discovered in the context of the topic, the writer's purpose, and the writer's ultimate message. Writers and readers of example essays must make a shift from chronological to logical thinking. A writer discussing variations in faces, for example, would be working with assorted memories of people, incidents, and age differences. All of these details will eventually take shape in some sort of statement about faces, but these observations would probably not follow a strictly chronological sequence.

The exercises here will help you experience the mental differences among the rhetorical modes we have studied so far and will also prepare you to make sense of details and examples through careful arrangement and rearrangement of them in your essay. In addition, these exercises will continue to give you more information about your mind's abilities and range.

1. In the photograph on page 161 by Naseeb Baroody, what kinds of examples do you see? Is this an example of simplicity or complexity? Good photography or bad photography? Make a list of at least five other ways this photograph could serve as an example.
2. For each sentence below, provide two to three examples that would illustrate the generalization:
   a. I really liked/disliked some of the movies released this year.
   b. Many career opportunities await a college graduate.
   c. Some companies make large sums of money by selling products with the names of professional sports teams on them.
3. Jot down five examples of a single problem on campus that bothers you. First, arrange these examples in an order that would convince the president

Example 161

© Dr. Naseeb Baroody

of your school that making some changes in this area would create a more positive learning environment. Second, organize your five examples in such a way that they would convince your parents that the learning environment at your current school cannot be salvaged and you should immediately transfer to another school.

READING AND WRITING EXAMPLE ESSAYS

A common criticism of college-level writers is that they often base their essays on unsupported generalizations, such as "All sports cars are unreliable." The guidelines discussed in this introduction will help you avoid this problem and use examples effectively to support your ideas.

As you read the essays in this chapter, take time to notice the degree of specificity the writers use to make various points. To a certain extent, the more examples you use in your essays, the clearer your ideas will be and the more your readers will understand and be interested in what you are saying.

Notice also that these writers know when to stop—when "more" becomes too much and boredom sets in for the reader. Most college students err by using too few examples, however, so we suggest that, when in doubt about whether or not to include another illustration, you should go ahead and add one.

Reading Example Essays

- What is the essay's context?
- What is the writer's main message?
- How do examples communicate this message?

Preparing to Read.   Before you begin reading the essays in this chapter, take some time to think about each author's title: What can you infer about Bill Cosby's attitude toward having children from his title "The Baffling Question"? What do you think is Richard Rodriguez's view of his past? In addition, try to discover the writer's audience and purpose at this point in the reading process; scanning the essay and surveying its synopsis in the Rhetorical Table of Contents will provide you with useful information for this task.

Also important as you prepare to read is information about the author and about how a particular essay was written. Most of this material is furnished for you in the biography preceding each essay. From it, you might learn why Harold Krents is qualified to write about blindness or why Brent Staples published "A Brother's Murder."

Finally, before you begin to read, take time to answer the Preparing to Read questions and to make some associations with the general subject of the essay: What do you know about your cultural and ethnic heritage (Richard Rodriguez)? What are some of your thoughts on friendship (Joel Stein)?

Reading.   As you first read these essays, record any ideas that come to mind. Make associations freely with the content of each essay, its purpose, its audience, and the facts about its publication. For example, try to learn why Cosby writes about having children or why Krents titles his essay "Darkness at Noon." At this point, you will probably be able to make some pretty accurate guesses about the audience each author is addressing. Creating a context for your reading—including the writer's qualifications; the essay's tone, purpose, and audience; and the publication data—is an important first step toward being able to analyze your reading material in any mode.

Each essay also contains questions at the bottom of the pages that guide you to think critically about the essay's subject and the claims the author is making about that topic. Answering these questions as you read will help you develop the skills to read critically and succeed in your other classes. Your responses will also help you generate ideas to build on as you continue to read. Ultimately, they help you build a bridge between your prereading thoughts and the exercises and writing assignments at the end of each essay.

Finally, after you have read an essay in this section once, preview the questions after the selection before you read it again. Let these questions focus your attention for your second reading.

Example   163

Rereading.   As you read the essays in this chapter for a second time, focus on the examples each writer uses to make his or her point: How relevant are these examples to the thesis and purpose of each essay? How many examples do the writers use? Do they vary the length of these examples to achieve different goals? Do the authors use examples their readers can easily identify with and understand? How are these examples organized in each case? Does this arrangement support each writer's purpose? For example, how relevant are Cosby's examples to his central idea? How many examples does Richard Rodriguez use to make each point? Does Krents vary the length of each of his examples to accomplish different purposes? How does Stein organize his examples? Does this arrangement help him accomplish his purpose? In what way? Does Staples use examples that everyone can identify with? How effective are his examples?

As you read, consider also how other rhetorical modes help each writer accomplish his or her purpose. What are these modes? How do they work along with examples to help create a coherent essay?

Last, answering the questions after each essay will help you check your grasp of its main points and will lead you from the literal to the analytical level in preparation for the discussion/writing assignments that follow.

For a thorough summary of reading tasks, you might want to consult the Reading Inventory at the end of Part I.

Writing Example Essays

- Draft a thesis statement.
- Choose relevant examples to support your thesis.
- Arrange your examples to prove your main point.

Preparing to Write.   Before you can use examples in an essay, you must first think of some. One good way to generate ideas is to use some of the prewriting techniques explained in Chapter 3 (pages 36–38) as you respond to the Preparing to Write questions that appear before the writing assignments for each essay. You should then consider these thoughts in conjunction with the purpose and audience specified in your chosen writing assignments. Out of these questions should come a number of good examples for your essay.

Writing.   In an example essay, a thesis statement or controlling idea will help you begin to organize your paper. (See page 41 for more information on thesis statements.) Examples become the primary method of organizing an essay when they actually guide the readers from point to point in reference to the writer's thesis statement. The examples you use should always be relevant to the thesis and purpose of your essay. If, for instance, the person talking about tennis players cited the practice schedules of only unknown players, her friend certainly would not be convinced of the truth of her statement about how hard internationally ranked athletes work at their game. To develop a topic principally with examples, you can use one extended example or several shorter examples, depending on the nature and purpose of your assertion. If you are attempting to prove that Americans are more health conscious now than they were twenty years ago, citing a few examples from your own neighborhood will not provide enough evidence to be convincing. If, however, you are simply commenting on a neighborhood health trend, you can legitimately refer to these local cases. Furthermore, always try to find examples with which your audience can identify so that they can follow your line of reasoning. If you want your parents to help finance an apartment, citing instances from the lives of current rock stars will probably not prove your point because your parents may not sympathize with these particular role models.

The examples you choose must also be arranged as effectively as possible to encourage audience interest and identification. If you are using examples to explain the imaginative quality of Disneyland, for instance, the most logical approach would probably be to organize your essay by degrees (i.e., from least to most imaginative or from most to least original). But if your essay uses examples to help readers visualize your bedroom, a spatial arrangement of the details (moving from one item to the next) might be easiest for your readers to follow. If the subject is a series of important events, like graduation weekend, the illustrations might most effectively be organized chronologically. As you will learn from reading the selections that follow, the careful organization of examples leads quite easily to unity and coherence in your essays. *Unity* is a sense of wholeness and interrelatedness that writers achieve by making sure all their sentences are related to the essay's main idea; *coherence* refers to logical development in an essay, with special attention to how well ideas grow out of one another as the essay develops. Unity and coherence produce good writing—and that, of course, helps foster confidence and accomplishment in school and in your professional life.

Rewriting.   As you reread your example essays, look closely at the choice and arrangement of details in relation to your purpose and audience:

- Have I included enough examples to develop each of my topics adequately?
- Are the examples I have chosen relevant to my thesis?
- Have I arranged these examples in a logical manner that my audience can follow?

For more detailed information on writing, see the Writing Inventory at the end of Part I.

Example   165

STUDENT ESSAY: EXAMPLES AT WORK

In the following essay, a student uses examples to explain and analyze her parents' behavior as they prepare for and enjoy their grandchildren during the Christmas holidays. As you read it, study the various examples the student writer uses to convince us that her parents truly undergo a transformation each winter.

Mom and Dad's Holiday Disappearing Act

General topic — Often during the winter holidays, people find surprises: Children discover the secret contents of brightly wrapped packages that have teased them for weeks; cooks are astonished by the wealth of smells and memories their busy kitchens can bring about; workaholics stumble upon the true joy of a few days' rest. *Details to capture holiday spirit*

Background information — My surprise over the past few winters has been the personality transformation my parents go through around mid-December as they change from Dad and Mom into Poppa and Granny. Yes, they become grandparents and are completely different from the people I know the other eleven and a half months of the year. *Thesis statement*

First point — The first sign of my parents' metamorphosis is the delight they take in visiting toy and children's clothing stores. These two people, who usually despise anything having to do with shopping malls, become crazed consumers. While they tell me to budget my money and shop wisely, they are buying every doll, dump truck, and velvet outfit in sight. And this is only the beginning of the holidays! *Examples relevant to thesis*

Transition — When my brother's children arrive, Poppa and Granny come into full form. First they throw out all ideas about a balanced diet for the grandkids. While we were raised in a house where everyone had to take two bites of broccoli, beets, or liver (foods that appeared quite often on our table despite constant groaning), the grandchildren never have to eat anything that does not appeal to them. Granny carries marshmallows in her pockets to bribe the littlest ones into following her around the house, while Poppa offers "surprises" of candy and cake to them all day long. Boxes of chocolate-covered cherries disappear while *Second point* *Humorous examples (organized from particular to general)* the bran muffins get hard and stale. The kids love all the sweets, and when the sugar revs up their energy levels, Granny and Poppa can always leave and do a bit more shopping or go to bed while my brother and sister-in-law try to deal with their supercharged, hyperactive kids.

Transition / *Third point*

Once the grandchildren have arrived, Granny and Poppa also seem to forget all of the responsibility lectures I so often hear in my daily life. If little Tommy throws a fit at a friend's house, he is "overwhelmed by the number of adults"; if Mickey screams at his sister during dinner, he is "developing his own personality"; if Nancy breaks Granny's vanity mirror (after being told twice to put it down), she is "just a curious child." But if I track mud into the house while helping to unload groceries, I become "careless"; if I scold one of the grandkids for tearing pages out of my calculus book, I am "impatient." If a grandchild talks back to her mother, Granny and Poppa chuckle at her spirit. If I mumble one word about all of this doting, Mom and Dad have a talk with me about petty jealousies.

Examples in the form of comparison

Transition to conclusion

When my nieces and nephews first started appearing at our home for the holidays a few years ago, I probably was jealous, and I complained a lot. But now I spend more time simply sitting back and watching Mom and Dad change into what we call the "Incredible Huggers." They enjoy their time with these grandchildren so much that I easily forgive them their Granny and Poppa faults.

Writer's attitude

Writer's analysis of situation

I believe their personality change is due to the lack of responsibility they feel for the grandkids: In their role as grandparents, they don't have to worry about sugar causing cavities or temporary failures of self-discipline turning into lifetime faults. Those problems are up to my brother and sister-in-law. All Granny and Poppa have to do is enjoy and love their grandchildren. They have all the fun of being parents without any of the attendant obligations. And you know what? I think they've earned the right to make this transformation—at least once a year.

Concluding remark / *Specific reference to introduction*

Example   167

Student Writer's Comments

To begin this essay, I listed examples of my parents' antics during the Christmas holidays as parents and as grandparents and then tried to figure out how these examples illustrated patterns of behavior. Next, I scratched out an outline pairing my parents' actions with what I thought were the causes of those actions. But once I sat down to write, I was completely stumped. I had lots of isolated ideas and saw a few patterns, but I had no notion of where this essay was going.

I thought I might put the theory that writing is discovery to the ultimate test and sit down to write out a very rough first draft. I wanted the introduction to be humorous, but I also wanted to maintain a dignified tone (so I wouldn't sound like a whiny kid!). I was really having trouble getting started. I decided to write down *anything* and then come back to the beginning later on. All of the examples and anecdotes were swimming around in my head wanting to be committed to paper. But I couldn't make sense of many of them, and I still couldn't see where I was headed. I found I needed my thesaurus and dictionary from the very beginning; they helped take the pressure off me to come up with the perfect word every time I was stuck. As I neared the middle of the paper, the introduction popped into my head, so I jotted down my thoughts and continued with the flow of ideas I needed for the body of my essay.

Writing my conclusion forced me to put my experiences with my parents into perspective and gave me an angle for revising the body of my essay. But my focus didn't come to me until I began to revise my entire paper. At that point, I realized I had never really tried to analyze how I felt toward my parents' actions or why they acted as they do during the Christmas holidays. I opened the conclusion with "I believe their [my parents'] personality change is due to" and sat in one place until I finished the statement with a reason that made sense out of all these years of frustration. It finally came to me: They act the way they do during the holidays because they don't have primary responsibility for their grandkids. It's a role they have never played before, and they are loving it. (Never mind how it is affecting me!) This basic realization led me to new insights about the major changes they go through during the holidays and ended up giving me a renewed appreciation of their behavior. I couldn't believe the sentence I wrote to close the essay: "I think they've earned the right to make this transformation—at least once a year." Holy cow! Writing this essay actually brought me to a new understanding of my parents.

Revising was a breeze. I felt as if I had just been through a completely draining therapy session, but I now knew what I thought of this topic and where my essay was headed. I dropped irrelevant examples, reorganized other details, and tightened up some of the explanations so they set up my conclusion more clearly. Both my parents and I were delighted with the results.

SOME FINAL THOUGHTS ON EXAMPLES

Although examples are often used to supplement and support other methods of development—such as cause/effect, comparison/contrast, and process analysis—the essays in this section focus principally on examples. A main idea is expressed in the introduction of each, and the rest of the essay provides examples to bolster that contention. As you read these essays, pay close attention to each author's choice and arrangement of examples; then try to determine which organizational techniques are most persuasive for each specific audience.

EXAMPLE IN REVIEW

Reading Example Essays

Preparing to Read
√ What assumptions can I make from the essay's title?
√ What do I think the general mood of the essay will be?
√ What is the essay's purpose and audience?
√ What does the synopsis tell me about the essay?
√ What can I learn from the author's biography?
√ Can I predict the author's point of view toward the subject?

Reading
√ What is the essay's context?
√ What is the writer's main message?
√ How do examples communicate this message?

Rereading
√ What examples help the author communicate the essay's message?
√ How are these examples organized?
√ What other rhetorical modes does the author use?

Writing Example Essays

Preparing to Write
√ What is my purpose?
√ Who is my audience?
√ What is the message I want to convey?

Writing
√ What is my thesis or controlling idea?
√ Do the examples I am choosing support this thesis?
√ Are these examples arranged as effectively as possible?

Rewriting
√ Have I included enough examples to develop each of my topics adequately?
√ Are the examples I have chosen relevant to my thesis?
√ Have I arranged these examples in a logical manner that my audience can follow?

(1937–   )

Question

>r, recording artist, and author Bill Cosby is undoubtedly
............America's best-loved entertainers. From his beginnings on the *I Spy*
television series through his *Fat Albert* years and his work on *Sesame Street,*
his eight Grammy awards for comedy albums, his commercials for everything
from Kodak film to Jell-O pudding, and his portrayal of the affable obste-
trician Cliff Huxtable on his immensely popular *The Cosby Show,* he has
retained his public persona of an honest and trustworthy storyteller intrigued
by the ironies in our everyday lives. After a series of hit movies in the 1970s,
Cosby decided to return to prime-time television in 1984: "I got tired of seeing TV shows that consisted of a car crash, a gunman, and a hooker talking
to a Black pimp. It was cheaper to do a series than to throw out my family's six television sets." At the peak of its success, *The Cosby Show* was seen
weekly by over sixty million viewers. Cosby's publications include *You Are
Somebody Special* (1978), *Fatherhood* (1986), *Time Flies* (1988), *Love and Marriage* (1989), and a children's book entitled *Friends of a Feather* (illustrated by
his daughter, Erika Cosby, 2003). He lives with his wife, Camille, in Los
Angeles, where he relaxes by playing an occasional game of tennis. Cosby
counsels student writers to look for the humor in life: "Through humor, you
can soften some of the worst blows that life delivers. Once you find laughter, no matter how painful your situation might be, you can survive it."

Preparing to Read

The following selection is from *Fatherhood,* which details the joys and frustrations of raising children. In this essay, he puts a comic spin on several serious issues connected with parenthood.

Exploring Experience: Before reading this piece, pause to consider the
effect parenthood has had or might have on your life: How did/would you
make the decision whether to have children? What variables were/would be
involved in this decision? What are/would be some of the difficulties involved
in raising children? Some of the joys? What memories do you have of your
own childhood?

Learning Online: Visit the U.S. Department of Health and Human Services
Web site located at www.hhs.gov, and select an article related to children or
new parents. What types of examples do the writers use to support their main
claims? While reading "The Baffling Question," consider how these examples
differ from the types of examples used by Bill Cosby.

So you've decided to have a child. You've decided to give up quiet 1
evenings with good books and lazy weekends with good music, intimate meals during which you finish whole sentences, sweet private times when you've savored the thought that just the two of you and your love are all you will ever need. You've decided to turn your sofas into trampolines and to abandon the joys of leisurely contemplating reproductions of great art for the joys of frantically coping with reproductions of yourselves. [1]

Why? 2

Poets have said the reason to have children is to give yourself immortality; and I must admit I did ask God to give me a son because I wanted someone to carry on the family name. Well, God did just that, and I now confess that there have been times when I've told my son not to reveal who he is. 3

"You make up a name," I've said. "Just don't tell anybody who you are." 4

Immortality? Now that I have had five children, my only hope is that 5
they all are out of the house before I die.

No, immortality was not the reason why my wife and I produced these 6
beloved sources of dirty laundry and ceaseless noise. And we also did not have them because we thought it would be fun to see one of them sit in a chair and stick out his leg so that another one of them running by was launched like Explorer I. After which I said to the child who was the launching pad, "Why did you do that?"

"Do what?" he replied. 7

"Stick out your leg." 8

"Dad, I didn't know my leg was going out. My leg, it does that a lot." 9

If you cannot function in a world where things like this are said, then you 10
better forget about raising children and go for daffodils.

My wife and I also did not have children so they could yell at each other 11
all over the house, moving me to say, "What's the problem?"

"She's waving her foot in my room," my daughter replied. 12

"And something like that *bothers* you?" 13

"Yes, I don't *want* her foot in my room." 14

"Well," I said, dipping into my storehouse of paternal wisdom, [2] "why 15
don't you just close the door?"

"Then I can't see what she's doing!" 16

Furthermore, we did not have the children because we thought it would 17
be rewarding to watch them do things that should be studied by the Menninger Clinic.

Thinking Critically

[1] What would you say are the top five reasons most people want to have children?

[2] What does Cosby mean by the phrase "my storehouse of paternal wisdom"? In what way are these words humorous in this context? Where else in the essay does the author use humor?

A Leading psychiatric hospital for treatment, research & education

"Okay," I said to all five one day, "go get into the car."   18

All five then ran to the same car door, grabbed the same handle, and spent   19
the next few minutes beating each other up. Not one of them had the intelligence to say, "Hey, *look*. There are three more doors." The dog, however, was
already inside.

And we did not have the children to help my wife develop new lines for   20
her face or because she had always had a desire to talk out loud to herself:
"Don't tell *me* you're *not* going to do something when I tell you to move!"
And we didn't have children so I could always be saying to someone, "Where's
my change?"

Like so many young couples, my wife and I simply were unable to project. ❸   21
In restaurants we did not see the small children who were casting their bread
on the water in the glasses the waiter had brought; and we did not see the
mother who was fasting because she was both cutting the food for one child
while pulling another from the floor to a chair that he would use for slipping
to the floor again. And we did not project beyond those lovely Saturdays of buying precious little things after leisurely brunches together. We did not see that
other precious little things would be coming along to destroy the first batch.

UNDERSTANDING DETAILS

1. According to Cosby, exactly what is "the baffling question"? Why is this question "baffling"?
2. If everyone felt as Cosby does about raising children, what kinds of people
   would have children?
3. List three important issues that Cosby believes couples should consider before
   they have children.
4. From Cosby's point of view, in what important ways do children change a couple's life?

READING CRITICALLY

5. Why do you think Cosby focuses on the problems children create in a couple's
   life? What effect does this approach have on his main point?
6. What does Cosby mean when he says, "You've decided . . . to abandon the
   joys of leisurely contemplating reproductions of great art for the joys of frantically coping with reproductions of yourselves" (paragraph 1)? Whom is he
   addressing?
7. Following Cosby's logic, why did he and his wife have children? What examples lead you to this conclusion?
8. In what way is the last sentence in this essay a good summary statement? What
   specific thoughts does it summarize?

Thinking Critically

❸ Do you think it's better for couples to have children in their twenties or thirties? Why?
Examine the advantages and disadvantages of this decision.

DISCOVERING RHETORICAL STRATEGIES

9. How does the first paragraph set the tone for the rest of the essay?
10. Cosby's primary strategy in this essay is irony. That is, he suggests reasons for having children by listing reasons *not* to have children. What effect is this approach likely to have on his readers?
11. How does Cosby use specific examples to create humor? Is his humor effective? Explain your answer.
12. Cosby is a master of choosing vivid examples to make his point. What other rhetorical strategies does Cosby use to develop his essay? Give examples of each.

MAKING CONNECTIONS

13. Compare Bill Cosby's comments about raising children with those made about our addiction to horror films by Stephen King in "Why We Crave Horror Movies." To what extent do these authors see our need for children and horror flicks as a kind of self-affirming masochism?
14. How seriously does Cosby intend his readers to take his "advice" about not having children? Do you see any connection between his point of view and that expressed by Jessica Mitford in "Behind the Formaldehyde Curtain"? How do both of these essays work through the rhetorical device of irony (i.e., saying the opposite of what they really mean)? Which essay is more effective? Explain your answer.
15. Contrast Cosby's rapport with his children with the parent–child relationships depicted in Lewis Sawaquat's "For My Indian Daughter," Sandra Cisneros's "Only daughter," Tamala Edwards's "Multi-Colored Families," and/or Michael Dorris's "The Broken Cord." Which parents do you think love their children most? Why do you believe this is true?

IDEAS FOR DISCUSSION/WRITING

Preparing to Write

Write freely about the art of parenthood: From your observations or experience, what are some of the principal problems and joys of parenthood? How is being a parent different from babysitting? What pleasant babysitting experiences have you had? What unpleasant experiences? What kind of child were you? What specific memories led you to this conclusion?

Choosing a Topic

1. *Learning Online:* Select a topic related to childhood on which you feel you have unique expertise. Use your Internet search from Preparing to Read as inspiration. Identify your own "baffling question" surrounding the topic, and write an essay that develops this problem. In organizing your essay, be especially aware of the types of examples you decide to use. Find facts and/or statistics online to develop your essay.
2. Write an essay for the general public explaining one particular problem or joy of parenthood. In your essay, mimic Cosby's humorous approach to the topic. Use several specific examples to make your point.

3. Write an editorial for your local newspaper on your own foolproof techniques for doing one of the following: (a) babysitting, (b) raising children, or (c) becoming a model child. Use specific examples to explain your approach.

4. Interview one or two relatives who are older than you; ask them about the type of child you were. Have them recall some particularly memorable details that characterized your behavior. Then write an essay explaining their predominant impressions of you. Use examples to support these impressions.

Before beginning your essay, you might want to consult the checklists on page 169.

RICHARD RODRIGUEZ   (1944–   )

Public and Private Language

Richard Rodriguez was raised in Sacramento, California, the son of industrious working-class Mexican immigrant parents. He attended parochial schools there and later continued his education at Stanford University, Columbia University, London's Warburg Institute, and, finally, the University of California at Berkeley, where he earned a Ph.D. in English Renaissance Literature. A writer and journalist, he is now Associate Editor of the Pacific News Service in San Francisco. "The Browning of America" is a phrase coined by Rodriguez to describe the cultural, racial, and ethnic blending of the population in the United States during the twentieth and twenty-first centuries. In 1982, he received wide critical acclaim for the publication of his autobiography, *Hunger of Memory: The Education of Richard Rodriguez*, which detailed his struggle to succeed in a totally alien culture. A regular contributor to the *Los Angeles Times,* he has also published essays in *New Republic, Time, Harper's, American Scholar, Columbia Forum,* and *College English.* His most recent books are *Days of Obligation: An Argument with My Mexican Father* (1992), an autobiographical study of Mexican immigrants in America, and *Brown: The Last Discovery of America* (2002). Asked to provide advice for students using *The Prose Reader,* Rodriguez explains, "There is no 'secret' to becoming a writer. Writing takes time—and patience, more than anything else. If you are willing to rewrite and rewrite and rewrite, you will become a good writer."

Preparing to Read

This essay was originally published in *Hunger of Memory,* an autobiography that Rodriguez wrote in 1982 about the experience of growing up in a culture alien to his cultural and ethnic heritage.

Exploring Experience: Before you actually read this essay, think about a time you tried to fit in somewhere: What were the circumstances? What did you do to fit in? Was your attempt successful? If you were unsuccessful, what went wrong? How important to you is "fitting in" or "assimilating" into a particular group? Why is assimilation important or unimportant to you? Explain your answer.

Learning Online: Visit the Language Games Web site (www.languagegames .org), and select an easy game in a language you don't speak: perhaps Spanish, French, German, or Italian. See how playing even a simple game, such as a word search or hangman, can be difficult when you're using vocabulary you are not familiar with. Consider this challenge as you read about Rodriguez's struggles with learning English.

Supporters of bilingual education today imply that students like me miss   1
a great deal by not being taught in their family's language. What they
seem not to recognize is that, as a socially disadvantaged child, I considered Spanish to be a private language. What I needed to learn in school
was that I had the right—and the obligation—to speak the public language
of *los gringos*. ◆ The odd truth is that my first-grade classmates could have
become bilingual, in the conventional sense of that word, more easily than
I. Had they been taught (as upper-middle-class children are often taught
early) a second language like Spanish or French, they could have regarded it
simply as that: another public language. In my case such bilingualism could
not have been so quickly achieved. What I did not believe was that I could
speak a single public language.

Without question, it would have pleased me to hear my teachers address   2
me in Spanish when I entered the classroom. I would have felt much less
afraid. I would have trusted them and responded with ease. But I would have
delayed—for how long postponed?—having to learn the language of public society. I would have evaded—and for how long could I have afforded to
delay?—learning the great lesson of school, that I had a public identity. ❷

Fortunately, my teachers were unsentimental about their responsibility.   3
What they understood was that I needed to speak a public language. So their
voices would search me out, asking me questions. Each time I'd hear them,
I'd look up in surprise to see a nun's face frowning at me. I'd mumble, not
really meaning to answer. The nun would persist, "Richard, stand up. Don't
look at the floor. Speak up. Speak to the entire class, not just to me!" But I
couldn't believe that the English language was mine to use. (In part, I did not
want to believe it.) I continued to mumble. I resisted the teacher's demands.
(Did I somehow suspect that once I learned public language my pleasing
family life would be changed?) Silent, waiting for the bell to sound, I
remained dazed, diffident, afraid.

Because I wrongly imagined that English was intrinsically a public lan-   4
guage and Spanish an intrinsically private one, I easily noticed the difference between classroom language and the language of home. At school,
words were directed to a general audience of listeners. ("Boys and girls.")
Words were meaningfully ordered. And the point was not self-expression
alone but to make oneself understood by many others. The teacher quizzed,
"Boys and girls, why do we use that word in this sentence? Could we think
of a better word to use there? Would the sentence change its meaning if the

---

Thinking Critically

❶ To what extent do you feel that immigrants to this country have a "right" and/or an
"obligation" to learn English?

❷ How is Rodriguez's "public identity" connected with learning the English language?

words were differently arranged? And wasn't there a better way of saying much the same thing?" (I couldn't say. I wouldn't try to say.)

Three months. Five. Half a year passed. Unsmiling, ever watchful, my 5 teachers noted my silence. They began to connect my behavior with the difficult progress my older sister and brother were making. Until one Saturday morning three nuns arrived at the house to talk to our parents. Stiffly, they sat on the blue living room sofa. From the doorway of another room, spying the visitors, I noted the incongruity—the clash of two worlds, the faces and voices of school intruding upon the familiar setting of home. I overheard one voice gently wondering, "Do your children speak only Spanish at home, Mrs. Rodriguez?" While another voice added, "That Richard especially seems so timid and shy."

That Rich-heard!   6

With great tact the visitors continued, "Is it possible for you and your 7 husband to encourage your children to practice their English when they are home?" Of course, my parents complied. What would they not do for their children's well-being? And how could they have questioned the Church's authority, which those women represented? ❸ In an instant, they agreed to give up the language (the sounds) that had revealed and accentuated our family's closeness. The moment after the visitors left, the change was observed. *"Ahora,* speak to us *en ingles,"* my father and mother united to tell us.

At first, it seemed a kind of game. After dinner each night, the family 8 gathered to practice "our" English. (It was still then *ingles,* a language foreign to us, so we felt drawn as strangers to it.) Laughing, we would try to define words we could not pronounce. We played with strange English sounds, often over-anglicizing our pronunciations. And we filled the smiling gaps of our sentences with familiar Spanish sounds. But that was cheating, somebody shouted. Everyone laughed. In school, meanwhile, like my brother and sister, I was required to attend a daily tutoring session. I needed a full year of special attention. I also needed my teachers to keep my attention from straying in class by calling out, *Rich-heard*—their English voices slowly prying loose my ties to my other name, its three notes. *Ri-car-do.* ❹ Most of all I needed to hear my mother and father speak to me in a moment of seriousness in broken—suddenly heartbreaking—English. The scene was inevitable: One Saturday morning I entered the kitchen where my parents were talking in Spanish. I did not realize that they were talking in Spanish however until, at the moment they saw me, I heard their voices change to speak English.

Thinking Critically

❸ What is the relationship between the nuns' request and their religious authority?

❹ How do the English and Spanish pronunciations of the author's first name help reinforce his distinction between public and private language?

Those *gringo* sounds they uttered startled me. Pushed me away. In that moment of trivial misunderstanding and profound insight, I felt my throat twisted by unsounded grief. I turned quickly and left the room. But I had no place to escape to with Spanish. (The spell was broken.) My brother and sisters were speaking English in another part of the house.

Again and again in the days following, increasingly angry, I was obliged   9
to hear my mother and father: "Speak to us *en ingles." (Speak).* Only then did I determine to learn classroom English. Weeks after, it happened: One day in school I raised my hand to volunteer an answer. I spoke out in a loud voice. And I did not think it remarkable when the entire class understood. That day, I moved very far from the disadvantaged child I had been only days earlier. The belief, the calming assurance that I belonged in public, had at last taken hold.

Shortly after, I stopped hearing the high and loud sounds of *los gringos.* A   10
more and more confident speaker of English, I didn't trouble to listen to *how* strangers sounded, speaking to me. And there simply were too many English-speaking people in my day for me to hear American accents anymore. Conversations quickened. Listening to persons who sounded eccentrically pitched voices, I usually noted their sounds for an initial few seconds before I concentrated on *what* they were saying. Conversations became content-full. Transparent. Hearing someone's *tone* of voice—angry or questioning or sarcastic or happy or sad—I didn't distinguish it from the words it expressed. Sound and word were thus tightly wedded. At the end of a day, I was often bemused, always relieved, to realize how "silent," though crowded with words, my day in public had been. (This public silence measured and quickened the change in my life.)

At last, seven years old, I came to believe what had been technically true   11
since my birth: I was an American citizen. [5]

But the special feeling of closeness at home was diminished by then. Gone   12
was the desperate, urgent, intense feeling of being at home: rare was the experience of feeling myself individualized by family intimates. We remained a loving family, but one greatly changed. No longer so close; no longer bound tight by the pleasing and troubling knowledge of our public separateness. Neither my older brother nor sister rushed home after school anymore. Nor did I. When I arrived home there would often be neighborhood kids in the house. Or the house would be empty of sounds.

Following the dramatic Americanization of their children, even my par-   13
ents grew more publicly confident. Especially my mother. She learned the

---

Thinking Critically

[5] Why do you think Rodriguez uses a one-sentence paragraph at this particular point in the essay?

names of all the people on our block. And she decided we needed to have a telephone installed in the house. My father continued to use the word *gringo*. But it was no longer charged with the old bitterness or distrust. (Stripped of any emotional content, the word simply became a name for those Americans not of Hispanic descent.) Hearing him, sometimes, I wasn't sure if he was pronouncing the Spanish word *gringo* or saying gringo in English.

Matching the silence I started hearing in public was a new quiet at home.   14
The family's quiet was partly due to the fact that, as we children learned more and more English, we shared fewer and fewer words with our parents. [6] Sentences needed to be spoken slowly when a child addressed his mother or father. (Often the parent wouldn't understand.) The child would need to repeat himself. (Still the parent misunderstood.) The young voice, frustrated, would end up saying, "Never mind"—the subject was closed. Dinners would be noisy with the clinking of knives and forks against dishes. My mother would smile softly between her remarks; my father at the other end of the table would chew and chew at his food, while he stared over the heads of his children.

My *mother!* My *father!* After English became my primary language, I no   15
longer knew what words to use in addressing my parents. The old Spanish words (those tender accents of sound) I had used earlier—*mama* and *papa*—I couldn't use anymore. They would have been too painful reminders of how much had changed in my life. On the other hand, the words I heard neighborhood kids call *their* parents seemed equally unsatisfactory. *Mother* and *Father; Ma, Papa, Pa, Dad, Pop* (how I hated the all-American sound of that last word especially)—all these terms I felt were unsuitable, not really terms of address for *my* parents. As a result, I never used them at home. Whenever I'd speak to my parents, I would try to get their attention with eye contact alone. In public conversations, I'd refer to "my parents" or "my mother and father."

My mother and father, for their part, responded differently, as their chil-   16
dren spoke to them less. She grew restless, seemed troubled and anxious at the scarcity of words exchanged in the house. It was she who would question me about my day when I came home from school. She smiled at small talk. She pried at the edges of my sentences to get me to say something more. (What?) She'd stopped her children's talking. By contrast, my father seemed reconciled to the new quiet. Though his English improved somewhat, he retired into silence. At dinner he spoke very little. One night his children and even his wife helplessly giggled at his garbled English pronunciation of

---

Thinking Critically

[6] Why does the author's home life become quieter?

the Catholic Grace before Meals. Thereafter he made his wife recite the prayer at the start of each meal, even on formal occasions, when there were guests in the house. Hers became the public voice of the family. [7] On official business, it was she, not my father, one would usually hear on the phone or in stores, talking to strangers. His children grew so accustomed to his silence that, years later, they would speak routinely of his shyness. (My mother would often try to explain: Both his parents died when he was eight. He was raised by an uncle who treated him like little more than a menial servant. He was never encouraged to speak. He grew up alone. A man of few words.) But my father was not shy, I realized, when I'd watch him speaking Spanish with relatives. Using Spanish, he was quickly effusive. Especially when talking with other men, his voice would spark, flicker, flare alive with sounds. In Spanish, he expressed ideas and feelings he rarely revealed in English. With firm Spanish sounds, he conveyed confidence and authority English would never allow him.

The silence at home, however, was finally more than a literal silence. Fewer   17
words passed between parent and child, but more profound was the silence that resulted from my inattention to sounds. At about the time I no longer bothered to listen with care to the sounds of English in public, I grew careless about listening to the sounds family members made when they spoke. Most of the time I heard someone speaking at home and didn't distinguish his sounds from the words people uttered in public. I didn't even pay much attention to my parents' accented and ungrammatical speech. At least not at home. Only when I was with them in public would I grow alert to their accents. Though, even then, their sounds caused me less and less concern. For I was increasingly confident of my own public identity.

I would have been happier about my public success had I not sometimes   18
recalled what it had been like earlier, when my family had conveyed its intimacy through a set of conveniently private sounds. Sometimes in public, hearing a stranger, I'd hark back to my past. A Mexican farm-worker approached me downtown to ask directions to somewhere. "Hijito . . . ?" he said. And his voice summoned deep longing. Another time, standing beside my mother in the visiting room of a Carmelite convent, before the dense screen which rendered the nuns' shadowy figures, I heard several Spanish-speaking nuns—their busy, singsong overlapping voices—assure us that yes, yes, we were remembered, all our family was remembered in their prayers. (Their voices echoed faraway family sounds.) Another day, a dark-faced old woman—her hand light on my shoulder—steadied herself against me as she

---

Thinking Critically

[7] Why did Rodriguez's mother become "the public voice" of the family?

boarded a bus. She murmured something I couldn't quite comprehend. Her Spanish voice came near, like the face of a never-before-seen relative in the instant before I was kissed. Her voice, like so many of the Spanish voices I'd hear in public, recalled the golden age of my youth. ◆⁸ Hearing Spanish then, I continued to be a careful, if sad, listener to sounds. Hearing a Spanish-speaking family walking behind me, I turned to look. I smiled for an instant, before my glance found the Hispanic-looking faces of strangers in the crowd going by.

UNDERSTANDING DETAILS

1. In what ways was Spanish a private language for Rodriguez?
2. What happened when Rodriguez's two worlds met through the nuns who visited his home?
3. What "spell" is Rodriguez referring to in paragraph 8: "The spell was broken." How was it broken?
4. How did the author finally assert his public self? What language was consistent with this identity?

READING CRITICALLY

5. How are language and identity connected for this author?
6. Why do you think Rodriguez didn't feel he had the right to use English as his language?
7. In the author's view, why was concentrating on "content-full" (paragraph 10) conversations good for him?
8. What does Rodriguez mean when he says, "This public silence measured and quickened the change in my life" (paragraph 10)?

DISCOVERING RHETORICAL STRATEGIES

9. Why do you think Rodriguez lets a single sentence stand as a paragraph in paragraph 11? What effect does this choice create in the essay?
10. Why did the family's mastery of English change the interaction of Rodriguez's family?
11. When in the essay does Rodriguez refer to the public confidence he and his family experience? What does he mean by this phrase? What is the context of each of the references to this notion?
12. Do you think the brief reference to the Spanish-speaking family is an effective conclusion to this essay? Why or why not?

Thinking Critically

◆⁸ How do the nuns' Spanish prayers remind the author of the "golden age" of his youth?

MAKING CONNECTIONS

13. Compare and contrast Rodriguez's devotion to his own cultural heritage to that expressed by Lewis Sawaquat ("For My Indian Daughter"), Firoozeh Dumas ("Leffingwell Elementary School"), Brent Staples ("A Brother's Murder"), Amy Tan ("Mother Tongue"), and/or Sucheng Chan ("You're Short, Besides!"). Which author is most intimately connected to his or her heritage? Why do you think this is so?

14. Which author is the best storyteller: Rodriguez, Firoozeh Dumas ("Leffingwell Elementary School"), Russell Baker ("The Saturday Evening Post"), or Malcolm X ("Learning to Read")? Why?

15. How would Tamala Edwards ("Multi-Colored Families"), Amy Tan ("Mother Tongue"), and/or Mary Pipher ("Beliefs About Families") feel about Rodriguez's growing estrangement from his parents due to their difficulties with English?

IDEAS FOR DISCUSSION/WRITING

Preparing to Write

Write freely about the importance of "fitting in" or "assimilating" in your life. To what degree is assimilation important to you? Why is it important? What does assimilation into a particular group mean to you? What is more important than assimilation in your life today? What is less important? What does assimilation signify to you? Why do you think it carries this level of priority?

Choosing a Topic

1. *Learning Online:* Go to the Center for Digital Storytelling Web site (www.storycenter.org/whatis.html), and read this short information page. Then view the two-minute digital story example by Thenmozhi Soundarajan called *Momnotmom*. Using that video as inspiration, choose one of your own family members, and consider what kind of digital story you could create as a tribute to that person. What memories would you include that would be good examples of his or her importance to you? In essay form, describe the video you would create, including as many specific details as possible. List the memories you would mention, the pictures you would use, and the background music you would select.

2. The board of education for your high school district is thinking of offering classes in several different languages that are spoken in your area. This would allow students who speak a second language at home to do their school work in that language as well. What would be the advantages of this approach? The disadvantages? Prepare a statement for a community meeting with the board arguing for or against this decision.

3. What specific actions create an intimacy in your family that matches the intimacy Rodriguez lost? Explain this intimacy to someone from another country and discuss its value in your life.

4. You have been asked by a group of friends to attend a concert with them. You really want to go because you like the group of friends and the performers. So you decide to ask your parents to give you the money for the trip. Use your best reasoning on one or both of your parents or guardians to get them to fund this request.

Before beginning your essay, you might want to consult the checklists on page 169.

Darkness at Noon

Raised in New York City, Harold Krents earned a B.A. and a law degree at Harvard, studied at Oxford University, worked as a partner in a Washington, D.C., law firm, was the subject of a long-running Broadway play, and wrote a popular television movie—all despite the fact that he was born blind. His "1-A" classification by a local draft board, which doubted the severity of his handicap, brought about the 1969 Broadway hit play *Butterflies Are Free* by Leonard Gershe. Krents once explained that he was merely the "prototype" for the central character: "I gave the story its inspiration—the play's plot is not my story; its spirit is." In 1972, Krents wrote *To Race the Wind,* which was made into a CBS-TV movie in 1980. During his career as a lawyer, Krents worked hard to expand legal protection for the handicapped and fought to secure their right to equal opportunity in the business world. He died in 1987 of a brain tumor.

Preparing to Read

In the following article, originally published in the *New York Times* in 1976, the author gives examples of different kinds of discrimination he has suffered because of his blindness.

Exploring Experience: As you prepare to read this essay, take a few minutes to think about disabilities or handicaps in general: Do you have a disability? If so, how are you treated by others? How do you feel others respond to your handicap? Do you know someone else who has a disability? How do you respond to that person? How do you think he or she wants to be treated? To what extent do you think disabilities should affect a person's job opportunities? What can be done to improve society's prejudices against the disabled?

Learning Online: In this essay, Harold Krents describes his frustrations with people's misconceptions about his disability. To gain a better understanding of his experience, go to www.nfb.org/nfb/Default.asp, the National Federation of the Blind's Web site for parents and teachers of blind children. Click "Publications," then "Future Reflections" for their magazine. Then select the most current issue, and pick a topic that interests you. Consider the experiences mentioned on the Web site as you read Krents's account.

om birth, I have never had the opportunity to see myself and   1
een completely dependent on the image I create in the eye of
erver.[1] To date it has not been narcissistic.

1ose who assume that since I can't see, I obviously also can-   2
..t hear. Very often people will converse with me at the top of their lungs,
enunciating each word very carefully. Conversely, people will also often whisper, assuming that since my eyes don't work, my ears don't either.

For example, when I go to the airport and ask the ticket agent for assis-   3
tance to the plane, he or she will invariably pick up the phone, call a ground
hostess and whisper: "Hi, Jane, we've got a 76 here." I have concluded that
the word "blind" is not used for one of two reasons: Either they fear that if
the dread word is spoken, the ticket agent's retina will immediately detach,
or they are reluctant to inform me of my condition of which I may not have
been previously aware.

On the other hand, others know that of course I can hear, but believe   4
that I can't talk. Often, therefore, when my wife and I go out to dinner, a
waiter or waitress will ask Kit if "*he* would like a drink" to which I respond
that "indeed *he* would."

This point was graphically driven home to me while we were in England.   5
I had been given a year's leave of absence from my Washington law firm to
study for a diploma in law degree at Oxford University. During the year I
became ill and was hospitalized. Immediately after admission, I was wheeled
down to the X-ray room. Just at the door sat an elderly woman—elderly I
would judge from the sound of her voice. "What is his name?" the woman
asked the orderly who had been wheeling me.

"What's your name?" the orderly repeated to me.   6
"Harold Krents," I replied.   7
"Harold Krents," he repeated.   8
"When was he born?"   9
"When were you born?"   10
"November 5, 1944," I responded.   11
"November 5, 1944," the orderly intoned.[2]   12

This procedure continued for approximately five minutes at which point   13
even my saint-like disposition deserted me. "Look," I finally blurted out,
"this is absolutely ridiculous. Okay, granted I can't see, but it's got to have
become pretty clear to both of you that I don't need an interpreter."

"He says he doesn't need an interpreter," the orderly reported to the woman.   14

Thinking Critically

1 What "image" do you create "in the eye of the observer"? To what extent is this image
dependent on visual stimuli?

2 Why is the exchange between Krents and the hospital orderly so funny?

The toughest misconception of all is the view that because I can't see, I 15
can't work. I was turned down by over forty law firms because of my blindness, even though my qualifications included a cum laude degree from Harvard College and a good ranking in my Harvard Law School class.

The attempt to find employment, the continuous frustration of being told 16
that it was impossible for a blind person to practice law, the rejection letters,
not based on my lack of ability but rather on my disability, will always remain
one of the most disillusioning experiences of my life.

I therefore look forward to the day, with the expectation that it is certain 17
to come, when employers will view their handicapped workers as a little
child did me years ago when my family still lived in Scarsdale.

I was playing basketball with my father in our backyard according to pro- 18
cedures we had developed. My father would stand beneath the hoop, shout,
and I would shoot over his head at the basket attached to our garage. Our
next-door neighbor, aged five, wandered over into our yard with a playmate.
"He's blind," our neighbor whispered to her friend in a voice that could be
heard distinctly by Dad and me. Dad shot and missed; I did the same. Dad
hit the rim; I missed entirely; Dad shot and missed the garage entirely. "Which
one is blind?" ❸ whispered back the little friend.

I would hope that in the near future when a plant manager is touring the 19
factory with the foreman and comes upon a handicapped and nonhandi-
capped person working together, his comment after watching them work will
be, "Which one is disabled?"

UNDERSTANDING DETAILS

1. According to Krents, what are three common misconceptions about blind people?
2. What important details did you learn about Krents's life from this essay? How
   does he introduce this information?
3. In what ways was Krents frustrated in his search for employment? Was he qualified for the jobs he sought? Why or why not?
4. What attitude toward the handicapped does Krents look forward to in the future?

READING CRITICALLY

5. What does Krents mean when he says that his self-image gained through the
   eyes of others "has not been narcissistic" (paragraph 1)? Why do you think this
   is the case?
6. What is Krents's attitude toward his handicap? What parts of his essay reveal
   that attitude?

Thinking Critically

❸ How does the author use humor in this essay to humanize the situation and put his readers
at ease?

✱ CUM Laude: With honors / A Latin honor to indicate level
of academic distinction
use – "he graduated Cum Laude"

7. How do you account for the reactions to his blindness that Krents relates in this essay? Are you aware of such behavior in yourself? In others?

8. Do you think we will ever arrive at the point in the working world that Krents describes in the last paragraph? How can we get there? What advantages or disadvantages might accompany such a change?

DISCOVERING RHETORICAL STRATEGIES

9. How does Krents organize the three main points in his essay? Why does he put them in this order? What is the benefit of discussing employment last?

10. Krents often offers specific examples in the form of dialogue or spoken statements. Are these effective ways to develop his main points? Explain your answer.

11. Krents establishes a fairly fast pace in this essay as he discusses several related ideas in a small amount of space. How does he create this sense of speed? What effect does this pace have on his essay as a whole?

12. Although the author's dominant rhetorical mode in this essay is example, what other strategies does he use to develop his ideas? Give examples of each of these strategies.

MAKING CONNECTIONS

13. Compare the employment discrimination faced by Krents because of his blindness with the racial and social discrimination suffered by Lewis Sawaquat ("For My Indian Daughter") and/or Tamala Edwards ("Multi-Colored Families"). Which person has been treated most unfairly by society? Explain your answer.

14. How similar is Krents's use of humor to that of Russell Baker ("The Saturday Evening Post"), Bill Cosby ("The Baffling Question"), and/or Marc Gellman ("Worry. Don't Be Happy")? Which author do you find most amusing? Why? Is humor used in a different way in Krents's essay than it is in the Cosby essay? If so, how?

15. How many examples does Krents use in his essay? Does Krents use more or fewer examples per page than Bill Cosby ("The Baffling Question"), Joel Stein ("You Are Not My Friend"), and/or Brent Staples ("A Brother's Murder")? How does the number of examples affect the believability of each author's argument?

IDEAS FOR DISCUSSION/WRITING

Preparing to Write

Write freely about disabilities: If you are disabled, what is your response to the world? Why do you respond the way you do? How does society respond to you? Are you pleased or not with your relationship to society in general? If you are not disabled, what do you think your attitude would be if you were disabled? How do you respond to disabled people? To what extent does your response depend upon the disability? Are you satisfied with your reaction to other people's disabilities? Are you prejudiced in any way against people with disabilities? Do you think our society as a whole demonstrates any prejudices toward the disabled? If so, how can we correct these biases?

Choosing a Topic

1. *Learning Online:* Select three of your favorite Web sites, and spend a few minutes visiting each one. Now return to them and consider how you would use the site if you were either blind or deaf. What accommodations, if any, have the Web sites made to assist differently abled users? Using Krents's article, the National Federation of the Blind's Web site (from Preparing to Read), and your experiences with these Web sites as examples, write an essay evaluating the accessibility of the Internet for those who are disabled. Following Krents's writing as an example, consider the effect of different ways of organizing your examples.

2. As a reporter for your campus newspaper, you have been assigned to study and write about the status of services for the disabled on your campus. Is your school equipped with parking for the handicapped? A sufficient number of ramps for wheelchairs? Transportation for the handicapped? Other special services for the handicapped? Interview some disabled students to get their views on these services. Write an example essay for the newspaper, explaining the situation.

3. With your eyes closed, take a walk through a place that you know well. How does it feel to be nearly sightless? What senses begin to compensate for your loss of vision? Write an essay for your classmates detailing your reactions. Use specific examples to communicate your feelings.

4. Do you have any phobias or irrational fears that handicap you in any way? Write a letter to a friend explaining one of these "handicaps" and your method of coping with it.

Before beginning your essay, you might want to consult the checklists on page 169.

JOEL STEIN   (1971–   )

You Are Not My Friend

One of America's funniest writers, Joel Stein was born in Edison, New Jersey, and attended J. P. Stevens High School, where his earliest literary efforts involved serving as editor of the student newspaper, *Hawkeye*. He then earned his B.A. and M.A. in English at Stanford University before moving to New York, where he began his journalistic career as a writer and researcher for *Martha Stewart Living* and later as a sports editor and columnist for *Time Out New York*. Stein is now a *Los Angeles Times* columnist and a regular contributor to *Time* magazine, where he has done a number of cover stories, including a very popular 1998 piece on basketball star Michael Jordan. He has also co-produced three TV pilots—an animated series for VH-1 and two for ABC—along with an animated show titled *Hey Joel*, which aired only in Canada and South Africa. Stein taught creative writing at Princeton University before moving to Los Angeles in 2005. One of his most controversial *Los Angeles Times* columns, "Warriors and Wusses," appeared on January 24, 2006, in which he argued that "it is a cop-out to oppose a war and yet claim to support the soldiers fighting it." Variously described as a "stunt journalist" and a "reblogger," he urges students to write about themselves as often as possible. "My whole career," he explains, "is a brilliant metacommentary on the solipsism and narcissism of my entire TV-addled, celebrity-obsessed generation. "

Preparing to Read

In the following essay, originally published in *Time* (October 15, 2007), Joel Stein talks about social networking in our lives today. He explains the issues connected with Internet friendships from the perspective of a participant in the relationships.

Exploring Experience: As you prepare to read this essay, take a few minutes to think about the friendships you are involved in: Do you have both Internet and non-Internet friendships? How are they alike? How do they differ? Which friendships do you enjoy the most? What do both mediums have to offer? Does one type of friendship take more time than the other? How do your various friendships benefit you?

Learning Online: Visit the technological Web site Engadget (www.engadget .com/). Scroll down, and look through the latest technological devices. Do you think all of them make communication easier? Are there any gadgets that try to improve communication, but might make it less personal? While reading Stein's article, think about the impact of these devices on friendships.

I n the pre-Internet days, neither of us would have even thought of call-   1
ing each other friends. [1] We'd have called ourselves friends of friends
who met once and yet, for some reason, kept sending each other gram-
matically challenged, inappropriately flirty letters with photos of ourselves attached. Police might have gotten involved. [2]

But now we're definitively friends, having taken a public vow of friend-   2
ship on friend-based websites, wearing metaphorical friendship bracelets on
the earnest Facebook, the punky MySpace, the careerist LinkedIn, and the suddenly very Asian Friendster. As if that wasn't enough friendship for you, some
of you have also asked me to be friends on the nerdy Twitter, the dorky-elitist
Doostang, and the Euro-trashy hi5. You message me and comment about me
and write on my walls and dedicate songs to me and invite me to join groups.
More than once you have taken it upon yourself to poke me.

This is hard to say to a friend, but our relationship is starting to take up   3
too much of my time. [3] It's weird that I know more about you than I do
about actual friends I hang out with in person—whom I propose we distinguish by calling "non-metafriends." In fact, I know more about you than
I know about myself. I have no idea what my favorite movie or song or TV
show is. Last I checked, they all involved Muppets.

Also, you're a bit aggressive in our friendship. Would a non-metafriend call   4
me up and say, "Hey! Guess what? I have a bunch of new pictures of me"?
Or tell me he'd colored in a map of all the places he'd ever been? Or inform
me, as Michael Hischorn did in his Facebook status update, that he "is not
making decisions, he's making surprises"? It's as if I suddenly met a new
group of people who were all in the special classes.

The horror is, I can't opt out. Just as I can't stop making money or my non-   5
metafriends will have more stuff than I do, I can't stop running up my tally
of MySpace friends or I'll look like a loser. Just as money made wealth quan-
tifiable, social networks have provided a metric for popularity. We all, oddly,
slot in at a specific ranking somewhere below Dane Cook.

I'm sure social networks serve many important functions that improve   6
our lives, like reconnecting us with old friends and finding out if people we
used to date are still good-looking. And social networks all have messaging
functions, which would be an excellent way to send information if no one
had invented email.

Thinking Critically

[1] How would you define the word "friend"? How does it compare to Stein's definition?

[2] In what ways has the Internet changed our social lives? Name another important contemporary influence on how we relate to each other.

[3] Consider how much time you devote to your friends. Do you wish you spent more or
less time with them? Why?

But really, these sites aren't about connecting and reconnecting. They're 7
a platform for self-branding. [4] Old people are always worrying that our
blogging and personal websites and MySpace profiles are taking away our privacy, but they clearly don't understand the word *privacy*. We're not sharing
things we don't want other people to know. We're showing you our best
posed, retouched photos. We're listing the Pynchon books we want you to
think we've read all the way through. We're allowing other people to write
whatever they want about us on our walls, unless we don't like it, in which
case we just erase it. If we had that much privacy in real life, the bathrooms
at that Minnesota airport would be empty.

And like the abrasively direct ads for tinctures and cleaning products at 8
the beginning of the advertising age, our self-branding is none too subtle.
We are a blunt lot, in our bikinis and our demands that our friends go
right now to check out our blog postings. We've gone 40 years back to sales
tactics predating irony, self-deprecation, and actual modesty. We are, as a
social network, all so awesome that we will soon not be able to type the
number 1, because we will have worn out the exclamation point that shares
its key.

Until we can build some kind of social network where we can present 9
our true, flawed selves—perhaps some genius can invent something that
takes place in a house over dinner with wine—I say we strip down our
online communities to just the important parts. With enough venture funding—
by which I mean the volunteer services of a dude who knows how to
build a website—I hope to launch TrueSocialStatus.com, on which users
are allowed to submit only their name, their occupation, a photo, the square
footage of their home, and a list of any celebrities they happen to know.
Then other people can vote, on a scale of 1 to 100, on how awesome they
are. At the end of the year, the ones with the most points are made home-
coming king and queen, which, if I remember correctly, should immediately send their scores plummeting. If nothing else, it should finally rid us
of Tila Tequila.

UNDERSTANDING DETAILS

1. What do you think is Stein's main reason for writing this essay?
2. What are the two types of friendships he discusses? Explain each in your
   own words.
3. What does Stein mean by the term "self-branding"?
4. How does Stein feel in general about Internet friendships?

Thinking Critically

[4] Define "self-branding." To what extent is self-branding part of friendship?

READING CRITICALLY

5. Why did Joel Stein join the Facebook population?
6. According to the author, what are the advantages of social networking? The disadvantages?
7. What relationship does Stein see between the identities people reveal on the Internet and their real selves?
8. Why does Stein believe that he can't drop out of his metafriend relationships?

DISCOVERING RHETORICAL STRATEGIES

9. Why does Stein start his essay with a reference to "pre-Internet days"? How does this choice prepare us for what he says?
10. List Stein's main points in this essay. Why do you think he deals with these topics in this particular order?
11. Describe Stein's intended audience in as much detail as possible. Why do you think he aims his essay at this particular group?
12. Explain Stein's title for his essay. Is this title an effective way to get the attention of his intended audience? Why or why not?

MAKING CONNECTIONS

13. Compare and contrast Joel Stein's use of examples with those provided by Harold Krents ("Darkness at Noon") and Brent Staples ("A Brother's Murder"). Which author's examples are most persuasive to you? Why?
14. Imagine that Stein was having a conversation about the impact of technology on our lives with Jay Walljasper ("Our Schedules, Our Selves"), Stephen King ("Why We Crave Horror Movies"), and Dave Grossman ("We Are Training Our Kids to Kill"). Which of these authors would argue most vehemently that modern technology is distorting our basic personalities? Why?
15. Stein's article about America's fascination with Facebook and other friend-based Web sites mirrors the fixation with illness described in Frank Furedi's "Our Unhealthy Obsession with Sickness" and the dependence on alcohol described in Michael Dorris's "The Broken Cord" and Barrett Seaman's "How Bingeing Became the New College Sport." Which of these addictions do you think is most detrimental to America today? Why?

IDEAS FOR DISCUSSION/WRITING

Preparing to Write

Write freely about your own friendships: Do you have metafriends and non-metafriends? What roles do your different friendships play in your life? Which of your friendships do you enjoy the most? Why do you enjoy these relationships? Are you currently on Facebook? Why did you make the decision to participate or not to participate in this electronic society? What do you think of yourself as a friend? How can you improve your role as a friend to others?

Choosing a Topic

1. *Learning Online:* Keeping in mind the newest technological devices you saw online (www.engadget.com/), think about how personal or impersonal your friendships are. Do you believe that technology has improved or impaired your relationships? Using examples from your own life, write an essay for or against increased use of technology in our personal lives.

2. As a college student, you see people approach friendship in different ways every day. Some students consider friends their first priority. Others don't rely on friendships as much as others. Some put equal value on friendship and the rest of their goals. Write an essay for your school newspaper explaining your observations about the different ways people establish friendships. Use carefully chosen examples to illustrate your observations. Consider both Internet and non-Internet friendships. You might even want to interview some of your peers about their friendships.

3. You have been asked to respond to a national survey on the role of the Internet in our lives. The organization conducting the survey wants to know the extent to which the Internet has helped or hindered you in achieving your goals. In a well-developed essay written for a general audience, explain the benefits and liabilities of the Internet in your life at present. Use specific examples to develop your essay.

4. Stein ends his essay with an example of a social network that he would like to launch. What do you think he is trying to convey with this ending? What is his "real" message at the end? Compose a different end for this essay, and explain its relationship to the rest of the essay and its implications for the audience. Use specific examples to support your opinion.

Before beginning your essay, you might want to consult the checklists on page 169.

A Brother's Murder

Brent Staples was the first of nine children born to a truck driver and a housewife in Chester, Pennsylvania, a factory town fifteen miles south of Philadelphia. He was educated at the Philadelphia Military College and Penn Morton College, eventually graduating from Widener College with honors. A prestigious Danforth Fellowship took him to the University of Chicago, where he earned a Ph.D. in Psychology. His brilliant memoir, *Parallel Time: Growing Up in Black and White* (published by Pantheon Books in 1994), was a finalist for the *Los Angeles Times* Book Award and a winner of the Anisfield-Wolff Award, which had been won previously by such luminaries as James Baldwin, Ralph Ellison, and Zora Neale Hurston. A past editor of the *New York Times* Book Review section and an assistant metropolitan editor, Staples currently writes on politics and culture for the *New York Times* editorial page. He is an avid gardener and is especially fond of roses. When asked to give some advice to college writers, he explains that "ninety percent of writing is rewriting. The simple declarative sentence is your best friend in the world."

Preparing to Read

"A Brother's Murder" was first published in an anthology of African-American writing entitled *Bearing Witness*. In this emotional account of his brother's death, Staples realizes many important truths about the role of violence among African-American men.

Exploring Experience: Before reading this essay, think for a few moments about violence in general: From your observations, which kinds of people are most violent? Why do these people use violence? What do you think is the cause of most violent acts? In your opinion, why is the crime rate so high in American society today? Can we do anything to reduce this crime rate? What are some of your constructive suggestions for controlling violence today? Which are most realistic?

Learning Online: Brent Staples uses personal examples to explore the causes and effects of youth violence in his hometown. Visit the "Building Blocks for Youth" Web site located at www.buildingblocksforyouth.org/. Click on the "Research" button, and read one of the online articles about violence in African-American communities. Consider the use of examples, such as statistics and dates, in the article as you read Brent Staples's essay.

It has been more than two years since my telephone rang with the news   1
that my younger brother Blake—just 22 years old—had been murdered.
The young man who killed him was only 24. Wearing a ski mask, he
emerged from a car, fired six times at close range with a massive .44 Mag-
num, then fled. The two had once been inseparable friends. A senseless
rivalry—beginning, I think, with an argument over a girlfriend—escalated
from posturing, to threats, to violence, to murder. The way the two were living, death could have come to either of them from anywhere. In fact, the as-
sailant had already survived multiple gunshot wounds from an incident much
like the one in which my brother lost his life.

As I wept for Blake, I felt wrenched backward into events and circum-   2
stances that had seemed light-years gone. Though a decade apart, we both
were raised in Chester, Pennsylvania, an angry, heavily black, heavily poor,
industrial city southwest of Philadelphia. There, in the 1960s, I was introduced
to mortality, not by the old and failing, but by beautiful young men who lay
wrecked after sudden explosions of violence. The first, I remember from my
14th year—Johnny, brash lover of fast cars, stabbed to death two doors from
my house in a fight over a pool game. The next year, my teen-age cousin,
Wesley, whom I loved very much, was shot dead. The summers blur. Milton,
an angry young neighbor, shot a crosstown rival, wounding him badly.
William, another teen-age neighbor, took a shotgun blast to the shoulder in
some urban drama and displayed his bandages proudly. His brother, Leonard,
severely beaten, lost an eye and donned a black patch. It went on.

I recall not long before I left for college, two local Vietnam veterans—one   3
from the Marines, one from the Army—arguing fiercely, nearly at blows
about which outfit had done the most in the war. The most killing, they
meant. Not much later, I read in a magazine article that set that dispute in a
context. In the story, a noncommissioned officer—a sergeant, I believe—
said he would pass up any number of affluent, suburban-born recruits to get
hard-core soldiers from the inner city. They jumped into the rice paddies with
"their manhood on their sleeves," I believe he said. These two items—the veterans arguing and the sergeant's words—still characterize for me the circumstances under which black men in their teens and 20's kill one another
with such frequency. With a touchy paranoia born of living battered lives, they
are desperate to be *real* men. ◆ Killing is only *machismo* taken to the extreme.
Incursions to be punished by death were many and minor, and they remain
so: they include stepping on the wrong toe, literally; cheating in a drug deal;

Thinking Critically

◆ What did wearing "their manhood on their sleeves" have to do with being "real" men for
Blake's group? What other actions or rituals might be more civilized and productive in
helping young people define themselves as "real"?

simply saying "I dare you" to someone holding a gun; crossing territorial lines in a gang dispute. My brother grew up to wear his manhood on his sleeve. And when he died, he was in that group—black, male, and in its teens and early 20's—that is far and away the most likely to murder or be murdered.

I left the East Coast after college, spent the mid- and late-1970's in Chicago   4
as a graduate student, taught for a time, then became a journalist. Within 10 years of leaving my hometown, I was overeducated and "upwardly mobile," ensconced on a quiet, tree-lined street where voices raised in anger were scarcely ever heard. [2] The telephone, like some grim umbilical, [3] kept me connected to the old world with news of deaths, imprisonings, and misfortune. I felt emotionally beaten up. Perhaps to protect myself, I added a psychological dimension to the physical distance I had already achieved. I rarely visited my hometown. I shut it out.

As I fled the past, so Blake embraced it. On Christmas of 1983, I traveled   5
from Chicago to a black section of Roanoke, Virginia, where he then lived. The desolate public housing projects, the hopeless, idle young men crashing against one another—these reminded me of the embittered town we'd grown up in. It was a place where once I would have been comfortable, or at least sure of myself. Now, hearing of my brother's forays into crime, his scrapes with police and street thugs, I was scared, unsteady on foreign terrain.

I saw Blake's romance with the street life, and the hustler image had flow-   6
ered dangerously. One evening that late December, standing in some Roanoke dive among drug dealers and grim, hair-trigger losers, I told him I feared for his life. He had affected the image of the tough he wanted to be. But behind the dark glasses and the swagger, I glimpsed the baby-faced toddler I'd once watched over. I nearly wept. I wanted desperately for him to live. The young think themselves immortal, and a dangerous light shone in his eyes as he spoke laughingly of making fools of the policemen who had raided his apartment looking for drugs. He cried out as I took his right hand. A line of stitches lay between the thumb and index finger. Kickback from a shotgun, he explained, nothing serious. Gunplay had become part of his life.

I lacked the language simply to say: Thousands have lived this for you and   7
died. [4] I fought the urge to lift him bodily and shake him. This place and the way you are living smells of death to me, I said. Take some time away, I said. Let's go downtown tomorrow and buy a plane ticket anywhere, take a bus

---

Thinking Critically

[2] How did Brent escape the claustrophobic environment of the ghetto, while his brother did not?

[3] How does the concept of mortality in paragraph 2 relate to the "grim umbilical" in paragraph 4?

[4] What does the author mean when he writes "Thousands have lived this for you and died"?

trip, anything to get away and cool things off. He took my alarm casually. We arranged to meet the following night—an appointment he would not keep. We embraced as though through glass. I drove away.

As I stood in my apartment in Chicago holding the receiver that evening   8
in February 1984, I felt as though part of my soul had been cut away. I questioned myself then, and I still do. Did I not reach back soon or earnestly enough for him? For weeks I awoke crying from a recurrent dream in which I chased him, urgently trying to get him to read a document I had, as though reading it would protect him from what had happened in waking life. His eyes shining like black diamonds, he smiled and danced just out of my grasp. When I reached for him, I caught only the space where he had been. ◆5

UNDERSTANDING DETAILS

1. What does Staples mean when he refers to his brother's death by saying, "The way the two were living, death could have come to either of them from anywhere" (paragraph 1)?
2. What stages did Staples's brother and his murderer go through before Blake was killed?
3. Why do you think Staples wrote this essay? What is his main point?
4. What did Staples learn about African-American males by examining his brother's life?

READING CRITICALLY

5. In what ways does Brent Staples's brother represent an important segment of the African-American male population?
6. Why did Staples create a distance between his present life and his past?
7. What examples does Staples use to prove his theory that "killing is only *machismo* taken to the extreme" (paragraph 3)? Do you agree with this conclusion? Can you think of any examples that demonstrate the opposite position?
8. What was "Blake's romance with the street life" (paragraph 6)?

DISCOVERING RHETORICAL STRATEGIES

9. Describe in as much detail as possible Staples's intended audience. Why do you think he aims his essay at this particular group?
10. In what way does Staples's recurring dream (paragraph 8) symbolize the author's relationship with his brother? How does this final paragraph sum up Staples's feelings about the plight of African-American males in American society today?

Thinking Critically

◆5 How did the "spaces" these two men lived in help shape their lives? Which spaces best define your life? To what extent do you become a different person when you move from one space to another?

11. In paragraph 7, Staples uses a simile (a special comparison between two unlike items, using *like* or *as*): "We embraced as though through glass." This image adds an extra dimension to Staples's description. Find another simile in this essay, and explain its effect on you.

12. This essay progresses most obviously through the use of examples. What other rhetorical strategies support this dominant mode? In what ways do they add to Staples's main point?

MAKING CONNECTIONS

13. Through hard work and a college education, Brent Staples was able to rise above the violent environment that contributed to his brother's death. Consider any of the following essays you have read, and explain how the central characters escaped their own difficult environments: Maya Angelou's "New Directions," Harold Krents's "Darkness at Noon," Alice Lesch Kelly's "Toughen Up!," and/or Wallerstein and Blakeslee's "Second Chances for Children of Divorce."

14. Examine Staples's essay through the lens of Ben Dattner's "Is Your Workplace Personality Out of (Birth) Order?" To what extent do Dattner's observations about birth order help explain the relationship between Staples and his brother?

15. How do Brent Staples's insights about the community in which his brother lived differ from the sense of "community" in the following essays: Tamala Edwards's "Multi-Colored Families," Scott Russell Sanders's "Homeplace," and/or Robert Ramirez's "The Barrio"?

IDEAS FOR DISCUSSION/WRITING

Preparing to Write

Write freely about your view of violence in the United States today: What is the source of most of this violence? How can we control violence in American society? Why do you think violence is increasing? How else might we channel our innate violent reactions? What other suggestions do you have for reducing violent crimes today?

Choosing Your Topic

1. *Learning Online:* Staples relates his painful experience to help explain the pervasiveness of youth violence. He selects personal examples rather than statistics or news stories to present his argument. Using www.buildingblocksforyouth .org/ (from Preparing to Read) as a starting point, choose an issue about which you feel strongly, and write an essay in which you argue your position using carefully selected, relevant examples. Try to clarify general concepts by using specific details as Staples does. Use the Internet to find statistics or case studies, if necessary, to support your argument.

2. Write an essay for a college-educated audience based on one of the following statements: "Current pressure in contemporary society causes most of the violence today" or "People's natural instincts cause most of the violence in contemporary society."

3. Interview some people about how they manage their anger: What do they do when they get mad? How do they control their reactions? Have they ever become violent? Then write an essay for the students in your English class explaining your findings.

4. According to Staples, the military frame of mind—the urge to kill—is at the heart of "the circumstances under which black men in their teens and 20's kill one another with such frequency" (paragraph 3). Do you agree or disagree with this statement? Write a well-developed essay, using examples from your experience, to support your opinion.

Before beginning your essay, you might want to consult the checklists on page 169.

Chapter Writing Assignments

Practicing Example

1. Think about some qualities that irritate you in other people's behavior (such as how someone drives, how someone talks on the phone, or how someone laughs). In an essay, use examples to explain a behavior that irritates you and the reason it bothers you so much.
2. Think about all the different roles people play, such as father, teacher, big brother, or sister. Who in your experience provides the best example of how this "role" should be performed? Write an essay that explains why this person is the best example of this role.
3. What do you do best as a writer? Which parts of the writing process do you seem to deal with most successfully? Taking examples from your own writing, compose an essay that discusses your strengths as a writer.

Exploring Ideas

4. Should the United States as a country promote the use of a single national language, or should we instead acknowledge and encourage the use of multiple languages? Write an essay that explores the advantages and/or disadvantages of either single or multiple languages in American society. As you write, use specific examples to support your position.
5. In what ways do all forms of the media use stereotypes? Choose a specific "type" (such as liberal, conservative, radical, athlete), and, using as many specific examples as possible, explain how the media help or hinder our understanding of a certain personality or issue.
6. Discuss a time when someone embarrassed you publicly. Describe what happened and how it affected you. What, if anything, did you learn from the experience?

Writing from Sources

For detailed information on writing from sources, see Part III.

7. Should governmental institutions and documents, such as schools, DMV agencies, and voting ballots, provide multilingual services? Research the issues surrounding this question, and find examples that support your position. Use your sources to argue for or against this practice in a documented essay.
8. Research the controversy surrounding privacy on networking Web sites. Do you think that lack of privacy creates a safety threat? Do authorities

have the right to use information you post against you? Take a position on this issue; then, citing examples from your research, write a documented essay arguing your case.

Analyzing Visual Images

© AP Wide World Photos

9. The photo shown here is entitled "Miracle on Ice" and reflects the moment the United States defeated, against all odds, the Russians in the 1980 Olympic games before going on to win the gold medal in ice hockey. This victory is an example of team members pulling together to accomplish a major goal and an improbable upset. Think of a time when you had to accomplish a difficult feat—against all odds—and needed others to help you overcome these obstacles. Write a narrative essay about this time, using specific examples to support your points.

10. Look at the picture on page 161 at the beginning of this chapter. How does it make you feel? Think about other places in your own city that make you feel the same way, and explain your response in a narrative essay. Remember to use specific examples to help illustrate your point.

Chapter 7

PROCESS ANALYSIS
Explaining Step by Step

Human nature is characterized by the perpetual desire to understand and analyze the process of living well. The best-seller list is always crowded with books on how to know yourself better, how to be assertive, how to become famous, how to survive a natural disaster, or how to be rich and happy—all explained in three easy lessons. Open almost any popular magazine, and you will find numerous articles on how to lose weight, how elections are run in this country, how to dress for success, how a political rally evolved, how to gain power, or how to hit a successful topspin backhand. People naturally gravitate toward material that tells them how something is done, how something happened, or how something works, especially if they think the information will help them improve their lives in a significant way.

DEFINING PROCESS ANALYSIS

A *process* is a procedure that follows a series of steps or stages; *analysis* involves taking a subject apart and explaining its components in order to better understand the whole. Process analysis, then, explains an action, a mechanism, or an event from beginning to end. It concentrates on either a mental or a physical operation: how to solve a chemistry problem, how to tune up your car, how John F. Kennedy was shot, how the telephone system works. In fact, the explanation of the writing process beginning on page 36 of this book is a good case in point: It divides writing into three inter-related verbal activities and explains how they each work—separately and together.

A process analysis can take one of two forms: (1) It can give directions, thereby explaining how to do something (directive), or (2) it can give information about how something happened or how something works (informative). The first type of analysis gives directions for a task the reader may wish to attempt in the future. Examples include how to make jelly, how to lose weight, how to drive to Los Angeles, how to assemble stereo equipment, how to make money, how to use a microscope, how to knit, how to resuscitate a dying relationship, how to win friends, how to discipline your child, and how to backpack.

The second type of analysis furnishes information about what actually occurred in specific situations or how something works. Examples include how Hiroshima was bombed, how certain Hollywood stars live, how the tax system works, how the movie *Chicago* was filmed, how Babe Ruth earned a place in the Baseball Hall of Fame, how gold was first discovered in California, how computers work, how a kibbutz functions, and how the Gulf War began. These subjects and others like them respond to a certain fascination we all have with mastering some processes and understanding the intricate details of others. They all provide us with opportunities to raise our own standard of living, either by helping us directly apply certain processes to our own lives or by increasing our understanding of how our complex world functions.

The following student paragraph analyzes the process of constructing a garden compost pit. Written primarily for people who might wish to make such a pit, this piece is directive rather than informative. Notice in particular the amount of detail the student calls upon to explain each stage of the process and the clear transitions she uses to guide us through her analysis.

No garden is complete without a functioning compost pit. Here's a simple, inexpensive way to make your garbage work for you! To begin with, make a pen out of hog wire or chicken wire, four feet long by eight feet wide by four feet high, splitting it down the middle with another piece of wire so that you end up with a structure that looks like a capital "E" on its side. This is a compost duplex. In the first pen, place a layer of soda ash, just sprinkled on the surface of the dirt. Then pile an inch or so of leaves, grass clippings, or sawdust on top of the soda ash. You're now ready for the exciting part. Start throwing in all the organic refuse from your kitchen (no meat, bones, or grease, please). After the food is a foot or so deep, throw in a shovelful of steer manure, and cover the entire mess with a thin layer of dirt. Then water it down. Continue this layering process until the pile is three to three-and-a-half feet high. Allow the pile to sit until it decomposes (from one month in warm climates to six months in colder weather). Next, take your pitchfork and start slinging the contents of pen one into pen two (which will land in reverse order, of course, with the top on the bottom and the bottom on the top). This ensures that everything will decompose evenly. Water this down and begin making a new pile in pen one. That's all there is to it! You now have a ready supply of fertilizer for your garden.

THINKING CRITICALLY THROUGH PROCESS ANALYSIS

Process analysis embodies clear, careful, step-by-step thinking that takes one of three different forms: chronological, simultaneous, or cyclical. The first follows a time sequence from "first this" to "then that." The second forces you to deal with activities or events that happen or happened at the same time, such as people quietly studying or just getting home from work when the major 1994 earthquake hit Los Angeles. And the third form of process analysis requires you to process information that is continuous, like the rising and setting of the sun. No other thinking pattern will force you to slow down as much as process analysis because the process you are explaining probably won't make any sense if you leave out even the slightest detail.

Good process analysis can truly help your reader see an event in a totally new light. An observer looks at a product already assembled or at a completed event and has no way of knowing without the help of a good process analysis how it got to this final stage. Such an analysis gives the writer or speaker as well as the observer a completely new way of "seeing" the subject in question. Separating process analysis from the other rhetorical modes lets you practice this method of thinking so that you will have a better understanding of the various mental procedures going on in your head. Exercising this possibility in isolation will help you feel its range and its intricacies so that you can become more adept at using it, fully developed, in combination with other modes of thought.

1. In the picture on page 204, the photographer manipulates our view by using a particular lens and by positioning the photo so that the man on the surfboard is almost in the middle of the scene. What are other ways we manipulate or influence people's views? Brainstorm about how you influence the views or ideas of people around you. What are your most effective techniques? Explain to someone else in class how you effectively influence people you know, or explain how to avoid unfairly manipulating or influencing others.

2. List as many examples of each type of process (chronological, simultaneous, and cyclical) as you can think of. Share your list with the class.

© Rick Doyle/CORBIS

3. Write a paragraph telling how *not* to do something. Practice your use of humor as a technique for creating interest in the essay by emphasizing the "wrong" way, for example, to wash a car or feed a dog.

READING AND WRITING PROCESS ANALYSIS ESSAYS

Your approach to a process analysis essay should be fairly straightforward. As a reader, you should be sure you understand the author's statement of purpose and then try to visualize each step as you go along. As a writer, you need to adapt the mechanics of the way you normally write to the demands of a process analysis paper, beginning with an interesting topic and a number of clearly explained ideas or stages. As usual, the intended audience determines the choice of words and the degree of detail.

Reading Process Analysis Essays

- Is the essay *directive* or *informative?*
- What is the author's general message?

Preparing to Read.   Preparing to read a process analysis essay is as uncomplicated as the essay itself. The title of Jay Walljasper's essay in this chapter, "Our Schedules, Our Selves," tells us exactly what we are going to learn about. Julia Bourland's title, "Getting Out of Debt (and Staying Out)," also lets us know what we are going to get. Scanning each selection to assess the author's audience will give you an even better idea of what to expect in these essays, while the synopsis of each in the Rhetorical Table of Contents will help focus your attention on its subject.

Also important as you prepare to read these essays are the qualifications of each author to write on their subject: Has he or she performed the task, worked with the mechanism, or seen the event? Is the writer's experience firsthand? When Jay Walljasper discusses "Our Schedules, Our Selves," is he writing from his personal experience? What is Jessica Mitford's experience with mortuaries? How does she know what goes on "Behind the Formaldehyde Curtain"? The biography preceding each essay will help you uncover this information and find out other publication details that will encourage you to focus on the material you are about to read.

Finally, before you begin reading, answer the prereading questions, and then do some brainstorming on the subject of the essay: What do you want to know about being "tough" (Alice Lesch Kelly)? How well do you read, and what do you think you can learn about the subject from Malcolm X?

Reading.   When you read the essays in this chapter for the first time, record your initial reactions to them. Consider the preliminary information you have been studying in order to create a context for each author's composition: What circumstances prompted Mitford's "Behind the Formaldehyde Curtain"? Why did Kelly write "Toughen Up!"? Who do you think is Bourland's target audience in "Getting Out of Debt (and Staying Out)"?

Included at the bottom of the pages of these essays are questions to help you think critically about the content and structure of each essay. These questions will provide ways for you to process the content and understand the structure of each essay so that you will be prepared to answer the questions and do the writing assignments at the end of the reading selections. They essentially help you build a mental bridge from the prereading activities that appear before each essay to those at the end of your reading assignments. Responding to these inquiries in writing will help you get the biggest benefit from this feature of the text because you will already have some thoughts on paper when you get your next writing task.

Also determine at this point whether the essay you are reading is *directive* (explaining how to do something) or *informative* (giving information about how something happened or how something works). This fundamental understanding of the author's intentions, along with a reading of the questions following the essay, will prepare you to approach the contents of each selection critically when you read it a second time.

Rereading.   As you reread these process analysis essays, look for an overview of the process at the beginning of the essay so you know where each writer is headed. The body of each essay, then, is generally a discussion of the stages of the process.

The central portion of an essay is often organized *chronologically* (as in Mitford's essay on current practices in mortuaries and Malcolm X's essay on his self-education), with clear transitions so that readers can easily follow the writer's train of thought. Other methods of organization are *cyclical* (such as the Kelly essay on toughening up and the Bourland essay on debt), describing a process that has no clear beginning or end, and *simultaneous* (such as the essay by Walljasper on organizing one's time), in which many activities occur at the same time with a clear beginning and end. Most of these essays discuss the process as a whole at some point. During this second reading, you will also benefit from discovering what rhetorical modes each writer uses to support his or her process analysis and why these rhetorical modes work effectively. What does Walljasper's cause/effect reasoning add to his essay on time management? And how do the descriptions in Mitford's essay on embalming heighten the horror of the American mortuary business? Do the examples that Malcolm X gives help explain how reading changed his life? How do all the rhetorical modes in each essay help create a coherent whole? After reading each essay for a second time, answer the questions that follow the selection to see if you are understanding your reading material on the literal, interpretive, and analytical levels before you take on the discussion/writing assignments.

For an overview of the entire reading process, you might consult the Reading Inventory at the end of Part I.

Writing Process Analysis Essays

- Provide an overview of the process.
- Draft a purpose statement or thesis.
- Make your essay *directive* or *informative*.
- Organize your essay chronologically, simultaneously, or cyclically.
- End with a description of the process as a whole.

Prewriting.   As you begin a process analysis assignment, you first need to become as familiar as you can with the action, mechanism, or event you are going to describe. If possible, try to go through the process yourself at least once or twice. If you can't actually carry out the procedure, going through the process mentally and taking notes is a good alternative. Then, try to read something about the process. After all this preparation (and careful consideration of your audience and purpose), you should be ready to brainstorm, freewrite, cluster, or use your favorite prewriting technique (see pages 36–38 of Chapter 3) in response to the prewriting questions before you start composing your paper.

Writing.   The essay should begin with an overview of the process or event to be analyzed. This initial section should introduce the subject, divide it into a number of recognizable steps, and describe the result once the process is complete. Your thesis in a process essay is usually a purpose statement that clearly and briefly explains your approach to the procedure you will discuss: "Building model airplanes can be divided into four basic steps" or "The American courts follow three stages in prosecuting a criminal case."

Next, a directive or informative essay should proceed logically through the various stages of the process, from beginning to end. The parts of a process usually fall nicely into chronological order, supported by such transitions as "at first," "in the beginning," "next," "then," "after that," and "finally." Some processes, however, are either simultaneous, forcing the writer to choose a more complex logical order for the essay (such as classification), or cyclical, requiring the writer to choose a starting point and then explain the cycle stage by stage. Playing the guitar, for example, involves two separate and simultaneous components that must work together: holding the strings against the frets with the fingers of one hand and strumming with the other hand. In analyzing this procedure, you would probably want to describe both parts of the process and then explain how the hands work together to produce music. An example of a cyclical process would be the changing of the seasons. To explain this concept to a reader, you would need to pick a starting point, such as spring, and describe the entire cycle, stage by stage, from that point onward.

In a process paper, you need to be especially sensitive to your intended audience, or they will not be able to follow your explanation. The amount of information, the number of examples and illustrations, and the terms to be defined all depend on the prior knowledge and background of your readers. A writer explaining to a group of amateur cooks how to prepare a soufflé would take an entirely different approach to the subject than he or she would if the audience were a group of bona fide chefs hoping to land jobs in elegant French restaurants. The professional chefs would need more sophisticated and precise explanations than their recreational counterparts, who would probably find such an approach tedious and complicated because of the extraneous details.

The last section of a process analysis paper should consider the process as a whole. If, for example, the writer is giving directions on how to build a model airplane, the essay might end with a good description or drawing of the plane. The informative essay on our legal system might offer a summary of the stages of judging and sentencing a criminal. And the essay on cooking a soufflé might finish with a photograph of the mouth-watering dish.

Rewriting.   In order to revise a process analysis essay, first make sure your main purpose is apparent throughout your paper:

• Is my purpose statement clear?

Next, you need to determine if your paper is aimed at the proper audience:

• Have I given my readers an overview of the process I am going to discuss?
• Do I go through the process step by step?
• At the end of the essay, do I help my readers see the process as a whole?

The Writing Inventory checklist at the end of Part I will give you further guidelines for writing, revising, and proofreading.

STUDENT ESSAY: PROCESS ANALYSIS AT WORK

The student essay that follows analyzes the process of using a "home permanent" kit. Notice that, once the student gives an overview of the process, she discusses the steps one at a time, being careful to follow a logical order (in this case, chronological) and to use clear transitions. Then, see how the end of the essay shows the process as a whole.

Follow the Simple Directions

Although fickle hairstylists in Paris and Hollywood decide what is currently "in," many romanticists disregard fashion and yearn for a mane of delicate tendrils. <u>Sharing this urge but resenting the cost, I opted</u> <u>for a "home perm" kit.</u> Any literate person with normal dexterity could follow illustrated directions, I reasoned, and the eight easy steps would energize my limp locks in less than two hours. "Before" and "after" photos of flawless models showed the metamorphosis one might achieve. Confidently, I assembled towels, rollers, hair clips, waving lotion, neutralizer, end papers, and a plastic cap. <u>While shampooing,</u> I chortled about my ingenuity and economy.

    <u>After towel-drying my hair, I applied the gooey, acidic</u> <u>waving lotion thoroughly. Then I wrapped an end paper</u> <u>around a parted section and rolled the first curl ("securely</u> <u>but not too tightly").</u> Despite the reassuring click of the fastened rollers, as I sectioned each new curl the previous one developed its own volition and slowly unrolled

Margin annotations:
Purpose statement for informative process analysis

Overview

First step (chronological order)

Transition

Second step

Third step

itself. Resolutely, I reapplied waving lotion and rewound—and rewound—each curl. <u>Since my hair was</u>   *Transition*
<u>already saturated, I regarded the next direction skepti-</u>
Fourth step   <u>cally: "Apply waving lotion to each curl."</u> Faithfully,
however, I complied with the instructions. <u>Ignoring the</u>   *Transition*
Fifth step   <u>fragile state of the fastened rollers, I then feigned assur-</u>
<u>ance and enclosed my entire head in a plastic cap.</u> In
forty minutes, chemical magic would occur.

Restless with anticipation, I puttered about the house; while absorbed in small chores, I felt the first few drops of lotion escape from the plastic tent. Stuffing wads of cotton around the cap's edges did not help, and the small drops soon became rivulets that left red streaks on my neck and face and splattered on the floor. (Had I overdone the waving lotion?) Ammonia fumes so permeated each room that I was soon asked to leave. Retreating to the bathroom, I opened the window and dreamed of frivolous new hairstyles.

Transition   <u>Finally, the waving time had elapsed; neutralizing</u>   *Sixth step*
<u>was next.</u> I removed my plastic cap, carefully heeding the caution: "Do not disturb curlers as you rinse waving lotion from hair." With their usual impudence, however, all the curlers soon bobbed in the sink; undaunted, I continued. "This next step is critical," warned the instructions. Thinking half-hearted curls were better than no curls at all, I poured the entire bottle of neutralizer on my hair. <u>After a drippy ten-</u>   *Transition*
Seventh   <u>minute wait, I read the next step: "Carefully remove</u>
step   <u>rollers."</u> <u>As this advice was superfluous, I moved anx-</u>   *Transition*
<u>iously to the finale: "Rinse all solution from your hair,</u>   *Eighth step*
<u>and enjoy your curls."</u>

Final   Lifting my head from the sink and expecting vi-
product   sions of Aphrodite, I saw instead Medusa's image in the mirror. Limp question-mark spirals fell over my eyes, and each "curl" ended in an explosion of steel-wool frizz. Reflecting on my ineptitude, I knew why the direction page was illustrated only with drawings. After washing a large load of ammonia-scented towels, I took two aspirin and called my hairdresser. <u>Some</u>   *Concluding*
<u>repair services are cheap at any price.</u>   *remark*

Student Writer's Comments

Any person with normal dexterity can probably do a successful perm, but I sure had trouble! I decided I wanted to communicate that trouble in my process analysis essay. When I was given this writing assignment, I knew immediately that I wanted to explain how to do a perm. But I didn't know how to handle the humor that had resulted from my misguided attempt to administer a perm to myself. Part of my response to this assignment resides deep within my personality (I'm a closet comedian), but part of it simply has to do with the relationship between me and permanents (actually, anything having to do with cosmetics). But as I started out on this project, I had no idea if I could mold the comedy into a step-by-step analysis of a process.

First, I went to the store and bought a brand-new home perm, so I could review the guidelines step by step. On a piece of paper, I listed the procedures for giving myself a perm. On another sheet of paper, I wrote down any stories or associations I had with each stage of the process. Some of the notes on the second sheet of paper took the form of full paragraphs, others a list of words and phrases, and still others a combination of lists and full sentences. I found myself laughing aloud at some of the memories the home perm directions triggered.

I knew I was writing a directive essay for someone who might actually want to try a home perm. After making my preliminary lists of ideas, I just let my natural sense of humor direct my writing. My overview and purpose statement came easily. Next, I went through the directions one by one, laughing at myself and the process along the way. Before I knew it, I found myself writing, "After washing a large load of ammonia-scented towels, I took two aspirin and called my hairdresser"—the perfect end, or so I thought, to my comedy of errors. I had written the whole first draft from start to finish without once surfacing for air.

When I reread my draft, I realized that the approach I had taken to this process analysis assignment was a satirical one. It allowed me to go through the proper procedure of giving myself a home perm while simultaneously poking fun at myself along the way. As I revised my essay, I tried to exaggerate some of the humorous sections that demonstrated my ineptness or my failure to follow the directions correctly, hoping they would communicate the true ridiculousness of this entire situation. After omitting some details and embellishing others, I came up with the current last sentence of the essay: "Some repair services are cheap at any price." This new concluding remark took the edge off the whiny tone of the previous sentence and brought the essay to an even lighter close than before. I ended up liking the way the humor worked in the essay, because besides accurately capturing my most recent process analysis experience, it made a potentially dull essay topic rather entertaining. My only problem now is that I'm still not sure I got all the frizz out of my hair!

SOME FINAL THOUGHTS ON PROCESS ANALYSIS

In this chapter, a single process dictates the development and organization of each of the essays that follow. Both directional and informational methods are represented here. Notice in particular the clear purpose statements that set the focus of the essays in each case, as well as the other rhetorical modes (such as narration, comparison/contrast, and definition) that are used to help support the writers' explanations.

PROCESS ANALYSIS IN REVIEW

Reading Process Analysis Essays

Preparing to Read
√ What assumptions can I make from the essay's title?
√ What do I think the general mood of the essay will be?
√ What is the essay's purpose and audience?
√ What does the synopsis tell me about the essay?
√ What can I learn from the author's biography?
√ Can I predict the author's point of view toward the subject?

Reading
√ Is the essay *directive* (explaining how to do something) or *informative* (giving information about how something happened)?
√ What is the author's general message?

Rereading
√ Does the author furnish an overview of the process?
√ How is the essay organized—chronologically, cyclically, or simultaneously?
√ What other rhetorical modes does the author use?

Writing Process Analysis Essays

Preparing to Write
√ What is my purpose?
√ Who is my audience?

Writing
√ Do I provide an overview of the process at the beginning?
√ Does my first paragraph introduce my subject, divide it into steps, describe the result of the process, and include a purpose statement as my thesis?
√ Is my process analysis essay either *directive* or *informative?*
√ Are the essay's details organized chronologically, simultaneously, or cyclically?
√ Does the essay end with the process as a whole?

Rewriting
√ Is my purpose statement clear?
√ Have I given my readers an overview of the process I am going to discuss?
√ Do I go through the process step by step?
√ At the end of the essay, do I help my readers see the process as a whole?

JAY WALLJASPER   (1955–   )

Our Schedules, Our Selves

An award-winning writer and speaker, Jay Walljasper is currently a senior fellow at the Project for Public Spaces, a nonprofit urban planning and design organization in New York City, and an editor of Onthecommons.org, a Web site devoted to drawing greater attention to all the important elements in society that everyone owns together. He is also an editor-at-large for *Ode Magazine*, a contributing writer for *National Geographic Traveler Magazine*, and a columnist for *Parks and Recreation* magazine. Specializing in urban, community, environmental, and travel issues, he has published articles in *Mother Jones*, *Preservation*, the *New Statesman*, *E Magazine*, the *Chicago Tribune Magazine*, and many other important journals and newspapers. Earlier in his career, he was the editor of the *Utne Reader* for fifteen years, a travel editor at *Better Homes and Gardens*, and a columnist for the British magazine *Resurgence*. He is also the author of two important books: *Visionaries: People and Ideas to Change Your Life* (2001) and *The Great Neighborhood Book: A Do-It-Yourself Guide to Place-making* (2007), each of which argues that we can change the world by starting with our own block. In his spare time, he loves to explore cities, cross-country ski, and haunt used bookstores. Asked to give advice to students using *The Prose Reader*, he explained that the best place for a writer to look for material "is in the differences you see in the world around you and how that world is reflected back to us in the media."

Preparing to Read

The following essay, originally published in the *Utne Reader* (January/February 2003), chronicles the extent to which most of us are "slaves" to our schedules, allowing our responsibilities to control our lives, and offers some concrete ideas for taking control of our lives away from the clock.

Exploring Experience: Before reading this essay, take a few minutes to think about how you schedule your days: How tightly do you schedule your time? Do you make lists of things you want to do every day? Do you usually accomplish more or less than you want in a typical day? How large a part of your life is your education? Are you able to say *no* to events you don't want to participate in? Are your personal life and your job or school activities in a healthy balance? If not, what could you do to create a more balanced life for yourself?

Learning Online: Conduct an Internet search for "time management advice," and notice how many Web sites are devoted to this topic. Explore one of the pertinent sites, and read the advice. Are these skills that you possess, or do you need help managing your time? Compare your life right now to your ideal schedule, and think about how you can improve your time management system.

D AMN! You're 20 minutes—no, more like half an hour—late for   1
your breakfast meeting, which you were hoping to scoot out of
early to make an 8:30 seminar across town. And, somewhere in
there, there's that conference call. Now, at the last minute, you have to be at
a 9:40 meeting. No way you can miss it. Let's see, the afternoon is totally
booked, but you can probably push back your 10:15 appointment and work
through lunch. That would do it. Whew! The day has barely begun, and already you are counting the hours until evening, when you can finally go
home and happily, gloriously, triumphantly, do nothing. You'll skip yoga class,
blow off the neighborhood meeting, ignore the piles of laundry and just
relax. Yes! . . . No! Tonight's the night of the concert. You promised Nathan
and Mara weeks ago that you would go. *DAMN!*

Welcome to the daily grind—a grueling 24-7 competition against the   2
clock that leaves even the winners wondering what happened to their lives. [1]
Determined and sternly focused, we march through each day obeying the
orders of our calendars. The idle moment, the reflective pause, serendipity of
any sort have no place in our plans. Stopping to talk to someone or slowing
down to appreciate a sunny afternoon will only make you late for your next
round of activities. From the minute we rise in the morning, most of us have
our day charted out. The only surprise is if we actually get everything done
that we had planned before collapsing into bed at night.

On the job, in school, at home, increasing numbers of North Americans are   3
virtual slaves to their schedules. Some of what fills our days are onerous obligations, some are wonderful opportunities, and most fall in between, but taken
together they add up to too much. Too much to do, too many places to be, too
many things happening too fast, all mapped out for us in precise quarter-hour
allotments on our cell phones or day planners. We are not leading our lives, but
merely following a dizzying timetable of duties, commitments, demands, and
options. How did this happen? Where's the luxurious leisure that decades of
technological progress was supposed to bestow upon us?

The acceleration of the globalized economy and the accompanying   4
decline of people having any kind of a say over wages and working conditions is a chief culprit. Folks at the bottom of the socio-economic ladder [2]
feel the pain most sharply. Holding down two or three jobs, struggling to pay
the bills, working weekends, no vacation time, little social safety net, they

---

Thinking Critically

[1] To what extent are you a slave to your schedule? When do you have free time? What is
your favorite leisure activity?

[2] What jobs are at the bottom of the "socio-economic ladder"? How do people move up
and down this ladder?

often feel out of control about everything happening to them. But even successful professionals, people who seem fully in charge of their destinies, feel the pinch. Doctors, for example, working impossibly crowded schedules under the command of HMOs, feel overwhelmed. Many of them are now seeking union representation, traditionally the recourse of low-pay workers.

The onslaught of new technology, which promised to set us free, has instead   5
ratcheted up the rhythms of everyday life. [3] Cell phones, email, and laptop computers instill expectations of instantaneous action. While such direct communication can loosen our schedules in certain instances (it's easier to shift around an engagement on short notice), overall they fuel the trend that every minute must be accounted for. It's almost impossible to put duties behind you now, when the boss or committee chair can call you at a rap show or sushi restaurant, and documents can be emailed to you on vacation in Banff or Thailand. If you are never out of the loop, then are you ever not working?

Our own human desire for more choices and new experiences also plays   6
a role. Just like hungry diners gathering around a bountiful smorgasbord, it's hard not to pile too many activities on our plates. An expanding choice of cultural offerings over recent decades and the liberating sense that each of us can fully play a number of different social roles (worker, citizen, lover, parent, artist, etc.) has opened up enriching and exciting opportunities. Spanish lessons? Yes. Join a volleyball team? Why not. Cello and gymnastics classes for the kids? Absolutely. Tickets to a blues festival, food and wine expo, and political fundraiser? Sure. And we can't forget to make time for school events, therapy sessions, protest rallies, religious services, and dinner with friends.

Yes, these can all add to our lives. But with only 24 hours allotted to us   7
each day, something is lost too. You don't just run into a friend anymore and decide to get coffee. You can't happily savor an experience because your mind races toward the next one on the calendar. In a busy life, nothing happens if you don't plan it, often weeks in advance. Our "free" hours become just as programmed as the work day. What begins as an idea for fun frequently turns into an obligation obstacle course. Visit that new barbecue restaurant. *Done!* Go to tango lessons. *Done!* Fly to Montreal for a long weekend. *Done!*

We've booked ourselves so full of prescheduled activities there's no time   8
left for those magic, spontaneous moments that make us feel most alive. [4] We seldom stop to think of all the experiences we are eliminating from our lives

---

Thinking Critically

[3] In what ways has new technology "ratcheted up the rhythms of everyday life"? Does your use of technology save you time or take time away from you?

[4] Do you agree with the author that "magic, spontaneous moments" make us feel most alive? Why or why not?

when we load up our appointment book. Reserving tickets for a basketball game months away could mean you miss out on the first balmy evening of spring. Five p.m. skating lessons for your children fit so conveniently into your schedule that you never realize it's the time all the other kids in the neighborhood gather on the sidewalk to play.

A few years back, radical Brazilian educator Paulo Freire was attending a 9 conference of Midwestern political activists and heard over and over about how overwhelmed people felt about the duties they face each day. Finally, he stood up and, in slow, heavily accented English, declared, "We are bigger than our schedules." The audience roared with applause.

Yes, we are bigger than our schedules. So how do we make sure our lives 10 are not overpowered by an endless roster of responsibilities? Especially in an age where demanding jobs, two-worker households or single-parent families make the joyous details of everyday life—cooking supper from scratch or organizing a block party—seem like an impossible dream? There is no set of easy answers, despite what the marketers of new convenience products would have us believe. But that doesn't mean we can't make real steps to take back our lives.

Part of the answer is political. So long as Americans work longer hours 11 than any other people on Earth, we are going to feel hemmed in by our schedules. ⑤ Expanded vacation time for everyone, including part-time and minimum wage workers, is one obvious and overdue solution. Shortening the work week, something the labor movement and progressive politicians successfully accomplished in the early decades of the 20th century, is another logical objective. There's nothing preordained about 40-hours on the job; Italy, France, and other European nations have already cut back working hours. An opportunity for employees outside academia to take a sabbatical every decade or so is another idea whose time has come. And how about more vacation and paid holidays? Let's start with Martin Luther King's birthday, Susan B. Anthony's birthday, and your own! Any effort to give people more clout in their workplaces—from strengthened unions to employee ownership—could help us gain much-needed flexibility in our jobs, and our lives.

On another front, how you think about time can make a big difference 12 in how you feel about your life. Note how some of your most memorable moments occurred when something in your schedule fell through. The canceled lunch that allows you to spend an hour strolling around town. Friday night plans scrapped for a bowl of popcorn in front of the fireplace. Don't be shy about shucking your schedule whenever you can get away with it. And

---

Thinking Critically

⑤ Why do you think Americans work longer hours than people in other countries? Do you think work hours vary from state to state? From one region of the country to another?

with some experimentation, you may find that you can get away with it a lot more than you imagined.

Setting aside some time on your calendar for life to just unfold in its own 13 surprising way can also nurture your soul. Carve out some nonscheduled hours (or days) once in a while and treat them as a firm commitment. And resist the temptation to turn every impulse or opportunity into another appointment. It's neither impolite nor inefficient to simply say, "let me get back to you on that tomorrow" or "let's check in that morning to see if it's still a good time." You cannot know how crammed that day may turn out to be, or how uninspired you might feel about another engagement, or how much you'll want to be rollerblading or playing chess or doing something else at that precise time.

In our industrialized, fast-paced society, we too often view time as just 14 another mechanical instrument to be programmed. But time possesses its own evershifting shape and rhythms and defies our best efforts to corral it within the tidy lines of our cell phones or datebooks. Stephan Rechtschaffen, author of *Time Shifting,* suggests you think back on a scary auto collision (or near miss) or spectacular night of lovemaking. Time seemed almost to stand still. ⬦⁶ You can remember everything in vivid detail. Compare that to an overcrammed week that you recall now only as a rapid-fire blur. Keeping in mind that our days expand and contract according to their own patterns is perhaps the best way to help keep time on your side.

UNDERSTANDING DETAILS

1. Explain in your own words the problem of letting your schedule control your life from Walljasper's point of view.
2. Walljasper divides the solutions to the problem he identifies into two categories. What are those categories?
3. List the solutions that Walljasper offers in each category.
4. Explain the final sentence of Walljasper's essay: "Keeping in mind that our days expand and contract according to their own patterns is perhaps the best way to help keep time on your side" (paragraph 14).

READING CRITICALLY

5. Name two major causes, according to Walljasper, of the time crunch we now live in.
6. Which of Walljasper's guidelines for managing your schedule could you benefit from most? How could it help you? Why do you have trouble in this area?

Thinking Critically

⬦⁶ When does time seem to move slowly? When does it move rapidly? Do you think we are most productive when time moves fast or slow?

7. Why does Walljasper advise us to slow down? What are the benefits of following this suggestion?

8. According to the author, how can we balance our personal and professional lives? How realistic are these ideas?

DISCOVERING RHETORICAL STRATEGIES

9. The author starts this essay with a realistic example from a twenty-first-century life. Is this an effective beginning? Why or why not? What are some alternative ways to start this essay?

10. How does Walljasper organize his techniques for managing our schedules? Is this order successful? Explain your answer.

11. How would you characterize the tone or general attitude of this essay? Is this an effective approach to the subject? Explain your answer.

12. What other rhetorical modes does Walljasper use to support this process analysis essay? Give examples of each of these modes.

MAKING CONNECTIONS

13. Pretend that you are Jay Walljasper giving advice to young Russell Baker ("The Saturday Evening Post"), who wants to become a good salesperson. Which of Walljasper's suggestions should Baker follow most earnestly? Why? Which of these suggestions would be most helpful in your own life?

14. Walljasper's essay analyzing the process of managing our time and Jessica Mitford's essay ("Behind the Formaldehyde Curtain") analyzing funeral customs both try to persuade us to adopt a certain opinion as they describe a process. Which essay is more convincing to you? Explain your answer in detail.

15. Walljasper's contention that many of us are "enslaved" by our schedules invites us to consider other types of addiction throughout this book. Examine any of the following essays you have read, and explain which of them involves a process that would be particularly challenging to overcome: Alice Lesch Kelly ("Toughen Up!"), Stephanie Ericsson ("The Ways We Lie"), Stephen King ("Why We Crave Horror Movies"), and/or Barrett Seaman ("How Bingeing Became the New College Sport").

IDEAS FOR DISCUSSION/WRITING

Preparing to Write

Write freely about various aspects of your daily schedule: Do you make realistic schedules for yourself from day to day? What benefits can you receive from giving yourself more free time? Can you identify any disadvantages that could result from more free time for you? How can you avoid the problems that the author identifies? Do you schedule yourself too tightly, or do you build in time to pursue spontaneous activities and free thoughts? How does being a student fit into the advice Walljasper gives?

Choosing a Topic

1. *Learning Online:* Think about the scheduling advice that you read in Preparing to Read and in Walljasper's article. Have you discovered any tips that would improve your daily routine? Write a process analysis essay about how you could incorporate this advice into your life. To what extent would you implement suggestions like taking longer vacations or spending more quality time with people? Make sure you are specific about how you would apply this scheduling guidance to your everyday life.

2. You have been asked by the editor of your campus newspaper to adapt Walljasper's suggestions to the life of a student. Write a process analysis essay adjusting Walljasper's guidelines to a college environment.

3. Interview someone in your class about his or her ability to use time wisely. Use Walljasper's guidelines to establish whether the person schedules himself or herself well. Then, direct a process analysis essay to this person, briefly evaluating his or her time-management skills and then offering suggestions for improvement.

4. In the typical life of a student, sometimes course obligations (study as much as you can every day) seem to conflict with the fundamental tenets for leading a quality life (relax and enjoy yourself). Do you think these two aspects of life are incompatible, or are there ways to reconcile the two? Write an essay for your classmates detailing a solution to this dilemma.

Before beginning your essay, you might want to consult the checklists on page 212.

JESSICA MITFORD   (1917–1996)

Behind the Formaldehyde Curtain

Once called "Queen of the Muckrakers" in a *Time* magazine review, Jessica Mitford has written scathing exposés of the Famous Writers' School, American funeral directors, television executives, prisons, a "fat farm" for wealthy women, and many other venerable social institutions. She was born in England into the gentry, immigrated to the United States, and later became a naturalized American citizen. After working at a series of jobs, she achieved literary fame at age forty-six with the publication of *The American Way of Death* (1963), which relentlessly shatters the image of funeral directors as "compassionate, reverent family-friends-in-need." Her other major works include *Kind and Unusual Punishment: The Prison Business* (1973); *Poison Penmanship: The Gentle Art of Muckraking* (1979), an anthology of her articles in the *Atlantic, Harper's,* and other periodicals covering a twenty-two-year time span; two volumes of autobiography, *Daughters and Rebels* (1960) and *A Fine Old Madness* (1977); and *The American Way of Birth* (1992). Superbly skilled in the techniques of investigative reporting, satire, and black humor, Mitford was described in a *Washington Post* article as "an older, more even-tempered, better-read Jane Fonda who has maintained her activism long past middle age." Her advice to students planning to write in this genre? "You may not be able to change the world, but at least you can embarrass the guilty."

Preparing to Read

The following essay, taken from *The American Way of Death,* clearly illustrates the ruthless manner in which Mitford exposes the greed and hypocrisy of the American mortuary business.

Exploring Experience: As you prepare to read this article, think for a few minutes about funeral customs in our society: Have you attended a funeral service recently? Which rituals seemed particularly vivid to you? What purpose did these symbolic actions serve? What other interesting customs are you aware of in American society? What purpose do these customs serve? What public images do these customs have? Are these images accurate? Do you generally approve or disapprove of these customs?

Learning Online: In this controversial essay, Jessica Mitford graphically describes the embalming process. Before reading her article, familiarize yourself with some technical mortuary terms by visiting HBO's "Six Feet Under" Web site (www.hbo.com/sixfeetunder). Select "Video" from the menu options to view farcical commercials that poke fun at the funeral industry.

The drama begins to unfold with the arrival of the corpse at the   1
mortuary.

Alas, poor Yorick! ◈ How surprised he would be to see how his   2
counterpart of today is whisked off to a funeral parlor and is in short order
sprayed, sliced, pierced, pickled, trussed, trimmed, creamed, waxed, painted,
rouged, and neatly dressed—transformed from a common corpse into a
Beautiful Memory Picture. This process is known in the trade as embalming and restorative art and is so universally employed in the United States and
Canada that the funeral director does it routinely, without consulting corpse
or kin. He regards as eccentric those few who are hardy enough to suggest
that it might be dispensed with. Yet no law requires embalming, no religious
doctrine commends it, nor is it dictated by considerations of health, sanitation, or even of personal daintiness. In no part of the world but in Northern
America is it widely used. The purpose of embalming is to make the corpse
presentable for viewing in a suitably costly container; and here too the funeral
director routinely, without first consulting the family, prepares the body for
public display.

Is all this legal? The processes to which a dead body may be subjected are   3
after all to some extent circumscribed by law. In most states, for instance,
the signature of next of kin must be obtained before an autopsy may be performed, before the deceased may be cremated, before the body may be turned
over to a medical school for research purposes; or such provision must be
made in the decedent's will. In the case of embalming, no such permission
is required nor is it ever sought. A textbook, *The Principles and Practices of
Embalming,* comments on this: "There is some question regarding the legality of much that is done within the preparation room." The author points out
that it would be most unusual for a responsible member of a bereaved family to instruct the mortician, in so many words, to "*embalm*" the body of a
deceased relative. The very term "embalming" is so seldom used that the
mortician must rely upon custom in the matter. The author concludes that
unless the family specifies otherwise, the act of entrusting the body to the
care of a funeral establishment carries with it an implied permission to go
ahead and embalm.

Embalming is indeed a most extraordinary procedure, and one must won-   4
der at the docility of Americans who each year pay hundreds of millions of
dollars for its perpetuation, blissfully ignorant of what it is all about, what is

---

Thinking Critically

◈ How do Mitford's description of the embalming process as a "drama" and her reference
to Shakespeare's *Hamlet* ("Alas, poor Yorick!") help set the tone for this essay?

done, how it is done. Not one in ten thousand has any idea of what actually takes place. Books on the subject are extremely hard to come by. They are not to be found in most libraries or bookshops.

In an era when huge television audiences watch surgical operations in the comfort of their living rooms, when, thanks to the animated cartoon, the geography of the digestive system [2] has become familiar territory even to the nursery school set, in a land where the satisfaction of curiosity about almost all matters is a national pastime, the secrecy surrounding embalming can, surely, hardly be attributed to the inherent gruesomeness of the subject. Custom in this regard has within this century suffered a complete reversal. In the early days of American embalming, when it was performed in the home of the deceased, it was almost mandatory for some relative to stay by the embalmer's side and witness the procedure. Today, family members who might wish to be in attendance would certainly be dissuaded by the funeral director. All others, except apprentices, are excluded by law from the preparation room.

A close look at what does actually take place may explain in large measure the undertaker's intractable reticence concerning a procedure that has become his major *raison d'être*. Is it possible he fears that public information about embalming might lead patrons to wonder if they really want this service? [3] If the funeral men are loath to discuss the subject outside the trade, the reader may, understandably, be equally loath to go on reading at this point. For those who have the stomach for it, let us part the formaldehyde curtain.

The body is first laid out in the undertaker's morgue—or rather, Mr. Jones is reposing in the preparation room—to be readied to bid the world farewell.

The preparation room in any of the better funeral establishments has the tiled and sterile look of a surgery, [4] and indeed the embalmer–restorative artist who does his chores there is beginning to adopt the term "dermasurgeon" (appropriately corrupted by some mortician-writers as "demisurgeon") to describe his calling. His equipment, consisting of scalpels, scissors, augers, forceps, clamps, needles, pumps, tubes, bowls, and basins, is crudely imitative of the surgeon's, as is his technique, acquired in a nine- or twelve-month post-high-school course in an embalming school. He is supplied by an advanced chemical industry with a bewildering array of fluids, sprays, pastes, oils, powders, creams, to fix or soften tissue, shrink or distend it as

---

Thinking Critically

[2] What does the author mean by the phrase "the geography of the digestive system"?

[3] Do you think this assertion is true? Why or why not?

[4] What does Mitford mean by the British term "surgery"? Find another example of British dialect in the essay?

needed, dry it here, restore the moisture there. There are cosmetics, waxes and paints to fill and cover features, even plaster of Paris to replace entire limbs. There are ingenious aids to prop and stabilize the cadaver: A Vari-Pose Head Rest, the Edwards Arm and Hand Positioner, the Repose Block (to support the shoulders during the embalming), and the Throop Foot Positioner, which resembles an old-fashioned stocks.

Mr. John H. Eckels, president of the Eckels College of Mortuary Science, 9 thus describes the first part of the embalming procedure: "In the hands of a skilled practitioner, this work may be done in a comparatively short time and without mutilating the body other than by slight incision—so slight that it scarcely would cause serious inconvenience if made upon a living person. It is necessary to remove the blood, and doing this not only helps in the disinfecting, but removes the principal cause of disfigurements due to discoloration."

Another textbook discusses the all-important time element: "The earlier 10 this is done, the better, for every hour that elapses between death and embalming will add to the problems and complications encountered. . . ." Just how soon should one get going on the embalming? The author tells us, "On the basis of such scanty information made available to this profession through its rudimentary and haphazard system of technical research, we must conclude that the best results are to be obtained if the subject is embalmed before life is completely extinct—that is, before cellular death has occurred. In the average case, this would mean within an hour after somatic death." 5 For those who feel that there is something a little rudimentary, not to say haphazard, about this advice, a comforting thought is offered by another writer. Speaking of fears entertained in early days of premature burial, he points out, "One of the effects of embalming by chemical injection, however, has been to dispel fears of live burial." How true; once the blood is removed, chances of live burial are indeed remote.

To return to Mr. Jones, the blood is drained out through the veins and 11 replaced by embalming fluid pumped in through the arteries. As noted in *The Principles and Practices of Embalming,* "every operator has a favorite injection and drainage point—a fact which becomes a handicap only if he fails or refuses to forsake his favorites when conditions demand it." Typical favorites are the carotid artery, femoral artery, jugular vein, subclavian vein. There are various choices of embalming fluid. If Flextone is used, it will produce a "mild, flexible rigidity. 6 The skin retains a velvety softness, the tissues are rubbery and pliable. Ideal for women and children." It may be blended with

---

Thinking Critically

5 What is the difference between "somatic death" and "cellular death"? Why is this distinction important to the funeral profession?

6 Why is the oxymoron "mild, flexible rigidity" humorous?

B. and G. Products Company's Lyf-Lyk tint, which is guaranteed to reproduce "nature's own skin texture . . . the velvety appearance of living tissue." Suntone comes in three separate tints: Suntan; Special Cosmetic Tint, a pink shade "especially indicated for young female subjects"; and Regular Cosmetic Tint, moderately pink.

About three to six gallons of a dyed and perfumed solution of formalde-   12
hyde, glycerin, borax, phenol, alcohol, and water is soon circulating through Mr. Jones, whose mouth has been sewn together with a "needle directed upward between the upper lip and gum and brought out through the left nostril," with the corners raised slightly "for a more pleasant expression." If he should be bucktoothed, his teeth are cleaned with Bon Ami and coated with colorless nail polish. His eyes, meanwhile, are closed with flesh-tinted eye caps and eye cement.

The next step is to have at Mr. Jones with a thing called a trocar. This is   13
a long, hollow needle attached to a tube. It is jabbed into the abdomen, poked around the entrails and chest cavity, the contents of which are pumped out and replaced with "cavity fluid." This done, and the hole in the abdomen sewn up, Mr. Jones's face is heavily creamed (to protect the skin from burns which may be caused by leakage of the chemicals), and he is covered with a sheet and left unmolested for a while. **7** But not for long—there is more, much more, in store for him. He has been embalmed, but not yet restored, and the best time to start the restorative work is eight to ten hours after embalming, when the tissues have become firm and dry.

The object of all this attention to the corpse, it must be remembered, is   14
to make it presentable for viewing in an attitude of healthy repose. **8** "Our customs require the presentation of our dead in the semblance of normality . . . unmarred by the ravages of illness, disease, or mutilation," says Mr. J. Sheridan Mayer in his *Restorative Art.* This is rather a large order since few people die in the full bloom of health, unravaged by illness and unmarked by some disfigurement. The funeral industry is equal to the challenge: "In some cases the gruesome appearance of a mutilated or disease-ridden subject may be quite discouraging. The task of restoration may seem impossible and shake the confidence of the embalmer. This is the time for intestinal fortitude and determination. Once the formative work is begun and affected tissues are cleaned or removed, all doubts of success vanish. It is surprising and gratifying to discover the results which may be obtained."

Thinking Critically

7 How do such phrases as "have at Mr. Jones with a thing called a trocar" and "left unmolested for a while" help Mitford satirize the embalming process?

8 What is ironic about the phrase "in an attitude of healthy repose"? Find at least one other example of irony.

The embalmer, having allowed an appropriate interval to elapse, returns to   15
the attack, but now he brings into play the skill and equipment of sculptor
and cosmetician. Is a hand missing? Casting one in plaster of Paris is a simple
matter. "For replacement purposes, only a cast of the back of the hand is necessary; this is within the ability of the average operator and is quite adequate."
If a lip or two, a nose or an ear should be missing, the embalmer has at hand
a variety of restorative waxes with which to model replacements. Pores and
skin texture are simulated by stippling with a little brush, and over this cosmetics are laid on. Head off? Decapitation cases are rather routinely handled. ⊘Ragged edges are trimmed, and head joined to torso with a series of
splints, wires, and sutures. It is a good idea to have a little something at the
neck—a scarf or a high collar—when time for viewing comes. Swollen
mouth: Cut out tissue as needed from inside the lips. If too much is removed,
the surface contour can easily be restored by padding with cotton. Swollen
necks and cheeks are reduced by removing tissue through vertical incisions
made down each side of the neck. "When the deceased is casketed, the pil-
low will hide the suture incisions. . . . As an extra precaution against leakage,
the suture may be painted with liquid sealer."

The opposite condition is more likely to present itself—that of emacia-   16
tion. His hypodermic syringe now loaded with massage cream, the embalmer
seeks out and fills the hollowed and sunken areas by injection. In this procedure the backs of the hands and fingers and the under-chin area should not
be neglected.

Positioning the lips is a problem that recurrently challenges the ingenu-   17
ity of the embalmer. Closed too tightly, they tend to give a stern, even disapproving expression. Ideally, embalmers feel, the lips should give the
impression of being ever so slightly parted, the upper lip protruding slightly
for a more youthful appearance. This takes some engineering, however, as the
lips tend to drift apart. Lip drift ⑩ can sometimes be remedied by pushing one
or two straight pins through the inner margin of the lower lip and then
inserting them between the two front upper teeth. If Mr. Jones happens to
have no teeth, the pins can just as easily be anchored in his Armstrong Face
Former and Denture Replacer. Another method to maintain lip closure is to
dislocate the lower jaw, which is then held in its new position by a wire run
through holes which have been drilled through the upper and lower jaws at
the midline. As the French are fond of saying, *il faut souffrir pour être belle.*

Thinking Critically

⊘ How did you respond to the following statement: "Decapitation cases are rather routinely
handled"? Analyze your emotional reaction.

⑩ How can funeral directors solve the problem of "lip drift"? What is the effect of such
vivid details in the essay?

If Mr. Jones had died of jaundice, the embalming fluid will very likely turn   18
him green. Does this deter the embalmer? Not if he has intestinal fortitude.
Masking pastes and cosmetics are heavily laid on, burial garments and casket
interiors are color-correlated with particular care, and Jones is displayed
beneath rose-colored lights. Friends will say "How *well* he looks." Death by
carbon monoxide, on the other hand, can be rather a good thing from the
embalmer's viewpoint: "One advantage is the fact that this type of discoloration is an exaggerated form of a natural pink coloration." This is nice
because the healthy glow is already present and needs but little attention. [11]

The patching and filling completed, Mr. Jones is now shaved, washed, and   19
dressed. Cream-based cosmetic, available in pink, flesh, suntan, brunette, and
blond, is applied to his hands and face, his hair is shampooed and combed
(and, in the case of Mrs. Jones, set), his hands manicured. For the horny-
handed son of toil special care must be taken; cream should be applied to
remove ingrained grime, and the nails cleaned. "If he were not in the habit
of having them manicured in life, trimming and shaping is advised for appearance—never questioned by kin."

Jones is now ready for casketing (this is the present participle of the verb   20
"to casket"). In this operation his right shoulder should be depressed slightly
"to turn the body a bit to the right and soften the appearance of lying flat
on the back." Positioning the hands is a matter of importance, and special rubber positioning blocks may be used. The hands should be cupped slightly
for a more lifelike, relaxed appearance. [12] Proper placement of the body
requires a delicate sense of balance. It should lie as high as possible in the casket, yet not so high that the lid, when lowered, will hit the nose. On the
other hand, we are cautioned, placing the body too low "creates the impression that the body is in a box."

Jones is next wheeled into the appointed slumber room where a few last   21
touches may be added—his favorite pipe placed in his hand or, if he was a
great reader, a book propped into position. (In the case of little Master Jones
a Teddy bear may be clutched.) Here he will hold open house for a few days,
visiting hours 10 A.M. to 9 P.M.

All now being in readiness, the funeral director calls a staff conference to   22
make sure that each assistant knows his precise duties. Mr. Wilber Kriege
writes, "This makes your staff feel that they are a part of the team, with a
definite assignment that must be properly carried out if the whole plan is to
succeed. You never heard of a football coach who failed to talk to his entire

---

Thinking Critically

[11] Why is death by carbon monoxide poisoning "a good thing from the embalmer's viewpoint"?

[12] Why would a mortician want to create "a more lifelike, relaxed appearance" in a corpse?
How does this phrase fit into the author's overall purpose in the essay?

team before they go on the field. They have drilled on the plays they are to execute for hours and days, and yet the successful coach knows the importance of making even the bench-warming third-string substitute feel that he is important if the game is to be won." The winning of *this* game is predicated upon glass-smooth handling of the logistics. The funeral director has notified the pallbearers whose names were furnished by the family, has arranged for the presence of clergyman, organist, and soloist, has provided transportation for everybody, has organized and listed the flowers sent by friends. In *Psychology of Funeral Service,* Mr. Edward A. Martin points out: "He may not always do as much as the family thinks he is doing, but it is his helpful guidance that they appreciate in knowing they are proceeding as they should. . . . The important thing is how well his services can be used to make the family believe they are giving unlimited expression to their own sentiment." [13]

The religious service may be held in a church or in the chapel of the   23 funeral home; the funeral director vastly prefers the latter arrangement, for not only is it more convenient for him but it affords him the opportunity to show off his beautiful facilities to the gathered mourners. After the clergyman has had his say, the mourners queue up to file past the casket for a last look at the deceased. The family is *never* asked whether they want an open-casket ceremony; in the absence of their instruction to the contrary, this is taken for granted. Consequently, well over 90 percent of all American funerals feature the open casket—a custom unknown in other parts of the world. [14] Foreigners are astonished by it. An English woman living in San Francisco described her reaction in a letter to the writer:

> I myself have attended only one funeral here—that of an elderly fellow worker of mine. After the service I could not understand why everyone was walking towards the coffin (sorry, I mean casket), but thought I had better follow the crowd. It shook me rigid to get there and find the casket open and poor old Oscar lying there in his brown tweed suit, wearing a suntan makeup and just the wrong shade of lipstick. If I had not been extremely fond of the old boy, I have a horrible feeling that I might have giggled. Then and there I decided that I could never face another American funeral—even dead.

The casket (which has been resting throughout the service on a Classic   24 Beauty Ultra Metal Casket Bier) is now transferred by a hydraulically operated device called Porto-Lift to a balloon-tired, Glide Easy casket carriage which will wheel it to yet another conveyance, the Cadillac Funeral Coach. This may be lavender, cream, light green—anything but

---

Thinking Critically

[13] What does the author mean by the phrase "giving unlimited expression to their own sentiment" when discussing the involvement of the deceased's family?

[14] How do you feel about "open casket" funeral ceremonies? Analyze your response to this custom.

black. Interiors, of course, are color-correlated, "for the man who cannot stop short of perfection."

At graveside, the casket is lowered into the earth. This office, once the pre- 25
rogative of friends of the deceased, is now performed by a patented mechanical lowering device. A "Life-time Green" artificial grass mat is at the ready to conceal the sere earth, and overhead, to conceal the sky, is a portable Steril Chapel Tent ("resists the intense heat and humidity of summer and the terrific storms of winter . . . available in Silver Grey, Rose, or Evergreen"). Now is the time for the ritual scattering of earth over the coffin, as the solemn words "earth to earth, ashes to ashes, dust to dust" are pronounced by the officiating cleric. This can today be accomplished "with a mere flick of the wrist with the Gordon Leak-Proof Earth Dispenser. No grasping of a handful of dirt, no soiled fingers. Simple, dignified, beautiful, reverent! The modern way!" The Golden Earth Dispenser (at $5) is of nickel-plated brass construction. It is not only "attractive to the eye and long wearing"; it is also "one of the 'tools' for building better public relations" if presented as "an appropriate non-commercial gift" to the clergyman. It is shaped something like a saltshaker.

Untouched by human hand, the coffin and the earth are now united. [15] 26

It is in the function of directing the participants through the maze of gad- 27
getry that the funeral director has assigned to himself his relatively new role of "grief therapist." He has relieved the family of every detail, he has revamped the corpse to look like a living doll, he has arranged for it to nap for a few days in a slumber room, he has put on a well-oiled performance in which the concept of *death* has played no part whatsoever—unless it was inconsiderately mentioned by the clergyman who conducted the religious service. He has done everything in his power to make the funeral a real pleasure for everybody concerned. He and his team have given their all to score an upset victory over death.

UNDERSTANDING DETAILS

1. List the major steps of the embalming process that the author reveals in this essay.
2. Why, according to Mitford, do funeral directors not want to make public the details of embalming? To what extent do you think their desire for secrecy is warranted?
3. Why isn't the permission of a family member needed for embalming? From Mitford's perspective, what does this custom reveal about Americans?
4. In what ways has embalming become the undertaker's *raison d'être*? How do American funeral customs encourage this procedure?

Thinking Critically

[15] Why do you think it's important for the coffin and the earth to be united "Untouched by human hand"? In what way is this comment ironic?

READING CRITICALLY

5. What is Mitford's primary purpose in this essay? Why do you think she has analyzed this particular process in such detail?

6. Explain the title of this essay.

7. Do you think the author knows how gruesome her essay is? How can you tell? What makes the essay so horrifying? How does such close attention to macabre detail help Mitford accomplish her purpose?

8. What does Mitford mean when she argues that the funeral director and his team "have given their all to score an upset victory over death" (paragraph 27)? Who or what is "the team"? Why does Mitford believe death plays no part in American burial customs?

DISCOVERING RHETORICAL STRATEGIES

9. Why does Mitford begin her essay with a one-sentence paragraph? Is it effective? Why or why not?

10. A euphemism is a deceptively pleasant term used in place of a straightforward, less pleasant one. In what way is "Beautiful Memory Picture" (paragraph 2) a euphemism? How are we reminded of this phrase throughout the essay? What other euphemisms can you find in this selection?

11. What tone does Mitford establish in the essay? What is her reason for creating this particular tone? What is your reaction to it?

12. What other rhetorical strategies does Mitford use besides gruesome examples and illustrations to make her point? Give examples of each of these different strategies.

MAKING CONNECTIONS

13. Imagine that Stephen King ("Why We Crave Horror Movies") has just read Mitford's essay on funeral customs. According to King, what would be the source of our fascination with these macabre practices? Why do essays like Mitford's both intrigue and repulse us at the same time?

14. Compare and contrast Mitford's use of examples with those used by Harold Krents ("Darkness at Noon"), Joel Stein ("You Are Not My Friend"), and/or Amy Tan ("Mother Tongue"). How often does each author use examples? What is the relationship between the frequency of examples in each essay and the extent to which you are convinced by the author's argument?

15. In this essay, Mitford lifts the curtain on certain bizarre funeral practices in much the same way that Judith Wallerstein and Sandra Blakeslee expose the trauma of divorce ("Second Chances for Children of Divorce"), Frank Furedi ("Our Unhealthy Obsession with Sickness") uncovers the abuses of the medical system, and Barbara Ehrenreich discloses the pleasures of combat ("The Ecstasy of War"). Which of these "exposés" that you have read seems most complete and devastating to you? Explain your answer.

IDEAS FOR DISCUSSION/WRITING

Preparing to Write

Write freely about a particularly interesting custom in America or in another country: Why does this custom exist? What role does it play in the society? What value does it have? What are the details of this custom? In what way is this custom a part of your life? Your family's life? What purpose does it serve for you? Is it worth continuing? Why or why not?

Choosing a Topic

1. *Learning Online:* Consider a task you find unpleasant, and write a farcical essay or commercial about it (like those at www.hbo.com/sixfeetunder mentioned in Preparing to Read). Make your piece as detailed as possible, offering stage directions and/or drawings for the essay or commercial if possible.
2. In a process analysis essay directed to your classmates, explain a custom you do not approve of. Decide on your tone and purpose before you begin to write.
3. In a process analysis essay directed to your classmates, explain a custom you approve of. Select a specific tone and purpose before you begin to write.
4. You have been asked to address a group of students at a college of mortuary science. In this role, you have an opportunity to influence the opinion of these students concerning the practice of embalming. Write a well-reasoned lecture to this group arguing either for or against the process of embalming.

Before beginning your essay, you might want to consult the checklists on page 212.

ALICE LESCH KELLY   (1963–   )

Toughen Up!

A Staten Island native, Alice Lesch Kelly earned her B.A. in Journalism at Syracuse and her M.A. in Creative Writing at Boston University. A very successful freelance writer specializing in health, nutrition, fertility, and mind/body issues, she has published articles in more than forty magazines and newspapers, including the *New York Times,* the *Los Angeles Times, Shape, Martha Stewart Living, Reader's Digest, Prevention, Woman's Day, Fit Pregnancy, Health,* and many others. She has also co-authored four books, the most popular of which is *Be Happy Without Being Perfect* with Alice Domar (2008). She currently lives in the Boston area, where she enjoys collecting vintage cookbooks. Asked to give advice to students using *The Prose Reader,* Kelly explained that "Writers need to know more than just how to write; they need to have expertise in a topic they'll write about, whether it's politics, music, health, religion, food, or anything else. Most publications are aimed at people who want to know more about specific subjects, and the more specialized expertise and experience you bring to the table, the more attractive you are to editors."

Preparing to Read

This essay, originally published in *Shape* (November 2004), has the following subtitle: "When the going gets rough, some of us fall apart, while others ride it out unscathed. Here's how to become more resilient in a crisis." Kelly asks five crucial questions that help determine exactly how tough we really are and then explains how to "toughen up!"

Exploring Experience: As you prepare to read this article, pause for a moment to consider your own ability to bounce back: Are you generally positive or negative? Do you complain while others get back on their feet? In your opinion, what qualities make a person strong? What makes others weak? Have you become more or less flexible with age? What is the primary reason for this change?

Learning Online: Use the Internet to look up some famous people you admire. Read their biographies to find out if they have faced any problems or difficult times in their lives. How did they overcome these obstacles? What resources did they use to persevere? Keep these stories in mind as you read Kelly's essay.

When the going gets rough, some of us fall apart, while others ride it out unscathed. Here's how to become more resilient in a crisis.

Two women who do similar work are laid off from their jobs. Their industry has been hit hard by economic troubles, and their prospects for finding new positions are few. They have comparable educations, career histories, and job experience. You might think they'd have about the same chance of landing on their feet, but they don't: A year later, one is unemployed, broke, and angry, while the other has branched out in an entirely new direction. It hasn't been easy, and she's not earning as much as she did at her old job. But she is excited and optimistic and looks back at her layoff as an unexpected opportunity to follow a new path in life.   1

We've all seen it: When adversity strikes, some people flourish, while others fall apart. ◆ What sets the survivors apart is their resilience—the ability to endure and even thrive under stressful conditions. "Some people are able to rise to the occasion," says Roberta R. Greene, Ph.D., a professor of social work at the University of Texas at Austin and editor of *Resiliency: An Integrated Approach to Practice, Policy, and Research* (National Association of Social Workers, 2002). "When a crisis emerges, they start moving in the direction of solving it."   2

Resilience is well worth cultivating. Instead of being overwhelmed by tough breaks, resilient people make the best of them. Instead of being crushed, they prosper. "Resilience helps you transform stressful circumstances from potential disasters into opportunities," says Salvatore R. Maddi, Ph.D., a founder of the Hardiness Institute, Inc. in Newport Beach, Calif. Resilient people improve their lives because they take control and work to positively influence what happens to them. They choose action rather than passivity and empowerment over powerlessness.   3

How resilient are you? In a blackout, would you be outside, complaining good-naturedly with your neighbors, or would you be sitting in the house moaning about how bad things always seem to happen to you? If you're the moaner, you should know that resilience can be learned. Sure, some people are born with an ability to bounce back, but experts promise that those of us who weren't can build the skills that carry resilient people through the toughest of times.   4

Ask yourself the following questions; the more "yes" answers you have, the more resilient you are. "No" answers indicate areas you may want to work on. Then follow our action plans to build your resilience.   5

Thinking Critically

◆ What special qualities help people flourish when adversity strikes? Do you think you have those qualities? Why or why not?

1. Did you grow up in a supportive family?

"Resilient people have parents, role models, and mentors who encouraged   6
them to believe they can do well," Maddi says. He and his colleagues discovered that many people who are high in resilience (or hardiness, as Maddi
calls it) grew up with parents and other adults who taught them coping skills
and emphasized that they possessed the power to transcend life's difficulties. ❷ Less-hardy adults grew up with similar stresses but much less support.

Plan of action

You can't change your childhood, but you can surround yourself with   7
the right kind of "family" now. Seek out supportive friends, relatives, neighbors, and coworkers, and avoid people who treat you badly. Reach out to your
support team, offering them assistance and encouragement on a regular basis.
Then, when difficulty strikes in your life, they will likely return the favor.

2. Do you embrace change?

Whether it's losing a job, going through a breakup, or moving to a new   8
city, the most difficult situations in life involve significant change. While less-
resilient people tend to be upset and threatened by change, those who are
highly resilient are more likely to embrace it and feel excited by and curious about new situations. They know—and accept—that change is a normal
part of life, and they look for creative ways to adapt to it. ❸

"Everyone I see who is resilient never stops being a playfully curious   9
child," says Al Siebert, Ph.D., director of The Resiliency Center in Portland,
Ore. and author of *The Survivor Personality: Why Some People Are Stronger,
Smarter, and More Skillful at Handling Life's Difficulties . . . and How You Can
Be, Too* (Berkley Publishing Group, 1996). "When something new comes
along, their brain opens outward."

Plan of action

Try to be more curious and open to change in small ways so that when   10
major changes come along, or you choose to make them, you will have built
up some positive experiences. "Highly resilient people ask lots of questions,
want to know how things work," Siebert says. "They wonder about things,
experiment, make mistakes, get hurt, laugh."

Thinking Critically

❷ To what extent did your parents teach you how to cope with failure? Can you remember
a time when you had to "transcend life's difficulties"? How successful were you in doing so?

❸ In what ways is change a "normal part of life"? What could we all do to improve our
ability to adapt to change?

After a breakup, for example, they take a long-planned vacation rather   11
than staying home and wishing the relationship hadn't ended. If you are
playful and curious, you're more likely to react to an unwanted situation by
asking yourself, "What do I need to do to fix this? How can I use what
happened to my advantage?"

3. Do you learn from past experiences?

When he staffs a suicide hotline, Robert Blundo, Ph.D., a licensed social   12
worker and an associate professor at the University of North Carolina at
Wilmington, asks troubled callers to reflect on how they've survived past
crises. By thinking about and learning from your past successes, he says, you
can pinpoint the skills and strategies that will help you endure new crises.
The same is true with failure: By considering your past mistakes, you can learn
to avoid making the same ones again. [4] "People who are high in hardiness
learn very well from failure," Maddi says.

Plan of action

When difficult situations arise, ask yourself what skills and coping mechanisms   13
you used to survive tough times in the past. What supported you? Was it asking a spiritual advisor for help? What made it possible for you to cope? Taking
long bike rides? Writing in your journal? Getting help from a therapist? And
after you do weather a storm, analyze what brought it on. Say you were fired
from your job. "Ask yourself, 'What is the lesson here? What early clues did I
ignore?'" Siebert advises. Then, figure out how you might have handled the situation better. Perhaps you could have asked your boss for better training or
paid more attention to a poor performance review. Hindsight is 20/20: Use it!

4. Do you take responsibility for your troubles?

People who lack resilience tend to pin their problems on other people or   14
outside events. They blame their spouse for a bad marriage, their boss for a
crummy job, their genes for a health problem. Certainly, if someone does something terrible to you, he or she is at fault. But resilient people try to separate
themselves from the person or event that hurt them and make an effort to
move on. "It's not the situation but how you respond to it that matters," Siebert
says. If you tie your well being to another person, then the only way you'll feel
better is if the person who hurts you apologizes, and in many cases, that's not

---

Thinking Critically

[4] To what extent do you think most people learn from their failures? Give an example to
support your opinion.

likely. "A victim blames the situation," Siebert says. "A resilient person takes responsibility and says, 'How I respond to this is what counts.' " **5**

Plan of action

Instead of thinking about how you can get back at someone for hurting   15
you, ask yourself, "How can I make things better for myself?" If the promotion you desperately wanted goes to someone else, don't sit home blaming your boss, watching TV, and fantasizing about quitting. Instead, focus on finding a new job or transferring to another position in your company. Work toward letting go of your anger; that will free you to move on.

5. Are you actively committed to being more resilient?

Resilient people are steadfast in their dedication to bouncing back. "There   16
has to be some sense that if you don't have resilience, you'll look for it, and that if you do have it, you'll develop more," Greene says. In other words, some people are more resilient simply because they decide to be, and because they recognize that no matter what the situation, they alone can decide whether to meet a challenge head-on or cave in to it.

Plan of action

Talk to friends who are good at recovering quickly from adversity to find   17
out what works for them, read books about surviving difficulties, and think ahead about how you might respond resiliently in certain situations. When trying events do arise, slow down and ask yourself how a resilient person would respond. If you need help shoring up your resilience, consider seeing a therapist or social worker.

Most of all, be confident that you can change. "Sometimes it feels like it's   18
the end of the world," Blundo says. "But if you can step outside the situation and see that it's not, you can survive. Remember that you always have choices."

UNDERSTANDING DETAILS

1. What is the main characteristic of most survivors in American society?
2. Based on the questions in this essay, how resilient are you? What are your weakest areas? Your strongest areas? Explain your answer in detail.
3. According to Kelly, how can we learn to be resilient?
4. How is learning from your past experiences an important part of resilience?

Thinking Critically

5 According to the author, what is the difference between a "victim" and a "resilient person"?

READING CRITICALLY

5. What is the principal purpose of this essay? To what extent do you think it accomplishes its goals? Explain your answer.
6. Why do resilient people "choose action rather than passivity and empowerment over powerlessness" (paragraph 3)?
7. According to the author, how can mistakes help us learn?
8. How can our specific responses to stressful situations help define our character?

DISCOVERING RHETORICAL STRATEGIES

9. How does Kelly start her essay? Is this an effective beginning? Why or why not?
10. Describe in detail Kelly's intended audience. How did you come to this conclusion?
11. Analyze the author's use of questions and recommendations throughout this essay. How does this form help us see the relationship of resilience and success?
12. Is remembering that "you always have choices" an effective ending for this essay? Explain your answer. In what ways does this quotation from Professor Blundo give the author's message credibility?

MAKING CONNECTIONS

13. What do you think Kelly means by the term "resilience"? Compare and contrast her definition of the word with the way other authors might define it: Malcolm Cowley ("The View From 80"), Maya Angelou ("New Directions"), Scott Russell Sanders ("Homeplace"), and/or Dave Grossman ("We Are Training Our Kids to Kill").
14. Which of the following essays do you think most clearly displays Kelly's definition of being "tough" in a crisis: "Notes from the Country Club" (Kimberly Wozencraft), "A Brother's Murder" (Brent Staples), "The Broken Cord" (Michael Dorris), and/or "Beauty: When the Other Dancer is the Self" (Alice Walker)?
15. Imagine that Alice Kelly, Gloria Steinem ("The Politics of Muscle"), and/or Barrett Seaman ("How Bingeing Became the New College Sport") are having a discussion about the role of adversity in America. To what extent would each say that adversity contributes to the moral and ethical decay of our country?

IDEAS FOR DISCUSSION/WRITING

Preparing to Write

Write freely about your impressions of success today: Do you feel successful? What makes someone successful? What makes someone unsuccessful? What are your goals in life? Do you think you can realistically reach them? Do you adjust easily to your circumstances? Do you learn from past experiences? Do you embrace change? What are the strongest influences on the decisions you make as a student? What qualities are you trying to develop as a person? Why do you think these characteristics will make you a better human being?

Choosing a Topic

1. *Learning Online:* Kelly uses process analysis to suggest ways an individual can become resilient and, therefore, more successful in society. Using the information you discovered in Preparing to Read from an Internet search on famous people, choose one person, and write a process analysis essay outlining his or her rise to fame. How did that person become successful?

2. Take one of Kelly's suggestions and develop it into an essay explaining how to accomplish this particular recommendation. Flesh out the essay with as many details as possible.

3. A lack of resilience is evident throughout many aspects of American society. Where do you see examples of inflexibility? How can rigidity become the motivating force behind an organization or event? Write an essay suggesting how a company or organization can fail because of a lack of resilience.

4. One of your friends who is still in high school has asked you for information about social activities in college. Write to this friend, using process analysis to explain how to survive college while having a life full of outside activities. Decide on a purpose and a point of view before you begin to write.

Before beginning your essay, you might want to consult the checklists on page 212.

Learning to Read

Born Malcolm Little in Omaha, Nebraska, the author later changed his name to Malcolm X when he joined the Nation of Islam in 1953. He explained his new name by saying that the "X" stood for what he had been and what he had become: "Ex-smoker, Ex-drinker, Ex-Christian, Ex-slave." The "X" also represented the unknown original names of the slaves from whom he descended, as opposed to the fictitious names, which would have been given by the slaves'"owners." A Boston street hustler in his youth, he was arrested in 1946 at the age of twenty on charges of breaking and entering, carrying firearms, and larceny and sentenced to eight years in prison, where he learned to read and became fascinated with the Nation of Islam's leader, Elijah Muhammad. Upon his release, he was a changed man, giving fervent, inspirational speeches and rising to the number-two person in Muhammad's organization, with which he later became disenchanted. He was also responsible for inspiring the famous heavyweight champion Cassius Clay to join the Nation of Islam and change his name to Muhammad Ali. In 1963, he began collaboration with Alex Haley (author of *Roots*) on *The Autobiography of Malcolm X,* which was published soon after his assassination two years later. Malcolm X will be remembered as a controversial, charismatic leader who advocated black pride, economic self-reliance, and political involvement. His advice to students is to get the best possible education, which he calls "our passport to the future." He goes on to say, "Tomorrow belongs to the people who prepare for it today."

Preparing to Read

This excerpt was first published in 1964 in *The Autobiography of Malcolm X,* written by Malcolm X and Alex Haley. It illustrates Malcolm X's view of the world that was fostered by his insatiable appetite for reading.

Exploring Experience: As you prepare to read this essay, think about one activity that defines you and your current life: What is that activity? How does it define you? How has this activity enriched your life? What have you gained from this activity that would otherwise not have enriched your life?

Learning Online: While he was in prison, Malcolm X was exposed to more books than ever before in his life. Today, we have free public libraries, but with the increasing popularity of the Internet, many books in their full-text forms are also available online. Visit the Bibliomania Web site at www.bibliomania .com, and examine the immense selection of fiction, drama, poetry, and short stories. Click on "Fiction," and scroll through the list of available novels. How many of them have you read? Consider the benefits of reading a book online compared to holding the book in your hands.

It was because of my letters that I happened to stumble upon starting to   1
acquire some kind of a homemade education.

I became increasingly frustrated at not being able to express what I   2
wanted to convey in letters that I wrote, especially those to Mr. Elijah
Muhammad. In the street, I had been the most articulate hustler out there—
I had commanded attention when I said something. But now, trying to write
simple English, I not only wasn't articulate, I wasn't even functional. How
would I sound writing in slang, the way I would *say* it, something such as
"Look, daddy, let me pull your coat about a cat, Elijah Muhammad—" ◀1

Many who today hear me somewhere in person, or on television, or those   3
who read something I've said, will think I went to school far beyond the
eighth grade. This impression is due entirely to my prison studies.

It had really begun back in the Charlestown Prison, when Bimbi first   4
made me feel envy of his stock of knowledge. Bimbi had always taken charge
of any conversation he was in, and I had tried to emulate him. But every book
I picked up had few sentences which didn't contain anywhere from one to
nearly all of the words that might as well have been in Chinese. When I just
skipped those words, of course, I really ended up with little idea of what the
book said. So I had come to the Norfolk Prison Colony still going through
only book-reading motions. Pretty soon, I would have quit even these
motions, unless I had received the motivation that I did.

I saw that the best thing I could do was get hold of a dictionary—to study,   5
to learn some words. I was lucky enough to reason also that I should try to
improve my penmanship. It was sad. I couldn't even write in a straight line.
It was both ideas together that moved me to request a dictionary along with
some tablets and pencils from the Norfolk Prison Colony school.

I spent two days just riffling uncertainly through the dictionary's pages.   6
I'd never realized so many words existed! I didn't know which words I needed
to learn. Finally, just to start some kind of action, I began copying.

In my slow, painstaking, ragged handwriting, I copied into my tablet every-   7
thing printed on that first page, down to the punctuation marks.

I believe it took me a day. Then, aloud, I read back, to myself, everything   8
I'd written on the tablet. Over and over, aloud, to myself, I read my own
handwriting.

I woke up the next morning, thinking about those words—immensely   9
proud to realize that not only had I written so much at one time, but I'd written words that I never knew were in the world. Moreover, with a little effort,

---

Thinking Critically

◀1 Under what circumstances do you communicate in slang? How powerful is this form of
written communication in those situations?

I also could remember what many of these words meant. I reviewed the words whose meanings I didn't remember. Funny thing, from the dictionary first page right now, that "aardvark" springs to my mind. The dictionary had a picture of it, a long-tailed, long-eared, burrowing African mammal, which lives off termites caught by sticking out its tongue as an anteater does for ants. [2]

I was so fascinated that I went on—I copied the dictionary's next page. And the same experience came when I studied that. With every succeeding page, I also learned of people and places and events from history. Actually the dictionary is like a miniature encyclopedia. Finally the dictionary's A section had filled a whole tablet—and I went on into the B's. That was the way I started copying what eventually became the entire dictionary. It went a lot faster after so much practice helped me to pick up handwriting speed. Between what I wrote in my tablet, and writing letters, during the rest of my time in prison I would guess I wrote a million words.   10

I suppose it was inevitable that as my word-base broadened, I could for the first time pick up a book and read and now begin to understand what the book was saying. [3] Anyone who has read a great deal can imagine the new world that opened. Let me tell you something: from then until I left that prison, in every free moment I had, if I was not reading in the library, I was reading on my bunk. You couldn't have gotten me out of books with a wedge. Between Mr. Muhammad's teachings, my correspondence, my visitors—usually Ella and Reginald—and my reading of books, months passed without my even thinking about being imprisoned. In fact, up to then, I never had been so truly free in my life. [4]   11

The Norfolk Prison Colony's library was in the school building. A variety of classes was taught there by instructors who came from such places as Harvard and Boston universities. The weekly debates between inmate teams were also held in the school building. You would be astonished to know how worked up convict debaters and audiences would get over subjects like "Should Babies Be Fed Milk?"   12

Available on the prison library's shelves were books on just about every general subject. Much of the big private collection that Parkhurst had willed to the prison was still in crates and boxes in the back of the library—thousands of old books. Some of them looked ancient: covers faded, old-time   13

Thinking Critically

[2] Have you ever browsed through the dictionary? Do you think this would be an effective way of increasing your vocabulary? Why or why not?

[3] What is the relationship between the author's newfound interest in words and his appetite for reading?

[4] How does reading make Malcolm X feel "truly free" even though he is still in prison?

parchment-looking binding. Parkhurst, I've mentioned, seemed to have been principally interested in history and religion. He had the money and the special interest to have a lot of books that you wouldn't have in general circulation. Any college library would have been lucky to get that collection.

As you can imagine, especially in a prison where there was heavy emphasis on rehabilitation, ◈ an inmate was smiled upon if he demonstrated an unusually intense interest in books. There was a sizable number of well-read inmates, especially the popular debaters. Some were said by many to be practically walking encyclopedias. They were almost celebrities. No university would ask any student to devour literature as I did when this new world opened to me, of being able to read and *understand*.   14

I read more in my room than in the library itself. An inmate who was known to read a lot could check out more than the permitted maximum number of books. I preferred reading in the total isolation of my own room.   15

When I had progressed to really serious reading, every night at about ten P.M. I would be outraged with the "lights out." It always seemed to catch me right in the middle of something engrossing.   16

Fortunately, right outside my door was a corridor light that cast a glow into my room. The glow was enough to read by, once my eyes adjusted to it. So when "lights out" came, I would sit on the floor where I could continue reading in that glow.   17

At one-hour intervals the night guards paced past every room. Each time I heard the approaching footsteps, I jumped into bed and feigned sleep. And as soon as the guard passed, I got back out of bed onto the floor area of that light-glow, where I would read for another fifty-eight minutes—until the guard approached again. That went on until three or four every morning. Three or four hours of sleep a night was enough for me. Often in the years in the streets I had slept less than that.   18

The teachings of Mr. Muhammad stressed how history had been "whitened"—when white men had written history books, the black man simply had been left out. Mr. Muhammad couldn't have said anything that would have struck me much harder. I had never forgotten how when my class, me and all of those whites, had studied seventh-grade United States history back in Mason, the history of the Negro had been covered in one paragraph, and the teacher had gotten a big laugh with his joke, "Negroes' feet are so big that when they walk they leave a hole in the ground."   19

This is one reason why Mr. Muhammad's teachings spread so swiftly *all* over the United States, among *all* Negroes, whether or not they became followers of Mr. Muhammad. The teachings ring true—to every Negro. You can   20

Thinking Critically

◈ Do you think prisons actually rehabilitate their inmates? Why or why not?

hardly show me a black adult in America—or a white one, for that matter—who knows from the history books anything like the truth about the black man's role. [6] In my own case, once I heard of the "glorious history of the black man," I took special pains to hunt in the library for books that would inform me on details about black history.

I can remember accurately the very first set of books that really impressed   21
me. I have since bought that set of books and have it at home for my children to read as they grow up. It's called *Wonders of the World*. It's full of pictures of archeological finds, statues that depict, usually, non-European people.

I found books like Will Durant's *Story of Civilization*. I read H. G. Wells'   22
Outline of History. *Souls of Black Folk* by W. E. B. DuBois gave me a glimpse into the black people's history before they came to this country. Carter G. Woodson's *Negro History* opened my eyes about black empires before the black slave was brought to the United States, and the early Negro struggles for freedom.

J. A. Rogers' three volumes of *Sex and Race* told about race mixing before   23
Christ's time; about Aesop being a black man who told fables; about Egypt's Pharaohs; about the great Coptic Christian Empires; about Ethiopia, the earth's oldest continuous black civilization, as China is the oldest continuous civilization.

Mr. Muhammad's teaching about how the white man had been created   24
led me to *Findings in Genetics* by Gregor Mendel. (The dictionary's G section was where I had learned what "genetics" meant.) I really studied this book by the Austrian monk. Reading it over and over, especially certain sections, helped me to understand that if you started with a black man, a white man could be produced; but starting with a white man, you never could produce a black man—because the white gene is recessive. And since no one disputes that there was but one Original Man, the conclusion is clear. [7]

During the last year or so, in the *New York Times,* Arnold Toynbee used the   25
word "bleached" in describing the white man. (His words were "White (i.e., bleached) human beings of North European origin. . . .") Toynbee also referred to the European geographic area as only a peninsula of Asia. He said there is no such thing as Europe. And if you look at the globe, you will see for yourself that America is only an extension of Asia. (But at the same time Toynbee is among those who have helped to bleach history. He has written that Africa was the only continent that produced no history. He won't write that again. Every day now, the truth is coming to light.)

Thinking Critically

[6] Return to Preparing to Read to find out when this essay was written. Do you think the author's conclusions about the lack of black history in textbooks are still true today?

[7] What is the author's argument concerning the relationship between the recessive nature of the white gene and the origins of life? What evidence does he offer to support his reasoning?

I never will forget how shocked I was when I began reading about slavery's   26
total horror. It made such an impact upon me that it later became one of my
favorite subjects when I became a minister of Mr. Muhammad's. The world's
most monstrous crime, the sin and the blood on the white man's hands, are
almost impossible to believe. Books like the one by Frederick Olmstead
opened my eyes to the horrors suffered when the slave was landed in the
United States. The European woman, Fannie Kimball, who had married a
Southern white slaveowner, described how human beings were degraded. Of
course I read *Uncle Tom's Cabin*. In fact, I believe that's the only novel I have
ever read since I started serious reading. ⁸

Parkhurst's collection also contained some bound pamphlets of the   27
Abolitionist Anti-Slavery Society of New England. I read descriptions of
atrocities, saw those illustrations of black slave women tied up and flogged
with whips; of black mothers watching their babies being dragged off,
never to be seen by their mothers again; of dogs after slaves, and of the
fugitive slave catchers, evil white men with whips and clubs and chains
and guns. I read about the slave preacher Nat Turner, who put the fear of
God into the white slavemaster. Nat Turner wasn't going around preaching pie-in-the-sky and "non-violent" freedom for the black man. There in
Virginia one night in 1831, Nat and seven other slaves started out at his
master's home and through the night they went from one plantation "big
house" to the next, killing, until by the next morning 57 white people
were dead and Nat had about 70 slaves following him. White people,
terrified for their lives, fled from their homes, locked themselves up in
public buildings, hid in the woods, and some even left the state. A small
army of soldiers took two months to catch and hang Nat Turner. Somewhere I have read where Nat Turner's example is said to have inspired John
Brown to invade Virginia and attack Harper's Ferry nearly thirty years later,
with thirteen white men and five Negroes.

I read Herodotus, "the father of History," or, rather, I read about him. And   28
I read the histories of various nations, which opened my eyes gradually, then
wider and wider, to how the whole world's white men had indeed acted
like devils, pillaging and raping and bleeding and draining the whole world's
nonwhite people. I remember, for instance, books such as Will Durant's story
of Oriental civilization, and Mahatma Gandhi's accounts of the struggle to
drive the British out of India.

Book after book showed me how the white man had brought upon the   29
world's black, brown, red, and yellow peoples every variety of the sufferings of
exploitation. I saw how since the sixteenth century, the so-called "Christian

---

Thinking Critically

⁸ Have you ever read *Uncle Tom's Cabin?* Why was this novel so interesting to Malcolm X?

trader" white man began to ply the seas in his lust for Asian and African empires, and plunder, and power. I read, I saw, how the white man never has gone among the non-white peoples bearing the Cross in the true manner and spirit of Christ's teachings—meek, humble, and Christ-like.

I perceived, as I read, how the collective white man had been actually   30
nothing but a piratical opportunist who used Faustian machinations to make his own Christianity his initial wedge in criminal conquests. ◆9 First, always "religiously," he branded "heathen" and "pagan" labels upon ancient non-white cultures and civilizations. The stage thus set, he then turned upon his non-white victims his weapons of war.

I read how, entering India—half a *billion* deeply religious brown people—   31
the British white man, by 1759, through promises, trickery and manipulations, controlled much of India through Great Britain's East India Company. The parasitical British administration kept tentacling out to half of the subcontinent. In 1857, some of the desperate people of India finally mutinied—and, excepting the African slave trade, nowhere has history recorded any more unnecessary bestial and ruthless human carnage than the British suppression of the non-white Indian people.

Over 115 million African blacks—close to the 1930s population of the   32
United States—were murdered or enslaved during the slave trade. And I read how when the slave market was glutted, the cannibalistic ◆10 white powers of Europe next carved up, as their colonies, the richest areas of the black continent. And Europe's chancelleries for the next century played a chess game of naked exploitation and power from Cape Horn to Cairo.

Ten guards and the warden couldn't have torn me out of those books. Not   33
even Elijah Muhammad could have been more eloquent than those books were in providing indisputable proof that the collective white man had acted like a devil in virtually every contact he had with the world's collective non-white man. I listen today to the radio, and watch television, and read the headlines about the collective white man's fear and tension concerning China. When the white man professes ignorance about why the Chinese hate him so, my mind can't help flashing back to what I read, there in prison, about how the blood forebears of this same white man raped China at a time when China was trusting and helpless. Those original white "Christian traders" sent into China millions of pounds of opium. By 1839, so many of the Chinese were addicts that China's desperate government destroyed twenty thousand chests of opium. The first Opium War was promptly declared by the white man. Imagine! Declaring war upon someone who objects to

---

Thinking Critically

◆9 With what "criminal conquests" does the author charge white men?
◆10 In what way were the white powers of Europe "cannibalistic"?

being narcotized! The Chinese were severely beaten, with Chinese-invented gunpowder.

The Treaty of Nanking made China pay the British white man for the destroyed opium; forced open China's major ports to British trade; forced China to abandon Hong Kong; fixed China's import tariffs so low that cheap British articles soon flooded in, maiming China's industrial development. 34

After a second Opium War, the Tientsin Treaties legalized the ravaging opium trade, legalized a British-French-American control of China's customs. China tried delaying that Treaty's ratification; Peking was looted and burned. 35

"Kill the foreign white devils!" was the 1901 Chinese war cry in the Boxer Rebellion. Losing again, this time the Chinese were driven from Peking's choicest areas. The vicious, arrogant white man put up the famous signs, "Chinese and dogs not allowed." 36

Red China after World War II closed its doors to the Western white world. Massive Chinese agricultural, scientific, and industrial efforts are described in a book that *Life* magazine recently published. Some observers inside Red China have reported that the world never has known such a hate-white campaign as is now going on in this non-white country where, present birth-rates continuing, in fifty more years Chinese will be half the earth's population. And it seems that some Chinese chickens will soon come home to roost, with China's recent successful nuclear tests. 37

Let us face reality. We can see in the United Nations a new world order being shaped, along color lines—an alliance among the non-white nations. [11] America's U.N. Ambassador Adlai Stevenson complained not long ago that in the United Nations "a skin game" was being played. He was right. He was facing reality. A "skin game" is being played. But Ambassador Stevenson sounded like Jesse James accusing the marshal of carrying a gun. Because who in the world's history ever has played a worse "skin game" than the white man? 38

Mr. Muhammad, to whom I was writing daily, had no idea of what a new world had opened up to me through my efforts to document his teachings in books. 39

When I discovered philosophy, I tried to touch all the landmarks of philosophical development. Gradually, I read most of the old philosophers, Occidental and Oriental. The Oriental philosophers were the ones I came to prefer; finally, my impression was that most Occidental philosophy had largely been borrowed from the Oriental thinkers. Socrates, for instance, traveled in Egypt. Some sources even say that Socrates was initiated into some of the Egyptian mysteries. Obviously Socrates got some of his wisdom among the East's wise men. 40

Thinking Critically

[11] Do you think this assertion is still true? Is a new world order "being shaped along color lines"? To what extent is this true in the Middle East? In other countries?

I have often reflected upon the new vistas that reading opened to me. [12]   41
I knew right there in prison that reading had changed forever the course of
my life. As I see it today, the ability to read awoke inside me some long
dormant craving to be mentally alive. I certainly wasn't seeking any degree,
the way a college confers a status symbol upon its students. My homemade
education gave me, with every additional book that I read, a little bit more
sensitivity to the deafness, dumbness, and blindness that was afflicting
the black race in America. Not long ago, an English writer telephoned me
from London, asking questions. One was, "What's your alma mater?" I told
him, "Books." You will never catch me with a free fifteen minutes in which
I'm not studying something I feel might be able to help the black man.

Yesterday I spoke in London, and both ways on the plane across the   42
Atlantic I was studying a document about how the United Nations pro-
poses to insure the human rights of the oppressed minorities of the world.
The American black man is the world's most shameful case of minority
oppression. What makes the black man think of himself as only an internal
United States issue is just a catch-phrase, two words, "civil rights." How is the
black man going to get "civil rights" before first he wins his human rights?
If American black man will start thinking about his *human* rights, and then
start thinking of himself as part of one of the world's greatest peoples, he
will see he has a case for the United Nations.

I can't think of a better case! Four hundred years of black blood and sweat   43
invested here in America, and the white man still has the black man begging
for what every immigrant fresh off the ship can take for granted the minute
he walks down the gangplank.

But I'm digressing. I told the Englishman that my alma mater was books,   44
a good library. Every time I catch a plane, I have with me a book that I want
to read—and that's a lot of books these days. If I weren't out here every day
battling the white man, I could spend the rest of my life reading, just satisfying
my curiosity—because you can hardly mention anything I'm not curious
about. I don't think anybody ever got more out of going to prison than I did.
In fact, prison enabled me to study far more intensively than I would have
if my life had gone differently and I had attended some college. I imagine
that one of the biggest troubles with colleges is there are too many distractions, too much panty-raiding, fraternities, and boola-boola and all of that.
Where else but prison could I have attacked my ignorance by being able to
study intensely sometimes as much as fifteen hours a day? [13]

Thinking Critically

[12] What "new vistas" did reading open for Malcolm X? What vistas has reading opened for you?

[13] What does Malcolm X think he gained by going to prison? How did the prison experience change his life?

UNDERSTANDING DETAILS

1. Why did Malcolm X start to educate himself?
2. What does Malcolm X mean by the phrase "homemade education" (paragraph 1)?
3. In what ways is the dictionary like an encyclopedia? What did Malcolm X learn from copying the dictionary pages?
4. Name three details that Malcolm X learned about "slavery's total horror" (paragraph 26)?

READING CRITICALLY

5. What does Malcolm X mean when he says, "Four hundred years of black blood and sweat invested here in America, and the white man still has the black man begging for what every immigrant fresh off the ship takes for granted the minute he walks down the gangplank" (paragraph 43)?
6. Why did reading make Malcolm X feel "truly free" (paragraph 11)?
7. Why do you think debating was so popular in prison?
8. How does Malcolm X characterize the relationship between whites and nonwhites in his reading? What is the main conflict according to the author?

DISCOVERING RHETORICAL STRATEGIES

9. Malcolm X starts this essay with a one-sentence paragraph. What effect does this beginning have on you?
10. In what way does Malcolm X feel white people misused Christianity in their treatment of the nonwhite population? How does the author use examples to make this case?
11. Malcolm X names actual books that he read and explains what impression they made on him. Is this an effective way to document his understanding of history? What do all these examples demonstrate? What other way could the author have explained his experience? Would this way have been more or less effective than giving examples from his reading?
12. In what way does Malcolm X make a comparison between African Americans and the Chinese?

MAKING CONNECTIONS

13. Compare and contrast Malcolm X's awakening about his ethnic and racial identity with similar experiences by Lewis Sawaquat ("For My Indian Daughter"), Sandra Cisneros ("Only daughter"), and/or Sucheng Chan ("You're Short, Besides!"). Which author seems most devoted to his or her personal identity? Why do you think this is so?
14. How does the act of reading bring enlightenment to Malcolm X, Sherman Alexie ("The Joy of Reading and Writing: Superman and Me"), and/or Richard Wright ("The Library Card")?
15. How is the time spent in prison different for Malcolm X and Kimberly Wozencraft ("Notes from the Country Club")? Which author used his or her time more effectively? Why do you think this is so?

IDEAS FOR DISCUSSION/WRITING

Preparing to Write

Write freely about the topics that stimulate your curiosity: What fuels this curiosity? How does this desire to learn and understand affect your development as a person? What would you be like without this basic curiosity?

Choosing a Topic

1. *Learning Online:* For a number of different reasons, publishers may no longer print books in hard copy someday. Even now, more and more reading material is being made available online. Write an essay about the process you would go through to read a novel online. What computer would you use? How would you take notes on what you read if you wanted to? Revisit the Bibliomania Web site (www.bibliomania.com) to get an idea of this experience.

2. What one activity captures you as a person? How does this activity represent you? Write an essay explaining to your classmates how this activity defines your personality.

3. Malcolm X is quite clear about how his view of the world took shape through a combination of prison and reading. Write an essay explaining what has contributed most dramatically to your perspective on life. What is that perspective? In what way does it make you a unique human being?

4. List five books, articles, essays, or comic books that you have read recently, and in a coherent essay, explain their effect on you and your view of the world.

Before beginning your essay, you might want to consult the checklists on page 212.

JULIA BOURLAND   (1970–   )

Getting Out of Debt (and Staying Out)

Born and raised in Dallas, Texas, Julia Bourland moved to California in 1989, where she graduated from Mills College with a B.A. in Political Science. A full-time writer, she is the author of two extremely popular books—*The Go-Girl Guide: Surviving Your 20s with Savvy, Soul, and Style* (2000) and *Hitched: The Go-Girl Guide to the First Year of Marriage* (2003)—along with numerous articles in such periodicals as *Bride's Magazine, Shape,* 7 × 7, *Parenting,* and many others. Her past positions include Senior Producer of the Relationships Channel at Women.com and Associate Editor of *Parenting* magazine. Bourland currently lives near San Francisco, where she is working on her third book. Recently married, she enjoys hiking, cycling, running, and practicing yoga. Her advice to students using *The Prose Reader* is to "allow yourself time every day just for unedited, free-flowing writing. Twenty minutes in the morning or evening can really open up any blockage you may be experiencing, especially knowing that this writing doesn't 'count.' By that, I mean that no one ever has to see it. Don't get out of the habit. It's like going to the gym—you've got to do it every day, or else you start mentally resisting it. Also, read other good writers for inspiration."

Preparing to Read

The following essay, from a book called *The Go-Girl Guide: Surviving Your 20s with Savvy, Soul, and Style,* offers extremely helpful advice for getting and staying out of debt. With national credit card interest payments in the trillions of dollars each year and with students getting multiple credit card offers even before they graduate, everyone can use a little help in this area.

Exploring Experience: As you prepare to read this essay, take a few minutes to think about money in general: Which do you enjoy more: making or spending money? Do you work? If so, do you feel you are paid fairly? Are you comfortable spending money? Do you ever buy on credit? Do you have trouble limiting your spending to the money you earn? How much difficulty do you have controlling your spending?

Learning Online: Visit the Motley Fool Web site (www.fool.com), and type "debt" into the search bar, or go to your campus financial-aid Web site. Read a few paragraphs describing ways to get out of debt or methods for paying student loans. How do the techniques suggested in these Web sites differ from Bourland's advice?

I'm going to make the bold assumption that you have incurred a little debt   1
during your great entrance into adulthood, from either student loans,
devilish credit cards, or that car loan you recently signed with its 36 easy
installment payments. If you haven't tasted debt, you are abnormally perfect
and un-American and can just skip on down to the next section on retirement planning and chill out until the rest of us catch up with you. ◆[1]

Some debt, such as student loans, is money well borrowed and an invest-   2
ment in your future. Because of their relatively low interest rates, manageable
(though seemingly eternal) repayment plans, and reasonable deferment
options, student loans should not be the source of midnight panic attacks
during your second semester of senior year, even if you've incurred thousands
and thousands of dollars to fund your education and still don't have a job that
suggests that all the debt was worth it. If you haven't graduated yet, toward
the end of your final semester, your college student loan officer will give
you all the dirty details of your repayment schedule (hopefully armed with
ample tissue for the tears that are certain to flood your contacts), as well as
tell you how to defer paying back your loans if you aren't employed by the
time your repayment grace period is up, as was my case. The cheery thing I
discovered about deferring repayment is that the groovy government actually paid the interest I owed during my six-month deferment. That's not the
case with all student loans, but you'll find that out when you start reading
the fine print.

If you're like me, you may have several loans to repay. Again, you proba-   3
bly got (or will get) the skinny from your financial aid administrator at college, but in case he or she is on drugs, I'll summarize. There are a few
consolidation plans that can make the whole process of paying back your
loans less horrifying. Consolidating means that you will be able to merge all
of your loans into one giant superloan that offers a low interest rate, as well
as various options for shortening or lengthening your repayment schedule
(which will increase or decrease the amount you owe each month, thereby
increasing or decreasing the amount of interest you ultimately end up paying). But the best reason to consolidate your loans is that you will receive only
one bill every month, which means you have to think and stress about all the
student loan money you owe only once every 30 days! I highly recommend
consolidation, if only for that.

If you have several loans from one financial institution, contact your lender   4
directly about its consolidation options, or try these two programs: Federal

---

Thinking Critically

◆[1] What does Bourland mean by the terms "devilish credit cards" and "un-American"? How
do they help set the tone and direction of her essay?

Direct Consolidation Loan Program (800-557-7392; www.ed.gov/directloan) and Student Loan Marketing Association (a.k.a. Sallie Mae) Smart Loan Account (800-524-9100; www.salliemae.com).

Student loans are much less threatening and guilt-provoking than credit   5
card debt, to which we 20-somethings are painfully vulnerable. ❷ There are so many things we want and need. Credit card companies seize upon our vulnerability, especially during college, sending us application after application with such enticing incentives as a *free water bottle, a two-pound bag of M & Ms, a 10% discount* on first purchases, *free checks* to spend anywhere we please, our very own *head shot* on the card, a *4.9% introductory interest rate,* and *bonus airline miles.* My first advice on the whole matter of credit card debt is to avoid it like the devil! I know many honest, smart girls who've become submerged in debt through the seductive power of plastic.

Our society once thrived without credit, so it *is* possible to stay out of debt   6
as we begin our adult lives. But since you will probably experiment with credit despite the danger, memorize these eight guidelines compliments of those who've battled the plastic demons:

#1: No Department Store Credit Cards

In-store credit usually carries a much higher interest rate than credit cards   7
issued by banks. If you don't pay your debt back right away, what you buy is going to cost you much more than you bargained for. The only exception is if you have money to pay off your debt as soon as the bill arrives, and signing up for a card gives you a substantial discount on your first purchase. In these cases, get the card (and discount), pay your bill in full, and immediately cancel the card and shred it into a million pieces, lest you be tempted to use it again without the discount and money to pay for it. Note: If the discount isn't more than $10 or 20, don't even bother, because when you sign on, you'll probably get put on some annoying direct-mail list that will be sold to a bunch of trashy companies who will send you junk mail every single day.

#2: One Card Only

The fewer little plastic rectangles you have, the less you'll be tempted to   8
live beyond your meager means (and the fewer hysteria-provoking bills ❸ you'll receive). Ideally, you should use your card only for items that you know you can pay off with your next paycheck or for unavoidable emergencies, like

---

Thinking Critically

❷ Why do you think "20-somethings" are so "painfully vulnerable" to credit card debt?

❸ Have you ever received a "hysteria-provoking" bill? What is the relationship the author is suggesting between credit cards and "hysteria-provoking bills"?

getting new brakes for your clunker or fillings for your insatiable sweet tooth. The ideal cards have fixed annual percentage rates ranging from 9 to 12 percent, or less if you can find them, no annual fee, and a grace period that doesn't start charging interest on what you buy until the bill's due date. If you are a conscientious customer, you will be inundated with appealing offers for new cards boasting Platinum status and $25,000 credit lines. When you receive these, gingerly toss them into the recycling bin. Opening them will only lead you into trouble. There is one exception to this rule, but I'll get to that when we talk about transferring balances. First, a few more basic tips.

#3: Use Your ATM Credit/Debit Card Instead

If you're diligent about balancing your checkbook, there's no reason to fear the credit card capabilities of your ATM card, which most banks are offering these days. Keep the receipt for whatever you purchase with your card as you would had you withdrawn money from the bank, and record the amount in your checkbook ledger as you would a check. Your debit card is just as convenient as a credit card, but your purchase won't accrue interest, which will save you money. Definitely use your debit card instead of a real credit card when grocery shopping or buying little things at the pharmacy, unless you like the idea of paying 18 percent interest on cereal and tampons. Trust your elders: the interest on all the little things makes them as costly as a raging girls' night out.   9

#4: Pay Back as Much as You Can, as Soon as You Can

If we take the *minimum* payment request on our monthly statements to heart, we may not pay off our account in full until we qualify for social security. That's because interest continues to accrue on our balance each month. If we don't pay off everything we owe, the remainder plus the interest we've amassed will be charged interest the following month and the month after that, which means our balance continues to grow at the speed of our card's annual percentage rate (APR) despite the fact that we pay our minimum due every month and have hidden our credit card in the closet under five shoe boxes. That's how credit card companies make so much money and why we should avoid getting into debt in every humanly possible (but legal) way.   10

If you have debt from several sources, pay back whatever has higher interest rates first—usually your credit cards—then tackle the typically lower-rated student loan and car loan debts. ◆ If your credit card debt is spiraling out of control, you could refinance your student or car loans so that you will owe   11

Thinking Critically

4 Do you know the interest rates you are paying on all your debts? Which is highest? Which is lowest? Why are these rates important?

less on them each month, using the extra money to pay off your credit cards. Then, when your costlier debts have been paid off (and cards dumped in the nearest incinerator), you can designate all your funds to paying back your temporarily neglected student and car loans as quickly as you can.

#5: Trash Those Credit Card Checks That Come with Your Statement, and Shun Cash Advances from the ATM

Both checks and cash advances will cost you dearly, since many card   12 companies tack on an additional finance charge to your bill when you use them, plus impose an interest rate for the amount you borrow that's much higher than the rate you have for normal purchases. That means that if you withdraw $100 from your card at a bank or ATM or use one of those checks for your rent, you'll be paying back your credit card company a lot more than the amount you borrowed.

#6: Switch to a Card with a Lower Interest Rate

I said earlier that you should throw away offers for additional credit cards,   13 and that is a good rule unless you are carrying a balance on a card (or cards) with an outrageous interest rate, say more than 12 percent. In that case, it's a good financial move to transfer your balance(s) to one card with the lowest rate you can find. Some offer temporary introductory interest rates as low as 2.9 percent on all transferred balances; when you apply, make sure you note the expiration date for those low rates on your calendar, and have another card offer lined up and ready to take on the load when the time comes. I know this sounds tedious, but careful organization and diligence will save you money as you attempt to pay the whole balance off.

If you play credit card musical chairs, keep three things in mind. [5] First,   14 some balance transfer offers have associated fees or finance charges that aren't exactly highlighted in their promotions. Always inquire about transfer fees, and try to talk them out of it; many issuers are willing to waive the fees upon request. Second, even after you transfer your balance in full, the account remains open. To close it, you must officially cancel. The issuing bank won't automatically cancel a zero-balance account, so if you don't, your access to that credit line will remain on your credit report. That could be problematic later on when you're applying for a mortgage and have thousands of dollars worth of potential debt in your financial profile—something that makes lenders skittish. The other reason to cancel is to avoid the temptation to start using that clean slate of credit that your old card suddenly presents. And the third caveat: when you transfer your balance, do not use this new card to purchase new things.

Thinking Critically
[5] What does the author mean by the term "credit card musical chairs"?

Declare it a debt repayment card only, and stick that shiny piece of plastic in the file where you keep your monthly statements. Here's why:

When you charge new items on a card that has adopted old debt, many card issuers apply a different (and uber-exorbitant) interest rate to those new purchases. The higher interest rate will remain on the amount of your new purchases until your entire debt has been repaid. Therefore, when you are trying to pay off a large debt, you should try to have two credit cards—one with a very low balance-transfer interest rate for your main debt and another with a reasonable interest rate on new purchases that you will use for emergencies only, since you are, after all, trying to get out of the hole, not rack up new debt. A good resource for finding low-rate, no-fee cards is a company called CardWeb.com, Inc., which publishes a newsletter called CardTrak that lists these desirable cards. You can access the newsletter and other credit card consumer information on its website (www.cardweb.com) or by calling (800) 344-7714.

#7: Apply for a Secured Credit Card If Your Credit Is Screwed

If you have damaged your credit rating by defaulting on a loan or debt, your main priority (besides coming up with a repayment plan that suits all your creditors) is to rebuild your credit. Secured credit cards can help. You give the issuer a certain sum of money up front, which is kept in an account for you as a security deposit. Depending on the terms of your agreement, you can then charge a specified amount on that card. Once you've proved that you can repay your debts in this secured way, you may be offered a new card with real credit that doesn't require you to put up money ahead of time. CardWeb.com, Inc. (cited in the previous entry) can provide a list of secured credit cards as well as low-rate, no-fee cards.

If you are in a bad situation and creditors are calling you about monster debt that you can't currently pay off, don't pack up and move to North Dakota, thinking creditors won't be able to find you—they will. A couple of nonprofit credit counseling organizations can help with debt-repayment planning assistance: Consumer Credit Counseling Services, associated with the National Foundation for Consumer Credit (800-388-2227; www.nfcc.org), and Debt Counselors of America (800-698-3782; www.dca.org).

#8: Check Your Credit Report

I've already expounded on why a clean credit report is so important, so I won't beat that dead horse, [6] but I will add that it's wise to check up on your report every now and then to make sure there are no surprises (or mistakes)

Thinking Critically

[6] What is the meaning of the metaphor "to beat a dead horse"?

that need mending. There are three agencies that compile credit reports, and they all get their information separately, so what one company says is part of your credit history may differ from what another company includes. You can get copies of your credit report from each company for $8 or less, depending on your state of residence. If you have had bad credit in the past but believe you've been exonerated (usually after seven years), you should make sure all three companies are showing you in the proper light.

The three agencies keeping tabs are Experian (formerly TRW) (888-397- 3742, www.experian.com/ecommerce/consumercredit.html); Equifax (800-685-1111, www.econsumer.equifax.com); and Trans Union (800-888-4213, www.transunion.com/Personal/PersonalSolutions.jsp).

19

UNDERSTANDING DETAILS

1. According to Bourland, what types of debts are worthwhile?
2. What does "consolidating loans" (paragraph 3) mean? What are the benefits of consolidating loans?
3. What are Bourland's eight guidelines for avoiding credit card debt? Summarize each guideline.
4. How can you check your credit rating?

READING CRITICALLY

5. Have you incurred any debts in your life so far? Explain your answer by giving specifics.
6. Why does Bourland think debts are a normal part of life?
7. Why are young adults especially vulnerable to credit card debt?
8. Which of Bourland's guidelines are most likely to help you now and in the future? Explain your answer.

DISCOVERING RHETORICAL STRATEGIES

9. How would you characterize the tone of this essay? What specific details bring you to this conclusion?
10. Who do you think is Bourland's primary audience in this essay? On what do you base your answer?
11. What method does Bourland use to organize her advice in this essay?
12. What other rhetorical strategies, besides process analysis, does Bourland use to strengthen her argument about handling debt? Give an example of each of these strategies.

MAKING CONNECTIONS

13. Compare and contrast the advice Julia Bourland provides about managing your money with similar suggestions by Jay Walljasper about managing your time. Which type of advice will be most useful to you in the future? Why do you think so?

14. How is Bourland's description of the process of staying out of debt similar to the process of embalming dead bodies described by Jessica Mitford in "Behind the Formaldehyde Curtain"? Which process seems most difficult to you? Explain your answer.

15. What advice would K. C. Cole ("Calculated Risks") give to Julia Bourland about the risks and rewards of money management? Which of these two authors would be more likely to make a big financial gamble in her life? Explain your answer.

IDEAS FOR DISCUSSION/WRITING

Preparing to Write

Write freely about your spending habits: Do you spend money wisely? Do you usually spend more than you make? How do you establish limits for your spending? Do you follow these limits? Have you built up a lot of debt? How do you plan to pay off this debt?

Choosing a Topic

1. *Learning Online:* Using Bourland's essay as a model, write an article entitled "How I Got into Debt," "How I Stay Out of Debt," or "How I Plan to Stay Out of Debt." Where applicable, cite websites that either provide additional resources or support your claims. Revisit Motley Fool (www.fool.com) or your campus financial-aid Web site to get started.

2. Debt is widespread in contemporary American society, especially among college students. As a result, your college newspaper is running a special series of articles focusing on debt in college. Find out as much as you can about this problem, its causes, and its solutions, and write an article for your campus newspaper on the various causes of student debt and some ways to avoid it.

3. Most people hope to find a job that fulfills and interests them as their lives progress. However, they generally don't start out with the job of their dreams. Write a letter to a high school student offering realistic advice on securing a good job during college.

4. Using Hansen's advice, explain what characterizes successful money management in your opinion. Direct your essay to college students.

Before beginning your essay, you might want to consult the checklists on page 212.

Chapter Writing Assignments

Practicing Process Analysis

1. Make a list of some of the activities you do well. Choose one activity, and think about exactly what you must do to perform this skill. Write an essay that describes to another person the process of doing this activity well. Be as specific and clear in your directions as you can.

2. Identify a task or responsibility that seems impossible for you to do well. What keeps you from performing this task with skill or efficiency? Write an essay that describes how to fail at this activity. Describe this method for failure in a humorous or sarcastic manner.

3. What is your best method for solving major life problems? Think of times in your life when you have had to solve a problem or make an important decision. Write an essay that explains to a person looking for problem-solving ideas the method you rely on when faced with important problems that need to be solved.

Exploring Ideas

4. How do you think your ability to manage money affects your daily life? Do you think this ability has mostly positive or negative effects on your lifestyle? Use specific examples to support your opinion.

5. Find a recent advertisement on television, in the newspaper, on a billboard, or on the radio that you think is especially successful. Examine this ad, and write an essay explaining its success. What makes it good? Whom does it reach? How effectively does it address its target population?

6. Should we "force" students to stay in school until the age of sixteen, or should we allow students who do not choose to go to school the right to drop out before they finish high school? Respond to these questions in an organized essay.

Writing from Sources

For detailed information on writing from sources, see Part III.

7. Choose a person in modern history who exhibited success in the face of adversity. Research his or her life. Is there anything notable about this person's early family life? What is his or her professional life like? From where does he or she draw motivation? How does this person handle hardship? Then, using examples from your research, write a documented essay explaining the qualities you believe foster and encourage success.

8. How do most people relax? What are the health benefits associated with relaxation? Consider the standard work week and vacation practices of the United States. How do they compare to those in other countries? Research this topic and present your evidence in a documented essay discussing the advantages or disadvantages of relaxation on a person's physical and mental health.

Analyzing Visual Images

© Michael Greco, www.visionlightgallery.com.

9. How do you achieve complete relaxation? Provide a step-by-step guide to accomplishing the kind of tranquility you see in the photograph.
10. Look at the picture on page 204 at the beginning of this chapter. Imagine having to explain the steps of surfing to someone who knows nothing about the sport. Think of a sport you know well, and try to explain the basic rules of that activity to someone who knows little or nothing about it.

Chapter 8

DIVISION/CLASSIFICATION
Finding Categories

Both division and classification play important roles in our everyday lives: Bureau drawers separate one type of clothing from another; kitchen cabinets and drawers organize food, dishes, and utensils into groups; grocery stores shelve similar items together so shoppers can easily locate what they want to buy; school notebooks with tabs help students divide up their academic lives; newspapers classify local and national events in order to organize a great deal of daily information for the general public; and our own personal classification systems assist us in separating what we like from what we don't so that we can have access to our favorite foods, our favorite cars, our favorite entertainment, our favorite people. The two processes of division and classification are so natural to us, in fact, that we sometimes aren't even aware that we are using them.

DEFINING DIVISION/CLASSIFICATION

Division and classification are actually mirror images of each other. Division is the basic feature of process analysis, which we studied in the last chapter; it moves from a general concept to subdivisions of that concept or from a single category to multiple subcategories. Classification works in the opposite direction, moving from specifics to a group with common traits or from multiple subgroups to a single, larger, and more inclusive category. These techniques work together in many ways: A college, for example, is *divided* into departments (single to multiple), whereas courses are *classified* by department (multiple to single); the medical field is *divided* into specialties, whereas doctors are *classified* by a single specialty; a cookbook is *divided* into chapters, whereas recipes are *classified* according to type; and athletics is *divided* into specific sports, whereas athletes are *classified* by the sport in which they participate. Division is the separation of an idea or an item into its basic parts, such as a home into rooms, a course into assignments, or a job into various duties or responsibilities; classification is the organization of items with similar features into a group or groups, such as finding all green-eyed people in a large group, omitting all carbohydrates from your diet, or watching only the track and field events during the Olympics.

Classification is an organizational system for presenting a large amount of material to a reader or listener. This process helps us make sense of the complex world we live in by letting us work with smaller, more understandable units of that world. Classification must be governed by some clear, logical purpose (such as focusing on all lower-division course requirements), which will then dictate the system of categories to be used. The plan of organization that results should be as flexible as possible, and it should illustrate the specific relationships of items in a group and of the groups themselves to one another.

As you already know, many different ways of classifying the same elements are possible. If you consider the examples at the outset of this chapter, you will realize that bureau drawers vary from house to house and even from person to person; that no one's kitchen is set up exactly the same way as someone else's; and that grocery stores have similar but not identical systems of classification. (Think, for instance, of the many different schemes for organizing dairy products, meats, foreign foods, etc.) In addition, your friends probably use a method different from yours to organize their school notebooks; different newspapers vary their presentation of the news; and two professors will probably teach the same course material in separate ways. We all have distinct and uniquely logical methods of classifying the elements in our own lives.

The following student paragraph about friends illustrates both division and classification. As you read it, notice how the student writer moves back and forth smoothly from general to specific and from multiple to single:

> The word friend *can refer to many different types of relationships. Close friends are "friends" at their very best: people for whom we feel respect, esteem, and, quite possibly, even love. We regard these people and their well being with kindness, interest, and goodwill; we trust them and will go out of our way to help them. Needless to say, we could all use at least one close friend. Next come*

"casual friends," people with whom we share a particular interest or activity. The investment of a great amount of time and energy in developing this type of friendship is usually not required, though casual friends often become close friends with the passage of time. The last division of "friend" is most general and is composed of all those individuals whose acquaintance we have made and who feel no hostility toward us. When one is counting friends, this group should certainly be included, since such friendships often develop into "casual" or "close" relationships. Knowing people in all three groups is necessary, however, because all types of friends undoubtedly help us live healthier, happier lives.

THINKING CRITICALLY THROUGH DIVISION/CLASSIFICATION

The thinking strategies of division and classification are the flip sides of each other: Your textbook is *divided* into chapters (one item divided into many), but chapters are *classified* (grouped) into sections or units. Your brain performs these mental acrobatics constantly, but to be as proficient at this method of thinking as possible, you need to be aware of the cognitive activities you go through. Focusing on these two companion patterns of thought will develop your skill in dealing with these complex schemes as it simultaneously increases your overall mental capabilities.

You might think of division/classification as a driving pattern that goes forward and then doubles back on itself in reverse. Division is a movement from a single concept to multiple categories, while classification involves gathering multiple concepts into a single group. Dividing and/or classifying helps us make sense of our subject by using categories to highlight similarities and differences. In the case of division, you are trying to find what differences break the items into separate groups; with classification, you let the similarities among the items help you put the material into meaningful categories. Processing your material in this way helps your readers see your particular subject in a new way and often brings renewed insights to both reader and writer.

Experimenting with division and classification is important to your growth as a critical thinker. It will help you process complex information so you can understand more fully your options for dealing with material in all subject areas. Practicing division and classification separate from other rhetorical modes makes you concentrate on improving this particular pattern of thinking before adding it to your expanding arsenal of critical thinking skills.

1. Describe the people, windows, and doors in the photograph on page 262 by Bill Carden. How could they be divided and classified into groups? What do you learn by looking at the photograph in this way?

© Bill Carden

2. Study the table of contents of a magazine that interests you. Into what sections is the magazine divided? What distinguishing features does each section have? Now study the various advertisements in the same magazine. What different categories would you use to classify these ads? List the ads in each category.
3. Make a chart classifying the English instructors at your school. Explain your classification system to the class.

READING AND WRITING DIVISION/CLASSIFICATION ESSAYS

Although writers of division/classification essays will probably use both division and classification in their essays, they should decide if they are primarily going to break down a topic into many separate parts or group together similar items into one coherent category; a writer's purpose will, of course, guide him or her in this decision. Readers must likewise recognize and understand which of these two parallel operations an author is using to structure an essay. Another important identifying feature of division/classification essays is an explanation (explicit or implicit) of the significance of a particular system of organization.

Reading Division/Classification Essays

• What is the essay's context?
• Does the essay divide and/or classify?

Preparing to Read.   As you approach the selections in this chapter, you should study all the material that precedes each essay so you can prepare yourself for your reading. First of all, what hints does the title give you about what you are going to read? To what extent does K. C. Cole reveal her attitude toward risks? Who do you think Judith Wallerstein and Sandra Blakeslee's audience is in "Second Chances for Children of Divorce"? Does Stephanie Ericsson's title give us any indication about her point of view in "The Ways We Lie"? Then see what you can learn from scanning each essay and reading its synopsis in the Rhetorical Table of Contents.

Also important as you prepare to read the essays in this chapter is your knowledge about each author and the conditions under which each essay was written: What does the biographical material tell you about Tamala Edwards's "Multi-Colored Families"? About Amy Tan's "Mother Tongue"? Knowing where these essays were first published will give you even more information about each author's purpose and audience.

Finally, before you begin to read, answer the Preparing to Read questions, and then think freely for a few minutes about the general topic: What do you want to know about children of divorce from Wallerstein and Blakeslee? What are some different types of lies you have told (Ericsson)?

Reading.   As you read each essay for the first time, write down your initial reactions to the topic itself, to the preliminary material, to the mood the writer sets, or to a specific incident in the essay. Make associations between the essay and your own experiences.

In addition, create a context for each essay by drawing on the preliminary material you just read about the essay: What is Tan implying about the relationship between language and culture, and why does she care about this relationship? What is significant about Edwards's point of view in "Multi-Colored Families"? According to Ericsson, why are some lies necessary? Also in this first reading, notice when the writers divided (split up) or classified (gathered together) their material to make their point.

At the bottom of the pages of these essays are several questions that will help you think critically about the topics in this chapter. They prompt you to understand the writers' reasoning and the structure of each essay. Your responses to these questions will give you ideas to use in response to the exercises and writing assignments after each essay, providing a "bridge" from the activities before to the tasks after each essay. Writing out your responses is always the way to get the most benefit out of these questions so that you have ideas to work with when you compose your own essays.

Finally, read the questions after each essay, and let them guide your second reading of the selection.

Rereading.   When you read these division/classification essays a second time, notice how the authors carefully match their dominant rhetorical approach (in this case, division or classification) to their purpose in a clear thesis. What, for example, is Cole's dominant rhetorical approach to her subject? How does this approach further her purpose? What other rhetorical strategies support her thesis? Then see how these writers logically present their division or classification systems to their readers, defining new categories as their essays progress. Finally, notice how each writer either implicitly or explicitly explains the significance or value of his or her division/classification system. How do Wallerstein and Blakeslee explain their system of organization? And how does Ericsson give her organizing principle significance? Now answer the questions after each essay to check your understanding and to help you analyze your reading in preparation for the discussion/writing topics that follow.

For a more complete survey of reading guidelines, you may want to consult the Reading Inventory at the end of Part I.

Writing Division/Classification Essays

- Decide on a purpose/thesis.
- Divide the subject into categories.
- Arrange the categories logically.
- Define each category.
- Explain the significance of your approach.

Preparing to Write.   You should approach a division/classification essay in the same way you have begun all your other writing assignments—with some kind of prewriting activity that will help you generate ideas, such as the Preparing to Write questions featured in this chapter. The prewriting techniques outlined in Chapter 3 on pages 36–38 can help you approach these questions imaginatively. Before you even consider the selection and arrangement of details, you need to explore your subject, choose a topic, and decide on a specific purpose and audience. The best way to explore your subject is to think about it, read about it, and then write about it. Look at it from all possible angles, and see what patterns and relationships emerge. To choose a specific topic, you might begin by listing any groups, patterns, or combinations you discover within your subject matter. Your purpose should take shape as you form your thesis, and your audience is probably dictated by the assignment. Making these decisions before you write will make the rest of your task much easier.

Writing.   As you begin to write, certain guidelines will help you structure your ideas for a division/classification essay:

1. First, declare an overall purpose for your division/classification.
2. Then divide the item or concept you are dealing with into categories.

3. Arrange these categories into a logical sequence.
4. Define each category, explaining the differences among your categories and demonstrating those differences through examples.
5. Explain the significance of your classification system (Why is it worth reading? What will your audience learn from it?).

All discussion in such an essay should reinforce the purpose stated at the beginning of your paper. Other rhetorical modes—such as narration, example, and comparison/contrast—will naturally be used to supplement your classification.

To make your division/classification as workable as possible, take special care that your categories do not overlap and that all topics fall into their proper places. If, for example, you were dividing/classifying all the jobs performed by students in your writing class, the categories of (1) indoor work and (2) outdoor work would probably be inadequate because some jobs fit into both categories. At a pizza parlor, a florist, or a gift shop, for example, a delivery person's time would be split between indoor and outdoor work. So you would need to alter the classification system to avoid this problem. The categories of (1) indoor work, (2) outdoor work, and (3) a combination of indoor and outdoor work would be much more useful for this task. Making sure your categories don't overlap will help make your classification essays more readable and more accurate.

Rewriting.   As you rewrite your division/classification essays, consider carefully the probable reactions of your readers to the form and content of your paper:

- Does my thesis communicate my purpose clearly?
- Have I divided my topic into separate categories?
- Are these categories arranged logically?
- Do I explain the significance of my classification system?

More guidelines for writing and rewriting are available in the Writing Inventory at the end of Part I.

STUDENT ESSAY: DIVISION/CLASSIFICATION AT WORK

The following student essay divides skiers into interesting categories based on their physical abilities. As you read it, notice how the student writer weaves the significance of his study into his opening statement of purpose. Also, pay particular attention to his logical method of organization and clear explanation of categories as he moves with ease from multiple to single and back to multiple again throughout the essay.

People on the Slopes

Subject When I first learned to ski, I was amazed by the shapes who whizzed by me and slipped down trails marked only by a black diamond signifying "most difficult," while others careened awkwardly down the "bunny slopes." These skiers, I discovered, could *Thesis statement* be divided into distinct categories—for my own entertainment and for the purpose of finding appropriate skiing partners.

Overall purpose

First category First are the "poetic skiers." They glide down the mountainside silently with what seems like no effort at *Definition* all. They float from side to side on the intermediate slopes, their knees bent perfectly above parallel skis, while their sharp skills allow them to bypass slower skiers with safely executed turns at remarkable speeds.

Supporting details

Second category The "crazy skiers" also get down the mountain quickly, but with a lot more noise attending their de- *Definition* scent. At every hill, they yell a loud "Yahoo!" and slam their skis into the snow. These go-for-broke athletes always whiz by faster than everyone else, and they especially seem to love the crowded runs where they can slide over the backs of other people's skis. I often find crazy skiers in mangled messes at the bottoms of steep hills, where they are yelling loudly, but not the famous "Yahoo!"

Supporting details (with humor)

After being overwhelmed by the crazy skiers, I *Transition* *Third category* am always glad to find other skiers like myself: "the average ones." We are polite on the slopes, concentrate on improving our technique with every run, and ski the beginner slopes only at the beginning of *Definition* the day to warm up. We go over the moguls (small hills) much more cautiously than the crazy or poetic skiers, but we still seek adventure with a little jump or two each day. We remain a silent majority on the mountain.

Supporting details (comparative)

Fourth category Below us in talent, but much more evident on the *Transition* mountainside, are what I call the "eternal beginners." These skiers stick to the same beginner slope almost *Definition* every run of every day during their vacation. Should they venture onto an intermediate slope, they quickly assume the snowplow position (a pigeon-toed stance) *Supporting details* and never leave it. Eternal beginners weave from one side of the run to the other and hardly ever fall, because they proceed so slowly; however, they do yell quite a bit at the crazies who like to run over the backs of their skis.

Transition Having always enjoyed people-watching, I have fun each time I am on the slopes observing the myriad of skiers around me. I use these observations to pick out **Significance of classification system** possible ski partners for myself and others. Since my mother is an eternal beginner, she has more fun skiing with someone who shares her interests than with my dad, who is a poetic skier with solitude on his mind. After taking care of Mom, I am free to find a partner I'll enjoy. My sister, the crazy skier of the family, just heads for the rowdiest group she can find! As the years go by and my talents grow, I am trusting my percep- **Concluding remarks** tions of skier types to help me find the right partner for life on and off the slopes. No doubt watching my fellow skiers will always remain an enjoyable pastime.

Student Writer's Comments

To begin this paper—the topic of which occurred to me as I flew over snow-capped mountains on a trip—I brainstormed. I jotted down the general groups of skiers I believed existed on the slopes and recorded characteristics of each group as they came to me. The ideas flowed quite freely at this point, and I enjoyed imagining the people I was describing. This prewriting stage brought back some great memories from the slopes that cluttered my thinking at times, but in most cases one useless memory triggered two or three other details or skiing stories that helped me make sense of my division/classification system.

I then felt ready to write a first draft but was having a lot of trouble coming up with a sensible order for my categories. So I just began to write. My categories were now clear to me, even though I wanted to work a little more on their labels. And the definitions of each category came quite naturally as I wrote. In fact, the ease with which they surfaced made me believe that I really had discovered some ultimate truth about types of skiers. I also had tons of details and anecdotes to work with from my brainstorming session. When I finished the body of my first draft (it had no introduction or conclusion yet), I realized that every paragraph worked nicely by itself—four separate category paragraphs. But these paragraphs didn't work together yet at all.

As I reworked the essay, I knew my major job was to reorganize my categories in some logical way and then smooth out the prose with transitions that would make the essay work as a unified whole. To accomplish this, I wrote more drafts of this single paper than I can remember writing for any other assignment. But I feel that the order and the transitions finally work now. The essay moves logically from type to type, and I think my transitions justify my arrangement along the way. My overall purpose came to me as I was reorganizing my categories, at which point I was able to write my introduction and conclusion. After I had put my purpose into words, the significance of my division/classification system became clear. I saved it, however, for the conclusion.

The most exciting part of this paper was realizing how often I had used these mental groupings in pairing my family and friends with other skiers. I had just never labeled, defined, or organized the categories I had created. Writing this paper helped me verbalize these categories and ended up being a lot of fun (especially when it was finished).

SOME FINAL THOUGHTS ON DIVISION/CLASSIFICATION

The essays collected in this chapter use division and/or classification as their primary organizing principle. All of these essays show both techniques at work to varying degrees. As you read these essays, you might also want to be aware of the other rhetorical modes that support these division/classification essays, such as description and definition. Finally, pay special attention to how these authors bring significance to their systems of classification and, as a result, to their essays themselves.

DIVISION/CLASSIFICATION IN REVIEW

Reading Division/Classification Essays

Preparing to Read
√ What assumptions can I make from the essay's title?
√ What do I think the general mood of the essay will be?
√ What is the essay's purpose and audience?
√ What does the synopsis tell me about the essay?
√ What can I learn from the author's biography?
√ Can I predict the author's point of view toward the subject?

Reading
√ What is the context of the essay?
√ Did the author divide or classify?

Rereading
√ How does division or classification help the author accomplish his or her purpose?
√ What other rhetorical strategies does the author use?
√ How does the writer explain the significance of his or her approach?

Writing Division/Classification Essays

Preparing to Write
√ What is my purpose?
√ Who is my audience?

Writing
√ Do I declare an overall purpose in my thesis?
√ Do I divide my subject into distinct categories?
√ Do I arrange the categories into a logical sequence?
√ Do I define each category?
√ Do I explain the significance of my approach?

Rewriting
√ Does my thesis communicate my purpose clearly?
√ Have I divided my topic into separate categories?
√ Are these categories arranged logically?
√ Do I explain the significance of my classification system?

TAMALA EDWARDS   (1971–   )

Multi-Colored Families

Born in Georgia and raised in Texas, Tamala Edwards earned her B.A. from Stanford University in International Relations, then worked for eight years as a staff writer in the Washington bureau of *Time* magazine, where she was principally responsible for covering presidential election campaigns and international news. In 2001, she joined World News Now, where she was an ABC News correspondent, anchor of ABC's *World News Now* and *World News This Morning*, and an embedded reporter during the Iraq War. Four years later, she moved to WPVI-TV/Channel 6 in Philadelphia, where she currently anchors the morning edition of Action News from 5 to 7 A.M. While at *Time* magazine, Edwards wrote stories on a number of controversial topics, including a piece entitled "Who Needs a Husband" about the changing dynamics surrounding love and marriage, along with articles about the fight over school funding, women in philanthropy, the Reform Party, sexual harassment, race relations, and mental illness. In her spare time, she likes to read, hike, cook, and watch movies. Edwards lives in Mount Airy, Pennsylvania, with her husband, Rocco Lugrine, an executive pastry chef at Miel Patisserie, who courted her with "tons of chocolates." Asked to give advice to students using *The Prose Reader*, Edwards said, "Read everything you can. There's no better way to absorb vocabulary, skill, sharpness, and context than to read it and have it soak into your memory banks, quietly seeping into the DNA of who you are as a writer, thinker, and speaker."

Preparing to Read

The following essay, originally published in *Time* magazine (May 3, 1999), examines the joys and challenges faced by multi-colored families in America. In this selection, the author gives the readers realistic approaches to this complex social issue.

Exploring Experience: Prior to reading this essay, consider the advantages and disadvantages of family life in general. How might these aspects be exacerbated by multi-racial or multi-ethnic differences and similarities? Are the social issues that surround multi-colored families changing? If so, in what ways? Are you a member of a multi-racial family? Do you know a multi-racial family? What are their greatest strengths? Their most difficult problems?

Learning Online: Adopting children internationally is often more difficult than adopting nationally. Go to the U.S. government's international adoption Web site (www.adoption.state.gov), and click on the Adoption Stats link to see how many children were adopted from different countries in recent years. Also, read about international adoption eligibility requirements. Do you know anyone who has had experience with international adoption? What difficulties have they faced because of it?

From the day Karen Katz brought her infant daughter Lena home, there 1
was a certain question she knew was coming. It finally came when
Lena was four; she turned to her mother and asked, "Mommy, how
come I'm not the same color as you?" Her heart stopped. Then Katz, who
is white, explained to her cinnamon-skinned, Guatemalan-born daughter
that they came from different countries. Over the years, Katz and her husband, Gary Richards, have consciously worked to minimize the distance between themselves and their daughter: taking a trip to Mexico to surround
Lena, now eight, with people who look like her and choosing to live in a
polyglot Manhattan neighborhood where she blends in easily. Nonetheless,
Lena sometimes seems to reject her dark skin, crying over her inability to
match her parents. But recently she's begun to explain proudly to strangers
her adopted status. "Which isn't to say we're home free now," says Katz. "It's
an ongoing conversation."

Dialogues about difference are going on in an increasing number of Amer- 2
ican households that have been made multi-racial through either intermar-
riage or transracial adoption. The Census Bureau estimates that there are
more than 1.3 million interracial marriages. Nearly a third of the children
adopted from the public foster-care system are placed with families of a different race. And in the past decade, the number of children adopted from
China, for example, has jumped from less than 200 to more than 4,000. You
see it even in Hollywood, where Steven Spielberg, Tom Cruise, and Michelle
Pfeiffer are parents of adopted nonwhite children. [1]

And like Katz, more and more parents are wrangling with tough ques- 3
tions: how to handle the external aspects—the stares, comments and other
public behaviors that arise when families look different—and perhaps more
important, how to handle the internal—the need to affirm the family bond
while helping a child craft a strong racial sense of self.

Dealing with Insensitivity

The spectrum of multi-racial families is broad but embraces some 4
common issues. For example, parents can't be as arbitrary in their choices
of neighborhoods, schools, play groups, or other social situations when they
have a mixed household. "For a child, it's easier to blend," says Mary Durr,
an executive with the Adoption Services Information Agency in Washington. She and other experts suggest searching out racially diverse communities—much as Susan Weiss, a Chicago social worker, had to do after

---

Thinking Critically

[1] What other Hollywood personalities have recently adopted children internationally? What
problems accompanied these adoptions?

acknowledging the negative racial remarks to which her adopted daughters, Indian-born Cathryn, 12, and Peruvian-born Amanda, 7, were subjected in the city. The family moved to a more mixed neighborhood in Oak Park, where, says Weiss, "there are so many parents and kids that don't 'match' that no one notices."

Despite such efforts to create a comforting environment, a trip to the 5 supermarket or McDonald's can be fraught with insensitive public behavior. People stare, children taunt, strangers ask rude questions. To be constantly asked, "Are you just the baby-sitter?" or "Do they look like their father?" can be trying, say those who have endured such questioning. "Some days I want to scream out, 'Leave us alone. My life is none of your business!'" rages Chicago drama teacher Jennifer Viets in *The Coffee Man and the Milk Maid*, a monologue about being the white mother of three biracial children.

In most cases screaming is the worst response, since it sends a message of 6 anger and tension to the child. Calm, assured answers ("We're blessed to be an adoptive family," "My husband is Chinese") disarm loaded questions and offer examples of coping behavior. "I had to model appropriate behavior and give answers I hope my children would use," says Nancy G. Brown, co-founder of Multi-racial Americans of Southern California [MASC] and mother of Nicole and Rachelle, two biracial black-and-white girls. Her daughters, now teenagers, handle questions with aplomb and simple, swift replies.

Harder to handle than the public incidents are sticky situations among 7 extended family and friends. Some cases are dire, like the grandparent who threatens to cease contact because of racial differences. But even the gray areas—family members who treat children differently or unwittingly make racist remarks—are tough. Limiting contact or forcing difficult conversations can be painful, but, says Faye Mandell, president of MASC, "parents must say, 'Treat them equally—or not at all.'"

But there are also grace notes, as in how time and communication can 8 resolve dicey situations. At first Kim Felder, a California family recruiter for adoptions with one biological child, encountered what she perceived as resistance from her parents to her intention to adopt transracially. She and her husband Carl decided to go ahead with the adoption and limit contact with Kim's parents. The following day, her parents explained that they were reacting to the prejudice they had faced as Italian immigrants—an experience they didn't want for their daughter. "They weren't prejudiced—they wanted to protect us," says Felder. "Now they're our biggest supporters." The Felders ultimately adopted four kids of varying African-American, Hispanic, and white backgrounds.

Having a child of a different or blended race also has a habit of shaking 9
up racial orientations. "I lost my white privilege; ❷ I began to experience
reactions from people," says Jennifer Viets. That can be difficult if there are
unresolved issues. Filippo Santoro, 34, an Italian American, is married to
Trayce, 36, an African American. But he grew up hearing blacks referred to
in derogatory terms. Even now, he admits, "Trayce still says I'm a racist."
These feelings make both parents more conscientious in the raising of biracial Philip, 2, and Lena, 6 months. "You find yourself," he says of his evolving handling of the race issue. Indeed, the experience of being part of a
multi-racial family invariably heightens awareness of racism and often inspires
parents to take action. Katz, for example, has written two children's books,
Over the Moon, on adoption, and *The Colors of Us*, on skin hues.

Drawing Your Own Boundaries

While some, such as Charles Byrd, editor of the webzine *Interracial Voice*, 10
argue that race is a false construct, few deny that it nonetheless acts as a
dividing line. Parenting a child who straddles that line means addressing not
only the question of "Who am I?" but also "Where do I belong?" ❸ —an
issue that parents must grapple with before they are swept away by the rapids
of everyday family living. "The father and mother have to get together on
what they're going to say so the child is not given two different spiels," says
Clayton Majete, a lecturer at New York City's Baruch College who studies
interracial families. He suggests waiting for the children to raise the issue
and then taking the time to deal with it.

Until recently, conventional wisdom typically classified a mixed-race child 11
as being of the same race as the minority parent. But that rule is being challenged as more interracial couples insist that their children be allowed to
claim all sides of their heritage—an approach that experts think makes for a
more settled, secure child.

It's an approach, however, that requires diligence on the part of the parents. 12
Project RACE (Reclassify All Children Equally)—a campaign started by
Ryan Graham, a biracial Florida teenager, and his mother Susan—has won
changes in the act on college-entrance-exam forms and some minor alterations in the U.S. Census form as well as on some local and state government
forms. But most of society has not yet taken to the concept of biracial identity.

Thinking Critically

❷ To what extent do you believe that white people are "privileged" in American society?
Can you think of any other groups that have special privileges in this country?

❸ Name three different societal groups you belong to. In which group are you most
comfortable? Why?

Most government forms don't include a multi-racial box, and it's usually up to the parent to make sure a child isn't compartmentalized. "I tell my kids that if somebody gives them a hard time about checking black and white, come get me, and I'll take care of it for them," says Edwin Darden, a Virginia father of two biracial kids who successfully pushed for a multi-racial box on his school-district forms.

Parents may prefer that children embrace their full racial heritage, and it   13
can be painful for, say, a white mother to see her biracial child choose to identify herself as black. But there are limits to parental influence, as well as immense pressure to choose sides. "One of the things we find is that in the teenage years, they stray from the teachings of their parents," says Darden, who has encountered this while running a local interracial-family support group. "It's too difficult to be different." Parents can offer their support and advice, but they should be ready to accept the child's decision on how to be classified.

Are You Ready?

In the past 10 years the number of people willing to consider transracial   14
adoptions has surged. [4] In 1972 the National Association of Black Social Workers made waves when it declared itself vehemently opposed to trans-racial placements. Representatives of the association argued that minority children need parents like them in order to form a strong sense of identity. While that view is shared by many officials in the foster-care system, there are now laws in place forbidding officials to use race as a routine consider-ation. And proponents of transracial placement have research behind them. "The bottom line is that these children grow up healthy and with ties to their culture," says sociologist Rita Simon.

Still, even those who assist in such placements advise that would-be parents   15
need to answer key questions. "How committed is one to making a child feel a part of a racial community as well as the family?" asks Gail Steinberg, co-director of Pact, a group that handles transracial adoptions. "Instead of looking with goo-goo eyes at an adorable child, prospective parents must raise their decision to an adult level."

It's wise, say experts, to review the decision with a transracial-adoption   16
specialist or to get hold of information like Pact's "Insider's Guide to Trans-racial Adoption," which tracks the stages of interracial adoption and explains how racial identity differs over time and between races. The 420-page man-ual poses some self-probing questions: Are you the retiring type, or do you naturally like to stand out? Do you need groups, or are you fine with

---

Thinking Critically

[4] Why do you think transracial adoptions have increased in the past ten years?

independence? If your "hard wire" traits lean toward the demure, then family life in a constant spotlight may not be a good idea.

Even if your heart is in the right place, there are practical hurdles to overcome. "Love is not enough," says Simon. "A child needs a sense of cultural identity and racial history." [5] Which church to join, what mall to shop in, which dentist to frequent are choices to be examined through a new perspective. And they are especially important to children from disadvantaged minority backgrounds. "You must surround them with people who look like them so they know they are as good as they can be and know what they can do," says Felder.   17

Another helpful step for parents of foreign-born children is to include the customs, language, and history of their birth land as part of the family tradition. While Katz waited to be allowed to take Lena home, she toured the girl's native village and took pictures to show her later. Families might also plan a trip to the child's birth country—or take advantage of summer camps sprouting up for multi-racial families, at which kids are given the chance to learn more about their culture and experience life as a majority. "It's a very emotional experience," says Gail Walton, director of one such camp, Hands Around the World, in Wheeling, Ill.   18

Just as important as helping a child with his uniqueness is affirming his current family ties. Unlike biological families, in which a child can see resemblances and grasp a genealogical connection, families formed by adoption have to take special steps to make a child feel secure. This can range from reaching out to religious leaders and extended family in order to help reaffirm the adopted child's inclusion, to keeping a watchful eye out for unhelpful, if well-intended, teasing ("My little Mexican one"). Lyn and Arthur Dobrin of Westbury, N.Y., adopted an African-American child, Kori, as a sibling to their biological son Eric. They devised a game they called Categories, in which Daddy and Eric were boys, Mommy and Kori were girls; Mommy and Daddy were adults, Eric and Kori were kids. The point was to show that there are many facets to each person—and that race is only one of them.   19

As they tend to be for all families, the years of adolescence and early adulthood are the most difficult. Extra effort and understanding are needed to defend against derogatory remarks about a child's looks or race. In later teen years, it's not easy for a white parent to explain to his dark-skinned daughter why other white parents don't want their sons to date her. Amy and Brad Russell of Mount Vernon, Iowa, refuse to let any of their seven multi-ethnic adopted kids use race as a crutch. They also know the struggle will be lifelong.   20

Thinking Critically

[5] What is the difference between "cultural identity" and "racial history"? How are these two concepts interrelated in our lives? Which has exerted the strongest influence on you?

"I'm going to have six young black men in the house," Amy says. "I worry for their emotional and physical safety."

Yet if there is a thread that runs through the many stories about mixed-race families, it is the amazing resilience of the kids. **6** As difficult as the questions about their identity may be, they swiftly find ways to right themselves and move on. That resilience should prove less necessary as they move into what is inexorably becoming the mainstream.   21

UNDERSTANDING DETAILS

1. What exactly is Edwards classifying in this essay? Explain her three categories.
2. What limitations do parents of multi-colored families have to accept?
3. What special questions do children in multi-racial families have to deal with?
4. What steps can parents of multi-ethnic children take to make them feel safe, secure, and confident?

READING CRITICALLY

5. Why do you think transracial adoptions have increased so dramatically in the past ten years? Explain your answer.
6. Which of Edwards's categories do you suppose is most difficult for the children? Explain your choice.
7. Why do you think "most of society has not yet taken to the concept of biracial identity" (paragraph 12)?
8. Why might acknowledging all aspects of a child's heritage rather than just the minority aspects produce a more secure child (paragraph 11)?

DISCOVERING RHETORICAL STRATEGIES

9. In what ways does Edwards use division and classification in this essay? How does she give significance or value to her system of organization? What other rhetorical techniques does she use to accomplish her purpose?
10. The author quotes many authorities on the subject of multi-colored families to help her make her point. Do you find these quotations, anecdotes, and examples effective or not? Explain your answer in detail.
11. What is Edwards's point of view toward multi-colored families in general?
12. Why do you think Edwards ends her essay with a reference to "the mainstream"? Is this an effective conclusion to her essay? Explain your answer.

MAKING CONNECTIONS

13. Compare and contrast Edwards's definition of a "family" with that expressed by Judith Wallerstein and Sandra Blakeslee ("Second Chances for Children of Divorce"), Ben Dattner ("Is Your Workplace Personality Out of (Birth) Order?"),

---

Thinking Critically

6 In what ways is resilience important in life? What support do you have for your statement?

Robert Ramirez (The Barrio"), Mary Pipher ("Beliefs About Families"), and/or Kim Severson ("I'm Not Willing to Settle for Crumbs"). Whose definition of a "family" would be most like yours? Why?

14. How do Tamala Edwards, K. C. Cole ("Calculated Risks"), and/or Stephanie Ericsson ("The Ways We Lie") use the process of division and classification to help explain their topics? Which author's method is easiest to follow? Why?

15. Imagine that Edwards is having a round-table discussion with the following authors about the evils of prejudice: Lewis Sawaquat ("For My Indian Daughter"), Firoozeh Dumas ("Leffingwell Elementary School"), Harold Krents ("Darkness at Noon"), Sucheng Chan ("You're Short, Besides!"), and Michael Dorris ("The Broken Cord"). Which author would you agree with most? Why?

IDEAS FOR DISCUSSION/WRITING

Preparing to Write

Write freely about various "multi-colored" events you have experienced. Do these instances have a different feel since you were a child? From your frame of reference, is American society more or less tolerant of multi-racial families and children? What specific details or comments bring you to this conclusion? What is your ethnic heritage? Do you know the details of all the cultures you represent? Do you think having knowledge about your heritage is important?

Choosing a Topic

1. *Learning Online:* Parent–child relationships come in many different forms. Think about the obstacles adoptive parents often encounter, especially if they have adopted internationally. Then revisit the government's website on international adoption to remember how difficult adoption can be (www.adoption.state .gov). Consider your own relationship with your parents. Now think about other parent–child relationships you have seen, either adoptive or biological. What are some of the differences that you notice? Write an essay analyzing different types of parent–child relationships.

2. Your English instructor has asked about your heritage. Respond to this question by classifying for him or her all the different ethnicities in your background. You might start this project by doing an Internet search of your family history. You can go back as far as you want. Then classify the results that you find, and discuss the characteristics of each classification. Decide on a point of view before you begin to write.

3. Your college newspaper is doing a series of articles on students who have come to your college from different countries. Interview a student whose culture interests you, and explain the primary rituals the student pursues by classifying them in an essay for other students to read.

4. If the daily activities we perform say something important about us, analyze yourself by writing an essay that classifies these different activities you carry out in a typical week. Discuss your choices as you proceed.

Before beginning your essay, you might want to consult the checklists on page 269.

K. C. COLE   (1946–   )

Calculated Risks

K. C. Cole spent her early childhood in Rio de Janeiro, then grew up in Port Washington, New York, and Shaker Heights, Ohio. After graduating from Barnard College with a B.A. in Political Science, she worked for Radio Free Europe as an editor and subsequently lived in Czechoslovakia, the Soviet Union, and Hungary. While working as a writer and editor at the *Saturday Review* in San Francisco, she developed a love for physics and started writing about science. In the 1970s, she became an editor at *Newsday*, for which she wrote personal essays on politics, humor, and women's issues. Her first book, *What Only a Mother Can Tell You*, was published in 1982; a collection of essays titled *Between the Lines* came out two years later. She has also written *Sympathetic Vibrations: Reflections on Physics as a Way of Life* (1985, with an introduction by Frank Oppenheimer), *The Universe and the Teacup* (1998), and *The Hole in the Universe* (2001). Since 1994, she has covered physical science for the *Los Angeles Times*, where she also writes the column Mind Over Matter. Her recreational activities include rollerblading, hiking, listening to Bach, and watching *Six Feet Under* and *Sex in the City*. Her advice to students using *The Prose Reader* is "to be passionate. There's no point in writing if you don't really care about what you say. And don't be afraid to make mistakes. If you don't make mistakes, you aren't taking enough risks."

Preparing to Read

The following essay first appeared in K. C. Cole's book entitled *The Universe and the Teacup: The Mathematics of Truth and Beauty* (1998). It suggests that the way we calculate risks in our lives doesn't make much sense.

Exploring Experience: As you prepare to read this article, take a few moments to think about how you analyze potential risks in your life: What constitutes a "risk" for you? What risks do you take every day? Do you take these risks readily and willingly? Give some examples. When do you avoid risks? Is taking risks a positive or negative force in your life? In what ways does taking risks influence your life? How does taking risks energize or diminish your actions?

Learning Online: To see how tolerant you are toward risks, visit www .queendom.com/tests/index.htm, and click on the "Attitude and Lifestyle tests" link to find the "risk-taking test." Take the online test to see how comfortable you are taking risks in your life. Keep your results in mind while reading the following article.

*N*ewsweek magazine plunged American women into a state of near panic some years ago when it announced that the chances of a college-educated thirty-five-year-old woman finding a husband was less than her chance of being killed by a terrorist. Although Susan Faludi made mincemeat of this so-called statistic in her book *Backlash*, the notion that we can precisely quantify risk has a strong hold on the Western psyche. ◆ Scientists, statisticians, and policy makers attach numbers to the risk of getting breast cancer or AIDS, to flying and food additives, to getting hit by lightning or falling in the bathtub.

Yet despite (or perhaps because of) all the numbers floating around, most people are quite properly confused about risk. I know people who live happily on the San Andreas Fault and yet are afraid to ride the New York subways (and vice versa). I've known smokers who can't stand to be in the same room with a fatty steak and women afraid of the side effects of birth control pills who have unprotected sex with strangers. Risk assessment is rarely based on purely rational considerations—even if people could agree on what those considerations were. We worry about negligible quantities of Alar in apples, yet shrug off the much higher probability of dying from smoking. We worry about flying, but not driving. We worry about getting brain cancer from cellular phones, although the link is quite tenuous. ◆ In fact, it's easy to make a statistical argument—albeit a fallacious one—that cellular phones prevent cancer, because the proportion of people with brain tumors is smaller among cell phone users than among the general population.

Even simple pleasures such as eating and breathing have become suspect. Love has always been risky, and AIDS has made intimacy more perilous than ever. On the other hand, not having relationships may be riskier still. According to at least one study, the average male faces three times the threat of early death associated with not being married as he does from cancer.

Of course, risk isn't all bad. Without knowingly taking risks, no one would ever walk out the door, much less go to school, drive a car, have a baby, submit a proposal for a research grant, fall in love, or swim in the ocean. It's hard to have any fun, accomplish anything productive, or experience life without taking on risks—sometimes substantial ones. Life, after all, is a fatal disease, and the mortality rate for humans, at the end of the day, is 100 percent.

Thinking Critically

◆ Do you think Cole is right in her assertion that most Americans try to "quantify risk" as much as possible? Explain your reasoning.

◆ What specific risks do you worry about most? Why do you worry about these particular risks?

Yet, people are notoriously bad at risk assessment. I couldn't get over 5 this feeling watching the aftermath of the crash of TWA Flight 800 and the horror it spread about flying, with the long lines at airports, the increased security measures, the stories about grieving families day after day in the newspaper, the ongoing attempt to figure out why and who and what could be done to prevent such a tragedy from happening again.

Meanwhile, tens of thousands of children die every day around the world 6 from common causes such as malnutrition and disease. That's roughly the same as a hundred exploding jumbo jets full of children every single day. ③ People who care more about the victims of Flight 800 aren't callous or ignorant. It's just the way our minds work. Certain kinds of tragedies make an impact; others don't. Our perceptual apparatus is geared toward threats that are exotic, personal, erratic, and dramatic. This doesn't mean we're ignorant, just human.

This skewed perception of risk has serious social consequences, however. 7 We aim our resources at phantoms, while real hazards are ignored. Parents, for example, tend to rate drug abuse and abduction by strangers as the greatest threats to their children. Yet hundreds of times more children die each year from choking, burns, falls, drowning, and other accidents that public safety efforts generally ignore. . . .

Even in terms of simple dollars, our policies don't make any sense. It's 8 well known, for example, that prenatal care for pregnant women saves enormous amounts of money—in terms of care infants need in the first year of life—and costs a pittance. Yet millions of low-income women don't get it.

Numbers are clearly not enough to make sense of risk assessment. Context counts, too. Take cancer statistics. It's always frightening to hear that 9 cancer is on the rise. However, at least one reason for the increase is simply that people are living longer—long enough to get the disease.

What you consider risky, after all, depends somewhat on the circumstances 10 of your life and lifestyle. People who don't have enough to eat don't worry about apples contaminated with Alar. People who face daily violence at their front door don't worry about hijackings on flights to the Bahamas. Attitudes toward risk evolve in cultural contexts and are influenced by everything from psychology to ethics to beliefs about personal responsibility.

In addition to context, another factor needed to see through the maze of 11 conflicting messages about risk is human psychology. For example, imminent risks strike much more fear in our hearts than distant ones; it's much harder to get a teenager than an older person to take long-term dangers like smoking seriously.

Thinking Critically

③ How effective is the author's "jumbo jet" analogy? What other analogy would be persuasive in this context?

Smoking is also a habit people believe they can control, which makes the 12
risk far more acceptable. ❹ (People seem to get more upset about the effects
of passive smoking than smoking itself—at least in part because smokers get
to choose, and breathers don't.)

As a general principle, people tend to grossly exaggerate the risk of any 13
danger perceived to be beyond their control, while shrugging off risks they
think they can manage. Thus, we go skiing and skydiving, but fear asbestos.
We resent and fear the idea that anonymous chemical companies are putting
additives into our food; yet the additives we load onto our own food—salt,
sugar, butter—are millions of times more dangerous.

This is one reason that airline accidents seem so unacceptable—because 14
strapped into our seats in the cabin, what happens is completely beyond our
control. In a poll taken soon after the TWA Flight 800 crash, an overwhelming majority of people said they'd be willing to pay up to fifty dollars
more for a round-trip ticket if it increased airline safety. Yet the same people
resist moves to improve automobile safety, for example, especially if it costs
money.

The idea that we can control what happens also influences whom we 15
blame when things go wrong. Most people don't like to pay the costs for
treating people injured by cigarettes or riding motorcycles because we think
they brought these things on themselves. Some people also hold these attitudes toward victims of AIDS or mental illness, because they think the illness
results from lack of character or personal morals. ❺

In another curious perceptual twist, risks associated with losing some- 16
thing and gaining something appear to be calculated in our minds according to quite different scales. In a now-classic series of studies, Stanford
psychologist Amos Tversky and colleague Daniel Kahneman concluded that
most people will bend over backward to avoid small risks, even if that means
sacrificing great potential rewards. "The threat of a loss has a greater impact
on a decision than the possibility of an equivalent gain," they concluded.

In one of their tests, Tversky and Kahneman asked physicians to choose 17
between two strategies for combating a rare disease, expected to kill 600
people. Strategy A promised to save 200 people (the rest would die), while
Strategy B offered a one-third probability that everyone would be saved, and
a two-thirds probability that no one would be saved. Betting on a sure thing,
the physicians choose A. But presented with the identical choice, stated
differently, they choose B. The difference in language was simply this: Instead

---
Thinking Critically
❹ What is the relationship between "control" and "risk"? Define each of these terms.
❺ Is the concept of risk somehow less meaningful if people are perceived to have brought
tragedy upon themselves? Why do you think this is the case?

of stating that Strategy A would guarantee 200 out of 600 saved lives, it stated that Strategy A would mean 400 sure deaths.

People will risk a lot to prevent a loss, in other words, but risk very little   18 for possible gain. Running into a burning house to save a pet or fighting back when a mugger asks for your wallet are both high-risk gambles that people take repeatedly in order to hang on to something they care about. [6] The same people might not risk the hassle of, say, fastening a seat belt in a car even though the potential gain might be much higher.

The bird in the hand always seems more attractive than the two in the   19 bush. Even if holding on to the one in your hand comes at a higher risk and the two in the bush are gold-plated.

The reverse situation comes into play when we judge risks of commis-   20 sion versus risks of omission. A risk that you assume by actually doing something seems far more risky than a risk you take by not doing something, even though the risk of doing nothing may be greater.

Deaths from natural causes, like cancer, are more readily acceptable than   21 deaths from accidents or murder. That's probably one reason it's so much easier to accept thousands of starving children than the death of one in a drive-by shooting. The former is an act of omission—a failure to step in and help, send food or medicine. The latter is the commission of a crime—somebody pulled the trigger.

In the same way, the Food and Drug Administration is far more likely to   22 withhold a drug that might help a great number of people if it threatens to harm a few; better to hurt a lot of people by failing to do something than act with the deliberate knowledge that some people will be hurt. Or as the doctors' credo puts it: First do no harm.

For obvious reasons, dramatic or exotic risks [7] seem far more dangerous   23 than more familiar ones. Plane crashes and AIDS are risks associated with ambulances and flashing lights, sex and drugs. While red dye #2 strikes terror in our hearts, that great glob of butter melting into our baked potato is accepted as an old friend. "A woman drives down the street with her child romping around in the front seat," says John Allen Paulos. "Then they arrive at the shopping mall, and she grabs the child's hand so hard it hurts, because she's afraid he'll be kidnapped."

Children who are kidnapped are far more likely to be whisked away by   24 relatives than strangers, just as most people are murdered by people they know.

Thinking Critically

[6] Who or what would you risk your life to save? Why would you make this choice?

[7] Define "exotic risk."

Familiar risks creep up on us like age and are often difficult to see until   25
it's too late to take action. Mathematician Sam C. Saunders of Washington
State University reminds us that a frog placed in hot water will struggle to
escape, but the same frog placed in cool water that's slowly warmed up will
sit peacefully until it's cooked. "One cannot anticipate what one does not perceive," he says, which is why gradual accumulations of risk due to lifestyle
choices (like smoking or eating) are so often ignored. We're in hot water, but
it's gotten hot so slowly that no one notices. [8]

To bring home his point, Saunders asks us to imagine that cigarettes are not   26
harmful—with the exception of an occasional one that has been packed with
explosives instead of tobacco. These dynamite-stuffed cigarettes look just like
normal ones. There's only one hidden away in every 18,250 packs—not a
grave risk, you might say. The only catch is, if you smoke one of those explosive cigarettes, it might blow your head off.

The mathematician speculates, I think correctly, that given such a situa-   27
tion, cigarettes would surely be banned outright. After all, if 30 million packs
of cigarettes are sold each day, an average of 1,600 people a day would die
in gruesome explosions. Yet the number of deaths is the same to be expected
from normal smoking. "The total expected loss of life or health to smokers
using dynamite-loaded (but otherwise harmless) cigarettes over forty years
would not be as great as with ordinary filtered cigarettes," says Saunders.

We can accept getting cooked like a frog, in other words, but not getting   28
blown up like a firecracker.

It won't come as a great surprise to anyone that ego also plays a role in the   29
way we assess risks. Psychological self-protection leads us to draw consistently
wrong conclusions. In general, we overestimate the risks of bad things happening to others, while vastly underrating the possibility that they will happen
to ourselves. [9] Indeed, the lengths people go to minimize their own perceived
risks can be downright "ingenious," according to Rutgers psychologist Neil
Weinstein. For example, people asked about the risk of finding radon in their
houses always rate their risk as "low" or "average," never "high." "If you ask them
why," says Weinstein, "they take anything and twist it around in a way that
reassures them. Some say their risk is low because the house is new; others,
because the house is old. Some will say their risk is low because their house is
at the top of a hill; others, because it's at the bottom of a hill."

Thinking Critically

[8] How does the author's analogy about a frog placed in hot water help us understand the
concept of "familiar risks"?

[9] Do you think Cole is right in her assertion that "we overestimate the risks of bad things
happening to others, while vastly underrating the possibility that they will happen to ourselves"? Explain your reasoning.

Whatever the evidence to the contrary, we think, "It won't happen to me." Weinstein and others speculate that this has something to do with preservation of self-esteem. We don't like to see ourselves as vulnerable. We like to think we've got some magical edge over the others. Ego gets involved especially in cases where being vulnerable to risk implies personal failure—for example, the risk of depression, suicide, alcoholism, drug addiction. "If you admit you're at risk," says Weinstein, "you're admitting that you can't handle stress. You're not as strong as the next person." 30

Average people, studies have shown, believe that they will enjoy longer lives, healthier lives, and longer marriages than the "average" person. Despite the obvious fact that they themselves are, well, average people too. According to a recent poll, 3 out of 4 baby boomers (those born between 1946 and 1964) think they look younger than their peers, and 4 out of 5 say they have fewer wrinkles than other people their age—a statistical impossibility. 31

Kahneman and Tversky studied this phenomenon as well and found that people think they'll beat the odds because they're special. This is no doubt a necessary psychological defense mechanism, or no one would ever get married again without thinking seriously about the potential for divorce. A clear view of personal vulnerability, however, could go a long way toward preventing activities like drunken driving. But then again, most people think they are better than average drivers—even when intoxicated. 32

We also seem to believe it won't happen to us if it hasn't happened yet. That is, we extrapolate from the past to the future. "I've been taking that highway at eighty miles per hour for ten years and I haven't crashed yet," we tell ourselves. This is rather like reasoning that flipping a coin ten times that comes up heads guarantees that heads will continue to come up indefinitely. 33

Curiously, one advertising campaign against drunken driving that was quite successful featured the faces of children killed by drunken drivers.[10] These children looked real to us. We could identify with them in the same way as we could identify with the people on TWA Flight 800. It's much easier to empathize with someone who has a name and a face than a statistic. 34

That explains in part why we go to great expense to rescue children who fall down mine shafts, but not children dying from preventable diseases. Economists call this the "rule of rescue."[11] If you know that someone is in danger and you know that you can help, you have a moral obligation to do so. If you don't know about it, however, you have no obligation. Columnist Roger Simon speculates that's one reason the National Rifle Association 35

Thinking Critically

[10] Why did the advertising campaign featuring the faces of children killed by drunk drivers work so well?

[11] What is the "rule of rescue"? Give examples from your own experience to prove or disprove the theory.

lobbied successfully to eliminate the program at the Centers for Disease Control that keeps track of gun deaths. If we don't have to face what's happening, we won't feel obligated to do anything about it.

Even without the complication of all these psychological factors, however, 36 calculating risks can be tricky because not everything is known about every situation. "We have to concede that a single neglected or unrecognized risk can invalidate all the reliability calculations, which are based on known risk," writes Ivar Ekeland. There is always a risk, in other words, that the risk assessment itself is wrong.

Genetic screening, like tests for HIV infection, has a certain probability of 37 being wrong. If your results come back positive, how much should you worry? If they come back negative, how safe should you feel?

The more factors involved, the more complicated the risk assessment 38 becomes. When you get to truly complex systems like nationwide telephone networks and power grids, worldwide computer networks and hugely complex machines like space shuttles, the risk of disaster becomes infinitely harder to pin down.[12] No one knows when a minor glitch will set off a chain reaction of events that will culminate in disaster. Potential risks in complex systems, in other words, are subject to exponential amplification.

Needless to say, the way a society assesses risk is very different from the way 39 an individual views the same choices. Whether or not you wish to ride a motorcycle is your own business. Whether society pays the bills for the thousands of people maimed by cycle accidents, however, is everybody's business. Any one of us might view our own survival on a transatlantic flight as more important than the needs of the nation's children. Governments, one presumes, ought to have a somewhat different agenda.

But how far does society want to go in strictly numerical accounting? It 40 certainly hasn't helped much in the all-important issue of health care, where an ounce of prevention has been proven again and again to be worth many pounds of cures. Most experts agree that we should be spending much more money preventing common diseases and accidents, especially in children. But no one wants to take health dollars away from precarious newborns or the elderly—where most of it goes. These are decisions that ultimately will not be made by numbers alone. Calculating risks only helps us to see more clearly what exactly is going on.

According to anthropologist Melvin Konner, author of *Why the* 41 *Reckless Survive,* our poor judgment about potential risks may well be the legacy of evolution.[13] Early peoples lived at constant risk from predators,

---

Thinking Critically
[12] What is the relationship between complexity and risk?
[13] Why is our poor judgment about potential risks "the legacy of evolution"?

disease, accidents. They died young. And in evolutionary terms, "winning" means not longevity, but merely sticking around long enough to pass on your genes to the next generation. Taking risks was therefore a "winning" strategy, especially if it meant a chance to mate before dying. Besides, decisions had to be made quickly. If going for a meal of ripe berries meant risking an attack from a saber-toothed tiger, you dove for the berries. For a half-starved cave dweller, this was a relatively simple choice. Perhaps our brains are simply not wired, speculates Konner, for the careful calculations presented by the risks of modern life.

UNDERSTANDING DETAILS

1. Why does Cole claim that people are basically confused about risk assessment (paragraph 2)?
2. What role does "context" play in our assessment of risks?
3. What three psychological factors affect people's perceptions of risk? Explain each in your own words.
4. How are the ways an individual calculates risk different from the ways society calculates risk?

READING CRITICALLY

5. What is the overall purpose of Cole's essay? How do you know? What clues make this purpose clear?
6. Why are faces and names more persuasive to us than statistics when considering risks in our own lives?
7. According to Cole, how do we form our own personal attitudes about risks? What does our lifestyle have to do with these attitudes?
8. Why does Cole think risk assessment is such a complex and difficult process?

DISCOVERING RHETORICAL STRATEGIES

9. Where in this essay does the author use division? Where does she use classification? Give specific examples. What other rhetorical modes does Cole use in her essay?
10. List the topic in each section of the body of this essay (paragraphs 9–40) (i.e., list one topic for each section). What advantages does this order have over other possible arrangements of the same ideas? How would the effect have been altered if Cole had changed the order of these ideas?
11. Why does Cole quote Melvin Kooner at the end of the essay: "Perhaps our brains are simply not wired, speculates Kooner, for the careful calculations presented by the risks of modern life" (paragraph 41)? What does this quote mean in the context of Cole's essay?
12. What point of view does Cole take in her article? What tone results from this point of view?

MAKING CONNECTIONS

13. If K. C. Cole were having a round-table discussion with Brent Staples ("A Brother's Murder"), Julia Bourland ("Getting Out of Debt (and Staying Out)"), and/or Michael Dorris ("The Broken Cord"), which of the four would speak most forcefully for the value and necessity of taking risks in life? Explain your answer.

14. What would Stephanie Ericsson ("The Ways We Lie") say about the kinds of lies we tell ourselves every day concerning the many risks we take? To what extent do you think K. C. Cole would agree with her?

15. Compare and contrast the way K. C. Cole divides and classifies types of risks with similar techniques of division and classification used by Tamala Edwards ("Multi-Colored Families").

IDEAS FOR DISCUSSION/WRITING

Preparing to Write

Write freely about the risks you take: What criteria do you use to decide whether or not to take a particular risk? What risks do you confront on a daily basis? What risks have you taken beyond your daily routine? Why do you take these risks? How often do you seek out risks? Which risks do you avoid most aggressively? Why? What do risks add or detract from your life?

Choosing a Topic

1. *Learning Online:* Visit your favorite online news source. What are today's most important headlines? How do they fit into K. C. Cole's categories of risk taking? Select a current event, and write an essay in which you analyze its actual risk using K. C. Cole's method of classification.

2. Use division/classification to explain the types of risks you deal with in your life. Divide the risks you face into categories, and then discuss those categories in an essay written for your English class. Make sure you decide on a purpose and a point of view before you begin to write.

3. How do you make decisions? Use division/classification to explain how you approach a decision and make up your mind. Decide on a purpose and point of view before you begin to write.

4. Write an essay for your classmates in which you convince them to take a specific risk that you have taken. This might be anything from riding a roller coaster to filling out a job application. Be creative in your essay.

Before beginning your essay, you might want to consult the checklists on page 269.

JUDITH WALLERSTEIN   (1921–   )
SANDRA BLAKESLEE   (1943–   )

Second Chances for Children of Divorce

Judith Wallerstein grew up in New York City, earned her Ph.D. at Lund University in Sweden, and now lives and works in Marin County, California, where she serves as Director of the Center for the Family in Transition. Since 1965, she has taught Psychology at the University of California at Berkeley, where she specializes in divorce and its effect on family members. Her first book, *Surviving the Breakup* (coauthored with Joan Kelly, 1980), analyzes the impact of divorce on young children in the family. Her next, *Second Chances: Men, Women, and Children a Decade After Divorce* (1989), is a study of the long-term effects of divorce on teenagers and young adults. Her most recent book, *The Unexpected Legacy of Divorce* (2000), is a study of the effects of divorce on children twenty-five years after their parents' breakup. She is currently hard at work on a study of happy marriages. An avid reader, she collects ideas the way "other people collect recipes." She advises college students to read as much as possible: "The first prerequisite a writer must have is a love of reading." Her coauthor on *Second Chances,* Sandra Blakeslee, was born in Flushing, New York, and earned her B.S. at Berkeley, where her specialty was Neurobiology. She is currently the West Coast science and medicine correspondent for the *New York Times.* Blakeslee goes mountain biking and running in her spare time. She and Wallerstein recently collaborated on a new book entitled *What About the Kids? Raising Your Children Before, During, and After Divorce* (2003). A former Peace Corps volunteer in Borneo, she advises students using *The Prose Reader* to travel as much as possible: "You need a wide range of experiences to be a good writer."

Preparing to Read

In the following essay from *Second Chances,* Wallerstein and Blakeslee classify the psychological tasks children who have suffered through the divorce of their parents must complete to free themselves from the past.

Exploring Experience: As you prepare to read this article, take a few minutes to think about the effects of divorce on yourself or someone you know: How close have you been to a divorce experience? What differences did you notice in the way adults and children responded to the same situation? Why do you think the divorce rate has been so high during the last fifty years?

Learning Online: Conduct an Internet search using the term *divorce statistics.* Keep in mind your findings when reading Wallerstein and Blakeslee's description of the different ways in which children are affected by divorce.

At each stage in the life cycle, children and adults face predictable and particular issues that represent the coming together of the demands of society and a biological and psychological timetable. Just as we physically learn to sit, crawl, walk, and run, we follow an equivalent progression in our psychological and social development. Each stage presents us with a sequence of tasks we must confront. We can succeed or fail in mastering them, to varying degrees, but everyone encounters the tasks. They begin at birth and end at death.

Children move upward along a common developmental ladder, although each goes it alone at his or her own pace. Gradually, as they pass through the various stages, children consolidate a sense of self. They develop coping skills, conscience, and the capacity to give and receive love.

Children take one step at a time, negotiating the rung they are on before they can move up to the next. They may—and often do—falter in this effort. The climb is not steady under the best of circumstances, and most children briefly stand still in their ascent. They may even at times move backward. Such regressions are not a cause for alarm; rather, they may represent an appropriate response to life's stresses. Children who fail one task are not stalled forever; they will go on to the next stage, although they may be weakened in their climb. Earlier failures will not necessarily imperil their capacity as adults to trust a relationship, make a commitment, hold an appropriate job, or be a parent—to make use of their second chances at each stage of development.

I propose that children who experience divorce face an additional set of tasks specific to divorce in addition to the normal developmental tasks of growing up. Growing up is inevitably harder for children of divorce because they must deal with psychological issues that children from well-functioning intact families do not have to face.

The psychological tasks of children begin as difficulties, escalate between the parents during the marriage, and continue through the separation and divorce and throughout the postdivorce years.

Task: Understanding the Divorce

The first and most basic task at the time of separation is for the children to understand realistically what the divorce means in their family and what its concrete consequences will be. Children, especially very young children, are thrown back on frightening and vivid fantasies of being abandoned, being

---

Thinking Critically

1 Try to remember a time when you "moved backward" in your social development. What were the long-term effects of this change on your life?

2 Why do you think growing up is more difficult for children of divorce?

placed in foster care, or never seeing a departed parent again, or macabre fantasies such as a mother being destroyed in an earthquake or a father being destroyed by a vengeful mother. All of these fantasies and the feelings that accompany them can be undone only as the children, with the parents' continuing help, begin to understand the reality and begin to adjust to the actual changes that the divorce brings.

The more mature task of understanding what led to the marital failure   7
awaits the perspective of the adolescent and young adult. Early on, most children regard divorce as a serious error, but by adolescence most feel that their parents never should have married. The task of understanding occurs in two stages. The first involves accurately perceiving the immediate changes that divorce brings and differentiating fantasy fears from reality. The second occurs later, when children are able at greater distance and with more mature understanding to evaluate their parents' actions and can draw useful lessons for their own lives. [3]

Task: Strategic Withdrawal

Children and adolescents need to get on with their own lives as soon as   8
possible after the divorce, to resume their normal activities at school and at play, to get back physically and emotionally to the normal tasks of growing up. Especially for adolescents who may have been beginning to spread their wings, the divorce pulls them back into the family orbit, where they may become consumed with care for siblings or a troubled parent. It also intrudes on their academic and social life, causing them to spend class time preoccupied with worry and to pass up social activities because of demands at home. This is not to say that children should ignore the divorce. Their task is to acknowledge their concern and to provide appropriate help to their parents and siblings, but they should strive to remove the divorce from the center of their own thoughts so that they can get back to their own interests, pleasures, problems, and peer relationships. To achieve this task, children need encouragement from their parents to *remain* children.

Task: Dealing with Loss

In the years following divorce, children experience two profound losses.   9
One is the loss of the intact family together with the symbolic and real protection it has provided. [4] The second is the loss of the presence of one parent, usually the father, from their daily lives.

Thinking Critically

[3] Explain one insight about your parents' relationship that you became aware of recently.

[4] What do you think is the difference between the "symbolic" and the "real" protection our family structure offers?

In dealing with these losses, children fall back on many fantasies to mask   10
their unhappiness. As we have seen, they may idealize the father as representative of all that is lacking in their current lives, thinking that if only he
were present, everything would be better.

The task of absorbing loss is perhaps the single most difficult task imposed   11
by divorce. At its core, the task requires children to overcome the profound
sense of rejection, humiliation, unlovability, and powerlessness they feel with
the departure of one parent. When the parent leaves, children of all ages
blame themselves. They say, "He left me because I was not lovable. I was not
worthy." They conclude that had they been more lovable, worthy, or different, the parent would have stayed. In this way, the loss of the parent and lowered self-esteem become intertwined.

To stave off these intensely painful feelings of rejection, children contin-   12
ually try to undo the divorce scenario, to bring their parents back together,
or to somehow win back the affection of the absent parent. ⑤ The explanation "Had he loved me, he would not have left the family" turns into a new
concern. "If he loved me, he would visit more often. He would spend more
time with me." With this in mind, the children not only are pained at the outset but remain vulnerable, sometimes increasingly, over the years. Many reach
out during adolescence to increase contact with the parent who left, again
to undo the sad scenario and to rebuild their self-esteem as well.

This task is easier if parents and children have a good relationship, within   13
the framework of a good visiting or joint custody arrangement.

Some children are able to use a good, close relationship with the visiting   14
parent to promote their growth within the divorced family. Others are able
to acknowledge and accept that the visiting parent could never become the
kind of parent they need, and they are able to turn away from blaming themselves. Still others are able to reject, on their own, a rejecting parent or to
reject a role model that they see as flawed. In so doing, these youngsters are
able to effectively master the loss and get on with their lives. ⑥

Task: Dealing with Anger

Divorce, unlike death, is always a voluntary decision for at least one of   15
the partners in a marriage. Everyone involved knows this. The child understands that divorce is not a natural disaster like an earthquake or tornado;
it is caused by the decision of one or both of the parents to separate. Its
true cause lies in the parents' failure to maintain the marriage, and someone
is culpable.

Thinking Critically

⑤ How and why do children "continually try to undo the divorce scenario"?

⑥ To what extent do you believe divorce is seen as a "loss" by the children of the relationship?

Given this knowledge, children face a terrible dilemma. They know that   16
their unhappiness has been caused by the very people charged with their
protection and care—their parents are the agents of their distress. Furthermore, the parents undertook this role voluntarily. This realization puts children in a dreadful bind because they know something that they dare not
express—out of fear, out of anxiety, out of a wish to protect their parents.

Children get angry at their parents, experiencing divorce as indifference   17
to their needs and perceiving parents sometimes realistically as self-centered
and uncaring, as preaching a corrupt morality, and as weak and unable to deal
with problems except by running away.

At the same time, children are aware of their parents' neediness, weak-   18
nesses, and anxiety about life's difficulties. Although children have little understanding of divorce, except when the fighting has been open and violent, they
fully recognize how unhappy and disorganized their parents become, and
this frightens them very much. Caught in a combination of anger and love,
the children are frightened and guilty about their anger because they love
their parents and perceive them as unhappy people who are trying to improve
their lives in the face of severe obstacles. Their concern makes it difficult
even to acknowledge their anger.

A major task, then, for children is to work through this anger, to recog-   19
nize their parents as human beings capable of making mistakes, and to respect
them for their real efforts and their real courage. ✦

Cooling of anger and the task of forgiveness go hand in hand with chil-   20
dren's growing emotional maturity and capacity to appreciate the various
needs of the different family members. As anger diminishes, young people are
better able to put the divorce behind them and experience relief. As children
forgive their parents, they forgive themselves for feeling anger and guilt and
for failing to restore the marriage. In this way, children can free themselves
from identification with the angry or violent parent or with the victim.

Task: Working Out Guilt

Young children often feel responsible for divorce, thinking that their mis-   21
behavior may have caused one parent to leave. Or, in a more complicated
way, they may feel that their fantasy wish to drive a wedge between their
mother and father has been magically granted. Many guilty feelings arise at
the time of divorce but dissipate naturally as children mature. Others persist, usually with roots in a profound continuing sense of having caused the
unthinkable—getting rid of one parent so as to be closer to the other.

Thinking Critically

✦ Have you ever tried to "work through" anger about something? How successful were you
in doing so?

Other feelings of guilt are rooted in children's realization that they were 22 indeed a cause of marital difficulty. Many divorces occur after the birth of a child, and the child correctly comprehends that he or she really did drive a wedge between the adults.

We see another kind of guilt in girls who, in identifying with their trou- 23 bled mothers, become afraid to surpass their mothers. These young women have trouble separating from their mothers, whom they love and feel sorry for, and establishing their own successful relationships with suitable young men. The children of divorce need to separate from guilty ties that bind them too closely to a troubled parent and to go on with their lives with compassion and love.

Task: Accepting the Permanence of the Divorce

At first, children feel a strong and understandable need to deny the divorce. 24 Such early denial may be a first step in the coping process. Like a screen that is alternately lowered and raised, the denial helps children confront the full reality of the divorce, bit by bit. They cannot take it in all at once.

Nevertheless, we have learned that five and even ten years after divorce, 25 some children and adolescents refuse to accept the divorce as a permanent state of affairs. They continue to hope, consciously or unconsciously, that the marriage will be restored, finding omens of reconciliation even in a harmless handshake or a simple friendly nod.

In accepting permanence, the children of divorce face a more difficult 26 task than children of bereavement. Death cannot be undone, but divorce happens between living people who can change their minds. A reconciliation fantasy[8] taps deep into children's psyches. Children need to feel that their parents will still be happy together. They may not overcome this fantasy of reconciliation until they themselves finally separate from their parents and leave home.

Task: Taking a Chance on Love

This is perhaps the most important task for growing children and for 27 society. Despite what life has dealt them, despite lingering fears and anxieties, the children of divorce must grow, become open to the possibility of success or failure, and take a chance on love. They must hold on to a realistic vision that they can both love and be loved.

This is the central task for youngsters during adolescence and at entry 28 into young adulthood. And as we have seen, it is the task on which so many

---

Thinking Critically

[8] What is a "reconciliation fantasy"?

children tragically flounder. Children who lose a parent through death must take a chance on loving with the knowledge that all people eventually die and that death can take away our loved ones at any time. Children who lose the intact family through divorce must also take a chance on love, knowing realistically that divorce is always possible but being willing nevertheless to remain open to love, commitment, marriage, and fidelity.

More than the ideology of hoping to fall in love and find commitment,   29
this task involves being able to turn away from the model of parents who could not stay committed to each other. While all the young people in our study were in search of romantic love, a large number of them lived with such a high degree of anxiety over fears of betrayal or of not finding love that they were entirely unable to take the kind of chances necessary for them to move emotionally into successful young adulthood.

This last task, taking a chance on love, ◆⁹ involves being able to venture,   30
not just thinking about it, and not thinking one way and behaving another. It involves accepting a morality that truly guides behavior. This is the task that occupies children of divorce throughout their adolescence. It is what makes adolescence such a critical and difficult time for them. The resolution of life's tasks is a relative process that never ends, but this last task, which is built on successfully negotiating all the others, leads to psychological freedom from the past. This is the essence of second chances for children of divorce.

UNDERSTANDING DETAILS

1. Name the seven categories into which Wallerstein and Blakeslee divide the psychological growth of the children of divorce. How long will it take most children to go through these stages?
2. Choose one of these tasks and explain it in your own words.
3. According to Wallerstein and Blakeslee, what is probably the most difficult task that results from divorce? Why do the authors believe this stage is so painful?
4. What did Wallerstein and Blakeslee find out about their subjects' ability to deal with love in their lives?

READING CRITICALLY

5. In your opinion, which of the emotional tasks that Wallerstein and Blakeslee describe is likely to be most traumatic in a child's life after a divorce? On what do you base your conclusion?

Thinking Critically

◆⁹ According to the authors, why is "taking a chance on love" tougher for children of divorce?

6. What is the relationship suggested in this essay between the parents' divorce and a child's sense of rejection?

7. In what ways does dealing with all facets of their anger create a problem for children of divorce? Do you know anyone who has worked through such a problem? Explain your answer in detail.

8. How might an understanding of the seven tasks discussed in this essay help people deal more effectively with children affected by divorce?

DISCOVERING RHETORICAL STRATEGIES

9. How do Wallerstein and Blakeslee organize their categories in this essay? Why do they place these tasks in this particular order?

10. What is the authors' general attitude toward divorce? What references in the essay reveal this point of view?

11. Describe the authors' intended audience. What makes you think they are directing their comments to this group?

12. What other rhetorical modes do Wallerstein and Blakeslee use in this essay besides division and classification? How do these other modes support the authors' division/classification system?

MAKING CONNECTIONS

13. Compare and contrast the love and support needed by children of divorce with the love and support provided naturally by the different types of families described in Mary Pipher's "Beliefs About Families."

14. What are the principal differences between Wallerstein and Blakeslee's prescriptions for how children can best cope with the death of their parents' relationships and the way in which funeral directors in Jessica Mitford's "Behind the Formaldehyde Curtain" try to help us endure the death of a friend or relative? Which coping mechanisms are the same? Which are different?

15. Wallerstein and Blakeslee divide their essay into seven "tasks" that must be accomplished by children of divorce. Find a division/classification essay in this section of *The Prose Reader* that has more subdivisions. Then, find one that has fewer. How does the number of subdivisions in a division/classification essay affect your ability to understand the author's entire argument? Which of these essays is the easiest to follow? Which is the most difficult? Why?

IDEAS FOR DISCUSSION/WRITING

Preparing to Write

Write freely about your thoughts on divorce and the effects of divorce on others: Do you know anyone who has gone through a divorce? How did the experience affect the couple getting divorced? How did it affect their friends, their relatives, and their children? How do you think the high divorce rate is affecting Americans in general? Why is the U.S. national divorce rate so high? What changes could we make to lower the divorce rate?

Choosing a Topic

1. *Learning Online:* What other important issues affect children? Visit the United Nations Children's Fund Web site (www.unicef.org), and explore issues affecting children internationally. Write an essay in which you either select a single issue and divide it into subsections or classify several different topics into a thematic order.

2. Assume that you are an expert on the variety and scope of college relationships. In an essay written for your classmates, divide your observations on different types of relationships into categories that will show students the full range of these associations in a college setting.

3. Because you have been involved with divorce in some way, you have been asked to submit to your college newspaper an editorial classifying the various ways in which different types of people react to divorce (husbands, wives, children, friends, and so on). You have been told to pay particular attention to the reactions of college students whose parents are going through or have gone through a divorce.

4. In an essay written for the general public, speculate about the reasons for the high national divorce rate. Use your own experience, interview others, or consult sources in the library to investigate the reasons for this trend. Suggest how we could solve this problem in the United States.

Before beginning your essay, you might want to consult the checklists on page 269.

AMY TAN   (1952–   )

Mother Tongue

In a very short time, Amy Tan has established herself as one of the foremost Chinese-American writers. Her first novel, *The Joy Luck Club* (1989), which was praised as "brilliant . . . a jewel of a book" by the *New York Times* Book Review, focuses on the lives of four Chinese women in pre-1949 China and their American-born daughters in modern-day California. Through a series of vignettes, Tan weaves together the dreams and sorrows of these mothers and daughters as they confront oppression in China and equally difficult cultural challenges in the new world of the United States. Like the protagonists in *The Joy Luck Club,* Tan's parents, a Baptist minister and a licensed vocational nurse, emigrated to America shortly before Tan's birth. She showed an early talent for writing when, at age eight, she won an essay contest (and a transistor radio) with a paper entitled "Why I Love the Library." Following the tremendous success of her first novel, Tan apparently had great difficulty writing her second book, *The Kitchen God's Wife* (1991). As she was working on it, she began grinding her teeth, which resulted in two broken molars and a sizable dental bill. "I am glad that I shall never again have to write a second book," the author has confessed. "Actually, I cannot recall any writer—with or without a splashy debut—who said the second book came easily." Successful film and stage adaptations of *The Joy Luck Club* in 1993 were followed by *The Chinese Siamese Cat* (1994), *The Hundred Secret Senses* (1995), *The Year of No Flood* (1996), *The Bonesetter's Daughter* (2001), *The Opposite of Fate: A Book of Musings* (2003), and *Saving Fish from Drowning* (2005).

Preparing to Read

In the following essay, originally published in *The Threepenny Review,* Amy Tan classifies the different "Englishes" she learned to use in her youth. These had a significant effect on her as she grew up to be a successful writer.

Exploring Experience: As you prepare to read this essay, take a few minutes to think about the different types of English that you use: How do you change your use of English when you relay the same message to different people? Why do you make these changes? Do you feel as if you do well in English class? On English tests? How could you become an even better writer and speaker of English than you already are?

Learning Online: To better understand Tan's cultural context, conduct an Internet search on the experience of Chinese immigrants in the United States. To start your search, you may want to visit "Becoming an American: The Chinese Experience" located at www.pbs.org/becomingamerican. Pay special attention to the Chinese-American women's experiences.

I am not a scholar of English or literature. I cannot give you much more   1
than personal opinions on the English language and its variations in this
country or others.

I am a writer. And by that definition, I am someone who has always loved   2
language. I am fascinated by language in daily life. I spend a great deal of my
time thinking about the power of language—the way it can evoke an emotion, a visual image, a complex idea, or a simple truth. Language is the tool
of my trade. And I use them all—all the Englishes I grew up with. **1**

Recently, I was made keenly aware of the different Englishes I do use. I   3
was giving a talk to a large group of people, the same talk I had already given
to half a dozen other groups. The nature of the talk was about my writing,
my life, and my book, *The Joy Luck Club*. The talk was going along well
enough, until I remembered one major difference that made the whole talk
sound wrong. My mother was in the room. And it was perhaps the first time
she had heard me give a lengthy speech, using the kind of English I have never
used with her. I was saying things like, "The intersection of memory upon
imagination" and "There is an aspect of my fiction that relates to thus-and-
thus"—a speech filled with carefully wrought grammatical phrases, bur-
dened, it suddenly seemed to me, with nominalized forms, past perfect tenses,
conditional phrases, all the forms of standard English that I had learned in
school and through books, the forms of English I did not use at home with
my mother.

Just last week, I was walking down the street with my mother, and I again   4
found myself conscious of the English I was using, the English I do use with
her. We were talking about the price of new and used furniture and I heard
myself saying this: "Not waste money that way." My husband was with us as
well, and he didn't notice any switch in my English. And then I realized why.
It's because over the twenty years we've been together I've often used the
same kind of English with him, and sometimes he even uses it with me. It
has become our language of intimacy, **2** a different sort of English that relates
to family talk, the language I grew up with.

So you'll have some idea of what this family talk I heard sounds like, I'll   5
quote what my mother said during a recent conversation which I videotaped and then transcribed. During this conversation, my mother was talking about a political gangster in Shanghai who had the same last name as her
family's, Du, and how the gangster in his early years wanted to be adopted
by her family, which was rich by comparison. Later, the gangster became

---

Thinking Critically

1 Why does Tan use the word "Englishes"? What is she referring to?

2 What does the author mean by the phrase "our language of intimacy"?

more powerful, far richer than my mother's family, and one day showed up at my mother's wedding to pay his respects. Here's what she said in part:

"Du Yusong having business like fruit stand. Like of the street kind. He is Du like Du Zong—but not Tsung-ming Island people. The local people call *putong,* the river east side, he belong to that side local people. That man want to ask Du Zong father take him in like become own family. Du Zong father wasn't look down on him, but didn't take seriously, until that man big like become a mafia. Now important person, very hard to inviting him. Chinese way, came only to show respect, don't stay for dinner. Respect for making big celebration, he shows up. Mean gives lots of respect. Chinese custom. Chinese social life that way. If too important won't have to stay too long. He come to my wedding. I didn't see, I heard it. I gone to boy's side, they have YMCA dinner, Chinese age I was nineteen." **❸**

You should know that my mother's expressive command of English belies how much she actually understands. She reads the *Forbes* report, listens to *Wall Street Week,* converses daily with her stockbroker, reads all of Shirley MacLaine's books with ease—all kinds of things I can't begin to understand. Yet some of my friends tell me they understand 50 percent of what my mother says. Some say they understand 80 to 90 percent. Some say they understand none of it, as if she were speaking pure Chinese. But to me, my mother's English is perfectly clear, perfectly natural. It's my mother tongue. Her language, as I hear it, is vivid, direct full of observation and imagery. That was the language that helped shape the way I saw things, expressed things, made sense of the world.

Lately, I've been giving more thought to the kind of English my mother speaks. Like others, I have described it to people as "broken" or "fractured" English. But I wince when I say that. It has always bothered me that I can think of no way to describe it other than "broken," as if it were damaged and needed to be fixed, as if it lacked a certain wholeness and soundness. I've heard other terms used, "limited English," for example. But they seem just as bad, as if everything is limited, including people's perceptions of the limited English speaker.

I know this for a fact, because when I was growing up, my mother's "limited" English limited *my* perception of her. **❹** I was ashamed of her English. I believed that her English reflected the quality of what she had to say. That is, because she expressed them imperfectly, her thoughts were imperfect. And I had plenty of empirical evidence to support me: the fact that people in department stores, at banks, and at restaurants did not take her seriously, did

6

7

8

9

Thinking Critically

❸ What is the author's main point here? Why did the gangster come to Tan's mother's wedding?

❹ How true is this in your life? To what extent do you judge others by their use of English?

not give her good advice, pretended not to understand her, or even acted as if they did not hear her.

My mother has long realized the limitations of her English as well. When   10
I was fifteen, she used to have me call people on the phone and pretend I was she. In this guise, I was forced to ask for information or even to complain and yell at people who had been rude to her. One time it was a call to her stockbroker in New York. She had cashed out her small portfolio, and it just so happened we were going to go to New York the next week, our very first trip outside California. I had to get on the phone and say in an adolescent voice that was not very convincing, "This is Mrs. Tan."

And my mother was standing in the back whispering loudly, "Why he don't   11
send me check, already two weeks late. So mad he lie to me, losing my money."

And then I said in perfect English, "Yes, I'm getting rather concerned.   12
You had agreed to send the check two weeks ago, but it hasn't arrived."

Then she began to talk more loudly. "What he want, I come to New York   13
tell him front of his boss, you cheating me?" And I was trying to calm her down, make her be quiet, while telling the stockbroker, "I can't tolerate any more excuses. If I don't receive the check immediately, I am going to have to speak to your manager when I'm in New York next week." And sure enough, the following week there we were in front of this astonished stockbroker, and I was sitting there red-faced and quiet, and my mother, the real Mrs. Tan, was shouting at his boss in her impeccable broken English. ⑤

We used a similar routine just five days ago, for a situation that was far less   14
humorous. My mother had gone to the hospital for an appointment, to find out about a benign brain tumor a CAT scan had revealed a month ago. She said she had spoken very good English, her best English, no mistakes. Still, she said, the hospital did not apologize when they said they had lost the CAT scan and she had come for nothing. She said they did not seem to have any sympathy when she told them she was anxious to know the exact diagnosis, since her husband and son had both died of brain tumors. She said they would not give her any more information until the next time and she would have to make another appointment for that. So she said she would not leave until the doctor called her daughter. She wouldn't budge. And when the doctor finally called her daughter, me, who spoke in perfect English—lo and behold—we had assurances the CAT scan would be found, promises that a conference call on Monday would be held, and apologies for any suffering my mother had gone through for a most regrettable mistake.

I think my mother's English almost had an effect on limiting my possi-   15
bilities in life as well. Sociologists and linguists probably will tell you that a

---

Thinking Critically

⑤ Why does Tan use the oxymoron "impeccable broken English" here? What does the phrase mean?

person's developing language skills are more influenced by peers. But I do think that the language spoken in the family, especially in immigrant families which are more insular, plays a large role in shaping the language of the child. ❻ And I believe that it affected my results on achievement tests, IQ tests, and the SAT. While my English skills were never judged as poor, compared to math, English could not be considered my strong suit. In grade school I did moderately well, getting perhaps B's, sometimes B-pluses, in English and scoring perhaps in the sixtieth or seventieth percentile on achievement tests. But those scores were not good enough to override the opinion that my true abilities lay in math and science, because in those areas I achieved A's and scored in the ninetieth percentile or higher.

This was understandable. Math is precise; there is only one correct   16
answer. ❼ Whereas, for me at least, the answers on English tests were always a judgment call, a matter of opinion and personal experience. Those tests were constructed around items like fill-in-the-blank sentence completion, such as "Even though Tom was _____, Mary thought he was _____." And the correct answer always seemed to be the most bland combinations of thoughts, for example, "Even though Tom was shy, Mary thought he was charming," with the grammatical structure "even though" limiting the correct answer to some sort of semantic opposites, so you wouldn't get answers like, "Even though Tom was foolish, Mary thought he was ridiculous." Well, according to my mother, there were very few limitations as to what Tom could have been and what Mary might have thought of him. So I never did well on tests like that.

The same was true with word analogies, pairs of words in which you were   17
supposed to find some sort of logical, semantic relationship—for example, "Sunset is to nightfall as _____ is to _____." And here you would be presented with a list of four possible pairs, one of which showed the same kind of relationship: *red* is to *stoplight, bus* is to *arrival, chills* is to *fever, yawn* is to *boring.* Well, I could never think that way. I knew what the tests were asking, but I could not block out of my mind the images already created by the first pair, *"sunset is to nightfall"*—and I would see a burst of colors against a darkening sky, the moon rising, the lowering of a curtain of stars. And all the other pairs of words—red, bus, stoplight, boring—just threw up a mass of confusing images, making it impossible for me to sort out something as logical as saying: "A sunset precedes nightfall" is the same as "a chill precedes a fever." The only way I would have gotten that answer right would have

---

Thinking Critically

❻ Do you think this is true? How has the English you heard as a child influenced your use of language today?

❼ Which subject do you like better—math or English? Which is more difficult for you? Why?

been to imagine an associative situation, for example, my being disobedient and staying out past sunset, catching a chill at night, which turns into feverish pneumonia as punishment, which indeed did happen to me.

I have been thinking about all this lately, about my mother's English, about achievement tests. Because lately I've been asked, as a writer, why there are not more Asian Americans represented in American literature. Why are there few Asian Americans enrolled in creative writing programs? Why do so many Chinese students go into engineering? Well, these are broad sociological questions I can't begin to answer. But I have noticed in surveys—in fact, just last week—that Asian students, as a whole, always do significantly better on math achievement tests than in English. And this makes me think that there are other Asian-American students whose English spoken in the home might also be described as "broken" or "limited." And perhaps they also have teachers who are steering them away from writing and into math and science, which is what happened to me. [8]   18

Fortunately, I happen to be rebellious in nature and enjoy the challenge of disproving assumptions made about me. I became an English major my first year in college, after being enrolled as pre-med. I started writing nonfiction as a freelancer the week after I was told by my former boss that writing was my worst skill and I should hone my talents toward account management.   19

But it wasn't until 1985 that I finally began to write fiction. And at first I wrote using what I thought to be wittily crafted sentences, sentences that would prove I had mastery over the English language. Here's an example from the first draft of a story that later made its way into *The Joy Luck Club,* but without this line: "That was my mental quandary in its nascent state." A terrible line, which I can barely pronounce.   20

Fortunately, for reasons I won't get into today, I later decided I should envision a reader for the stories I would write. And the reader I decided upon was my mother, because these were stories about mothers. So with this reader in mind—and in fact she did read my early drafts—I began to write stories using all the Englishes I grew up with: the English I spoke to my mother, which for lack of a better term might be described as "simple"; the English she used with me, which for lack of a better term might be described as "broken"; my translation of her Chinese, which could certainly be described as "watered down"; and what I imagined to be her translation of her Chinese if she could speak in perfect English, her internal language, [9]   21

Thinking Critically

[8] To what extent do you think ethnic bias exists in the career advice students receive in high school and college?

[9] What does Tan mean when she refers to her mother's "internal language"?

and for that I sought to preserve the essence, but neither an English nor a Chinese structure. I wanted to capture what language ability tests can never reveal: her intent, her passion, her imagery, the rhythms of her speech, and the nature of her thoughts.

Apart from what any critic had to say about my writing, I knew I had suc- 22 ceeded where it counted when my mother finished reading my book and gave me her verdict: "So easy to read."

UNDERSTANDING DETAILS

1. What do you think is Tan's main reason for writing this essay?
2. What are the four "Englishes" that Tan grew up with? Explain each in your own words.
3. What is Tan referring to when she uses the term "mother tongue"?
4. How did Tan feel about her mother's "limited English" in the past?

READING CRITICALLY

5. How did Amy Tan become a writer? In what way did her rebellious nature help her make this decision?
6. How do all the Englishes Tan grew up with help her as a writer? Explain your answer.
7. What relationship does Tan see between achievement test scores and actual abilities?
8. Why did Tan choose her mother as the audience she envisions when she writes?

DISCOVERING RHETORICAL STRATEGIES

9. Why does Tan actually quote some of her mother's language early in her essay? What effect does this example have on you as a reader?
10. Tan discusses these types of English in a specific order. Explain this progression, and discuss whether it is effective in achieving her overall purpose.
11. Describe Tan's intended audience in as much detail as possible. Why do you think she aims her essay at this particular group?
12. What other rhetorical strategies does Tan use to help make her point? Give examples of each of these strategies.

MAKING CONNECTIONS

13. Compare and contrast Amy Tan's relationship with her mother and the parent–child relationships examined in any or all of the following essays: Lewis Sawaquat's "For My Indian Daughter," Firoozeh Dumas's "Leffingwell Elementary School," Russell Baker's "The Saturday Evening Post," and/or Wallerstein and Blakeslee's "Second Chances for Children of Divorce."

14. In her essay, Tan describes her love of English and her avocation as a writer despite her relatively weak performance on English achievement tests as a child. Examine the manner in which other people exceeded the expectations placed on them as expressed in Maya Angelou's "New Directions," Russell Baker's "The Saturday Evening Post," Harold Krents's "Darkness at Noon," and/or Alice Walker's "Beauty: When the Other Dancer Is the Self."

15. Discuss the theme of "the limitations of language" as it appears in any of the following essays you have read: "Mother Tongue," Stephanie Ericsson's "The Ways We Lie," Mary Roach's "Meet the Bickersons," and/or Sherman Alexie's "The Joy of Reading and Writing: Superman and Me."

IDEAS FOR DISCUSSION/WRITING

Preparing to Write

Write freely about your own abilities in English: Do you feel you use more than one version of English? How does your oral English differ from your written English? Is English your first language? What do you think of yourself as a writer? As a reader? How well do you perform on English achievement tests?

Choosing a Topic

1. *Learning Online:* Tan refers to the ways in which family, culture, and education affect how she speaks and writes. Using recent emails you have written, examine the "different Englishes" and other languages you use when communicating with diverse audiences. For example, what words do you use when writing to your friends, your family, or your teachers? How do your language choices differ in each instance? What social pressures affect your use of "different Englishes"? Write an essay that examines your different uses of English and/or other languages. Consider your reasons for using various words when communicating with different people. Use specific examples from your emails to support and develop your essay.

2. As a college student, you see different people approaching their writing assignments in different ways every day. Some students get right down to work. Others procrastinate until the last minute. Some write in spurts until they have finished the task. Write an essay for your school newspaper explaining your observations about the different ways people write. Use carefully chosen examples to illustrate your observations. You might even want to interview some of your peers about their writing rituals.

3. Pretend that your college newspaper is running a special issue distinguishing among different generations of students. In a coherent essay written for the readers of this newspaper, classify the students of your generation in some logical, interesting fashion. Remember that classification is a rhetorical movement from "many" to "one." Group the members of your generation by some meaningful guidelines or general characteristics that you establish. Be sure to decide on a purpose and a point of view before you begin to write.

4. In her essay, Tan refers to the fact that her teachers steered her "away from writ-
    ing and into math and science" (paragraph 18) primarily because of her test
    scores. But she believes her test scores were not an accurate measurement of her
    ability in English because of her background in the language. Do you think
    test scores are ever used inappropriately to advise students? Do you think these
    scores are the best way we currently have to measure ability and aptitude? Direct
    your comments to the general public, and use several specific examples to sup-
    port your opinion.

Before beginning your essay, you might want to consult the checklists on page 269.

STEPHANIE ERICSSON   (1953–   )

The Ways We Lie

Born in Dallas, Stephanie Ericsson grew up in San Francisco and lived in London, Spain, New York, and Los Angeles before settling in Minneapolis, Minnesota, where she currently lives with her two children. Following a filmmaking degree in college, she worked in advertising and then became a screenwriter's assistant and later a writer of situation comedies. After overcoming substance abuse problems, she published *Shamefaced: The Road to Recovery* (1985) and *Women of AA: Recovering Together* (1985). When she was 32 years old, her husband died suddenly of a heart attack while she was two and a half months pregnant, thereby inspiring a number of journal entries and two frank and wrenching books on grief: *Companion Through the Darkness: Inner Dialogues on Grief* (1993) and *Companion into the Dawn: Inner Dialogues on Loving* (1994). Defining grief as "the constant reawakening that things are now different," she argues that it "shears away the masks of normal life and forces brutal honesty out of your mouth before propriety can stop you. It shoves away friends and scares away so-called friends and rewrites your address book for you." Her unique prose style is a very effective combination of her own diary entries mixed with brief essays that vividly chronicle wrenching emotions of grief. A frequent speaker on the subject of loss, Ericsson has written extensively on human psychology and the mental and physical repercussions of addiction and deceit.

Preparing to Read

In this essay, first published in the *Utne Reader,* Stephanie Ericsson categorizes the different types of lies we all tell in an attempt to portray the reality we live in and clarify how lying affects our social morality.

Exploring Experience: As you prepare to read this selection, consider how often you lie or stretch the truth in a typical day: Do you find that you don't tell the truth in every situation? When do you stretch the truth? Why do you do it? What are the consequences of these lies? Do you feel guilty when you don't tell the whole truth? Why do you think you feel this way?

Learning Online: Visit the Blifaloo Web site selection "How to Detect Lies" (www.blifaloo.com/info/lies.php), and read this short article on the common signs of deception. According to the essay, what are some of the physical gestures, facial expressions, and verbal indicators that people display when they are lying? Have you ever been aware of these indicators in yourself or someone else? You also might read the companion article "Eye Direction and Lying" (www.blifaloo.com/info/lies_eyes.php).

The bank called today and I told them my deposit was in the mail, even though I hadn't written a check yet. It'd been a rough day. The baby I'm pregnant with decided to do aerobics on my lungs for two hours, our three-year-old daughter painted the living-room couch with lipstick, the IRS put me on hold for an hour, and I was late to a business meeting because I was tired.

I told my client that traffic had been bad. When my partner came home, his haggard face told me his day hadn't gone any better than mine, so when he asked, "How was your day?" I said, "Oh, fine," knowing that one more straw might break his back. A friend called and wanted to take me to lunch. I said I was busy. Four lies in the course of a day, none of which I felt the least bit guilty about.

We lie. We all do. We exaggerate, we minimize, we avoid confrontation, we spare people's feelings, we conveniently forget, we keep secrets, we justify lying to the big-guy institutions. Like most people, I indulge in small falsehoods and still think of myself as an honest person. Sure I lie, but it doesn't hurt anything. Or does it? ❶

I once tried going a whole week without telling a lie, and it was paralyzing. I discovered that telling the truth all the time is nearly impossible. It means living with some serious consequences: The bank charges me $60 in overdraft fees, my partner keels over when I tell him about my travails, my client fires me for telling her I didn't feel like being on time, and my friend takes it personally when I say I'm not hungry. There must be some merit to lying.

But if I justify lying, what makes me any different from slick politicians or the corporate robbers who raided the S&L industry? Saying it's okay to lie one way and not another is hedging. I cannot seem to escape the voice deep inside me that tells me: When someone lies, someone loses.

What far-reaching consequences will I, or others, pay as a result of my lie? ❷ Will someone's trust be destroyed? Will someone else pay my penance because I ducked out? We must consider the *meaning of our actions*. Deception, lies, capital crimes, and misdemeanors all carry meanings. *Webster's* definition of *lie* is specific:

1. a false statement or action especially made with the intent to deceive;
2. anything that gives or is meant to give a false impression.

A definition like this implies that there are many, many ways to tell a lie. Here are just a few.

Thinking Critically

❶ Do you think lying "doesn't hurt anything"? Have you ever been harmed by a lie?

❷ Have your lies ever hurt another person? How did the situation make you feel?

The White Lie

A man who won't lie to a woman has very little consideration for her feelings.

—*Bergen Evans*

The white lie assumes that the truth will cause more damage than a sim-   8
ple, harmless untruth. Telling a friend he looks great when he looks like hell
can be based on a decision that the friend needs a compliment more than a
frank opinion. But, in effect, it is the liar deciding what is best for the lied
to. Ultimately, it is a vote of no confidence. It is an act of subtle arrogance
for anyone to decide what is best for someone else.

Yet not all circumstances are quite so cut and dried. Take, for instance, the   9
sergeant in Vietnam who knew one of his men was killed in action but listed
him as missing so that the man's family would receive indefinite compensation instead of the lump sum pittance the military gives widows and children. His intent was honorable. Yet for twenty years this family kept their
hopes alive, unable to move on to a new life. ❸

Façades

Et tu, Brute?

—*Caesar*

We all put up façades to one degree or another. When I put on a suit to   10
go to see a client, I feel as though I am putting on another face, obeying the
expectation that serious businesspeople wear suits rather than sweatpants. But
I'm a writer: Normally, I get up, get the kid off to school, and sit at my computer in my pajamas until four in the afternoon. When I answer the phone,
the caller thinks I'm wearing a suit (though the UPS man knows better).

But façades can be destructive because they are used to seduce others into   11
an illusion. For instance, I recently realized that a former friend was a liar.
He presented himself with all the right looks and the right words and offered
lots of new consciousness theories, fabulous books to read, and fascinating
insights. Then I did some business with him, and the time came for him to
pay me. He turned out to be all talk and no walk. I heard a plethora of reasonable excuses, including in-depth descriptions of the big break around the
corner. In six months of work, I saw less than a hundred bucks. When I confronted him, he raised both eyebrows and tried to convince me that I'd heard
him wrong, that he'd made no commitment to me. A simple investigation into
his past revealed a crowded graveyard of disenchanted former friends. ❹

Thinking Critically

❸ Do you approve of the sergeant's lie? Why or why not?

❹ What does the metaphor "a crowded graveyard of disenchanted former friends" mean to
you? Where else does the author use metaphors?

Ignoring the Plain Facts

Well, you must understand that Father Porter is only human.

—A Massachusetts Priest

In the '60s, the Catholic Church in Massachusetts began hearing com-   12
plaints that Father James Porter was sexually molesting children. Rather
than relieving him of his duties, the ecclesiastical authorities moved him
from one parish to another between 1960 and 1967, actually providing him
with a fresh supply of unsuspecting families and innocent children to abuse.
After treatment in 1967 for pedophilia, he went back to work, this time in
Minnesota. The new diocese was aware of Father Porter's obsession with
children, but they needed priests and recklessly believed treatment had cured
him. More children were abused until he was relieved of his duties a year
later. By his own admission, Porter may have abused as many as a hundred
children.

Ignoring the facts may not in and of itself be a form of lying, but con-   13
sider the context of this situation. If a lie is a false action done with the
intent to deceive, then the Catholic Church's conscious covering for Porter
created irreparable consequences. The church became a co-perpetrator with
Porter.

Deflecting

When you have no basis for an argument, abuse the plaintiff.

—Cicero

I've discovered that I can keep anyone from seeing the true me by being   14
selectively blatant. I set a precedent of being up-front about intimate issues,
but I never bring up the things I truly want to hide; I just let people assume
I'm revealing everything. It's an effective way of hiding. ⑤

Any good liar knows that the way to perpetuate an untruth is to deflect   15
attention from it. When Clarence Thomas exploded with accusations that the
Senate hearings were a "high-tech lynching," he simply switched the focus
from a highly charged subject to a radioactive subject. Rather than defending himself, he took the offensive and accused the country of racism. It was
a brilliant maneuver. Racism is now politically incorrect in official circles—
unlike sexual harassment, which still rewards those who can get away with it.

Some of the most skilled deflectors are passive-aggressive people who,   16
when accused of inappropriate behavior, refuse to respond to the accusations.
This you-don't-exist stance infuriates the accuser, who, understandably,

---

Thinking Critically

⑤ What does the term "deflecting" mean? How does this differ from the white lie?

screams something obscene out of frustration. The trap is sprung and the act of deflection successful, because now the passive aggressive person can indignantly say, "Who can talk to someone as unreasonable as you?" The real issue is forgotten and the sins of the original victim become the focus. Feeling guilty of name-calling, the victim is fully tamed and crawls into a hole, ashamed. I have watched this fighting technique work thousands of times in disputes between men and women, and what I've learned is that the real culprit is not necessarily the one who swears the loudest.

Omission

The cruelest lies are often told in silence.

—*R. L. Stevenson*

Omission involves telling most of the truth minus one or two key facts 17 whose absence changes the story completely. You break a pair of glasses that are guaranteed under normal use and get a new pair, without mentioning that the first pair broke during a rowdy game of basketball. Who hasn't tried something like that? But what about omission of information that could make a difference in how a person lives his or her life?

For instance, one day I found out that rabbinical legends tell of another 18 woman in the Garden of Eden before Eve. I was stunned. The omission of the Sumerian goddess Lilith from Genesis—as well as her demonization by ancient misogynists as an embodiment of female evil—felt like spiritual robbery. I felt like I'd just found out my mother was really my stepmother. To take seriously the tradition that Adam was created out of the same mud as his equal counterpart, Lilith, redefines all of Judeo-Christian history.

Some renegade Catholic feminists introduced me to a view of Lilith that 19 had been suppressed during the many centuries when this strong goddess was seen only as a spirit of evil. Lilith was a proud goddess who defied Adam's need to control her, attempted negotiations, and when this failed, said adios and left the Garden of Eden.

This omission of Lilith from the Bible was a patriarchal strategy to keep 20 women weak. Omitting the strong-woman archetype of Lilith from Western religions and starting the story with Eve the Rib has helped keep Christian and Jewish women believing they were the lesser sex for thousands of years.

Stereotypes and Clichés

Where opinion does not exist, the status quo becomes stereotyped and all originality is discouraged.

—*Bertrand Russell*

Stereotype and cliché serve a purpose as a form of shorthand. [6] Our need 21
for vast amounts of information in nanoseconds has made the stereotype
vital to modern communication. Unfortunately, it often shuts down original thinking, giving those hungry for the truth a candy bar of misinforma-
tion instead of a balanced meal. The stereotype explains a situation with just
enough truth to seem unquestionable.

All the "isms"—racism, sexism, ageism, et al.—are founded on and fueled 22
by the stereotype and the cliché, which are lies of exaggeration, omission, and
ignorance. They are always dangerous. They take a single tree and make it a landscape. They destroy curiosity. They close minds and separate people. The single mother on welfare is assumed to be cheating. Any black male could tell you
how much of his identity is obliterated daily by stereotypes. Fat people, ugly
people; beautiful people, old people, large-breasted women, short men, the
mentally ill, and the homeless man could tell you how much more they are like
us than we want to think. I once admitted to a group of people that I had a
mouth like a truck driver. Much to my surprise, a man stood up and said, "I'm
a truck driver, and I never cuss." Needless to say, I was humbled.

Groupthink

Who is more foolish, the child afraid of the dark, or the man afraid of the light?
—Maurice Freehill

Irving Janis, in *Victims of Group Think,* defines this sort of lie as a psycho- 23
logical phenomenon within decision-making groups in which loyalty to the
group has become more important than any other value, with the result that
dissent and the appraisal of alternatives are suppressed. If you've ever worked
on a committee or in a corporation, you've encountered groupthink. [7] It
requires a combination of other forms or lying—ignoring facts, selective
memory, omission, and denial, to name a few.

The textbook example of groupthink came on December 7, 1941. From 24
as early as the fall of 1941, the warnings came in, one after another, that
Japan was preparing for a massive military operation. The navy command
in Hawaii assumed Pearl Harbor was invulnerable—the Japanese weren't
stupid enough to attack the United States' most important base. On the
other hand, racist stereotypes said the Japanese weren't smart enough to
invent a torpedo effective in less than 60 feet of water (the fleet was docked
in 30 feet); after all, US technology hadn't been able to do it.

Thinking Critically

[6] In what way are stereotype and cliché a "form of shorthand"?

[7] What is "groupthink"? Have you ever been involved in it?

On Friday, December 5, normal weekend leave was granted to all the   25
commanders at Pearl Harbor even though the Japanese consulate in Hawaii
was busy burning papers. Within the tight, good-ole-boy cohesiveness of the
US command in Hawaii, the myth of invulnerability stayed well entrenched.
No one in the group considered the alternatives. The rest is history. ◆⁸

Out-and-Out Lies

The only form of lying that is beyond reproach is lying for its own sake.
—Oscar Wilde

Of all the ways to lie, I like this one the best, probably because I get tired   26
of trying to figure out the real meanings behind things. At least I can trust
the bald-faced lie. I once asked my five-year-old nephew, "Who broke the
fence?" (I had seen him do it.) He answered, "The murderers." Who could
argue?

At least when this sort of lie is told it can be easily confronted. As the   27
person who is lied to, I know where I stand. The bald-faced lie doesn't toy
with my perceptions—it argues with them. It doesn't try to refashion reality, it tries to refute it. *Read my lips. . . .* No sleight of hand. No guessing. If
this were the only form of lying, there would be no such things as floating
anxiety or the adult–children–of–alcoholics movement.

Dismissal

Pay no attention to that man behind the curtain! I am the Great Oz!
—The Wizard of Oz

Dismissal is perhaps the slipperiest of all lies. Dismissing feelings, percep-   28
tions, or even the raw facts of a situation ranks as a kind of lie that can do as
much damage to a person as any other kind of lie.

The roots of many mental disorders can be linked back to the dismissal   29
of reality. Imagine that a person is told from the time she is a tot that her perceptions are inaccurate. *"Mommy, I'm scared."* "No you're not, darling." *"I
don't like that man next door, he makes me feel icky."* "Johnny, that's a terrible thing
to say, of course you like him. You go over there right now and be nice to
him."

I've often mused over the idea that madness is actually a sane reaction to   30
an insane world. ◆⁹ Psychologist R. D. Laing supports this hypothesis in *Sanity,
Madness and the Family,* an account of his investigation into the families of

---

Thinking Critically

◆⁸ What does "history" mean in this context?

◆⁹ Do you agree that "madness is actually a sane reaction to an insane world"? Why or why not?

schizophrenics. The common thread that ran through all of the families he studied was a deliberate, staunch dismissal of the patient's perceptions from a very early age. Each of the patients started out with an accurate grasp of reality, which, through meticulous and methodical dismissal, was demolished until the only reality the patient could trust was catatonia.

Dismissal runs the gamut. Mild dismissal can be quite handy for forgiving the foibles of others in our day-to-day lives. Toddlers who have just learned to manipulate their parents' attention sometimes are dismissed out of necessity. Absolute attention from the parents would require so much energy that no one would get to eat dinner. But we must be careful and attentive about how far we take our "necessary" dismissals. Dismissal is a dangerous tool, because it's nothing less than a lie.   31

Delusion

We lie loudest when we lie to ourselves.

—Eric Hoffer

I could write the book on this one. Delusion, a cousin of dismissal, is the tendency to see excuses as facts. It's a powerful lying tool because it filters out information that contradicts what we want to believe. Alcoholics who believe that the problems in their lives are legitimate reasons for drinking rather than results of the drinking offer the classic example of deluded thinking. Delusion uses the mind's ability to see things in myriad ways to support what it wants to be the truth.   32

But delusion is also a survival mechanism we all use. If we were to fully contemplate the consequences of our stockpiles of nuclear weapons or global warming, we could hardly function on a day-to-day level. We don't want to incorporate that much reality into our lives because to do so would be paralyzing.   33

Delusion acts as an adhesive to keep the status quo intact. It shamelessly employs dismissal, omission, and amnesia, among other sorts of lies. Its most cunning defense is that it cannot see itself.   34

The liar's punishment [...] is that he cannot believe anyone else.

—George Bernard Shaw

These are only a few of the ways we lie. Or are lied to. As I said earlier, it's not easy to entirely eliminate lies from our lives. No matter how pious we may try to be, we will still embellish, hedge, and omit to lubricate the daily machinery of living. [10] But there is a world of difference between telling   35

Thinking Critically

[10] In what way do lies "lubricate the daily machinery of living"?

functional lies and living a lie. Martin Buber once said, "The lie is the spirit committing treason against itself." Our acceptance of lies becomes a cultural cancer that eventually shrouds and reorders reality until moral garbage becomes as invisible to us as water is to a fish.

How much do we tolerate before we become sick and tired of being sick   36
and tired? When will we stand up and declare our *right* to trust? When do we stop accepting that the real truth is in the fine print? Whose lips do we read this year when we vote for president? When will we stop being so reticent about making judgments? When do we stop turning over our personal power and responsibility to liars?

Maybe if I don't tell the bank the check's in the mail I'll be less tolerant   37
of the lies told to me every day. A country song I once heard said it all for me: "You've got to stand for something or you'll fall for anything."

UNDERSTANDING DETAILS

1. According to Ericsson, why do we all lie?
2. What are the ten types of lies the author delineates?
3. How do we justify lying in our lives?
4. Why does Ericsson claim that telling the truth all the time is "nearly impossible" (paragraph 4)?

READING CRITICALLY

5. What are some of the consequences Ericsson is referring to at the beginning of this essay?
6. Which of these types of lies do you tell most often? Why do you resort to them?
7. Which of these types of lies would you say is most damaging? Why is this so?
8. What is the difference between "telling functional lies and living a lie" (paragraph 35)?

DISCOVERING RHETORICAL STRATEGIES

9. What do the quotes that the author uses to introduce each type of lie add to the explanations of each category?
10. Why does Ericsson end her essay with lyrics from a song? What do they mean? What significance do they have in this essay?
11. What does the definition from *Webster's* dictionary add to Ericsson's essay?
12. What other rhetorical strategies does the author use besides division/classification?

MAKING CONNECTIONS

13. To what extent would Ericsson and/or Jessica Mitford ("Behind the Formaldehyde Curtain") agree on the need for "façades" in life?

14. Read Ericsson's section on "Stereotypes and Clichés," and then analyze Malcolm Cowley's "The View from 80," Sandra Cisneros's "Only daughter," Gloria Steinem's "The Politics of Muscle," and/or Sucheng Chan's "You're Short, Besides!" in terms of how much each of these authors has suffered from being a member of a group that society sometimes stereotypes.

15. Contrast the ways in which Ericsson, Tamala Edwards ("Multi-Colored Families"), and/or K. C. Cole ("Calculated Risks") divide their various topics.

IDEAS FOR DISCUSSION/WRITING

Preparing to Write

Write freely about the role of lies in your life: What types of lies do you tell most often? Why do you tell these lies? How are these lies necessary to your life? How do you justify these lies? Would telling the truth all the time have any negative consequences for you? If so, what would these consequences be?

Choosing a Topic

1. *Learning Online:* At the bottom of the Blifaloo article "How to Detect Lies" (www.blifaloo.com/info/lies.php) is a section inviting readers to post comments. Read the comments that others have posted, and then write a response that you would like to post in response to the article.

2. A friend found out you lied to him or her and demands an explanation. Instead of talking to your friend, you decide to write an explanation of the history of the lie, your justification for this lie, and an apology (if appropriate).

3. Write an essay explaining and analyzing our behavior when we lie. Use information you learned from Ericsson and your own experience when appropriate.

4. John Webster once said, "There is nothing so powerful as truth—and often nothing so strange." What does this statement mean to you? Write an essay to Ericsson explaining this concept.

Before beginning your essay, you might want to consult the checklists on page 269.

Chapter Writing Assignments

Practicing Division/Classification

1. Do you think public schools should teach students ethics and personal values? If so, which values should schools teach in order to produce "good citizens"? Classify these values in an essay, and explain how these categories would have fit into your high school curriculum.

2. What problems are most destructive to a healthy relationship? Choose a specific type of relationship (friend, spouse, parent–child), and write an essay discussing various categories of problems that can cause the most trouble in this type of relationship. Explain why the qualities you identify would be destructive in the kind of relationship you describe.

3. Think about the ideal _____ (fill in the blank with one of the many roles we play every day [for example, wife, husband, teacher, student, friend, or cousin]). List the qualities that person needs. What categories do these qualities fall into? Why are these characteristics ideal? Write an essay explaining the categories you have developed for the role you chose to discuss.

Exploring Ideas

4. We all have bad habits, but few people know how to break them. What advice do you have for people who want to change their behavior in some important way or break a bad habit? How do you know your method works?

5. Explain a cultural tradition we are in danger of losing in society today. Discuss the value of the tradition itself and the ways this tradition is changing, along with the value and effects of this change. Make sure you discuss this topic in an unbiased way.

6. How do a person's cultural views and beliefs affect the educational process? In what ways does our current system of education acknowledge, hinder, or ignore our diverse cultural backgrounds? In a well-developed essay, discuss how our educational system successfully or unsuccessfully deals with our various cultural differences. Are the categories in your essay distinct from one another? What rhetorical strategies support your essay?

Writing from Sources

For detailed information on writing from sources, see Part III.

7. What are the differences among public, private, and international adoption? Classify these types of adoption based on their requirements. Consider the advantages and disadvantages of each type—for example, the

financial commitment involved and the psychological obstacles that adoptive parents should be prepared to face. Find one or two credible sources that discuss circumstances surrounding adoption and use them in a research-based essay.

8. Environmental awareness has become very important in recent years. Research environmentalism to find different ways that people and businesses are responding to the crisis of climate change. Write a documented essay that recommends the best ways to be "green" in the twenty-first century.

Analyzing Visual Images

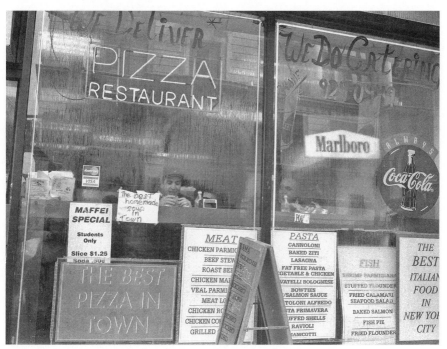

Dave Beckerman Photography

9. This photo classifies the food available at this restaurant. Choose a common topic like food, houses, or clothing (or another subject that interests you), and discuss in essay form how someone might classify the items in that category. For example, someone could discuss types of cars according to the characteristics of the people who are likely to buy them.

10. Look at the picture on page 262 at the beginning of this chapter. What do you think these people are doing? Why are they here? Consider the various reasons people might be in this particular place, and write an essay classifying them according to your assumptions.

Chapter 9

COMPARISON/CONTRAST
Discovering Similarities and Differences

Making comparisons is such a natural and necessary part of our everyday lives that we often do so without conscious effort. When we were children, we compared our toys with those of our friends, we contrasted our height and physical development to other children's, and we constantly evaluated our happiness in comparison with that of our parents and childhood companions. As we grew older, we habitually compared our dates, teachers, parents, friends, cars, and physical attributes. In college, we learn about anthropology by writing essays on the similarities and differences between two African tribes, about political science by contrasting the Republican and Democratic platforms, about business by comparing annual production rates, and about literature by comparing Shakespeare with Marlowe or Browning with Tennyson. Comparing and contrasting various elements in our lives helps us make decisions, such as which course to take or which house to buy, and it justifies preferences that we already hold, such as liking one city more than another or loving one person more than the next. In these ways and in many others, the skillful use of comparison and contrast is clearly essential to our social and professional lives.

DEFINING COMPARISON/CONTRAST

Comparison and contrast allow us to understand one subject by putting it next to another. Comparing involves discovering likenesses or similarities, whereas contrasting is based on finding differences. Like division and classification, comparison and contrast are generally considered part of the same process, because we usually have no reason for comparing unless some contrast is also involved. Each technique implies the existence of the other. For this reason, the word *compare* is often used for both techniques.

Comparison and contrast are most profitably applied to two items that have something in common, such as cats and dogs or cars and motorcycles. A discussion of cats and motorcycles, for example, would probably not be very rewarding or stimulating because they do not have much in common. If more than two items are compared in an essay, they are still most profitably discussed in pairs: for instance, motorcycles and cars, cars and bicycles, or bicycles and motorcycles.

An analogy is an extended, sustained comparison. Often used to explain unfamiliar, abstract, or complicated thoughts, this rhetorical technique adds energy and vividness to a wide variety of college-level writing. The process of analogy differs slightly from comparison/contrast in three important ways: Comparison/contrast begins with subjects from the same class and places equal weight on both of them. In addition, it addresses both the similarities and the differences of these subjects. Analogy, conversely, seldom explores subjects from the same class and focuses principally on one familiar subject in an attempt to explain another, more complex one. Furthermore, it deals only with similarities, not with contrasts. A comparison/contrast essay, for example, might study two veterans' ways of coping with the trauma of the War in Iraq by pointing out the differences in their methods as well as the similarities. An analogy essay might use the familiar notion of a fireworks display to reveal the chilling horror of the lonely hours after dark during this war: "Nights in Bagdad were similar to a loud, unending fireworks display. We had no idea when the next blast was coming, how loud it would be, or how close. We cringed in terror after dark, hoping the next surprise would not be our own death." In this example, rather than simply hearing about an event, we participate in it through this highly refined form of comparison.

The following student paragraph compares and contrasts married and single life. As you read it, notice how the author compares similar social states and, in the process, justifies her current lifestyle:

> *Recently I saw a bumper sticker that read, "It used to be wine, women, and song, and now it's beer, the old lady, and TV." Much truth may be found in this comparison of single and married lifestyles. When my husband and I*

used to date, for example, we'd go out for dinner and drinks and then maybe see a play or concert. Our discussions were intelligent, often ranging over global politics, science, literature, and other lofty topics. He would open doors for me, buy me flowers, and make sure I was comfortable and happy. Now, three years later, after marriage and a child, the baby bottle has replaced the wine bottle, the smell of diapers wipes out the scent of roses, and our nights on the town are infrequent, cherished events. But that's all right. A little bit of the excitement and mystery may be gone, but these intangible qualities have given way to a sturdy, dependable trust in each other and a quiet confidence about our future together.

THINKING CRITICALLY THROUGH COMPARISON/CONTRAST

Comparison and contrast are basic to a number of different thought processes. We compare and contrast quite naturally on a daily basis, but all of us would benefit greatly from being more aware of these companion strategies in our own writing. They help us not only in perceiving our environment but also in understanding and organizing large amounts of information.

The basic skill of finding similarities and differences will enhance your ability to create accurate descriptions, to cite appropriate examples, to present a full process analysis, and, of course, to classify and label subjects. It is a pattern of thought that is essential to more complex thinking strategies, so perfecting the ability to use it is an important step in your efforts to improve your critical thinking.

Once again, we are going to practice this strategy in isolation to get a strong sense of its mechanics before we combine it with other rhetorical modes. Isolating this mode will make your reading and writing even stronger than they are now, because the individual parts of the thinking process will be more vigorous and effective, thus making your academic performance more powerful than ever.

1. Make a list of the similarities and differences in the photograph on page 321. What messages or ideas do you think the photographer is able to communicate through this photograph?
2. Find magazine ads that use comparison/contrast to make a point or sell a product. What is the basis of each comparison? How effective or ineffective is each comparison?
3. Have you ever been to the same place twice? Think for a moment about how the first and second visits to this place differed. How were they similar? What were the primary reasons for the similarities and differences in your perceptions of these visits?

© Zach Gold/CORBIS

READING AND WRITING COMPARISON/CONTRAST ESSAYS

Many established guidelines regulate the development of a comparison/contrast essay and should be taken into account from both the reading and the writing perspectives. All good comparative studies serve a specific purpose. They attempt either to examine their subjects separately or to demonstrate the superiority of one over the other. In evaluating two different types of cars, for example, a writer might point out the amazing gas mileage of one model and the smooth handling qualities of the other or the superiority of one car's gas mileage over that of another. Whatever the intent, comparison/contrast essays need to be clear and logical and have a precise purpose.

Reading Comparison/Contrast Essays

- What is the writer comparing?
- What is the essay's thesis?
- How is the essay organized?

Preparing to Read. As you begin reading this chapter, pull together as much preliminary material as possible for each essay so you can focus your attention and have the benefit of prior knowledge before you start to read. In particular, you should try to discover what is being compared or contrasted and why. From the title of his essay, can you tell what Ben Dattner is comparing in "Is Your Workplace Personality Out of (Birth) Order"? What does William Ouchi's title "Japanese and American Workers: Two Casts of Mind" suggest to you? From glancing at the essay itself and reading the synopsis in the Rhetorical Table of Contents, what do you think Sucheng Chan's essay will try to accomplish?

Also, before you begin to read these essays, try to discover information about the author and about the conditions under which each essay was written. Why is Ouchi qualified to write about Japanese and American workers? How does he reveal his background in his essay? What is Gloria Steinem's stand on women's bodybuilding? To what extent do you expect her opinions on this topic to color her comparison of women's past and present physical strength?

Finally, just before you begin to read, answer the Preparing to Read questions, and then make some free associations with the general topic of each essay: For example, what do you think are some of the comparisons and contrasts in "Homeplace" (Scott Russell Sanders)? What is your general view on women's bodybuilding (Gloria Steinem)?

Reading. As you read each comparison/contrast essay for the first time, be sure to record your own feelings and opinions. Some of the issues presented in this chapter are highly controversial. You will often have strong reactions to them, which you should try to write down as soon as possible.

In addition, you may want to comment on the relationships among the preliminary essay material, the author's stance in the essay, and the content of the essay itself. For example, what motivated Sanders to write "Homeplace"? Who is his primary audience? What is Chan's tone in "You're Short, Besides!" and how does it advance her purpose? Answers to questions such as these will provide you with a context for your first reading of these essays and will assist you in preparing to analyze the essays in more depth on your second reading.

Critical thinking questions are provided with each essay at the bottom of the pages in this chapter. If you dig in and try to answer each one, they will lead you to higher levels of thinking on these particular issues. They are designed to bridge the gap in understanding between the prereading and postreading activities surrounding each essay. Writing your responses to these questions will provide you with the best opportunity to learn how to think analytically about these topics.

At this point in the chapter, you should make certain you understand each author's thesis and then take a close look at his or her principal method of organization: Is the essay arranged (1) point by point, (2) subject by subject, (3) as a combination of these two, or (4) as separate discussions of similarities and differences between two subjects? (See the chart on page 325 for an illustration of these options.) Last, preview the questions that follow the essay before you read it again.

Rereading.   When you read these essays a second time, you should look at the comparison or contrast much more closely than you have up to now. First, look in detail at the writer's method of organization (see the chart on page 325). How effective is it in advancing the writer's thesis?

Next, you should consider whether each essay is fully developed and balanced: Does Dattner compare similar items? Does Sanders discuss the same elements of his subjects? Does Ouchi deal with all aspects of the comparison between Japanese and American workers? Is Steinem's treatment of her subjects well balanced? And does Chan give her audience enough specific details to clarify the extent of her comparison? Do all the writers in this chapter use well-chosen transitions so you can move smoothly from one point to the next? Also, what other rhetorical modes support each comparison/contrast in this chapter?

Finally, the answers to the questions after each selection will let you evaluate your understanding of the essay and help you analyze its contents in preparation for the discussion/writing topics that follow.

For a more thorough inventory of the reading process, refer to the Reading Inventory at the end of Part I.

Writing Comparison / Contrast Essays

- Draft a thesis.
- Choose items in the same category.
- Introduce your subjects and your reason for comparing them.
- Include the limits of your discussion.
- Organize your essay.
- Balance the treatment of your subjects.

Preparing to Write.   As you consider various topics for a comparison/contrast essay, you should answer the Preparing to Write questions that precede the assignments and then use the prewriting techniques explained in Chapter 3 (pp. 36–38) to generate even more ideas on these topics.

As you focus your attention on a particular topic, keep the following suggestions in mind:

1. Always compare/contrast items in the same category (e.g., compare two professors, but not a professor and a swimming pool).
2. Have a specific purpose or reason for writing your essay.

3. Discuss the same qualities of each subject (if you evaluate the teaching techniques of one professor, do so for the other professor as well).
4. Use as many pertinent details as possible to expand your comparison/contrast and to accomplish your stated purpose.
5. Deal with all aspects of the comparison that are relevant to the purpose.
6. Balance the treatment of the different subjects of your comparison (i.e., don't spend more time on one than on another).
7. Determine your audience's background and knowledge so that you will know how much of your comparison should be explained in detail and how much can be skimmed over.

Next, in preparation for a comparison/contrast project, you might list all the elements of both subjects that you want to compare. This list can then help you give your essay structure as well as substance. At this stage in the writing process, the task may seem similar to pure description, but a discussion of two subjects in relation to one another rapidly changes the assignment from description to comparison.

Writing.   The introduction of your comparison/contrast essay should (1) clearly identify your subjects, (2) explain the basis of your comparison/contrast, and (3) state your purpose and the overall limits of your particular study. Identifying your subject is, of course, a necessary and important task in any essay. Similarly, justifying the elements you will be comparing and contrasting creates interest and gives your audience some specifics to look for in the essay. Finally, your statement of purpose, or thesis (for example, to prove that one professor is superior to another), should include the boundaries of your discussion. You cannot cover all the reasons for your preference in one short essay, so you must limit your consideration to three or four basic categories (perhaps teaching techniques, the clarity of the assignments given, classroom attitude, and grading standards). The introduction is the place to make all these limits known.

You can organize the body of your paper in one of four ways: (1) a point-by-point, or alternating, comparison; (2) a subject-by-subject, or divided, comparison; (3) a combination of these two methods; or (4) a division between the similarities and differences.

The point-by-point comparison evaluates both subjects in terms of each category. If the issue, for example, is which of two cars to buy, you might discuss both models' gasoline mileage first; then, their horsepower; next, their ease in handling; and, finally, their standard equipment. Following the second method of organization, subject by subject, you would discuss the gasoline mileage, horsepower, ease in handling, and standard equipment of car A first and then follow the same format for car B. The third option would allow you to introduce, say, the standard equipment of each car point by point (or car

Point by Point	**Subject by Subject**
MPG, car A MPG, car B Horsepower, car A Horsepower, car B Handling, car A Handling, car B Equipment, car A Equipment, car B	MPG, car A Horsepower, car A Handling, car A Equipment, car A MPG, car B Horsepower, car B Handling, car B Equipment, car B

Combination	**Similarities/Differences**
Equipment, car A Equipment, car B ———— MPG, car A Horsepower, car A Handling, car A MPG, car B Horsepower, car B Handling, car B	Similarities: MPG, cars A & B Differences: Horsepower, cars A & B Handling, cars A & B Equipment, cars A & B

by car) and then to explain the other features in your comparison (miles per gallon, horsepower, and ease in handling) subject by subject. To use the last method of organization, you might discuss the similarities between the two models first and the differences second (or vice versa). If the cars you are comparing have similar miles–per–gallon (MPG) ratings but completely different horsepower, steering systems, and optional equipment, you could discuss the gasoline mileage and then emphasize the differences by mentioning them later in the essay. If, instead, you are trying to emphasize the fact that the MPG ratings of these models remain consistent despite their differences, then reverse the order of your essay.

When confronted with the task of choosing a method of organization for a comparison/contrast essay, you need to find the pattern that best suits your purpose. If you want single items to stand out in a discussion, for instance, the best choice will be the point-by-point system; it is especially appropriate for long essays but has a tendency to turn into an exercise in listing if you don't pay careful attention to your transitions. If, however, the subjects themselves (rather than the itemized points) are the most interesting feature of your essay, you should use the subject-by-subject comparison; this system is particularly good for short essays in which the readers can retain what was said about one subject while they read about a second subject. Through this second method of organization, each subject becomes a unified whole, an approach to an essay that is generally effective unless the theme becomes awkwardly divided into two separate parts. You must also remember, if you choose this second method of organization, that the second (or last) subject is in the most emphatic position because that is what your readers will have seen most recently. The final two options for organizing a comparison/contrast essay give you some built-in flexibility so that you can create emphasis and attempt to manipulate reader opinion simply by the structure of your essay.

Using logical transitions in your comparison/contrast essays will establish clear relationships between the items in your comparisons and will also move your readers smoothly from one topic to the next. If you wish to indicate comparisons, use such words as *like, as, also, in like manner, similarly,* and *in addition;* to signal contrasts, try *but, in contrast to, unlike, whereas,* and *on the one hand/on the other hand.*

The conclusion of a comparison/contrast essay summarizes the main points and states the deductions drawn from those points. As you choose your method of organization, remember not to get locked into a formulaic approach to your subjects, which will adversely affect the readability of your essay. To avoid making your reader feel like a spectator at a verbal table tennis match, be straightforward, honest, and patient as you discover and recount the details of your comparison.

Rewriting.   When you review the draft of your comparison/contrast essay, you need once again to make sure that you communicate your purpose as effectively as possible to your intended audience. Two guidelines previously mentioned should help you accomplish this goal:

• Does my thesis state the purpose and limits of my study?

You will also need to pay close attention to the following in the development of your essay:

• Do I compare/contrast items from the same general category?
• Do I discuss the same qualities of each subject?
• Do I balance the treatment of my topics?
• Do I organize your essay as effectively as possible?
• Does my conclusion summarize and analyze my main points?

For further information on writing and revising your comparison/contrast essays, consult the Writing Inventory at the end of Part I.

STUDENT ESSAY: COMPARISON/CONTRAST AT WORK

The following student essay compares the advantages and disadvantages of macaroni and cheese versus tacos in the life of a harried college freshman. As you read it, notice that the writer states his intention in the first paragraph and then expands his discussion with appropriate details to produce a balanced essay. Also, try to determine what effect he creates by using two methods of organization: first subject by subject, then point by point.

Dormitory Chef

Topics

To this day, I will not eat either macaroni and cheese or tacos. No, it's not because of any allergy; it's because *Basis of comparison* during my freshman year at college, I prepared one or the other of these scrumptious dishes more times than I care to remember. <u>However, my choice of which culinary delight to cook on any given night was not as simple a decision as one might imagine</u>.

Thesis statement: Purpose and limits of comparison

Paragraph on Subject A: Macaroni and cheese Macaroni and cheese has numerous advantages for the dormitory chef. <u>First of all, it is inexpensive</u>. No matter how poor one may be, there's probably enough change under the couch cushion to buy a box at the market. All that starch for only $5.29. What a bargain! *Point 2 (Preparation)* <u>Second, it can be prepared in just one pan</u>. This is especially important given the meager resources of the average dorm kitchen. <u>Third, and perhaps most important, macaroni and cheese is odorless</u>. By odorless, I mean that no one else can smell it. It is a well-known fact that dorm residents hate to cook and that they love nothing better than to wander dejectedly around the kitchen with big, sad eyes after someone else has been cooking. But with macaroni and cheese, no enticing aromas are going to find their way into the nose of any would-be mooch.

Point 1 (Price)

Point 3 (Odor)

Paragraph on Subject B: Tacos Tacos, <u>on the other hand</u>, are a different matter altogether. For the dorm cook, <u>the most significant difference is obviously the price</u>. To enjoy tacos for dinner, the adventurous dorm gourmet must purchase no fewer than five ingredients from the market: corn tortillas, beef, lettuce, tomatoes, and cheese. Needless to say, this is a major expenditure. <u>Second, the chef *Point 2 (Preparation)* must adroitly shuffle these ingredients back and forth among his or her very limited supply of pans and bowls. And finally, tacos smell great</u>. That wouldn't be

Transition

Point 1 (Price)

Point 3 (Odor)

a problem if the tacos didn't also smell great to about twenty of the cook's newest—if not closest—friends, who appear with those same pathetic, starving eyes mentioned earlier. When this happens, the cook will be lucky to get more than two of his own creations.

Subject B

Tacos, then, wouldn't stand much of a chance if they didn't outdo macaroni and cheese in one area: taste. Taste is almost—but not quite—an optional requirement in the opinion of a frugal dormitory hash-slinger. Taste is just important enough so that tacos are occasionally prepared, despite their disadvantages. **Transition** / **Subject A**

Paragraph on Point 4: Taste

Transition

But tacos have other advantages besides their taste. With their enticing, colorful ingredients, they even look good. The only thing that can be said about the color of macaroni and cheese is that it's a color not found in nature. **Subject B** / **Subject A**

Paragraph on Point 5: Color

Transition

On the other hand, macaroni and cheese is quick. It can be prepared in about ten minutes, while tacos take more than twice as long. And there are occasions—such as final exam week—when time is a scarce and precious resource. **Subject A** / **Subject B**

Paragraph on Point 6: Time

Transition

As you can see, quite a bit of thinking went into my choice of food in my younger years. These two dishes essentially got me through my freshman year and indirectly taught me how to make important decisions (like what to eat). But I still feel a certain revulsion when I hear their names today. **Summary** / **Concluding statement**

Analysis

Student Writer's Comments

I compare and contrast so many times during a typical day that I took this rhetorical technique for granted. In fact, I had overlooked it completely. The most difficult part of writing this essay was finding two appropriate subjects to compare. Ideally, I knew they should be united by a similarity. So I brainstormed to come up with some possible topics. Then, working from this list of potential subjects, I began to freewrite to see if I could come up with two topics in the same category on which I could write a balanced comparison. Out of my freewriting came this reasoning: Macaroni and cheese and tacos, in reality, are two very different kinds of food from the same category. Proving this fact is easy and might even result in an interesting essay. Their similar property of being popular dorm foods unites the two despite their differences and also gives me two important reasons for writing the comparison: to discover why they are both popular dorm delicacies and to determine which one has more advantages for my particular purposes. In proportion to writing and revising, I spent most of my time choosing my topic, brainstorming, freewriting, and rebrainstorming to make sure I could develop every aspect of my comparison adequately. Most of my prewriting work took the form of two columns in which I recorded my opinions on the choice between macaroni and cheese versus tacos.

Sitting down to mold my lists into an essay posed an entirely new set of problems. From the copious notes I had taken, I easily wrote the introductory paragraph, identifying my topics, explaining the basis of my comparison/contrast, and stating the purpose and limits of my study (my thesis statement). But now that I faced the body of the essay, I needed to find the best way to organize my opinions on these two dorm foods: point by point, subject by subject, a combination of these two, or a discussion of similarities and differences?

I wrote my first draft discussing my topics point by point. Even with an occasional joke and a few snide comments interjected, the essay reminded me of a boring game of ping-pong with only a few attempts at changing the pace. I started over completely with my second draft and worked through my topics subject by subject. I felt this approach was better, but not quite right for my particular purpose and audience. I set out to do some heavy-handed revising.

Discussing my first three points (price, preparation, and odor) subject by subject seemed to work quite well. I was actually satisfied with the first half of my discussion of these two subjects. But the essay really started to get sluggish when I brought up the fourth point: taste. So I broke off my discussion there and rewrote the second half of my essay point by point, dealing with taste, color, and time each in its own paragraph. This change gave my essay the new direction it needed to keep the readers' attention and also offered me some new insights into my comparison. Then I returned to the beginning of my essay and revised it for readability, adding transitions and making sure the paper now moved smoothly from one point or subject to the next. Finally, I added my final paragraph including a brief summary of my main points and an explanation of the deductions I had made. My concluding remark ("But I still feel a certain revulsion when I hear their names today.") came to me as I was putting the final touches on this draft.

What I learned from writing this particular essay is that comparison/contrast thinking, more than thinking in other rhetorical modes, is much like a puzzle. I really had to spend an enormous amount of time thinking through, mapping out, and rethinking my comparison before I could start to put my thoughts in essay form. The results are rewarding, but I sure wore out a piece of linoleum on the den floor on the way to my final draft.

SOME FINAL THOUGHTS ON COMPARISON/CONTRAST

The essays in this section demonstrate various methods of organization as well as a number of distinct stylistic approaches to writing a comparison/contrast essay. As you read these selections, pay particular attention to the clear, well-focused introductions; the different logical methods of organization; and the smooth transitions between sentences and paragraphs.

COMPARISON/CONTRAST IN REVIEW

Reading Comparison/Contrast Essays

Preparing to Read
√ What assumptions can I make from the essay's title?
√ What do I think the general mood of the essay will be?
√ What is the essay's purpose and audience?
√ What does the synopsis tell me about the essay?
√ What can I learn from the author's biography?
√ Can I predict the author's point of view toward the subject?

Reading
√ What is the writer comparing?
√ What is the essay's thesis?
√ How is the essay organized?

Rereading
√ Is the writer's method of organization effective?
√ Is the essay fully developed?
√ What other rhetorical strategies does the author use?

Writing Comparison/Contrast Essays

Preparing to Write
√ What is my purpose?
√ Who is my audience?

Writing
√ Did I draft a thesis?
√ Am I comparing items in the same general category?
√ Does my introduction (1) identify my subjects, (2) explain the basis of my comparison, and (3) state the purpose and limits of my study?
√ Does my thesis include the boundaries of my discussion?
√ Is my paper organized point by point, subject by subject, as a combination of the two, or as a discussion of similarities and differences?
√ Do I balance the treatment of my subjects?

Rewriting
√ Does my thesis state the purpose and limits of my study?
√ Do I compare/contrast items from the same general category?
√ Do I discuss the same qualities of each subject?
√ Do I balance the treatment of my topics?
√ Do I organize my essay as effectively as possible?
√ Does my conclusion summarize and analyze my main points?

BEN DATTNER   (1969–   )

Is Your Workplace Personality Out of (Birth) Order?

A specialist in business consulting and group dynamics, Ben Dattner has his B.A. in Psychology from Harvard University and his Ph.D. in Industrial and Organizational Psychology from New York University. After graduating from NYU, he worked at the Republic National Bank of New York as an assistant to the CEO and then as Director of Human Resources at Blink.com before founding his own firm, Dattner Consulting, which specializes in helping corporate and nonprofit organizations develop a more successful understanding of the impact of individual psychology and group dynamics on job performance. He has written articles and blogs on a number of fascinating topics, including narcissism and fairness in the workplace, the impact of trust on negotiation, and organizational environments. Frequently quoted in the press, Dattner has been interviewed often on CNN and CNBC and is the workplace consultant on *Morning Edition* on National Public Radio. He is also an adjunct professor in the industrial and organizational psychology Master's Degree Program at New York University's Graduate School of Arts and Sciences. An avid reader, Dattner loves to travel, watch movies, and study architecture. When asked to give advice to students using *The Prose Reader*, he explains that "all good writing starts with an outline" and counsels student writers to "pay particular attention to the sequence of sentences within your paragraphs. Try to find ways," he suggests, "to make your written work as concise, clear, and logical as possible."

Preparing to Read

The following essay was originally published on the *Psychology Today* blog (June 2, 2008). In it, Dattner examines the effect of birth order on personality and achievement.

Exploring Experience: As you prepare to read this article, take a few moments to consider birth order in families you know: What special qualities do firstborns have in these families? What characteristics do the youngest siblings share? What do middle children that you know have in common? How do parents generally treat their oldest children? How do the oldest children usually feel about the youngest? How do the middle children fit into the picture? What does sibling rivalry have to do with the feelings siblings have for each other? How do you think these characteristics might transfer to the workplace?

Learning Online: In preparing to read this essay on personality differences created by birth order, go to the following child development Web site to see a chart comparing birth order and personality (www.childdevelopmentinfo .com/development/birth_order.htm). Under the "Development" link, click on "Birth Order," and look at the typical characteristics of each position. Do you fit the description of your birth order?

Birth order goes in and out of style in academic psychology, but is a perennial favorite in popular psychology. *Time* magazine recently featured a cover story about the general implications of birth order, and *USA Today* ran an article about the impact of sibling structure on business leadership.

Academic research has shown that accurate predictions about personality can be made based on birth order (whether a person is first-born, second-born, middle or only child, or twin). Yet birth order is an often-overlooked variable in the workplace and is rarely considered in personnel decisions.

In his 1996 book, *Born to Rebel*, MIT Professor Frank Sulloway uses the framework of evolutionary psychology to explain why sibling rivalry and strategies for gaining emotional, physical, and intellectual resources from parents during childhood are critical determinants of adult personality. According to this theory, sibling rivalry is the most direct kind of competition in evolution, and personalities are formed as siblings strive to occupy and defend different niches within the family in order to survive. Although Sulloway does not cite studies that focus on the business world, it is possible to make inferences based on his general findings and to find anecdotal support for these inferences.

As children, first-borns strive to emulate and please their parents and often dominate and care for their younger siblings. Parents tend to delegate responsibility to first-borns, who identify with their parents and with authority. Therefore, relative to their younger siblings, first-born children tend to be more extraverted and confident, more conformist and conservative, more conscientious and academically inclined, and more dominant and authoritarian.

First-borns, over represented among CEOs and political leaders, are likely to be relatively more comfortable and successful in situations where they can execute within an existing structure, leveraging their achievement orientation to incrementally build businesses and their attention to detail to ensure quality control. An example of an ambitious and successful first-born is Leonard Lauder of Estee Lauder, who took over a small business from his parents and used a disciplined approach to grow it into one of the world's largest cosmetics companies.

First-borns are likely to be least comfortable in situations that require radical change or innovation, in self-managing teams where roles and status are fluid and ambiguous or in expatriate assignments where they need to adapt to a foreign culture. Additionally, first-borns may be uncomfortable when they are required to work in subordinate roles. A case in point is Michael Ovitz, who did not succeed at Disney partly because he was not able

---

Thinking Critically

Do you have siblings? If so, what was your birth order in your family? To what extent do you think it accounts for your basic personality?

to work as Michael Eisner's number two. Because second-born children enter a family system in which the first-born niche is already taken, their incentive is to be different and to create their own niche. [2]

Second-born children, relative to their older siblings, tend to be more flexible and open to new experiences, more empathic and altruistic, more creative and innovative, and more rebellious, liberal and interested in foreign cultures, and more concerned with justice and fairness. Gordon Moore of Intel and Lou Gerstner of IBM are two examples of later-borns who were able to challenge the industry or corporate status quo and transform their organizations in order to adjust to rapid change.   7

Because as children they have less to lose by taking risks, second-borns also tend to be more comfortable taking risks, as was super-successful hedge fund manager George Soros, who made his fortune by making bold bets, like his $10 billion bet against the English Pound in the early 1990's. Because they are more interested in foreign cultures, later-borns are likely to be more comfortable in international assignments. Leonard Lauder's younger brother, Ronald, sought a career outside of the family business and served as ambassador to Austria.   8

Middle siblings, who lack the dominance of first-borns and the higher degree of attention given to last-borns are in a precarious situation and therefore must learn to be diplomatic and political in order to get their way. Relative to their siblings, middle children tend to be more diplomatic and politically skilled, and good at negotiation and compromise. Carly Fiorina, who initially triumphed in the highly political and contentious merger of Hewlett-Packard and Compaq, is an example of a successful middle-born child who was able to bring together disparate constituencies, even though she was not able to retain her leadership role after the merger.   9

Only children tend to resemble first-borns and are achievement-oriented and motivated to please their parents. [3] For example, Jack Welch often describes how pleasing his working-class parent was a major source of motivation throughout his career.   10

Twins are more similar to and have a lower degree of sibling rivalry with each other than with other siblings and, therefore, may resemble first-born, middle children, or youngest siblings, depending on how many older or younger siblings they have.   11

Also worth considering is the respective birth order of partners or members of a team. A successful partnership might involve a later-born who creates an   12

Thinking Critically

[2] What other family dynamics, in addition to birth order, might account for the way we behave? Name five different familial stimuli, and then rank them in the order of their influence on human behavior.

[3] According to Dattner, why do "only children" tend to resemble first-borns? Do you agree with the author's assessment? Why or why not?

innovative new vision and a first-born who executes according to this vision. Bill Gates and Steve Ballmer provide a good example of such a partnership.

There can be exceptions to the general pattern of birth order and per- 13
sonality. Moderating variables such as gender, temperament, physical characteristics, socio-economic class, family size, and degree of conflict between siblings and parents can alter the basic impact of birth order on personality. For example, first-born siblings who have a high degree of conflict with their parents can rebel and take on certain attributes that are usually associated with younger siblings, and their younger siblings may take on attributes usually associated with first-borns.

Another example of a way in which birth order can fail as a predictor of 14
behavior is if the first-born sibling is disabled or shy, the younger sibling may take on some first-born personality characteristics. Multiple marriages and half- and step-siblings can also have a significant moderating effect on the relationship between birth order and personality. In conclusion, there are consistent and enduring differences in personality between people who occupied different niches in their families. 4

While birth order may not be an infallible predictor of attitudes or 15
behavior in the workplace, there are no infallible predictors of job performance.

UNDERSTANDING DETAILS

1. Explain in your own words how birth order can be used as a predictor of personality.
2. List the characteristics that oldest children share; then list characteristics of the youngest children. What patterns do you see?
3. According to Dattner, how can considering birth order help a company with its hiring process?
4. From examples in this article, explain the differences between family position and personality in the workplace.

READING CRITICALLY

5. What is Dattner's purpose in this essay? How does he go about achieving this purpose?
6. Why do you think birth order is "rarely considered in personnel decisions" (paragraph 2)?

Thinking Critically

4 If you were the CEO of a large company, would you allow your personnel department to consider birth order in its hiring procedures? Explain your reasoning. What is the legality of such a practice?

7. In what ways can first-borns be uncomfortable on the job? Give some examples of these types of situations that are not mentioned in Dattner's article.

8. What does the author mean when he says, "While birth order may not be an infallible predictor of attitudes or behavior in the workplace, there are no infallible predictors of job performance" (paragraph 15)?

DISCOVERING RHETORICAL STRATEGIES

9. Which of the four main methods of organizing a comparison/contrast essay does Dattner use? How many paragraphs does the author spend on each part of his comparison? Why do you think he spends this amount of time on each?

10. Do the author's transitions help you move through the essay with understanding and focus? Explain your answer by giving some examples from the essay.

11. Dattner uses examples to help him prove his point about birth order. In what ways do these illustrations advance the author's argument? What do they add to the discussion?

12. Who do you think is Dattner's audience for this essay? What features of the essay bring you to this conclusion?

MAKING CONNECTIONS

13. How is Ben Dattner's method of comparison/contrast different from that of Gloria Steinem in "The Politics of Muscle" and Sucheng Chan in "You're Short, Besides!"? Which author's argument is most persuasive to you? Why?

14. Ben Dattner, Sandra Cisneros ("Only daughter"), Tamala Edwards ("Multi-Colored Families"), and Mary Pipher ("Beliefs About Families") all discuss interpersonal dynamics within the family structure. Which essay gave you the most insight into your own family? Explain your answer.

15. Dattner argues that birth order often plays a major role in determining the relative success of siblings within the same family. To what extent do you think the following authors would agree with him: Russell Baker ("The Saturday Evening Post"), Brent Staples ("A Brother's Murder"), Tamala Edwards ("Multi-Colored Families"), and/or Alice Walker ("Beauty: When the Other Dancer Is the Self")?

IDEAS FOR DISCUSSION/WRITING

Preparing to Write

Write freely about the effects of birth order from your personal experience: List some successful people you know; then label them by their birth order. What patterns do you notice? What qualities do your most successful friends share? Do you think parents treat their oldest children differently than their youngest? In what ways? How might these differences affect these children? What is your birth order in your family? Do you fit the author's description in this essay? In what ways?

Choosing a Topic

1. *Learning Online:* What is your birth order in your own family? Revisit the online source that describes different personality characteristics related to birth order (www.childdevelopmentinfo.com/development/birth_order.htm). Keeping in mind Dattner's evaluation of birth order, write an essay comparing your personality to that of a sibling's. If you are an only child, compare yourself with a friend of yours.

2. Based on material from Dattner's essay, compare and/or contrast two of your friends based on the birth order in their families. What insights does Dattner give you into their character? Into their work ethic? Into their lifestyle?

3. Analyze your relationship with two different people based on their birth order. How influential have they been in your life? What characteristics of theirs affected your behavior most? Based on Dattner's discussion, do you think these influences had anything to do with birth order? Explain your answer in a well-developed essay.

4. In response to Dattner's blog entry, choose one of his claims about birth order, and launch an argument in your own blog entry for or against his point based on your personal experience. In addition to using your personal experience, support your argument with elements from this article and/or other sources.

Before beginning your essay, you might want to consult the checklists on page 331.

SCOTT RUSSELL SANDERS   (1945–   )

Homeplace

Scott Sanders has been connected to many places in his life. Born in Memphis, he descended from a father related to cotton farmers in Mississippi and a mother from an immigrant doctor's family in Chicago. He studied Physics and English at Brown University, then earned his Ph.D. in English at Cambridge University in England. Since 1971, he has been a professor of English at Indiana University, where he has won a number of teaching awards. His fiction and essays have been published in a wide variety of journals, including *Audubon, Harper's, North American Review, Georgia Review,* and *Resurgence.* He has also been Literary Editor of *The Cambridge Review,* Fiction Editor for *The Minnesota Review,* a columnist for the *Chicago Sun-Times,* and a contributing editor for *Audubon.* Among his nineteen books are *Wilderness Plots* (1983), *Blow* (1985), *Bad Man Ballad* (1986), *The Paradise of Bombs* (1987), *In Limestone Country* (1991), *Staying Put* (1993), and *The Force of Spirit* (2000). His most recent book is *A Private History of Awe* (2006), which is simultaneously a coming-of-age memoir, a love story, and a spiritual testament. Like most of his other written work, it celebrates the triumph of social justice, the search for divine truth, and the sense of community so lacking in our busy modern lives. He and his wife, Ruth, a biochemist, live in Bloomington in the White River Valley. His advice to student writers is to use the essay as "a process of discovery. It is a medium for asking questions, for investigating the world, for exploring."

Preparing to Read

This essay was first published in 1992 in a journal called *Orion.* In it, Sanders addresses the innate desire in our culture to keep moving, exploring, and growing.

Exploring Experience: As you prepare to read this essay, consider your natural inclination to move or to stay in the same place: Do you feel genuinely connected to the place you call "home," or are you always looking for a chance to move? What value do you derive from settling down? From staying on the move? Do you feel you are working with or against our culture? In what ways? Do you think this culture varies by geographic region? Explain your answer.

Learning Online: In his essay, Sanders points out that the United States has created more transportation systems than any other nation in the world. Visit the *America on the Move* project sponsored by the Smithsonian National Museum of American History (americanhistory.si.edu/onthemove). Take some time to view the pictures and read the history of American transportation.

As a boy in Ohio, I knew a farm family, the Millers, who suffered from three tornadoes. The father, mother, and two sons were pulling into their driveway after church when the first tornado hoisted up their mobile home, spun it around, and carried it off. With the insurance money, they built a small frame house on the same spot.

Several years later, a second tornado peeled off the roof, splintered the garage, and rustled two cows. The Millers rebuilt again, raising a new garage on the old foundation and adding another story to the house. That upper floor was reduced to kindling by a third tornado, which also pulled out half the apple trees and slurped water from the stock pond. Soon after that I left Ohio, snatched away by college as forcefully as by any cyclone. Last thing I heard, the family was preparing to rebuild yet again. **1**

Why did the Millers refuse to move? I knew them all enough to say they were neither stupid nor crazy. Plain stubbornness was a factor. These were people who, once settled, might have remained at the volcano or on the bank of a flood-prone river or beside an earthquake fault. They had relatives nearby, helpful neighbors, jobs and stores and schools within a short drive, and those were all good reasons to stay. But the main reason, I believe, was that the Millers had invested so much of their lives in the land, **2** planting orchards and gardens, spreading manure on the fields, digging ponds, building sheds, seeding pastures. Out back of the house were groves of walnuts, hickories, and oaks, all started by hand from acorns and nuts. April through October, perennial flowers in the yard pumped out a fountain of blossoms. This farm was not just so many acres of dirt, easily exchanged for an equal amount elsewhere; it was a particular place, intimately known, worked on, dreamed over, cherished.

Psychologists tell us that we answer trouble with one of two impulses, either fight or flight. I believe that the Millers exhibited a third instinct, that of staying put. They knew better than to fight a tornado, and they chose not to flee. Their commitment to the place may have been fool hardy, but it was also grand. I suspect that most human achievements worth admiring are the result of such devotion.

The Millers dramatize a choice we are faced with constantly: whether to go or stay, whether to move to a situation that is safer, richer, easier, more attractive, or to stick where we are and make what we can of it. If the shine goes off our marriage, our house, our car, do we trade it for a new one? If the fertility leaches out of our soil, the creativity out of our job, the money

---

Thinking Critically

1 Why do you think the family kept rebuilding their home? Would you have done the same thing? Why or why not?

2 What does "invested" mean in this context?

out of our pocket, do we start over somewhere else?[3] There are voices enough, both inner and outer, urging us to deal with difficulties by pulling up stakes and heading for new territory. I know them well, for they have been calling to me all my days. I wish to raise here a contrary voice, to say a few words on behalf of staying put, learning the ground, going deeper.

Claims for the virtues of moving on are familiar and seductive to Americans, this nation founded by immigrants and shaped by restless seekers. From the beginning, our heroes have been sailors, explorers, cowboys, prospectors, speculators, backwoods ramblers, rainbow chasers, vagabonds of every stripe. Our Promised Land has always been over the next ridge or at the end of the trail, never under our feet. In our national mythology, the worst fate is to be trapped on a farm, in a village, in the sticks, in some dead-end job or unglamorous marriage or played-out game.

Stand still, we are warned, and you die. Americans have dug the most canals, laid the most rails, built the most roads and airports of any nation. In a newspaper I read that, even though our sprawling system of interstate highways is crumbling, politicians think we should triple its size. Only a populace drunk on driving,[4] a populace infatuated with the myth of the open road, could hear such a proposal without hooting.

Novelist Salman Rushdie chose to leave his native India for England, where he has written a series of brilliant books from the perspective of a cultural immigrant. In his book of essays *Imaginary Homelands* he celebrates the migrant sensibility: "The effect of mass migrations has been the creation of radically new types of human being: people who root themselves in ideas rather than places,[5] in memories as much as in material things." He goes on to say that "to be a migrant is, perhaps, to be the only species of human being free of the shackles of nationalism (to say nothing of its ugly sister, patriotism)." Lord knows we could do with less nationalism (to say nothing of its ugly siblings, racism, religious sectarianism, and class snobbery). But who would pretend that a history of migration has immunized the United States against bigotry? And even if, by uprooting ourselves, we shed our chauvinism, is that all we lose?

In this hemisphere, many of the worst abuses—of land, forests, animals, and communities—have been carried out by "people who root themselves in ideas rather than places." Migrants often pack up their visions and values with the rest of their baggage and carry them along. The Spaniards devastated Central and South America by imposing on this New World the

Thinking Critically

[3] How does creativity "leach" out of a job? Give an example.
[4] Do you agree that our society is "drunk on driving"? In what ways is this metaphor especially true?
[5] Do you root yourself in ideas or in places? What is the difference?

religion, economics, and politics of the old. Colonists brought slavery with them to North America, along with smallpox and Norway rats. The Dust Bowl of the 1930s was caused not by drought but by the transfer onto the Great Plains of farming methods that were suitable to wetter regions. The habit of our industry and commerce has been to force identical schemes onto differing locales, as though the mind were a cookie cutter and the land were dough.

I quarrel with Rushdie because he articulates as eloquently as anyone the 10 orthodoxy that I wish to counter: the belief that movement is inherently good, staying put is bad; that uprooting brings tolerance, while rootedness breeds intolerance; that to be modern, enlightened, fully of our time is to be displaced. Wholesale displacement may be inevitable in today's world; but we should not suppose that it occurs without disastrous consequences for the earth and for ourselves. People who root themselves in places are likelier to know and care for those places than are people who root themselves in ideas. When we cease to be migrants and become inhabitants, ⑥ we might begin to pay enough heed and respect to where we are. By settling in, we have a chance of making a durable home for ourselves, our fellow creatures, and our descendants.

The poet Gary Snyder writes frequently about our need to "inhabit" a 11 place. One of the key problems in American society now, he points out, is people's lack of commitment to any given place:

> Neighborhoods are allowed to deteriorate, landscapes are allowed to be strip-mined, because there is nobody who will live there and take responsibility; they'll just move on. The reconstruction of a people and a life in the United States depends on people, neighborhood by neighborhood, county by county, deciding to stick it out and make it work where they are rather than flee.

But if you stick in one place, won't you become a stick-in-the-mud? If you stay put, won't you be narrow, backward, dull? You might. I have met ignorant people who never moved; and I have also met ignorant people who never stood still. Committing yourself to a place does not guarantee that you will become wise, but neither does it guarantee that you will become parochial.

To become intimate with your home region, to know the territory as 12 well as you can, to understand your life as woven into the local life does not prevent you from recognizing and honoring the diversity of other places, cultures, ways. On the contrary, how can you value other places if you do not

---

Thinking Critically

⑥ Do you agree with the author's assertion that when we "cease to be migrants" we "become inhabitants"?

have one of your own? If you are not yourself placed, then you wander the world like a sightseer, a collector of sensations, with no gauge for measuring what you see. Local knowledge is the grounding for global knowledge. Those who care about nothing beyond the confines of their parish are in truth parochial, and are at least mildly dangerous to their parish; on the other hand, those who *have* no parish, those who navigate ceaselessly among postal zones and area codes, those for whom the world is only a smear of highways and bank accounts and stores, [7] are a danger not just to their parish but to the planet.

Since birth, my children have regularly seen images of the earth as viewed   13
from space, images that I first encountered when I was in my 20s. Those photographs show vividly what in our sanest moments we have always known— that the earth is a closed circle, lovely and rare. On the wall beside me as I write is a poster of the big blue marble encased in its white swirl of clouds. That is one pole of my awareness; but the other pole is what I see through my window. I try to keep both in sight at once.

For all my convictions, I still have to wrestle with the fear—in myself, in   14
my children, and even in some of my neighbors—that our place is too remote from the action. This fear drives many people to pack their bags and move to some resort or burg they have seen on television, leaving behind what they learn to think of as the boondocks. I deal with my own unease by asking just what action I am remote from—a stock market? a debating chamber? a drive-in mortuary? The action that matters, the work of nature and community, goes on everywhere.

Since Copernicus, we have known better than to see the earth as the cen-   15
ter of the universe. Since Einstein, we have learned that there is no center; or alternatively, that any point is as good as any other for observing the world. I find a kindred lesson in the words of the Zen master Thich Nhat Hanh: "This spot where you sit is your own spot. It is on this very spot and in this very moment that you can become enlightened. You don't have to sit beneath a special tree in a distant land." If you stay put, your place may become a holy center, [8] not because it gives you special access to the divine, but because in your stillness you hear what might be heard anywhere.

I think of my home ground as a series of nested rings, with house and fam-   16
ily and marriage at the center, surrounded by the wider and wider hoops of neighborhood and community, the bioregion within walking distance of my

---

Thinking Critically

[7] What does Sanders mean when he refers to the world as a "smear of highways and bank accounts and stores"? What does the word "smear" imply in this context?

[8] How can your place "become a holy center" if you "stay put"? Paraphrase this concept in your own words.

door, the wooded and rocky hills of southern Indiana, the watershed of the Ohio Valley, and so on outward—and inward—to the ultimate source.

The longing to become an inhabitant rather than a drifter sets me against the current of my culture, which nudges everyone into motion. [9] Newton taught us that a body at rest tends to stay at rest, unless it is acted on by an outside force. We are acted on ceaselessly by outside forces—advertising, movies, magazines, speeches—and also by the inner force of biology. I am not immune to their pressure. Before settling in my present home, I lived in seven states and two countries, tugged from place to place in childhood by my father's work and in early adulthood by my own. This itinerant life is so common among the people I know that I have been slow to conceive of an alternative. Only by knocking against the golden calf of mobility, which looms so large and shines so brightly, have I come to realize that it is hollow. Like all idols, it distracts us from what is truly divine.   17

I am encouraged by the words of a Crow elder, quoted by Gary Snyder in *The Practice of the Wild:* "You know, I think if people stay somewhere long enough—even white people—the spirits will begin to speak to them. It's the power of the spirits coming up from the land. The spirits and the old powers aren't lost, they just need people to be around long enough and the spirits will begin to influence them."   18

As I write this, I hear the snarl of earth movers and chain saws a mile away destroying a farm to make way for another shopping strip. I would rather hear a tornado, whose damage can be undone. The elderly woman who owned the farm had it listed in the National Register, then willed it to her daughters on condition they preserve it. After her death, the daughters, who live out of state, had the will broken, so the land could be turned over to the chain saws and earth movers. The machines work around the clock. Their noise wakes me at midnight, at three in the morning, at dawn. The roaring abrades my dreams. The sound is a reminder that we are living in the midst of a holocaust. I do not use the word lightly. The earth is being pillaged, and every one of us, willingly or grudgingly, is taking part. We ask how sensible, educated, supposedly moral people could have tolerated slavery or the slaughter of Jews. Similar questions will be asked about us by our descendants, to whom we bequeath an impoverished planet. They will demand to know how we could have been party to such waste and ruin. [10]   19

What does it mean to be alive in an era when earth is being devoured, and in a country that has set the pattern for that devouring? What are we   20

Thinking Critically

[9] According to the author, how does our culture "nudge" everyone into motion?

[10] Do you agree with Sanders that the mistreatment of our planet is similar to the horrors of slavery and the holocaust? Why or why not?

called to do? I think we are called to the work of healing, both inner and outer: healing of the mind through a change in consciousness, healing of the earth through a change in our lives. We can begin that work by learning how to inhabit a place.

"The man who is often thinking that it is better to be somewhere else than   21
where he is excommunicates himself," we are cautioned by Thoreau, that notorious stay-at-home. The metaphor is religious: To withhold yourself from where you are is to be cut off from communion with the source. It has taken me half a lifetime of searching to realize that the likeliest path to the ultimate ground leads through my local ground. I mean the land itself, with its creeks and rivers, its weather, seasons, stone outcroppings, and all the plants and animals that share it. I cannot have a spiritual center without having a geographical one; I cannot live a grounded life without being grounded in a place.

In belonging to a landscape, one feels a rightness, an at-homeness, a knit-   22
ting of self and world. ⓣ This condition of clarity and focus, this being fully present, is akin to what the Buddhists call mindfulness, what Christian contemplatives refer to as recollection, what Quakers call centering down. I am suspicious of any philosophy that would separate this-worldly from other-worldly commitment. There is only one world, and we participate in it here and now, in our flesh and our place.

UNDERSTANDING DETAILS

1. Why does Sanders believe the Millers didn't move—even after three tornadoes devastated their house?
2. What is associated with a commitment to place for the author?
3. According to Sanders, how does being committed to a place help us appreciate other places and cultures?
4. What does Sanders mean when he says, "By settling in, we have a chance of making a durable home for ourselves, our fellow creatures, and our descendants" (paragraph 10)?

READING CRITICALLY

5. How does being committed to a place work against our heritage in the United States?
6. What does Sanders imply about the difference between a commitment to place and a commitment to ideas?
7. What is the significance of the move from migrants to inhabitants in the American culture?
8. In paragraph 12, Sanders says, "Local knowledge is the grounding for global knowledge." Do you agree or disagree with this statement? Explain your answer.

Thinking Critically

ⓣ What does the author mean by "a knitting of self and world"?

DISCOVERING RHETORICAL STRATEGIES

9. Explain the title of this selection.
10. Is the story about the Millers an effective beginning for this essay?
11. Sanders divides his essay into four sections. What is the main idea of each section?
12. What rhetorical strategies besides comparison/contrast does Sanders use to make his point?

MAKING CONNECTIONS

13. How is Sanders's devotion to the sense of place echoed in the following essays: Ray Bradbury's "Summer Rituals," John McPhee's "The Pines," and/or Firoozeh Dumas's "Leffingwell Elementary School"?
14. In what important ways does Sanders's comparison/contrast technique differ from that of William Ouchi ("Japanese and American Workers: Two Casts of Mind"), Gloria Steinem ("The Politics of Muscle"), and/or Sucheng Chan ("You're Short, Besides!")?
15. Compare and contrast the resilience of the Millers (paragraphs 1–3) in Sanders's essay with similar stories of persistence in Maya Angelou's "New Directions," Harold Krents's "Darkness at Noon," Alice Lesch Kelly's "Toughen Up!," and/or Malcolm X's "Learning to Read."

IDEAS FOR DISCUSSION/WRITING

Preparing to Write

Write freely about your desire or lack of desire for change: How many times have you moved to a new residence during your life so far? Have you moved by choice or by necessity? Do you welcome major changes in your life? Do you make commitments easily? Do these commitments last? What is your strongest current commitment? Will this commitment ever change? What leads you to this conclusion?

Choosing a Topic

1. *Learning Online:* Take the brief online travel quiz sponsored by Travel-Journal (www.travel-journal.org/quiz), and find out your "travel personality." After receiving the results of the quiz, write an essay describing the type of traveler you are. Compare the quiz results with your own self-evaluation to determine the accuracy of the quiz.
2. Someone is considering moving into your neighborhood. In preparation for talking to this neighbor, record your thoughts in essay form about whether or not this would be a good idea.
3. Compare and contrast your level of commitment with that of someone else whom you know very well.
4. Are you more committed to places or ideas? Defend your choice in a well-developed essay modeled on Sanders's selection.

Before beginning your essay, you might want to consult the checklists on page 331.

WILLIAM OUCHI   (1943–   )

Japanese and American Workers: Two Casts of Mind

Born in Honolulu, Hawaii, William Ouchi is an internationally known expert on business management—particularly on the relationship between U.S. and Japanese corporations. Ouchi was educated at Williams College, Stanford University, and the University of Chicago; since then, he has taught in business programs at several major U.S. universities, most recently at the Anderson Graduate School of Management at UCLA, where he is Vice Dean and Faculty Director of the Executive Education Program. The author has also served as Associate Study Director for the National Opinion Research Center and as a business consultant for many of America's most successful companies. He has written three books on organization and management: *Theory Z: How American Business Can Meet the Japanese Challenge* (1981) is a thorough analysis of the differences between U.S. and Japanese industrial productivity; *The M-Form Society: How American Teamwork Can Recapture the Competitive Edge* (1984) is the result of a three-year study by a team of sixteen researchers led by Ouchi; and *Organizational Economics* (1986) is a textbook coedited with Jay Barney. His latest book is titled *Making Schools Work: A Revolutionary Plan to Get Your Children the Education They Need* (2003). He advises students using *The Prose Reader* to spend plenty of time revising their material. "No one writes a good first draft," he explains. "You must continue to revise your work till you understand exactly what you want to say and you have constructed a group of sentences that say it clearly." Ouchi lives with his wife and three children in Santa Monica, California, where he enjoys playing golf as frequently as his busy schedule allows.

Preparing to Read

The following essay, excerpted from *Theory Z*, compares and contrasts Japan's collective work ethic with Americans' spirit of individualism.

Exploring Experience: As you prepare to read this essay, think about your own work ethic: When you study, for example, do you prefer working alone or with a group of people? What kinds of jobs have you held during your life? Did they stress individual or collective behavior? Were you often rewarded for individual achievement, or did you work mostly within a group? In what sort of work environment are you most productive? Most satisfied?

Learning Online: Select an industry such as cars or electronics. Find Web sites for an American company and a Japanese company in your chosen industry. Try to access the companies' mission statements; then think about ways in which their company philosophies are both similar and different.

Perhaps the most difficult aspect of the Japanese for Westerners to com-   1
prehend is the strong orientation to collective values, ❶ particularly a
collective sense of responsibility. Let me illustrate with an anecdote
about a visit to a new factory in Japan owned and operated by an American
electronics company. The American company, a particularly creative firm,
frequently attracts attention within the business community for its novel approaches to planning, organizational design, and management systems. As a
consequence of this corporate style, the parent company determined to make
a thorough study of Japanese workers and to design a plant that would combine the best of East and West. In their study they discovered that Japanese
firms almost never make use of individual work incentives, such as piecework
or even individual performance appraisal tied to salary increases. They concluded that rewarding individual achievement and individual ability is always a good thing.

In the final assembly area of their new plant long lines of young Japanese   2
women wired together electronic products on a piece-rate system: The
more you wired, the more you got paid. About two months after opening,
the head foreladies approached the plant manager. "Honorable plant manager," they said humbly as they bowed, "we are embarrassed to be so forward, but we must speak to you because all of the girls have threatened to
quit work this Friday." (To have this happen, of course, would be a great disaster for all concerned.) "Why," they wanted to know, "can't our plant have
the same compensation system as other Japanese companies? When you
hire a new girl, her starting wage should be fixed by her age. An eighteen-
year-old should be paid more than a sixteen-year-old. Every year on her
birthday, she should receive an automatic increase in pay. The idea that any
one of us can be more productive than another must be wrong, because
none of us in final assembly could make a thing unless all of the other people in the plant had done their jobs right first. To single one person out as
being more productive is wrong and is also personally humiliating to us." The
company changed its compensation system to the Japanese model. ❷

Another American company in Japan had installed a suggestion system   3
much as we have in the United States. Individual workers were encouraged
to place suggestions to improve productivity into special boxes. For an
accepted idea the individual received a bonus amounting to some fraction
of the productivity savings realized from his or her suggestion. After a period

---

Thinking Critically

❶ What does the term "collective values" mean in this context? How important is this phrase
in Japanese culture?

❷ Why were the workers humiliated? How did the plant solve the problem?

of six months, not a single suggestion had been submitted. The American managers were puzzled. They had heard many stories of the inventiveness, the commitment, and the loyalty of Japanese workers, yet not one suggestion to improve productivity had appeared.

The managers approached some of the workers and asked why the   4
suggestion system had not been used. The answer: "No one can come up with a work improvement idea alone. We work together, and any ideas that one of us may have are actually developed by watching others and talking to others. If one of us was singled out for being responsible for such an idea, it would embarrass all of us." The company changed to a group suggestion system, in which workers collectively submitted suggestions. Bonuses were paid to groups which would save bonus money until the end of the year for a party at a restaurant or, if there was enough money, for family vacations together. The suggestions and productivity improvements rained down on the plant. ③

One can interpret these examples in two quite different ways. Perhaps the   5
Japanese commitment to collective values is an anachronism that does not fit with modern industrialism but brings economic success despite that collectivism. Collectivism seems to be inimical to the kind of maverick creativity exemplified in Benjamin Franklin, Thomas Edison, and John D. Rockefeller. Collectivism does not seem to provide the individual incentive to excel which has made a great success of American enterprise. Entirely apart from its economic effects, collectivism implies a loss of individuality, a loss of the freedom to be different, to hold fundamentally different values from others.

The second interpretation of the examples is that the Japanese collec-   6
tivism is economically efficient. It causes people to work well together and to encourage one another to better efforts. Industrial life requires interdependence of one person on another. ④ But a less obvious but far-reaching implication of the Japanese collectivism for economic performance has to do with accountability.

In the Japanese mind, collectivism is neither a corporate or individual   7
goal to strive for nor a slogan to pursue. Rather, the nature of things operates so that nothing of consequence occurs as a result of individual effort. Everything important in life happens as a result of teamwork or collective effort. Therefore, to attempt to assign individual credit or blame to results is unfounded. A Japanese professor of accounting, a brilliant scholar trained at

---

Thinking Critically

③ How did the shift to a "group suggestion system" affect morale and productivity at the plant? Why was this simple change so successful?

④ To what extent is this concept of "interdependence" developed at your college? At your job? What are its advantages and disadvantages?

Carnegie-Mellon University who teaches now in Tokyo, remarked that the status of accounting systems in Japanese industry is primitive compared to those in the United States. Profit centers, transfer prices, and computerized information systems are barely known even in the largest Japanese companies, whereas they are commonplace in even small United States organizations. Though not at all surprised at the difference in accounting systems, I was not at all sure that the Japanese were primitive. In fact, I thought their system a good deal more efficient than ours.

Most American companies have basically two accounting systems. One   8
system summarizes the overall financial state to inform stockholders, bankers, and other outsiders. That system is not of interest here. The other system, called the managerial or cost accounting system, exists for an entirely different reason. ◈ It measures in detail all of the particulars of transactions between departments, divisions, and key individuals in the organization, for the purpose of untangling the interdependencies between people. When, for example, two departments share one truck for deliveries, the cost accounting system charges each department for part of the cost of maintaining the truck and driver, so that at the end of the year, the performance of each department can be individually assessed, and the better department's manager can receive a larger raise. Of course, all of this information processing costs money, and furthermore may lead to arguments between the departments over whether the costs charged to each are fair.

In a Japanese company a short-run assessment of individual perfor-   9
mance is not wanted, so the company can save the considerable expense of collecting and processing all of that information. Companies still keep track of which department uses a truck how often and for what purposes, but like-minded people can interpret some simple numbers for themselves and adjust their behavior accordingly. Those insisting upon clear and precise measurement for the purpose of advancing individual interests must have an elaborate information system. Industrial life, however, is essentially integrated and interdependent. No one builds an automobile alone, no one carries through a banking transaction alone. In a sense the Japanese value of collectivism fits naturally into an industrial setting, whereas the Western individualism provides constant conflicts. The image that comes to mind is of Chaplin's silent film Modern Times in which the apparently insignificant hero played by Chaplin successfully fights against

---

Thinking Critically
◈ Why do most American companies have two systems of accounting? How is the Japanese system different?

the unfeeling machinery of industry. Modern industrial life can be aggravating, even hostile, or natural: All depends on the fit between our culture and our technology. ⑥

The *shinkansen* or "bullet train" speeds across the rural areas of Japan giv-   10
ing a quick view of cluster after cluster of farmhouses surrounded by rice paddies. This particular pattern did not develop purely by chance, but as a consequence of the technology peculiar to the growing of rice, the staple of the Japanese diet. The growing of rice requires construction and maintenance of an irrigation system, something that takes many hands to build. More importantly, the planting and the harvesting of rice can only be done efficiently with the cooperation of twenty or more people. The "bottom line" is that a single family working alone cannot produce enough rice to survive, but a dozen families working together can produce a surplus. Thus the Japanese have had to develop the capacity to work together in harmony, no matter what the forces of disagreement or social disintegration, in order to survive.

Japan is a nation built entirely on the tips of giant, suboceanic volcanoes. ⑦   11
Little of the land is flat and suitable for agriculture. Terraced hillsides make use of every available square foot of arable land. Small homes built very close together further conserve the land. Japan also suffers from natural disasters such as earthquakes and hurricanes. Traditionally homes are made of light construction materials, so a house falling down during a disaster will not crush its occupants and also could be quickly and inexpensively rebuilt. During the feudal period until the Meiji restoration of 1868, each feudal lord sought to restrain his subjects from moving from one village to the next for fear that a neighboring lord might amass enough peasants with which to produce a large agricultural surplus, hire an army, and pose a threat. Apparently bridges were not commonly built across rivers and streams until the late nineteenth century, since bridges increased mobility between villages.

Taken all together, this characteristic style of living paints the picture of a   12
nation of people who are homogeneous with respect to race, history, language, religion, and culture. ⑧ For centuries and generations these people have lived in the same village next door to the same neighbors. Living in close proximity and in dwellings which gave very little privacy, the Japanese survived through their capacity to work together in harmony. In this situation, it was inevitable that the one most central social value which emerged, the one value without which the society could not continue, was that an individual does not matter.

Thinking Critically

⑥ What do you think the author means by "the fit between our culture and our technology"?

⑦ What is the relationship between Japan's geography and its business practices?

⑧ Explain the effect of homogeneity on business.

To the Western soul this is a chilling picture of society. Subordinating 13 individual tastes to the harmony of the group and knowing that individual needs can never take precedence over the interests of all is repellent to the Western citizen. But a frequent theme of Western philosophers and sociologists is that individual freedom exists only when people willingly subordinate their self-interests to the social interest. A society composed entirely of self-interested individuals is a society in which each person is at war with the other, a society which has no freedom. This issue, constantly at the heart of understanding society, comes up in every century, and in every society, whether the writer be Plato, Hobbes, or B. F. Skinner. The question of understanding which contemporary institutions lie at the heart of the conflict between automatism and totalitarianism remains. In some ages, the kinship group, the central social institution, mediated between these opposing forces to preserve the balance in which freedom was realized; in other times the church or the government was most critical. Perhaps our present age puts the work organization as the central institution.

In order to complete the comparison of Japanese and American living 14 situations, consider a flight over the United States. Looking out of the window high over the state of Kansas, we see a pattern of a single farmhouse surrounded by fields, followed by another single homestead surrounded by fields. In the early 1800s in the state of Kansas there were no automobiles. Your nearest neighbor was perhaps two miles distant; the winters were long, and the snow was deep. Inevitably, the central social values were self-reliance and independence. Those were the realities of that place and age that children had to learn to value.

The key to the industrial revolution was discovering that non-human 15 forms of energy substituted for human forms could increase the wealth of a nation beyond anyone's wildest dreams. But there was a catch. To realize this great wealth, non-human energy needed huge complexes called factories with hundreds, even thousands of workers collected into one factory. Moreover, several factories in one central place made the generation of energy more efficient. Almost overnight, the Western world was transformed from a rural and agricultural country to an urban and industrial state. 9 Our technological advance seems to no longer fit our social structure: In a sense, the Japanese can better cope with modern industrialism. While Americans still busily protect our rather extreme form of individualism, the Japanese hold their individualism in check and emphasize cooperation.

Thinking Critically

9 How was the Western world transformed overnight "from a rural and agricultural country to an urban and industrialized state"? What effect did this have on our business practices?

UNDERSTANDING DETAILS

1. Describe in your own words the two different philosophies Ouchi is comparing in this essay.
2. What is Ouchi's main point in this essay? Where does he introduce his purpose?
3. According to the author, what is the most difficult aspect of the Japanese business ethic for Westerners to understand?
4. Why does "collectivism" work better for the Japanese than for the Americans? What is its history in Japan? How is it different from Western "individualism"?

READING CRITICALLY

5. What is Ouchi's personal opinion of the two value systems he is comparing? At what points does he reveal his preference?
6. Why does the author introduce the origins of American and Japanese living conditions?
7. Which set of business values do you prefer after reading Ouchi's comparison? Explain the reasons for your preference.
8. In what ways is the "work organization" the middle ground between automatism and totalitarianism today? Give examples of this observation from your own experience.

DISCOVERING RHETORICAL STRATEGIES

9. How does Ouchi organize this essay? Outline the main points he covers for each subject.
10. Why do you think the author introduces the two anecdotes at the outset of this essay? How do these stories help Ouchi achieve his purpose?
11. Who do you think is the author's intended audience? How much knowledge about these two subjects does he assume they have? What evidence can you give to support your answer?
12. What other rhetorical strategies besides comparison and contrast does Ouchi use to achieve his purpose in this essay? Give examples of each strategy.

MAKING CONNECTIONS

13. Ouchi argues persuasively that geography has played a major role in Japan's orientation toward "collective" values. Scarcity of land and crowded conditions have forced Japanese citizens to work together harmoniously in ways that seem alien to our concept of self-reliance and independence born on the wide-open American frontier. In what similar ways does geography play a part in the essays by John McPhee ("The Pines"), Firoozeh Dumas ("Leffingwell Elementary School"), and/or Scott Russell Sanders ("Homeplace")?
14. Imagine that Ouchi, Robert Ramirez ("The Barrio"), and Mary Pipher ("Beliefs About Families") are having a conversation about the importance of cooperation among people who live close together. What would these authors

say are the principal difficulties of achieving such necessary cooperation? What would they say are the main rewards? How "cooperative" is the neighborhood in which you live? Do you wish it were more so? Why or why not?

15. Compare the suggestions made by Ouchi and Jay Walljasper ("Our Schedules, Our Selves") concerning how American businesses could work more effectively and efficiently. What ideas would you like to share with our business leaders to help make American industry more productive?

IDEAS FOR DISCUSSION/WRITING

Preparing to Write

Write freely about the work ethic that characterizes your immediate environment—at school, at home, or on the job: How do the people in each of these environments feel about one another? How do you feel about them? When are you most productive in these environments? What are the circumstances? Do you work better individually or collectively? Why?

Choosing a Topic

1. *Learning Online:* Have you observed differences in perspective based on age, gender, or culture outside the business arena? How do these differences in perspective affect individual or collective behavior? Select an online magazine whose audience would be interested in your observations. Using Ouchi's technique of alternating comparisons, prepare an article that compares and contrasts these differences in perspective and analyzes their effect on individual and/or collective behavior.

2. Would you prefer to live your social life individually or collectively (as Ouchi defines the two methods)? Explain your preference to a friend, comparing the advantages and disadvantages of both situations. What implications does your preference have? Be sure to make your purpose as clear as possible.

3. Would you rather work in a factory that follows the Japanese or the American method of organization as outlined by Ouchi? Explain your preference to your best friend or your immediate supervisor at work. Compare the advantages and disadvantages of both situations. What implications does your preference have? Be sure to make your purpose as clear as possible.

4. *Leisure* magazine has asked you to compare work and leisure from a college student's point of view. Consider the advantages and disadvantages of each. Be sure to decide on a purpose before you begin to write your comparison.

Before beginning your essay, you might want to consult the checklists on page 331.

GLORIA STEINEM   (1934–   )

The Politics of Muscle

Once described as a writer with "unpretentious clarity and forceful expression," Gloria Steinem is one of the foremost organizers and champions of the modern women's movement. She was born in Toledo, Ohio, earned a B.A. at Smith College, and pursued graduate work in Political Science at the universities of Delhi and Calcutta in India before returning to the United States to begin a freelance career in journalism. One of her earliest and best-known articles, "I Was a Playboy Bunny," was a witty exposé of the entire Playboy operation written in 1963 after she had worked undercover for two weeks in the New York City Playboy Club. In 1968 she and Clay Felker founded *New York* magazine; then, in 1972, they started *Ms.* magazine, which sold out its entire 300,000-copy run in eight days. Steinem's subsequent publications have included *Outrageous Acts and Everyday Rebellions* (1983), *Marilyn: Norma Jean* (1986), *Bedside Book of Self-Esteem* (1989), and *Moving Beyond Words* (1994). An articulate and passionate spokesperson for feminist causes, Steinem has been honored nine times by the *World Almanac* as one of the twenty-five most influential women in the United States.

Preparing to Read

Taken from the author's newest book, *Moving Beyond Words*, "The Politics of Muscle" is actually an introduction to a longer essay entitled "The Strongest Woman in the World," which celebrates the virtues of women's bodybuilding champion Bev Francis.

Exploring Experience: As you prepare to read this essay, examine for a few minutes your own thoughts about the associations Americans make with weakness and strength in both men and women: Which sex do you think of as stronger? In the United States, what does strength have to do with accomplishment? With failure? Do these associations vary for men and women? What does weakness suggest in American culture? Do these suggestions vary for men and women? What are the positive values Americans associate with muscles and strength? With helplessness and weakness? What are the negative values Americans associate with muscles and strength? With helplessness and weakness? What connections have you made from your experience between physical strength and gender roles?

Learning Online: Read expert opinions about Gloria Steinem by conducting an Internet search using the terms "Perspectives of Gloria Steinem." As you read these perspectives, consider the ways Steinem uses her writing for social and political activism.

Icome from a generation of women who didn't do sports. Being a cheer-   1
leader or a drum majorette was as far as our imaginations or role models could take us. Oh yes, there was also being a strutter—one of a group
of girls (and we were girls then) who marched and danced and turned cart-
wheels in front of the high school band at football games. Did you know that
big football universities actually gave strutting scholarships? That shouldn't
sound any more bizarre than football scholarships, yet somehow it does.
Gender politics strikes again.

But even winning one of those rare positions, the stuff that dreams were   2
made of, was more about body display than about the considerable skill they
required. **1** You could forget about trying out for them if you didn't have the
right face and figure, and my high school was full of girls who had learned
to do back flips and twirl flaming batons, all to no avail. Winning wasn't
about being the best in an objective competition or achieving a personal
best, or even about becoming healthy or fit. It was about *being chosen.*

That's one of many reasons why I and other women of my generation   3
grew up believing—as many girls still do—that the most important thing
about a female body is not what it does but how it looks. The power lies not
within us but in the gaze of the observer. In retrospect, I feel sorry for the
protofeminist gym teachers who tried so hard to interest us in half-court
basketball and other team sports thought suitable for girls in my high school,
while we worried about the hairdo we'd slept on rollers all night to achieve.
Gym was just a stupid requirement you tried to get out of, with ugly gym
suits whose very freedom felt odd on bodies accustomed to being constricted
for viewing. **2** My blue-collar neighborhood didn't help much either, for it
convinced me that sports like tennis or golf were as remote as the country
clubs where they were played—mostly by men anyway. That left tap dancing and ballet as my only exercise, and though my dancing school farmed us
out to supermarket openings and local nightclubs, where we danced our
hearts out in homemade costumes, those events were about display too, about
smiling and pleasing and, even during the rigors of ballet, about looking
ethereal and hiding any muscles or strength.

My sports avoidance continued into college, where I went through shock   4
about class and wrongly assumed athletics were only for well-to-do prep
school girls like those who brought their own lacrosse sticks and riding
horses to school. With no sports training to carry over from childhood—and
no place to become childlike, as we must when we belatedly learn basic
skills—I clung to my familiar limits. Even at the casual softball games where

---

Thinking Critically

1 What does Steinem mean by the term "body display"?

2 To what extent are women's bodies still "constricted for viewing" today?

Ms. played the staffs of other magazines, I confined myself to cheering. As the *Ms.* No Stars, we prided ourselves on keeping the same lineup, win or lose, and otherwise disobeying the rules of the jockocracy, so I contented myself with upsetting the men on the opposing team by cheering for their female team members. [3] It's amazing how upset those accustomed to conventional divisions can become when others refuse to be divided by them.

In my case, an interest in the politics of strength had come not from my own experience but from observing the mysterious changes in many women around me. Several of my unathletic friends had deserted me by joining gyms, becoming joggers, or discovering the pleasure of learning to yell and kick in self-defense class. Others who had young daughters described the unexpected thrill of seeing them learn to throw a ball or run with a freedom that hadn't been part of our lives in conscious memory. On campuses, I listened to formerly anorexic young women who said their obsession with dieting had diminished when they discovered strength as a third alternative to the usual fat-versus-thin dichotomy. [4] Suddenly, a skinny, androgynous, "boyish" body was no longer the only way to escape the soft, female, "victim" bodies they associated with their mothers' fates. Added together, these examples of before-and-after-strength changes were so dramatic that the only male analogues I could find were Vietnam amputees whose confidence was bolstered when they entered marathons in wheelchairs or on artificial legs, or paralyzed accident survivors whose sense of themselves was changed when they learned to play wheelchair basketball. Compared to their handicapped female counterparts, however, even those men seemed to be less transformed. Within each category, women had been less encouraged to develop whatever muscle and skills we had.

Since my old habits of ignoring my body and living inside my head weren't that easy to break, it was difficult to change my nonathletic ways. Instead, I continued to learn secondhand from watching my friends, from reading about female strength in other cultures, and from asking questions wherever I traveled.

Though cultural differences were many, there were political similarities in the way women's bodies were treated that went as deep as patriarchy itself. Whether achieved through law and social policy, as in this and other industrialized countries, or by way of tribal practice and religious ritual, as in older cultures, an individual woman's body was far more subject to other people's rules than was that of her male counterpart. Women always seemed to be owned to some degree as the means of reproduction. And as possessions,

---

Thinking Critically

[3] What do you think the author means by a "jockocracy"? What are some of its "rules"?

[4] In what way is "strength" a "third alternative to the usual fat-versus-thin dichotomy"?

women's bodies then became symbols of men's status, [5] with a value that was often determined by what was rare. Thus, rich cultures valued thin women, and poor cultures valued fat women. Yet all patriarchal cultures valued weakness in women. How else could male dominance survive? In my own country, for example, women who "belong" to rich white men are often thinner (as in "You can never be too rich or too thin") than those who "belong" to poor men of color; yet those very different groups of males tend to come together in their belief that women are supposed to be weaker than men; that muscles and strength aren't "feminine."

If I had any doubts about the psychological importance of cultural emphasis on male/female strength difference, listening to arguments about equality put them to rest. Sooner or later, even the most intellectual discussion came down to men's supposedly superior strength as a justification for inequality, whether the person arguing regretted or celebrated it. What no one seemed to explore, however, was the inadequacy of physical strength as a way of explaining oppression in other cases. Men of European origin hadn't ruled in South Africa because they were stronger than African men, and blacks hadn't been kept in slavery or bad jobs in the United States because whites had more muscles. On the contrary, males of the "wrong" class or color were often confined to laboring positions precisely because of their supposedly greater strength, just as the lower pay females received was often rationalized by their supposedly lesser strength. [6] Oppression has no logic— just a self-fulfilling prophecy, justified by a self-perpetuating system.

The more I learned, the more I realized that belief in great strength differences between women and men was itself part of the gender mindgame. In fact, we can't really know what those differences might be, because they are so enshrined, perpetuated, and exaggerated by culture. They seem to be greatest during the childbearing years (when men as a group have more speed and upper-body strength, and women have better balance, endurance, and flexibility) but only marginal during early childhood and old age (when females and males seem to have about the same degree of physical strength). Even during those middle years, the range of difference *among* men and *among* women is far greater than the generalized difference *between* males and females as groups. In multiracial societies like ours, where males of some races are smaller than females of others, judgments based on sex make even less sense. Yet we go right on assuming and praising female weakness and male strength.

Thinking Critically

[5] In what ways are women's bodies "symbols of men's status"?

[6] According to the author, what is the relationship between muscles and social class? Do you agree with this assertion? Why or why not?

But there is a problem about keeping women weak, even in a patriarchy.   10
Women are workers, as well as the means of reproduction. Lower-class
women are especially likely to do hard physical labor. So the problem
becomes: How to make sure female strength is used for work but not for
rebellion? The answer is: Make women ashamed of it. Though hard work
requires lower-class women to be stronger than their upper-class sisters, for
example, those strong women are made to envy and imitate the weakness of
women who "belong" to, and are the means of reproduction for, upper-class
men—and so must be kept even *more* physically restricted if the lines of race
and inheritance are to be kept "pure." That's why restrictive dress, from the
chadors, or full-body veils, of the Middle East to metal ankle and neck rings
in Africa, from nineteenth-century hoop skirts in Europe to corsets and high
heels here, started among upper-class women and then sifted downward as
poor women were encouraged to envy or imitate them. So did such bodily
restrictions as bound feet in China, or clitoridectomies and infibulations in
much of the Middle East and Africa, both of which practices began with
women whose bodies were the means of reproduction for the powerful, and
gradually became generalized symbols of femininity. [7] In this country, the
self-starvation known as anorexia nervosa is mostly a white, upper-middle-
class, young-female phenomenon, but all women are encouraged to envy a
white and impossibly thin ideal.

Sexual politics are also reflected through differing emphases on the repro-   11
ductive parts of women's bodies. Whenever a patriarchy wants females to
populate a new territory or replenish an old one, big breasts and hips become
admirable. Think of the bosomy ideal of this country's frontier days, or the
zaftig, Marilyn Monroe–type figure that became popular after the population losses of World War II. As soon as increased population wasn't desirable
or necessary, hips and breasts were deemphasized. Think of the Twiggy look
that arrived in the 1960s.

But whether bosomy or flat, *zaftig* or thin, the female ideal remains weak,   12
and it stays that way unless women ourselves organize to change it. Suffrag-
ists shed the unhealthy corsets that produced such a tiny-waisted, big-breasted
look that fainting and smelling salts became routine. Instead, they brought in
bloomers and bicycling. Feminists of today are struggling against social pressures that exalt siliconed breasts but otherwise stick-thin silhouettes. Introducing health and fitness has already led to a fashion industry effort to
reintroduce weakness with the waif look, but at least it's being protested.

Thinking Critically

[7] How are "bound feet" and "clitoridectomies" in other cultures symbols of femininity?
Name some symbols of femininity in American culture today.

The point is: Only when women rebel against patriarchal standards does female muscle become more accepted. [8]

For these very political reasons, I've gradually come to believe that society's   13
acceptance of muscular women may be one of the most intimate, visceral measures of change. Yes, we need progress everywhere, but an increase in our physical strength could have more impact on the everyday lives of most women than the occasional role model in the boardroom or in the White House.

UNDERSTANDING DETAILS

1. According to Steinem, what is "gender politics" (paragraph 1)?
2. In what ways does Steinem equate "winning" with "being chosen" (paragraph 2)? Why is this an important premise for her essay?
3. What does Steinem mean when she says, "Oppression has no logic" (paragraph 8)? Explain your answer in detail.
4. In what ways does "power" lie with the observer rather than within the female?

READING CRITICALLY

5. Why does Steinem call the female body a "victim" body (paragraph 5)? What did girls' mothers have to do with this association?
6. Do you agree with the author that a woman's body is "far more subject to other people's rules than . . . that of her male counterpart" (paragraph 7)? Explain your answer, giving examples from your own experience.
7. What is Steinem implying about the political overtones connected with female weakness and male strength? According to Steinem, why are these judgments so ingrained in American social and cultural mores?
8. What are Steinem's reasons for saying that "society's acceptance of muscular women may be one of the most intimate, visceral measures of change" (paragraph 13)? Do you agree with this statement? Explain your reaction in detail.

DISCOVERING RHETORICAL STRATEGIES

9. Who do you think is Steinem's intended audience for this essay? On what do you base your answer?
10. In your opinion, what is Steinem's primary purpose in this essay? Explain your answer in detail.
11. How appropriate is the title of this essay? What would be some possible alternate titles?
12. What rhetorical modes support the author's comparison/contrast? Give examples of each.

Thinking Critically

[8] Why will female muscle become more accepted when women rebel against patriarchal standards? Do you agree with this assertion? Why or why not?

MAKING CONNECTIONS

13. To what extent would Mary Pipher ("Beliefs About Families"), Alice Walker ("Beauty: When the Other Dancer Is the Self"), and/or Barbara Ehrenreich ("The Ecstasy of War") agree with Gloria Steinem's assertion that "the most important thing about a female body is not what it does but how it looks" (paragraph 3)? Do you agree or disagree with this assertion? Give at least three reasons for your opinion.

14. If Steinem is correct that American women have not traditionally found power in their muscles, where have they found it? If you were able to ask Sandra Cisneros ("Only daughter") this same question, what do you think her response would be? With whom would you agree more? Explain your answer.

15. How would Lyn Mikel Brown and Meda Chesney-Lind ("Bad Girls, Bad Girls, Whatcha Gonna Do?") feel about the revolution in women's bodybuilding Steinem describes, which is bringing renewed power and strength to women of all ages? To what extent might they see this trend as an antidote to the growing epidemic of "girlfighting"?

IDEAS FOR DISCUSSION/WRITING

Preparing to Write

Write freely about the definition and role of strength and weakness in American society: What does strength generally mean in American society? What does weakness mean? What associations do you have with both modes of behavior? Where do these associations come from? What are the political implications of these associations? The social implications? In what ways are strength and weakness basic to the value system in American culture?

Choosing a Topic

1. *Learning Online:* Gloria Steinem organizes her comparison of males and females around the issue of "muscle." What other comparisons can be made between men and women? Visit both an online men's magazine and an online women's magazine, and examine the headings. Find an issue that is explored in both magazines, and write an essay that analyzes their similarities and differences. Following Steinem's example, organize your analysis around a single issue, and include your own perspective where appropriate.

2. Compare two different approaches to the process of succeeding in a specific job or activity. Develop your own guidelines for making the comparison; then, write an essay for your fellow students about the similarities and differences you have observed between these two different approaches. Be sure to decide on a purpose and a point of view before you begin to write.

3. Interview your mother and your father about their views on physical strength in their separate family backgrounds. If you have grandparents or stepparents, interview them as well. Then compare and contrast these various influences in your life. Which of them are alike? Which are different? How have you personally dealt with these similarities and differences? Be sure to decide on a purpose and a point of view before you begin to write.

4. In her essay, Steinem argues that "an increase in our [women's] physical strength could have more impact on the everyday lives of most women than the occasional role model in the boardroom or in the White House" (paragraph 13). Do you agree with the author? Write an essay to be published in your hometown newspaper explaining your views on this issue.

Before beginning your essay, you might want to consult the checklists on page 331.

SUCHENG CHAN   (1941–   )

You're Short, Besides!

Sucheng Chan was born in the Peoples' Republic of China and immigrated to the United States in 1957 at the age of sixteen. Following a B.A. at Swarthmore College, an M.A. from the University of Hawaii, and a Ph.D. at the University of California, Berkeley, she held a number of prestigious academic positions, including Assistant Professor of History at Sonoma State University; Professor of History and Provost of Oakes College at the University of California, Santa Cruz; and Professor of Global Studies and Chair of Asian Studies at the University of California, Santa Barbara, where she is now a distinguished Professor Emeritus. Chan currently lives in Santa Barbara, where she continues to publish books and articles in the field of Asian Studies. Among her many influential books are *This Bittersweet Soil* (1986), *Asian Americans: An Interpretive History* (1990), *Entry Denied: Exclusion and the Chinese Community in America* (1991), *Peoples of Color in the American West* (1994), *Not Just Victims: Conversations with Cambodian Community Leaders in the United States* (2003), and *In Defense of Asian American Studies* (2005). Her advice to students using *The Prose Reader* is to "read as much good writing as you can and be sure to read different genres of writing. That will help you pick up (often subconsciously) the sounds and rhythms of felicitous prose. Of course, writing classes also help."

Preparing to Read

The following essay, from *Making Space, Making Soul: Creative Perspectives by Women of Color,* edited by Gloria Anzalvúa (1990), gives us many valuable insights into the life of a handicapped person. In it, the author presents a resilient self-concept that had to be adjusted several times to cope with new circumstances.

Exploring Experience: As you prepare to read this essay, examine for a few minutes your own ideas about the handicapped: If you are handicapped, how would your life be different as an able-bodied person? If you are able-bodied, how would your life be different as a handicapped person? How physically independent could you be in either situation? Is physical independence important to you? In what ways? How dependent are you on others in your daily life? Does this dependence bother you in any way? To what extent are your goals in life influenced by your dependence on other people?

Learning Online: Visit the "Americans with Disabilities" Web site (www.ada .gov), and spend a few moments exploring some of the issues people with disabilities frequently face. When reading Sucheng Chan's article, consider how she presents her experience and compares the differences in Asian and American perspectives.

When asked to write about being a physically handicapped Asian- 1
American woman, I considered it an insult. ❶ After all, my ac-
complishments are many, yet I was not asked to write about any
of them. Is being handicapped the most salient feature about me? The fact
that it might be in the eyes of others made me decide to write the essay as
requested. I realized that the way I think about myself may differ considerably from the way others perceive me. And maybe that's what being physically handicapped is all about.

I was stricken simultaneously with pneumonia and polio at the age of 2
four. Uncertain whether I had polio of the lungs, seven of the eight doctors
who attended me—all practitioners of Western medicine—told my parents
they should not feel optimistic about my survival. A Chinese fortune teller
my mother consulted also gave a grim prognosis, but for an entirely different reason: I had been stricken because my name was offensive to the gods. ❷
My grandmother had named me "grandchild of wisdom," a name that the
fortune teller said was too presumptuous for a girl. So he advised my parents to change my name to "chaste virgin." All these pessimistic predictions
notwithstanding, I hung onto life, if only by a thread. For three years, my body
was periodically pierced with electric shocks as the muscles of my legs atro-
phied. Before my illness, I had been an active, rambunctious, precocious, and
very curious child. Being confined to bed was thus a mental agony as great
as my physical pain. Living in war-torn China, I received little medical attention; physical therapy was unheard of. But I was determined to walk. So one
day, when I was six or seven, I instructed my mother to set up two rows of
chairs to face each other so that I could use them as I would parallel bars. I
attempted to walk by holding my body up and moving it forward with my
arms while dragging my legs along behind. Each time I fell, my mother
gasped, but I badgered her until she let me try again. After four nonambu-
latory years, I finally walked once more by pressing my hands against my
thighs so my knees wouldn't buckle.

My father had been away from home during most of those years because 3
of the war. When he returned, I had to confront the guilt he felt about my
condition. In many East Asian cultures, there is a strong folk belief that a
person's physical state in this life is a reflection of how morally or sinfully he
or she lived in previous lives. Furthermore, because of the tendency to view
the family as a single unit, it is believed that the fate of one member can be
caused by the behavior of another. Some of my father's relatives told him that

---

Thinking Critically

❶ Why was Chan insulted when she was asked to write about being a "physically handicapped Asian-American woman"?

❷ In what ways was Chan's name "offensive to the gods"?

my illness had doubtless been caused by the wild carousing he did in his youth. A well-meaning but somewhat simple man, my father believed them.

Throughout my childhood, he sometimes apologized to me for having to   4
suffer retribution for his former bad behavior. This upset me; it was bad enough that I had to deal with the anguish of not being able to walk, but to have to assuage his guilt as well was a real burden! In other ways, my father was very good to me. He took me out often, carrying me on his shoulders or back, to give me fresh air and sunshine. He did this until I was too large and heavy for him to carry. And ever since I can remember, he has told me that I am pretty. ❸

After getting over her anxieties about my constant falls, my mother decided   5
to send me to school. I had already learned to read some words of Chinese at the age of three by asking my parents to teach me the sounds and meaning of various characters in the daily newspaper. But between the ages of four and eight, I received no education since just staying alive was a full-time job. Much to her chagrin, my mother found no school in Shanghai, where we lived at the time, which would accept me as a student. Finally, as a last resort, she approached the American School, which agreed to enroll me only if my family kept an *amah* (a servant who takes care of children) by my side at all times. The tuition at the school was twenty U.S. dollars per month—a huge sum of money during those years of runaway inflation in China—and payable only in U.S. dollars. My family afforded the high cost of tuition and the expense of employing a full-time *amah* for less than a year.

We left China as the Communist forces swept across the country in vic-   6
tory. We found an apartment in Hong Kong across the street from a school run by Seventh-Day Adventists. By that time I could walk a little, so the principal was persuaded to accept me. An *amah* now had to take care of me only during recess when my classmates might easily knock me over as they ran about the playground.

After a year and a half in Hong Kong, we moved to Malaysia, where my   7
father's family had lived for four generations. There I learned to swim in the lovely warm waters of the tropics and fell in love with the sea. On land I was a cripple; in the ocean I could move with the grace of a fish. ❹ I liked the freedom of being in the water so much that many years later, when I was a graduate student in Hawaii, I became greatly enamored with a man just because he called me a "Polynesian water nymph."

Thinking Critically

❸ Why was Chan pleased that her father often told her she was pretty? What does this reaction reveal about the relationship between Chan and her father?

❹ Why did the author fall in love with the sea? How did the sea make her feel?

As my overall health improved, my mother became less anxious about all 8 aspects of my life. She did everything possible to enable me to lead as normal a life as possible. I remember how once some of her colleagues in the high school where she taught criticized her for letting me wear short skirts. They felt my legs should not be exposed to public view. My mother's response was, "All girls her age wear short skirts, so why shouldn't she?"

The years in Malaysia were the happiest of my childhood, even though I 9 was constantly fending off children who ran after me calling, "*Baikah! Baikah!*" ("Cripple! Cripple!" in the Hokkien dialect commonly spoken in Malaysia). The taunts of children mattered little because I was a star pupil. I won one award after another for general scholarship as well as for art and public speaking. Whenever the school had important visitors, my teacher always called on me to recite in front of the class.

A significant event that marked me indelibly occurred when I was twelve. 10 That year my school held a music recital, and I was one of the students chosen to play the piano. I managed to get up the steps to the stage without any problem, but as I walked across the stage, I fell. Out of the audience, a voice said loudly and clearly, "Ayah! A *baikah* shouldn't be allowed to perform in public." I got up before anyone could get on stage to help me and, with tears streaming uncontrollably down my face, I rushed to the piano and began to play. Beethoven's "Für Elise" had never been played so fiendishly fast before or since, but I managed to finish the whole piece. That I managed to do so made me feel really strong. I never again feared ridicule. ⑤

In later years I was reminded of this experience from time to time. During my fourth year as an assistant professor at the University of California at 11 Berkeley, I won a distinguished teaching award. Some weeks later I ran into a former professor who congratulated me enthusiastically. But I said to him, "You know what? I became a distinguished teacher by *limping* across the stage of Dwinelle 155!" (Dwinelle 155 is a large, cold classroom that most colleagues of mine hate to teach in.) I was rude not because I lacked graciousness but because this man, who had told me that my dissertation was the finest piece of work he had read in fifteen years, had nevertheless advised me to eschew a teaching career.

"Why?" I asked. 12

"Your leg . . ." he responded. 13

"What about my leg?" I said, puzzled. 14

"Well, how would you feel standing in front of a large lecture class?" 15

"If it makes any difference, I want you to know I've won a number of 16 speech contests in my life, and I am not the least bit self-conscious about

---

Thinking Critically

⑤ How did finishing her piano solo give the author strength?

speaking in front of large audiences. . . . Look, why don't you write me a letter of recommendation to tell people how brilliant I am and let *me* worry about my leg!"

This incident is worth recounting only because it illustrates a dilemma   17
that handicapped persons face frequently: those who care about us sometimes get so protective that they unwittingly limit our growth. **6** This former professor of mine had been one of my greatest supporters for two decades. Time after time, he had written glowing letters of recommendation on my behalf. He had spoken as he did because he thought he had my best interests at heart; he thought that if I got a desk job rather than one that required me to be a visible, public person, I would be spared the misery of being stared at.

Americans, for the most part, do not believe as Asians do that physically   18
handicapped persons are morally flawed. But they are equally inept at interacting with those of us who are not able-bodied. Cultural differences in the perception and treatment of handicapped people are most clearly expressed by adults. **7** Children, regardless of where they are, tend to be openly curious about people who do not look "normal." Adults in Asia have no hesitation in asking visibly handicapped people what is wrong with them, often expressing their sympathy with looks of pity, whereas adults in the United States try desperately to be polite by pretending not to notice.

One interesting response I often elicited from people in Asia but have   19
never encountered in America is the attempt to link my physical condition to the state of my soul. Many a time while living and traveling in Asia people would ask me what religion I belonged to. I would tell them that my mother is a devout Buddhist, that my father was baptized a Catholic but has never practiced Catholicism, and that I am an agnostic. Upon hearing this, people would try strenuously to convert me to their religion so that whichever God they believed in could bless me. If I would only attend this church or that temple regularly, they urged, I would surely get cured. **8** Catholics and Buddhists alike have pressed religious medallions into my palm, telling me if I would wear these, the relevant deity or saint would make me well. Once while visiting the tomb of Muhammad Ali Jinnah in Karachi, Pakistan, an old Muslim, after finishing his evening prayers, spotted me, gestured toward my legs, raised his arms heavenward, and began a new round of prayers, apparently on my behalf.

Thinking Critically

6 In what way did Chan's professor "unwittingly limit" her growth? Have you ever had a similar experience?

7 How do adults in Asia and America differ in their treatment of handicapped people? Which approach is better in your opinion? Why?

8 What is the relationship between religion and better health in these examples? Do you agree with this relationship? Why or why not?

In the United States adults who try to act "civilized" toward handicapped   20
people by pretending they don't notice anything unusual sometimes end up
ignoring handicapped people completely. In the first few months I lived in
this country, I was struck by the fact that whenever children asked me what
was the matter with my leg, their adult companions would hurriedly shush
them up, furtively look at me, mumble apologies, and rush their children
away. After a few months of such encounters, I decided it was my responsibility to educate these people. So I would say to the flustered adults, "It's
okay, let the kid ask." Turning to the child, I would say, "When I was a little
girl, no bigger than you are, I became sick with something called polio. The
muscles of my leg shrank up and I couldn't walk very well. You're much
luckier than I am because now you can get a vaccine to make sure you never
get my disease. So don't cry when your mommy takes you to get a polio vaccine, okay?" Some adults and their little companions I talked to this way
were glad to be rescued from embarrassment; others thought I was strange.

Americans have another way of covering up their uneasiness: they become   21
jovially patronizing. Sometimes when people spot my crutch, they ask if I've
had a skiing accident. When I answer that unfortunately it is something less
glamorous than that they say, "I bet you *could* ski if you put your mind to it!"
Alternately, at parties where people dance, men who ask me to dance with
them get almost belligerent when I decline their invitation. They say, "Of
course you can dance if you *want* to!" Some have given me pep talks about
how if I would only develop the right mental attitude, I would have more
fun in life. [9]

Different cultural attitudes toward handicapped persons came out clearly   22
during my wedding. My father-in-law, as solid a representative of middle
America as could be found, had no qualms about objecting to the marriage
on racial grounds, but he could bring himself to comment on my handicap
only indirectly. He wondered why his son, who had dated numerous high
school and college beauty queens, couldn't marry one of them instead of
me. My mother-in-law, a devout Christian, did not share her husband's prejudices, but she worried aloud about whether I could have children. [10] Some
Chinese friends of my parents, on the other hand, said that I was lucky to
have found such a noble man, one who would marry me despite my handicap. I, for my part, appeared in church in a white lace wedding dress I had
designed and made myself—a miniskirt!

Thinking Critically

[9] Define "right mental attitude" in the context of this essay. Why do some people say that
the "right mental attitude" could help Chan have more fun in life?

[10] What is the difference in reactions to Chan by her mother-in-law and father-in-law?
How do you account for this difference?

How Asian Americans treat me with respect to my handicap tells me a   23
great deal about their degree of acculturation. Recent immigrants behave just
like Asians in Asia; those who have been here longer or who grew up in the
United States behave more like their white counterparts. I have not encountered any distinctly Asian American pattern of response. What makes the
experience of Asian American handicapped people unique is the duality of
responses we elicit.

Regardless of racial or cultural background, most handicapped people   24
have to learn to find a balance between the desire to attain physical independence and the need to take care of ourselves by not overtaxing our bodies. In my case. I've had to learn to accept the fact that leading an active life
has its price. Between the ages of eight and eighteen. I walked without using
crutches or braces, but the effort caused my right leg to become badly mis-
aligned. Soon after I came to the United States, I had a series of operations
to straighten out the bones of my right leg; afterwards, though my leg looked
straighter and presumably better, I could no longer walk on my own. Initially
my doctors fitted me with a brace, but I found wearing one cumbersome and
soon gave it up. I could move around much more easily—and more important, faster—by using one crutch. One orthopedist after another warned me
that using a single crutch was a bad practice. 11 They were right. Over the
years my spine developed a double-S curve, and for the last twenty years I
have suffered from severe, chronic back pains, which neither conventional
physical therapy nor a lighter work load can eliminate.

The only thing that helps my backaches is a good massage, but the sooth-   25
ing effect lasts no more than a day or two. Massages are expensive, especially
when one needs them three times a week. So I found a job that pays better,
but at which I have to work longer hours, consequently increasing the physical strain on my body—a sort of vicious circle. When I was in my thirties,
my doctors told me that if I kept leading the strenuous life I did, I would be
in a wheelchair by the time I was forty. They were right on target: I bought
myself a wheelchair when I was forty-one. But being the incorrigible character that I am, I use it only when I am *not* in a hurry!

It is a good thing, however, that I am too busy to think much about my   26
handicap or my backaches because pain can physically debilitate as well as
cause depression. And there are days when my spirits get rather low. What
has helped me is realizing that being handicapped is akin to growing old at
an accelerated rate. The contradiction I experience is that often my mind
races along as though I'm only twenty while my body feels about sixty. But
fifteen or twenty years hence, unlike my peers who will have to cope with

---

Thinking Critically

11 Why was using a single crutch a bad practice?

aging for the first time, I shall be full of cheer because I will have already fought, and I hope won, that battle long ago.

Beyond learning how to be physically independent and, for some of us,   27
living with chronic pain or other kinds of discomfort, the most difficult thing a handicapped person has to deal with, especially during puberty and early adulthood, is relating to potential sexual partners. Because American culture places so much emphasis on physical attractiveness, a person with a shriveled limb, or a tilt to the head, or the inability to speak clearly, experiences great uncertainty—indeed trauma—when interacting with someone to whom he or she is attracted. My problem was that I was not only physically handicapped, small, and short, but worse, I also wore glasses and was smarter than all the boys I knew! Alas, an insurmountable combination. **12** Yet somehow I have managed to have intimate relationships, all of them with extraordinary men. Not surprisingly, there have also been countless men who broke my heart—men who enjoyed my company "as a friend," but who never found the courage to date or make love with me, although I am sure my experience in this regard is no different from that of many able-bodied persons.

The day came when my backaches got in the way of having an active sex   28
life. Surprisingly, that development was liberating because I stopped worrying about being attractive to men. No matter how headstrong I had been, I, like most women of my generation, had had the desire to be alluring to men ingrained into me. And that longing had always worked like a brake on my behavior. When what men think of me ceased to be compelling, I gained greater freedom to be myself. **13**

I've often wondered if I would have been a different person had I not   29
been physically handicapped. I really don't know, though there is no question that being handicapped has marked me. But at the same time I usually do not *feel* handicapped—and consequently, I do not *act* handicapped. People are therefore less likely to treat me as a handicapped person. There is no doubt, however, that the lives of my parents, sister, husband, other family members, and some close friends have been affected by my physical condition. They have had to learn not to hide me away at home, not to feel embarrassed by how I look or react to people who say silly things to me, and not to resent me for the extra demands my condition makes on them. Perhaps the hardest thing for those who live with handicapped people is to know when and how to offer help. There are no guidelines applicable to all

---

Thinking Critically

12 How many "handicaps" does Chan imply she has? Which do you think was the most difficult for her to cope with? Why?

13 How did Chan begin to gain greater freedom to be herself when she stopped worrying about what men thought of her?

situations. My advice is, when in doubt, ask, but ask in a way that does not smack of pity or embarrassment. Most important, please don't talk to us as though we are children.

So, has being physically handicapped been a handicap? It all depends on   30
one's attitude. Some years ago, I told a friend that I had once said to an affirmative action compliance officer (somewhat sardonically, since I do not believe in the head count approach to affirmative action) that the institution which employs me is triply lucky because it can count me as non–white, female and handicapped. He responded, "Why don't you tell them to count you four times? . . . Remember, you're short, besides!"

UNDERSTANDING DETAILS

1. What "folk belief" (paragraph 3) did Chan's family use to explain the cause of her condition?
2. How was Chan finally able to walk after four years of not walking?
3. What specific event enabled the author to tolerate ridicule without fear?
4. In what ways have Chan's friends and family had to adjust to her condition?

READING CRITICALLY

5. What is Chan comparing in this essay? Explain three topics that she discusses in her comparison.
6. According to Chan, why do most handicapped people need to "find a balance between the desire to attain physical independence and the need to take care of ourselves by not overtaxing our bodies" (paragraph 24)? Explain your answer.
7. How does Chan plan to win the battle against aging before her peers take it on?
8. Why was giving up on sex a liberating experience for Chan? Explain your answer.

DISCOVERING RHETORICAL STRATEGIES

9. In what way does the background information Chan gives us in the first paragraph set up the entire essay? Explain your answer.
10. Who do you think is Chan's intended audience? On what evidence do you base your answer?
11. What is the author's attitude toward her subject in this essay? What details in the essay reveal this point of view?
12. Which rhetorical modes does Chan use to support her comparison? How effective are these choices in fulfilling her purpose?

MAKING CONNECTIONS

13. Imagine that Chan, Harold Krents ("Darkness at Noon"), and/or Alice Walker ("Beauty: When the Other Dancer Is the Self") are having a discussion about

whether their physical disability has been a "handicap" to them. Which of these authors do you think would feel least handicapped by his or her disability? Why?

14. Chan, Amy Tan ("Mother Tongue"), and William Ouchi ("Japanese and American Workers: Two Casts of Mind") all exhibit distinctively Eastern views of life. In what ways do these authors share similar philosophies? How are they different?

15. How do Chan's comparison/contrast techniques differ from those used by Gloria Steinem ("The Politics of Muscle")?

IDEAS FOR DISCUSSION/WRITING

Preparing to Write

Write freely about your own physical independence: If you are handicapped, how "independent" do you feel? If you are able-bodied, are you aware of your physical independence? How much do you value your independence? In what ways is it a part of your identity? What would happen if your independence were threatened or taken away? How is physical independence related to your identity?

Choosing a Topic

1. *Learning Online:* Find another Web site (besides the "Americans with Disabilities" site from Preparing to Read) that addresses either a specific disability or disabilities in general. First, identify their commonalities, and then compare the ways in which they are different. Write an essay comparing the two Web sites' approaches and perspectives toward disability. Following Chan's example, integrate your perspective into your examples.

2. As if you are writing for a magazine popular with your peers, explain some specific elements in your ideal life by comparing and contrasting them to those aspects in other people's lives. Is your ideal based on anyone's life in particular? In what way is he or she a role model for you? Does this person play an active role in helping you achieve your ideal existence?

3. Write a comparison essay explaining your attraction to the types of people you date or have married. Why do you like these people? What do your feelings about this type of person tell other people about you?

4. Discuss the concepts of independence and dependence by comparing these ideas to one another. Give examples to support your main points.

Before beginning your essay, you might want to consult the checklists on page 331.

Chapter Writing Assignments

Practicing Comparison/Contrast

1. Compare one feature of your culture to the same aspect of someone else's culture. Make sure you are not making random or biased judgments but are exploring similarities, differences, and their significance.

2. Compare the styles of two different writers in *The Prose Reader*. First, identify the major features of each writer's style. Then narrow your ideas to a few points of comparison. For example, perhaps one writer is serious and another funny; one writer may write long, complex sentences, while another writes mostly simple sentences. Discuss the effects each essay has on its readers based on these specific differences in style.

3. Discuss the major differences between two views of a political issue or between two political candidates. Identify the main sources of the differences, and then defend the point of view you believe is most reasonable.

Exploring a Theme

4. What does being "an individual" mean? How important is individualism to you personally? When might being an individual clash with the needs of society? Identify and discuss a situation in which individualism and the needs of society might conflict. If such a conflict occurs, which needs should prevail and why?

5. Identify a disturbing trend that you see in American society. Describe this trend in an essay, providing examples from your observations and experiences.

6. Think about a business or organization that is not what it appears to be. Then write an essay explaining the differences between the image this business or organization projects and the way it actually functions. Include specific examples to illustrate the differences between its image and the reality experienced by its customers or clients.

Writing from Sources

For detailed information on writing from sources, see Part III.

7. Compare the typical family dynamics of today with those of another era. How is today's family different from one in another period? What does research say about the family life of another century or another decade in this century? After consulting a few sources, compare and contrast the characteristics of families from two different eras.

8. In the last century, the United States saw radical changes in societal norms, such as the civil rights movement, women's suffrage, and equal rights for persons with disabilities. Did these groups gain recognition through legislative means or civil disobedience? Research two of these movements, and write a documented essay comparing and contrasting the tactics behind their success.

Analyzing Visual Images

© Dave Beckerman Photography

9. Based on the photo above, we can see that couples behave very differently. Compare a relationship you have had with a relationship you've seen, such as your parents' relationship or marriage, a previous relationship in which you were involved, or the relationship of someone else you know that seems very different from your own.
10. Look at the picture on page 321 at the beginning of the chapter. Do you think the woman in the photograph is holding up a picture of herself or someone else, possibly a daughter or sister? Explain your answer by discussing the different comparisons/contrasts you considered in order to reach your conclusion.

Chapter 10

DEFINITION
Limiting the Frame
of Reference

Definitions help us function smoothly in a complex world. All effective communication, in fact, is continuously dependent on our unique human ability to understand and employ accurate definitions of a wide range of words, phrases, and abstract ideas. If we did not work from a set of shared definitions, we would not be able to carry on coherent conversations, write comprehensible letters, or respond to even the simplest radio and television programs. Definitions help us understand basic concrete terms (such as *automobiles, laser beams*, and *gross national product*), discuss various events in our lives (such as snowboarding, legal proceedings, and a Cinco de Mayo celebration), and grasp difficult abstract ideas (such as democracy, ambition, and resentment). The ability to comprehend definitions and use them effectively helps us keep our oral and written level of communication accurate and accessible to a wide variety of people.

DEFINING DEFINITION

Definition is the process of explaining a word, object, or idea in such a way that the reader (or listener) knows as precisely as possible what we mean. A good definition sets up intellectual boundaries by focusing on the special qualities of a word or phrase that set it apart from other, similar words or phrases. Clear definitions always give the writer and the reader a mutual starting point on the sometimes bumpy road to successful communication.

Definitions vary from short, dictionary-length summaries to longer, "extended" accounts that determine the form of an entire essay. Words or ideas that require expanded definitions are usually abstract, complex, or unavoidably controversial; they generally bear many related meanings or many shades of meaning. Definitions can be *objective* (technically precise and generally dry) or *subjective* (colored with personal opinion), and they can be used to instruct, to entertain, or to accomplish a combination of these two fundamental rhetorical goals.

In the following paragraph, a student defines *childhood* by putting it into perspective with other important stages of life. Though mostly entertaining, the paragraph is also instructive as the student objectively captures the essence of this phase of human development:

> *Childhood is a stage of growth somewhere between infancy and adolescence. Just as each developmental period in our lives brings new changes and concerns, childhood serves as the threshold to puberty—the time we learn to discriminate between good and bad, right and wrong, love and lust. Childhood is neither a time of irresponsible infancy nor responsible adulthood. Rather, it is marked by duties that we don't really want, challenges that excite us, feelings that puzzle and frighten us, and limitless opportunities that help us explore the world around us. Childhood is a time when we solidify our personalities in spite of pressures to be someone else.*

THINKING CRITICALLY THROUGH DEFINITION

Definitions are building blocks in communication that help us make certain we are functioning from the same understanding of terms and ideas. They give us a foundation to work from in both reading and writing. Definitions force us to think about meanings and word associations that make other logical strategies stronger and easier to work with.

The process of thinking through our definitions forces us to come to some understanding about a particular term or concept we are mentally wrestling with. Articulating that definition helps us move to other modes of thought and higher levels of understanding. Practicing definitions in isolation to get a feel for them is much like separating the skill of pedaling from the process of riding a bike. The better you get at pedaling, the more natural the rest of the cycling process becomes. The following exercises ask you to practice definitions in a number of different ways. Being more conscious of what definition entails will make it more useful to you in both your reading and your writing.

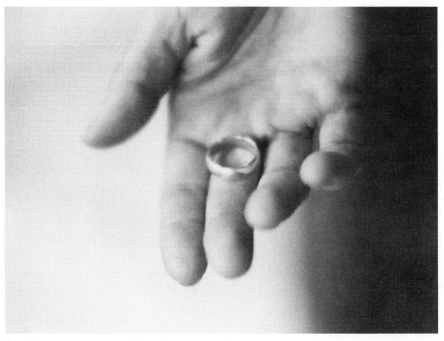

© Mel Curtis/Getty Images—Photodisc

1. What does the ring in this photograph mean? Identify at least three ways in which people could define this ring. Write your definitions as precisely as possible, and share one with your class.
2. Define in one or two sentences one of the concrete words and one of the abstract words listed here.
   Concrete: *cattle, book, ranch, water, gum*
   Abstract: *freedom, progress, equality, fairness, boredom*
   What were some of the differences between the processes you went through to explain the concrete word and the abstract word? What can you conclude from this brief exercise about the differences in defining abstract and concrete words?
3. Define the word *grammar*. Consult a dictionary, several handbooks, and maybe even some friends to get their views on the word's meaning. Then write a humorous definition of *grammar* that consolidates all these views into a single definition.

READING AND WRITING DEFINITION ESSAYS

Extended definitions, which may range from two or three paragraphs to an entire essay, seldom follow a set pattern of development or organization. Instead, as you will see from the examples in this chapter, they draw on a number of different techniques to help explain a word, object, term, concept, or phenomenon.

Reading Definition Essays

- What is the essay's context?
- How is the definition introduced?
- Is the essay objective or subjective?
- What other rhetorical modes support the definition?

Preparing to Read. As you begin to read each of the definition essays in this chapter, take some time to consider the author's title and the synopsis of the essay in the Rhetorical Table of Contents: What do you think Marc Gellman's attitude is in "Worry. Don't Be Happy"? What do you sense is the general mood of Mary Pipher's "Beliefs About Families"? How much can you learn about Lyn Mikel Brown and Meda Chesney-Lind's topic from their title, "Bad Girls, Bad Girls, Watcha Gonna Do?"

Equally important as you prepare to read is scanning an essay and finding information from its prefatory material about the author and the circumstances surrounding the composition of the essay. What can you learn from Claudia Wallis and Sonia Steptoe about our schools? And what do you think is Robert Ramirez's purpose in his definition of the barrio?

Last, as you prepare to read these essays, answer the prereading questions before each essay, and then spend a few minutes thinking freely about the general subject of the essay at hand: What do you want to know from Pipher about families? What interests you about aggressive behavior in others (Brown and Chesney-Lind)?

Reading. As you read a definition essay, as with all essays, be sure to record your initial reactions to your reading material. What are some of your thoughts or associations in relation to each essay?

As you get more involved in the essay, reconsider the preliminary material so you can create a context within which to analyze what the writer is saying: What is Gellman's purpose in writing "Worry. Don't Be Happy"? Does his tone effectively support that purpose? Who do you think is Ramirez's primary audience? Do you think his essay will effectively reach that group of people? In what ways are Wallis and Steptoe qualified to write about schools?

Throughout each essay in this chapter are provocative questions at the bottom of the pages meant to guide you to analysis and critical thinking. These questions ask you to consider the authors' ideas as they relate to one another and to your own experience. Your responses to these questions will then give you thoughtful material to work with on the tasks after each essay. These questions essentially bridge the gap between the prereading questions and the activities after each essay. Writing down your thoughts will be especially beneficial to you as you gather your own ideas together in response to a writing assignment.

Finally, determine at this point whether the author's treatment of his or her subject is predominantly objective or subjective. Then, make sure you understand the main points of the essay on the literal, interpretive, and analytical levels by reading the questions that follow.

Rereading.   When you read these definition essays for a second time, check to see how each writer actually sets forth his or her definition: Does the writer put each item in a specific category with clear boundaries? Do you understand how the item being defined is different from other items in the same category? Did the author name the various components of the item, explain its etymology (linguistic origin and history), discuss what it is not, or perform a combination of these tasks?

To evaluate the effectiveness of a definition essay, you need to reconsider the essay's primary purpose and audience. If Gellman is trying to get the general reader to reconsider the role of happiness in our lives, how effective is he? In like manner, is Pipher successful in communicating to the same audience the value of the family unit?

Especially applicable is the question of what other rhetorical strategies help the author communicate this purpose. What other modes does Ramirez use to help him define the barrio? Through what other modes do Brown and Chesney-Lind define "bad girls"?

For an inventory of the reading process, you can review the Reading Inventory at the end of Part I.

Writing Definition Essays

- Compose a thesis statement.
- Approach the definition creatively.
- Define the word or concept.
- Use other rhetorical strategies to support your definition.

Preparing to Write.   As with other essays, you should begin the task of writing a definition essay by answering the prewriting questions featured in this text and then exploring your subject and generating other ideas. (See the explanation of various prewriting techniques on pages 36–38 of Chapter 3.)

Be sure you know what you are going to define and how you will approach your definition. You should then focus on a specific audience and purpose as you approach your writing assignment.

Writing.   The next step toward developing a definition essay is usually to describe the general category to which the word belongs and then to contrast the word with all other words in that group. To define *exposition,* for example, you might say that it is a type of writing. Then, to differentiate it from other types of writing, you could go on to say that its main purpose is to "expose," or present, information, as opposed to rhetorical modes such as description and narration, which describe and tell stories. In addition, you might want to cite some expository methods such as example, process analysis, division/classification, and comparison/contrast.

Yet another way to begin a definition essay is to provide a term's etymology. Tracing a word's origin often illuminates its current meaning and usage as well. *Exposition,* for example, comes from the Latin *exponere,* meaning "to put forth, set forth, display, declare, or publish" (*ex* = out; *ponere* = to put or place). This information can generally be found in any good dictionary or encyclopedia.

Another approach to defining a term is to explain what it does *not* mean. For example, *exposition* is not creative writing. By limiting the readers' frame of reference in these various ways, you are helping to establish a working definition for the term under consideration.

Finally, rhetorical methods that we have already studied, such as description, narration, example, process analysis, division/classification, and comparison/contrast, are particularly useful to writers in expanding their definitions. To clarify the term *exposition,* you might **describe** the details of an expository theme, **narrate** a story about the wide use of the term in today's classroom, or **give examples** of assignments that would produce good expository writing. In other situations, you could **analyze** various writing assignments and discuss the **process** of producing an expository essay, **classify** exposition apart from creative writing and then **divide** it into categories similar to the headings of this book, or **compare** and **contrast** it with creative writing. Writers also use definition quite often to support other rhetorical modes.

Rewriting.   Reviewing and revising a definition essay is a relatively straightforward task:

- Have I chosen an effective beginning for my paper?
- Did I create a reasonable context for my definition?
- Have I used appropriate rhetorical strategies to develop my ideas?
- Have I achieved my overall purpose as effectively as possible?

Other guidelines to direct your writing and revising appear in the Writing Inventory at the end of Part I.

STUDENT ESSAY: DEFINITION AT WORK

In the following essay, a student defines "the perfect yuppie." Notice how the writer puts this term in a category and then explains the limits of that category and the uniqueness of this term within the category. To further inform her audience about the features of "yuppiedom," the student calls on the word's etymology, its dictionary definition, an itemization of the term's basic characteristics, a number of examples that explain those characteristics, and, finally, a general discussion of causes and effects that regulate a yuppie's behavior.

The Perfect Yuppie

Many people already know that <u>the letters YUP stand for "young urban professional.</u>" *Young* in this context is understood to mean fortyish; *urban* often means suburban; and *professional* means most definitely college-educated. Double the *P* and add an *I* and an *E* at the end, and you get <u>*yuppie*</u>—that 1980s' bourgeois, the marketers' darling, and the 1960s' inheritance. But let's not generalize. <u>Not every forty-year-old suburban college graduate qualifies as a yuppie. Nor is every yuppie in his or her forties.</u> True yuppiness involves much more than the words that make up the acronym. Being the little sister of a couple of yups, I am in an especially good position to define the perfect yuppie. I watched two develop.

The essence of yuppiness is generally <u>new money</u>. In the yuppie's defense, I will admit that most yuppies have worked hard for their money and social status. Moreover, the baby boom of which they are a part has caused a glut of job seekers in their age bracket, forcing them to be competitive if they want all the nice things retailers have designed for them. But with new money comes <u>an interesting combination of wealth, naiveté, and pretentiousness.</u>

For example, most yuppies worthy of the title have long ago <u>traded in their fringed suede jackets for fancy fur coats.</u> Although they were animal rights activists in the 1960s, they will not notice the irony of this change. In fact, they may be shameless enough to <u>parade in</u>

Margin annotations:
- General category of word being defined
- Limitations set
- Writer's credibility
- Cause/Effect
- General characteristic
- Specific example
- Etymology/dictionary definition
- Subject
- Why the dictionary definition is inadequate
- General characteristic
- Cause/Effect

their fur coats—fashion-show style—for friends and Specific example
family. Because of their "innocence," yuppies generally will not see the vulgarity of their actions.

General charac-teristic Because they are often quite wealthy, yuppies <u>tend to have a lot of "things."</u> They are simply overwhelmed by the responsibility of spending all that money. For example, <u>one yup I know has fourteen pairs of sun-</u> Specific example <u>glasses and seven watches</u>. She, her husband, and their three children own at least <u>twenty collections of every-</u> Specific example <u>thing from comic books to Civil War memorabilia</u>. Most yuppies have so much money that I often wonder why the word "yuppie" does not have a dollar sign in it somewhere.

General charac-teristic Perhaps in an effort to rid themselves of this financial burden, <u>all good yuppies go to Europe</u> as soon Cause/ Effect as possible. Not Germany or France or Portugal, mind you, but Europe. They do not know what they are doing there and thus generally spend much more Cause/ Effect money than they need to—but, after all, no yuppie ever claimed to be frugal. Most important, they <u>bring</u> <u>home slides of Europe and show them</u> to everyone they know. A really good yuppie will forget and show you his or her slides more than once. Incidentally, when everyone has seen the slides of Europe twice, the yuppie's next stop is Australia.

General charac-teristic A favorite pastime of yuppies is having <u>wine-tasting</u> <u>parties</u> for their yuppie friends. At these parties, they must <u>make a great to-do about tasting the wine</u>, cup- Specific example ping their faces over the glass with their palms (as if they were having a facial), and even sniffing the cork, for goodness sake. I once knew a yuppie who <u>did not</u> Specific example <u>understand that a bottle of wine could not be rejected</u> <u>simply because he found he "did not like that kind."</u> Specific example <u>Another enjoyed making a show of having his wife</u> <u>choose and taste the wine occasionally, which they</u> <u>both thought was adorable.</u>

What it is not <u>Some yuppie wanna-bes drive red or black BMWs,</u> but don't let them fool you. A genuine, hard-core yuppie will usually <u>own a gold or silver Volvo station</u> General charac-teristic <u>wagon</u>. In this yuppie-mobile, the yuppie wife will chauffeur her young yupettes to and from <u>their mod-</u> Specific examples <u>eling classes, track meets, ballet, the manicurist, and</u>

boy scouts, for the young yuppie is generally as com-   *Cause/*
petitive and socially active as his or her parents. On   *Effect*
the same topic, one particularly annoying trait of yuppie parents is bragging about their yupettes. You will
General   know yuppies by the fact that they <u>have the smartest,</u>
charac-   <u>most talented children in the world.</u> They <u>will show</u>
teristic   <u>you their kids' report cards, making sure you notice</u>   *Specific*
<u>any improvements from last quarter.</u>   *example*

    Perhaps I have been harsh in my portrayal of the
perfect yuppie, and, certainly, I will be accused by some
Division/   of stereotyping. But consider this: I never classify peo-   *General*
Classifi-   ple as yuppies who do not so classify themselves. <u>The</u>   *charac-*
cation   <u>ultimate criterion for being yuppies is that they will</u>   *teristic and*
<u>always proudly label themselves as such.</u>   *concluding*
statement

Student Writer's Comments

The most difficult part about writing this definition essay was choosing
a topic. I knew it had to be a word or phrase with different shades of meaning, but it also had to be either something I knew more about than the
average person or something I had an unusual perspective on. I figured *yuppie*
was a good word, not only because it has different meanings for different
people, but also because it is an acronym, and acronyms tend to be greater
than the sum of their parts.

    I started by looking the word up in the dictionary and writing down its
etymology (which I later referred to in my opening sentence). I then used
freewriting to record the various meanings and natural associations I have
with the word *yuppie,* which helped me discover relationships between these
meanings and associations. I felt my mind wandering freely over all aspects
of this word as I filled up pages and pages of freewriting. I then felt as if I
had enough material to work with, so I began to write a draft of my essay.

    I started writing the essay from the beginning, a process that was a real
novelty for me. After citing the etymology of my word and placing it in a general category, I explained why the dictionary definition was inadequate. Then,
I let the general characteristics I associate with the word take me step by step
through the essay. As I wrote, I found myself mentally reorganizing my prewriting notes so that I could stay slightly ahead of my actual writing. I kept looping back and forth into my notes, looking for the next best characters to
introduce, then writing, then going back to my notes again. I generated my
entire first draft this way and revised the order only slightly in my final draft.

    As I reworked my essay before handing it in, I added some humor from
my own experience with my older sisters and looked closely at other

rhetorical modes I had used to support my definition. Naturally, I had scattered examples throughout my essay and had discussed causes and effects quite openly. I revised my paper to make some of the connections I had in mind clearer by either adding transitions or explaining the relationships in other words. I found that this process lengthened my essay quite a bit as I revised. I also worked on the essay at this point to bring out a secondary point I had in mind, which is that some yuppies have lost the 1960s values they once had but often don't even realize it.

I spent the remainder of my time on my conclusion, which I rewrote from scratch four times. I finally ended up directly addressing the classification of yuppies, at which point I stumbled on the ultimate criterion for being a yuppy: "They will always proudly label themselves as such." When I reached this insight, I knew my paper was finished, and I was content with the results. I also realized that rewriting the conclusion so many times had given me a headache, but the pain was worth it.

SOME FINAL THOUGHTS ON DEFINITION

The following selections feature extended definitions whose main purpose is to explain a specific term or idea to their readers. Each essay in its own way helps its audience identify with various parts of the definitions, and each successfully communicates the unique qualities of the term or idea in question. Notice what approaches to definition each writer takes and how these approaches limit the readers' frame of reference in the process of effective communication.

DEFINITION IN REVIEW

Reading Definition Essays

Preparing to Read
√ What assumptions can I make from the essay's title?
√ What do I think the general mood of the essay will be?
√ What is the essay's purpose and audience?
√ What does the synopsis tell me about the essay?
√ What can I learn from the author's biography?
√ Can I predict the author's point of view toward the subject?

Reading
√ What is the essay's context?
√ How is the definition introduced?
√ Is the essay objective or subjective?
√ What other rhetorical modes support the thesis?

Rereading
√ How does the author lay out the definition?
√ What is the essay's main purpose and audience?
√ What other rhetorical strategies does the author use?

Writing Definition Essays

Preparing to Write
√ Do I know what I am going to define and how I will approach my topic?
√ Who is my audience?

Writing
√ Did I compose a thesis statement?
√ Does the beginning of my essay suit my purpose?
√ Do I use effective strategies to define my word or concept effectively?
√ What rhetorical strategies do I use to expand my definition essay?

Rewriting
√ Have I chosen an effective beginning for my paper?
√ Did I create a reasonable context for my definition?
√ Have I used appropriate rhetorical strategies to develop my ideas?
√ Have I achieved my overall purpose as effectively as possible?

MARC GELLMAN   (1947–   )

Worry. Don't Be Happy.

One of America's most revered religious leaders, Rabbi Marc Gellman earned his Ph.D. in Philosophy from Northwestern University and then completed a six-year rabbinical program at Hebrew Union College in only three years. Since 1981, he has been Senior Rabbi at Temple Beth Torah in Dix Hills, New York, where he is involved in a wide range of activities that help people come to terms with their own spirituality. His many books include *Where Does God Live* (1992), *Does God Have a Big Toe: Stories About Stories in the Bible* (1993), *How Do You Spell God: Answers to the Big Questions from Around the World* (1998), *God's Mailbox: More Stories About Stories in the Bible* (1998), *Always Wear Clean Underwear: And Other Ways Parents Say I Love You* (2000), *Bad Stuff in the News: A Family Guide to Handling the Headlines* (2002), and *Someday You'll Thank Me for This!: And Other Annoying (But True) Life Lessons* (2007). In addition, he writes a weekly *Newsweek* column, The Spiritual State, and with Monsignor Thomas Hartman produces a nationally syndicated advice column and a daily television program, *The God Squad*, which is broadcast to over fifteen million homes. An avid golfer, Rabbi Gellman also contributes articles to *Golf Digest* magazine. Asked to give advice to college writers, the author encourages students to consistently ask themselves the following question: "What if what everybody says and believes is flat out wrong?" Continuing, he explains that "examining unexamined clichés can give a new perspective on the truth and a deeper insight into language and its proper meaning."

Preparing to Read

The following essay, originally published in *Newsweek* (October 5, 2006), attempts to explain the relationship among happiness, pleasure, and goodness. Gellman supports his definition with stories, examples, comparisons, and a discussion of causes and effects that helps us understand the role of happiness in our lives.

Exploring Experience: As you prepare to read this essay, pause a few moments to think about any associations you make with the word *happiness:* When are you naturally happy? When are you sad? What makes you worry? How are worry and happiness related in your life? How do you create happiness in your life? Does happiness ever become selfish for you? Where do good deeds fit into your life in relation to happiness and worry?

Learning Online: In preparing to read this essay, look online at some other definitions of happiness at www.pursuit-of-happiness.org/projects.aspx. Whose understanding of happiness do you relate to most? Keep these definitions in mind while reading Gellman's essay.

A popular but false saying we hear all the time is, "All I want is that my children should be happy." The most obvious reason this wish is wrong is that very bad people can be very happy. Sinners can be smiling, and saints can be tormented. In fact, this is often the case. I learned from the comics the truth about superheroes, which is that they are hardly ever happy, while the supervillains are hardly ever sad. ① The Joker is always smiling, and Batman is always morose. Superman is constantly depressed about his inability to eliminate all evil while Lex Luthor exults in his every act of carnage and murder.

In the real world, happy saints are also rare. King, Gandhi, and Schweitzer lived with troubled souls but were nonetheless able to achieve a level of surpassing goodness. Gangs exult after killing a rival gang member, and as the Twin Towers were smoking and people were jumping from the windows, some jihadist sympathizers were jumping up and down in delirious happiness at the deaths of infidels. Because terrible people can be happy, saying that all you want is for your children to be happy is either foolish or evil. Why would your only wish for your children be their ability to possess the same pleasurable feelings that are also felt by the worst criminals and creeps of our world?

Why is it that bad people can be happy? The reason is that happiness as defined by our culture has become just a synonym for pleasure, and anyone can feel pleasure. A good meal, a winning team, a fabulous vacation can make even the biggest criminal feel just as happy as the most noble hero. The problem is the linkage between happiness and pleasure. Feeling good has no natural connection to doing good. But it does in the teachings of Hinduism, Buddhism, Sikhism, Judaism, Christianity, and Islam, as well as in the good and decent lives of those who do not find their life's guidance from ancient-wisdom traditions. For all these people, happiness is linked to goodness, not pleasure.

The reason we have an obesity epidemic in this country is not because we eat too much and exercise too little. It's because we eat what gives us pleasure. Sugar and fat taste better than celery and tofu. You can learn to love lettuce, and you can learn to give peas a chance, but it takes time. On the other hand, the pleasure of chocolate ice cream is instantaneous. The reason we have to force kids to exercise is because it is more pleasurable to sit on your tush and play videogames than it is to run around and sweat. True happiness, the kind of happiness we ought to wish for our children and for ourselves, is almost always the result of doing hard but good things over and over. ②

Thinking Critically

① To what extent do you think this statement is true? Can you think of a happy superhero? What about an unhappy villain? Why are villains often happier than superheroes?

② Name a "hard but good thing" you have done. Did this action make you happy? Why or why not?

Let me ask my married readers, "Has being married made you happier?" Studies by Ed Deiner show that after a honeymoon period, most people are no more satisfied with life after marriage than they were before. Being married is not always pleasurable, but it ought to make you happy because marriage is a hard good thing, and true happiness only comes from doing hard good things.

Let me ask parents, "Did having children make you happy?" In Judaism, having children is the fulfillment of the very first commandment from God to Adam in the Garden of Eden, "be fruitful and multiply." However, their term for raising children was, *tzar gidul banim,* "The agony of raising children."

You just have to decide where true happiness comes from. Does it come from pleasure, or does it come from goodness? The choice you make about this is the single most important one you will ever make in your life. It will determine whether you become a creep or a mensch.

And one last thing: money will not buy you happiness. ◆3 Now I know some of you with a cynical streak don't buy this theory. You may be followers of the great philosopher Spike Milligan who teaches in his Las Vegas lounge act, "Money can't buy you happiness, but it does bring you a more pleasant form of misery." Or perhaps you follow the teachings of Rabbi Henny Youngman, who once said, "What's the use of happiness? It can't buy you money." Once you make enough to meet the basic needs of life, more money does not make you discernibly happier. This is why the rabbis teach, "Who is rich? The one who is happy with his lot."

Happiness for our culture is pleasure, and pleasure is selfish. Happiness for Judaism is goodness, and goodness is transcending. Pleasure points us inward while goodness points us to each other and God. ◆4

I'll end with a story: David and Dana were in my office for premarital counseling, and I asked her what qualities David possessed that made her happy. She told me this story: On a blazing hot summer day, they were approaching the Triborough Bridge when they saw a man selling newspapers. David opened the window, bought all the man's papers, and said to him, "Go home. It's way too hot for you to be standing out here." So how about this saying: "All I wish is that on a hot day my children will buy all the papers."

Now if that is what you mean, if that is what you want for your children and for the children of your children, well, that's what I want for my children, too, and that is what God wants for all his children.

Thinking Critically

◆3 Can money make us happy? Why or why not?

◆4 Do you agree with the author that "Pleasure points us inward while goodness points us to each other and God"? Is this maxim uniquely "Jewish," or would other religions embrace it too?

UNDERSTANDING DETAILS

1. What is Gellman defining in this essay?
2. According to Gellman, in what ways can bad people be happy and good people be unhappy?
3. Why, according to Gellman, do we have an obesity problem in the United States?
4. For Gellman, what does doing "hard good things" (paragraph 5) have to do with happiness?

READING CRITICALLY

5. Define *happiness* after reading Gellman's essay.
6. Do you agree with Gellman that "pleasure is selfish" (paragraph 9)?
7. How are happiness and goodness related in the American culture? In your life?
8. Will you take Gellman's advice in this essay?

DISCOVERING RHETORICAL STRATEGIES

9. Why in his title does Gellman tell his readers to worry? How does this title give us a clue to his overall purpose?
10. To whom is Gellman writing this essay? Circle any groups he speaks to directly.
11. What is the tone of this essay? What details bring you to this decision?
12. What rhetorical strategies, besides definition, does Gellman use in this essay? Give examples of each strategy.

MAKING CONNECTIONS

13. Compare and contrast the ways in which any of the following authors you have read limit the frame of reference in his or her definition essay: Marc Gellman ("Worry. Don't Be Happy"), Robert Ramirez ("The Barrio"), and/or Mary Pipher ("Beliefs About Families").
14. Imagine that Rabbi Gellman is having a discussion about the search for happiness with the following other authors: Ray Bradbury ("Summer Rituals"), Bill Cosby ("The Baffling Question"), and/or K. C. Cole ("Calculated Risks"). Whose definition of "happiness" would be closest to your own? Why?
15. To what extent do you think any of the following authors you have read would agree with Rabbi Gellman about the importance of "doing hard good things" in life: Russell Baker ("The Saturday Evening Post"), Alice Lesch Kelly ("Toughen Up!"), and/or Claudia Wallis and Sonia Steptoe ("How to Bring Our Schools Out of the 20th Century")?

IDEAS FOR DISCUSSION/WRITING

Preparing to Write

Write freely about the different relationships in your family: What special qualities characterize each of these family members? Whom do you like the best? How many different roles do you play in your family (e.g., father/mother, son/daughter, brother/sister, husband/wife)? Which of these roles do you like best? Why? What makes some of your relationships with family members better than others? To what extent are you able to control these relationships?

Choosing a Topic

1. *Learning Online:* Revisit some other definitions of happiness online (www .pursuit-of-happiness.org/projects.aspx). Consider your own thoughts about happiness. Do you want popularity, financial success, a strong family life? Write an essay defining your own idea of happiness.

2. In an essay written for your classmates, explain the role of defining in our writing. Why is being able to define an important ability? What general role does defining play in writing?

3. Using the process of definition, explain an important quality of American culture in relation to society in general.

4. Choose one of the definitional techniques explained in the introduction to this chapter, and, in an essay written for the general public, define the word *pleasure* in the context of a well-developed, logically organized society. Introduce your main topic at the beginning of your essay; then explain and illustrate it clearly as your essay progresses. You may use other definition techniques in addition to your main choice.

Before beginning your essay, you might want to consult the checklists on page 384.

ROBERT RAMIREZ   (1949–   )

The Barrio

Robert Ramirez was born and raised in Edinburg, a southern Texas town near the Mexican border in an area that has been home to his family for almost two hundred years. After graduating from the University of Texas–Pan American, he taught Freshman Composition and worked for a while as a photographer. For the next several years, he was a salesman, reporter, and announcer/anchor for the CBS affiliate station KGBT-TV in Harlingen, Texas. His current job has brought him full circle, back to the University of Texas–Pan American, where he serves as a development officer responsible for alumni fundraising. He loves baseball and once considered a professional career, but he now contents himself with bike riding, swimming, and playing tennis. A conversion to the Baha'i faith in the 1970s has brought him much spiritual happiness. When asked to give advice to students using *The Prose Reader,* Ramirez responded, "The best writing, like anything else of value, requires a great deal of effort. Rewriting is 90 percent of the process. Sometimes, if you are fortunate, your work can take on a life of its own, and you end up writing something important that astounds and humbles you. This is what happened with 'The Barrio,' which is much better than the essay I originally intended. There's an element of the divine in it, as there is in all good writing."

Preparing to Read

First titled "The Woolen Sarape," Ramirez's essay was written while he was a student at the University of Texas–Pan American. His professor, Edward Simmens, published it in an anthology entitled *Pain and Promise: The Chicano Today* (1972). In it, the author defines the exciting, colorful, and close-knit atmosphere typical of many Hispanic *barrios,* or communities.

Exploring Experience: As you prepare to read this essay, take a few moments to think about a place that is very special to you: What are its physical characteristics? What memories are connected to this place for you? What kinds of people live there? What is the relationship of these people to each other? To people in other places? Why is this place so special to you? Is it special to anyone else?

Learning Online: Gain a stronger perspective on Robert Ramirez's definition of home by visiting the Web site for the PBS series *American Family* (www.pbs .org/Americanfamily). Click on the link for "Cisco's Journal" to see an artistic interpretation of life in the barrio.

The train, its metal wheels squealing as they spin along the silvery tracks, 1
rolls slower now. Through the gaps between the cars blinks a street-
lamp, and this pulsing light on a barrio street corner beats slower, like
a weary heartbeat, until the train shudders to a halt, the light goes out, and the
barrio is deep asleep.

Throughout Aztlán (the Nahuatl term meaning "land to the north"), 2
trains grumble along the edges of a sleeping people. From Lower California,
through the blistering Southwest, down the Rio Grande to the muddy Gulf,
the darkness and mystery of dreams ❶ engulf communities fenced off by
railroads, canals, and expressways. Paradoxical communities, isolated from the
rest of the town by concrete columned monuments of progress, and yet
stranded in the past. They are surrounded by change. It eludes their reach,
in their own backyards, and the people, unable and unwilling to see the
future, or even touch the present, perpetuate the past.

Leaning from the expressway or jolting across the tracks, one enters a 3
different physical world permeated by a different attitude. The physical
dimensions are impressive. It is a large section of town which extends for fifteen blocks north and south along the tracks, and then advances eastward,
thinning into nothingness beyond the city limits. Within the invisible (yet sensible) walls of the barrio are many, many people living in too few houses. The
homes, however, are much more numerous than on the outside.

Members of the barrio describe the entire area as their home. It is a home, 4
but it is more than this. The barrio is a refuge from the harshness and the cold-
ness of the Anglo world. ❷ It is a forced refuge. The leprous people are isolated from the rest of the community and contained in their section of town.
The stoical pariahs of the barrio accept their fate, and from the angry seeds
of rejection grow the flowers of closeness between outcasts, not the thorns
of bitterness and the mad desire to flee. There is no want to escape, for the
feeling of the barrio is known only to its inhabitants, and the material needs
of life can also be found here.

The *tortillería* fires up its machinery three times a day, producing steam- 5
ing, round, flat slices of barrio bread. In the winter, the warmth of the tortilla
factory is a wool sarape in the chilly morning hours, but in the summer, it
unbearably toasts every noontime customer.

The *panadería* sends its sweet messenger aroma down the dimly lit street, 6
announcing the arrival of fresh, hot, sugary *pan dulce.*

Thinking Critically

❶ What does Ramirez mean by the "mystery of dreams"? What is mysterious about dreams?

❷ In what ways might the "Anglo world" be harsh and cold to Ramirez? Give examples from
your own experience.

The small corner grocery serves the meal-to-meal needs of customers, and 7
the owner, a part of the neighborhood, willingly gives credit to people unable
to pay cash for foodstuffs.

The barbershop is a living room with hydraulic chairs, radio, and televi- 8
sion, where old friends meet and speak of life as their salted hair falls aimlessly about them.

The pool hall is a junior level country club where 'chucos, strangers in 9
their own land, get together to shoot pool and rap, while veterans, unaware
of the cracking, popping balls on the green felt, complacently play dominoes
beneath rudely hung *Playboy* foldouts.

The *cantina* is the night spot of the barrio. It is the country club and the 10
den where the rites of puberty are enacted. Here the young become men. ❸
It is in the taverns that a young dude shows his *machismo* through the quantity of beer he can hold, the stories of *rucas* he has had, and his willingness
and ability to defend his image against hardened and scarred old lions.

No, there is no frantic wish to flee. It would be absurd to leave the famil- 11
iar and nervously step into the strange and cold Anglo community when
the needs of the Chicano can be met in the barrio.

The barrio is closeness. From the family living unit, familial relationships 12
stretch out to immediate neighbors, down the block, around the corner, and
to all parts of the barrio. The feeling of family, a rare and treasurable sentiment, pervades and accounts for the inability of the people to leave. The
barrio is this attitude manifested on the countenances of the people, on the
faces of their homes, and in the gaiety of their gardens.

The color-splashed homes arrest your eyes, arouse your curiosity, and 13
make you wonder what life scenes are being played out in them. The flimsy,
brightly colored, wood-frame houses ignore no neon-brilliant color. Houses
trimmed in orange, chartreuse, lime green, yellow, and mixtures of these and
other hues beckon the beholder to reflect on the peculiarity of each home.
Passing through this land is refreshing like Brubeck, not narcoticizing like
revolting rows of similar houses, which neither offend nor please.

In the evenings, the porches and front yards are occupied with men calmly 14
talking over the noise of children playing baseball in the unpaved extension
of the living room, while the women cook supper or gossip with female
neighbors as they water the *jardines*. The gardens mutely echo the expressive
verses of the colorful houses. The denseness of multicolored plants and trees
gives the house the appearance of an oasis or a tropical isand hideaway,
sheltered from the rest of the world.

Thinking Critically
❸ What relationship does the author imply between drinking and maturity?

Fences are common in the barrio, but they are fences and not the walls   15
of the Anglo community. ④ On the western side of town, the high wooden
fences between houses are thick, impenetrable walls, built to keep the neighbors at bay. In the barrio, the fences may be rusty, wire contraptions or thick
green shrubs. In either case you can see through them and feel no sense of
intrusion when you cross them.

Many lower-income families of the barrio manage to maintain a com-   16
fortable standard of living through the communal action of family members
who contribute their wages to the head of the family. Economic need creates interdependence and closeness. Small barefooted boys sell papers on
cool, dark Sunday mornings, deny themselves pleasantries, and give their
earnings to *mamá*. The older the child, the greater the responsibility to help
the head of the household provide for the rest of the family.

There are those, too, who for a number of reasons have not achieved a rel-   17
ative sense of financial security. Perhaps it results from too many children
too soon, but it is the homes of these people and their situation that numbs
rather than charms. Their houses, aged and bent, oozing children, are fissures
in the horn of plenty. Their wooden homes may have brick-pattern asbestos
tile on the outer walls, but the tile is not convincing.

Unable to pay city taxes or incapable of influencing the city to live up to   18
its duty to serve all the citizens, the poorer barrio families remain trapped in
the nineteenth century and survive as best they can. The backyards have
well-worn paths to the outhouses, which sit near the alley. Running water
is considered a luxury in some parts of the barrio. Decent drainage is usually unknown, and when it rains, the water stands for days, an incubator of
health hazards and an avoidable nuisance. Streets, costly to pave, remain rough,
rocky trails. Tires do not last long, and the constant rattling and shaking grind
away a car's life and spread dust through screen windows.

The houses and their *jardines,* the jollity of the people in an adverse   19
world, the brightly feathered alarm clock pecking away at supper and cautiously eyeing the children playing nearby, produce a mystifying sensation
at finding the noble savage alive in the twentieth century. ⑤ It is easy to
look at the positive qualities of life in the barrio and look at them with a
distantly envious feeling. One wishes to experience the feelings of the barrio and not the hardships. Remembering the illness, the hunger, the feeling of time running out on you, the walls, both real and imagined, reflecting
on living in the past, one finds his envy becoming more elusive, until it has
vanished altogether.

Thinking Critically

④ According to Ramirez, how are "fences" different from "walls"?

⑤ What is a "noble savage"? How does the author use the term in this context?

Back now beyond the tracks, the train creaks and groans, the cars jostle 20
each other down the track, and as the light begins its pulsing, the barrio,
with all its meanings, greets a new dawn with yawns and restless stretchings.

UNDERSTANDING DETAILS

1. Define the barrio in your own words.
2. What is the difference between fences in the barrio and in the Anglo
   community?
3. In Ramirez's view, what creates "interdependence and closeness" (paragraph 16)?
   How does this phenomenon work in the barrio?
4. According to Ramirez, why are the houses in the barrio so colorful? What do you
   think is the relationship between color and happiness in the barrio?

READING CRITICALLY

5. Why does Ramirez call the people in the barrio "leprous" (paragraph 4)?
6. What does the author mean when he says, "The barrio is closeness" (paragraph 12)?
   How does this statement compare with the way you feel about your neighborhood? Why can't people leave the barrio?
7. Why might people look at the barrio with "a distantly envious feeling" (paragraph 19)?
   What other feelings may alter or even erase this sense of envy?
8. In what ways does the barrio resemble the communal living of various social
   groups in the 1960s?

DISCOVERING RHETORICAL STRATEGIES

9. How does Ramirez use the train to help him define the barrio? In what ways
   would the essay be different without the references to the train?
10. Ramirez uses metaphors masterfully throughout this essay to help us under-
    stand the internal workings of the barrio. He relies on this technique espe-
    cially in paragraphs 4 through 10. For example, a metaphor that explains
    how relationships develop in the barrio is "The stoical pariahs of the barrio
    accept their fate, and from the angry seeds of rejection grow the flowers of
    closeness between outcasts, not the thorns of bitterness and the mad desire
    to flee" (paragraph 4). In this garden metaphor, "rejection" is likened to
    "angry seeds," "closeness between outcasts" to "flowers," and "bitterness" to
    "thorns." Find four other metaphors in these paragraphs, and explain how the
    comparisons work. What are the familiar and less familiar items in each com-
    parison?
11. What tone does Ramirez establish in this essay? How does he create this
    tone?
12. The dominant method the author uses to organize his essay is definition. What
    other rhetorical strategies does Ramirez use to support his definition?

MAKING CONNECTIONS

13. Compare and contrast the "feeling of family" described by Ramirez with that depicted by Sandra Cisneros ("Only daughter"), Tamala Edwards (Multi-Colored Families"), and/or Mary Pipher ("Beliefs About Families").

14. Ramirez does a wonderful job of creating a sensual experience in his essay as he chronicles the vivid sights, sounds, smells, tastes, and textures of life in the barrio. In the same way, Ray Bradbury ("Summer Rituals") and John McPhee ("The Pines") appeal to our senses in their descriptive essays. Which author's prose style (of the essays you have read) do you find most sensual? Explain your answer.

15. While Ramirez defines the "barrio" through description, Marc Gellman ("Worry. Don't Be Happy") defines his principal topic in another fashion. How do the two authors differ in constructing their definitions? Which technique do you find most persuasive? Explain your answer.

IDEAS FOR DISCUSSION/WRITING

Preparing to Write

Write freely about a place that is special to you: Describe this place from your perspective. Is this place special to anyone else? Describe this place from someone else's perspective. How do these descriptions differ? What characteristics differentiate this place from other places? What makes this place special to you? Use some metaphors to relay to your readers your feelings about certain features of this place. Do you think this place will always be special to you? Why or why not?

Choosing a Topic

1. *Learning Online:* What does the term *home* mean to you? Using "Cisco's Journal" (from Preparing to Read), create a virtual tour of a place you have lived. Describe each room, the neighborhood, or the region. Develop your definition of *home* so that the reader can walk with you through each detail.

2. Ramirez's definition of the barrio demonstrates a difference between an insider's view and an outsider's view of the same location. In an essay for your classmates, define your special place from both the inside and the outside. Then discuss the similarities and differences between these two points of view.

3. In essay form, define the relationships among the people who are your extended family. These could be people from your neighborhood, your school, your job, or a combination of places. How did these relationships come about? Why are you close to these people? Why are these people close to you? To each other?

4. What primary cultural or social traditions have made you what you are today? In an essay written to a close friend, define the two or three most important traditions you practiced as a child, and explain what effects they had on you.

Before beginning your essay, you might want to consult the checklists on page 384.

CLAUDIA WALLIS   (1956–   )
SONJA STEPTOE   (1960–   )

How to Bring Our Schools Out of the 20th Century

A Phi Beta Kappa graduate of Yale University, Claudia Wallis began working at *Time* magazine as a medical writer in 1979, then moved up rapidly in the corporate ranks to Senior Editor and now Editor-at-Large. She has written more than twenty cover stories, including "How to Make Your Kid a Better Student," "Faith and Healing," "Attention Deficit Disorder," "Pills for the Mind," and many others. She has also been responsible for dozens of *Time* covers, such as those for "Who Was Jesus?," "Sex in America," and "Women: The Road Ahead." Sonja Steptoe, a *Time* magazine senior correspondent, earned her B.A. at the University of Missouri and her law degree at Duke before taking editorial jobs at the *Wall Street Journal* and *Sports Illustrated*. Among the many celebrities she has interviewed are Billy Graham, Kenneth Starr, Gloria Steinem, and Rick Warren; she has also covered the 9/11 tragedy, the basketball point-shaving scandal at Arizona State University, and the Mike Tyson rape trial (where she frequently appeared on Court TV as an expert analyst). With Jackie Joyner-Kersee, she coauthored *A Kind of Grace: The Autobiography of the World's Greatest Female Athlete* and wrote *A Guide to Women's Golf* with LPGA Hall of Famer Carol Mann. Steptoe advises aspiring student writers to "learn as much as possible about liberal arts subjects, such as economics, history, and philosophy, which will enliven your writing and protect you from . . . people with agendas."

Preparing to Read

This essay first appeared in *Time* magazine in 2006. In it, Wallis and Steptoe define what they believe should be the key elements of K-12 education in the twenty-first century, along with their reasons and some suggestions for accomplishing these goals as they outline them.

Exploring Experience: As you prepare to read this essay, think about your own education: How was your high school experience different from your college experience? Were you ready for your college responsibilities? What subjects were you most prepared for in college? Do you believe your high school taught you how to think critically? Are you able to compete technologically with your peers? What competencies that were missing from your background do you wish you had when you started college?

Learning Online: In this article, Wallis and Steptoe refer to McNealy's Web site www.curriki.org. Visit and explore this site. How can online tools such as this be helpful to students and teachers? Keep this in mind while reading the article.

There's a dark little joke exchanged by educators with a dissident   1
streak: Rip Van Winkle awakens in the 21st century after a hundred-
year snooze and is, of course, utterly bewildered by what he sees.
Men and women dash about, talking to small metal devices pinned to their
ears. Young people sit at home on sofas, moving miniature athletes around
on electronic screens. Older folk defy death and disability with metronomes
in their chests and with hips made of metal and plastic. Airports, hospitals,
shopping malls—every place Rip goes just baffles him. But when he finally
walks into a schoolroom, the old man knows exactly where he is. "This is a
school," he declares. "We used to have these back in 1906. Only now the
blackboards are green." ❶

American schools aren't exactly frozen in time, but considering the   2
pace of change in other areas of life, our public schools tend to feel like
throwbacks. ❷ Kids spend much of the day as their great-grandparents once
did: sitting in rows, listening to teachers lecture, scribbling notes by hand, reading from textbooks that are out of date by the time they are printed. A yawning chasm (with an emphasis on yawning) separates the world inside the
schoolhouse from the world outside.

For the past five years, the national conversation on education has focused   3
on reading scores, math tests, and closing the "achievement gap" between
social classes. This is not a story about that conversation. This is a story about
the big public conversation the nation is *not* having about education, the
one that will ultimately determine not merely whether some fraction of our
children get "left behind" but also whether an entire generation of kids will
fail to make the grade in the global economy because they can't think their
way through abstract problems, work in teams, distinguish good information
from bad, or speak a language other than English.

[In 2006], the conversation burst onto the front page, when the New   4
Commission on the Skills of the American Workforce, a high-powered, bipar-
tisan assembly of Education Secretaries and business, government, and other
education leaders released a blueprint for rethinking American education
from pre-K to 12 and beyond to better prepare students to thrive in the
global economy. While that report includes some controversial proposals,
there is nonetheless a remarkable consensus among educators and business
and policy leaders on one key conclusion: we need to bring what we teach
and how we teach into the 21st century.

Right now we're aiming too low. Competency in reading and math—the   5
focus of so much No Child Left Behind (NCLB) testing—is the meager

---

Thinking Critically

❶ Why do you think the authors begin their essay with a joke? How does this story about
Rip Van Winkle help set the tone for the rest of the article?

❷ Is your own high school "frozen in time"? What suggestions do you have to improve it?

minimum. Scientific and technical skills are, likewise, utterly necessary but insufficient. Today's economy demands not only a high-level competence in the traditional academic disciplines but also what might be called 21st century skills. Here's what they are:

Knowing more about the world.   Kids are global citizens now, even in   6
small-town America, and they must learn to act that way. Mike Eskew, CEO of UPS, talks about needing workers who are "global trade literate, sensitive to foreign cultures, conversant in different languages"—not exactly strong points in the U.S., where fewer than half of high school students are enrolled in a foreign-language class and where the social-studies curriculum tends to fixate on U.S. history.

Thinking outside the box.   Jobs in the new economy—the ones that won't   7
get outsourced or automated—"put an enormous premium on creative and innovative skills, seeing patterns where other people see only chaos," says Marc Tucker, an author of the skills-commission report and president of the National Center on Education and the Economy. ❸ Traditionally that's been an American strength, but schools have become less daring in the back-to-basics climate of NCLB. Kids also must learn to think across disciplines, since that's where most new breakthroughs are made. It's interdisciplinary combinations— design and technology, mathematics and art—"that produce YouTube and Google," says Thomas Friedman, the best-selling author of *The World Is Flat.*

Becoming smarter about new sources of information.   In an age of over-   8
flowing information and proliferating media, kids need to rapidly process what's coming at them and distinguish between what's reliable and what isn't. "It's important that students know how to manage it, interpret it, validate it, and how to act on it," says Dell executive Karen Bruett, who serves on the board of the Partnership for 21st Century Skills, a group of corporate and education leaders focused on upgrading American education.

Developing good people skills.   EQ, or emotional intelligence, is as   9
important as IQ for success in today's workplace. "Most innovations today involve large teams of people," says former Lockheed Martin CEO Norman Augustine. "We have to emphasize communication skills, the ability to work in teams and with people from different cultures."

Can our public schools, originally designed to educate workers for agrar-   10
ian life and industrial-age factories, make the necessary shifts? ❹ The skills commission will argue that it's possible only if we add new depth and rigor to our curriculum and standardized exams, redeploy the dollars we spend on

---

Thinking Critically

❸ What does the phrase "thinking outside the box" mean in this context? Why is this a good approach to education?

❹ How have high school students changed in the past 100 years?

education, reshape the teaching force, and reorganize who runs the schools. But without waiting for such a revolution, enterprising administrators around the country have begun to update their schools, often with ideas and support from local businesses. The state of Michigan, conceding that it can no longer count on the ailing auto industry to absorb its poorly educated and low-skilled workers, is retooling its high schools, instituting what are among the most rigorous graduation requirements in the nation. Elsewhere, organizations like the Bill and Melinda Gates Foundation, the Carnegie Foundation for the Advancement of Teaching, and the Asia Society are pouring money and expertise into model programs to show the way.

What It Means to Be a Global Student

Quick! How many ways can you combine nickels, dimes, and pennies to get 20¢? That's the challenge for students in a second-grade math class at Seattle's John Stanford International School, and hands are flying up with answers. The students sit at tables of four manipulating play money. One boy shouts "10 plus 10"; a girl offers "10 plus 5 plus 5," only it sounds like this: *"Ju, tasu, go, tasu, go."* Down the hall, third-graders are learning to interpret charts and graphs showing how many hours of sleep people need at different ages. *"¿Cuantas horas duerme un bebé?"* asks the teacher Sabrina Storlie.   11

This public elementary school has taken the idea of global education and run with it. All students take some classes in either Japanese or Spanish. Other subjects are taught in English, but the content has an international flavor. The school pulls its 393 students from the surrounding highly diverse neighborhood and by lottery from other parts of the city. Generally, its scores on state tests are at or above average, although those exams barely scratch the surface of what Stanford students learn.   12

Before opening the school seven years ago, principal Karen Kodama surveyed 1,500 business leaders on which languages to teach (plans for Mandarin were dropped for lack of classroom space) and which skills and disciplines. "No. 1 was technology," she recalls. Even first-graders at Stanford begin to use PowerPoint and Internet tools. "Exposure to world cultures was also an important trait cited by the executives," says Kodama, so that instead of circling back to the Pilgrims and Indians every autumn, children at Stanford do social-studies units on Asia, Africa, Australia, Mexico, and South America. Students actively apply the lessons in foreign language and culture by video-conferencing with sister schools in Japan, Africa, and Mexico, by exchanging messages, gifts and joining in charity projects. 📀   13

Thinking Critically

📀 Do you think you would have enjoyed going to Seattle's John Stanford International School? Why or why not? How is it different from the grade school you attended?

Stanford International shows what's possible for a public elementary 14
school, although it has the rare advantage of support from corporations like
Nintendo and Starbucks, which contribute to its $1.7 million-a-year bud-
get. Still, dozens of U.S. school districts have found ways to orient some of
their students toward the global economy. Many have opened schools that
offer the international baccalaureate (I.B.) program, a rigorous, off-the-shelf
curriculum recognized by universities around the world and first introduced
in 1968—well before globalization became a buzzword.

To earn an I.B. diploma, students must prove written and spoken profi- 15
ciency in a second language, write a 4,000-word, college-level research paper,
complete a real-world service project, and pass rigorous oral and written subject exams. Courses offer an international perspective, so even a lesson on the
American Revolution will interweave sources from Britain and France with
views from the Founding Fathers. "We try to build something we call international mindedness," says Jeffrey Beard, director general of the International
Baccalaureate Organization in Geneva, Switzerland. "These are students who
can grasp issues across national borders. They have an understanding of nuances
and complexity and a balanced approach to problem solving." Despite stringent certification requirements, I.B. schools are growing in the U.S.—from
about 350 in 2000 to 682 today. The U.S. Department of Education has a
pilot effort to bring the program to more low-income students.

Real Knowledge in the Google Era

Learn the names of all the rivers in South America. That was the assign- 16
ment given to Deborah Stipek's daughter Meredith in school, and her mom,
who's dean of the Stanford University School of Education, was not
impressed. "That's silly," Stipek told her daughter. "Tell your teacher that if
you need to know anything besides the Amazon, you can look it up on
Google." Any number of old-school assignments—memorizing the battles of
the Civil War or the periodic table of the elements—now seem faintly absurd.
That kind of information, which is poorly retained unless you routinely use
it, is available at a keystroke. Still, few would argue that an American child
shouldn't learn the causes of the Civil War or understand how the periodic
table reflects the atomic structure and properties of the elements. As school
critic E.D. Hirsch Jr. points out in his book, *The Knowledge Deficit*, kids need
a substantial fund of information just to make sense of reading materials
beyond the grade-school level. Without mastering the fundamental building
blocks of math, science, or history, complex concepts are impossible. [6]

Thinking Critically

[6] What principal skills and abilities do you think today's high school students need in order
to be successful in life?

Many analysts believe that to achieve the right balance between such core   17
knowledge and what educators call "portable skills"—critical thinking, making connections between ideas, and knowing how to keep on learning—
the U.S. curriculum needs to become more like that of Singapore, Belgium,
and Sweden, whose students out-perform American students on math and
science tests. Classes in these countries dwell on key concepts that are taught
in depth and in careful sequence, as opposed to a succession of forgettable
details so often served in U.S. classrooms. Textbooks and tests support this
approach. "Countries from Germany to Singapore have extremely small textbooks that focus on the most powerful and generative ideas," says Roy Pea,
co-director of the Stanford Center for Innovations in Learning. These might
be the key theorem in math, the laws of thermodynamics in science, or the
relationship between supply and demand in economics. America's bloated
textbooks, by contrast, tend to gallop through a mind-numbing stream of topics and subtopics in an attempt to address a vast range of state standards.

Depth over breadth and the ability to leap across disciplines are exactly   18
what teachers aim for at the Henry Ford Academy, a public charter school
in Dearborn, Mich. This fall, 10th-graders in Charles Dershimer's science
class began a project that combines concepts from earth science, chemistry,
business, and design. After reading about Nike's efforts to develop a more
environmentally friendly sneaker, students had to choose a consumer product, analyze and explain its environmental impact, and then develop a plan
for re-engineering it to reduce pollution costs without sacrificing its commercial appeal. Says Dershimer: "It's a challenge for them and for me."

A New Kind of Literacy

The juniors in Bill Stroud's class are riveted by a documentary called *Loose*   19
Change unspooling on a small TV screen at the Baccalaureate School for
Global Education, in urban Astoria, N.Y. The film uses 9/11 footage and
interviews with building engineers and Twin Towers survivors to make an
oddly compelling if paranoid case that interior explosions unrelated to the
impact of the airplanes brought down the World Trade Center on that fate-
ful day. Afterward, the students—an ethnic mix of New Yorkers with their
own 9/11 memories—dive into a discussion about the elusive nature of truth.

Raya Harris finds the video more convincing than the official version of   20
the facts. Marisa Reichel objects. "Because of a movie, you are going to
change your beliefs?" she demands. "Just because people heard explosions
doesn't mean there were explosions. You can say you feel the room spinning, but it isn't." This kind of discussion about what we know and how we
know it is typical of a theory knowledge class, 7 a required element for an

---

Thinking Critically

7 What do the authors mean by a "theory knowledge class"? Which of your past or
current classes fit this category?

international-baccalaureate diploma. Stroud has posed this question to his class on the blackboard: "If truth is difficult to prove in history, does it follow that all versions are equally acceptable?"

Throughout the year, the class will examine news reports, websites, pro-   21
paganda, history books, blogs, even pop songs. The goal is to teach kids to be discerning consumers of information and to research, formulate and defend their own views, says Stroud, who is founder and principal of the four-year-old public school, which is located in a repurposed handbag factory.

Classes like this, which teach key aspects of information literacy, remain   22
rare in public education, but more and more universities and employers say they are needed as the world grows ever more deluged with information of variable quality. Last year, in response to demand from colleges, the Educational Testing Service unveiled a new, computer-based exam designed to measure information-and-communication-technology literacy. A pilot study of the test with 6,200 high school seniors and college freshmen found that only half could correctly judge the objectivity of a website. "Kids tend to go to Google and cut and paste a research report together," says Terry Egan, who led the team that developed the new test. "We kind of assumed this generation was so comfortable with technology that they know how to use it for research and deeper thinking," says Egan. "But if they're not taught these skills, they don't necessarily pick them up."

Learning 2.0

The chairman of Sun Microsystems was up against one of the most   23
vexing challenges of modem life: a third-grade science project. Scott McNealy had spent hours searching the Web for a lively explanation of electricity that his son could understand. "Finally I found a very nice, animated, educational website showing electrons zooming around and tests after each section. We did this for about an hour and a half and had a ball—a great father-son moment of learning. All of a sudden we ran out of runway because it was a site to help welders, and it then got into welding." For McNealy the experience, three years ago, provided one of life's *aha!* moments: "It made me wonder why there isn't a website where I can just go and have anything I want to learn, K to 12, online, browser based and free."

His solution: draw on the Wikipedia model to create a collection of online   24
courses that can be updated, improved, vetted, and built upon by innovative teachers, who, he notes, "are always developing new materials and methods of instruction because they aren't happy with what they have." And who better to create such a site than McNealy, whose company has led the way in designing open-source computer software? He quickly raised some money,

created a nonprofit and—*voilà!*—Curriki.org [8] made its debut January 2006 and has been growing fast. Some 450 courses are in the works, and about 3,000 people have joined as members. McNealy reports that a teenager in Kuwait has already completed the introductory physics and calculus classes in 18 days.

Curriki, however, isn't meant to replace going to school but to supplement it and offer courses that may not be available locally. It aims to give teachers classroom-tested content materials and assessments that are livelier and more current and multimedia-based than printed textbooks. Ultimately, it could take the Web 2.0 revolution to school, closing that yawning gap between how kids learn at school and how they do everything else. Educators around the country and overseas are already discussing ways to certify Curriki's online course work for credit.

Some states are creating their own online courses. "In the 21st century, the ability to be a lifelong learner will, for many people, be dependent on their ability to access and benefit from online learning," says Michael Flanagan, Michigan's superintendent of public instruction, which is why Michigan's new high school graduation requirements, which roll out next year, include completing at least one course online.

A Dose of Reality

Teachers need not fear that they will be made obsolete. They will, however, feel increasing pressure to bring their methods—along with the curriculum—into line with the way the modern world works. That means putting a greater emphasis on teaching kids to collaborate and solve problems in small groups and apply what they've learned in the real world. [9] Besides, research shows that kids learn better that way than with the old chalk-and-talk approach.

At suburban Farmington High in Michigan, the engineering-technology department functions like an engineering firm, with teachers as project managers, a Ford Motor Co. engineer as a consultant, and students working in teams. The principles of calculus, physics, chemistry, and engineering are taught through activities that fill the hallways with a cacophony of nailing, sawing, and chattering. The result: the kids learn to apply academic principles to the real world, think strategically, and solve problems.

Thinking Critically

[8] What kind of information can you find on the website Curriki.org?

[9] Do you think today's high schools should encourage students to collaborate with other students and apply what they are learning to the real world? Why or why not?

Such lessons also teach students to show respect for others as well as to   29
be punctual, be responsible, and work well in teams. Those skills were badly
missing in recently hired high school graduates, according to a survey of
over 400 human-resource professionals conducted by the Partnership for
21st Century Skills. "Kids don't know how to shake your hand at graduation," says Rudolph Crew, superintendent of the Miami-Dade school system.
Deportment, he notes, used to be on the report card. Some of the nation's
more forward-thinking schools are bringing it back. It's one part of 21st century education that sleepy old Rip would recognize.

UNDERSTANDING DETAILS

1. In what ways do Wallis and Steptoe think U.S. students are deficient as they
   prepare to function in the global economy?
2. In 2006, what did the New Commission on the Skills of the American Workforce agree had to happen in education to make our children competitive for
   jobs in the future?
3. List the skills the authors agree are twenty-first-century skills our students need
   to survive in the future world of work. Then explain each skill in your own
   words.
4. According to this article, what competencies does a global student need?

READING CRITICALLY

5. Read the article again, and underline the authors' thesis in one color and their
   topic sentences in another color.
6. In your opinion, how are "portable skills" (paragraph 17) useful in today's
   society?
7. From your experience in life so far, what role does "information literacy" (paragraph 22) play in the world today?
8. What do Wallis and Steptoe mean when they say, "A yawning chasm (with an
   emphasis on yawning) separates the world inside the schoolhouse from the
   world outside" (paragraph 2)?

DISCOVERING RHETORICAL STRATEGIES

9. What is the main purpose of this essay? Does it achieve this purpose in your
   opinion?
10. Who is the audience for this essay? How did you come to that conclusion?
11. Wallis and Steptoe organize their definition essay from problem to solution.
    Do you think this organization in an effective way to present this topic? Do the
    headings help you progress through the essay?
12. What other rhetorical modes do Wallis and Steptoe draw on to develop their
    definition? Do these choices help them achieve their purpose? Explain your
    answer.

MAKING CONNECTIONS

13. Which of the following authors would agree most enthusiastically with Wallis and Steptoe that America's schools are failing their students: Brent Staples ("A Brother's Murder"), Malcolm X ("Learning to Read"), and/or Lyn Mikel Brown and Meda Chesney-Lind ("Bad Girls, Bad Girls, Whatcha Gonna Do")?

14. To what extent would any of the following authors you have read claim with Wallis and Steptoe that today's students need to know more about the world around them: Firoozeh Dumas ("Leffingwell Elementary School"), William Ouchi ("Japanese and American Workers: Two Casts of Mind"), and/or Sucheng Chan ("You're Short, Besides")? Who would be most supportive of the "globalization" of our curriculum? Why? Would you agree?

15. How would the definition of "literacy" found in this article differ from that expressed by Russell Baker ("The Saturday Evening Post"), K. C. Cole ("Calculated Risks"), and/or Richard Wright ("The Library Card")?

IDEAS FOR DISCUSSION/WRITING

Preparing to Write

Write freely about the importance of education in the United States today: What role does education play in our society? How can the quality of education help or hinder our society? What can we do to control the quality of education? What can we do to control the quality of the students we produce? How can we test for the abstract competencies we need our students to have? What suggestions do you have for changing your educational experience so far?

Choosing a Topic

1. *Learning Online:* Revisit www.curriki.org to review an example of an online tool for teachers and students. Have you ever taken an online class? Think about the ideal balance between face-to-face and computer-based learning, and then write an essay defining this class. Do you think the classroom is a necessary element for learning?

2. As a graduate of your high school, you have been asked by the Board of Education to define twelveth-grade competency. The Board has asked you to include in your prepared statement an explanation of the skills and abilities students should possess when they leave high school and a summary of why these competencies are important.

3. Do you agree with Wallis and Steptoe that students need a global education to be successful in today's society—whether as an everyday citizen or a CEO of a major company? Answer this question in a well-developed essay directed to the authors.

4. How do you think we will be able to test the abstract skills our students need to compete in the contemporary workplace? Who is this testing for? Do we need testing at all? Take a stand on testing, and develop your argument in an essay.

Before beginning your essay, you might want to consult the checklists on page 384.

MARY PIPHER   (1947–   )

Beliefs about Families

The oldest of seven children, Mary Pipher was born in Springfield, Missouri. She earned her B.A. in Cultural Anthropology at the University of California, Berkeley, and her Ph.D. in Clinical Psychology at the University of Nebraska. Currently a professor in the graduate clinical training program at the University of Nebraska, she became a writer only after her children had been raised, declaring that "Writing has been the great gift of my middle years. It is my reason to wake up in the morning." Her first book, *Hunger Pains: The Modern Woman's Tragic Quest for Thinness* (1987), was followed by *Reviving Ophelia: Saving the Selves of Adolescent Girls* (1994), an enormously influential study of the world of teenage girls. Her most recent books are *The Shelter of Each Other: Rebuilding Our Families* (1996), which examines family relationships in America today; *Another Country: Navigating the Emotional Terrain of Our Elders* (1999), an analysis of how the United States isolates and misunderstands its senior citizens; *The Middle of Everywhere: The World's Refugees Come to Our Town* (2002); *Letters to a Young Therapist: The Art of Mentoring* (2003); and *Writing to Change the World* (2006). An avid outdoorswoman who loves hiking, backpacking, and watching sunsets, Pipher has the following words for students using *The Prose Reader:* "What all good writers have in common is a yearning to communicate."

Preparing to Read

The following essay from *The Shelter of Each Other: Rebuilding Our Families* attempts to define the notion of "family" in contemporary society.

Exploring Experience: As you prepare to read this essay, take a few moments to think about the role family plays in your life: Are you close to your biological family? Are you a part of any other groups that function like a family? How do they work? Are you aware of your roles in these various groups? What is the relationship betwen your role in your immediate family and your personal goals?

Learning Online: To gain a perspective on the varied media representations of "family," go to the TV Land Web site (www.tvland.com). Choose "shows" from the menu, and then select the "Leave It to Beaver" link from the alphabetized list. Peruse the episode descriptions, sound bytes, and photos from the sitcom. Contrast this family with the one portrayed in *American Beauty.* Visit the Internet Movie Database Web site (www.imdb.com), enter "American Beauty" into the search field, and view the movie trailer. Consider how these "families" relate to Pipher's definition as you read her essay.

Whén I speak of families, I usually mean biological families. There is a power in blood ties that cannot be denied. ❶ But in our fragmented, chaotic culture, many people don't have biological families nearby. For many people, friends become family. Family is a collection of people who pool resources and help each other over the long haul. Families love one another even when that requires sacrifice. Family means that if you disagree, you still stay together.

Families are the people for whom it matters if you have a cold, are feuding with your mate or training a new puppy. Family members use magnets to fasten the newspaper clippings about your bowling team on the refrigerator door. They save your drawings and homemade pottery. They like to hear stories about when you were young. They'll help you can tomatoes or change the oil in your car. They're the people who will come visit you in the hospital, will talk to you when you call with "a dark night of the soul" and will loan you money to pay the rent if you lose your job. Whether or not they are biologically related to each other, the people who do these things are family. ❷

If you are very lucky, family is the group you were born into. But some are not that lucky. When Janet was in college, her parents were killed in a car wreck. In her early twenties she married, but three years later she lost her husband to leukemia. She has one sister, who calls mainly when she's suicidal or needs money. Janet is a congresswoman in a western state, a hard worker and an idealist. Her family consists of the men, women, and children she's grown to depend on in the twenty-five years she's lived in her community. Except for her beloved dog, nobody lives with her. But she brings the cinnamon rolls to one family's Thanksgiving dinner and has a Mexican fiesta for families at her house on New Year's Eve. She attends Bar Mitzvahs, weddings, school concerts, and soccer matches. She told me with great pride, "When I sprained my ankle skiing last year, three families brought me meals."

I think of Morgan, a jazz musician who long ago left his small town and rigid, judgmental family. He had many memories of his father whipping him with a belt or making him sleep in the cold. Once he said to me, "I was eighteen years old before anyone ever told me I had something to offer." Indeed he does. He plays the violin beautifully. He teaches improvisation and jazz violin and organizes jazz events for his town. His family is the family of musicians and music lovers that he has built around him over the years.

Thinking Critically

❶ What does Pipher mean when she says, "There is a power in blood ties that cannot be denied"?

❷ What is your definition of "family"? How is it different from Pipher's?

If you are very unlucky, you come from a nuclear family that didn't care [3] Curtis, who as a boy was regularly beaten by his father, lied about his age so that he could join the Navy at sixteen. Years later he wrote his parents and asked if he could return home for Christmas. They didn't answer his letter. When I saw him in therapy, I encouraged him to look for a new family, among his cousins and friends from the Navy. Sometimes cutoffs, tragic as they are, are unavoidable. **5**

I think of Anita, who never knew her father and whose mother abandoned her when she was seven. Anita was raised by an aunt and uncle, whom she loved very much. As an adult she tracked down her mother and tried to establish a relationship, but her mother wasn't interested. At least Anita was able to find other family members to love her. She had a family in her aunt and uncle. **6**

Family need not be traditional or biological. But what family offers is not easily replicated. Let me share a Sioux word, *tiospaye,* which means the people with whom one lives. The *tiospaye* is probably closer to a kibbutz than to any other Western institution. The *tiospaye* gives children multiple parents, aunts, uncles and grandparents. It offers children a corrective factor for problems in their nuclear families. If parents are difficult, there are other adults around to soften and diffuse the situation. Until the 1930s, when the *tiospaye* began to fall apart with sale of land, migration and alcoholism, there was not much mental illness among the Sioux. When all adults were responsible for all children, people grew up healthy. **7**

What *tiospaye* offers and what biological family offers is a place that all members can belong to regardless of merit. Everyone is included regardless of health, likability or prestige. What's most valuable about such institutions is that people are in by virtue of being born into the group. People are in even if they've committed a crime, been a difficult person, become physically or mentally disabled or are unemployed and broke. That ascribed status was what Robert Frost valued when he wrote that home "was something you somehow hadn't to deserve." [4] **8**

Many people do not have access to either a supportive biological family or a *tiospaye.* They make do with a "formed family." Others simply prefer a community of friends to their biological families. The problem with formed families is they often have less staying power. They might not take you in, give you money if you lose a job or visit you in a rest home if you are paralyzed **9**

Thinking Critically

[3] Why does the author think that people who come from families that don't care for them are "unlucky"?

[4] Why does the author quote from the poet Robert Frost? What special insight does this quotation bring to Pipher's essay?

in a car crash. My father had a stroke and lost most of his sight and speech. Family members were the people who invited him to visit and helped him through the long tough years after his stroke. Of course, there are formed families who do this. With the AIDS crisis, many gays have supported their friends through terrible times. Often immigrants will help each other in this new country. And there are families who don't stick together in crisis. But generally blood is thicker than water. Families come through when they must.

Another problem with formed families is that not everyone has the skills   10
to be included in that kind of family. Friendship isn't a product that can be obtained for cash. People need friends today more than ever, but friends are harder to make in a world where people are busy, moving, and isolated. Some people don't have the skills. They are shy, abrasive, or dull. Crack babies have a hard time making friends, as do people with Alzheimer's. Formed families can leave many people out.

From my point of view the issue isn't biology. Rather the issues are com-   11
mitment and inclusiveness. I don't think for most of us it has to be either/or. A person can have both a strong network of friends and a strong family. ⑤ It is important to define family broadly so that all kinds of families, such as single-parent families, multigenerational families, foster families and the families of gays are included. But I agree with David Blankenberg's conclusion in his book *Rebuilding the Nest:* "Even with all the problems of nuclear families, I will support it as an institution until something better comes along."

Americans hold two parallel versions of the family—the idealized ver-   12
sion and the dysfunctional version. The idealized version portrays families as wellsprings of love and happiness, loyal, wholesome, and true. This is the version we see in *Leave It to Beaver* or *Father Knows Best*. The dysfunctional version depicts families as disturbed and disturbing, and suggests that salvation lies in extricating oneself from all the ties that bind. Both versions have had their eras. In the 1950s the idealized version was at its zenith. Extolling family was in response to the Depression and war, which separated families. People who had been wrenched away from home missed their families and thought of them with great longing. They idealized how close and warm they had been.

In the 1990s the dysfunctional version of family seems the most influen-   13
tial. This belief system goes along with the culture of narcissism, which sells people the idea that families get in the way of individual fulfillment.

Thinking Critically

⑤ Which is more important to you now: "a strong network of friends" or "a strong family"? Which group do you think will be more important to you twenty years from now? Explain your answer.

Currently, many Americans are deeply mistrustful of their own and other people's families. Pop psychology presents families as pathology-producing. Talk shows make families look like hotbeds of sin and sickness. Day after day people testify about the diverse forms of emotional abuse that they suffered in their families. Movies and television often portray families as useless impediments.

In our culture, after a certain age, children no longer have permission to love their parents. We define adulthood as breaking away, disagreeing and making up new rules. ⑥ Just when teenagers most need their parents, they are encouraged to distance themselves from them. A friend told me of walking with her son in a shopping mall. They passed some of his friends, and she noticed that suddenly he was ten feet behind, trying hard not to be seen with her. She said, "I felt like I was drooling and wearing purple plaid polyester." Later her son told her that he enjoyed being with her, but that his friends all hated their parents and he would be teased if anyone knew he loved her. He said, "I'm confused about this. Am I supposed to hate you?"   14

This socialized antipathy toward families is unusual. Most cultures revere and respect family. In Vietnam, for example, the tender word for lover is "sibling." In the Kuma tribe of Papua New Guinea, family members are valued above all others. Siblings are seen as alter egos ⑦ essential parts of the self. The Kuma believe that mates can be replaced, but not family members. Many Native American tribes regard family members as connected to the self. To be without family is to be dead.   15

From the Greeks, to Descartes, to Freud and Ayn Rand, Westerners have valued the independent ego. But Americans are the most extreme. Our founders were rebels who couldn't tolerate oppression. When they formed a new government they emphasized rights and freedoms.   16

American values concerning independence may have worked better when we lived in small communities surrounded by endless space. But we have run out of space and our outlaws live among us. At one time the outlaw mentality was mitigated by a strong sense of community. Now the values of community have been superseded by other values.   17

We have pushed the concept of individual rights to the limits. Our laws let adults sell children harmful products. But laws are not our main problem. People have always been governed more by community values than by laws. ⑧ Ethics, rather than laws, determine most of our behavior. Unwritten   18

Thinking Critically

⑥ Do you agree with Pipher that adulthood in our culture means "breaking away, disagreeing and making up new rules"? Why or why not?

⑦ Do you have a sibling? In what sense is he or she an "alter ego"?

⑧ What is the difference between "community values" and "laws"? Give an example of each.

rules of civility—for taking turns, not cutting in lines, holding doors open for others and lowering our voices in theaters—organize civic life. Unfortunately, those rules of civility seem to be crumbling in America. We are becoming a nation of people who get angry when anyone gets in our way.

Rudeness is everywhere in our culture. Howard Stern, G. Gordon Liddy, and Newt Gingrich are rude. It's not surprising our children copy them. Phil Donahue and Jay Leno interrupt, and children learn to interrupt. A young man I know was recently injured on a volleyball court. The player who hurt him didn't apologize or offer to help him get to an emergency room. An official told him to get off the floor because he was messing it up with his blood and holding up the game. I recently saw an old man hesitate at a busy intersection. Behind him drivers swore and honked. He looked scared and confused as he turned into traffic and almost wrecked his car. At a festival a man stood in front of the stage, refusing to sit down when people yelled out that they couldn't see. Finally another man wrestled him to the ground. All around were the omnipresent calls of "Fuck You." Over coffee a local politician told me she would no longer attend town meetings. She said, "People get out of control and insult me and each other. There's no dialogue, it's all insults and accusations." 19

We have a crisis in meaning in our culture. The crisis comes from our isolation from each other, from the values we learn in a culture of consumption and from the fuzzy, self-help message that the only commitment is to the self and the only important question is—Am I happy? We learn that we are number one and that our own immediate needs are the most important ones. The crisis comes from the message that products satisfy and that happiness can be purchased. 20

We live in a money-driven culture. ◉ But the bottom line is not the only line, or even the best line for us to hold. A culture organized around profits instead of people is not user friendly to families. We all suffer from existential flu, as we search for meaning in a culture that values money, not meaning. Everyone I know wants to do good work. But right now we have an enormous gap between doing what's meaningful and doing what is reimbursed. 21

UNDERSTANDING DETAILS

1. How does Pipher define *families?* What particular activities characterize a "family" member?
2. What do "commitment and inclusiveness" (paragraph 11) have to do with being in a family?

Thinking Critically

◉ Do you agree that we live in a "money-driven culture"? Explain your answer.

3. According to Pipher, what are the two parallel versions of the family and when were they dominant?
4. According to Pipher, what poses the biggest problem to the integrity of the family as a unit?

READING CRITICALLY

5. In what way does the Sioux word *tiospaye* (paragraph 7) describe the traits of a family?
6. According to Pipher, why do "people need friends today more than ever" (paragraph 10)?
7. What is difficult about "formed families" (paragraph 10)?
8. Do you agree with Pipher that we have "a crisis of meaning in our culture" (paragraph 20)? Explain your answer in detail.

DISCOVERING RHETORICAL STRATEGIES

9. Why does the author introduce the stories of Janet, Morgan, Curtis, and Anita?
10. What do you think Pipher's purpose is in this essay?
11. Pipher approaches her definition from many different angles before suggesting that American culture is facing a crisis in understanding and agreeing on what a family is. How do her various definitions support her statement about a crisis? Explain your answer.
12. What rhetorical modes support the author's definition? Give examples of each.

MAKING CONNECTIONS

13. Which parts of Mary Pipher's definition of "family" would Ray Bradbury ("Summer Rituals"), Judith Wallerstein and Sandra Blakeslee ("Second Chances for Children of Divorce"), and/or Robert Ramirez ("The Barrio") most agree with? Explain your answer.
14. Imagine that Russell Baker ("The Saturday Evening Post"), Mary Roach ("Meet the Bickersons"), and/or Mary Pipher are discussing the extent to which people in a family have to compromise. Which author would you probably agree with and why?
15. Compare and contrast the ways in which Marc Gellman ("Worry. Don't Be Happy"), Robert Ramirez ("The Barrio"), and/or Lyn Mikel Brown and Meda Chesney-Lind ("Bad Girls, Bad Girls, Whatcha Gonna Do?") begin their definition essays.

IDEAS FOR DISCUSSION/WRITING

Preparing to Write

Write freely about the qualities that constitute a good family member: How do you recognize a good family member? What characterizes him or her? Do you personally appreciate your biological family? Are you a part of other families? If so, what are the characteristics of these families? Why is some type of family important to our well-being? What role does the notion of family play in your self-definition?

Choosing a Topic

1. *Learning Online:* Conduct an Internet research on international representations of "family." Start with the United Nations Children's Fund (UNICEF) Web site (www.unicef.org). Use terms such as "family practices" to begin your search. Write an essay in which you expand Pipher's definition of *family* to include at least three detailed examples of global family practices. Use Pipher's developed example of Sioux customs as a model for your expanded descriptions.
2. Write an essay for your classmates defining "a family" that you belong to.
3. In a well-organized essay, use examples to define the dysfunctional family as it exists today. Be as specific as possible.
4. The relationship between family and individual has changed since your parents were in school. Explain to them the current relationship between you and your family. What are the connections between your personal goals and your role in your immediate family?

Before beginning your essay, you might want to consult the checklists on page 384.

LYN MIKEL BROWN   (1956–   )

MEDA CHESNEY–LIND   (1947–   )

Bad Girls, Bad Girls, Whatcha Gonna Do?

Lyn Mikel Brown is a professor of Women's Studies, Education, and Human Development at Colby College in Waterville, Maine. She earned her Ed.D. from Harvard University's Graduate School of Education. Her first book (written with Carol Gilligan), *Meeting at the Crossroads* (1992), was a *New York Times* Notable Book of the Year, while her second, *Raising Their Voices: The Politics of Girls' Anger* (1998), offered a study of how girls express anger. She is currently finishing a book on girls' friendships tentatively titled *Girlfighting: Betrayal, Teasing, and Rejection Among Girls.* Her hobbies include "raising a preteen daughter," creating perennial gardens, and talking with close friends. When asked to provide advice for students using *The Prose Reader,* Brown said to "take time each day to breathe, reflect, and sit with your feelings. Write a little every day, be brave, and dare to move out of your comfort zone." Meda Chesney-Lind earned her B.A. at Whitman College and her M.A. and Ph.D. at the University of Hawaii. She is currently a professor of Women's Studies at the University of Hawaii at Manoa, where she has published three books on women and crime—*Girls, Delinquency, and Juvenile Justice* (1992, with Randall Shelden), *The Female Offender* (1997), and *Female Gangs in America* (1999, with John Hagedorn)—plus over fifty articles on related topics. Her recreational activities include walking and haunting thrift shops. She advises student writers to "trust your instincts in order to become better writers, which also requires patience, discipline, and a healthy sense of humor."

Preparing to Read

This essay was first published on a Web site called "Critical Criminology" ("Criticrim" for short). In it, the authors analyze the causes and effects of female aggression in society today.

Exploring Experience: As you prepare to read this essay, consider how our society deals with anger in girls: What do you think are the general causes of this anger? Should we make girls control this anger or allow them to vent their frustration? What are some acceptable ways of expressing anger? What are some of the social consequences of expressing one's anger?

Learning Online: StopHazing.org is a popular online site that deals with many types of hazing—in schools, in fraternity and sorority groups, in the military, and in athletics. Read the article entitled "Myths and Facts About Hazing" at www.stophazing.org/mythsandfacts.html. Six common myths are outlined in the article. Do you think any of these "myths" are true?

Suddenly the world is filled with nasty girls. [1] "Girls just want to be mean," the *New York Times Magazine* announced last year as a slew of new books on girls' relational aggression told us how "to tame them," to use the *Times'* own words. 1

Girls will be (backstabbing, catty) girls—the latest flavor de jour of the American media's love affair with "bad" girls. Hardly a new idea in a country that grew up reading Longfellow's poem about his daughter: "When she was good, she was very very good, but when she was bad she was horrid." 2

Now comes the ultimate girl fight in living color. Full-scale "savagery in the Chicago suburbs," *Newsweek* called it. Junior girls from the privileged Glenbrook North High School paid for the right to be hazed by seniors at the annual powder puff football game. After the beatings and humiliations ended, five girls were sent to the hospital, one with a broken ankle, another with a concussion so serious it caused memory loss, another to receive 10 stitches in her scalp. 3

As authors who write about girls' anger, aggression and violence, we are troubled, for reasons that are obvious and some that are less so. Violence that girls perpetrate on other girls, whether it's emotional or physical, is cause for concern. But the media frenzy that greeted the lurid and voyeuristic video of girls fighting other girls is also problematic. In fact, it signals another major issue for those concerned about girls' development. Girls grow up in a world that has long encouraged them to turn their rage against one another—and then likes to be in the audience for the fight. Like the Glenbrook parents, they might even supply the beer. 4

Girls' anger has a long history of being dismissed ("she's just a bitch," "it must be PMS") and trivialized ("you're beautiful when you're angry"). [2] Girls violence is generally either ignored entirely or sensationalized and sexualized. Girlfighting, in particular, is often presented as a spectacle (consider mud or Jello wrestling) enjoyed for its eroticism as much as its entertainment value (think Jerry Springer). 5

The hazing we watched up-close and personal, over and over again, was horrifying, but questions about how and why the episode gripped the nation are at least as troubling. Who was it watching the events unfold on the field? Why was it caught on videotape to begin with? How was it passed on to cable and network television? Who made the decision to run it repeatedly? Why was it international news? 6

Thinking Critically

[1] Does the essay's first sentence catch your attention? Why or why not?

[2] Do you agree with the authors that anger among girls is often dismissed or trivialized? Why do you think this is so?

Girlfighting as spectator sport. Again.   7

Why, when boys perpetrate 80 percent of serious violence in the U.S., is   8
this the story that captivates us—and helps define a generation of girls?

In the shock and awe, we've missed the point. The school principal suggests   9
this is just kids with "old scores to settle." That doesn't tell us enough and,
worse, it fudges the real issues.

This was girls fighting over boyfriends and popularity. The seniors used   10
words like "bitches," "wimps," and "sluts" to shame the juniors into staying
on the field. In what many think of as post-feminist America, ❸ it's not popular to raise issues of power and subordination, but the fact that girls are
fighting other girls in front of videotaping boys, is hardly insignificant. That
girls used sexist and misogynistic language to control other girls during and
after the event and that their fights were primarily for boys' attention and
favor is a symptom of deeper cultural problems. As with many girl fights, boys
are both the "cause" of girl's violence and the real audience.

We need to ask harder, more critical questions about why girls are fight-   11
ing. Why embrace insults that ratify the sexual double standard? Why is
strength in women always devalued as "bitchiness?" Why the endless competition among girls for male approval? And why fight each other instead of
against a culture still rife with sexism and violence toward women?

Girlfighting gets acted out horizontally on other girls because this is the   12
safest and easiest outlet for their outrage and frustration. Girls are essentially
accessing and mimicking the male violence they sometimes know all too
well; and they are choosing victims that are societally approved—other
girls. ❹ This pattern of horizontal aggression has long characterized subordinate groups since it manages the inevitable anger in the group being
controlled without jeopardizing the overall structure of male privilege.

Girls' violence also served one additional purpose. It's not uncommon for   13
the targets of that violence to, themselves, be the group members that are
challenging the rigid norms of girlhood. Why, for example, wouldn't the
girlfighters go after those "girly girls" that the media continuously tells them
are weak, vapid, and stupid? From the evil head cheerleaders in the Disney
Channel's *Kim Possible* and *Lizzie McGuire*, to *The Man Show's* Juggy Squad
on Comedy Central, to *Thong Song* wannabes, these girls make easy targets.

Girls who take out other girls for being "dykes," "hos," and "bitches" can   14
prove they are different, worth taking seriously, a force to contend with. No
wimps, wusses, or victims here. But this posturing is short-lived protection at
best, because selling out other girls this way only continues a climate of misogyny,
and any wrong move can quickly turn the perpetrator into a victim.

Thinking Critically

❸ What do the authors mean by the phrase "post-feminist America" in this context?

❹ Why are girls choosing other girls as victims?

The problem is not girls; the problem is a culture that denigrates, 15 commodifies, and demoralizes women [5] and then gets a kick out of watching the divide and conquer consequences.

There's an old saying, "men kill their weak, women kill their strong." If 16 we would give girls legitimate avenues to power, value their minds as much as their bodies, they'd be less likely to go down those nasty, underhanded or openly hostile roads, less likely to take their legitimate rage out on other girls. Let's face it, "meanness" and other covert aggressions are, in the final analysis, weapons of the weak; horizontal violence ultimately ratifies boy not girl power. When we join with girls to create real pathways to power and possibility, we'll have a lot less to video tape, and we'd have a lot more to be proud of both in ourselves and in our daughters.

UNDERSTANDING DETAILS

1. Explain the basic problem that Brown and Chesney-Lind are addressing.
2. In what way is "girlfighting" a spectator sport in American society?
3. How can boys be both the cause and the audience for girls' violence?
4. What do the authors suggest to solve the problem of female anger and aggression?

READING CRITICALLY

5. Why did the media's reaction to the "girlfighting" bother the authors? What are the implications of these fights? Their social consequences?
6. From your own experience, in what ways is girls' anger "dismissed"?
7. Why is American society fascinated by girls' fighting?
8. Why do the authors believe that girls choose other girls to vent their rage on?

DISCOVERING RHETORICAL STRATEGIES

9. List the main points the authors make. Why do the authors address these points in this particular order?
10. Who do you think is the intended audience of this essay?
11. What rhetorical modes do the authors draw on to produce this essay? Give an example of each strategy.
12. How would you characterize the tone of this essay?

MAKING CONNECTIONS

13. To what extent do you think that Brown and Chesney-Lind would agree with Sandra Cisneros ("Only daughter"), Gloria Steinem ("The Politics of Muscle"), and/or Kim Severson ("I'm Not Willing to Settle for Crumbs") about the need for traditional roles for women in today's society? With which author would you most likely agree? Why?

Thinking Critically

[5] Do you believe our culture "denigrates, commodifies, and demoralizes" women? What does each of these terms mean?

14. Compare and contrast the opinions of Brown and Chesney-Lind with Stephen King ("Why We Crave Horror Movies") and/or Dave Grossman ("We Are Training Our Kids to Kill") about the level of violence in the United States today, its causes, and its effects on our society.

15. Write an essay entitled "Bad Boys, Bad Boys, Whatcha Gonna Do?" using examples taken from essays by Brent Staples ("A Brother's Murder"), Dave Grossman ("We Are Training Our Kids to Kill"), and/or Barbara Ehrenreich ("The Ecstasy of War").

IDEAS FOR DISCUSSION/WRITING

Preparing to Write

Write freely about the anger in U.S. society today: What events or actions are likely to bring anger to the surface? What are some acceptable ways of expressing anger? Why is girls' anger more sensational than boys' anger? How does society react to anger and aggression from these two groups? What are the consequences of any type of anger? Why is anger so difficult to control?

Choosing a Topic

1. *Learning Online:* Most schools have anti-hazing policies, many of which are available online. In an Internet search, type in the name of your school and then "hazing policy" to find the guidelines enforced on your campus. If you cannot find your own school's policy, you can broaden your search and read one from another school (such as Fort Hays State University's at www.fhsu.edu/staffairs/hazing.shtml). Using the online policy statement for information, write an essay including a definition of what you consider unacceptable student behavior and a statement explaining the appropriate penalty for students who display such behavior. Be as specific as possible.

2. Imagine that you are the head counselor at your high school and you have noticed a serious increase in aggression from both male and female students at your school. You call an assembly to discuss this issue and make students realize the seriousness of their behavior. Because you have very little time with them, you write your speech out in the form of an essay on the day before you deliver it. What could you say to make the students look closely at their anger and change their behavior?

3. *Psychology Today* has asked you, as an adolescent psychologist, to write an essay analyzing the differences and similarities between girls' anger and boys' anger in high school. They need you to write two to three typed pages for their journal.

4. Having survived high school, you are in a position of being able to advise younger students. In a well-developed essay, give a younger girl whom you know some advice about managing anger during her high school years.

Before beginning your essay, you might want to consult the checklists on page 384.

Chapter Writing Assignments

Practicing Definition

1. Identify a term people use to describe you (for example, *trustworthy, sloppy,* or *athletic*). In a well-developed essay, define this term as clearly as you can, and discuss whether or not it accurately represents you. Support your claim with carefully chosen details.
2. In what ways do our families define us? How do our families shape who we are and who we have become? In an essay, define the concept of family by explaining how your family members relate to each other.
3. Think of an object you value greatly. For example, a ring might represent a special relationship. Then, in essay form, explain what this object says about you. Why is it your favorite? What does it mean to you?

Exploring Ideas

4. Have you ever felt jealous? What do you think are the most common sources of jealousy? Do you think that jealousy is mostly a productive or unproductive emotion? Write an essay discussing the main qualities of jealousy. What do most people need to know about this feeling?
5. Think of all the "communities" to which you belong (for example, school, church, neighborhood, friends). Choose one that is really important to you, and, in an essay, identify the major features of this community. What makes this community so important in your life?
6. In essay form, describe an ugly part of your campus or city, and explore some important ways this place could be improved or changed. What effects do you think these changes might have on your community or campus? How did you come to this conclusion?

Writing from Sources

For detailed information on writing from sources, see Part III.

7. Choose a modern technological device that you rely on, such as a computer, cell phone, or automobile. Research its evolvement from inception to the product you know and use today. Write an essay, citing two to three sources, that outlines the origin, stages of development, and obstacles surrounding the device you have chosen.
8. Different cultures throughout history have had many divergent ideals. Choose a culture other than your own, and research the defining characteristics of happiness. Is happiness connected to spiritual, moral, or

physical contentment? You may want to look at how the definition of happiness has evolved within one culture over time. Write an essay supported by your research that defines the elements required for happiness.

Analyzing Visual Images

© Reuters/Anthony Correla/Landov LLC.

9. The photo above was taken shortly after 9/11. Looking at this picture carefully, how would you characterize the scene in words—confusion, rescue efforts, heroes, terrorism? Explore the associations you have with this photograph, and then write an essay in which you clearly define one of these terms. Use examples to clarify your definition.
10. Look at the picture on page 376 at the beginning of this chapter. Why do you think the man is holding this ring? Based on your answer, what do you think this ring signifies—love, honor, deceit, betrayal? Write an essay that explains how this picture captures the word you associate with it.

Chapter 11

CAUSE/EFFECT
Tracing Reasons and Results

Wanting to know why things happen is one of our earliest, most basic instincts: Why can't I go out, Mommy? Why are you laughing? Why won't the dog stop barking? Why can't I swim faster than my big brother? These questions, and many more like them, reflect the innately inquisitive nature that dwells within each of us. Closely related to this desire to understand *why* is our corresponding interest in *what* will happen in the future as a result of some particular action: What will I feel like tomorrow if I stay up late tonight? How will I perform in the track meet Saturday if I practice all week? What will be the result if I mix together these two potent chemicals? What will happen if I turn in my next English assignment two days early?

A daily awareness of this intimate relationship between causes and effects allows us to begin to understand the complex and interrelated series of events that make up our lives and the lives of others. For example, trying to understand the various causes of the conflict between Palestine and Israel teaches us about international relations; knowing our biological reactions to certain foods helps us make decisions about what to eat; understanding the interrelated reasons for the outbreak of World War II offers us insight into historical trends and human nature; knowing the effects of sunshine on various parts of our bodies helps us make decisions about how much ultraviolet exposure we can tolerate and what suntan lotion to use; and understanding

421

the causes of the United States' most recent recession will help us respond appropriately to the next economic crisis we encounter. More than anything else, tracing causes and effects teaches us how to think clearly and react intelligently to our multifaceted environment.

In college, you will often be asked to use this natural interest in causes and effects to analyze particular situations and to discern general principles. For example, you might be asked some of the following questions on essay exams in different courses:

Anthropology: Why did the Mayan culture disintegrate?

Psychology: Why do humans respond to fear in different ways?

Biology: How do lab rats react to caffeine?

History: What were the positive effects of the Spanish-American War?

Business: Why did so many computer manufacturing companies go bankrupt in the early 1980s?

Your ability to answer such questions will depend in large part on your skill at understanding cause/effect relationships.

DEFINING CAUSE/EFFECT

Cause/effect analysis requires the ability to look for connections between different elements and to analyze the reasons for those connections. As the name implies, this rhetorical mode has two separate components: cause and effect. A particular essay might concentrate on cause (Why do you live in a dorm?), on effect (What are the resulting advantages and disadvantages of living in a dorm?), or on some combination of the two. In working with causes, we are searching for any circumstances from the past that may have caused a single event; in looking for effects, we seek occurrences that took place after a particular event and resulted from that event. Like process analysis, cause/effect makes use of our intellectual ability to analyze. Process analysis addresses *how* something happens, whereas causal analysis discusses *why* it happened and *what* the result was. A process analysis paper, for example, might explain how to advertise more effectively to increase sales, whereas a cause/effect study would discover that three specific elements contributed to an increase in sales: effective advertising, personal service, and selective discounts. The study of causes and effects, therefore, provides many different and helpful ways for humans to make sense of and clarify their views of the world.

Looking for causes and effects requires an advanced form of thinking. It is more complex than most rhetorical strategies we have studied because it can exist on a number of different and progressively more difficult levels. The most accurate and effective causal analysis accrues from digging for the real or ultimate causes or effects, as opposed to those that are merely superficial or immediate. Actress Angela Lansbury would have been out of work on an episode of the television show *Murder, She Wrote,* for example, if her character had stopped her investigation at the immediate cause of death (slipping in the bathtub) rather than searching diligently for the *real* cause (an overdose of cocaine administered by an angry companion, which resulted in the slip in the tub). Similarly, voters would be easy to manipulate if they considered only the immediate effects of a tax increase (a slightly higher tax bill) rather than the ultimate benefits that would result (the many years of improved education their children would receive because of the specialized programs allowed by such an increase). Only the discovery of the actual reasons for an event or an idea will lead to the logical and accurate analysis of causes and effects important to a basic understanding of various aspects of our lives.

Faulty reasoning assigns causes to a sequence of actions without adequate justification. One such logical fallacy is called *post hoc, ergo propter hoc* ("after this, therefore because of this"): The fact that someone lost a job after walking under a ladder does not mean that the two events are causally related; by the same token, if we get up every morning at 5:30 A.M., just before the sun rises, we cannot therefore conclude that the sun rises *because* we get up (no matter how self-centered we are!). Faulty reasoning also occurs when we oversimplify a particular situation. Most events are connected to a multitude of causes and effects. Sometimes one effect has many causes: A student may fail a history exam because she's been working two part-time jobs, she was sick, she didn't study hard enough, and she found the instructor very boring. One cause may also have many effects. If a house burns down, the people who lived in it will be out of a home. If we look at such a tragic scene more closely, however, we may also note that the fire traumatized a child who lived there, helped the family learn what good friends they had, encouraged the family to double their future fire insurance, and provided the stimulus they needed to make a long-dreamed-of move to another city. One event has thus resulted in many interrelated effects. Building an argument on insecure foundations or oversimplifying the causes or effects connected with an event will seriously hinder the construction of a rational essay. No matter what the nature of the cause/effect analysis, it must always be based on clear observation, accurate facts, and rigorous logic.

In the following paragraph, a student writer analyzes some of the causes and effects connected with the controversial issue of euthanasia. Notice how he makes connections and then analyzes those connections as he consistently explores the immediate and ultimate effects of being able to stretch life beyond its normal limits through new medical technology:

> *Along with the many recent startling advancements in medical technology have come a number of complex moral, ethical, and spiritual questions that beg to be answered. We now have the ability to prolong the life of the human body for a very long time. But what rights do patients and their families have to curtail cruel and unusual medical treatment that stretches life beyond its normal limits? This dilemma has produced a ripple effect in society. Is the extension of life an unquestionable goal in itself, regardless of the quality of that life? Modern scientific technology has forced doctors to reevaluate the exact meaning and purpose of their profession. For example, many medical schools and undergraduate university programs now routinely offer classes on medical ethics—an esoteric and infrequently taught subject only a few years ago. Doctors and scholars alike are realizing that medical personnel alone cannot be expected to decide on the exact parameters of life. In like manner, the judicial process must now evaluate the legal complexities of mercy killings and the rights of patients to die with dignity and without unnecessary medical intervention. The insurance business, too, wrestles with the catastrophic effects of new technology on the costs of today's hospital care. In short, medical progress entails more than microscopes, chemicals, and high-tech instruments. If we are to develop as a thoughtful, just, and merciful society, we must consider not only the physical well-being of our nation's patients, but their emotional, spiritual, and financial status as well.*

THINKING CRITICALLY THROUGH CAUSE/EFFECT

Thinking about causes and effects is one of the most advanced mental activities that we perform. It involves complex operations that we must think through carefully, making sure all connections are reasonable and accurate. Unlike other rhetorical patterns, cause/effect thinking requires us to see specific relationships between two or more items. To practice this strategy, we need to look for items or events that are causally related—that is, one that has caused the other. Then, we can focus on either the causes (the initial stimuli), the effects (the results), or a combination of the two.

Searching for causes and effects requires a great deal of digging that is not necessary for most of the other modes. Cause/effect necessitates the ultimate in investigative work. The mental exertion associated with this thinking strategy is sometimes exhausting, but it is always worth going through when you discover relationships that you never saw before or when you uncover links in your reasoning that were previously unknown or obscure to you.

If you've ever had the secret desire to be a private eye or an investigator of any sort, practicing cause/effect reasoning can be lots of fun. It forces you to see relationships among multiple items and then to make sense of those connections. Completing exercises in this skill by itself will once again help you perfect the logistics of cause/effect thinking before you mix and match it with other thinking strategies.

© Sam Shere/UPI/Corbis Bettmann

1. In Sam Shere's famous 1937 photo of the *Hindenburg* bursting into flames, we can see that this voyage of the Zeppelin from Germany to the United States ended in disaster. Ninety-seven people were aboard when the Hindenberg went down, and none of them expected to die. Think of other examples of technological inventions or changes that resulted in an outcome different from what people expected. Identify the expectations, the actual results, and what can be learned from these results.

2. Choose a major problem you see in our society, and list what you think are the main causes of this problem on one side of a piece of paper and the effects on the other side. Compare the two lists to see how they differ. Then, compare and contrast your list with those written by other students.

3. What "caused" you to become a student? What influences led you to this choice at this point in your life? How has being a student affected your life? List several overall effects.

READING AND WRITING CAUSE/EFFECT ESSAYS

Causal analysis is usually employed for one of three main purposes: (1) to prove a specific point (such as the necessity for stricter gun control), in which case the writer generally deals totally with facts and with conclusions drawn from those facts; (2) to argue against a widely accepted belief (for example, the assertion that cocaine is addictive), in which case the writer relies principally on facts, with perhaps some pertinent opinions; or (3) to speculate on a theory (for instance, why the crime rate is higher in most major cities than it is in rural areas), in which case the writer probably presents hypotheses and opinions along with facts. This section will explore these purposes in cause/effect essays from the standpoint of both reading and writing.

Reading Cause/Effect Essays

- What is the essay's thesis?
- What are the real causes and effects?
- What are the author's assertions?

Preparing to Read.   As you set out to read the essays in this chapter, begin by focusing your attention on the title and the synopsis of the essay you are about to read and by scanning the essay itself: What do you think Stephen King is going to talk about in "Why We Crave Horror Movies"? What does the synopsis in the Rhetorical Table of Contents tell you about Michael Dorris's "The Broken Cord" or about Sherman Alexie's "The Joy of Reading and Writing: Superman and Me"?

Also, at this stage in the reading process, you should try to learn as much as you can about the author of the essay and the reasons he or she wrote it. Ask yourself questions like the following: What is King's intention in "Why We Crave Horror Movies"? Who is Mary Roach's intended audience in "Meet the Bickersons"? And what is Alice Walker's point of view in "Beauty: When the Other Dancer Is the Self"?

Finally, before you begin to read, answer the prereading questions for each essay and then consider the proposed essay topic from a variety of perspectives: For example, concerning Alexie's topic, how important to you is reading and/or writing? Which segments of American society are most aware of the value of these skills? Which the least? What do you want to know from Roach about people and arguing? Do you have a desire to understand relationships better?

Reading.   As you read each essay in this chapter for the first time, record your spontaneous reactions to it, drawing as often as possible on the preliminary material you already know: What do you think of horror movies (King)? What is Dorris suggesting about babies with fetal alcohol syndrome? Have you experienced an addiction of any kind? Why did Roach choose the title she did?

Whenever you can, try to create a context for your reading: What is the tone of Alexie's comments about reading and writing? How does this tone help him communicate with his audience? What do you think Walker's purpose is in her essay concerning her childhood accident? How clearly does she get this purpose across to you?

Also, during this reading, note the essay's thesis and check to see if the writer thoroughly explores all possibilities before settling on the primary causes and/or effects of a particular situation; in addition, determine whether the writer clearly states the assertions that naturally evolve from a discussion of the topic.

At the bottom of the essay's pages in this chapter are some questions that will help you process this reading material critically or analytically. These questions are designed to provide a bridge that will connect your thoughts before you read the essay with your tasks at the end of your reading by helping you see relationships among ideas that will lead you to higher levels of thinking. Recording your answers in writing is the best way to approach these questions, but your instructor might have some other guidelines for you.

Finally, read the questions following each essay to get a sense of the main issues and strategies in the selection.

Rereading.   When you reread these essays, you should focus mainly on the writer's craft. Notice how the authors narrow and focus their material, how they make clear and logical connections between ideas in their essays, how they support their conclusions with concrete examples, how they use other rhetorical modes to accomplish their cause/effect analysis, and how they employ logical transitions to move us smoothly from one point to another. Most important, however, ask yourself if the writer actually discusses the real causes and/or effects of a particular circumstance: What does King say are the primary reasons people crave horror movies? According to Roach, why do many couples have trouble in their marriages? What are the primary causes and effects of Walker's childhood injury?

For a thorough outline of the reading process, consult the Reading Inventory at the end of Part I.

Writing Cause/Effect Essays

- State your purpose in your thesis.
- Explore all causes and effects.
- Use concrete evidence.
- Summarize and draw conclusions.

Preparing to Write.   Beginning a cause/effect essay requires—as does any other essay—exploring and limiting your subject, specifying a purpose, and identifying an audience. The Preparing to Write questions before the essay assignments, coupled with the prewriting techniques outlined on pages 36–38, encourage you to consider specific issues related to your reading. The assignments themselves will then help you limit your topic and determine a particular purpose and audience for your message. For cause/effect essays, determining a purpose is even more important than usual, because your readers can get hopelessly lost unless your analysis is clearly focused.

Writing.   For all its conceptual complexity, a cause/effect essay can be organized quite simply. The introduction generally presents the subject(s) and states the purpose of the analysis in a clear thesis. The body of the paper then explores all relevant causes and/or effects, typically progressing either from least to most influential or from most to least influential. Finally, the concluding section summarizes the various cause/effect relationships established in the body of the paper and clearly states the conclusions that can be drawn from those relationships.

The following additional guidelines should assist you in producing an effective cause/effect essay in all academic disciplines:

1. Narrow and focus your material as much as possible.
2. Consider all possibilities before assigning real or ultimate causes or effects.
3. Show connections between ideas by using transitions and key words—such as *because, reasons, results, effects,* and *consequences*—to guide your readers smoothly through your essay.
4. Support all inferences with concrete evidence.
5. Be as objective as possible in your analysis so that you don't distort logic with personal biases.
6. Understand your audience's opinions and convictions so that you know what to emphasize in your essay.
7. Qualify your assertions to avoid overstatement and oversimplification.

These suggestions apply to both cause/effect essay assignments and exam questions.

Rewriting.   As you revise your cause/effect essays, ask yourself the following important questions:

- Is my thesis stated clearly at the outset of my paper?
- Does it include my subject and my purpose?
- Do I explore all relevant causes and/or effects?
- Do I accomplish my purpose as effectively as possible?

- Do I use logical reasoning throughout the essay?
- Do I state clearly the conclusions that can be drawn from my paper?

More specific guidelines for writing and revising your essays appear in the Writing Inventory at the end of Part I.

STUDENT ESSAY: CAUSE/EFFECT AT WORK

In the following essay, the student writer analyzes the effects of contemporary television soap operas on young people: Notice that she states her subject and purpose at the beginning of the essay and then presents a combination of facts and opinions in her exploration of the topic. Notice also that, in her analysis, the writer is careful to draw clear connections between her perceptions of the issue and various objective details in an attempt to trace the effects of this medium in our society today. At the end of her essay, look at her summary of the logical relationships she establishes in the body of the essay and her statements about the conclusions she draws from these relationships.

Distortions of Reality

Background   Television's contributions to society, positive and negative, have been debated continually since this piece of technology invaded the average American household in the 1950s. Television has brought an un-limited influx of new information, ideas, and cultures into our homes. However, based on my observations of my thirteen-year-old cousin, Katie, and her friends, I think we need to take a closer look at the effects of soap operas on adolescents today. The distortions of reality portrayed on these programs are frighteningly misleading and, in my opinion, can be very confusing to young people.   Thesis statement

Transition   During the early 1990s, the lifestyle of the typical soap opera "family" has been radically transformed from comfortable pretentiousness to blatant and unrealistic decadence. The characters neither live nor dress like the majority of their viewers, who are generally middle-class Americans. These television families live in large, majestic homes that are flawlessly decorated. The actors are often adorned in beautiful designer clothing, fur coats, and expensive jewelry, and this opulent lifestyle is sustained by people with no visible means of income. Very few of the characters seem to "work" for a living. When they do, upward   First distortion of reality

Concrete examples

mobility—without the benefit of the proper education or suitable training—and a well-planned marriage come quickly.

Transition　　From this constant barrage of conspicuous consumption, my cousin and her friends seem to have a *First effect* distorted view of everyday economic realities. I see Katie and her group becoming obsessed with the ap-*Concrete* pearance of their clothes and possessions. I frequently *examples* hear them criticize their parents' jobs and modest homes. With noticeable arrogance, these young adolescents seem to view their parents' lives as "failures" when compared to the effortless, luxurious lifestyles portrayed in the soaps.

Transition　　One of the most alluring features of this genre is its masterful use of deception. Conflicts between characters in soap operas are based on secrecy and misin-*Concrete* formation. Failure to tell the truth and to perform *examples* honorable deeds further complicates the entangled lives and love affairs of the participants. But when the *Second* truth finally comes out and all mistakes and misdeeds *distortion of* become public, the culprits and offenders hardly ever *reality* suffer for their actions. In fact, they appear to leave the scene of the crime guilt-free.

Transition　　Regrettably, Katie and her friends consistently express alarming indifference to this lack of moral in-*Concrete* tegrity. In their daily viewing, they shrug off *examples* underhanded scenes of scheming and conniving, and they marvel at how the characters manipulate each other into positions of powerlessness or grapple in distasteful love scenes. I can only conclude that contin-*Second* ued exposure to this amoral behavior is eroding the *effect* fundamental values of truth and fidelity in these kids.

Transition　　Also in the soaps, the powers-that-be conveniently *Third* disregard any sense of responsibility for wrongdoing. *distortion of* Characters serve jail terms quickly and in relative *reality* comfort. Drug or alcohol abuse does not mar any-*Concrete* one's physical appearance or behavior, and poverty is *examples* virtually nonexistent. Usually, the wrongdoer's position, wealth, and prestige are quickly restored—with little pain and suffering.

　　Adolescents are clearly learning that people can act *Third effect* without regard for the harmful effects of their actions

<u>on themselves and others when they see this type of behavior go unpunished</u>. Again, I notice the result of this delusion in my cousin. Recently, when a businessman in our community was convicted of embezzling large sums of money from his clients, Katie was outraged because he was sentenced to five years in prison, unlike her daytime TV "heartthrob," who had been given a suspended sentence for a similar crime. With righteous indignation, Katie claimed that the victims, many of whom had lost their entire savings, should have realized that any business investment involves risk and the threat of loss. Logic and common sense evaded Katie's reasoning as she insisted on comparing television justice with real-life jurisprudence.

Concrete examples

The writers and producers of soap operas argue that the shows are designed to entertain viewers and are not meant to be reflections of reality. Theoretically, this may be true, but I can actually see how these soap operas are affecting my cousin and her crowd. Although my personal observations are limited, I cannot believe they are unique or unusual. <u>Too many young people think that they can amass wealth and material possessions without an education, hard work, or careful financial planning; that material goods are the sole measure of a person's success in life; and that honesty and integrity are not necessarily admirable qualities.</u>

Ultimate effect

<u>Soap operas should demonstrate a realistic lifestyle and a responsible sense of behavior.</u> The many hours adolescents spend in front of the television can obviously influence their view of the world. As a society, we cannot afford the consequences resulting from the distortions of reality portrayed every day in these shows.

Proposed solution

Student Writer's Comments

In general, writing this essay was not as easy as I had anticipated during my prewriting phase. Although I was interested in and familiar with my topic, I had trouble fitting all the pieces together: matching causes with effects, examples with main points, and problems with solutions.

My prewriting activities were a combination of lists and journal entries that gave me loads of ideas and phrasing to work with in my drafts. From this initial thinking exercise, I created an informal outline of the points I wanted to make. I played with the order of these topics for a while and then began to write.

Because I had spent so much time thinking through various causal relationships before I began to write, I generated the first draft with minimal pain. But I was not happy with it. The examples that I had chosen to support various points I wanted to make did not fit as well as they could, and the whole essay was scattered and incoherent. Although all writing requires support and focus, I realized that a cause/effect essay demands special attention to the relationship between specific examples and their ultimate causes and/or effects. As a result, I had to begin again to revise my sprawling first draft.

I spent my first revising session on the very sloppy introduction and conclusion. I felt that if I could tighten up these parts of the essay, I would have a clearer notion of my purpose and focus. I am convinced now that the time I spent on the beginning and ending of my essay really paid off. I rewrote my thesis several times until I finally arrived at the statement in the draft printed here. This final thesis statement gave me a clear sense of direction for revising the rest of my paper.

I then worked through my essay paragraph by paragraph, verifying that the examples and illustrations I cited supported as effectively as possible each of my points. I made sure that the causes and effects were accurately paired, and I reorganized sections of the essay that didn't yet read smoothly. I put the final touches on my conclusion and handed in my paper—with visions of causes, effects, and soap opera characters still dancing around in my head.

SOME FINAL THOUGHTS ON CAUSE/EFFECT

The essays in this chapter deal with both causes and effects in a variety of ways. As you read each essay, try to discover its primary purpose and the ultimate causes and/or effects of the issue under discussion. Note also the clear causal relationships that each author sets forth on solid foundations supported by logical reasoning. Although the subjects of these essays vary dramatically, each essay exhibits the basic elements of effective causal analysis.

CAUSE/EFFECT IN REVIEW

Reading Cause/Effect Essays

Preparing to Read
√ What assumptions can I make from the essay's title?
√ What do I think the general mood of the essay will be?
√ What is the essay's purpose and audience?
√ What does the synopsis tell me about the essay?
√ What can I learn from the author's biography?
√ Can I predict the author's point of view toward the subject?

Reading
√ What is the essay's thesis?
√ What are the real causes and/or effects?
√ What are the author's assertions?

Rereading
√ How does the writer narrow and focus the essay?
√ Does the writer make clear and logical connections between the ideas?
√ What concrete examples support the author's conclusions?
√ Does the writer discuss the real causes and effects?

Writing Cause/Effect Essays

Preparing to Write
√ What is my purpose?
√ Who is my audience?

Writing
√ Do I state my purpose in my thesis?
√ Do I explore all causes and effects?
√ Do I use concrete evidence?
√ Do I summarize and draw conclusions?

Rewriting
√ Is my thesis stated clearly at the outset of my paper?
√ Does it include my subject and my purpose?
√ Do I explore all relevant causes and/or effects?
√ Do I accomplish my purpose as effectively as possible?
√ Do I use logical reasoning throughout the essay?
√ Do I state clearly the conclusions that can be drawn from my paper?

STEPHEN KING   (1947–   )

Why We Crave Horror Movies

"People's appetites for terror seem insatiable," Stephen King once remarked, an insight that may help justify his phenomenal success as a writer of horror fiction since the mid-1970s. His books have sold over one hundred million copies, and the movies made from them have generated more income than the gross domestic product of several small countries. After early jobs as a janitor, a laundry worker, and a high school English teacher in Portland, Maine, King turned to writing full time following the spectacular sales of his first novel, *Carrie* (1974), which focuses on a shy, socially ostracized young girl who takes revenge on her cruel classmates through newly developed telekinetic powers. King's subsequent books have included *The Shining* (1976), *Firestarter* (1980), *Cujo* (1981), *Christine* (1983), *Pet Sematary* (1983), *Misery* (1987), *The Stand* (1990), *The Waste Lands* (1992), *Delores Claiborne* (1993), *Desperation* (1996), *Bag of Bones* (1999), *Dreamcatcher* (2001), and *The Dark Tower V: Wolves of the Calla* (2003). Asked to explain why readers and moviegoers are so attracted to his tales of horror, King explained that most people's lives "are full of fears—that their marriage isn't working, that they aren't going to make it on the job, that society is crumbling all around them. But we're really not supposed to talk about things like that, and so they don't have any outlets for all those scary feelings. But the horror writer can give them a place to put their fears." A cheerful though somewhat superstitious person, King, who now lives in Bangor, Maine, admits to doing most of his best writing during the morning hours. "You think I want to write this stuff at night?" he once asked a reviewer.

Preparing to Read

This essay, originally published in *Playboy* magazine, attempts to explain why horror movies satisfy our most basic instincts.

Exploring Experience: As you prepare to read this article, consider your thoughts on the emotional condition of people in the United States: How emotionally healthy are Americans? Were they more emotionally healthy twenty years ago? A century ago? What makes a society emotionally healthy? Emotionally unhealthy? How can a society maintain good health? What is the relationship between emotional health and a civilized society?

Learning Online: Conduct an Internet search on two recently released horror movies. Use the title of the film as well as the phrase "movie trailer" as your search terms. Find links that allow you to watch each film's preview trailer. How do you feel after watching the trailers? Do you like or dislike this type of film?

I think that we're all mentally ill; those of us outside the asylums only hide   1
it a little better—and maybe not all that much better, after all. We've all
known people who talk to themselves, people who sometimes squinch
their faces into horrible grimaces when they believe no one is watching,
people who have some hysterical fear—of snakes, the dark, the tight place,
the long drop . . . and, of course, those final worms and grubs that are waiting so patiently underground. ◆

When we pay our four or five bucks and seat ourselves at tenth-row center   2
in a theater showing a horror movie, we are daring the nightmare.

Why? Some of the reasons are simple and obvious. To show that we can,   3
that we are not afraid, that we can ride this roller coaster. ◆ Which is not to
say that a really good horror movie may not surprise a scream out of us at
some point, the way we may scream when the roller coaster twists through
a complete 360 or plows through a lake at the bottom of the drop. And horror movies, like roller coasters, have always been the special province of the
young; by the time one turns 40 or 50, one's appetite for double twists or
360-degree loops may be considerably depleted.

We also go to reestablish our feelings of essential normality; the horror   4
movie is innately conservative, even reactionary. Freda Jackson as the horrible melting woman in *Die, Monster, Die!* confirms for us that no matter how
far we may be removed from the beauty of a Robert Redford or a Diana
Ross, we are still light-years from true ugliness.

And we go to have fun.   5

Ah, but this is where the ground starts to slope away, isn't it? Because this   6
is a very peculiar sort of fun, indeed. The fun comes from seeing others men-
aced—sometimes killed. One critic has suggested that if pro football has
become the voyeur's version of combat, then the horror film has become the
modern version of the public lynching.

It is true that the mythic, "fairy-tale" horror film intends to take away the   7
shades of gray. . . . It urges us to put away our more civilized and adult
penchant for analysis and to become children again, seeing things in pure
blacks and whites. It may be that horror movies provide psychic relief on this
level because this invitation to lapse into simplicity, irrationality, and even
outright madness is extended so rarely. We are told we may allow our emotions a free rein . . . or no rein at all.

If we are all insane, then sanity becomes a matter of degree. If your insanity   8
leads you to carve up women, like Jack the Ripper or the Cleveland Torso

---

Thinking Critically

◆ What are the worms and grubs waiting for? What tone does this detail help create in the
essay?

◆ How does King use the image of a roller coaster as a metaphor here? What does the roller
coaster represent?

Murderer, we clap you away in the funny farm (but neither of those two amateur-night surgeons was ever caught, heh-heh-heh); if, on the other hand, your insanity leads you only to talk to yourself when you're under stress or to pick your nose on your morning bus, then you are left alone to go about your business . . . though it is doubtful that you will ever be invited to the best parties.

The potential lyncher is in almost all of us [3] (excluding saints, past and   9
present; but then, most saints have been crazy in their own ways), and every now and then, he has to be let loose to scream and roll around in the grass. Our emotions and our fears form their own body, and we recognize that it demands its own exercise to maintain proper muscle tone. Certain of these emotional muscles are accepted—even exalted—in civilized society; they are, of course, the emotions that tend to maintain the status quo of civilization itself. Love, friendship, loyalty, kindness—these are all the emotions that we applaud, emotions that have been immortalized in the couplets of Hallmark cards and in the verses (I don't dare call it poetry) of Leonard Nimoy.

When we exhibit these emotions, society showers us with positive   10
reinforcement; we learn this even before we get out of diapers. When, as children, we hug our rotten little puke of a sister and give her a kiss, all the aunts and uncles smile and twit and cry, "Isn't he the sweetest little thing?" Such coveted treats as chocolate-covered graham crackers often follow. But if we deliberately slam the rotten little puke of a sister's fingers in the door, sanctions follow—angry remonstrance from parents, aunts, and uncles; instead of a chocolate-covered graham cracker, a spanking.

But anticivilization emotions [4] don't go away, and they demand periodic   11
exercise. We have such "sick" jokes as, "What's the difference between a truck-load of bowling balls and a truckload of dead babies?" (You can't unload a truckload of bowling balls with a pitchfork . . . a joke, by the way, that I heard originally from a ten-year-old.) Such a joke may surprise a laugh or a grin out of us even as we recoil, a possibility that confirms the thesis: If we share a brotherhood of man, then we also share an insanity of man. None of which is intended as a defense of either the sick joke or insanity but merely as an explanation of why the best horror films, like the best fairy tales, manage to be reactionary, anarchistic, and revolutionary all at the same time.

The mythic horror movie, like the sick joke, has a dirty job to do. It delib-   12
erately appeals to all that is worst in us. It is morbidity unchained, our most base instincts let free, our nastiest fantasies realized . . . , and it all happens,

---

Thinking Critically

[3] Do you agree with the author that a "potential lyncher" lurks inside all of us? Why or why not?

[4] What are "anticivilization emotions"? Give an example, and explain how it fits into this category.

fittingly enough, in the dark. For those reasons, good liberals often shy away from horror films. For myself, I like to see the most aggressive of them— *Dawn of the Dead,* for instance—as lifting a trap door in the civilized forebrain and throwing a basket of raw meat to the hungry alligators swimming around in that subterranean river beneath.

Why bother? Because it keeps them from getting out, man. It keeps them   13 down there and me up here. It was Lennon and McCartney who said that all you need is love, and I would agree with that.

As long as you keep the gators fed.   14

UNDERSTANDING DETAILS

1. Why, in King's opinion, do civilized people enjoy horror movies?
2. According to King, in what ways are horror movies like roller coasters?
3. According to King, how are horror films like public lynchings?
4. What is the difference between "emotions that tend to maintain the status quo of civilization" (paragraph 9) and "anticivilization emotions" (paragraph 11)?

READING CRITICALLY

5. How can horror movies "reestablish our feelings of essential normality" (paragraph 4)?
6. What is "reactionary, anarchistic, and revolutionary" (paragraph 11) about fairy tales? About horror films?
7. Why does the author think we need to exercise our anticivilization emotions? What are some other ways we might confront these emotions?
8. Explain the last line of King's essay: "As long as you keep the gators fed" (paragraph 14).

DISCOVERING RHETORICAL STRATEGIES

9. What is the cause/effect relationship that King notes in society between horror movies and sanity?
10. Why does King begin his essay with such a dramatic statement as "I think that we're all mentally ill" (paragraph 1)?
11. Who do you think is the author's intended audience for this essay? Describe them in detail. How did you come to this conclusion?
12. What different rhetorical strategies does King use to support his cause/effect analysis? Give examples of each.

MAKING CONNECTIONS

13. Apply Stephen King's definition of *horror* to such frightening experiences as the preparation of a dead body for its funeral (Jessica Mitford, "Behind the Formaldehyde Curtain") and/or caring for a child with fetal alcohol syndrome (Michael Dorris, "The Broken Cord"). In what way is each of these events "horrible"? What are the principal differences between watching a horror movie and living through a real-life horror?

14. In this essay, King gives us important insights into his own writing process, especially into how horror novels and movies affect their audiences. Compare and contrast his revelation of the techniques of his trade with those advanced by Amy Tan ("Mother Tongue"), Roger Rosenblatt ("I am Writing Blindly"), and/or Rita Mae Brown ("Writing as a Moral Act"), all of whom discuss the writing process. Whose comments are most helpful to you? Explain your answer.

15. Compare King's remarks about "fear" with similar insights into the topic by such other authors as Alice Lesch Kelly ("Toughen Up"), Alice Walker ("Beauty: When the Other Dancer Is the Self"), and/or Barbara Ehrenreich ("The Ecstasy of War"). How would each of these writers define the term differently? With which author's definition would you most likely agree? Explain your answer.

IDEAS FOR DISCUSSION/WRITING

Preparing to Write

Write freely about how most people maintain a healthy emotional attitude: How would you define emotional well-being? When are people most emotionally healthy? Most emotionally unhealthy? What do your friends and relatives do to maintain a healthy emotional life? What do you do to maintain emotional health? What is the connection between our individual emotional health and the extent to which our society is civilized?

Choosing a Topic

1. *Learning Online:* King's essay focuses on the benefits of watching horror films. What are other practices we have that on the surface may seem silly or trivial but that actually serve an important purpose? Select one such practice, and write an essay in which you identify its causes and effects. Conduct an Internet search on your topic, and use credible references to support your theories. Try to use relevant, vivid imagery, as King does, to engage your audience.

2. Think of a release other than horror films for our most violent emotions. Is it an acceptable release? Write an essay for the general public explaining the relationship between this particular release and our "civilized" society.

3. If you accept King's analysis of horror movies, what role in society do you think other types of movies play (e.g., love stories, science-fiction movies, and comedies)? Choose one type, and explain its role to your college composition class.

4. Your psychology instructor has asked you to explain your opinions on the degree of sanity or insanity in the United States at present. In what ways are we sane? In what ways are we insane? Write an essay for your psychology instructor explaining in detail your observations along these lines.

Before beginning your essay, you might want to consult the checklists on page 433.

MICHAEL DORRIS   (1945–1997)

The Broken Cord

Michael Dorris, a descendant of Modoc Native Americans and Irish and French settlers, grew up in Kentucky and Montana. He earned his B.A. at Georgetown University and his M.A. at Yale and was for many years a professor of Anthropology and Native-American Studies at Dartmouth, where he was also head of the Native-American Studies Program. His training was quite eclectic. "I came to cultural anthropology," he has explained, "by way of an undergraduate program in English and classics and a Master's Degree in history of the theater." He was also a Guggenheim Fellow (1978), a Rockefeller Fellow (1985), a member of the Smithsonian Institution Council, a National Endowment for the Humanities consultant, a National Public Radio commentator, and a member of the editorial board of the *American Indian Culture and Research Journal* during his distinguished academic career. His many publications include *Native Americans: Five Hundred Years After* (1975); a bestselling novel, *A Yellow Raft in Blue Water* (1987); *The Broken Cord* (1989), a work of nonfiction that won the Heartland Prize, the Christopher Medal, and the National Book Critics Circle Award; *Morning Girl* (1992), a book of short stories; and two more novels, *Working Men* (1993) and *Rooms in the House of Stone* (1993). Dorris also coauthored several books with his wife, Louise Erdrich, including *Route Two and Back* (1991), a collection of travel essays. Prior to his death, he advised student writers to "work at as many kinds of jobs as possible while they are young and keep daily journals of their experiences and impressions."

Preparing to Read

The following excerpt from *The Broken Cord* details some of Dorris's frustrations in raising his adopted son, Adam, who suffered from fetal alcohol syndrome until his death in 1991.

Exploring Experience: As you prepare to read this article, take a few moments to think about your own physical and mental growth: What do you know about your birth? How did you develop as a child? Are you reaching your physical and mental potential? How do you know? Are there any barriers between you and this potential? What are they? How can you surmount them? How will you maintain your potential?

Learning Online: Go to the national Web site for Fetal Alcohol Syndrome (www.nofas.org), and find facts and photos about this condition described so vividly in Dorris's essay.

Adam's birthdays are, I think, the hardest anniversaries, even though as   1
an adoptive father I was not present to hear Adam's first cry, to feel
the aspirated warmth of his body meeting air for the first time. I was
not present to count his fingers, to exclaim at the surprise of gender, to be
comforted by the hope at the heart of his new existence.

From what I've learned, from the sum of gathered profiles divided by the   2
tragedy of each case, the delivery of my premature son was unlikely to have been
a joyous occasion. Most fetal alcohol babies emerge not in a tide, the facsimile
of saline, primordial, life-granting sea, but instead enter this world tainted with
stale wine. Their amniotic fluid literally reeks of Thunderbird or Ripple, and the
whole operating theater stinks like the scene of a three-day party. Delivery room
staff who have been witness time and again tell of undernourished babies thrown
into delirium tremens when the cord that brought sustenance and poison is
severed. ◆ Nurses close their eyes at the memory. An infant with the shakes, as
cold turkey as a raving derelict deprived of the next fix, is hard to forget.

Compared to the ideal, Adam started far in the hole, differently from the   3
child who began a march through the years without the scars of fetters on
his ankles, with eyes and ears that worked, with nothing to carry except
what he or she collected along the path.

Adam's birthdays are reminders for me. For each celebration commemo-   4
rating that he was born, there is the pang, the rage, that he was not born
whole. I grieve for what he might have, what he should have been. I magnify
and sustain those looks of understanding or compassion or curiosity that fleet
across his face, fast as a breeze, unexpected as the voice of God—the time he
said to me in the car, the words arising from no context I could see, "Kansas
is between Oklahoma and Texas." But when I turned in amazement, agreeing loudly, still ready after all these years to discover a buried talent or passion
for geography, for anything, that possible person had disappeared.

"What made you say that?" I asked.   5

"Say what?" he answered. "I didn't say anything."   6

The sixteenth birthday, the eighteenth. The milestones. The driver's license,   7
voting, the adult boundary-marker birthdays. The days I envisioned while
watching the mail for the response to my first adoption application, the days
that set forth like distant skyscrapers as I projected ahead through my years
of fatherhood. I had given little specific consideration to what might come
between, but of those outstanding days I had been sure. They were the pillars
I followed, the oases of certainty. Alone in the cabin in Alaska or in the basement apartment near Franconia while I waited for the definition of the rest

---

Thinking Critically

◆ Why is it ironic that the umbilical cord brings both "sustenance and poison"?

of my life to commence, I planned the elaborate cake decorations for those big birthdays, the significant presents I would save to buy. Odd as it may seem, the anticipation of the acts of letting Adam go began before I even knew his name. ❷ I looked forward to the proud days on which the world would recognize my son as progressively more his own man. Those were among the strongest hooks that bonded me to him in my imagination.

As each of these anniversaries finally came and went, nothing like I   8
expected them to be, I doubly mourned. First, selfishly, for me, and second for Adam, because he didn't know what he was missing, what he had already missed, what he would miss. I wanted to burst through those birthdays like a speeding train blasts a weak gate, to get past them and back into the anonymous years for which I had made no models, where there were no obvious measurements, no cakes with candles that would never be lit.

It was a coincidence that Adam turned twenty-one as this book neared   9
completion, but it seemed appropriate. On the morning of his birthday, I rose early and baked him a lemon cake, his favorite, and left the layers to cool while I drove to Hanover to pick him up. His gifts were wrapped and on the kitchen table—an electric shaver, clothes, a Garfield calendar. ❸ For his special dinner he had requested tacos, and as always I had reserved a magic candle—the kind that keeps reigniting no matter how often it is blown out—for the center of his cake.

I was greeted at Adam's house by the news that he had just had a seizure,   10
a small one this time, but it had left him groggy. I helped him on with his coat, bent to tie his shoelace, all the while talking about the fun we would have during the day. He looked out the window. Only the week before he had been laid off from his dishwashing job. December had been a bad month for seizures, some due to his body's adjustment to a change in dosage and some occurring because Adam had skipped taking medicine altogether. The bowling alley's insurance carrier was concerned and that, combined with an after-Christmas slump in business, decided the issue. Now he was back at Hartford for a few weeks while Ken Krambert and his associates sought a new work placement. I thought perhaps Adam was depressed about this turn of events, so I tried to cheer him up as we drove south on the familiar road to Cornish.

"So, Adam," I said, making conversation, summoning the conventional   11
words, "do you feel any older? What's good about being twenty-one?"

He turned to me and grinned. There *was* something good.   12

"Well," he answered, "now the guys at work say I'm old enough to drink."   13

Thinking Critically

❷ Why does Dorris anticipate "letting Adam go" before he even knows his name?

❸ How does the odd combination of an electric shaver and a Garfield calendar help us understand Adam's condition?

His unexpected words kicked me in the stomach. They crowded every   14
thought from my brain.

"Adam, you can't," I protested. "I've told you about your birth-mother,   15
about your other father. Do you remember what happened to them?" I knew
he did. I had told him the story several times, and we had gone over it
together as he read, or I read to him, parts of this book.

Adam thought for a moment. "They were sick?" he offered finally. "That's   16
why I have seizures?"

"No, they weren't sick. They died, Adam. They died from drinking. If you   17
drank, it could happen to you." My memory played back all the statistics
about sons of alcoholic fathers and their particular susceptibility to substance
abuse. "It would not mix well with your medicine."

Adam sniffed, turned away, but not before I recognized the amused   18
disbelief in his expression. He did not take death seriously, never had. It was
an abstract concept out of his reach and therefore of no interest to him.
Death was less real than Santa Claus—after all, Adam had in his album a
photograph of himself seated on Santa Claus's lap. Death was no threat, no
good reason to refuse his first drink.

My son will forever travel through a moonless night with only the roar   19
of wind for company. ◆ Don't talk to him of mountains, of tropical beaches.
Don't ask him to swoon at sunrises or marvel at the filter of light through
leaves. He's never had time for such things, and he does not believe in them.
He may pass by them close enough to touch on either side, but his hands are
stretched forward, grasping for balance instead of pleasure. He doesn't wonder where he came from, where he's going. He doesn't ask who he is, or
why. Questions are a luxury, the province of those at a distance from the
periodic shock of rain. Gravity presses Adam so hard against reality that he
doesn't feel the points at which he touches it. A drowning man is not separated from the lust for air by a bridge of thought—he is one with it—and
my son, conceived and grown in an ethanol bath, lives each day in the act
of drowning. For him there is no shore.

UNDERSTANDING DETAILS

1. Why are Adam's birthdays difficult for Dorris?
2. What are some of the problems Adam was born with?
3. Why will Adam never reach his full potential?
4. In what ways did Dorris feel Adam's birthdays would be "oases of certainty"
   (paragraph 7)? How did the actual celebrations differ from these expectations?

Thinking Critically

◆ Explain this metaphor in your own words: "My son will forever travel through a moonless night with only the roar of wind for company."

READING CRITICALLY

5. Why does Dorris "doubly" mourn (paragraph 8) his son's birthdays? Explain your answer.
6. In what way was "the definition of the rest of [Dorris's] life" (paragraph 7) connected with his son's birthdays?
7. In what way is death like Santa Claus for Adam? Explain your answer.
8. What does Dorris mean when he says "Questions are a luxury" for his son (paragraph 19)?

DISCOVERING RHETORICAL STRATEGIES

9. At what points in this essay does Dorris either directly or indirectly analyze the causes of Adam's behavior? When does he study its effects (on either himself or his son)? Divide a piece of paper in half. List the causes of Adam's behavior on one side and the effects on the other. Record the paragraph references in each case. Then, discuss the pattern that emerges from your two lists. Does Dorris give more attention to the causes or the effects of Adam's behavior? Why do you think the author develops his essay around this particular emphasis?
10. Dorris uses several comparisons to help his readers understand what raising a child with fetal alcohol syndrome is like. Look, for example, at paragraph 19, in which he compares Adam's life to "a moonless night" and to "the act of drowning." Find two other vivid comparisons in this essay. What do all these comparisons add to the essay? What effect do they have on the essay as a whole?
11. What tone does Dorris establish in his essay? Describe it in three or four well-chosen words. How does he create this tone? What effect does this particular tone have on you as a reader?
12. What rhetorical strategies does Dorris use to support his cause/effect analysis? Give examples of each.

MAKING CONNECTIONS

13. Contrast Dorris's definition of "addiction" with the definitions in any of the following essays that discuss other addictive topics: Kimberly Wozencraft's "Notes from the Country Club," Jay Walljasper's "Our Schedules, Our Selves," and/or Stephen King's "Why We Crave Horror Movies." What specific substance is addictive in these essays? Which addiction do you think would be most difficult to recover from? Explain your answer.
14. Love and concern for a child is the principal topic of Dorris's essay, as it is in Lewis Sawaquat's "For My Indian Daughter," Russell Baker's "The Saturday Evening Post," Bill Cosby's "The Baffling Question," and Judith Wallerstein and Sandra Blakeslee's "Second Chances for Children of Divorce." If we were able to get all these authors together in a roundtable discussion about parent–child relationships, do you think they would agree on any of the issues? If so, what would these areas of agreement be for the essays you have read?
15. Birthdays are milestones in Dorris's essay, just as they are for Malcolm Cowley in "The View from 80." What are the principal differences in the ways each author celebrates these birthdays? Why do these differences exist?

IDEAS FOR DISCUSSION/WRITING

Preparing to Write

Write freely about the process of growing up and reaching your potential: What special problems did you experience while growing up? How did you deal with these problems? How did your parents deal with these problems? Do you feel you are heading toward your full potential, or have you already reached it? How do you plan to reach or maintain your potential? What experiences or people have disappointed you mainly because they were not what you expected? What were their shortcomings? Can these shortcomings be remedied? What effects do such shortcomings have on society as a whole?

Choosing a Topic

1. *Learning Online:* In his article, Dorris personalizes the effects of alcoholism on unborn children. Conduct an Internet search on other threats to infant and child health. To begin your search, you may want to visit the Centers for Disease Control and Prevention's Web site (www.cdc.gov). Choose a topic that interests you, and write an article for your campus's student health Web site. Describe the causes and effects of your chosen topic. Find a way to personalize your essay so that it will strike a nerve with your intended audience.

2. In a conversation with your mother, father, or another close relative, explain what problems you found most difficult as you were growing up, and speculate about the causes of those problems. In dialogue form, record the conversation as accurately as possible. Add an introduction, a conclusion, and an explanation of your discussion in order to mold the conversation into an essay.

3. In the last paragraph of his essay, Dorris implies that his son is slowly drowning in his birth-mother's alcohol abuse. This essay is Dorris's process of grieving about "what [his son] was missing, what he had already missed, what he would miss" (paragraph 8). In an essay of your own, explain something (a process, a person, an event, a relationship, or an activity) that disappointed you mainly because your expectations weren't met. What were the principal reasons for your disappointment? What were the effects of your disappointment? What could have changed the situation?

4. Many forms of addiction and abuse plague our society at present. In an essay written for your composition class, choose one of these problems and speculate on its primary causes and effects in society today. As often as possible, give specific examples to support your observations.

Before beginning your essay, you might want to consult the checklists on page 433.

SHERMAN ALEXIE   (1966–   )

The Joy of Reading and Writing: Superman and Me

A Spokane/Coeur d'Alene Indian, Sherman Alexie grew up on a reservation in Wellpinit, Washington, where he read voraciously as a child. Despite suffering seizures due to his hydrocephalic birth, he excelled in school, eventually attending Gonzaga University on a scholarship. Later, while a student at Washington State University, he stumbled into a poetry workshop and fell in love with writing, which became his life's work. His first two poetry collections, *The Business of Fancydancing* (1991) and *I Would Steal Horses* (1993), led to a collection of short stories, *The Lone Ranger and Tonto Fistfight in Heaven* (1993), which won several prestigious awards. After dabbling in stand-up comedy, Alexie wrote his first novel, *Reservation Blues* (1995), which was soon followed by *Indian Killer* (1996), described by the author as "a feel-good novel about interracial murder." His first movie, *Smoke Signals* (1999), won the Filmmaker's Trophy at the Sundance Film Festival. Additional publications include *Old Shirts and New Skins* (1993), *First Indian on the Moon* (1993), *Water Flowing Home* (1995), *The Summer of Black Widows* (1996), and *Ten Little Indians* (2003). Proud of his Native American heritage, Alexie has admitted that he isn't trying to speak for everybody: "I'm one individual heavily influenced by my tribe. And good art doesn't come out of assimilation—it comes out of tribalism." His advice for college writers is to "read, read, read. I always ask students, 'What's your favorite book? If you aren't carrying a book around with you, then you're doomed.'"

Preparing to Read

This essay was first published in a collection of essays on reading called *Most Wonderful Books*. In it, the author, Sherman Alexie, describes his love affair with books and explains their role in his success.

Exploring Experience: As you prepare to read this essay, think about how important reading is in your life: What types of books do you read? What percentage of your reading is for school? For pleasure? Do you enjoy reading? What does leisure reading do for you? How are reading and writing related for you? Are you a good writer? How do you account for your writing ability?

Learning Online: Sherman Alexie's enthusiasm about learning and writing has led him to become a very passionate spokesman for education. Using Google's search engine (www.google.com), click on the "Images" tab to conduct a picture search. Use the author's name, "Sherman Alexie," and view several pictures of Alexie addressing various audiences. He humorously describes himself as a "Banana Republic kind of Indian." Consider these pictures as you read his essay, and listen to the voice in his writing.

I learned to read with a *Superman* comic book. Simple enough, I suppose. 1
I cannot recall which particular Superman comic book I read, nor can I
remember which villain he fought in that issue. I cannot remember the
plot nor the means by which I obtained the comic book. What I can
remember is this: I was three years old, a Spokane Indian boy living with his
family on the Spokane Indian Reservation in eastern Washington state. We
were poor by most standards, but one of my parents usually managed to find
some minimum-wage job or another, which made us middle-class by reservation standards. I had a brother and three sisters. We lived on a combination
of irregular paychecks, hope, fear, and government surplus food. ◆

My father, who is one of the few Indians who went to Catholic school 2
on purpose, was an avid reader of westerns, spy thrillers, murder mysteries,
gangster epics, basketball player biographies, and anything else he could find.
He bought his books by the pound at Dutch's Pawn Shop, Goodwill, Salvation Army, and Value Village. When he had extra money, he bought new novels at supermarkets, convenience stores and hospital gift shops. Our house was
filled with books. They were stacked in crazy piles in the bathroom,
bedrooms, and living room. In a fit of unemployment-inspired creative
energy, my father built a set of bookshelves and soon filled them with a random assortment of books about the Kennedy assassination, Watergate, the
Vietnam War, and the entire twenty-three-book series of the Apache westerns. My father loved books, and since I loved my father with an aching
devotion, I decided to love books as well. ◆

I can remember picking up my father's books before I could read. The 3
words themselves were mostly foreign, but I still remember the exact moment
when I first understood, with a sudden clarity, the purpose of a paragraph.
I didn't have the vocabulary to say "paragraph," but I realized that a paragraph
was a fence that held words. ◆ The words inside a paragraph worked together
for a common purpose. They had some specific reason for being inside the
same fence. This knowledge delighted me. I began to think of everything in
terms of paragraphs. Our reservation was a small paragraph within the United
States. My family's house was a paragraph, distinct from the other paragraphs
of the LeBrets to the north, the Fords to our south, and the Tribal School to
the west. Inside our house, each family member existed as a separate paragraph

---

Thinking Critically

◆ What do "irregular paychecks, hope, fear, and government surplus food" tell us about
Alexie's childhood?

◆ How do you feel about books? What is your favorite novel? Your favorite comic book?
Your favorite poet? Your favorite play?

◆ Do you believe this is a good definition of a "paragraph"? Can you define a "sentence"
in a similar way?

but still had genetics and common experiences to link us. Now, using this logic, I can see my changed family as an essay of seven paragraphs: mother, father, older brother, the deceased sister, my younger twin sisters, and our adopted little brother.

At the same time I was seeing the world in paragraphs, I also picked up   4
the *Superman* comic book. Each panel, complete with picture, dialogue, and narrative, was a three-dimensional paragraph. In one panel, Superman breaks through a door. His suit is red, blue, and yellow. The brown door shatters into many pieces. I look at the narrative above the picture. I cannot read the words, but I assume it tells me that "Superman is breaking down the door." Aloud, I pretend to read the words and say, "Superman is breaking down the door." Words, dialogue, also float out of Superman's mouth. Because he is breaking down the door, I assume he says, "I am breaking down the door." Once again, I pretend to read the words and say aloud, "I am breaking down the door." In this way, I learned to read.

This might be an interesting story all by itself. A little Indian boy teaches   5
himself to read at an early age and advances quickly. He reads *Grapes of Wrath* in kindergarten when other children are struggling through Dick and Jane. If he'd been anything but an Indian boy living on the reservation, he might have been called a prodigy. But he is an Indian boy living on the reservation and is simply an oddity. ❹ He grows into a man who often speaks of his childhood in the third-person, as if it will somehow dull the pain and make him sound more modest about his talents.

A smart Indian is a dangerous person, widely feared and ridiculed by   6
Indians and non-Indians alike. I fought with my classmates on a daily basis. They wanted me to stay quiet when the non-Indian teacher asked for answers, for volunteers, for help. We were Indian children who were expected to be stupid. Most lived up to those expectations inside the classroom but subverted them on the outside. They struggled with basic reading in school but could remember how to sing a few dozen powwow songs. They were monosyllabic in front of their non-Indian teachers but could tell complicated stories and jokes at the dinner table. They submissively ducked their heads when confronted by a non-Indian adult but would slug it out with the Indian bully who was ten years older. As Indian children, we were expected to fail in the non-Indian world. Those who failed were ceremonially accepted by other Indians and appropriately pitied by non-Indians.

I refused to fail. I was smart. I was arrogant. I was lucky. I read books late   7
into the night, until I could barely keep my eyes open. I read books at recess,

---

Thinking Critically

❹ What is the difference between a "prodigy" and an "oddity" in the context of the reservation?

then during lunch, and in the few minutes left after I had finished my classroom assignments. I read books in the car when my family traveled to powwows or basketball games. In shopping malls, I ran to the bookstores and read bits and pieces of as many books as I could. I read the books my father brought home from the pawnshops and secondhand. I read the books I borrowed from the library. I read the backs of cereal boxes. I read the newspaper. I read the bulletins posted on the walls of the school, the clinic, the tribal offices, the post office. I read junk mail. I read auto-repair manuals. I read magazines. I read anything that had words and paragraphs. I read with equal parts joy and desperation. I loved those books, but I also knew that love had only one purpose. I was trying to save my life. 5

Despite all the books I read, I am still surprised I became a writer. I was   8 going to be a pediatrician. These days, I write novels, short stories, and poems. I visit schools and teach creative writing to Indian kids. In all my years in the reservation school system, I was never taught how to write poetry, short stories, or novels. I was certainly never taught that Indians wrote poetry, short stories, and novels. Writing was something beyond Indians. I cannot recall a single time that a guest teacher visited the reservation. There must have been visiting teachers. Who were they? Where are they now? Do they exist? I visit the schools as often as possible. The Indian kids crowd the classroom. Many are writing their own poems, short stories, and novels. They have read my books. They have read many other books. They look at me with bright eyes and arrogant wonder. They are trying to save their lives. Then there are the sullen and already defeated Indian kids who sit in the back rows and ignore me with theatrical precision. The pages of their notebooks are empty. They carry neither pencil nor pen. They stare out the window. They refuse and resist. "Books," I say to them. "Books," I say. I throw my weight against their locked doors. 6 The door holds. I am smart. I am arrogant. I am lucky. I am trying to save our lives.

UNDERSTANDING DETAILS

1. How did Alexie learn to read? Why was it important to him?
2. How were life and paragraphs related for Alexie?
3. In what ways is the author unique in his own cultural environment?
4. How are reading and writing related for the author?

Thinking Critically

5 Why does the author think that books will save his life? In what ways do you agree with him? In what ways do you disagree?

6 In what sense does Alexie throw his weight against the students' "locked doors"? Why does he do this?

READING CRITICALLY

5. Why is a smart Indian "a dangerous person" (paragraph 6)? Explain your answer in detail.
6. What did reading have to do with the author's success in life?
7. Why did many Indian children fail in the classroom but succeed on the streets?
8. In what ways can books save lives?

DISCOVERING RHETORICAL STRATEGIES

9. Explain the title of this essay.
10. Alexie starts this essay with background information about his family. Is this an effective beginning? Why or why not?
11. What rhetorical modes does Alexie use to tell his story?
12. What is the main message Alexie is trying to communicate? Does he get his message across effectively? Explain your answer.

MAKING CONNECTIONS

13. Compare and contrast Alexie's love of books with that expressed by Malcolm X in "Learning to Read." Which author's life has been most changed by the act of reading? Why do you think this is so?
14. Which of the following authors overcame the most discrimination and hardship in his or her life: Alexie, Sandra Cisneros ("Only daughter"), Harold Krents ("Darkness at Noon"), Sucheng Chan ("You're Short, Besides!"), and/or Alice Walker ("Beauty: When the Other Dancer Is the Self")?
15. How do Alexie, Stephen King ("Why We Crave Horror Movies"), Michael Dorris ("The Broken Cord"), and/or Mary Roach ("Meet the Bickersons") use the cause/effect rhetorical mode differently?

IDEAS FOR DISCUSSION/WRITING

Preparing to Write

Write freely about the role of reading and writing in your life: How do they help you? Do they hinder you in any way? How are they related for you? Which one do you enjoy more? Which one is your stronger suit? Why do you think this is the case? In your opinion, can someone be a good writer, but not a good reader? Can someone be a good reader, but not a good writer? Explain your reasoning.

Choosing a Topic

1. *Learning Online:* In his essay, Alexie explains that when he was a child Indian children were not expected to be smart. No matter what other people said, however, he continued to pursue learning because he truly loved it. Think of an important quality about yourself that would surprise other people. It may be a passion you care deeply about, a secret talent you are especially proud of, or even a goal you have for the future. Write a short essay about this "unexpected

characteristic" that you could post on your MySpace profile or your Facebook page.

2. Compose an autobiography of your memories about reading, starting with your earliest recollections. Retrace your experiences with reading up to the present, including the kinds of books you have read, the circumstances surrounding your reading experiences, the people who read to you, the places where you read, your feelings about reading, and your current reading habits.

3. Compose a writing autobiography of your memories about writing, starting with your earliest recollections about writing. Retrace your experiences with writing up to the present, including the types of writing you do, the circumstances surrounding your writing experiences, the people or companies you write to, the places where you write, your feelings about writing, and your current writing habits.

4. Analyze the relationship between reading and writing, using your experience and the stories of others to support your main points.

Before beginning your essay, you might want to consult the checklists on page 433.

Meet the Bickersons

A native of Hanover, New Hampshire, Mary Roach received her B.A. in Psychology from Wesleyan University, then worked as a copy editor and a public relations consultant for the San Francisco Zoo. Following five years in the business world, she began her career as a freelance writer after deciding that "it was a lot easier to write the stuff in the first place than to clean it up after someone else had written it." She has been a contributor for many years to the "Diversions" section of the *San Francisco Examiner Sunday Magazine,* focusing on such quirky, interesting topics as drive-in movies and old black-and-white photo booths. She is currently a contributing editor for such well-known periodicals as *Health, Discover, Wired, Muse* (the Smithsonian Museum's children's magazine), and *SALON.com* (an online journal). Her most recent book is *Stiff: The Curious Lives of Human Cadavers* (2003). Roach now lives in San Francisco, where her hobbies include bird watching, reading, and traveling. Asked to give advice to students using *The Prose Reader,* she claims, "People think writing is harder than it is. They tie themselves up in knots over it. Good writing is really just talking on paper. If it were difficult to do, I would not be that successful at it."

Preparing to Read

The following humorous essay, originally published in *Health* magazine, explains different strategies for arguing among couples. The title "Meet the Bickersons" is drawn from an extremely popular American radio comedy (1946–1951) starring Don Ameche and Frances Langford, which was later made into a TV series of the same name.

Exploring Experience: Before you read this essay, think for a moment about how important arguing fairly is to you: Do you argue fairly? Do you expect your partner to argue fairly? What are the qualities of a fair argument? Do you argue with other people? Are you able to control your temper? Do you feel better after you argue? Why or why not? When is arguing most worthwhile? When is it never worthwhile? Do you have any special ground rules for arguing with the people you love?

Learning Online: Visit About.com (www.about.com), and type "Why do couples fight?" into the search field. Read a short article about why couples fight. Consider the format and content of this article as you read Mary Roach's essay. Why is Roach's presentation more effective?

P sychologists have long said it's possible to predict whether a couple will   1
stay happily married simply by looking at how they fight. This did
not bode well for yours truly, who got married not too long ago.
Pretty much all I'd learned about spousal arguing came from *The Newlywed
Game,* which taught us 1) that the proper form of conflict resolution is to
hit your partner over the head with a large piece of poster board and 2) that
most problems can be resolved with the acquisition of a brand-new washer
and dryer or a gift pack of Turtle Wax.

I've been told I'm defensive—"like a cornered mongoose" were the exact   2
words. I've also been criticized for being sarcastic, overreacting, and crying
too easily. I don't deny these things (though if you were to accuse me of
them in the heat of battle, you can be sure I would—vehemently, and with
pointy little teeth bared).

I had a boyfriend who tried to change me. He asked me to use a therapy   3
technique called "active listening," a mainstay of many modern marriage
counselors. ◆ It's supposed to make you a more fair, less combative arguer.
I (and here's something you couldn't see coming) objected to this, stating that
I was already an active listener. My ex countered that deep sighs, nostril
flares, pacing, and storming from the room did not qualify. Active listening
means focusing carefully on what your partner is saying, as though there
were going to be a test, because, in fact, there is. You are required to paraphrase your beloved's misguided rantings—sorry, feelings—beginning with
the phrase "What I hear you saying is. . . ."

I agreed to try it. He went first. Minutes passed. Fortunately, we were on   4
the phone at the time, which allowed me to scribble notes. He finished and
fell silent.

"What I hear you saying," I began, "is that you think I'm defensive, and I don't   5
allow you to feel what you're feeling and that makes you incredibly . . . trun-
cated, wait, flat-footed?"

"Frustrated."   6

"Of course."   7

"You're cheating," he said. "You're writing things down."   8

"Am not."   9

Nothing—not counseling, not even Turtle Wax—was going to save that   10
relationship.

With Ed, I was determined to do things right and asked a friend with a   11
degree in counseling for advice. She encouraged me to use "I" statements
because "you" statements put people on the defensive. For instance, one does
not say to one's beloved, "You never do the dishes, you self-centered pea

---

Thinking Critically

◆ What do you think the term "active listening" means in this context?

brain." One says, "I feel angry and taken advantage of when the people I love leave their dishes for me, especially when it was those people who dirtied them in the first place and ate the leftovers they knew darn well I was planning to have for lunch." ❷

Another suggested technique was validation, in which each partner makes an effort to endorse the other's feelings: "I can see why you'd be upset with my failing to wash one small dish and eating an eighth of a taco. I would be, too, if I were an oversensitive, petty person who only focuses on the negative."

A while back I put all these techniques to work. We were driving, and I had failed to notice a stop sign, which even the most vigilant driver will do from time to time. Am I right? Ed did not fail to notice the stop sign, as was evinced by his slamming of the imaginary brakes on his side of the car. "When you constantly remark upon my driving irregularities," I began, "I feel scrutinized and inadequate, and by the way, who was it that nearly got us killed by turning into traffic outside Costco?"

Ed was unperturbed by the Costco barb. What got him was the I-feel-blah-dee-blah business. "Why don't you just get mad and call me a back-seat driver, and that'd be that?"

Later that evening I tried to explain what I'd learned about "you" statements and active listening and validating feelings. Ed listened carefully. Then he took my hand in his. "When you talk about things like this, I feel, let me see, like throwing up. How was that?"

Shortly after, Ed left a newspaper clipping on my desk. It described a university study in which 130 newlywed pairs were videotaped arguing and then tracked for six years. It turns out the couples who stayed married had seldom used techniques like active listening and validation. The researcher was "shocked" to find that the happy couples fought like normal people— getting angry, clearing the air, and making up. (Their spats, however, were tinged with soothing and humor.)

This was one instance in which I was glad to be proved wrong. So thrilled was I at the prospect of never again having to begin a sentence with "What I hear you saying is" that I made a vow on the spot that the next time Ed got mad at me, I would not get defensive.

It happened on a Saturday afternoon. I had thrown away a set of circa-1970 stereo speakers that Ed had wanted to keep because they might come in handy for taking up space in the basement for the next ten years. It didn't go quite the way I'd envisioned. I heard myself lambasting Ed for having gone through the garbage, checking up on what I'd junked. "You're scrutinizing me!"

Thinking Critically

❷ What is the difference between an "I" statement and a "You" statement? Which do you use most frequently when you're arguing with a loved one? Why?

Ed looked flabbergasted. "You toss things without even asking!"   19

The bell rang, and we withdrew to our corners. ❸ Around dinnertime, I   20
appeared in the kitchen with the speakers, dusted and polished. Ed, in turn,
promised not to supervise my spring cleaning. He asked me to let him know
when I caught him checking over something I'd done. "I'm not even aware
of it. So please tell me." He smiled sweetly. "And then I'll deny it."

UNDERSTANDING DETAILS

1. What is "active listening" (paragraph 3)? What verbal technique did Roach
   learn as an active listener?
2. Explain the technique of "validation" in your own words.
3. Does Roach think she is too defensive? What animal did someone compare
   her defensiveness to?
4. What did a university study learn about the argumentative habits of 130 newlywed couples? How did Roach feel about the findings of this study?

READING CRITICALLY

5. According to psychologists, how does the way couples fight affect the survival
   of their marriages?
6. Why was Roach trying different strategies for getting along with her partner?
7. Who is Ed? Why was Roach trying so hard to make her relationship with Ed
   work?
8. What does Roach mean when she says about the first boyfriend, "Nothing—
   not counseling, not even Turtle Wax—was going to save that relationship" (paragraph 10)?

DISCOVERING RHETORICAL STRATEGIES

9. List the causes and effects that this essay studies.
10. What is the general mood of Roach's essay?
11. Roach begins her essay with some references to the *Newlywed Game*. What do
    the poster board, a washer and dryer, and Turtle Wax have to do with that game?
    Do you think this is an effective way to start her essay? Explain your answer.
12. What other rhetorical strategies support this cause/effect essay? Give examples
    of each.

MAKING CONNECTIONS

13. Compare and contrast Roach's conclusions about successful communication
    within a relationship with similar advice provided in Wallerstein and Blakeslee's

---

Thinking Critically

❸ What metaphor for fighting is the author using here? How effective is this comparison?

"Second Chances for Children of Divorce" and/or Mary Pipher's "Beliefs About Families."

14. Analyze Roach's prescription for dealing with anger in light of the following essays: Lewis Sawaquat's "For My Indian Daughter," Brent Staples's "A Brother's Murder," and/or Michael Dorris's "The Broken Cord."

15. Compare Roach's use of humor in her essay to similar anecdotes in Russell Baker's "The Saturday Evening Post," Joel Stein's "You're Not My Friend," and/or Bill Cosby's "The Baffling Question."

IDEAS FOR DISCUSSION/WRITING

Preparing to Write

Write freely about your views on arguing: Do you know how to argue? Have you ever been sorry for anything you said while you were arguing? Do you argue with your parents differently than you argue with your friends? With your boyfriend/girlfriend/spouse? Why do you argue? What do you try to accomplish when you argue? Does arguing usually make you feel better or worse? Is it difficult to make up after you argue? How do you make up?

Choosing a Topic

1. *Learning Online:* What are some other techniques, besides fair fighting, necessary for maintaining healthy relationships? Choose an issue such as compromise, honesty, or communication, and reflect on your experience with this topic. Then write an essay in which you explore the cause and effect of positive—and negative—uses of this technique. Roach supports her personal observations with case studies. Strengthen your essay by using case studies and statistics that you have found online.

2. Your college newspaper is accepting essays on your interests in life. Write an essay for the newspaper explaining in detail your most passionate interest. Cover both the causes and effects of this interest. (This interest does not have to be related to school matters.)

3. Your college counselor/adviser wants to know if you consider yourself emotionally healthy. In a detailed essay written for this counselor, who is writing a letter of recommendation for you, explain why you are or are not in good emotional health. What events, attitudes, or activities have played a part in developing your mental health?

4. Americans seem to be obsessed with their health these days. Why do you think this is so? How did this obsession start? Explain your reasoning in an essay to your peers.

Before beginning your essay, you might want to consult the checklists on page 433.

ALICE WALKER   (1944–   )

Beauty: When the Other Dancer Is the Self

Born in Eatonton, Georgia, and educated at Spelman College and Sarah Lawrence College, Alice Walker is best known for her Pulitzer Prize–winning novel *The Color Purple* (1983), which was later made into an immensely popular movie of the same title. The book details a young African-American woman's search for self-identity within a world contaminated by racial prejudice and family crisis. Most of Walker's other novels and collections of short stories echo the same theme, and most share the "sense of affirmation" featured in *The Color Purple* that overcomes the anger and social indignity suffered by so many of her characters. The author's many other publications include *In Love and Trouble: Stories of Black Women* (1973), *Meridian* (1976), *You Can't Keep a Good Woman Down* (1981), *In Search of Our Mothers' Gardens* (1983), *Living by the Word* (1988), *To Hell with Dying* (1988), *The Temple of My Familiar* (1989), *Possessing the Secret of Joy* (1992), *Everyday Use* (1994), *Alice Walker Banned* (1996), *By the Light of My Father's Smile* (1998), *The Way Forward Is with a Broken Heart* (2000), *Absolute Trust in the Goodness of the Earth: New Poems* (2003), and *Now Is the Time to Open Your Heart* (2004). Walker—who has been a professor and writer-in-residence at Wellesley College, the University of Massachusetts, the University of California at Berkeley, and Brandeis University—currently lives in Mendocino, California. To writers, she gives the following advice: "I'm not sure a bad person can write a good book. If art doesn't make us better, then what on earth is it for?"

Preparing to Read

The following essay, from *In Search of Our Mothers' Gardens,* focuses on young Alice Walker's reaction to being blinded in one eye as a result of an accident with a BB gun.

Exploring Experience: As you begin to read this essay, take a few minutes to consider the role of physical appearance in our lives: Do you find that you often judge people based on their physical appearance? Do you feel that people judge you based on your appearance? What other characteristics play a part in your judgment of others? How important are good looks to you? Why do they carry this importance for you? What specific people affect the way you feel about yourself?

Learning Online: In her essay, Alice Walker describes concerns about her own appearance. Look for pictures of Walker online: Do a Google search, and use *Alice Walker* as your search term. Consider your opinions of her appearance as you read her essay.

It is a bright summer day in 1947. My father, a fat, funny man with
beautiful eyes and a subversive wit, is trying to decide which of his eight
children he will take with him to the county fair. My mother, of course,
will not go. She is knocked out from getting most of us ready: I hold my neck
stiff against the pressure of her knuckles as she hastily completes the braid-
ing and then beribboning of my hair.

My father is the driver for the rich old white lady up the road. Her name   2
is Miss Mey. She owns all the land for miles around, as well as the house in
which we live. All I remember about her is that she once offered to pay my
mother thirty-five cents for cleaning her house, raking up piles of her mag-
nolia leaves, and washing her family's clothes, and that my mother—she of
no money, eight children, and a chronic earache—refused it. But I do not
think of this in 1947. I am two and a half years old. I want to go everywhere
my daddy goes. I am excited at the prospect of riding in a car. Someone has
told me fairs are fun. That there is room in the car for only three of us
doesn't faze me at all. Whirling happily in my starchy frock, showing off my
biscuit-polished patent-leather shoes and lavender socks, tossing my head in
a way that makes my ribbons bounce, I stand, hands on hips, before my
father. "Take me, Daddy," I say with assurance; "I'm the prettiest!" ❶

Later, it does not surprise me to find myself in Miss Mey's shiny black car,   3
sharing the back seat with the other lucky ones. Does not surprise me that
I thoroughly enjoy the fair. At home that night I tell the unlucky ones all I
can remember about the merry-go-round, the man who eats live chickens,
and the teddy bears, until they say: that's enough, baby Alice. Shut up now,
and go to sleep.

It is Easter Sunday, 1950. I am dressed in a green, flocked, scalloped-hem   4
dress (handmade by my adoring sister, Ruth) that has its own smooth satin
petticoat and tiny hot-pink roses tucked into each scallop. My shoes, new
T-strap patent leather, again highly biscuit-polished. I am six years old and
have learned one of the longest Easter speeches to be heard that day, totally
unlike the speech I said when I was two: "Easter lilies/pure and white/ blos-
som in/the morning light." When I rise to give my speech I do so on a great
wave of love and pride and expectation. People in the church stop rustling
their new crinolines. They seem to hold their breath. I can tell they admire
my dress, but it is my spirit, bordering on sassiness (womanishness), they
secretly applaud. ❷

Thinking Critically

❶ What does the emphasis on clothing here and elsewhere in the essay tell us about the
author's childhood memories?

❷ What is the relationship between "sassiness" and "womanishness"? Why does the church
congregation applaud this spirit?

"That girl's a little *mess*," they whisper to each other, pleased.   5

Naturally I say my speech without stammer or pause, unlike those who   6
stutter, stammer, or, worst of all, forget. This is before the word "beautiful"
exists in people's vocabulary, but "Oh, isn't she the *cutest* thing!" frequently
floats my way. "And got so much sense!" they gratefully add . . . for which
thoughtful addition I thank them to this day.

It was great fun being cute. But then, one day, it ended. ❸   7

I am eight years old and a tomboy. I have a cowboy hat, cowboy boots,   8
checkered shirt and pants, all red. My playmates are my brothers, two and four
years older than I. Their colors are black and green, the only difference in the
way we are dressed. On Saturday nights we all go to the picture show, even
my mother; Westerns are her favorite kind of movie. Back home, "on the
ranch," we pretend we are Tom Mix, Hopalong Cassidy, Lash LaRue (we've
even named one of our dogs Lash LaRue); we chase each other for hours
rustling cattle, being outlaws, delivering damsels from distress. Then my parents decide to buy my brothers guns. These are not "real" guns. They shoot
"BBs," copper pellets my brothers say will kill birds. Because I am a girl, I do
not get a gun. Instantly I am relegated to the position of Indian. Now there
appears a great distance between us. They shoot and shoot at everything with
their new guns. I try to keep up with my bow and arrows.

One day while I am standing on top of our makeshift "garage"—pieces   9
of tin nailed across some poles—holding my bow and arrow and looking out
toward the fields, I feel an incredible blow in my right eye. I look down just
in time to see my brother lower his gun.

Both brothers rush to my side. My eye stings, and I cover it with my hand.   10
"If you tell," they say, "we will get a whipping. You don't want that to happen,
do you?" I do not. "Here is a piece of wire," says the older brother, picking it up
from the roof; "say you stepped on one end of it and the other flew up and hit
you." The pain is beginning to start. "Yes," I say. "Yes, I will say that is what happened." If I do not say this is what happened, I know my brothers will find ways
to make me wish I had. But now I will say anything that gets me to my mother.

Confronted by our parents we stick to the lie agreed upon. They place me   11
on a bench on the porch, and I close my left eye while they examine the
right. There is a tree growing from underneath the porch that climbs past the
railing to the roof. It is the last thing my right eye sees. ❹ I watch as its trunk,
its branches, and then its leaves are blotted out by the rising blood.

Thinking Critically

❸ Why does Walker use italics here and elsewhere? At which moments in the essay does she
use them?

❹ Why is it significant that a tree is the last thing the author sees with her injured right eye?

I am in shock. First there is intense fever, which my father tries to break   12
using lily leaves bound around my head. Then there are chills: my mother tries
to get me to eat soup. Eventually, I do not know how, my parents learn what
has happened. A week after the "accident" they take me to see a doctor.
"Why did you wait so long to come?" he asks, looking into my eye and
shaking his head. "Eyes are sympathetic," he says. "If one is blind, the other
will likely become blind too."

This comment of the doctor's terrifies me. But it is really how I look that   13
bothers me most. Where the BB pellet struck there is a glob of whitish scar
tissue, a hideous cataract, on my eye. Now when I stare at people—a favorite
pastime, up to now—they will stare back. Not at the "cute" little girl, but at
her scar. For six years I do not stare at anyone, because I do not raise my head.

Years later, in the throes of a mid-life crisis, I ask my mother and sister whether   14
I changed after the "accident." "No," they say, puzzled. "What do you mean?"

What do I mean?   15

I am eight and, for the first time, doing poorly in school, where I have been   16
something of a whiz since I was four. ⑤ We have just moved to the place
where the "accident" occurred. We do not know any of the people around
us because this is a different county. The only time I see the friends I knew
is when we go back to our old church. The new school is the former state
penitentiary. It is a large stone building, cold and drafty, crammed to over-
flowing with boisterous, ill-disciplined children. On the third floor there is
a huge circular imprint of some partition that has been torn out.

"What used to be here?" I ask a sullen girl next to me on our way past it   17
to lunch.

"The electric chair," says she. ⑥   18

At night I have nightmares about the electric chair and about all the peo-   19
ple reputedly "fried" in it. I am afraid of the school, where all the students
seem to be budding criminals.

"What's the matter with your eye?" they ask, critically.   20

When I don't answer (I cannot decide whether it was an "accident" or   21
not), they shove me, insist on a fight.

My brother, the one who created the story about the wire, comes to my   22
rescue. But then brags so much about "protecting" me, I become sick.

After months of torture at the school, my parents decide to send me back   23
to our old community, to my old school. I live with my grandparents and the

---

Thinking Critically

⑤ How does time pass in the essay? Why does the author choose these particular moments
to help tell her story?

⑥ How did the former presence of an electric chair help characterize Walker's new school?

teacher they board. But there is no room for Phoebe, my cat. By the time my grandparents decide there *is* room, and I ask for my cat, she cannot be found. Miss Yarborough, the boarding teacher, takes me under her wing and begins to teach me to play the piano. But soon she marries an African—a "prince," she says—and is whisked away to his continent.

At my old school there is at least one teacher who loves me. She is the 24 teacher who "knew me before I was born" and bought my first baby clothes. It is she who makes life bearable. It is her presence that finally helps me turn on the one child at the school who continually calls me "one-eyed bitch." One day I simply grab him by his coat and beat him until I am satisfied. It is my teacher who tells me my mother is ill.

My mother is lying in bed in the middle of the day, something I have never 25 seen. She is in too much pain to speak. She has an abscess in her ear. I stand looking down on her, knowing that if she dies, I cannot live. She is being treated with warm oils and hot bricks held against her cheek. Finally a doctor comes. But I must go back to my grandparents' house. The weeks pass but I am hardly aware of it. All I know is that my mother might die, my father is not so jolly, my brothers still have their guns, and I am the one sent away from home.

"You did not change," they say. 26

Did I imagine the anguish of never looking up? 27

I am twelve. When relatives come to visit I hide in my room. My cousin 28 Brenda, just my age, whose father works in the post office and whose mother is a nurse, comes to find me. "Hello," she says. And then she asks, looking at my recent school picture, which I did not want taken, and on which the "glob," as I think of it, is clearly visible, "You still can't see out of that eye?"

"No," I say, and flop back on the bed over my book. 29

That night, as I do almost every night, I abuse my eye. I rant and rave at 30 it, in front of the mirror. I plead with it to clear up before morning. I tell it I hate and despise it. I do not pray for sight. I pray for beauty. 🔶

"You did not change," they say. 31

I am fourteen and baby-sitting for my brother Bill, who lives in Boston. 32 He is my favorite brother, and there is a strong bond between us. Understanding my feelings of shame and ugliness he and his wife take me to a local hospital, where the "glob" is removed by a doctor named O. Henry. There is still a small bluish crater where the scar tissue was, but the ugly white stuff is gone. Almost immediately I become a different person from the girl who

---

Thinking Critically

🔶 Why does the author pray every night for beauty rather than sight? Which is more important to her? Why?

does not raise her head. **8** Or so I think. Now that I've raised my head I win the boyfriend of my dreams. Now that I've raised my head I have plenty of friends. Now that I've raised my head classwork comes from my lips as faultlessly as Easter speeches did, and I leave high school as valedictorian, most popular student, and *queen,* hardly believing my luck. Ironically, the girl who was voted most beautiful in our class (and was) was later shot twice through the chest by a male companion, using a "real" gun, while she was pregnant. But that's another story in itself. Or is it?

"You did not change," they say.   33

It is now thirty years since the "accident." A beautiful journalist comes to   34
visit and to interview me. She is going to write a cover story for her magazine that focuses on my latest book. "Decide how you want to look on the cover," she says. "Glamorous, or whatever."

Never mind "glamorous," it is the "whatever" that I hear. Suddenly all I   35
can think of is whether I will get enough sleep the night before the photography session: if I don't, my eye will be tired and wander, as blind eyes will.

At night in bed with my lover I think up reasons why I should not appear   36
on the cover of a magazine. "My meanest critics will say I've sold out," I say. "My family will now realize I write scandalous books."

"But what's the real reason you don't want to do this?" **9** he asks.   37

"Because in all probability," I say in a rush, "my eye won't be straight."   38

"It will be straight enough," he says. Then, "Besides, I thought you'd made   39
your peace with that."

And I suddenly remember that I have.   40

I remember: 41

I am talking to my brother Jimmy, asking if he remembers anything   42
unusual about the day I was shot. He does not know I consider that day the last time my father, with his sweet home remedy of cool lily leaves, chose me, and that I suffered and raged inside because of this. "Well," he says, "all I remember is standing by the side of the highway with Daddy, trying to flag down a car. A white man stopped, but when Daddy said he needed somebody to take his little girl to the doctor, he drove off."

I remember: 43

I am in the desert for the first time. I fall totally in love with it. I am so over-   44
whelmed by its beauty, I confront for the first time, consciously, the meaning

---

Thinking Critically

8 In what ways does Walker change when the scar tissue is removed from her eye?

9 Why doesn't the author want to be photographed?

of the doctor's words years ago: "Eyes are sympathetic. If one is blind, the other will likely become blind too." I realize I have dashed about the world madly, looking at this, looking at that, storing up images against the fading of the light. *But I might have missed seeing the desert!* The shock of that possibility—and gratitude for over twenty-five years of sight—sends me literally to my knees. Poem after poem comes—which is perhaps how poets pray. ⑩

ON SIGHT

I am so thankful I have seen
The Desert
And the creatures in the desert
And the desert Itself.
The desert has its own moon
Which I have seen
With my own eye.
There is no flag on it.

Trees of the desert have arms
All of which are always up
That is because the moon is up
The sun is up
Also the sky
The stars
Clouds
None with flags.

If there were flags, I doubt
the trees would point.
Would you?

But mostly, I remember this: 45

I am twenty-seven, and my baby daughter is almost three. Since her birth 46
I have worried about her discovery that her mother's eyes are different from other people's. Will she be embarrassed? I think. What will she say? Every day she watches a television program called *Big Blue Marble.* It begins with a picture of the earth as it appears from the moon. It is bluish, a little battered-looking, but full of light, with whitish clouds swirling around it. Every time I see it I weep with love, as if it is a picture of Grandma's house. One day when I am putting Rebecca down for her nap, she suddenly focuses on my eye. Something inside me cringes, gets ready to try to protect myself. All children are cruel about physical differences, I know from experience, and that they don't always mean to be is another matter. I assume Rebecca will be the same.

But no-o-o-o. She studies my face intently as we stand, her inside and me 47
outside her crib. She even holds my face maternally between her dimpled

---

Thinking Critically

⑩ What do you think Walker means when she says that writing poems is "how poets pray"?

little hands. Then, looking every bit as serious and lawyerlike as her father, she says, as if it may just possibly have slipped my attention: "Mommy, there's a *world* in your eye." (As in, "Don't be alarmed, or do anything crazy.") And then, gently, but with great interest: "Mommy, where did you *get* that world in your eye?"

For the most part, the pain left then. (So what, if my brothers grew up to   48
buy even more powerful pellet guns for their sons and to carry real guns themselves. So what, if a young "Morehouse man" once nearly fell off the steps of Trevor Arnett Library because he thought my eyes were blue.) Crying and laughing I ran to the bathroom, while Rebecca mumbled and sang herself off to sleep. Yes indeed, I realized, looking into the mirror. There *was* a world in my eye. And I saw that it was possible to love it: that in fact, for all it had taught me of shame and anger and inner vision, I *did* love it. **11** Even to see it drifting out of orbit in boredom, or rolling up out of fatigue, not to mention floating back at attention in excitement (bearing witness, a friend has called it), deeply suitable to my personality, and even characteristic of me.

That night I dream I am dancing to Stevie Wonder's song "Always" (the   49
name of the song is really "As," but I hear it as "Always"). As I dance, whirling and joyous, happier than I've ever been in my life, another bright-faced dancer joins me. We dance and kiss each other and hold each other through the night. The other dancer has obviously come through all right, as I have done. **12** She is beautiful, whole and free. And she is also me.

UNDERSTANDING DETAILS

1. What time frame in the author's life does this essay cover?
2. What is the focal point of the essay? What activities lead up to this "accident"? What are the long-term effects of this "accident"?
3. In what ways does Walker think her life changed after she was shot in the eye?
4. Describe the author's relationship with her brothers, before and after the accident.

READING CRITICALLY

5. Why is Walker devastated by the scar tissue in her eye? Which bothers her more, the scar tissue or the blindness? Explain your answer.
6. Which of the people introduced in the essay (other than her family members) mean the most to her? List them in order of importance. Then explain why each is important in this cause/effect essay.

Thinking Critically

11 What event enables Walker to begin loving her eye?

12 Who is "the other dancer"? How is she related to the author?

7. List the changes that Walker mentions in her actions and personality. Then analyze these changes by discussing their causes and effects.

8. Why is Rebecca's declaration "Mommy, there's a *world* in your eye" (paragraph 47) so important to the author? What changes in Walker result from this particular encounter with her daughter?

DISCOVERING RHETORICAL STRATEGIES

9. Why do you think Walker wrote this essay? What was she trying to accomplish by writing it?

10. How does Walker use blank spaces between her paragraphs? In what ways does this spacing contribute to her essay?

11. Why does Walker put the sentences "It was great fun being cute. But then, one day, it ended" (paragraph 7) by themselves in italics?

12. Explain the emotional ups and downs in the essay. How does Walker's language change in each case?

MAKING CONNECTIONS

13. Walker's essay centers on a single momentous event, the blinding of her right eye, that affected her life from the instant it happened. Similarly significant events shape the lives of the principal characters in Ray Bradbury's "Summer Rituals," Sandra Cisneros's "Only daughter," and Michael Dorris's "The Broken Cord." Compare and contrast the extent to which each of these events influenced the characters in the essays you read.

14. One of Walker's primary themes involves the eventual acceptance of who we are in life. Find the same theme in Malcolm Cowley's "The View from 80," Lewis Sawaquat's "For My Indian Daughter," and/or Richard Rodriguez's "Hunger of Memory"; then decide which of these authors seems most content with his or her own self-image. How did you come to this conclusion?

15. The relationship between Walker's original injury and the shyness and insecurity that resulted from it imply a negative cause/effect connection. Find an essay in this chapter of the book that implies a positive connection between a cause and its effect. How are the two essays different? How are they the same?

IDEAS FOR DISCUSSION/WRITING

Preparing to Write

Write freely about your self-esteem and the role of self-esteem in the life of college students: How important is self-esteem to you personally? To your academic performance? What affects your self-esteem most? Why do these events affect you? Do they help or hinder your self-esteem? What elements affect the self-esteem of other students you know? Of friends of yours? Of relatives? What effects have you observed in college students that result from low self-esteem? In friends? In relatives? How do you control your self-esteem? Do you recommend this method to others?

Choosing a Topic

1. *Learning Online:* Despite her concerns about the wound in her eye, photographs of Alice Walker are published in several places on the Internet. (See the results of your Internet search before you read this essay.) How do you feel about having your picture published on the Internet? Do you have any insecurities about your appearance? Write an essay in which you explore these feelings. With Walker's essay as a model, use vivid description in your analysis of the causes of these insecurities and their effects on other aspects of your life.

2. Low self-esteem can cause a number of serious problems in different aspects of college students' lives. Conduct a study of the causes and effects of low self-esteem in the lives of several students at your school. Write an essay for the college community explaining these causes and effects.

3. Your campus newspaper is printing a special issue highlighting the psychological health of different generations of college students. Interview some people who represent a generation other than your own. Then characterize the students in this generation for the newspaper. In essay form, introduce the features you have discovered, and then discuss their causes and effects.

4. Some people believe self-esteem is a result of peer groups; others say that it is a result of one's family environment. What do you think? *Time* magazine is soliciting student reactions on this issue and has asked for your opinion. Where do you stand on this question? Give specific examples that support your opinion. Respond in essay form.

Before beginning your essay, you might want to consult the checklists on page 433.

Chapter Writing Assignments

Practicing Cause/Effect

1. Think about a time in your life when you had definite, clear expectations of an event or experience. Where did these expectations come from? Were they high or low? Were they fulfilled or not? If not, what went wrong? Explain the situation surrounding this experience in a coherent essay.

2. Brainstorm about some challenges or difficult times you have faced. Then describe the most important challenge you have overcome. Explain why this experience was so difficult and what helped you face and conquer it.

3. What do you believe are the major causes of violence in American society? Write an essay that explains why the causes you cite are real or valid. Can you propose any possible solutions to the predicament you describe?

Exploring Ideas

4. How does our reading help us perceive the world? Do you think short stories, plays, and poems help us understand people's behavior and feelings? Write an essay responding to these questions.

5. Compare your memory of a particular childhood experience with that of another family member. How accurately do you both seem to remember this same event? What do you think accounts for the differences in what we remember about various events? What do these differences say about us? Write an essay exploring these questions, using the event from your childhood to support your discussion.

6. Television has been blamed for causing violent behavior, shortening attention spans, and exposing young people to sexually explicit images. Should we as a society monitor what appears on television more closely, or should parents be responsible for censoring what their children watch? Write an essay that takes a stand on this issue.

Writing from Sources

For detailed information on writing from sources, see Part III.

7. Substance abuse can materialize in several ways. Choose one form of substance abuse to research, and examine the ways it can affect individuals in their personal lives, their workplace, and their relationships. Then write an essay citing two or three sources that discuss the effects that you researched.

8. How does the way the media portrays body image affect the average American? What types of people are most susceptible to negative

reaction? Can you think of any positive portrayals in the media? While thinking about these questions, research the connection between the media's portrayal of body image and eating and psychological disorders that women and men face today. Write an essay discussing the cause/effect relationship between the media and body image using evidence from your research.

Analyzing Visual Images

© Dave Beckerman Photography

9. Examine the photo above and think about the roads that we travel in our lives. Discuss a time when you decided to take a different road, and explain the effect this change had on your life.

10. Look at the picture on page 425 at the beginning of this chapter, which depicts the famous Zeppelin *Hindenburg* (one of the largest airships ever) bursting into flames in 1937. You might be interested in researching the causes and effects of this disaster at en.wikipedia.org/wiki/Hindenburg_disaster. Consider other similar disasters that changed the way people think about traveling, and write an essay explaining all the causes and effects that were connected with this change.

Chapter 12

ARGUMENT AND PERSUASION
Inciting People to Thought or Action

Almost everything we do or say is an attempt to persuade. Whether we dress up to impress a potential employer or argue openly with a friend about an upcoming election, we are trying to convince various people to see the world our way. However, some aspects of life are particularly dependent on persuasion. Think, for example, of all the television, magazine, and billboard ads we see urging us to buy certain products or of the many impassioned appeals we read and hear on such controversial issues as school prayer, abortion, gun control, and nuclear energy. Religious leaders devote their professional lives to convincing people to live a certain way and believe in certain religious truths, whereas scientists and mathematicians use rigorous logic and natural law to convince us of other hypotheses. Politicians make their living persuading voters to elect them and then support them throughout their terms in office. In fact, anyone who wants something from another person or agency, ranging from federal money for a research project to a new bicycle for Christmas, must use some form of persuasion to get what he or she desires. The success or failure of this type of communication is easily determined: If the people being addressed change their actions or attitudes in favor of the writer or speaker, the attempt at persuasion has been successful.

DEFINING ARGUMENT AND PERSUASION

The terms *argument* and *persuasion* are often used interchangeably, but one is actually a subdivision of the other. Persuasion names a purpose for writing. To persuade your readers is to convince them to think, act, or feel a certain way. Much of the writing you have been doing in this book has persuasion as one of its goals: A description of an African tribe might have a "dominant impression" you want your readers to accept; in an essay comparing various ways of celebrating Thanksgiving, you might try to convince your readers to believe that these similarities and differences actually exist; and in writing an essay exam on the causes of the Vietnam War, you are trying to convince your instructor that your reasoning is clear and your conclusions sound. In a sense, some degree of persuasion propels all writing.

More specifically, however, the process of persuasion involves appealing to one or more of the following: to reason, to emotion, or to a sense of ethics. An *argument* is an appeal predominantly to your readers' reason and intellect. You are working in the realm of argument when you deal with complex issues that are debatable; opposing views (either explicit or implicit) are a basic requirement of argumentation. But argument and persuasion are taught together because good writers are constantly blending these three appeals and adjusting them to the purpose and audience of a particular writing task. Although reason and logic are the focus of this chapter, you need to learn to use all three methods of persuasion as skillfully as possible to write effective essays.

An appeal to reason relies on logic and intellect and is usually most effective when you are expecting your readers to disagree with you in some way. This type of appeal can help you change your readers' opinions or influence their future actions through the sheer strength of logical validity. If you want to argue, for example, that pregnant women should refrain from smoking cigarettes, you could cite abundant statistical evidence that babies born to mothers who smoke have lower birth weights, more respiratory problems, and a higher incidence of sudden infant death syndrome than the children of nonsmoking mothers. Because smoking clearly endangers the health of the unborn child, reason dictates that mothers who wish to give birth to the healthiest possible babies should avoid smoking during pregnancy.

Emotional appeals, however, attempt to arouse your readers' feelings, instincts, senses, and biases. Used most profitably when your readers already agree with you, this type of essay generally validates, reinforces, and/or incites in an effort to get your readers to share your feelings or ideas. In order to urge our lawmakers to impose stricter jail sentences for alcohol abuse, you might describe a recent tragic accident involving a local twelve-year-old girl who was killed by a drunk driver as she rode her bicycle to school one morning.

By focusing on such poignant visual details as the condition of her mangled bike, the bright red blood stains on her white dress, and the anguish on the faces of parents and friends, you could build a powerfully persuasive essay that would be much more effective than a dull recitation of impersonal facts and nationwide statistics.

An appeal to ethics, the third technique writers often use to encourage readers to agree with them, involves cultivating a sincere, honest tone that will establish your reputation as a reliable, qualified, experienced, well-informed, and knowledgeable person whose opinions on the topic under discussion are believable because they are ethically sound. Such an approach is often used in conjunction with logical or emotional appeals to foster a verbal environment that will result in minimal resistance from its readers. Premier golfer Tiger Woods is a master at creating this ethical, trustworthy persona as he tries to persuade television viewers to buy Nike products. In fact, the old gag question "Would you buy a used car from this man?" is our instinctive response to all forms of attempted persuasion, whether the salesperson is trying to sell us Puppy Chow or gun control, hair spray or school prayer. The more believable we are as human beings, the better chance we will have of convincing our audience.

The following student paragraph is directed primarily toward the audience's logical reasoning ability. Notice that the writer states her assertion and then gives reasons to convince her readers to change their ways. The student writer also brings both emotion and ethics into the argument by choosing her words and examples with great precision.

Have you ever watched a pair of chunky thighs, a jiggling posterior, and an extra-large sweatshirt straining to cover a beer belly and thought, "Thank God I don't look like that! I'm in pretty good shape . . . for someone my age." Well, before you become too smug and self-righteous, consider what kind of shape you're really in. Just because you don't look like Shamu the whale doesn't mean you're in good condition. What's missing, you ask? Exercise. You can diet all day, wear the latest slim-cut designer jeans, and still be in worse shape than someone twice your age if you don't get a strong physical workout at least three times a week. Exercise is not only good for you, but it can also be fun—especially if you find a sport that makes you happy while you sweat. Your activity need not be expensive: Jogging, walking, basketball, tennis, and handball are not costly, unless you're seduced by the glossy sheen of the latest sporting fashions and accessories. Most of all, however, regular exercise is important for your health. You can just as easily drop dead from a sudden heart attack in the middle of a restaurant when you're slim and trim as when you're a slob. Your heart and lungs need regular workouts to stay healthy. So do yourself a favor, and add some form of exercise to your schedule. You'll feel better and live longer, and your looks will improve, too!

THINKING CRITICALLY THROUGH ARGUMENT AND PERSUASION

Argument and persuasion require you to present your views on an issue through logic, emotion, and good character in such a way that you convince an audience of your point of view. This rhetorical mode comes at the end of this book because it is an extremely complex and sophisticated method of reasoning. The more proficient you become with this strategy of thinking and presenting your views, the more you will get what you want out of life (and out of school). Winning arguments means getting the pay raises you need, the refund you deserve, and the grades you've worked so hard for.

In a successful argument, your logic must be flawless. Your conclusions should be based on clear evidence, which must be organized in such a way that it builds to an effective, convincing conclusion. You should constantly have your purpose and audience in mind as you build your case; at the same time, issues of emotion and good character should support the flow of your logic.

Exercising your best logical skills is extremely important to all phases of your daily survival—in and out of the classroom. Following a logical argument in your reading and presenting a logical response to your course work are the hallmarks of a good student. Right now, put your best logic forward and work on your reasoning and persuasive abilities in the following series of exercises. Isolate argument/persuasion from the other rhetorical strategies so that you can practice it and strengthen your ability to argue before you combine it with other methods.

© Charles Moore/Black Star

1. Charles Moore uses the photograph on page 471 to document how the police in Birmingham, Alabama, used a dog to harass a peaceful protester in a 1963 civil rights struggle. Identify another social struggle or protest that you believe is important. Brainstorm about the many views people might hold about this issue. Choose one and identify the types of evidence you would need to support this view, the resolutions you might offer, and the concessions you would be willing to make to resolve the issue. Make a five- to ten-minute presentation arguing your point to your class or to a small group in your class.

2. Bring to class two magazine ads—one that tries to sell a product and another that tries to convince the reader that a particular action or product is wrong or bad (unhealthy, misinterpreted, politically incorrect, etc.). How does each ad appeal to the reader's logic? How does the advertiser use emotion and character in his or her appeal?

3. Fill in the following blanks: The best way to _____ is to _____. (For example, "The best way to lose weight is to exercise.") Then list ways you might use to persuade a reader to see your point of view in this statement.

READING AND WRITING ARGUMENT/PERSUASION ESSAYS

Although persuasive writing can be approached essentially in three different ways—logically, emotionally, and/or ethically—our stress in this chapter is on logic and reason, because they are at the heart of most college writing. As a reader, you will see how various forms of reasoning and different methods of organization affect your reaction to an essay. Your stand on a particular issue will control the way you process information in argument and persuasion essays. As you read the essays in this chapter, you will also learn to recognize emotional and ethical appeals and the different effects they create. In your role as a writer, you need to be fully aware of the options available to you as you compose. Although the basis of your writing will be logical argument, you will see that you can learn to control your readers' responses to your essays by choosing your evidence carefully, organizing it wisely, and seasoning it with the right amount of emotion and ethics—depending on your purpose and audience.

Reading Argument/Persuasion Essays

- What is the author's main assertion or thesis?
- What ideas do you agree with?
- What ideas do you disagree with?
- What appeals does the author use?

Preparing to Read.   As you prepare to read the essays in this chapter, spend a few minutes browsing through the preliminary material for each selection: What does Frank Furedi's title, "Our Unhealthy Obsession with Sickness," prepare you for? What can you learn from scanning Barrett Seaman's essay, "How Bingeing Became the New College Sport," and reading the synopsis of Dave Grassman's essay ("We Are Training Our Kids to Kill") in the Rhetorical Table of Contents?

Also, you should bring to your reading as much information as you can from the authors' biographies: Why do you think Dave Grossman writes about violence and the media? Does he have the proper qualifications to teach us about how "We Are Training Our Kids to Kill"? What perspective does the photo essay ("Tag, You're It!") take? What is the source of Kim Severson's interest in gay marriage ("I'm Not Willing to Settle for Crumbs")? For the essays in this chapter that present several viewpoints on an argument (on immigration and DNA testing), what biographical details prepare us for each writer's stand on the issue? Who were the original audiences for these opposing viewpoints?

Last, before you read these essays, try to generate some ideas on each topic so that you can take the role of an active reader. In this text, the Preparing to Read questions will help you get ready for this task. Then, you should speculate further on the general subject of the essay: How do you think binge drinking is affecting American society? What would you change about the approach taken in the United States to this controversial topic? What would you continue? What are the main arguments related to gay marriage? What side do you think Severson is on? Where do you stand on the subject?

Reading.   Be sure to record your spontaneous reactions to the persuasive essays in this chapter as you read them for the first time: What are your opinions on each subject? Why do you hold these opinions? Be especially aware of your responses to the essays representing opposing viewpoints at the end of the chapter; know where you stand in relation to each side of the issues here.

Use the preliminary material before an essay to help you create a framework for your responses to it: What motivated Furedi to publish his arguments on illness? What makes Grossman so knowledgeable about children and TV violence? Which argument on immigration do you find most convincing? On postconviction DNA testing?

Throughout each essay in the chapter are questions at the bottom of the pages that further critical thinking. They essentially bridge the gap between the inquiries before each essay and the exercises after the essays. If you answer these questions as they appear in the text, you will be building a framework of understanding that you can draw on when you finally get to the writing assignments at the end of each reading. Putting your responses in writing is the most beneficial way to make the material your own in a way that just thinking about the questions can't accomplish.

Your main job at this stage of reading is to determine each author's primary assertion or proposition (thesis statement) and to create an inquisitive environment for thinking critically about the essay's ideas. In addition, take a look at the questions after each selection to make sure you are picking up the major points of the essay.

Rereading.   As you reread these persuasive essays, notice how the writers integrate their appeals to logic, to emotion, and to ethics. Also, pay attention to the emphasis the writers place on one or more appeals at certain strategic points in the essays: What combination of appeals does Dave Grossman use in "We Are Training Our Kids to Kill"? In what way does the tone of his writing support what he is saying? How does he establish this tone? Which appeal is most prominent in the photo essay? What questions do you have in reference to the three essays on DNA testing? What questions do the authors leave unanswered?

Also, determine what other rhetorical strategies help these writers make their primary points. How do these strategies enable each writer to establish a unified essay with a beginning, a middle, and an end?

Then answer the questions after each reading selection to make certain you understand the essay on the literal, interpretive, and analytical levels in preparation for the discussion/writing assignments that follow.

For a list of guidelines for the entire reading process, see the Reading Inventory at the end of Part I.

Writing Argument/Persuasion Essays

- Write a debatable thesis.
- Justify the significance of the issue.
- Choose evidence for your thesis.
- Organize your essay effectively.
- Use logical, ethical, and pathetic appeals.
- Conclude with a summary and recommendations.

Preparing to Write.   The first stage of writing an essay of this sort involves, as usual, exploring and then limiting your topic. As you prepare to write your persuasive paper, first try to generate as many ideas as possible— regardless of whether they appeal to logic, emotion, or ethics. To do this, review the prewriting techniques on pages 36–38, and answer the Preparing to Write questions. Then choose a topic. Next, focus on a purpose and a specific audience before you begin to write.

Writing.   Most persuasive essays should begin with an assertion or a proposition stating what you believe about a certain issue. This thesis should generally be phrased as a debatable statement, such as, "If individual states reinstituted the death penalty, Americans would notice an immediate drop in violent crimes." At this point in your essay, you should also justify the significance of the issue you will be discussing: "Such a decline in the crime rate would affect all our lives and make this country a safer place in which to live."

The essay should then support your thesis in a variety of ways. This support may take the form of facts, figures, examples, opinions by recognized authorities, case histories, narratives/anecdotes, comparisons, contrasts, or cause/effect studies. This evidence is most effectively organized from least to most important when you are confronted with a hostile audience (so that you can lead your readers through your reasoning step by step) and from most to least important when you are facing a supportive audience (so that you can build on their loyalty and enthusiasm as you advance your thesis). In fact, you will be able to engineer your best support if you know your audience's opinions, feelings, and background before you write your essay, so that your intended "target" is as clear as possible. The body of your essay will undoubtedly consist of a combination of logical, emotional, and ethical appeals—all leading to some final summation or recommendation.

The concluding paragraph of a persuasive essay should restate your main assertion (in terms slightly different from your original statement) and should offer some constructive recommendations about the problem you have been discussing (if you haven't already done so). This section of your paper should clearly bring your argument to a close in one final attempt to move your audience to accept or act on the viewpoint you present. Let's look more closely now at each of the three types of appeals used in such essays: logical, emotional, and ethical.

To construct a *logical* argument, you have two principal patterns available to you: inductive reasoning or deductive reasoning. The first encourages an audience to make what is called an "inductive leap" from several particular examples to a single, useful generalization. In the case of the death penalty, for instance, you might cite a number of examples, figures, facts, and case studies illustrating the effectiveness of capital punishment in various states, thereby leading up to your firm belief that the death penalty should be reinstituted. Used most often by detectives, scientists, and lawyers, the process of inductive reasoning addresses the audience's ability to think logically by moving them systematically from an assortment of selected evidence to a rational and ordered conclusion.

In contrast, deductive reasoning moves its audience from a broad, general statement to particular examples supporting that statement. In writing such an essay, you would present your thesis statement about capital punishment first and then offer clear, orderly evidence to support that belief. Although the mental process we go through in creating a deductive argument is quite sophisticated, it is based on a three-step form of reasoning called the *syllogism,* which most logicians believe is the foundation of logical thinking. The traditional syllogism has

> *A major premise:* All humans fear death.
>
> *A minor premise:* Criminals are humans.
>
> *A conclusion:* Therefore, criminals fear death.

As you might suspect, this type of reasoning is only as accurate as its original premises, so you need to be sure your premises are true so your argument will be valid.

In constructing a logical argument, you should take great care to avoid several types of fallacies in reasoning found most frequently in lower-division college papers. Fallacies occur when you use faulty evidence, when you misrepresent your evidence, or when you use evidence that is irrelevant to your argument. Avoiding fallacies is important because readers who discover a fallacy or problem in logic are likely to question the writer's credibility and perhaps even the writer's interpretation of other evidence. While the following is not an exhaustive list, these fallacies illustrate why most writers purposely try to avoid using fallacious or faulty reasoning:

Hasty Generalization: When we present a claim that is based on too few examples, we are making a hasty generalization. For example, if we state that students never get enough sleep, we are committing this fallacy. To avoid these kinds of blanket statements, writers need to qualify their claims so they are accurate: Many students don't get enough sleep.

Non Sequitur: A *non sequitur* occurs when we make a statement that does not logically follow the previous statement. Some people say, for example, "That car she just bought is very expensive. She must be rich." This second sentence is not a conclusion we can draw from the first sentence.

Either/Or Fallacy: Writers commit the either/or fallacy when they present an argument as if only two views exist, but actually other views are possible as well. For example, someone might argue that a person could not protest the war in Iraq and still be a patriotic American. A citizen can express a negative view about one policy and still be patriotic, so the explanation of two sides only (supporting the war or being unpatriotic) is an example of the either/or fallacy.

False Cause and Effect: This logical flaw involves making a causal argument based solely on chronology. To avoid this fallacy, the cause must be proved: "First, the group of politicians criticized the war; then the terrorists bombed a building in Baghdad. See what happens when we criticize the war!"

False Authority: An appeal to a false authority occurs when a writer cites an example or opinion of someone who is not an expert in the field. Having an actor advertise a product unrelated to his or her career is an example of this fallacy. When writers choose an expert, they must make sure the person can actually offer a relevant and meaningful testimonial or perspective.

Begging the Question: This is circular logic. For example, skydiving is dangerous because it is not safe. To avoid this fallacy, bring new information into the explanation: Skydiving is dangerous because a lot can go wrong on the way down to the ground.

Bandwagon: This fallacy is based on the false logic that some action is preferable because it is supported by many people. Examples often occur in advertising when companies claim that their product is the best because so many people are using it.

If you build your argument on true statements and abundant, accurate evidence, your essay will be effective, and your argument is likely to be persuasive. Avoiding fallacies is also easier when you thoroughly examine your evidence and carefully present supporting ideas and information to your reader. As a writer, you have the ultimate responsibility to find credible evidence and to present it in a well-reasoned and clear essay.

Persuading through *emotion* necessitates controlling your readers' instinctive reactions to what you are saying. You can accomplish this goal in two different ways: (1) by choosing your words with even greater care than usual and (2) by using figurative language whenever appropriate. In the first case, you must be especially conscious of using words that have the same general denotative (or dictionary) meaning but bear decidedly favorable or unfavorable connotative (or implicit) meanings. For example, notice the difference between *slender* and *scrawny, patriotic* and *chauvinistic,* or *compliment* and *flattery.* Your careful attention to the choice of such words can help readers form visual images with certain positive or negative associations that subtly encourage them to follow your argument and adopt your opinions. Second, the effective use of figurative language—especially similes and metaphors—makes your writing more vivid, thus triggering your readers' senses and encouraging them to accept your views. Both of these techniques will help you manipulate your readers into the position of agreeing with your ideas.

Ethical appeals, which establish you as a reliable, well-informed person, are accomplished through (1) the tone of your essay and (2) the number and type of examples you cite. Tone is created through deliberate word choice: Careful attention to the mood implied in the words you use can convince your readers that you are serious, friendly, authoritative, jovial, or methodical—depending on your intended purpose. In like manner, the examples you supply to support your assertions can encourage readers to see you as experienced, insightful, relaxed, or intense. In both of these cases, winning favor for yourself will usually also gain approval for your opinions.

Rewriting.   To rework your persuasive essays, you should play the role of your readers and impartially evaluate the different appeals you have used to accomplish your purpose:

- Is my thesis statement clear?
- Is the main thrust of my essay an appeal to reason?
- Have I chosen examples carefully to support my thesis statement?
- Does my conclusion restate my argument, make a recommendation, and bring my essay to a close?

You should also look closely at the way your appeals work together in your essay:

- When I use logic, is that section of my paper arranged according to either inductive or deductive reasoning?
- Is that the most effective order to achieve my purpose?
- In appealing to the emotions, have I chosen my words with proper attention to their denotative and connotative effects?

Any additional guidance you may need as you write and revise your persuasive essays is furnished on pages 41–46 of Chapter 3.

STUDENT ESSAY: ARGUMENT AND PERSUASION AT WORK

The following student essay uses all three appeals to make its point about the power of language in shaping our view of the world. First, the writer sets forth her character references (ethical appeal) in the first paragraph, after which she presents her thesis and its significance in paragraph 2. The support for her thesis is a combination of logical and emotional appeals, heavy on the logical, as the writer moves her paragraphs from general to particular in an effort to convince her readers to adopt her point of view and adjust their language use accordingly.

The Language of Equal Rights

Ethical appeal   Up front, I admit it. I've been a card-carrying feminist since junior high school. I want to see an Equal Rights Amendment to the U.S. Constitution, equal pay for equal—and comparable—work, and I go dutch on dates. Furthermore, I am quite prickly on the subject of language. I'm one of those people who bristles at terms like *lady doctor* (you know they don't mean a gynecologist), *female policeman* (a paradox), and *mankind* instead of *humanity* (are they really talking about me?).

<aside>Emotional appeal</aside>

Many people ask "How important are mere words, anyway? You know what we really mean." A question like this ignores the symbolic and psychological importance of language. What words "mean" can go beyond what a speaker or writer consciously intends, reflecting personal and cultural biases that run so deep that most of the time we aren't even aware they exist. "Mere words" are incredibly important: They are our framework for seeing and understanding the world.

<aside>Assertion or thesis statement</aside>

<aside>Significance of assertion</aside>

Man, we are told, means woman as well as man, just as *mankind* supposedly stands for all of humanity. In the introduction of a sociology textbook I recently read, the author was anxious to demonstrate his awareness of the controversy over sexist language and to assure his female readers that, despite his use of noninclusive terms, he was not forgetting the existence or importance of women in society. He was making a conscious decision to continue to use *man* and *mankind* instead of *people, humanity,* etc., for ease of expression and aesthetic reasons. "Man" simply sounds better, he explained. I flipped through the table of contents and found "Man and Society," "Man and Nature," "Man and Technology," and, near the end, "Man and Woman." At what point did *Man* quit meaning *people* and start meaning men again? The writer was obviously unaware of the answer to this question, because it is one he would never think to ask. Having consciously addressed the issue only to dismiss it, he reverted to form.

<aside>Logical appeal</aside>

<aside>Examples organized deductively</aside>

<aside>Emotional appeal</aside>

The very ambiguity of *man* as the generic word for our species ought to be enough to combat any arguments that we keep it because we all "know what it means" or because it is both traditional and sounds better. And does it really sound all that much better, or are we just more used to it, more comfortable? Our own national history proves that we can be comfortable with a host of words and attitudes that strike us

<aside>Logical appeal</aside>

<aside>Examples organized deductively</aside>

as unjust and ugly today. A lot of white folks probably thought that Negroes were getting pretty stuffy and picky when they began to insist on being called *blacks.* <u>After all, weren't there more important things to worry about, like civil rights</u>? But black activists recognized the emotional and symbolic significance of having a name that was parallel to the name that the dominant race used for itself—a name equal in dignity, lacking that vaguely alien, anthropological sound. After all, whites were called *Caucasians* only in police reports, textbooks, and autopsies. *Negro* may have sounded better to people in the bad old days of blatant racial bigotry, but we adjusted to the word *black* and have now moved on to *African American,* and more and more people of each race are adjusting to the wider implications and demands of practical, as well as verbal, labels.

Emotional appeal

<u>In a world where *man* and *human* are offered as synonymous terms, I don't think it is a coincidence that women are still vastly underrepresented in positions of money, power, and respect</u>. Children grow up learning a language that makes maleness the norm for anything that isn't explicitly designated as female, giving little girls a very limited corner of the universe to picture themselves in. Indeed, the language that nonfeminists today claim to be inclusive was never intended to cover women in the first place. "One man, one vote" and "All men are created equal" meant just that. Women had to fight for decades to be included even as an afterthought; it took constitutional amendments to convince the government and the courts that women are human too.

Logical appeal

Examples organized deductively

The message is clear. <u>We have to start speaking about people, not men, if we are going to start thinking in terms of both women and men. A "female man" will never be the equal of her brother.</u>

Conclusion/ restatement

Student Writer's Comments

The hardest task for me in writing this essay was coming up with a topic! The second hardest job was trying to be effective without getting preachy, strident, or wordy. I wanted to persuade an audience that would no doubt include the bored, the hostile, and the indifferent, and I was worried about losing their attention.

I chose my topic after several prewriting sessions that generated numerous options for me to write about. I stumbled on the idea of sexist language in one of these sessions and then went on to generate new material on this particular topic. Eventually satisfied that I had enough ideas to stay with this topic, I doubled back and labeled them according to each type of appeal.

Even before I had written my thesis, I had a good idea of what I wanted to say in this essay. I began working from an assertion that essentially remained the same as I wrote and revised my essay. It's more polished now, but its basic intention never changed.

To create my first draft, I worked from my notes, labeled by type of appeal. I let the logical arguments guide my writing, strategically introducing emotional and ethical appeals as I sensed they would be effective. I appealed to ethics in the beginning of the essay to establish my credibility, and I appealed to the readers' emotions occasionally to vary my pace and help my argument gain momentum. I was fully aware of what I was doing when I moved from one appeal to another. I wrote from a passionate desire to change people's thinking about language and its ability to control our perceptions of the world.

Next, I revised my entire essay several times, playing the role of different readers with dissimilar biases in each case. Every time I worked through the essay, I made major changes in the introduction and the conclusion as well. At this point, I paid special attention to the denotation, connotation, and tone of my words (especially highly charged language) and to the examples I had chosen to support each point I decided to keep in my argument. Though I moved a lot of examples around and thought of better ones in some cases, I was eventually happy with the final product. I am especially pleased with the balance of appeals in the final draft.

SOME FINAL THOUGHTS ON ARGUMENT AND PERSUASION

As you can tell from the selections that follow, the three different types of persuasive appeals usually complement one another in practice. Most good persuasive essays use a combination of these methods to achieve their purposes. Good persuasive essays also rely on various rhetorical modes we have already studied—such as example, process analysis, division/classification, comparison/contrast, definition, and cause/effect—to advance their arguments. In the following essays, you will see a combination of appeals and a number of different rhetorical modes at work.

ARGUMENT AND PERSUASION IN REVIEW

Reading Argument/Persuasion Essays

Preparing to Read

√ What assumptions can I make from the essay's title?
√ What do I think the general mood of the essay will be?
√ What is the essay's purpose and audience?
√ What does the synopsis tell me about the essay?
√ What can I learn from the author's biography?
√ Can I predict the author's point of view toward the subject?

Reading

√ What is the author's main assertion or thesis?
√ What ideas do I agree with?
√ What ideas do I disagree with?
√ What appeals does the author use?

Rereading

√ How does the writer integrate the appeals in the essay?
√ What is the tone of the essay? How does the author establish this tone?
√ What other rhetorical strategies does the author use?

Writing Argument/Persuasion Essays

Preparing to Write

√ Do I narrow and focus my material as much as possible?
√ What is my purpose?
√ Do I understand my audience's background?

Writing

√ Did I write a debatable thesis?
√ Do I justify the significance of the issue?
√ Did I choose evidence that supports my thesis?
√ Is my essay organized effectively for what I am trying to accomplish?
√ Do I use a combination of logical, ethical, and emotional appeals?
√ Do I conclude with a summary and recommendations?

Rewriting

√ Is my thesis statement clear?
√ Is the main thrust of my essay an appeal to reason?
√ Have I chosen examples carefully to support my thesis statement?
√ Does my conclusion restate my argument, make a recommendation, and bring my essay to a close?

FRANK FUREDI   (1947–   )

Our Unhealthy Obsession with Sickness

An extremely prolific author, Frank Furedi was born in Hungary, immigrated to England, and earned both his master's degree and doctorate at the School of Oriental and African Studies of London University. In the 1970s, under the pseudonym "Frank Richards," he was the cofounder and chairman of the Revolutionary Communist Party in Britain. Currently a professor of Sociology at the University of Kent, he has written fourteen books, including *The Soviet Union Demystified* (1986), *The Mau Mau War in Perspective* (1989), *Mythical Past, Elusive Future: History and Society in an Anxious Age* (1991), *Culture of Fear: Risk Taking and the Morality of Low Expectation* (1997), *Paranoid Parenting* (2001), and *The Politics of Fear: Beyond Left and Right* (2005). His most recent publication, *Invitation to Terror* (2007), is focused on the "culture of risk" that has developed following the terrorist attacks on 9/11. He also writes articles for the Web journal *Spiked Online* and does frequent media interviews, in which he often decries what he describes as the "dumbing down" of society. He advises student writers "not to obsess about the actual act of writing. Spend most of your time working on what it is you are trying to say."

Preparing to Read

This selection, written by Frank Furedi, was first delivered as a speech at a health conference and then published in *Spiked Online* (March 23, 2005). In it, Furedi explains the problems with our new concentration in society today on illness rather than wellness. (This essay contains British spellings.)

Exploring Experience: Before you read this essay, think about your approach to your health and the health of others: Do you focus unnecessarily on your health problems? Are health issues a part of your daily conversation? Does your health play a major part in your definition as a person? What do you make of the new focus on "wellness" in our daily affairs?

Learning Online: Visit and explore the U.S. Department of Health and Human Services Web site at healthfinder.gov/. Do you think the government should be responsible for providing this information? Is it beneficial or not to have information like this readily available to the public?

W e live in a world where illnesses are on the increase. The distin- 1 guishing feature of the twenty-first century is that health has become a dominant issue, both in our personal lives and in public life. It has become a highly politicised issue too and an increasingly important site of government intervention and policymaking. With every year that passes, we seem to spend more and more time and resources thinking about health and sickness. I think there are four possible reasons for this.

First, there is the imperative of **medicalisation**. When the concept of 2 medicalisation was first formulated, in the late 1960s and early 1970s, it referred to a far narrower range of phenomena than is the case today, and it was linked to the actions of a small number of professionals rather than having the all-pervasive character that it does now.

Essentially, the term medicalisation means that problems we encounter 3 in everyday life are reinterpreted as medical ones. So problems that might traditionally have been defined as existential—that is, the problems of existence—have a medical label attached to them. Today, it is difficult to think of any kind of human experience that doesn't come with a health warning or some kind of medical explanation. ❶

It is not only the experience of pain or distress or disappointment or 4 engagement with adversity that is medicalised and seen as potentially traumatic and stress-inducing; even human characteristics are medicalised now. Consider shyness. It is quite normal to be shy; there are many circumstances where many of us feel shy and awkward. Yet shyness is now referred to as "social phobia." And, of course, when a medical label is attached to shyness, it is only a matter of time before a pharmaceutical company comes up with a "shyness pill." Pop these pills, and you too can become the life and soul of the party! ❷

One of my hobbies is to read press releases informing us of the existence 5 of a new illness, the "illness of the week," if you like. Recently I received one that said, "Psychologists say that love sickness is a genuine disease and needs more awareness and diagnoses. Those little actions that are normally seen as the symptoms of the first flush of love—buying presents, waiting by the phone, or making an effort before a date—may actually be signs of a deep-rooted problem to come. Many people who suffer from love sickness cannot cope with the intensity of love and have been destabilised by falling in love or suffer on account of their love being unrequited. . . ."

Of course, an intense passion can and does have an impact upon our 6 bodies. But when even love can be seen as the harbinger of illness, what aspect of our lives can be said to be illness-free? What can we possibly do

---

Thinking Critically

❶ What does the author mean by the term "medicalisation"? Give an example of this process.

❷ Why do you think we medicate personality traits?

that will not apparently induce some sickness or syndrome? Medicalisation no longer knows any limits. It is so intrusive that it can impact on virtually any of our experiences, creating a situation where illness is increasingly perceived as normal.

This leads to my second point—there is now a **presupposition that illness is as normal as health**. Earlier theories of medicalisation still considered illness to be the exception; now, being ill is seen as a normal state, possibly even more normal than being healthy. We are all now seen as being *potentially* ill; that is the default state we live in today.   7

This can be glimpsed in the increasing use of the term "wellness," with well men's clinics and well women's clinics. "Wellness," another relatively recent concept, is a peculiar term. It presupposes that being well is not a natural or normal state. After all, there are no such things as "sunshine clinics" or "evening clinics"; such normal things do not normally need an institution attached to them. And why would you have to visit a wellness clinic if you were well anyway? It makes little sense.   8

Wellness has become something you have to work on, something to aspire to and achieve. ❸ This reinforces the presupposition that not being well—or being ill—is the normal state. That is what our culture says to us now: you are not okay; you are not fine; you are potentially ill. The message seems to be that if you do not subscribe to this project of keeping well, you will revert to being ill.   9

In supermarkets, especially in middle-class neighbourhoods, buying food has become like conducting a scientific experiment. Individuals spend hours looking at how many carbohydrates there are, whether it's organic, natural, holistic. Spending time reading labels is one way of doing your bit to keep well.   10

Being potentially ill is now so prevalent that we have reached a situation where illness becomes a part of our identity, part of the human condition. Some of us might not flaunt it, walking around saying, "I've got a gum disease" or "I've got a bad case of athlete's foot." That doesn't sound very sexy and is unlikely to go down well at the dinner table. But it has become acceptable to talk openly about other illnesses—to declare that you are a cancer survivor or to flaunt a disability. As we normalise illness, our identity becomes inextricably linked to illness. So it is normal to be ill, and to be ill is normal.   11

The nature of illness changes when it becomes part of our identity. ❹   12
When we invest so much emotion in an illness, when it becomes such a

---

Thinking Critically

❸ How can we achieve "wellness" in our lives? Name three specific actions that can make us or keep us "well."

❹ Do you have an illness that has become part of your identity? If so, how does it affect your daily life?

large aspect of our lives through the illness metaphor, we start to embrace it, and it can be very difficult to let go of that part of our identity. This is why illness tends to become more durable and last longer. Sickness is no longer a temporary episode: it is something that, increasingly, afflicts one for life. You are scarred for life, with an indelible stamp on your personality. This can be seen in the idea of being a cancer survivor or some other kind of survivor; we are always, it seems, in remission. The illness remains part of us and shapes our personality.

As this happens, illnesses start to acquire features that are no longer neg- 13
ative. In the past, illness was seen as a bad thing. Today you can read illness diaries in the *Guardian* and other newspapers and magazines. We often hear the phrase: "I've learned so much about myself through my illness." It becomes a pedagogic experience: "I may have lost a leg and half my brain cells, but I'm learning so much from this extremely unique experience." It's almost like going to university, something positive, to be embraced, with hundreds of books telling us how to make the most of the experience of sickness.

We are not simply making a virtue out of a necessity; rather we are con- 14
sciously *valuing* illness. From a theoretical standpoint, we might view illness as the first order concept and wellness as the second order concept. Wellness is subordinate, methodologically, to the state of being ill.

The third influence is today's cultural script, the cultural narrative that 15
impacts on our lives, which increasingly **uses health to make sense of the human experience**. The more uncertainty we face, the more difficult we find it to make statements of moral purpose, the more ambiguous we feel about what is right and wrong, then the more comfortable we feel using the language of health to make sense of our lives. At a time of moral and existential uncertainty, health has become an important idiom through which to provide guidance to individuals.

This is now so prevalent that we no longer even notice when we are 16
doing it. For example, we no longer tell teenagers that pre-marital sex is good or bad or sinful. Instead we say that pre-marital sex is a health risk. Sex education programmes teach that you will be emotionally traumatised if pressured into having sex and will be generally healthier if you stay at home and watch TV instead.

There are few clear moral guidelines that can direct our behaviour today, 17
but we have become very good at using health to regulate people's lives in an intrusive and systematic fashion. Even medicine and food have acquired moral connotations. So some drugs are said to be bad for the environment, while others, especially those made with a natural herb, are seen as being morally superior. Organic food is seen as "good," not only in nutritional terms, but in moral terms. Junk food, on the other hand, is seen as evil.

If you look at the language that is used to discuss health and medicine or obese people and their body shapes, it isn't just about health: we are making moral statements. A fat person is considered to have a serious moral problem, rather than simply a health one. [5] As we become morally illiterate, we turn to health to save us from circumstances where we face a degree of moral or spiritual disorientation.

18

The fourth influence is **the politicisation of health**. Health has become a focus of incessant political activity. Politicians who have little by way of beliefs or passions and don't know what to say to the public, are guaranteed a response if they say something health-related. Some also make a lot of money from the health issue, from pharmaceutical companies to alternative health shops to individual quacks selling their wares. All are in the business, essentially, of living off today's health-obsessed cultural sentiment.

19

Governments today do two things that I object to in particular. First they encourage introspection, telling us that unless men examine their testicles, unless we keep a check on our cholesterol level, then we are not being responsible citizens. You are letting down yourself, your wife, your kids, everybody. We are encouraged continually to worry about our health. As a consequence, public health initiatives have become, as far as I can tell, a threat to public health. [6] Secondly, governments promote the value of *health seeking*. We are meant always to be seeking health for this or that condition. The primary effect of this, I believe, is to make us all feel more ill.

20

Here's a prediction—Western societies are not going to overcome the crisis of healthcare; it is beyond the realms of possibility. No matter what policies government pursue or how much money they throw at the problem, even if they increase health expenditure fourfold, the problem will not go away. As long as the normalisation of illness [7] remains culturally affirmed, more and more of us are likely to identify ourselves as sick and will identify ourselves as sick for a growing period of time. The solution to this problem lies not in the area of policymaking, or even medicine, but in the cultural sphere.

21

UNDERSTANDING DETAILS

1. What does Furedi see as the reasons for our obsession with health today?
2. What are "illness diaries"? How might they affect our approach to health issues?
3. What are the consequences of society's new state of mind that illness is normal?
4. According to Furedi, what is the solution to this new focus on illness?

Thinking Critically

[5] Do you consider obesity to be a "moral" or "spiritual" problem? Explain your reasoning.

[6] Why does the author say that public health initiatives have become "a threat to public health"? What are some other ironies in the health profession?

[7] What does Furedi mean by "the normalization of illness"? Which illnesses seem most "normal" to you?

READING CRITICALLY

5. Read the essay again, and draw lines in the body of the essay to separate his four main points. Then give examples from your own experience for each of his categories.
6. Why do you think health has become a dominant issue in American society today?
7. Do you agree with Furedi that we are "seen as being *potentially* ill" (paragraph 7) today? Explain your answer.
8. From your own experience, give some examples of wellness being subordinate to illness.

DISCOVERING RHETORICAL STRATEGIES

9. In what order does Furedi introduce the reasons in his argument? Is this an effective order? Explain your answer in detail.
10. Who do you think was Furedi's original audience? Explain your answer.
11. What rhetorical strategies does the author use to advance his argument? Give an example of each one you find.
12. What is the tone of this essay?

MAKING CONNECTIONS

13. Examine Furedi's essay in light of Jessica Mitford's "Behind the Formaldehyde Curtain." To what extent do current funeral practices attempt to erase the "illnesses" we suffer in life?
14. Imagine that Furedi was having a round-table discussion about "sickness" with the following authors: Malcolm Cowley ("The View from 80"), Harold Krents ("Darkness at Noon"), Sucheng Chan ("You're Short, Besides!"), and/or Michael Dorris ("The Broken Cord"). Which of these people could most successfully argue that his or her infirmity should be treated as an "illness." Would you agree? Why or why not?
15. Compare and contrast the use of cause/effect in essays by the following authors: Furedi, Stephen King ("Why We Crave Horror Movies"), and/or Michael Dorris ("The Broken Cord"). Who uses this rhetorical technique most skillfully? Why?

IDEAS FOR DISCUSSION/WRITING

Preparing to Write

Write freely about our approach to health in the United States: Where is your focus in reference to Furedi's argument—on illness or wellness? Why do you think that is your focus? Is your focus different from that of other members of your family? From that of your friends?

Choosing a Topic

1. *Learning Online:* Do you agree with Furedi's argument about our preoccupation with disease? Revisit the U.S. Department Health and Human Services Web site at healthfinder.gov/ to review how involved the U.S. government is in our healthcare. Do you think that the government should be involved in health education and care, or should it be considered a personal matter? Write an essay arguing for or against government involvement in the healthcare industry.

2. You have been asked to speak to a group of high school students about your perception of health in the United States. What do you want to tell them? What will be your dominant message? Write out a draft of your speech.

3. We are especially consumed today with psychological disorders, like depression, stress, anxiety, and the like, conditions that Furedi called "existential" (paragraph 3). Do you think these are conditions that should be treated like diseases or everyday emotional problems? Gather your thoughts on this question, and present them in the form of a well-reasoned argumentative essay.

4. Do you agree with Furedi's main point that we are obsessed with illness? Write a response to this selection in the form of an essay of your own.

Before beginning your essay, you might want to consult the checklists on page 482.

BARRETT SEAMAN   (1946–   )

How Bingeing Became the New College Sport

Almost forty years after he graduated from Hamilton College as an undergraduate, former White House Correspondent and Editor at *Time* magazine
Barrett Seaman recently returned to his alma mater and visited twelve other
colleges and universities to investigate the culture of residential college campuses in the United States. The result was *Binge: What Your College Student Won't
Tell You* (2005), an unvarnished look at undergraduate life in the early twenty-
first century. After two and a half years of living with students in dormitories
at Harvard, Middlebury, Duke, Stanford, the University of Virginia, and other
prominent schools, Seaman turned his journalist's eye on such controversial
topics as binge drinking, casual sex, date rape, "pregaming," and other colle-
giate rites of passage that, in his opinion, have grown more reckless and impersonal since his graduation from Hamilton in 1967. Now a trustee at the college
and the father of three daughters who recently earned their B.A. degrees,
Seaman became fascinated with the topic after he accepted an early retirement
package from *Time* following the 2001 merger between America Online and
Time Warner. Today's college students, he argues, are plagued by anxieties and
live in a culture drenched with alcohol and disconnected from the adult world
around them. He also decries the decline in academic rigor and the lack of
meaningful contact between today's students and their professors, particularly
at large research institutions. The author lives in Irvington, New York.

Preparing to Read

This essay was first published in *Time* magazine in August 2005. In it, Barrett Seaman argues that the twenty-one-year-old drinking age in our country is the cause of many serious problems.

Exploring Experience: Before you read this essay, consider what you know
about the drinking habits of college students: Does underage drinking occur
at your college? Why does it occur? Do students drink excessively? If so, what
do they gain from excessive drinking? Are there other rules that are broken
in college? What are they? What are their risks? Where do you stand on the
enforcement of these rules?

Learning Online: Take a few minutes to visit the College Drinking Prevention
Web site (www.collegedrinkingprevention.gov), and browse the articles, charts,
and video clips addressing alcohol abuse in colleges across the United States.
Familiarize yourself with the extent of the problem and the consequences faced
by the students and their campuses.

In the coming weeks, millions of students will begin their fall semester 1 of college, with all the attendant rituals of campus life: freshman orientation, registering for classes, rushing by fraternities and sororities, and, in a more recent nocturnal college tradition, "pregaming" in their rooms.

Pregaming is probably unfamiliar to people who went to college before 2 the 1990s. But it is now a common practice among 18-, 19- and 20-year-old students who cannot legally buy or consume alcohol. It usually involves sitting in a dorm room or an off-campus apartment and drinking as much hard liquor as possible before heading out for the evening's parties. ❶ While reporting for my book *Binge,* I witnessed the hospitalization of several students for acute alcohol poisoning. Among them was a Hamilton College freshman who had consumed 22 shots of vodka while sitting in a dorm room with her friends. Such hospitalizations are routine on campuses across the nation. By the Thanksgiving break of the year I visited Harvard, the university's health center had admitted nearly 70 students for alcohol poisoning.

When students are hospitalized—or worse yet, die from alcohol poison- 3 ing, which happens about 300 times each year—college presidents tend to react by declaring their campuses dry or shutting down fraternity houses. But tighter enforcement of the minimum drinking age of 21 is not the solution. It's part of the problem.

Over the past 40 years, the U.S. has taken a confusing approach to the 4 age-appropriateness of various rights, privileges and behaviors. It used to be that 21 was the age that legally defined adulthood. On the heels of the student revolution of the late '60s, however, came sweeping changes: the voting age was reduced to 18; privacy laws were enacted that protected college students' academic, health and disciplinary records from outsiders, including parents; and the drinking age, which had varied from state to state, was lowered to 18.

Then, thanks in large measure to intense lobbying by Mothers Against 5 Drunk Driving, Congress in 1984 effectively blackmailed states into hiking the minimum drinking age to 21 by passing a law that tied compliance to the distribution of federal-aid highway funds—an amount that will average $690 million per state this year. ❷ There is no doubt that the law, which achieved full 50-state compliance in 1988, saved lives, but it had the unintended consequence of creating a covert culture around alcohol as the young adult's forbidden fruit.

Thinking Critically

❶ What is "pregaming"? Have you ever participated in it?

❷ What was the relationship between raising the drinking age to twenty-one and the distribution of federal highway funds?

Drinking has been an aspect of college life since the first Western uni-   6
versities in the 14th century. My friends and I drank in college in the 1960s—
sometimes a lot but not so much that we had to be hospitalized. Veteran
college administrators cite a sea change in campus culture that began, not
without coincidence, in the 1990s. It was marked by a shift from beer to
hard liquor, consumed not in large social settings, since that is now illegal,
but furtively and dangerously in students' residences.

In my reporting at colleges around the country, I did not meet any pres-   7
idents or deans who felt that the 21-year age minimum helps their efforts to
curb the abuse of alcohol on their campuses. Quite the opposite. They
thought the law impeded their efforts since it takes away the ability to monitor and supervise drinking activity.

What would happen if the drinking age was rolled back to 18 or 19? Ini-   8
tially, there would be a surge in binge drinking as young adults savored their
newfound freedom. But over time, I predict, U.S. college students would
settle into the saner approach to alcohol I saw on the one campus I visited
where the legal drinking age is 18: Montreal's McGill University, which
enrolls about 2,000 American undergraduates a year. ❸ Many, when they
first arrive, go overboard, exploiting their ability to drink legally. But by
midterms, when McGill's demanding academic standards must be met, the vast
majority have put drinking into its practical place among their priorities.

A culture like that is achievable at U.S. colleges if Congress can muster the   9
fortitude to reverse a bad policy. If lawmakers want to reduce drunk driving,
they should do what the Norwegians do: throw the book at offenders no
matter what their age. Meanwhile, we should let the pregamers come out of
their dorm rooms so that they can learn to handle alcohol like the adults we
hope and expect them to be.

UNDERSTANDING DETAILS

1. What is "pregaming" according to this essay?
2. What does Seaman believe is the main cause of binge drinking?
3. How does the twenty-one-year drinking age cause problems for colleges?
4. What is the legal drinking age in Montreal, Canada? How do the students
    respond to this law at McGill University?

READING CRITICALLY

5. In what ways has alcohol become "the young adult's forbidden fruit" (paragraph 5)?
6. Do you agree with the author that lowering the drinking age would encour-
    age students to put drinking in their lives into perspective? Explain your answer.

Thinking Critically

❸ What would be the short-term result of lowering the drinking age to 18? The long-term
result? Would you be in favor of reducing the drinking age? Why or why not?

7. Why do you think alcohol consumption is so prevalent on U.S. college campuses?

8. In your opinion, what would be the ideal drinking age in the United States? Explain your reasoning.

DISCOVERING RHETORICAL STRATEGIES

9. Seaman starts his essay with a list of real activities that take place on most college campuses. Is this an effective beginning? Why or why not?

10. List Seaman's topics and make an outline of his essay. Does he cover all the important ideas on this subject?

11. How does the specific reference to McGill University in Montreal affect you? What does it do for the essay?

12. What is the thesis of this essay? Where does this thesis statement appear?

MAKING CONNECTIONS

13. Imagine that Seaman, Michael Dorris ("The Broken Cord"), and/or Dave Grossman ("We Are Training Our Kids to Kill") are discussing how tough it is to break an addiction. Which of these addictions do you think would be most difficult to stop? Why?

14. Compare and contrast Seaman's use of examples with those employed by Brent Staples ("A Brother's Murder"), Jessica Mitford ("Behind the Formaldehyde Curtain"), and/or Amy Tan ("Mother Tongue"). Who uses examples most skillfully? Why do you think this is so?

15. Do you think Michael Dorris ("The Broken Cord") would agree with Seaman that the drinking age ought to be lowered? Whose side would you be on? Why?

IDEAS FOR DISCUSSION/WRITING

Preparing to Write

Write freely about the risks students take in college today: What dangers are most common at your college? Which of these is connected with a law? Why do you think students take risks in college? In what ways is the whole college experience ripe for risk-taking? What risks have you taken in college? Were they worth the danger? Why did you take these risks? Would you take them again? Why or why not?

Choosing a Topic

1. *Learning Online:* Imagine that one of your close friends was recently involved in a "pregaming" party at someone's house before a football game. During the party, your friend drank too much alcohol, lost consciousness, and ended up spending the night passed out in a back bedroom. Your friend does not remember several events that happened that evening, and this seriously worries you. Write an email to your friend explaining your concern and persuading him or her to pay more attention to the dangers of alcohol abuse. Use Internet sources you discovered in Preparing to Read to bolster your argument.

2. Your old high school has noticed an increase in drinking before high school dances and other social events. Since you used to hold a seat in the student government, your high school has asked you to come back to your school and talk to the seniors about drinking. What will you say? Since this is such a sensitive issue, the school officials have asked to see a copy of your speech before you deliver it. Prepare your talk, being aware that you need to win the students' trust as you also give them realistic warnings.

3. From what you have observed in college so far, analyze the behavior of your peers. How do they generally manage themselves on your campus during the week? How does that change on the weekend? How do you fit into this "routine"? Explain your observations in an essay to your English instructor.

4. What risks have you taken in your life? Why did you take them? Are you glad you did? Why or why not? Focusing on your own behavior, analyze your attitude toward taking risks. What are the advantages? The disadvantages? Use your experiences and observations to support your analysis.

Before beginning your essay, you might want to consult the checklists on page 482.

DAVE GROSSMAN   (1956–   )

We Are Training Our Kids to Kill

Lieutenant Colonel Dave Grossman is a retired professor of Psychology and Military Science and a former U. S. Army Ranger who has recently founded a new field of scientific study he calls "killology," which investigates how and why people kill each other during wartime, the psychological costs of battle, the root causes of violent crime, and the process of healing that victims of violence must go through (see www.killology.com). Following a B.S. at Columbus College in Georgia (where he was elected to Phi Beta Kappa) and an M.Ed. at the University of Texas, Grossman joined the army, where he rose quickly through the ranks to Lieutenant Colonel and served as a professor at both the United States Military Academy at West Point and as Chair of the Department of Military Science at Arkansas State University. The author of three books—*On Killing: The Psychological Cost of Learning to Kill in War and Society* (1995), *Stop Teaching Our Kids to Kill: A Call to Action Against TV, Movie, and Video Game Violence* (with Gloria deGaetano, 1999), and *On Combat* (2004)—he spends nearly three hundred days on the road each year consulting and giving workshops about combat and violence. He also writes military science fiction and will soon publish a new book entitled *The Two-Space War*. His advice to students using *The Prose Reader* is to avoid a steady diet of violent visual images, which "will lobotomize the brain and make thinking and writing more difficult. If you cleanse your mind (particularly the frontal cortex) with periods of contemplation and reading, you will become a much better writer."

Preparing to Read

The following controversial essay, originally published in the *Saturday Evening Post* in July/August 1999, contains a clear, well-reasoned analysis of the dangers connected with violence on TV and in video games. The author, Dave Grossman, is especially concerned with the way in which these media sources actually train our children to kill.

Exploring Experience: Before you read this essay, think about your views on violence in the media: Do you think watching violence on television and in the movies or playing video games can lead to violent acts? How useful are movie ratings for violence and sex? At what age do you think children should be able to see violence without adult supervision or censorship? Who do you think should control the violence children are exposed to? To what extent should we censor violence in the media? What specific types of violent behavior should be regulated in the media? What should not be censored?

Learning Online: Go to your favorite online news source. How many of the headlines describe violent acts? Consider this information while reading Grossman's argument.

I am from Jonesboro, Arkansas. I travel the world training medical, law en-   1
forcement, and U.S. military personnel about the realities of warfare. I try
to make those who carry deadly force keenly aware of the magnitude of
killing. Too many law enforcement and military personnel act like "cowboys," never stopping to think about who they are and what they are called
to do. I hope I am able to give them a reality check.

So here I am, a world traveler and an expert in the field of "killology," ¹   2
when the (then) largest school massacre in American history happens in my
hometown of Jonesboro, Arkansas. That was the March 24, 1998, schoolyard
shooting deaths of four girls and a teacher. Ten others were injured, and two
boys, ages 11 and 13, were jailed, charged with murder.

Virus of Violence

To understand the why behind Littleton, Jonesboro, Springfield, Pearl,   3
and Paducah, and all the other outbreaks of this "virus of violence," ² we
need to first understand the magnitude of the problem. The per capita murder rate doubled in this country between 1957—when the FBI started keeping track of the data—and 1992. A fuller picture of the problem, however,
is indicated by the rate at which people are attempting to kill one another—
the aggravated assault rate. That rate in America has gone from around 60 per
100,000 in 1957 to over 440 per 100,000 in 2002. As bad as this is, it would
be much worse were it not for two major factors.

The first is the increased imprisonment of violent offenders. The prison   4
population in America nearly quintupled between 1975 and 2002. According
to criminologist John A. DiIulio, "dozens of credible empirical analyses . . .
leave no doubt that the increased use of prisons averted millions of serious
crimes." ³ If it were not for our tremendous imprisonment rate (the highest
of any industrialized nation), the aggravated assault rate and the murder rate
would undoubtedly be even higher.

The second factor keeping the murder rate from being even worse is med-   5
ical technology. According to the U.S. Army Medical Service Corps, a wound
that would have killed nine out of ten soldiers in World War II, nine out of
ten could have survived in Vietnam. Thus, by a very conservative estimate, if
we still had a 1940-level medical technology today, our murder rate would
be ten times higher than it is. The murder rate has been held down by the

---

Thinking Critically

[1] What do you think the term "killology" means?

[2] What does Grossman mean by the "virus of violence" in our country? In what ways is this
problem like a disease?

[3] Do you agree with the assertion that "the increased use of prisons averted millions of
serious crimes"? Explain your reasoning.

development of sophisticated lifesaving skills and techniques, such as helicopter medevacs, 911 operators, paramedics, CPR, trauma centers, and medicines.

Today, both our assault rate and murder rate are at phenomenally high 6 levels. Both are increasing worldwide. In Canada, according to their Center for Justice, per capita assaults increased almost fivefold between 1964 and 2002, attempted murder increased nearly sevenfold, and murders doubled. Similar trends can be seen in other countries in the per capita violent crime rates reported to Interpol between 1977 and 2002. In Australia and New Zealand, the assault rate increased approximately fourfold, and the murder rate nearly doubled in both nations. The assault rate tripled in Sweden and approximately doubled in Belgium, Denmark, England and Wales, France, Hungary, the Netherlands, and Scotland. Meanwhile, all these nations had an associated (but smaller) increase in murder.

This virus of violence is occurring worldwide. The explanation for it has 7 to be some new factor that is occurring in all of these countries. There are many factors involved, and none should be discounted: for example, the prevalence of guns in our society. But violence is rising in many nations with Draconian gun laws. And though we should never downplay child abuse, poverty, or racism, there is only one new variable present in each of these countries that bears the exact same fruit: media violence presented as entertainment for children. ❹

Killing Is Unnatural

Before retiring from the military, I spent almost a quarter of a century as 8 an army infantry officer and a psychologist, learning and studying how to enable people to kill. Believe me, we are very good at it. But it does not come naturally; you have to be taught to kill. And just as the army is conditioning people to kill, we are indiscriminately doing the same thing to our children, but without the safeguards.

After the Jonesboro killings, the head of the American Academy of Pediatrics Task Force on Juvenile Violence came to town and said that children 9 don't naturally kill. It is a learned skill. And they learn it from abuse and violence in the home and, most pervasively, from violence as entertainment in television, the movies, and interactive video games.

Killing requires training because there is a built-in aversion to killing one's 10 own kind. ❺ I can best illustrate this fact by drawing on my own military research into the act of killing.

Thinking Critically

❹ How much violence do you think the average six-year-old child sees on television each day? What do you think is the cumulative effect of watching it for many years?

❺ Do you think this is true? Do most people have an innate aversion to killing other human beings? Explain your reasoning.

We all know how hard it is to have a discussion with a frightened or   11
angry human being. Vasoconstriction, the narrowing of the blood vessels,
has literally closed down the forebrain—that great gob of gray matter that
makes one a human being and distinguishes one from a dog. When those
neurons close down, the midbrain takes over and your thought processes
and reflexes are indistinguishable from your dog's. If you've worked with
animals, you have some understanding of what happens to frightened
human beings on the battlefield. The battlefield and violent crime are in
the realm of midbrain responses.

Within the midbrain, there is a powerful, God-given resistance to killing   12
your own kind. Every species, with a few exceptions, has a hardwired resistance to killing its own kind **⑥** in territorial and mating battles. When animals
with antlers and horns fight one another, they head-butt in a nonfatal fashion. But when they fight any other species, they go to the side to gut and gore.
Piranhas will turn their fangs on anything, but they fight one another with
flicks of the tail. Rattlesnakes will bite anything, but they wrestle one another.
Almost every species has this hard-wired resistance to killing its own kind.

When we human beings are overwhelmed with anger and fear, we slam   13
head-on into that midbrain resistance that generally prevents us from killing.
Only sociopaths—who by definition don't have that resistance—lack this
innate violence immune system.

Throughout all human history, when humans have fought each other, there   14
has been a lot of posturing. Adversaries make loud noises and puff themselves
up, trying to daunt the enemy. There is a lot of fleeing and submission. Ancient
battles were nothing more than great shoving matches. It was not until one
side turned and ran that most of the killing happened, and most of that was
stabbing people in the back. All of the ancient military historians report that
the vast majority of killing happened in pursuit when one side was fleeing.

In more modern times, the average firing rate was incredibly low in Civil   15
War battles. British author Paddy Griffith demonstrates in his book *The Battle Tactics of the Civil War* that the killing potential of the average Civil War regiment was anywhere from five hundred to a thousand men per minute. The
actual killing rate was only one or two men per minute per regiment. At
the Battle of Gettysburg, of the 27,000 muskets picked up from the dead
and dying after the battle, 90 percent were loaded. This is an anomaly, because
it took 90 percent of their time to load muskets and only 5 percent to fire.
But even more amazing, of the thousands of loaded muskets, over half had
multiple loads in the barrel—one had 23 loads in the barrel. **⑦**

Thinking Critically

⑥ What does the phrase "hardwired resistance" mean in this context?

⑦ What do all these statistics imply about the willingness of Civil War soldiers to fire their
muskets?

In reality, the average man would load his musket and bring it to his shoulder, but he could not bring himself to kill. He would be brave, he would stand shoulder to shoulder, he would do what he was trained to do; but at the moment of truth, he could not bring himself to pull the trigger. And so he lowered the weapon and loaded it again. Of those who did fire, only a tiny percentage fired to hit. The vast majority fired over the enemy's head.   16

During World War II, U.S. Army Brig. Gen. S. L. A. Marshall had a team   17
of researchers study what soldiers did in battle. For the first time in history, they asked individual soldiers what they did in battle. They discovered that only 15 to 20 percent of the individual riflemen could bring themselves to fire at an exposed enemy soldier.

That is the reality of the battlefield. Only a small percentage of soldiers   18
are able and willing to participate. Men are willing to die. They are willing to sacrifice themselves for their nation; but they are not willing to kill. It is a phenomenal insight into human nature; but when the military became aware of that, they systematically went about the process of trying to fix this "problem." From the military perspective, a 15 percent firing rate among riflemen is like a 15 percent literacy rate among librarians. And fix it the military did. By the Korean War, around 55 percent of the soldiers were willing to fire to kill. And by Vietnam, the rate rose to over 90 percent.

The method in this madness: desensitization.   19

How the military increases the killing rate of soldiers in combat is instruc-   20
tive because our culture today is doing the same thing to our children. The training methods militaries use are brutalization, classical conditioning, operant conditioning, and role modeling. I will explain each of these in the military context and show how these same factors are contributing to the phenomenal increase of violence in our culture.

Brutalization and desensitization are what happens at boot camp. From   21
the moment you step off the bus, you are physically and verbally abused: countless push-ups, endless hours at attention or running with heavy loads, while carefully trained professionals take turns screaming at you. [8] Your head is shaved; you are herded together naked and dressed alike, losing all individuality. This brutalization is designed to break down your existing mores and norms and force you to accept a new set of values that embraces destruction, violence, and death as a way of life. In the end, you are desensitized to violence and accept it as a normal and essential survival skill in your brutal new world.

Something very similar to this desensitization toward violence is hap-   22
pening to our children through violence in the media—but instead of

---

Thinking Critically

[8] What do you think is the relationship between brutalization and desensitization in armed forces training?

18-year-olds, it begins at the age of 18 months when a child is first able to discern what is happening on television. At that age, a child can watch something happening on television and mimic that action. But it isn't until children are six or seven years old that the part of the brain kicks in that lets them understand where information comes from. Even though young children have some understanding of what it means to pretend, they are developmentally unable to distinguish clearly between fantasy and reality. [9]

When young children see somebody shot, stabbed, raped, brutalized, degraded, or murdered on TV, to them it is as though it were actually happening. To have a child of three, four, or five watch a "splatter" movie, learning to relate to a character for the first 90 minutes and then in the last 30 minutes watch helplessly as that new friend is hunted and brutally murdered, is the moral and psychological equivalent of introducing your child to a friend, letting her play with that friend, and then butchering that friend in front of your child's eyes. And this happens to our children hundreds upon hundreds of times.   23

Sure, they are told, "Hey, it's all for fun. Look, this isn't real; it's just TV." And they nod their little heads and say OK. But they can't tell the difference. Can you remember a point in your life or in your children's lives when dreams, reality, and television were all jumbled together? That's what it is like to be at that level of psychological development. That's what the media are doing to them.   24

The *Journal of the American Medical Association* published the definitive epidemiological study on the impact of TV violence. The research demonstrated what happened in numerous nations after television made its appearance as compared to nations and regions without TV. The two nations or regions being compared are demographically and ethnically identical; only one variable is different: the presence of television. In every nation, region, or city with television, there is an immediate explosion of violence on the playground, and within 15 years there is a doubling of the murder rate. Why 15 years? That is how long it takes for the brutalization of a three-to five-year-old to reach the "prime crime age." That is how long it takes for you to reap what you have sown when you brutalize and desensitize a three-year-old. [10]   25

Today the data linking violence in the media to violence in society are superior to those linking cancer and tobacco. Hundreds of sound scientific   26

Thinking Critically

[9] According to the author, at what age are children able to understand the difference between fantasy and reality? How does this affect their reaction to televised violence?

[10] How is the brutalization and desensitization of soldiers in training different from the indoctrination of a three-year-old through televised violence?

studies demonstrate the social impact of brutalization by the media. The *Journal of the American Medical Association* concluded that "the introduction of television in the 1950s caused a subsequent doubling of the homicide rate, i.e., long-term childhood exposure to television is a causal factor behind approximately one half of the homicides committed in the United States, or approximately 10,000 homicides annually." The article went on to say that "if, hypothetically, television technology had never been developed, there would today be 10,000 fewer homicides each year in the United States, 70,000 fewer rapes, and 700,000 fewer injurious assaults" (June 10, 1992).

Classical Conditioning

Classical conditioning is like the famous case of Pavlov's dogs they teach in Psychology 101. The dogs learned to associate the ringing of the bell with food, and once conditioned, the dogs could not hear the bell without salivating. 27

The Japanese were masters at using classical conditioning with their soldiers. Early in World War II, Chinese prisoners were placed in a ditch on their knees with their hands bound behind them. And one by one, a select few Japanese soldiers would go into the ditch and bayonet "their" prisoner to death. This is a horrific way to kill another human being. Up on the bank, countless other young soldiers would cheer them on in their violence. Comparatively few soldiers actually killed in these situations, but by making the others watch and cheer, the Japanese were able to use these kinds of atrocities to classically condition a very large audience to associate pleasure with human death and suffering. [11] Immediately afterwards, the soldiers who had been spectators were treated to sake, the best meal they had in months, and to so-called comfort girls. The result? They learned to associate committing violent acts with pleasure. 28

The Japanese found these kinds of techniques to be extraordinarily effective at quickly enabling very large numbers of soldiers to commit atrocities in the years to come. Operant conditioning (which we will look at shortly) teaches you to kill, but classical conditioning is a subtle but powerful mechanism that teaches you to like it. [12] 29

This technique is so morally reprehensible that there are very few examples of it in modern U.S. military training, but there are some clear-cut examples of it being done by the media to our children. What is happening to our 30

Thinking Critically

[11] How and why did the World War II Japanese army teach its soldiers to "associate pleasure with human death and suffering"?

[12] What is the difference between "operant conditioning" and "classical conditioning"? Which do you think is more sinister? Which is more powerful?

children is the reverse of the aversion therapy portrayed in the movie *A Clockwork Orange.* In *A Clockwork Orange,* a brutal sociopath, a mass murderer, is strapped to a chair and forced to watch violent movies while he is injected with a drug that nauseates him. So he sits and gags and retches as he watches the movies. After hundreds of repetitions of this, he associates violence with nausea. And it limits his ability to be violent.

We are doing the exact opposite: Our children watch vivid pictures of human suffering and death, and they learn to associate it with their favorite soft drink and candy bar, or their girlfriend's perfume. 31

After the Jonesboro shootings, one of the high-school teachers told me how her students reacted when she told them about the shootings at the middle school. "They laughed," she told me with dismay. A similar reaction happens all the time in movie theaters when there is bloody violence. The young people laugh and cheer and keep right on eating popcorn and drinking pop. We have raised a generation of barbarians who have learned to associate violence with pleasure, like the Romans cheering and snacking as the Christians were slaughtered in the Colosseum. **13** 32

The result is a phenomenon that functions much like AIDS, a phenomenon I call AVIDS—Acquired Violence Immune Deficiency Syndrome. AIDS has never killed anybody. It destroys your immune system, and then other diseases that shouldn't kill you become fatal. Television violence by itself does not kill you. It destroys your violence immune system and conditions you to derive pleasure from violence. And once you are at close range with another human being and it's time for you to pull that trigger, Acquired Violence Immune Deficiency Syndrome can destroy your midbrain resistance. 33

Operant Conditioning

The third method the military uses is operant conditioning, a very powerful repetitive procedure of stimulus-response, stimulus-response. A benign example is the use of flight simulators to train pilots. An airline pilot in training sits in front of a flight simulator for endless hours; when a particular warning light goes on, he is taught to react in a certain way. When another warning light goes on, a different reaction is required. Stimulus-response, stimulus-response, stimulus-response. One day the pilot is actually flying a jumbo jet; the plane is going down, and 300 people are screaming behind him. He is wetting his seat cushion, and he is scared out of his wits; but he does the right thing. Why? Because he has been conditioned to respond reflexively to this particular crisis. 34

Thinking Critically

13 Do you agree with the author when she says "we have raised a generation of barbarians who have learned to associate violence with pleasure"? Why or why not?

When people are frightened or angry, they will do what they have been [35] conditioned to do. In fire drills, children learn to file out of the school in orderly fashion. One day there is a real fire, and they are frightened out of their wits; but they do exactly what they have been conditioned to do, and it saves their lives. 14

The military and law enforcement community have made killing a con- [36] ditioned response. This has substantially raised the firing rate on the modern battlefield. Whereas infantry training in World War II used bull's-eye targets, now soldiers learn to fire at realistic, man-shaped silhouettes that pop into their field of view. That is the stimulus. The trainees have only a split second to engage the target. The conditioned response is to shoot the target, and then it drops. Stimulus-response, stimulus-response, stimulus-response—soldiers or police officers experience hundreds of repetitions. Later, when soldiers are on the battlefield or a police officer is walking a beat and somebody pops up with a gun, they will shoot reflexively and shoot to kill. We know that 75 to 80 percent of the shooting on the modern battlefield is the result of this kind of stimulus-response training.

Now, if you're a little troubled by that, how much more should we be [37] troubled by the fact that every time a child plays an interactive point-and-shoot video game, he is learning the exact same conditioned reflex and motor skills?

I was an expert witness in a murder case in South Carolina offering mit- [38] igation for a kid who was facing the death penalty. I tried to explain to the jury that interactive video games had conditioned him to shoot a gun to kill. He had spent hundreds of dollars on video games learning to point and shoot, point and shoot. One day he and his buddy decided it would be fun to rob the local convenience store. They walked in, and he pointed a snub-nosed .38 pistol at the clerk's head. The clerk turned to look at him, and the defendant shot reflexively from about six feet. The bullet hit the clerk right between the eyes—which is a pretty remarkable shot with that weapon at that range—and killed this father of two. Afterward, we asked the boy what happened and why he did it. It clearly was not part of the plan to kill the guy—it was being videotaped from six different directions. He said, "I don't know. It was a mistake. It wasn't supposed to happen."

In the military and law-enforcement worlds, the right option is often [39] not to shoot. But you never, ever put your money in that video machine with the intention of not shooting. There is always some stimulus that sets you off. And when he was excited, and his heart rate went up, and vaso-constriction closed his forebrain down, this young man did exactly what he

---

Thinking Critically

14 What are some other positive results of "operant conditioning"?

was conditioned to do: he reflexively pulled the trigger, shooting accurately just like all those times he played video games.

This process is extraordinarily powerful and frightening. The result is ever 40 more "homemade" sociopaths who kill reflexively. Our children are learning how to kill and learning to like the idea of killing; and then we have the audacity to say, "Oh my goodness, what's wrong?" **15**

One of the boys involved in the Jonesboro shootings (and they are just 41 boys) had a fair amount of experience shooting real guns. The other one, to the best of our knowledge, had almost no experience shooting. Between them, those two boys fired 27 shots from a range of over 100 yards, and they hit 15 people. That's pretty remarkable shooting. We run into these situations often—kids who have never picked up a gun in their lives pick up a real gun and are incredibly accurate. Why? Video games.

UNDERSTANDING DETAILS

1. According to Grossman, what is the "virus of violence" (paragraph 3)?
2. What evidence does the author use to argue that "killing is unnatural"?
3. What three methods does the military use to train its soldiers to kill?
4. How does Grossman claim we are training our children to kill?

READING CRITICALLY

5. What two factors does the author believe control the murder rate in the United States? How do these factors affect this rate?
6. How are the techniques used in video games similar to those taught in military training?
7. How did the U.S. military train more soldiers to actually fire their guns?
8. How can we control this epidemic of violence that Grossman outlines?

DISCOVERING RHETORICAL STRATEGIES

9. What do you think Grossman's purpose is in this essay?
10. Who do you think would be most interested in this essay?
11. What effect do you think this essay will have on parents?
12. Describe the writer's point of view in a complete sentence.

MAKING CONNECTIONS

13. To what extent would Grossman, Brent Staples ("A Brother's Murder"), Lyn Mikel Brown and Meda Chesney-Lind ("Bad Girls, Bad Girls, Whatcha Gonna Do?"), and/or Barbara Ehrenreich ("The Ecstasy of War") agree that violence

---

Thinking Critically

15 In what ways does the author indict all of us in the creation of "homemade sociopaths"?

is encoded in our human DNA? What outside influences, according to these authors, make us a more violent culture? Which of the three authors makes the most convincing case for his or her point of view? Explain your answer.

14. Imagine a conversation between Grossman, Kimberly Wozencraft ("Notes from the Country Club"), and/or Malcolm X ("Learning to Read") about the relationship between societal pressures and incarceration. Why do you think our jails are so crowded? What can be done about this massive increase in the U.S. prison population?

15. How do you think Bill Cosby ("The Baffling Question"), Robert Ramirez ("The Barrio"), and/or Mary Pipher ("Beliefs About Families") would each respond to Grossman's implication that parents need to be more vigilant in monitoring what their children watch on television? What is your own opinion on this issue?

IDEAS FOR DISCUSSION/WRITING

Preparing to Write

Write freely about your feelings concerning censorship: Should violence on TV be censored in any way? Why or why not? At what age can children safely watch violence in the media? Do you believe a relationship exists between watching violence and acting in a violent manner? Who is most responsible for restricting or editing the violence that children see?

Choosing a Topic

1. *Learning Online:* What is the most popular current video game? How violent is it? Do you believe that video games, movies, television shows, or popular music influence youth violence? In a Google search, type "violence and video games" into the search box, and read some of the opinions on this subject. Write an argument in which you take a position regarding this controversial issue. Following Grossman's style, use several different types of examples to support your claims.

2. *Time* magazine has asked you to respond directly to Grossman's article. Do you think his argument about the relationship between children and video games is reasonable? Give specific examples to support your contention.

3. As an apprentice at a TV station, you have been asked to represent your age group by giving your opinion on the network's inclusion of violence in their programming. What is your opinion concerning TV violence? In what ways do you think your opinion represents the consensus of U.S. society as a whole?

4. Research and describe the censorship practices of another country. Explain specifically how that country's views on censorship are carried out in practice. Give as many examples as possible to support your explanation.

Before beginning your essay, you might want to consult the checklists on page 482.

I'm Not Willing to Settle for Crumbs

Born in Eau Claire, Wisconsin, Kim Severson earned her B.A. in Journalism at Michigan State University before turning to a career in newspaper writing. Currently a staff writer for the Dining Section of the *New York Times,* she previously wrote about cooking and the culture of food for the *San Francisco Chronicle,* following a seven-year stint as an editor and reporter at the *Anchorage Daily News* in Alaska. Before writing about food full-time, she covered crime, education, social services, and government activities for several daily newspapers on the West Coast. The author of two books—*The New Alaska Cookbook* (2001) and *The Trans Fat Solution: Cooking and Shopping to Eliminate the Deadliest Fat from Your Diet* (2003)—Severson has won several regional and national awards for news and feature writing, including the Casey Medal for Meritorious Journalism for her work on childhood obesity in 2002 and four James Beard awards for food writing. Her hobbies include cooking (no surprise there!), reading, and playing softball in Brooklyn, where she lives with her partner, Katia Hetter. Her advice to students using *The Prose Reader* is to "always keep a notebook for moments of inspiration. Keep writing down any important ideas and thoughts that you have. You will inevitably forget that great idea if it's not in the notebook."

Preparing to Read

This article was originally published in *Newsweek* in 2005. In it, Kim Severson uses personal anecdotes to argue for equal rights for gay couples in marriage.

Exploring Experience: As you prepare to read this essay, consider your views on marriage: What does marriage signify in our society? Why do many people consider marriage "sacred"? What does that mean in this context? Who should be allowed to get married? Should anyone be prohibited from getting married? Why is the institution of marriage important to some and unimportant to others? Where do you stand on the issue of gay marriage?

Learning Online: Visit a retail Web site that features products specifically tailored to same-sex wedding ceremonies, such as www.gayweddings.com or www.pinkproducts.co.uk. Browse through the products available (e.g., invitations, cake toppers, reception favors, and guest books). Compare these products to those used in traditional heterosexual weddings. Can you think of other items that should be offered?

Tag, You're It!

The following selection is a pictorial essay compiled from "tagging," or graffiti, in various cities throughout the United States.

Preparing to Read

Tagging is an illegal practice that marks a building or structure with the identity of a person or group through graphics of some sort. Most of the graphics make statements—some in aesthetically appealing ways, others with very unappealing results.

Exploring Experience: Before you read this essay, think about your views on graffiti: Do you have any direct experience with graffiti as either a creator or an observer? What is that experience? Why do you think graffiti is illegal? Where have you seen graffiti? What messages does graffiti send? Is the graffiti you have seen artistic or not? Do you think people should be allowed to express themselves through graphics in public places? Explain your answer.

Learning Online: Go to www.graffiti.org, and look for graffiti from your city or from a city near you. What is your general opinion of the graffiti pictured on this site?

New York

12A

Miami

Los Angeles

Dallas

Chicago

Atlanta

Seattle

UNDERSTANDING DETAILS

1. Define graffiti from the examples presented here.
2. What two characteristics do the examples of graffiti in this photo essay have in common?
3. Choose a picture from the photo essay, and explain it to the class. Do the colors help convey any part of the message?
4. Which of these examples of graffiti do you like best? Explain your choice.

READING CRITICALLY

5. Why do you think graffiti is so popular in urban settings?
6. Why is graffiti illegal?

7. Do you think graffiti defiles its location?
8. Are these examples typical of graffiti in places near you?

DISCOVERING RHETORICAL STRATEGIES

9. Can pictures be read like words? Explain your answer.
10. Who pays attention to graffiti?
11. Do you think we should furnish legal outlets in the United States for these modes of expression? Explain your answer.
12. What rhetorical strategies are at work in these pictures? Give examples of each.

MAKING CONNECTIONS

13. Compare and contrast the examples of graffiti in this essay. Which looks most like something you might have produced? Explain your answer.
14. Imagine that Brent Staples ("A Brother's Murder"), Robert Ramirez ("The Barrio"), and/or the people who created the pictures in this photo essay were discussing the importance of graffiti. Who would argue most strongly that graffiti is a reputable art form? Explain your answer.
15. How is developing the ability to read pictures in this photo essay different from discovering how to read books in Malcolm X's "Learning to Read" and/or Richard Wright's "The Library Card"?

IDEAS FOR DISCUSSION /WRITING

Preparing to Write

Write freely about your views on graffiti: What is your experience with graffiti? What do you think of graffiti in general? Why do people create graffiti? Why do you think graffiti is illegal? Should any form of it be legal? Are there any benefits to graffiti?

Choosing a Topic

1. *Learning Online:* Go to the Web site you consulted earlier (www.graffiti.org), and create your own photo essay that deals with graffiti in your area. Choose your pictures carefully with an eye toward your thesis or controlling idea: What do you want to say with your essay? Following your graphic essay, write three discussion questions to focus the readers' attention on your primary message.
2. Your old high school has asked you to talk to its senior class about the topic of graffiti. What constitutes "graffiti" in your opinion? What should we do to control the production of graffiti? Write a well-developed essay on this issue.
3. Can graffiti ever be art? If so, when is this possible? If not, why not?
4. Do you think this type of self-expression should be allowed in public places? If so, explain your reasoning, and provide a solution for finding legal avenues for it. If you believe it should not be allowed, explain why, and provide effective ideas for preventing the production of graffiti.

Before beginning your essay, you might want to consult the checklists on page 482.

There is such a sweet light in the face of the straight people who want   1
me to get married. It starts with that sparkly, conspiratorial smile.
They squeeze my arm, leaning in like a favorite auntie. "So," they say,
"are you going to Massachusetts?"

I can barely stand the kick to the curb I'm about to deliver.   2

I would love nothing more than to marry my partner. I love this girl. I   3
want the dinner and the dance and the promise of her Social Security check
if, God forbid, she dies young. I want a joint tax return and the family discount at the health club.

I also want some return for the years I've spent giving straight people   4
wedding presents. I want everyone at the office to gasp at my engagement
ring and pitch in for a bad bakery cake to celebrate. I want the magic of the
day I was conditioned to hope for. ❶

That's not going to happen by going to Massachusetts, where same-sex   5
marriage has been legal since 2003. Sure, I might get the cake and a little slice
of symbolism, but any legal or financial advantage would dissolve once we
left the state. For gay couples like us, marriage is about collecting paper. ❷

Our commitment is measured by the size of our legal files, which grow   6
each time we move to a new state or accumulate property or struggle to
ensure that one person's retirement account will go to the other.

Say my girlfriend and I did take what would be an unquestionably roman-   7
tic trip to Massachusetts. We'd have to start our married life off with a lie,
since you have to declare your intention to live there. We'd have to wait
three days for a license, then get a certificate saying we don't have syphilis and
listen to a lecture on AIDS (a nice bit of equality with our straight brothers
and sisters). For the drive, we'd stock the glove compartment with our medical powers of attorney and hospital authorization forms. That way, if we got
in a car accident and one of us needed to get into the other's hospital room
or make some hard decisions, we wouldn't get shut out while doctors tried
to reach our parents.

Then there's the general power of attorney, which is good, all-round   8
backup. We'd also tuck in the New York City domestic-partnership certificate we got at city hall. It cost us $1 more than the license straight people
buy, for reasons I can't suss out. (My girlfriend says it doesn't really give us
much except the right to visit each other in Rikers. Still, it might work in
a pinch.) All this, on top of the regular pressures of finding a hall, someone
to do the ceremony, and a florist.

Thinking Critically

❶ When did you first suspect that this essay was written by a gay author? What textual clues
led you to this conclusion?

❷ Why is marriage "about collecting paper" for Severson and her partner?

Even if we did decide that one more piece of paper might actually make   9
us married, the government wouldn't care. Consider, for example, our medical insurance. She is covered by the domestic-partnership benefits of my
job. That's great, until you run headfirst into the federal tax law. Because the
Feds don't think gay weddings are real, even if we did get married I'd still have
to pay taxes on an extra $9,370.20—what her medical coverage is worth.

Don't get me wrong. I applaud the right-thinking folks in Massachusetts,   10
Vermont and Canada. I appreciate the recent battle in Connecticut, where
we get something that looks a lot like marriage but isn't called that. This is
a civil-rights battle rooted in love, and it's moving quickly.

I'm grateful that in the Blue States and some of the Red it's not cool to   11
fire me from my job based on my sexual orientation. Except for one incident at a weird resort near Kansas City, Mo., my girlfriend and I have never
been hassled when we've asked for a double bed. Even high schools have
gay–straight alliances now. The only gay–straight alliance at my school was
when the straight kids called me a lezzie.

I understand the emotional draw of a legally sanctioned ceremony. We   12
were living in San Francisco when gay marriage started breaking out all over
city hall one Friday afternoon in the winter of last year. My girlfriend was
covering it for the daily paper, and she called me to come watch what was
a historic moment.

I saw people on the steps of the beaux-arts building, weeping and kiss-   13
ing. On that glorious day, it felt as if I could have what all my straight friends
had. I hadn't known how heavy the oppression was until it was lifted, even
for a moment.

We didn't get married. My girlfriend believed that as a journalist, she   14
couldn't be a part of a story she was writing about. (The old journalistic-
objectivity excuse—like I haven't heard that before.) She didn't buy my
argument that straight, married people shouldn't be able to cover it then,
either.

The truth was, we didn't want to rush it. Isn't the whole point of getting   15
married to have your brothers make stupid toasts and your mother cry and your
friends swear to help keep you together when you're falling apart—to craft a
public sharing of love? ❸ Marriage is not about driving to a place where you
don't live or settling for a ceremony that will be recognized only there.

It's my wedding, damn it. I don't want the crumbs. ❹ I want the whole cake.   16

Thinking Critically

❸ Why does the author want "to craft a public sharing of love"? In what ways is this desire
different from the feelings of straight couples?

❹ What does Severson mean when she explains that she doesn't want "the crumbs"? How does
this metaphor work in the context of the essay? Is it an effective conclusion for her essay?

UNDERSTANDING DETAILS

1. What reasons does Severson give for wanting to get married?
2. What is the "little slice of symbolism" Severson is referring to in paragraph 5?
3. In what ways is marriage for gay couples about "collecting paper" (paragraph 5)?
4. Why does Severson believe a Massachusetts marriage is not for her?

READING CRITICALLY

5. In your opinion, who should be allowed to marry?
6. In what ways is gay marriage "a civil-rights battle rooted in love" (paragraph 10)?
7. What do you think is "the emotional draw of a legally sanctioned ceremony" that Severson refers to in paragraph 12?
8. Explain the last paragraph of Severson's essay.

DISCOVERING RHETORICAL STRATEGIES

9. Explain the title of this essay.
10. Severson uses the word "oppression" in paragraph 13. Define this word in the context of gay rights.
11. Is developing her argument with personal examples and anecdotes effective for this topic, or would a more objective essay be more persuasive?
12. How effective is Severson's argument that she wants "the whole cake" (paragraph 16) effective? Explain your answer.

MAKING CONNECTIONS

13. Compare and contrast the quality of love portrayed by Severson, Judith Waller-stein and Sandra Blakeslee ("Second Chances for Children of Divorce"), and/or Mary Roach ("Meet the Bickersons").
14. Do you think that Mary Pipher ("Beliefs About Families") and/or Tamala Edwards ("Multi-Colored Families") would agree with Severson that a gay couple would make a good "family"? Why or why not?
15. How do Severson, Richard Rodriguez ("Public and Private Language"), Jessica Mitford ("Behind the Formaldehyde Curtain"), and/or Amy Tan ("Mother Tongue") use specific details to help advance their arguments? Which author is most skilled at this technique? Why do you think this is so?

IDEAS FOR DISCUSSION/WRITING

Preparing to Write

Write freely about your views on gay marriage: Is marriage an important ritual to you? Why or why not? Should the institution of marriage be denied to anyone? What do you think is the main reason people decide to get married? How important is marriage to society? Explain your answer. Why is marriage important to some people and not to others? Are there any rituals important to you that you were not allowed to participate in? Why were you excluded? Did the decision make sense to you? How did it make you feel?

Choosing a Topic

1. *Learning Online:* Revisit the retail Web site for Pink Products (www.pinkproducts .co.uk). Imagine that you are running a similar company that sells all types of wedding products. However, you would like to make as much profit as possible by attracting both straight and gay couples. Create a one-page advertisement or marketing brochure featuring your products. Design it in such a way that it would appeal to both audiences.
2. Write an argument either for or against gay marriage. Before you start writing, gather some information on this topic from the Internet. Then support your position with appropriate evidence.
3. How does disappointment make us stronger? Choose an activity or event that you were excluded from even though participating in it was important to you, and write an essay discussing the activity and explaining how the disappointment made you a stronger person.
4. You have been asked by the local Psychology Club to be on a panel debating the advantages and disadvantages of marriage in society today. You decide to write out your thoughts before the panel presentation. In essay form, argue for or against marriage as an important institution in our society. What are your reasons? What will be the reasons of the opposition? Can you anticipate and counter the opposition? Explore all angles of this issue so you are well prepared for the debate.

Before beginning your essay, you might want to consult the checklists on page 482.

OPPOSING VIEWPOINTS

Immigration

The following essays take opposite views on the question of immigration controls. The first, by Michael Scott, argues in favor of more stringent restraint on immigration into the United States. Scott is a graduate of the UCLA School of Management currently employed as a national sales manager for a high-tech electronics firm. His interest in immigration began twelve years ago when he stumbled upon nearly one hundred illegal aliens hiding in the scrub brush in Newport Beach, California. His advice to students using *The Prose Reader* is to concentrate on topics they feel passionate about: "The first draft of an essay should come straight from the heart or gut. Don't worry about spelling or punctuation at that early stage. Just let it all hang out. Then go back and smooth everything out to create the finished product."

Richard Raynor, who takes the other side of the immigration question, is a British-born journalist and Cambridge graduate who has published six novels, among them *The Elephant* (1992), *The Blue Suit: Memoir of a Crime* (1995), *Los Angeles Without a Map* (1997), and *The Cloud Sketcher* (2001, soon to be made into a movie starring Brad Pitt). His advice for aspiring authors is to "write about the kinds of things you like to read, something that will make you want to turn the page. As John Cleese says in a Monty Python sketch, 'it's not just getting the right number of words—it's getting them in the right order.'"

Preparing to Read

The following essays were first published in *The Social Contract* (2000) and *New York Times Magazine* (1996) respectively. They take opposing viewpoints on the many complex issues associated with illegal immigration.

Exploring Experience: Before you begin to read these essays, think about immigration and its effect on society: How do you feel about illegal immigration? Whom should we stop from entering our borders? Whom should we let through? Why is immigration such a major issue in the United States? What do immigrants generally bring to the United States? What do they take from our country? Do you worry about the expense of illegal aliens? What other issues concern you about this topic?

Learning Online: Visit the Generation Engage Web site (www.Generation Engage.org), and click on the Video Library link. Choose "Browse by Issue," and then scroll on the left to "Immigration" to hear current facts and opinions on immigration. Pay special attention to the issues surrounding illegal immigrants. Consider how each writer uses evidence to develop his argument.

MICHAEL SCOTT   (1948–   )

America Must Take Stronger Measures to Halt Illegal Immigration

In 1991, I accidentally stumbled upon a botched illegal immigration oper-   1
ation on a nearby Southern California beach—in broad daylight. Nearly
one-hundred illegal immigrants were hiding in a few tiny gullies, partially
protected by a cadre of lookouts, presumably waiting for transportation to
get them to their destinations. Neither the local police nor Los Angeles
Immigration and Naturalization Service (INS) showed much concern. This
resulted in my researching the background and realities of illegal immigration, and the more I learned, the worse it got. We've got a ticking time bomb
on our hands, [1] made worse by legions of government officials who just
slumber on or push their heads deeper into the sand to curry favor with
those who support this relentless invasion. Just as bad, lots of Americans have
been sucker-punched into inaction by threats of being called "racist," "bigot"
and sundry yada yada.

Then, in 1999, I had a conversation with Arizona rancher Roger Barnett,   2
whose property is under year-round siege by hordes of illegal aliens. His
Chochise County border sector is overwhelmed by about 475,000 illegal
aliens annually. Although Barnett has apprehended over 1000 illegal aliens
on his property and turned them over to the Border Patrol, he's anything
but a vigilante. Roger has lived in Douglas, Arizona, all of his 50-some years
and is infuriated by the on-going destruction of his property caused by
incessant swarms of illegal immigrants, as well as by the repeated failures of
the INS to stem this relentless flood. [2] Barnett and his neighbors have had
it with an unmerciful stealth migration that generates mountains of rotting
garbage, piles of discarded diapers, food containers and plastic water bottles,
and sundry filth everywhere—exacerbated by the stench of excrement, poisoned (or throat-slit) pets and livestock, and lots of stolen property that
wasn't tied down.

Of special ire is Barnett's 80-year-old widowed neighbor who lives behind   3
her chain-link fence, with a shotgun and pistol always near by, and who's afraid
to come out at night and challenge the hoards who have ruined her crops and

---

Thinking Critically

[1] Do you agree that illegal immigration in this country is a "ticking time bomb"? Why or
why not?

[2] How do the metaphors "incessant swarms" and "relentless flood" help the author make his
point?

garden and made her a virtual prisoner in her own home. She's afraid to buy more guard dogs since the last two were poisoned, probably by "coyotes."

Costs of Illegal Immigration

One look at the ravages of illegal immigration in California is enough to   4
make most Americans sick. At least 40 percent of the nation's 6 million illegal immigrants are here. From a base of 2.4 million illegal immigrants already present, they just keep coming—120,000 net new illegals each year into California (300,000 nationally), and the horrendous social costs just keep rising. There are 408,000 illegal immigrant K–12 students to educate at a cost to California taxpayers of approximately $2.2 billion annually, for example. Never mind that these students can't work, drive, or vote once they graduate, unless they obtain fraudulent documents.

Taxpayers subsidize 96,000 illegal immigrant births in statewide county   5
hospitals (200,000 nationally) at a yearly cost of $352 million. Then we have annual [welfare] costs for these new citizen children of nearly $552 million. Add another $557 million to incarcerate 23,000 illegal alien felons in California, plus $60 million health care costs for various services, and we're over $3.7 billion annually—out of our pockets and against our overwhelming opposition to such outrages. ❸

Eliminating this brutal migratory devastation involves two basic actions—   6
enforcing our own immigration laws and accepting the ugly reality that "we've met the enemy and it is us."

Enforcing the Law

Three fundamental law enforcement steps must be taken to break the   7
back of illegal immigration. First, our borders must be sealed. No more baloney about how difficult this might be. The INS instituted a Border Patrol crackdown in 1994 in the El Paso sector and then took it to San Diego a year later. In 1993, 90 percent of all illegal aliens crossed at border cities. Today [in 2000], two-thirds cross in remote areas. In 1994, in the San Diego sector, 42 percent of all illegals surged through a 14-mile-corridor near Imperial Beach. Another 22.6 percent entered in and around El Paso. Both sectors are now almost impregnable, as these flows have become trickles. So today's illegals are going where it's easier to get across, like Douglas, Arizona. The inescapable conclusion is that the crackdown has succeeded where sufficient resources have been applied. This isn't a matter of insufficient resources or wherewithal; it's a matter of insufficient willpower, as well as a writing-off of those individuals and organizations who want illegal immigration to succeed.

Thinking Critically

❸ Why do you think the alleged costs of illegal immigration are used so often to argue against it?

The next critical law enforcement step is to prosecute employers who 8
hire illegal aliens. ◆ The Justice Department is hardly lifting a finger in this
area. If there were no jobs, most illegal aliens would leave, or most wouldn't
come in the first place. The fantasy of illegal immigration cheerleaders that
the economy would collapse without illegal labor simply doesn't wash. Since
when don't we enforce laws (or break them) in accordance with our own
standards of right and wrong? I sometimes speed on California interstates,
and I'm prepared for the fines if caught. But this doesn't excuse me from punishment nor the California Highway Patrol (CHP) from enforcement.

This baloney about the need for "guest workers" is pure bunk. Both the 9
California Division of Labor and the General Accounting Office (GAO)
have confirmed there are currently two farm workers for every agricultural
job in California. This glut of farm workers has depressed agricultural wages
over the past twenty years, in inflation adjusted terms, by 20 percent and
spawned deplorable working conditions.

Job opportunities for low-skilled workers have been declining for three 10
decades. The continued influx of low-skilled, uneducated immigrants has
depressed earnings and limited opportunities. Income disparity has widened
as a result of too many low-skilled workers pursuing too few jobs.

A University of California (Davis) agricultural economist (and several 11
other noted researchers) published "Poverty Amid Prosperity," a compilation of research findings on "The processes of immigration and its unexamined impacts on cities and towns" (July 1997; The Urban Institute Press).
They offered the following analysis of the impact of farm worker wage
increases on both grower expenses and the price of food:

> And suppose that the entire cost of higher farm wages is passed on to consumers, so that
> the annual cost of the farm labor used to produce the fresh fruit consumed by the aver-
> age American household rises from $8.60 to $13 and the cost of farm labor rises from
> $10.20 to $15. If these increased farm labor costs were completely passed on to con-
> sumers, spending on fresh fruits and vegetables eaten at home for a typical 2.6 person
> consumer unit would increase by less than $10, from $270 to almost $280.

I'd welcome the opportunity to pay higher consumer prices to rid our land 12
of illegal immigrants. ◆ We'd lift an enormous financial albatross from our
backs and provide better educational opportunities for thousands of American kids to receive the full attention of teachers in schools crowded with the
children of illegal immigrants.

Thinking Critically

◆ Why does the author criticize employers who hire illegal aliens?

◆ Would you be willing to pay higher prices for consumer items such as food in order to
"rid our land of illegal immigrants"? Why or why not? Do you think most people would
agree with you?

Americans Willing to Work

Finally, to address perhaps the biggest lie of all—that Americans won't do   13
the work that illegals perform—the truth is that uneducated and unskilled
Americans won't live in garages with multiple families and endure similar
hardships to take on backbreaking work at below minimum wages. Get rid
of illegal immigrants, and wages would have to rise to attract those native-
born and legal residents who lack the skills and education to do much else. **6**

About deportation. With the exception of illegal alien felons incarcerated   14
in various prisons and those illegals caught by the border patrol (at the border), deportations are virtually nonexistent. Yet there are six million illegal
aliens in this country. We could make a huge deportation dent in this stealth
population if we only had the commitment and determination to do so.
Once again, it's a national administration attempting to curry favor with the
wrong people.

About "we've met the enemy and they are us," some conservatives and   15
liberals support Cardinal Roger Mahony's statement, "the right to immigrate is more fundamental than that of nations to control their borders"—
conservatives because they get their jollies from exploiting cheap labor and
liberals because it gives them another opportunity to smother someone
with compassion. Added to these afflictions are the wishes of politicians
to get reelected by ducking issues and the hidden agendas of opportunists
and ideologues to advance their causes.

Proposition 187

Let's look at California's Proposition 187. This was a 1994 ballot initiative   16
that barred illegal immigrant access to public social services, including education and public health care services, except emergency care. In November
of 1994, 59 percent of the California electorate voted for Proposition 187.
Of California's 58 counties, 49 voted yes.

The day after Proposition 187 passed, a federal court in Los Angeles and   17
a state court in San Francisco barred enforcement of most of its provisions.
A federal judge kept this bottled up for nearly $3\frac{1}{2}$ years before voiding it.
Immediately thereafter the State of California appealed the decision, but
because a conniving governor was soon thereafter elected—a person opposed
to Proposition 187—he saw to it that the initiative never reached the
Supreme Court through the appellate process.

Just before Governor Gray Davis strangled Proposition 187 in April 1999,   18
he said with the most angelic of faces, "If this (Proposition 187) were a piece

---

Thinking Critically

6 Do you agree with the author that a decrease in the number of illegal immigrants would
prompt a rise in wages for unskilled American workers? Why or why not?

of legislation, I would veto it. But it's not. It's an initiative, passed by nearly 60 percent of the voters through a process specifically designed to go over the heads of the legislature and the governor. If officials choose to selectively enforce only the laws they like, our system of justice will not long endure." Davis then walked off the press conference stage and betrayed the people of California by stabbing them in the back.

Our Own Worst Enemies

Then there's the shameful AFL-CIO [labor union] clamor for amnesty for   19
6 million illegal aliens, hoping lots of them will become union members. ⬥
The AFL-CIO is attempting to line their pockets with membership dues over the short run, while rolling the dice with the futures of American work-ers. All this will do is end control of our borders and unleash terrible wage depression pressures on millions of American workers as hordes of foreign-ers surge across unprotected borders looking for American jobs.

We've clearly become our own worst enemies and will suffer a terrible   20
fate unless we end this madness. A series of national administrations have buried their collective heads in the sand and ignored the acrid odors of the white hot burning fuse attached to the illegal immigration time bomb. There just aren't enough Roger Barnetts around, and that's what's necessary for us to retake our country. Just remember folks, the only card your opponents hold in their hands is the race-baiting card, the threat of calling you a racist or a bigot. But the collective votes of an ignored and aggrieved articulate voting population are the strongest cards of all, and if you chose to play them, it's a slam-dunk for the good guys.

Illegal immigration is repudiated by our laws, by the facts, and by most   21
Americans. So, one more time folks, let's seal our borders, deport all illegal aliens, prosecute any employer hiring illegals, throw the rascals out who live on the Planet Beltway and kowtow to the illegal immigration lobby, and begin to pay close attention to the calamity that awaits us unless we do all of these things.

Thinking Critically

⬥ According to Scott, why are labor unions in favor of amnesty for illegal aliens? Who would profit most from such an action?

RICHARD RAYNOR   (1955–   )

Illegal Immigration Does Not Threaten America

M aria T. bites her nails. At 31, with five children, she's one of the 1.7 1
million immigrants now estimated to be living in California illegally. She speaks almost no English, even though she has been in
America for more than eight years. In her clean and sparsely furnished living room, her kids—Gustavo (11), Mario (7), Maribel (6), Cesar (5) and Joan
(4)—are in front of the TV, laughing first at "Home Improvement," then at
"The Simpsons."

The refrigerator is almost empty; it contains only a gallon of milk, some 2
Kool-Aid, a few tortillas. Her life is frugal, a devotion to the future of her children. Though there are three bedrooms in the apartment, all five sleep with
her because she hates to let them out of her sight. Since she has no car and
can rarely afford the bus, the family walks everywhere, Maria leading the
way like Mother Goose with the kids behind toting Batman and Pocahon-
tas backpacks. On a typical day she walks six miles, shuttling between her
apartment and the local school in Van Nuys. ◆

For her, as for so many, the decision to make the journey to El Norte was 3
the beginning of an epic. Gustavo was 3 at the time, Mario was 8 months,
and she was 5 months pregnant with Maribel. Maria crossed the border with
the help of a "coyote," a guide, but when she arrived in San Diego the woman
who'd paid for her brothers' crossings didn't have any money this time. Maria
was kept a slave in the coyote's house. He beat and raped her until, after three
months, her brother raised $300, half the sum agreed for the crossing, and the
coyote let her go.

She stayed with her brother in Los Angeles, the Pico-Union district, and 4
it was here that Maribel was born. "I'd come out of labor and I was staring
at the wall and I said to my sister-in-law, 'Look, she's there.' She said, 'Who?'
I said, 'The Virgin Mary.' She said, 'There's nothing there. You're crazy.' But
it was true all the same. For eight months the Virgin would appear to me.
She made me strong." ◆

"At first, I had to beg for food. Sometimes I did day work for Latinos, for 5
$10 a day. I'd take off into the city on the bus, not really knowing where I
was going and get off to beg on the streets. I'm ashamed of that."

Thinking Critically

◆ Instead of beginning his essay with statistics, Raynor starts with a brief case study of a typical illegal immigrant. Is this tactic effective or not? Explain your answer.

◆ How does the author connect religion with the desire to immigrate to America?

Slowly, she clawed her way up. It is in so many ways a classic immigrant's   6
tale, although she has been the beneficiary not just of her own drive, but
also of something equally important—welfare. She's here illegally, with fake
ID, and she doesn't work. She receives $723 in cash and $226 in food stamps,
and Section 8 takes care of more than two-thirds of her $1,000 rent (high,
because landlords know illegals won't complain).

It's a myth, however, that anyone can come over the border and start milk-   7
ing the system. Only Medicaid and limited food benefits are available to illegal immigrants, and most don't apply for these because they fear detection
by the Immigration and Naturalization Service (I.N.S.). Maria T. gets what
she does because of her children who were born here. ❸

Local, state, and federal governments spend about $11.8 billion a year   8
educating legal and illegal immigrant children, according to the Urban Institute, a nonpartisan research organization, compared with the $227 billion
spent to educate all children. Generally, this is more than offset by the taxes
that legal and illegal immigrant families pay—$70.3 billion a year, the Urban
Institute says—while receiving $42.9 billion in total services. Illegal immi-
grants pay $7 billion in taxes.

Maria T., however, represents the nightmare scenario—an illegal immigrant   9
who's sucking money from the system and putting nothing back. Even so,
it's not clear that she's a villain. She hopes one day to go to work herself. She
hopes and believes that her bright children will become outstanding. She
believes in America.

Fears of Strangers

My wife, from Finland, has a green card; I'm English, in the process of   10
applying for one myself; our son was born an American. When we moved
into our house in Venice, Calif., one of our neighbors, an elderly white
woman with whom we're now very friendly, said, "No Americans live on our
block anymore."

Maybe she had the jitters about new neighbors, or maybe there was some-   11
thing else at play. I knew that her father had been born in Germany and had
journeyed to Detroit, where she was born. I wanted to say that logically,
therefore, our son is every bit as American as she is. But in any debate about
nationality, I know, logic fades fast.

My own father once traced our family tree back to 1066, when one Baron   12
de Rainier sailed from Normandy to help conquer England. Since then,
give or take the occasional Irish excursion, my progenitors were all born

---

Thinking Critically

❸ How do you feel about the legality of granting automatic citizenship to U.S.–born children of illegal immigrants? Do you agree with Raynor on this point?

within a hundred or so miles of one another in the north of England. So, when I came to America and found that nearly everyone was from somewhere else if they stepped back a generation or two, I found myself thrilled and oddly at ease. It explained America's drive, its generosity and up-for-anything energy. As (novelist Herman) Melville wrote, "We are not a nation, so much as a world."

Not everyone sees things this way. Many have drawn a line behind which   13
they stand, true Americans, fearful and angry about the erosion of their identity. With unintended irony they talk of themselves as "natives." ◆ On immigration, they argue that enough is enough, that the borders must be secured
and a drastic cutback enforced. Those who are allowed in, they say, must be
professionals or skilled workers because the others—mobs of unskilled, third-
world peasants—drain resources and take jobs. They cost billions and dilute
the gene pool. They are mutating the face of America.

California itself, for instance, passed an anti-immigrant measure with scary   14
ease. In 1994's state election nearly 60 percent voted for Proposition 187, the
so-called Save-Our-State initiative, which sought to deny public education,
nonemergency health care and welfare to illegal immigrants. By linking illegal immigration to joblessness and crime, Pete Wilson revived his flagging
gubernatorial campaign and was swept back into office, even though, as an exit
poll showed, few who voted for 187 actually thought it was going to work.

Wilson was avid for votes and a reaction and he got both. Many illegal   15
Latinos, fearful of deportation, refused to go near schools and emergency
rooms. There was immigrant bashing and hate mail. Since the Republicans
took control of the United States House and Senate, moreover, it seems as
though all Washington has been grandstanding on the issue. Dozens of
immigration-related bills were introduced.

Many of the proposals are mean-spirited and, to a lot of observers, wrong-   16
headed. One would impose a tax on employers who hire legal aliens. Others would deny citizenship to children born in this country to illegals or
eliminate some categories of family immigration. The anti-immigration
forces have done an excellent job of creating an atmosphere of crisis in which
the debate has focused on how to slow the "flood" of immigration, legal and
illegal. But illegal immigration should not be folded over to scapegoat legals
as well. The real point is that there isn't any immigration crisis.

How Many Immigrants?

"The perception is that immigration is out of control," says Joel Kotkin,   17
author of *Tribes* and a fellow at the Pepperdine University Institute of Public

---

Thinking Critically
◆ Who are the true "natives" of America, according to Raynor? What does the word "native"
mean in this context?

Policy. "It isn't. [5] If you say to most Americans, 'We have 800,000 legal immigrants a year,' they're going to reply, 'Hey, that's not so bad.' And this is the truth of the situation. But it's somehow been demonized so that people think there are millions coming across the border."

The Border Patrol logged 1,094,718 apprehensions in 1994. On page 26   18
of his *Alien Nation,* a leading restrictionist, Peter Brimelow, writes that legal immigration is "overwhelmed by an estimated 2 to 3 million illegal entries into the country in every recent year." He goes on to note, correctly, that many of these illegal entrants go back home and that some trundle to and fro across the border every day. By page 33, however, he's writing "a remarkable 2 to 3 million illegal immigrants may have succeeded in entering the country in 1993."

Within seven pages illegal entrants have mysteriously become illegal immigrants, attached to that hyperbolic two to three million, a figure vigorously   19
disputed by I.N.S., which regards as preposterous the idea that for every border crosser caught another three get away. Indeed, throughout the 1970's there were some eight million border apprehensions and during that time, according to the best estimates of I.N.S., about one million illegals came to reside—eight apprehensions per illegal immigrant.

So how many illegals are coming in and staying each year now? The Urban   20
Institute says 250,000 to 300,000. The Center for Immigration Studies, a conservative research group, says 400,000, while I.N.S. says 300,000. The Census Bureau until recently guessed 200,000 to 400,000; now it agrees with the I.N.S.

The 300,000 figure is considered firm because it was based on the years   21
following 1988, when the I.N.S. started to process the genuinely reliable data it amassed following the 1986 amnesty for illegals. Too much of this and the eyes glaze over, but the gist is, the further you get from 1988, the flakier the statistics become. And the argument over the number of illegal immigrants is nothing compared with the furor over how much they cost. [6]

The fact is, no one knows for sure; there is simply no up-to-date research.   22
"The issue has caught political fire," Papademetriou says. "But serious academics haven't got out into the field yet. They're reluctant to play into the hands of the politicians."

Immigration is in the spotlight not because of money but because it so   23
impinges on issues like race, the role of government, national identity, and change. Name an issue and you can hook it to immigration. One side looks at crime, failing schools, and soaring welfare spending and sees too many

---

Thinking Critically

[5] Do you believe that immigration is "out of control"? Why or why not?

[6] The author attacks the notion that illegal immigration is costly to Americans, yet provides no statistics to support his point. Does this tactic help or hurt his argument?

immigrants. The other sees America, the greatest nation on earth, built on the backs of immigrants and still benefiting enormously from the brains, energy, and determination (not to speak of low wages) of the next generation of newcomers. Right now the debate is more emotional than informed. It's all temper tantrums and red–hot sound bites.

Fear of Latinos

When people complain about immigration, about the alien "flood," it's Latin 24
Americans they mean, who from their entry points in California and Miami are fanning out through the country. There's concern about the small minority, who are criminals, and the seeming reluctance of these people to learn English. ⑦ Mixed in with this is the prejudice summarized by D. H. Lawrence in *Mornings in Mexico*. They are other, he concluded; they are dirty; I don't trust them and they stink. There's also the suggestion that Latinos are lazy, though everywhere you look in Los Angeles you see evidence to the contrary.

A Demand for Labor

Historically, immigration has been tolerated, even encouraged during 25
labor shortages. Labor migration has been going on for centuries, and it's hard to see how 300,000 or so illegal immigrants per year will make or break the American economy. Indeed, in Los Angeles they're most likely an asset. The number of illegals in California is thought to be growing by 125,000 a year—hardly an economic catastrophe in a state of 31 million. In Los Angeles, where 80,000 jobs were created last year, it's a definite plus. The city has a thirst for people who will work for $5 or even $3 an hour.

The legal Chinese immigrants who have revitalized the San Gabriel Val- 26
ley, the Latinos who are opening businesses in depressed areas of South Los Angeles, and the Russians and Iranians who are opening businesses all over are the principal reasons the city is so different from, say, Detroit. Says Joel Kotkin, "The only place where American society is evolving is where the immigrant influx is strong. Cities would have no future without them. But if you're sitting in Idaho, it looks different."

The Race Issue

Pro-immigration forces have tended to keep their focus tight on the eco- 27
nomic issues because they sense that Americans don't want to be told they're racist. Nobody does. Yet, one of the problems with the immigration issue is

---

Thinking Critically

⑦ How do you feel about the alleged reluctance of many immigrants to learn English?

that it does impinge on the race issue and thus appeals temptingly and dangerously to the worst side of all of us. **8**

A central argument of Brimelow's "Alien Nation" is that America has always had an essential nature, an ethnic core, and that it's white. He writes that "the first naturalization law, in 1790, stipulated that an applicant must be a 'free white person.' Blacks became full citizens only after the Civil War." 28

He goes on, "Maybe America should not have been like this. But it was." And now, "Americans are being tricked out of their own identity." 29

Reading this, I'm overcome with a weird looking-glass giddiness. Someone's trying to change the rules here, to wipe a rag over history. **9** America's identity is precisely that of mutation, its power drawn from an energetic and quite fearless ability to adapt and win. Its national book, after all, is *The Adventures of Huckleberry Finn,* about a beautiful and dangerous river that never stops changing. 30

An Immigrant Nation

America is an immigrant nation, indeed, a nation of strangers. I like it that way, though the arguments in favor of the idea are not merely sentimental and historical. Corporate interests value immigration for something that troubles us—keeping wages lower, and these days not just at the level of busboys and dayworkers. 31

The American economy is in relatively good shape and has pretty much the legal immigration it needs. The system isn't broken, doesn't need fixing—and certainly not in the ways that are now being proposed. Illegal immigration is touchier. Listening to academics makes it easy to forget the racially inflamed brush fire that is the debate in California. 32

Recent polls show a surprising sympathy even for illegal immigrants, provided they otherwise play by the rules: work, get documentation, learn English. Only 20 percent say immigrants take jobs away from citizens, and 69 percent say they do work that citizens don't necessarily want and that needs to be done. Few say that the American-born children of illegals should be deprived of education and welfare, let alone their citizenship. The message here is a sensible one: beef up the Border Patrol; deport criminals; don't break up families; target labor-enforcement at bad-guy sweatshop employers and make an effort to deal with temporary visa overstays, who surprisingly make up as much as 50 percent of all illegals; supply Federal assistance to heavily impacted areas such as Los Angeles; and forget the idea of a national verification system or an identification card. 33

Thinking Critically

8 Do you feel that most people who oppose illegal immigration are racists? Why or why not?

9 Explain the metaphor referring to someone trying to "wipe a rag over history"?

Ultimately, this is a debate about values, not money. This is about how   34
America feels about itself. [10]

UNDERSTANDING DETAILS

1. What are Scott ("America Must Take Stronger Measures to Halt Illegal Immigration") and Raynor ("Illegal Immigration Does Not Threaten America") each saying about illegal immigration in these two essays?
2. What arguments can you think of to supplement both of their essays?
3. What three basic steps does Scott say must be taken through law enforcement to stop illegal immigration? Explain each in detail.
4. What does Raynor mean when he says, "Ultimately, this is a debate about values, not money. This is about how America feels about itself" (paragraph 34)?

READING CRITICALLY

5. Which stand on this particular argument is most convincing to you? Which examples or statistics seem most persuasive? Explain your reactions to each of these two positions.
6. Would you agree to pay higher prices "to rid our land of illegal immigrants" (Scott, paragraph 12)?
7. What do you think Melville means by the words "We are not a nation, so much as a world" (Raynor, paragragh 12)? Do you agree with this statement?
8. How might the opinions in these two essays be reconciled? Can you make a compromise prediction that combines both these views of the world?

DISCOVERING RHETORICAL STRATEGIES

9. Who do you think is the intended audience for each of these essays? Are there any important differences between these audiences, in your opinion?
10. These two authors make their points with slightly different writing voices. Describe the tone or mood of each essay, and explain whether you think that particular voice is most effective for the author's purpose.
11. How does the organization of the two essays differ? What is the general organizing principle in each case?
12. What other rhetorical strategies does each essay use to make its point? Give examples of each strategy.

MAKING CONNECTIONS

13. Briefly summarize the arguments advanced by Scott and Raynor about immigration. Which point of view comes closest to your own? Explain your reasoning.
14. If Scott and Raynor were having a conversation with Kimberly Wozencraft ("Notes from the Country Club") about the difficulties in enforcing laws against

---

Thinking Critically

[10] What do you think the author's last sentence means? Is it an effective conclusion?

illegal aliens versus those concerning drug abuse, which issue would the authors say receives less attention from our legal system? Would you agree? What does this disparity in justice tell us about laws in the United States? About the power of special interest groups?

15. Imagine that Scott and Raynor are having a round-table discussion about the topic of illegal immigration with Sandra Cisneros ("Only daughter"), Richard Rodriguez ("Public and Private Language"), Amy Tan ("Mother Tongue"), and/or Sucheng Chan ("You're Short, Besides!"). Which of these authors would speak most vigorously in favor of having the United States truly integrated with people from many different countries? What specific skills and abilities do immigrants bring to the United States? Do you think the alleged strain on our economy and infrastructure is worth the contributions these immigrants make to our country? Why or why not?

IDEAS FOR DISCUSSION/WRITING

Preparing to Write

Write freely about your views on the role of immigrants in the United States: What do immigrants offer America? In what ways do immigrants weaken our country? What is your general view of immigrants? Who should be allowed to enter our national borders? What guidelines would you put on immigrants? Why would you establish these guidelines? Explain your answers in as much detail as possible.

Choosing a Topic

1. *Learning Online:* Which of the two arguments was presented most effectively? Regardless of your personal feelings about the issue, evaluate which argument presented its case most persuasively. Write an editorial essay for your favorite online news source, in which you evaluate both articles and argue that one's presentation is more effective. Be sure to use specific details to support your claims. Use the Generation Engage Web site from Preparing to Read to help you make your case.

2. Whether or not we should pay for the education of illegal aliens has been an issue in politics for quite some time. What is your opinion on this issue? Use facts and statistics from these two essays to support your point of view.

3. Many sociologists and politicians who have studied immigration claim that the issue ultimately centers on race. Do you agree with this contention? Present your own argument on this statement, supporting your opinion with persuasive examples and facts.

4. Your local library is sponsoring a writing contest with a first place prize of $1,000. All contestants must write a 500-word essay on the following topic: "How does understanding other cultures help make us better human beings?" Write an essay on this topic that would win the first-place award.

Before beginning your essay, you might want to consult the checklists on page 482.

OPPOSING VIEWPOINTS

Postconviction DNA Testing

The following three essays each offer a different viewpoint on the controversial question of whether DNA testing should be used consistently in legal cases. Tim O'Brien, who argues that the use of DNA should be encouraged, is an attorney and award-winning journalist who covered the Supreme Court for more than twenty-two years. He also served as the principal Washington correspondent for CNN's *Moneyline News Hour*. James Dao, who suggests in his article that DNA testing is helpful in some cases and not in others, is a reporter for the *New York Times* who has covered a wide variety of political and social events. And Peter Roff, who argues against the widespread use of DNA testing, is a Senior Political Analyst with United Press International. He is also the editor of the Daily Enterprise, a blog for the Free Enterprise Fund. DNA testing was pioneered by Sir Alec Jeffreys at the University of Leicester in 1985. Also called "genetic fingerprinting," it identifies subtle differences in DNA sequencing that can be used to help determine guilt or innocence in a court of law, confirm paternity, and establish biogeographic and ethnic heritage.

Preparing to Read

Each of the next three essays takes a different stand on DNA: One talks about using DNA to prove someone's innocence; the second tells us how DNA testing cleared one convict and implicated another; and the third argues for limiting DNA testing on previously convicted prisoners.

Exploring Experience: This series of essays deals with the advantages and disadvantages of DNA testing. As you prepare to read these essays, share with the rest of your class what you know about DNA testing: What are its advantages and disadvantages? What is the source of your information? Why is DNA testing such an interesting feature of most investigations? What makes it so interesting?

Learning Online: Visit the "Facts and Figures" page of the Web site for the National Coalition Against the Death Penalty (NCADP) at www.ncadp.org/ facts_figures.html. Scroll through the charts and tables of statistics regarding the number of death penalty executions that have taken place over the last several years. Note the number of people currently on death row in each state, and pay particular attention to the disparity according to race. Do any of these numbers surprise you? What are your thoughts about this information?

TIM O'BRIEN   (1946–   )

Postconviction DNA Testing Should Be Encouraged

My editors and I thought it was a good story: the black, one-eyed, 1
homosexual rapist who claimed it was a case of mistaken identity.
P.S.: He also walked with a limp. ❶

The U.S. Supreme Court had agreed to review the case in its 1988 term, 2
because it had raised an important constitutional question: Do the police
have any obligation to preserve potentially exculpatory evidence?

The Case of Larry Youngblood

The defendant, Larry Youngblood, had been convicted of abducting a 3
10-year-old boy from a church carnival and repeatedly sodomizing him.
Youngblood had argued that if the police had preserved semen samples
taken from the boy's clothing, DNA tests would have shown they had
arrested the wrong man.

Never mind that the tests in question weren't ordinarily available at the 4
time of the trial (although they are now routine). Never mind that Youngblood fit the description provided by the victim or that the traumatized child
also identified Youngblood in court as the perpetrator. Never mind that the
evidence appeared so overwhelming that it took the jury only 40 minutes
to convict Youngblood and send him on his way to a 10-year prison term.

The legal issue the case raised was significant; it was to resonate years later 5
in the O.J. Simpson case[1] and doubtless many other lesser cases. In my heart,
I questioned the judgment of the public defenders who would bring such
an important issue to the Supreme Court with such an obviously guilty
defendant. If, as Oliver Wendell Holmes put it, hard cases make bad law, then
what do bad cases make? ❷

But public defenders Dan Davis and Carol Witteis seemed less concerned 6
with the precedent the court might set than with winning freedom for their
client. Could they possibly believe he was really innocent? Yes, without a doubt,
they both said. Defense lawyers can believe, or appear to believe, anything.

Supreme Court justices are supposed to decide cases on the basis of the 7
law, but like all humans, they too can be influenced by the facts. And the

---

Thinking Critically

❶ Do you think this is a good beginning to the essay? Why or why not?
❷ What does this Oliver Wendell Holmes maxim mean to you? Paraphrase it in your own
words.

facts in this case couldn't have been worse for Youngblood. Moreover, he lived alone, had a history of mental illness and had had previous run-ins with the law.

As expected, the Supreme Court upheld Youngblood's conviction, decid- 8 ing his fate with exceptional speed, just as the jury had two years earlier. Only three justices dissented, with the late Harry Blackmun writing that "the Constitution requires a fair trial, not merely a 'good faith' try at a fair trial."

Mistaken Identity

A good story? We didn't know the half of it. [In August 2000] Young- 9 blood's conviction was vacated—thrown out by the Pima County Superior Court in Tucson. While the small amount of semen that was preserved was insufficient for reliable testing at the time of the appeal, new testing procedures that only recently became available were conducted by the Tucson police. They showed conclusively what attorneys Witteis and Davis knew all along: The police really did have the wrong man. It was a case of mistaken identity. 3

Youngblood may have been less a victim of bad facts than of societal biases 10 that can seep into and poison the criminal justice process. Could his race have been a factor? His multiple disabilities, mental and physical? His perceived sexual orientation? The fact that he had been accused of a horrendous crime that cried out for retribution?

There is no scientific way to quantify the effects of these illicit consider- 11 ations in Youngblood's case, nor anyone else's for that matter. And the Supreme Court, in another case, has ruled that even a statistical probability of bias is insufficient to set aside a conviction, even a death sentence. DNA testing, by providing statistical proof of innocence (or guilt), may be the only way to effectively offset invidious biases.

Yet at every turn prosecutors are resisting the use of DNA tests whenever 12 it might mean reopening an old case. There are now hundreds of inmates on death row who claim DNA tests would show they were not guilty of the crimes for which they were convicted. Most, perhaps even all, are mistaken. But in light of what happened to Larry Youngblood, the complaints that such tests are too expensive and time-consuming or that a jury's verdict must be accorded finality ring hollow indeed. The Tucson police have graciously conceded that it was "unfortunate" Youngblood spent so much time incarcerated for a crime he didn't commit, but they say they did what they thought was right at the time. Youngblood is angry to have been robbed of "the best part of my life," and he wants to sue the police. All agree it should not have happened.

Thinking Critically

3 How did the newly analyzed DNA evidence save this particular defendant?

To prevent it from happening again, courts must be receptive to any cred-   13
ible claim that new tests might prove the actual innocence of one who has
already been convicted. Had Larry Youngblood been charged with first degree
murder, he'd probably be dead now. ◆

Note

1. In 1995 former football star O.J. Simpson was found not guilty of mur-
   dering his ex-wife and her friend. Controversies over evidence had been
   a significant factor in the murder trial.

Thinking Critically

◆ How convincing is this single example? Would you vote to require DNA testing for all
such offenses based on this one case? Why or why not?

JAMES DAO   (1942–   )

In Same Case, DNA Clears Convict and Finds Suspect

In his final years in prison, Kirk Bloodsworth had a passing acquaintance 1
with a fellow inmate, Kimberly Shay Ruffner. Mr. Bloodsworth, a prison
librarian, delivered books to Mr. Ruffner. Sometimes they lifted weights
together. But Mr. Bloodsworth said Mr. Ruffner seemed to behave "kind of
peculiar" when they were together.

Mr. Bloodsworth may now know the reason why. This morning, the police 2
in Baltimore County charged Mr. Ruffner in the murder and rape of a
9-year-old in 1984, Dawn Hamilton, the very crime that Mr. Bloodsworth
was serving time for when he met Mr. Ruffner.

"I'm so happy," said Mr. Bloodsworth, 43, a fisherman from Cambridge, 3
Md. "This tells the world that I'm innocent."

The charges against Mr. Ruffner open a new chapter in a case that has 4
become a prime example of the two-edged nature of DNA testing: not only
as a means of clearing the wrongly accused, but also of identifying new sus-
pects in cold cases. ◆1

In 1993, Mr. Bloodsworth became the first person in the nation con- 5
victed in a death penalty case to be exonerated through DNA testing, which
eliminated him as a source of semen stains on the girl's underpants. He had
served nine years in prison, including two on death row, when he was released
by a judge and pardoned by the governor.

Last spring, a Baltimore County forensic biologist who was studying evi- 6
dence from the case found stains on a sheet that had not been analyzed, a
spokesman for the Police Department said. Investigators conducted DNA
tests on the stains and ran the results through a national database last month.
Mr. Ruffner's name popped up.

The police did not have to go far to charge Mr. Ruffner. He was still 7
serving time for attempted rape and attempted murder in the prison in Baltimore where he had met Mr. Bloodsworth.

Defense lawyers say they hope the dual use of DNA evidence in the case 8
will reduce resistance among prosecutors to allow prisoners to challenge
convictions with DNA tests. They say the case demonstrates that DNA can
not only prove innocence, but also pinpoint culprits. ◆2

Thinking Critically

◆1 What is the "two-edged nature" of DNA testing? In which of these two situations is DNA
testing more valuable? Explain your reasoning.

◆2 In this particular case, how did DNA testing "prove innocence" and "pinpoint" a culprit?

"Maryland, and the nation, would be remiss if we did not learn from 9 today's news," said Peter Loge, director of the Criminal Justice Reform Education Fund, which has championed Mr. Bloodsworth's case.

The new charges were filed at a crucial time in a debate in Florida over 10 a law from 2001 that will soon bar prisoners from seeking DNA testing for old cases. The law set Oct. 1 as the deadline for such requests. It also allows the destruction of DNA evidence, except in death penalty cases.

Defense lawyers contend that the Hamilton case clearly shows how DNA 11 can be used to reopen cold cases. If a law like Florida's had been in effect in Maryland 12 years ago, they say, Mr. Bloodsworth would still be behind bars.

"This should be a cautionary tale to those in Florida who are insisting on 12 this deadline for destroying biological evidence," said Barry Scheck, codirector of the Innocence Project at the Benjamin L. Cardozo Law School in Manhattan. "It's a law enforcement calamity."

Many prosecutors contend that DNA testing, though reliable, is not a 13 sure-fire way to prove innocence where there is other evidence of guilt. DNA testing, they say, should be seen as only one piece of a bigger evidentiary puzzle. ❸

"I don't know of many people in my business who don't see the accuracy 14 of DNA testing," George W. Clarke, deputy district attorney for San Diego County, said. "It's more the significance of those results. Those questions aren't about to go away."

For Mr. Bloodsworth, today's developments had a far more personal sig- 15 nificance. Though he was pardoned a decade ago, he said some people had continued to view him as a child murderer. Worse, he feared that prosecutors remained convinced of his guilt and might try to bring new charges against him.

So after the assistant state's attorney who had prosecuted him, Ann Brobst, 16 called him on Thursday night to ask for a meeting, Mr. Bloodsworth and his wife could not sleep.

"We were prepared for anything," Mr. Bloodsworth's lawyer, Deborah 17 Crandall, said.

Instead, in a meeting this morning at a Burger King, Ms. Brobst told Mr. 18 Bloodsworth of the DNA evidence against Mr. Ruffner and apologized for wrongly prosecuting him. Mr. Bloodsworth, who has become an outspoken advocate for reforming federal death penalty laws, said he cried and then hugged Ms. Brobst.

In an interview, the state's attorney for Baltimore County, Sandra A. O'Con- 19 nor, said that the police and prosecutors had acted responsibly in the case,

---

Thinking Critically

❸ Do you agree that DNA testing should be seen "as only one piece of a bigger evidentiary puzzle," or should it be the most important evidence in a court case?

but that DNA technology did not exist at the time of Mr. Bloodsworth's trial. What did exist were the statements of five witnesses who said they saw him with the girl on the day she was killed.

"Obviously," Ms. O'Connor said, "the system failed in the case of 20 Mr. Bloodsworth." ◆4

Thinking Critically

◆4 How often do you think our judicial system fails? What are the most serious flaws of this system? What can we do about them?

PETER ROFF   (1966–   )

Postconviction DNA Testing Should Not Be Encouraged

To deprive an individual of their liberty—even for a short time—is to   1
limit their most basic freedom. It is a serious matter and should be
done with the utmost care. The Anglo-American system of jurispru-
dence gives every benefit of every doubt to the accused. At trial, the state must
prove guilt beyond a reasonable doubt while the accused is presumed to be
innocent.

What Justice Oliver Wendell Holmes said in defense of the Fourth Amend-   2
ment is generally true where the free exercise of liberty is at issue: "It is less
evil that some criminals should escape than that the government should play
an ignoble part (in gathering evidence)." ◆

This does not, however, require evidence be re-examined years after the   3
fact because the science changes.

Prisons Full of Innocent People?

Technology may have advanced to the point where certain types of evi-   4
dence may conclusively identify a guilty party. This is just part of the entire
equation, admittedly an important part. Yet the idea that many of the
inmates on death row or serving long sentences could be freed by new
DNA evidence has been ingrained in the American mind by Hollywood.
While dramatic, it is hardly true and runs counter to the argument, most
often heard from inmates and their lawyers that the prisons are full of innocent people, wrongfully convicted.

While the presence of DNA at a crime scene can be used to establish   5
guilt in a court of law, the converse is not automatically true. The absence of
a particular individual's DNA at a crime scene is not alone proof of their
innocence. ◆ Prosecutors and legislators arguing against the unlimited opportunity for taxpayer-funded DNA tests in pursuit of the exoneration of convicted felons are correct in their objections.

It is the entire body of evidence that must be considered, not just the   6
results of lab tests performed on old clothing.

Thinking Critically

◆ What does "ignoble" mean? Paraphrase this quotation in your own words. Do you agree
with it? Why or why not?

◆ Can you think of a recent court case where the absence of DNA was an important piece
of the evidence? How might the case have turned out if DNA had been available?

Doubtful Evidence

The rights of the accused are protected in the courtroom, often at the   7
expense of the victims'. Physical evidence, eyewitness testimony and evidence
often circumstantial in nature but attesting to means, motive, and opportunity
are considered during trial under accepted rules of evidence. Can that chain
of evidence still be as reliable 10, 15, or 20 years after the fact? It is doubtful. ❸

Can the state, fairly and years later, represent the interests of the victim and   8
society as a whole if the judicial system lets doubt—which increases over
time—adhere to the benefit of the accused, especially when DNA tests often
produce more doubt than proof?

In the same way repeated death penalty appeals slowed the wheels of jus-   9
tice for many years these DNA requests will tax the already overburdened
legal system, depriving the victims and the wrongfully accused of their day
in court in a timely manner.

The requests for these tests amount more to lawyerly shams rather [than   10
to] efforts to overcome justice denied. The state is right to limit them.

UNDERSTANDING DETAILS

1. According to Tim O'Brien, what facts worked against Youngblood in his trial?
2. How did "the system" fail in Bloodsworth's case (Dao, paragraph 20)?
3. What is Roff's main argument in his essay?
4. Explain Oliver Wendell Holmes's comment in paragraph 2 of the Roff essay: "It is less evil that some criminals should escape than that the government should play an ignoble part (in gathering evidence)."

READING CRITICALLY

5. Why does Tim O'Brien say that Youngblood would probably be dead if he were charged with first-degree murder?
6. Why was the Hamilton case (Dao) a landmark in DNA testing?
7. Why would Bloodsworth still be behind bars if the Florida law about DNA testing were applied to Maryland?
8. In what ways are death penalty appeals and DNA requests similar?

DISCOVERING RHETORICAL STRATEGIES

9. In paragraph 4, O'Brien writes a series of sentences starting with "Never mind." What effect does this group of sentences have on the rest of the essay? How does this paragraph stand apart from the other paragraphs?
10. Is the opening paragraph of the Dao essay effective? Why or why not?
11. Roff includes two subheadings in his essay. In what ways do they help you move logically through this essay?

Thinking Critically

❸ What point is the author making about the length of time from the original crime and the reliability of the evidence?

12. Why does Roff refer to Hollywood in his essay?

MAKING CONNECTIONS

13. Briefly summarize the arguments advanced by O'Brien, Dao, and Roff concerning the use of DNA testing. Which point of view comes closest to your own? Why?
14. Compare and contrast the ways in which all three authors use examples in their essays. Who do you think uses examples most skillfully? Why do you think this is so?
15. Imagine that Kimberly Wozencraft ("Notes from the Country Club") and/or Brent Staples ("A Brother's Murder") were having a discussion with O'Brien, Dao, and Roff about the necessity of presenting physical evidence in a court of law. Which authors would argue most forcefully that such evidence must be displayed before a conviction can be attained? Why?

IDEAS FOR DISCUSSION/WRITING

Preparing to Write

Write freely about your knowledge of DNA testing after reading these essays: What are its advantages? Its disadvantages? Its limitations? Why is the public so interested in its use? Do you think DNA testing will deter criminals in any way?

Choosing a Topic

1. *Learning Online:* The National Coalition Against the Death Penalty has a very interesting fact sheet entitled "Innocence" found online at www.ncadp .org/fact_sheet4.html. It begins with general statistics regarding the number of people on death row who have been exonerated. Then the fact sheet highlights stories about specific individuals who were wrongly convicted because DNA testing was not available at the time of their trials. Notice the appeals to logic (logos) in the overall statistics and the appeals to emotion and character (pathos and ethos) in the individual stories. Choose one of the personal stories to use for information, and write a letter to a defense attorney requesting that he or she reopen the case to consider new DNA evidence. Try to incorporate all three appeals—to logos, pathos, and ethos—in your letter.
2. DNA testing is sensationalized on *CSI* television shows to the point that real-life juries often expect such conclusive evidence when they serve on a case. How might these expectations affect our judicial system? To what extent does Hollywood actually influence what goes on in our courtrooms? Argue for or against putting these unrealistic shows on the air.
3. You have been asked to write a response to Roff's essay for publication as a companion piece. Using his format, develop your own argument for or against limiting DNA testing. Research this issue on the Internet a bit before you begin to write.
4. Americans are currently fascinated with investigative TV shows. *CSI, Law and Order,* and *Forensic Files* are at the top of the Neilsen ratings. Do you see any connection between the increasing popularity of these shows and the violent crime rate in the United States today? Take a stand for or against the airing of this type of show as it relates to crime.

Before beginning your essay, you might want to consult the checklists on page 482.

Chapter Writing Assignments

Practicing Argument/Persuasion

1. What are the primary issues involved in the legalization of gay marriage? Where do you stand on this controversial topic? Why do you hold this opinion? Write an essay arguing for or against legalizing gay marriage.

2. Many people argue that the media actually run the elections in the United States. What is your opinion on this issue? What should be the role of the media in the political arena? How should we force them to limit themselves to this role? In what ways do the media help us understand certain important issues? In what ways do they hinder our understanding? Write an essay in which you argue for a specific relationship between the media and politics, including elections, referendums, and bond issues. Support your position with concrete details.

3. Look up the term *immigration* in the dictionary. Ask a variety of people about their positive and negative responses to immigration. Write an essay in which you explain your position on immigration, using your interviews as background and support.

Exploring Ideas

4. Do you think people are prone to violence because of inborn qualities or because of learned behavior? Why are some people violent while others are not? Where, in your opinion, does this difference come from—nature or nurture?

5. Do you think any limits should be put on free speech? If so, what should these limits be? If not, why not? What is the reasoning behind your opinion? Write an essay supporting your position with examples.

6. American society often argues about whether voting materials and other government documents should be printed in multiple languages. Does this practice work against the principle of speaking only one language in the United States? Write an essay that explains your opinion on this issue. Be sure to include specific examples to support your argument.

Writing from Sources

For detailed information on writing from sources, see Part III.

7. Consider the different belief systems and practices associated with holistic and Western medicines. Which approach do you think is the healthiest? Citing research from two to three sources, write a well-documented essay arguing your position on this topic.

8. Binge drinking has become almost epidemic among today's teens and college students. Think of another problem that young people in the United States are battling, such as eating disorders or obesity. Research the topic, and then write a convincing essay that discusses the importance of this issue and the actions you feel are necessary to solve the problem.

Analyzing Visual Images

© AP Wide World Photos

9. Choose a current issue and design several slogans that would effectively argue your point of view. Discuss in essay form how effectively these slogans would persuade others.
10. Look at the picture on page 471 at the beginning of this chapter, which captures the Civil Rights movement and the struggle for equal rights. Many today would argue that racism is no longer an issue and that equal rights have, in fact, been granted to all races, genders, religious sects, etc. Argue for or against this statement, using examples from your own experience, including your reading and observations, to support your claim.

Chapter 13

THINKING, READING, AND WRITING IN DIFFERENT LITERARY FORMS
Combining Rhetorical Modes

In each of the preceding chapters, we have examined a single rhetorical mode to focus attention on how that pattern works in both reading and writing. In this final chapter, we consider the topics of thinking, reading, and writing through four different literary genres.

Our primary purpose in this text has been to show how thinking, reading, and writing work together as fine machinery to help all of us function as intelligent and productive human beings. Part I analyzes the relationships among thinking, reading, and writing, while Part II demonstrates the crucial interdependence of these skills and ends with this chapter, which includes two essays, two short stories, and three poems—all featuring topics related to thinking, reading, and writing.

These final reading selections are offered here as a review of your work in this text, so let your mind run freely through this material as you recall in a leisurely way what you have learned in the previous chapters. These readings bring together the theoretical framework of this book as they illustrate how thinking, reading, and writing inform each other and work together to make meaning. They also integrate the rhetorical patterns in such a way that each reading selection is a complex blend of the various modes, thereby providing a perfect summary of the topics and strategies you have been studying throughout this text.

ESSAYS

ROGER ROSENBLATT   (1940–   )

"I Am Writing Blindly"

Besides the newsworthy revelation of Lieut. Captain Dimitri 1
Kolesnikov's dying message to his wife recovered from the husk of the
sunken submarine *Kursk*—that 23 of the 118 crewmen had survived
in an isolated chamber for a while, in contradiction to claims by Russian officials that all had perished within minutes of the accident—there was the
matter of writing the message in the first place.

In the first place, in the last place, that is what we people do—write mes- 2
sages to one another. We are a narrative species. We exist by storytelling—
by relating our situations—and the test of our evolution may lie in getting
the story right.

What Kolesnikov did in deciding to describe his position and entrapment, 3
others have also done—in states of repose or terror. When a JAL airliner went
down in 1985, passengers used the long minutes of its terrible, spiraling descent
to write letters to loved ones. When the last occupants of the Warsaw Ghetto
had finally seen their families and companions die of disease or starvation, or
be carried off in trucks to extermination camps, and there could be no doubt
of their own fate, still they took scraps of paper on which they wrote poems,
thoughts, fragments of lives, rolled them into tight scrolls, and slipped them
into the crevices of the ghetto walls.

Why did they bother? With no countervailing news from the outside 4
world, they assumed the Nazis had inherited the earth; that if anyone discovered their writings, it would be their killers, who would snicker and toss
them away. They wrote because, like Kolesnikov, they had to. The impulse was
in them, like a biological fact.

So enduring is this storytelling need that it shapes nearly every human 5
endeavor. Businesses depend on the stories told of past failures and successes
and on the myth of the mission of the company. In medicine, doctors increasingly rely on a patient's narrative of the progress of an ailment, which is
inevitably more nuanced and useful than the data of machines. In law, the
same thing. Every court case is a competition of tales told by the prosecu-
tor and defense attorney; the jury picks the one it likes best.

All these activities derive from essential places in us. Psychologist Jerome 6
Bruner says children acquire language in order to tell the stories that are
already in them. We do our learning through storytelling processes. The man
who arrives at our door is thought to be a salesman because his predecessor

was a salesman. When the patternmaking faculties fail, the brain breaks down. Schizophrenics suffer from a loss of story.

The deep proof of our need to spill, and keep on spilling, lies in reflex, often in desperate circumstances. A number of years ago, Jean-Dominique Bauby, the editor of *Elle* magazine in Paris, was felled by a stroke so destructive that the only part of his body that could move was his left eyelid. Flicking that eyelid, he managed to signal the letters of the alphabet, and proceeded to write his autobiography, *The Diving Bell and the Butterfly,* with the last grand gesture of his life.   7

All this is of acute and consoling interest to writers, whose odd existences are ordinarily strung between asking why we do it and doing it incessantly. The explanation I've been able to come up with has to do with freedom. You write a sentence, the basic unit of storytelling, and you are never sure where it will lead. The readers will not know where it leads either. Your adventure becomes theirs, eternally recapitulated in tandem—one wild ride together. Even when you come to the end of the sentence, that dot, it is still strangely inconclusive. I sometimes think one writes to find God in every sentence. But God (the ironist) always lives in the next sentence.   8

It is this freedom of the message sender and receiver that connects them— sailor to wife, the dying to the living. Writing has been so important in America, I think, because communication is the soul and engine of democracy. To write is to live according to one's terms. If you ask me to be serious, I will be frivolous. Magnanimous? Petty. Cynical? I will be a brazen believer in all things. Whatever you demand I will not give you—unless it is with the misty hope that what I give you is not what you ask for but what you want.   9

We use this freedom to break the silence, even of death, even when—in the depths of our darkest loneliness—we have no clear idea of why we reach out to one another with these frail, perishable chains of words. In the black chamber of the submarine, Kolesnikov noted, "I am writing blindly." Like everyone else.   10

RITA MAE BROWN   (1944–   )

Writing as a Moral Act

L anguage is decanted and shared. If only one person is left alive speak- 1
ing a language—the case with some American Indian languages—the
language is dead. Language takes two and their multiples.

Speaking is a social contract. You and I agree to exchange sounds whose 2
organized noises represent agreed-upon symbols. *Cat* means the same thing
to you as it does to me. It doesn't mean a thing to a Portuguese person. You
might think of a sleek tiger cat, and I might be thinking of a long-haired red
cat, but we are in sync about the species. If you want to get fancy you could
say feline (Latin again) but we're in the same ballpark.

Up to this point we are in agreement. We are cooperating as two indi- 3
viduals conceding to civilization. Literacy, or even simple speech, is the starting point of civilization. The unspoken truth is that we are unequal; we are
different. If you and I were exactly the same, a pair of identical strangers, we
wouldn't need to speak to one another or to write. You'd know what I was
thinking and vice versa. All communication rests upon inequality. That's the
sheer excitement of it. I don't know what you think. I can't wait to find out.
Language is the common thread by which we explore our differences and,
if we are both lucky and mature, the thread that will bring us to a form of
agreement or at least understanding.

Therefore it is imperative that people write and speak the truth. There can 4
be no community if a person is not as good as her/his word. How easy to
write that and how hard to put it in practice. You, my reader, whoever you
are, know things that will disturb others. You must tell. Camus said, "It is
immoral not to tell."

Again we can split hairs. A dear friend of mine has put on ten pounds. Do 5
I say, "Gee, Frank, you're fat as a toad" (the truth) or "Frank, you look wonderful." It may be wonderful to see him, but he still looks fat. I'll choose to
make my friend feel better.

If Frank, involved in a sordid affair with the wife of another friend of 6
mine, asks my opinion, I'll tell him the truth. "Either she leaves him and goes
to you, or you leave her. Don't mess with married people."

Telling the truth should be simple. Writing the truth should be even eas- 7
ier because you don't have to look your listener/reader in the eye. Writing
the truth is far more treacherous. The act of putting words down on paper
gives them a glamour and permanence not associated with speech. Writing,
to most everyone, is a more serious act than speaking.

Every generation produces those people—writers, composers, plastic 8
artists, and even the re-creative artists—who shatter social convention and tell
the truth. They aren't saying "Here I am." They are saying "Here you are."
The "you" is both individual and plural. In the case of *Oedipus Rex* or *Crime
and Punishment,* this recognition can be horrifying. In the case of *The Birds*
or *School for Scandal* it can be deliciously funny.

If this is prevented from happening (as in Stalin's Soviet Union, Hitler's 9
Germany, Botha's South Africa) the civilization begins to die from the inside
out. There may be a plethora of books in such nations but they aren't upsetting. They merely entertain. Art must both entertain and provoke.

If people refrain from telling what they know, how long before they 10
actively lie? Is there not a subtle and corrosive connection between withholding the truth and lying? You are as sick as you are secret.

If you don't believe that words will be followed by deeds, how can you 11
trust anyone? How can you form a community? When language no longer
corresponds to reality, any form of betrayal and misconduct are to be
expected.

Writers are the moral purifiers of the culture. We may not be pure our- 12
selves, but we must tell the truth, which is a purifying act. Therefore it is
impossible for a real fiction writer to be the mouthpiece for a political cause.
A writer should, as should any citizen, cherish his or her political beliefs but
that's not the same as being a propagandist.

By political beliefs I am not talking about the American two-party sys- 13
tem. The Republican party is a study in unlimited vandalism, and the
Democratic party presides over the cadaver of liberalism. The difference
between Republicans and Democrats is the difference between syphilis
and gonorrhea. Political beliefs are stronger than that. The separation of
church and state is a political belief. Affirming or repudiating capital punishment is a political belief. The desire for a state-controlled economy is not
only a political belief, in some nations it's a religion. You get the difference.
Our political parties skate over the political fashions that are current.
Opportunism wears many masks.

Since politicians seek to conceal the truth in order to dupe the public, 14
every writer alive is critical of whatever political system s/he lives in. Not
everyone in politics is bad and politics is a necessary evil, *but* politics is never
ever about the truth. Politics seeks to conceal; Art, to reveal.

The severest blasts in Russia or in our own country are directed at peo- 15
ple the state considers expendable. First, writers get it because they are potentially dangerous. Scientists run into walls only if they become critical of the
uses of science by the government. If they shut up and continue as the hired
help, they're okay. In our country, we are too sophisticated to put writers in

jail. It looks bad. Also, we are very fortunate in that most of our elected officials are semi-illiterate, and therefore they don't even know what we're writing. Should a writer happen to become disturbing and powerful enough to come to the attention of our civic worthies, then the fur flies. A politician will cite the offending author and make a stink. His acolytes will press to have the subversive texts banned from the libraries. (Actually, the acolytes control the politician. S/he usually responds to their pressure.) Loathsome as it is, such talk does get into the newspapers, and once publicity attaches itself to a book, the sales shoot upward. Bless the narrow-minded! You can survive that. You'll know when you're really in Dutch when the IRS hounds you. You think a highly placed government official wouldn't stoop that low? You think the IRS is not a punitive instrument of whatever administration is current? You also believe in the tooth fairy, don't you?

Communist and fascist nations recognize the power of writers. They   16
imprison them or drive them out of their homeland. The United States of America, no matter how absurd and contradictory our various administrations, has drawn the line here. When push comes to shove, we defend the First Amendment. By defending the First Amendment we are defending writers. Buried in the marrow of our collective bones is the recognition that we must know the truth about ourselves. Even the most bigoted American hates a liar. Despite our economic struggle, far better to be a writer here than elsewhere.

Morality is involved in issues other than lying or withholding informa-   17
tion. What happens when the word is substituted for the deed? Some act of faith is always involved in the connection between theory and action. To write and talk and not produce the action is to destroy faith. Once again, community becomes impossible.

The best example I can think of for this phenomenon involves the protest   18
movements of the late 1960s and early 1970s. While the Nazis committed unspeakable acts (I mean unspeakable—they had no word for what they were doing), the New Left and the Women's Movement spoke incessantly but committed few acts. This seems to be a hallmark of leftist politics: the substitution of the word for the deed. Yes, some things got accomplished, but compare it to the dedicated raising of money by the New Right and the intelligent daily application of those funds, and you quickly grasp the difference.

The New Right has few writers. The New Left was top-heavy with them.   19
From the New Left true fiction writers emerged, leaving behind the restrictions of ideology and moving toward a wider embrace of human experience but, I hope, imbued with a belief in justice, equality, and innovation. To date, not one decent fiction writer has emerged from the New Right.

I was one of those people to emerge from the New Left. I recall the early   20
days of the movement. The blind were leading the blind with great excitement into walls, into ravines, into the waiting rifles at Jackson and Kent State.

These anguished memories are then supplanted with pride; we did help to end a war which was ill-conceived. We wrested a few changes from the system for the nonwhite, and we created the conditions for the removal of a President who may have committed criminal acts. From this haunted terrain sprang a generation of scribblers. Perhaps the New Right will fool me yet and bring forth fiction writers capable of making us see ourselves as we really are. One thing is certain: That writer or those writers will get clobbered by their former associates. The Right suffers little dissent.

Some writers maintain that they are apolitical. A worm is apolitical; a human   21 being is not. If you live in a political system and do not seek to make it better, you are still a product of that system. Your lack of involvement is a political statement. All Art rests on a political foundation but it need not concern itself with politics.

Go back to *The Iliad*. Achilles has plopped his butt in his tent and won't   22 fight. Agamemnon took a damsel awarded to Achilles for his battle prowess. Briseis was her name, and Achilles, although in love with Patroclus, a man, wanted the girl. Why not eat your cake and have it too? The Greeks were not as ravaged by sexual definitions as we are. Agamemnon, as head of the armed forces (think of him as Eisenhower during World War II), could take this woman. He had the power but he didn't have the right. Achilles, by our standards, should set aside personal ego and fight for his people. Achilles, by Greek standards, is absolutely right. His first allegiance is to his honor. This conflict between the need of the individual to be sovereign and the need of the community to triumph/survive provides the context for the unfolding drama. *The Iliad* has a political basis but you can read it without giving politics a thought.

Even *Alice's Adventures in Wonderland* rests on a political foundation. It can   23 be read as a glorious fantasy, or it can be read as a comment on the powerlessness of a child, of children in society. You don't have to choose—you can read it on many levels, including reading it as a drug trip.

Both *The Iliad* and *Alice in Wonderland* ring true. People read them today   24 with as much pleasure as people derived from them when they were first written. A work lives like that if it is morally true.

You bring to a book your past, your system of beliefs. First, you read a book   25 and answer that book with those beliefs. If you are a student of literature, you will study the environment of the writer, and then you'll read the book again, setting aside your values. When you've finished the second reading you can engage the writer's beliefs with your own. Reading is an active moral and intellectual exchange. If you aren't reading books that challenge you, you're reading the wrong books.

If you aren't writing books that challenge you, keep writing. It takes years   26 to get there. I know the book I wanted to write, the challenging, lyrical work I dreamed about. You know only the book I wrote. I am acutely aware of the gap between desire and performance. Lash me though you might, you'll never hit me as hard as I hit myself, for only I know the full extent of my failure.

Morality shifts. Infanticide was acceptable to the Greeks. It isn't accept-   27 able to us. Your work will reflect your implied faiths and fears. Without your being necessarily conscious of it, your work reflects your society. Here's an example. Since *The Iliad,* Western writers have treated common experience as comic relief. This attitude depends on a clear class structure in which the superior classes, aristocrats, are assumed better than the inferior classes. When the middle classes began to assert themselves, this shifted. Chaucer in *The Canterbury Tales* presents sympathetic middle-class characters. Some are comic, and some are not, but none of them is heroic. A great revolution took place on the page. This accelerated over time. Shakespeare used all the classes, to his and our great profit.

Eventually, middle-class people developed the leisure in which to write, and   28 what did they do? They wrote about themselves. As the Industrial Revolution wears on, their literature takes over. The middle-class character is not a king or a landed aristocrat but a lawyer or a doctor perhaps. Chekhov comes to my mind instantly. The tendency to present ordinary people (an assumption in itself—are there ordinary people?) as vaguely comic still exists but it isn't as strict a literary convention as it was for a good two thousand years.

When you reject inferiority at the lowest level, you topple the whole   29 structure of dominance. The shift in literature, beginning with Chaucer, reflected real life and, in turn, had an impact upon real life. No longer were kings and queens so important. They were replaced with parliaments or by revolutions. They were replaced on the page. Morally, there's nothing wrong with having a king for your form of government or for your literary hero, but as an American I bet you don't write about one.

This struggle for literary representation bubbles over the decades. Today,   30 the lower classes, thanks to programs to get them into colleges, are producing literature. The class in control of the arts, the middle class, finds itself besieged from below. Not only are the lower classes becoming literate, non-white and non-Christians have acquired the skills to create English literature. Stick around—the show is just beginning!

As Shakespeare arrived at a creative imbalance between the passing   31 medieval world and the coming modern world (Bacon, Newton, Descartes), so we are at a similar overlap between the nation–state and global interdependence, between men and women, between whites and nonwhites, between the Christian world and science, the Christian world and the non-Christian world, between spiritual concerns and material ones. Like Shakespeare we find ourselves in a time where the future, so thrilling to the nonrigid, terrifies the rigid. Every action has an equal and opposite reaction. Every cultural/social push forward is followed by people organizing to hold back the hands of time. Those men who were willing to kill you if you thought the earth revolved around the sun instead of believing Ptolemy are still here. Those people, like Elizabeth I, who killed their political enemies are here too. Like Shakespeare, you've got to try to make sense of it. You don't have to explain it. He didn't. You need to use it, use every bit of it. This overlap and straining of divergent world views is a gift. Don't ask to live in tranquil times. Literature doesn't grow there.

FICTION

RICHARD WRIGHT   (1908–1960)

The Library Card

One morning I arrived early at work and went into the bank lobby 1
where the Negro porter was mopping. I stood at a counter and
picked up the Memphis *Commercial Appeal* and began my free
reading of the press. I came finally to the editorial page and saw an article
dealing with one H. L. Mencken. I knew by hearsay that he was the editor of the *American Mercury,* but aside from that I knew nothing about him.
The article was a furious denunciation of Mencken, concluding with one,
hot, short sentence: Mencken is a fool.

I wondered what on earth this Mencken had done to call down upon 2
him the scorn of the South. The only people I had ever heard denounced
in the South were Negroes, and this man was not a Negro. Then what ideas
did Mencken hold that made a newspaper like the *Commercial Appeal* casti-
gate him publicly? Undoubtedly he must be advocating ideas that the South
did not like. Were there, then, people other than Negroes who criticized the
South? I knew that during the Civil War the South had hated northern
whites, but I had not encountered such hate during my life. Knowing no
more of Mencken than I did at that moment, I felt a vague sympathy for him.
Had not the South, which had assigned me the role of a nonman, cast at
him its hardest words?

Now, how could I find out about this Mencken? There was a huge library 3
near the riverfront, but I knew that Negroes were not allowed to patronize
its shelves any more than they were the parks and playgrounds of the city. I
had gone into the library several times to get books for the white men on
the job. Which of them would now help me to get books? And how could
I read them without causing concern to the white men with whom I
worked? I had so far been successful in hiding my thoughts and feelings from
them, but I knew that I would create hostility if I went about the business
of reading in a clumsy way.

I weighed the personalities of the men on the job. There was Don, a Jew; 4
but I distrusted him. His position was not much better than mine and I knew
that he was uneasy and insecure; he had always treated me in an offhand, ban-
tering way that barely concealed his contempt. I was afraid to ask him to help
me get books; his frantic desire to demonstrate a racial solidarity with the
whites against Negroes might make him betray me.

Then how about the boss? No, he was a Baptist and I had the suspicion 5
that he would not be quite able to comprehend why a black boy would
want to read Mencken. There were other white men on the job whose attitudes showed clearly that they were Kluxers or sympathizers, and they were
out of the question.

There remained only one man whose attitude did not fit into an anti- 6
Negro category, for I had heard the white men refer to him as a "Pope lover."
He was an Irish Catholic and was hated by the white Southerners. I knew
that he read books, because I had got him volumes from the library several
times. Since he, too, was an object of hatred, I felt that he might refuse me
but would hardly betray me. I hesitated, weighing and balancing the impon-
derable realities.

One morning I paused before the Catholic fellow's desk. 7

"I want to ask you a favor," I whispered to him. 8

"What is it?" 9

"I want to read. I can't get books from the library. I wonder if you'd let 10
me use your card?"

He looked at me suspiciously. 11

"My card is full most of the time," he said. 12

"I see," I said and waited, posing my question silently. 13

"You're not trying to get me into trouble, are you, boy?" He asked, star- 14
ing at me.

"Oh, no sir." 15

"What book do you want?" 16

"A book by H. L. Mencken." 17

"Which one?" 18

"I don't know. Has he written more than one?" 19

"He has written several." 20

"I didn't know that." 21

"What makes you want to read Mencken?" 22

"Oh, I just saw his name in the newspaper," I said. 23

"It's good of you to want to read," he said. "But you ought to read the right 24
things."

I said nothing. Would he want to supervise my reading? 25

"Let me think," he said. "I'll figure out something." 26

I turned from him and he called me back. He stared at me quizzically. 27

"Richard, don't mention this to the other white men," he said. 28

"I understand," I said. "I won't say a word." 29

A few days later he called me to him. 30

"I've got a card in my wife's name," he said. "Here's mine." 31

"Thank you, sir." 32

"Do you think you can manage it?"   33

"I'll manage fine," I said.   34

"If they suspect you, you'll get in trouble," he said.   35

"I'll write the same kind of notes to the library that you wrote when you   36
sent me for books," I told him. "I'll sign your name."

He laughed.   37

"Go ahead. Let me see what you get," he said.   38

That afternoon I addressed myself to forging a note. Now, what were the   39
names of books written by H. L. Mencken? I did not know any of them. I
finally wrote what I thought would be a foolproof note: *Dear Madam: Will
you please let this nigger boy*—I used the word "nigger" to make the librarian
feel that I could not possibly be the author of the note—*have some books by
H. L. Mencken?* I forged the white man's name.

I entered the library as I had always done when on errands for whites, but   40
I felt that I would somehow slip up and betray myself. I doffed my hat, stood
a respectful distance from the desk, looked as unbookish as possible, and
waited for the white patrons to be taken care of. When the desk was clear
of people, I still waited. The white librarian looked at me.

"What do you want, boy?"   41

As though I did not possess the power of speech, I stepped forward and   42
simply handed her the forged note, not parting my lips.

"What books by Mencken does he want?" she asked.   43

"I don't know, ma'am," I said, avoiding her eyes.   44

"Who gave you this card?"   45

"Mr. Falk," I said.   46

"Where is he?"   47

"He's at work, at the M——— Optical Company," I said. "I've been in   48
here for him before."

"I remember," the woman said. "But he never wrote notes like this."   49

Oh, God, she's suspicious. Perhaps she would not let me have the books?   50
If she had turned her back at that moment, I would have ducked out the door
and never gone back. Then I thought of a bold idea.

"You can call him up, ma'am," I said, my heart pounding.   51

"You're not using these books, are you?" she asked pointedly.   52

"Oh, no, ma'am. I can't read."   53

"I don't know what he wants by Mencken," she said under her breath.   54

I knew now that I had won; she was thinking of other things and the race   55
question had gone out of her mind. She went to the shelves. Once or twice
she looked over her shoulder at me, as though she was still doubtful. Finally
she came foreward with two books in her hand.

"I'm sending him two books," she said. "But tell Mr. Falk to come in next time,   56
or send me the names of the books he wants. I don't know what he wants to read."

I said nothing. She stamped the card and handed me the books. Not dar- 57
ing to glance at them, I went out of the library, fearing that the woman
would call me back for further questioning. A block away from the library
I opened one of the books and read a title: *A Book of Prefaces.* I was nearing
my nineteenth birthday and I did not know how to pronounce the word
"preface." I thumbed the pages and saw strange words and strange names. I
shook my head, disappointed. I looked at the other book; it was called
Prejudices. I knew what that word meant; I had heard it all my life. And right
off I was on guard against Mencken's books. Why would a man want to call
a book *Prejudices?* The word was so stained with all my memories of racial
hate that I could not conceive of anybody using it for a title. Perhaps I had
made a mistake about Mencken? A man who had prejudices must be wrong.

When I showed the books to Mr. Falk, he looked at me and frowned. 58

"That librarian might telephone you," I warned him. 59

"That's all right," he said. "But when you're through reading those books, 60
I want you to tell me what you get out of them."

That night in my rented room, while letting the hot water run over my 61
can of pork and beans in the sink, I opened *A Book of Prefaces* and began to
read. I was jarred and shocked by the style, the clear, clean, sweeping sentences. Why did he write like that? And how did one write like that? I pictured the man as a raging demon, slashing with his pen, consumed with hate,
denouncing everything American, extolling everything European or German,
laughing at the weaknesses of people, mocking God, authority. What was
this? I stood up, trying to realize what reality lay behind the meaning of the
words. . . . Yes, this man was fighting, fighting with words. He was using
words as a weapon, using them as one would use a club. Could words be
weapons? Well, yes, for here they were. Then, maybe, perhaps, I could use
them as a weapon? No. It frightened me. I read on and what amazed me was
not what he said, but how on earth anybody had the courage to say it.

Occasionally I glanced up to reassure myself that I was alone in the room. Who 62
were these men about whom Mencken was talking so passionately? Who was
Anatole France? Joseph Conrad? Sinclair Lewis, Sherwood Anderson, Dostoevski,
George Moore, Gustave Flaubert, Maupassant, Tolstoy, Frank Harris, Mark Twain,
Thomas Hardy, Arnold Bennett, Stephen Crane, Zola, Norris, Gorky, Bergson,
Ibsen, Balzac, Bernard Shaw, Dumas, Poe, Thomas Mann, O. Henry, Dreiser,
H. G. Wells, Gogol, T. S. Eliot, Gide, Baudelaire, Edgar Lee Masters, Stendhal,
Turgenev, Huneker, Nietzsche, and scores of others? Were these men real? Did
they exist or had they existed? And how did one pronounce their names?

I ran across many words whose meanings I did not know, and I either 63
looked them up in a dictionary or, before I had a chance to do that,
encountered the word in a context that made its meaning clear. But what
strange world was this? I concluded the book with the conviction that I

had somehow overlooked something terribly important in life. I had once tried to write, had once reveled in feeling, had let my crude imagination roam, but the impulse to dream had been slowly beaten out of me by experience. Now it surged up again and I hungered for books, new ways of looking and seeing. It was not a matter of believing or disbelieving what I read, but of feeling something new, of being affected by something that made the look of the world different.

As dawn broke I ate my pork and beans, feeling dopey, sleepy. I went to work, but the mood of the book would not die; it lingered, coloring everything I saw, heard, did. I now felt that I knew what the white men were feeling. Merely because I had read a book that had spoken of how they lived and thought, I identified myself with that book. I felt vaguely guilty. Would I, filled with bookish notions, act in a manner that would make the whites dislike me? 64

I forged more notes and my trips to the library became frequent. Reading grew into a passion. My first serious novel was Sinclair Lewis's *Main Street*. It made me see my boss, Mr. Gerald, and identify him as an American type. I would smile when I saw him lugging his golf bags into the office. I had always felt a vast distance separating me from the boss, and now I felt closer to him, though still distant. I felt now that I knew him, that I could feel the very limits of his narrow life. And this had happened because I had read a novel about a mythical man called George F. Babbitt. 65

The plots and stories in the novels did not interest me so much as the point of view revealed. I gave myself over to each novel without reserve, without trying to criticize it; it was enough for me to see and feel something different. And for me, everything was something different. Reading was like a drug, a dope. The novels created moods in which I lived for days. But I could not conquer my sense of guilt, my feeling that the white men around me knew that I was changing, that I had begun to regard them differently. 66

Whenever I brought a book to the job, I wrapped it in newspaper—a habit that was to persist for years in other cities and under other circumstances. But some of the white men pried into my packages when I was absent and they questioned me. 67

"Boy, what are you reading those books for?" 68

"Oh, I don't know, sir." 69

"That's deep stuff you're reading, boy." 70

"I'm just killing time, sir." 71

"You'll addle your brains if you don't watch out." 72

I read Dreiser's *Jennie Gerhardt* and *Sister Carrie* and they revived in me a vivid sense of my mother's suffering; I was overwhelmed. I grew silent, wondering about the life around me. It would have been impossible for me to have told anyone what I derived from these novels, for it was nothing less than 73 a sense of life itself. All my life had shaped me for the realism, the natural-ism of the modern novel, and I could not read enough of them.

Steeped in new moods and ideas, I bought a ream of paper and tried to 74 write; but nothing would come, or what did come was flat beyond telling. I discovered that more than desire and feeling were necessary to write and I dropped the idea. Yet I still wondered how it was possible to know people sufficiently to write about them? Could I ever learn about life and people? To me, with my vast ignorance, my Jim Crow station in life, it seemed a task impossible of achievement. I now knew what being a Negro meant. I could endure the hunger; I had learned to live with hate. But to feel that there were feelings denied me, that the very breath of life itself was beyond my reach, that more than anything else hurt, wounded me. I had a new hunger.

In buoying me up, reading also cast me down, made me see what was pos- 75 sible, what I had missed. My tension returned, new, terrible, bitter, surging, almost too great to be contained. I no longer *felt* that the world about me was hostile, killing; I *knew* it. A million times I asked myself what I could do to save myself, and there were no answers. I seemed forever condemned, ringed by walls.

I did not discuss my reading with Mr. Falk, who had lent me his library 76 card; it would have meant talking about myself and that would have been too painful. I smiled each day, fighting desperately to maintain my old behavior, to keep my disposition seemingly sunny. But some of the white men dis-cerned that I had begun to brood.

"Wake up there, boy!" Mr. Olin said one day. 77

"Sir!" I answered for the lack of a better word. 78

"You act like you've stolen something," he said. 79

I laughed in the way I knew he expected me to laugh, but I resolved to 80 be more conscious of myself, to watch my every act, to guard and hide the new knowledge that was dawning within me.

If I went north, would it be possible for me to build a new life then? But 81 how could a man build a life upon vague, unformed yearnings? I wanted to write and I did not even know the English language. I bought English gram-mars and found them dull. I felt that I was getting a better sense of the lan-guage from novels than from grammars. I read hard, discarding a writer as soon as I felt that I had grasped his point of view. At night the printed page stood before my eyes in sleep.

Mrs. Moss, my landlady, asked me one Sunday morning: 82

"Son, what is this you keep on reading?" 83

"Oh, nothing. Just novels." 84

"What you get out of 'em?" 85

"I'm just killing time," I said. 86

"I hope you know your own mind," she said in a tone which implied 87 that she doubted if I had a mind.

I knew of no Negroes who read the books I liked and I wondered if any   88
Negroes ever thought of them. I knew that there were Negro doctors,
lawyers, newspapermen, but I never saw any of them. When I read a Negro
newspaper I never caught the faintest echo of my pre-occupation in its pages.
I felt trapped and occasionally, for a few days, I would stop reading. But a
vague hunger would come over me for books, books that opened up new
avenues of feeling and seeing, and again I would forge another note to the
white librarian. Again I would read and wonder as only the naïve and unlet-
tered can read and wonder, feeling that I carried a secret, criminal burden
about with me each day.

That winter my mother and brother came and we set up housekeeping,   89
buying furniture on the installment plan, being cheated and yet knowing
no way to avoid it. I began to eat warm food and to my surprise found that
regular meals enabled me to read faster. I may have lived through many illnesses and survived them, never suspecting that I was ill. My brother obtained
a job and we began to save toward the trip north, plotting our time, setting
tentative dates for departure. I told none of the white men on the job that
I was planning to go north; I knew that the moment they felt I was thinking of the North they would change toward me. It would have made them
feel that I did not like the life I was living, and because my life was completely
conditioned by what they said or did, it would have been tantamount to
challenging them.

I could calculate my chances for life in the South as a Negro fairly clearly   90
now.

I could fight the southern whites by organizing with other Negroes, as my   91
grandfather had done. But I knew that I could never win that way; there
were many whites and there were but few blacks. They were strong and we
were weak. Outright black rebellion could never win. If I fought openly I
would die and I did not want to die. News of lynchings were frequent.

I could submit and live the life of a genial slave, but that was impossible.   92
All of my life had shaped me to live by my own feelings, and thoughts. I
could make up to Bess and marry her and inherit the house. But that, too,
would be the life of a slave; if I did that, I would crush to death something
within me, and I would hate myself as much as I knew the whites already
hated those who had submitted. Neither could I ever willingly present myself
to be kicked, as Shorty had done. I would rather have died than do that.

I could drain off my restlessness by fighting with Shorty and Harrison. I   93
had seen many Negroes solve the problem of being black by transfering their
hatred of themselves to others with a black skin and fighting them. I would
have to be cold to do that, and I was not cold and I could never be.

I could, of course, forget what I had read, thrust the whites out of my   94
mind, forget them; and find release from anxiety and longing in sex and

alcohol. But the memory of how my father had conducted himself made that course repugnant. If I did not want others to violate my life, how could I voluntarily violate it myself?

I had no hope whatever of being a professional man. Not only had I been 95 so conditioned that I did not desire it, but the fulfillment of such an ambition was beyond my capabilities. Well-to-do Negroes lived in a world that was almost as alien to me as the world inhabited by whites.

What, then, was there? I held my life in my mind, in my consciousness each 96 day, feeling at times that I would stumble and drop it, spill it forever. My reading had created a vast sense of distance between me and the world in which I lived and tried to make a living, and that sense of distance was increasing each day. My days and nights were one long, quiet, continuously contained dream of terror, tension, and anxiety. I wondered how long I could bear it.

JESSICA ANYA BLAU   (1963–   )

Red-Headed

I had no idea what I was going to do after college, no idea what I should   1
do in my life. I had been a French major and had thought of working
for Club Med on some French-speaking island somewhere. But I was in
love. My boyfriend, Ricardo, hadn't graduated yet, and I wasn't willing to
leave him behind.

   That summer Ricardo got an internship at a hospital in Oakland,   2
California (he was pre-med and planned on becoming a cardiologist), so we
moved from Berkeley to Oakland where we lived in an art deco apartment
building near Lake Merritt, a man-made lake in the middle of the city. Our
side of the lake hadn't been gentrified yet. There was what we called a
Drug-in-the-Box across the street: at a sidewalk level window, people walked
by all times of day and night, stuck their hand in the window, then walked
away. The only thing we ever saw of the Drug-in-the-Box dealer was his
arm: lean, sinewy, quick as a biting snake. Next door were pay-by-the-week
apartments. Someone called 911 from that building at least three or four
times a week. At the little market on the first floor, a security man with a gun
in his holster stood day and night. We heard gunfire a few times, and Ricardo
once found himself down on the ground with two police guns pointed at
his head when he was in the market buying a soda and was mistaken for the
guy who was hiding behind the canned goods aisle.

   Late one fall night we heard screams and looked out our window to find   3
a man beating up a woman in the parking lot. Ricardo hid behind the slats
of the blinds, lowered his voice three octaves and yelled, "LEAVE HER
ALONE; I'M CALLING THE POLICE." The guy stopped what he was
doing. He and the woman straightened themselves up and looked in the
direction of our window, both of them squinting to find where the voice had
come from.

   "MIND YOUR OWN BUSINESS," the woman finally yelled. "THIS   4
DON'T HAVE NOTHING TO DO WITH YOU!"

   When the man shifted his shoulders and head a bit, like he was trying to   5
sniff out our scent, we shut the window and latched it, ran to the front door
to make sure it was locked, and secreted ourselves in the bedroom with the
door shut.

   About a month after we moved in, the manager of our apartment build-   6
ing died—an old woman who, I had been told, marched out into the hallway each Christmas and plopped a small plastic decorated tree on top of
the radiator. The owner of the building asked if I wanted to be the new

manager. Ricardo and I would get free rent, our utilities and phone bill paid, and a small salary. I wouldn't have to do the maintenance work; there was a man for that. I'd just have to direct the maintenance man, collect the rents, and rent out vacant apartments. This is how I ended up with my first post-college job.

What the building owner didn't tell me about was the old woman with   7
a beehive hairdo (apartment 3F) who wanted her place sprayed for roaches so often that the hallway outside her door smelled like the chimney out-pourings from a factory in Elizabeth, New Jersey. He didn't tell me about the Viet Nam vet (2E) who had several calendars with pictures of naked women on his walls. He asked to use my bathroom once when he was dropping off the rent check and peed a wreath of yellow urine on the seat. The owner also failed to mention the alcoholic who rented a basement studio (B1), vomited on his walls, and had cartoons playing on his TV all day. And then there were the users and dealers. The stuttering crack addict, Frank O'Malley (B6), once came to our door in his neon orange skivvy underpants. With a cigarette wag-ging in one hand, he repeated one phrase over and over again, as if his brain were stuck like a car spinning its wheels to get out of a muddy ditch: "I want my cccccc-cable television! I want my ccccc-cable television!"

The Cherokee Indian man, Rex (1E), was as gentle and sweet as a llama,   8
but always paid his rent late because his crack-addicted girlfriend often stole his social security checks, leaving him penniless. For a quarter you could eat a great big meal at the church down the street, Rex told me. I gave him a quarter every day, so even if he wasn't up on his rent, he was up on his meals. Once, Ricardo and I went to dinner at the church with Rex. We wanted to see if the meal was as great as he raved it was. Ricardo concurred. I found it inedible.

Rikki (4D) was an androgynously thin man with black Shirley Temple   9
curls, who claimed he was living off savings. Rikki had three brand new cars (a Mercedes, BMW, and SAAB) and the showroom furniture off the floor of Emporium Capwells. He paid the rent in cash, and when I told him I didn't want that much cash in the apartment he brought me a check every month, written out in his hand, on a check book that had a name other than his. One day a plain white truck pulled up, and four enormous men carried out the contents of Rikki's apartment and drove away in the Mercedes and BMW. Rikki came to our door, sweat glossing his face like oil, as he jangled his keys. He had to get out of town quick, that second in fact, and would Ricardo and I be interested in buying the SAAB for ten-thousand dollars—it was brand new, had all the extras. Ricardo told him we'd buy it for five hundred dollars. Rikki laughed, but came back ten hours later with the keys. This is how Ricardo and I got our first car. Until then we both took buses or the BART train to get around.

Ricardo liked everyone in the building—he was the kind of person who   10
could see the good in anyone. He even liked the maintenance man, Ed, who
called him Cubano, even though Ricardo wasn't Cuban. Ricardo explained
to Ed one day that he was from Texas and his family was from Mexico. Ed
slitted-up his baggy eyes, looked Ricardo up and down, and said, "I lived in
Miami for ten years, Ricardo, and I know a Cuban when I see one." It's true
Ricardo looked like a modern-day Ricky Ricardo—square head, hair as
black as oil, and light brown eyes that reminded me of suede. But he'd never
even met anyone from Cuba.

Ricardo and I would often lie in bed at night laughing as I told him about   11
all my encounters with the tenants that day. He claimed that he couldn't fall
asleep until he had heard at least one story about someone in the building.

The only person who could get Ricardo upset was the stumpy, grey-faced   12
woman in apartment 4B. Like me, her name was Rachel. At least once a
week, she called me on the phone and said in her wavering, operatic voice,
"Hi Rachel, *this* is Rachel!" And then she would go on to chronicle all the
Jews she had met in her life and how each one had betrayed her in some way.
She always capped this rant by saying, "And the red-headed Jews are the
worst Jews!"

I am red-headed. And I'm Jewish. But there is nothing on me that states   13
that I am Jewish. In fact, people often think I'm Irish—I even have green eyes.
But unlike Ricardo, who, with his beautiful brown skin and his name, *Ricardo
Gonzales,* is clearly Hispanic, I am not clearly anything.

Rachel told me about the red-headed Jew who sold her a car in 1964. It   14
never ran properly, and when she drove it off the lot it was immediately
worth less than half what she paid for it. She told me about the red-headed
Jew who sold her a mattress in 1985 that had springs that would carve circles into your back while you slept. She told me about the carpet, the couch,
the encyclopedia set, and dishes she had bought from red-headed Jews. It
seemed that everywhere Rachel went during her seven decades on this
planet, there were red-headed Jews who were trying to rip her off. I wanted
to say to her, "Rachel, if all the red-headed Jews in the world are liars and
cheats, why do you keep buying things from them?" But I never did.

Ricardo wanted me to tell Rachel that I was Jewish. He wanted me to   15
point out that perhaps some of these red-headed salesmen weren't Jews at all.
And he wanted me to ask her if she hadn't noticed that swindling salesmen
come in every form, color, and size. Ricardo himself once got ripped off by
an overweight albino Texan who sold him a color TV that made everything
pink or green. "The guy was wearing a cross," Ricardo told me. "Tell Rachel
that there was no way he was a red-headed Jew!" But I never said anything.
I took Rachel's rent checks and listened to her talk about how much she
hated the red-headed Jew who owned the building because he had raised the

rent after he put a new laundry room in the basement. And I took Rachel's phone calls and listened patiently through the litany of the red-headed Jews. I knew all the characters and circumstances in each story she had created about her life. If I had been an artist, I could have drawn the scenes perfectly. And in the peaceful dark of our bedroom each night, I relayed it all to Ricardo with exacting detail.

Once, when I was telling Ricardo the story Rachel had told me earlier 16
in the day (a red-headed Jewish dentist had pulled out her good teeth, replaced them with caps, while letting her bad teeth lie rotting, bloody, and throbbing in her mouth), he threw up both his hands and stopped me.

"Rachel," he said. "You have to *do* something about this woman!" 17

"What am I going to do?" I said. "Even if I tell her I'm Jewish, I'll never 18
get her to see the world differently. She'll just make up some story about me, and I'll be another person on her list of evil red-headed Jews."

"But you have to *do* something!" That was Ricardo. He was always doing 19
things. He was on his way to medical school to learn things, to do things, to heal people, to save the world one heart at a time. But I wasn't like that. I wasn't doing things to people so much as I was watching them, listening to them, recording them in my mind and in my memory.

"Well write it down, at least," Ricardo said. I wrote all the time, in jour- 20
nals and diaries that I had kept up since the time I could form letters in cursive. And I wrote letters to friends, to my family, to Ricardo—each word in a messy slant on yellow blue-lined paper. No one wrote back, but I didn't mind. I understood that sitting down and writing a letter isn't as easy for everyone else as it is for me.

That week, I wrote a short story called, "Red-Headed," about a young 21
Jewish woman who was managing an apartment building where there was a wizened, old tenant named Rachel who hated all the Jews. I sent the story out to twelve different literary magazines. Each one rejected it. And when I sat down and rewrote the story over and over again in spite of the rejections, I realized that not only was I a red-headed Jew, I was also a writer.

POETRY

BILLY COLLINS   (1941–   )

Books

From the heart of this dark, evacuated campus   1
I can hear the library humming in the night,
a choir of authors murmuring inside their books
along the unlit, alphabetical shelves,
Giovanni Pontano next to Pope, Dumas next to his son,   5
each one stitched into his own private coat,
together forming a low, gigantic chord of language.

I picture a figure in the act of reading,
shoes on a desk, head tilted into the wind of a book,
a man in two worlds, holding the rope of his tie   10
as the suicide of lovers saturates a page,
or lighting a cigarette in the middle of a theorem.
He moves from paragraph to paragraph
as if touring a house of endless, paneled rooms.

I hear the voice of my mother reading to me   15
from a chair facing the bed, books about horses and dogs,
and inside her voice lie other distant sounds,
the horrors of a stable ablaze in the night,
a bark that is moving toward the brink of speech.

I watch myself building bookshelves in college,   20
walls within walls, as rain soaks New England,
or standing in a bookstore in a trench coat.

I see all of us reading ourselves away from ourselves,

straining in circles of light to find more light
until the line of words becomes a trail of crumbs   25
that we follow across a page of fresh snow;
when evening is shadowing the forest
and small birds flutter down to consume the crumbs,
we have to listen hard to hear the voices
of the boy and his sister receding into the woods.   30

ROBERT FRANCIS   (1901–1987)

Catch

Two boys uncoached are tossing a poem together,   1
Overhand, underhand, backhand, sleight of hand, every hand,
Teasing with attitudes, latitudes, interludes, altitudes,
High, make him fly off the ground for it, low, make him stoop,
Make him scoop it up, make him as-almost-as-possible miss it,   5
Fast, let him sting from it, now, now, fool him slowly,
Anything, everything tricky, risky, nonchalant,
Anything under the sun to outwit the prosy,
Over the tree and the long sweet cadence down,
Over his head, make him scramble to pick up the meaning,   10
And now, like a posy, a pretty one plump in his hands.

Glass

Words of a poem should be glass   1
But glass so simple-subtle its shape
Is nothing but the shape of what it holds.

A glass spun for itself is empty,
Brittle, at best Venetian trinket.   5
Embossed glass hides the poem or its absence.

Words should be looked through, should be windows.
The best words were invisible.
The poem is the thing the poet thinks.

If the possible were not,   10
And if the glass, only the glass,
Could be removed, the poem would remain.

Chapter Writing Assignments

Practicing Thinking, Reading, and Writing

1. In her essay, Rita Mae Brown claims, "Reading is an active moral and intellectual exchange." In what way is reading an "exchange"? How does this notion make reading more interesting and worthwhile? Write an essay in which you explain how to engage in different types of reading material that a college student encounters. Anticipate questions that another student might ask.

2. Think about the details of your own writing process, and list all the activities, routines, rituals, and crises you go through to produce a good piece of writing. Then write a humorous essay that makes fun of your own writing process. Through satire, guide students to an understanding of the features of a good, functional writing process.

3. Discuss in an essay the differences between fiction, such as short stories and novels, and non-fiction, such as informational essays and excerpts from your college textbooks. How is each kind of reading important for a college student? What can we learn from each genre?

Exploring Ideas

4. In what ways do you believe television, video games, movies, computers, and other technology have affected reading? In an essay written to other college students, identify the ways technology has improved and/or decreased the reading skills of a particular group of people (for example, college students, children, people on the job).

5. If thought is at least partly language based, how does our ability to use language influence our ability to think? Can we have a thought that we have no language to express? Write an essay that explores the effect language skills have on our ability to think.

6. Choose a word that has changed over a period of time. Think about what it meant originally and the connotations or meanings it has acquired over time. How do changes in our words reflect changes in our thinking? Write an essay that explores the way changes in language reflect changes in thought, using the initial word you chose as an example.

Part III

Reference
Reading and Writing
from Sources

R-1 Introducing the Documented Essay

We use sources every day in both formal and informal situations. For example, we might explain the source of a phone message or refer to an instructor's comments in class. We may use someone else's opinion in an essay or quote an expert to prove a point. We cite sources both in speaking and in writing through summary, paraphrase, and direct quotation. Most of your college instructors will ask you to write papers using sources so they can see how well you understand the course material. The use of sources in academic papers requires you to understand what you have read and to integrate this reading material with your own opinions and observations—a process that demands a high level of skill in thinking, reading, and writing.

R-1.1 DEFINING DOCUMENTED ESSAYS

Documented essays provide you with the opportunity to perform sophisticated and exciting exercises that draw on the thinking, reading, and writing abilities you have built up over the course of your academic career. They also require you to put all the rhetorical modes to work at their most analytical level. Documented essays demonstrate the process of analytical thinking at its best in different disciplines. In the academic world, documented essays are also called *research papers, library papers,* and *term papers.* They are generally written for one of three reasons: (1) to **report,** (2) to **interpret,** or (3) to **analyze.**

The most straightforward, uncomplicated type of documented essay **reports** information, as in a survey of problems that children have in preschool. The second type of documented essay both presents and **interprets** its findings. It examines a number of different views on a specific issue and weighs these views in drawing its own conclusions. A topic that might fall into this category would be whether children who have attended preschool are more sociable than those who have not. After considering evidence on both sides, the writer would draw his or her own conclusions on this topic. A documented essay that **analyzes** a particular topic presents a hypothesis, tests the hypothesis, and analyzes or evaluates its conclusions. This type of essay calls for the most advanced form of critical thinking. It might look, for example, at the reasons preschool children are more or less socially adaptable than nonpreschool children. At its most proficient, this type of writing requires a sophisticated degree of evaluation that encourages you to judge your reading, evaluate your sources, and ultimately scrutinize your own reasoning ability as the essay takes shape. Each of these types of research papers calls for a higher level of thinking, and each evolves from the previous category. In other words, interpreting requires some reporting, and analyzing draws on both reporting and interpreting.

R-1.2 SAMPLE DOCUMENTED PARAGRAPH

In the following paragraph, a student uses sources to report on, interpret, and analyze the problem of solid waste disposal in the United States. Notice how the student writer draws his readers into the essay with a commonly used phrase about America and then questions the validity of its meaning. The student's opinions give shape to the paragraph, while his use of sources helps identify the problem and support his contentions as he uses several rhetorical modes to prove his point.

> "America the Beautiful" is a phrase used to describe the many wonders of nature found throughout our country. America's natural beauty will fade, however, if solutions to our solid waste problems are not discovered soon. America is a rich nation socially, economically, and politically. But these very elements may be the cause of America's wastefulness. Americans now generate approximately 160 million tons of solid waste a year—$3\frac{1}{2}$ pounds per person per day. We live in a consumer society where "convenience," "ready-to-use," and "throw-away" are words that spark the consumer's attention (Cook 60). However, many of the products associated with these words create a large part of our problem with solid waste (Grossman 39). We are running out of space for our garbage. The people of America are beginning to produce responses to this problem. Are we too late? A joint effort from individuals, businesses, government industries, and local, state, and federal governments is necessary to establish policies and procedures to combat this war on waste. The problem requires not one solution, but a combination of solutions involving technologies and people working together to provide a safe and healthy environment for themselves and future generations.

R-1.3 DOCUMENTED ESSAY REFERENCE CHART

A documented essay is really just an essay with supporting material that comes from outside sources. The following chart compares a standard essay and a research paper.

Standard Essay		Research paper
Introduction with thesis statement	⟷	Introduction with thesis statement
Body paragraphs with facts and personal experience to support thesis statement	⟷	Body paragraphs with documented evidence to support thesis statement
Concluding paragraph	⟷	Concluding paragraph

Keep this outline in mind as you read how to construct a good documented essay. Laying out some clear guidelines is the best place to start.

R-2 Reading a Documented Essay

You should read a documented essay in much the same way that you read any essay. In all cases, you should prepare to read, read, and then reread several times—each with a slightly different purpose. The main difference is that you are paying attention to not only what the writer concludes but also how the writer's sources support that conclusion.

R-2.1 PREPARING TO READ A DOCUMENTED ESSAY

As you approach a documented essay, you should first take a few minutes to look at the preliminary material for each selection: What can you learn from scanning Ehrenreich's essay ("The Ecstasy of War") or from reading the synopsis in the Rhetorical Table of Contents? What does Barbara Ehrenreich's title, "The Ecstasy of War," prepare you to read?

Also, you should learn as much as you can from the author's biography: What is Ehrenreich's interest in war? What biographical details prepare us for her approach to this topic? Does she have the proper qualifications to write about this subject?

Another important part of preparing to read a documented essay is surveying the sources cited. Turn to the end of the essay and look at the sources. What publications does Ehrenreich draw from? Are these books and magazines well respected? Do you recognize any of the authorities she quotes?

Last, before you read these essays, try to generate some ideas on each topic so you can participate as fully as possible in your reading. The Preparing to Read questions will get you ready for this task. Then, try to speculate further on the topic of each essay: What is the connection for Ehrenreich between war and ecstasy? What does this relationship tell us about human nature in general?

R-2.2 READING A DOCUMENTED ESSAY

As you read to the professional essay in this chapter, you should respond to both the research and the writing. Record your responses as you read the essay for the first time: What are your reactions to the information you are reading? Are the sources appropriate? How well do they support the author's main points?

Use the preliminary material before the essay to help you create a framework for your responses to it: What motivated Ehrenreich to publish her essay on war? Do you find her argument convincing? Who was her primary audience when the essay was first published? In what ways is the tone of her essay appropriate for that audience?

Your main job at this stage is to determine the essay's primary assertion (thesis statement), note the sources that support this thesis, and begin to ask yourself questions about the essay so you can respond critically to your reading. Annotate the essay with your personal reactions, and make sure you understand all the author's vocabulary.

As in previous chapters, carefully crafted questions at the bottom of the pages of the essay will guide you from prereading predictions to higher levels of critical thinking in preparation for your writing assignments at the end of the selection. These questions are especially helpful with more complex reading tasks like the ones in this chapter. The essay in this chapter is similar to the material you will read in your other courses throughout your college experience. The questions at the bottom of these pages will essentially teach you how to approach this type of reading and understand it in all its complexity. Read these questions, but don't answer them until your second reading.

After you have read the essay for the first time, summarize its main ideas in some fashion. The form of this task might be anything from a succinct written summary to a drawing of the main ideas as they connect with one another. You could outline the ideas to get an overview of the piece; draw a graph or map of the topics in the essay (in much the same way that a person would draw a map of an area for someone unfamiliar with a particular destination); or write a traditional summary of the ideas to check your understanding of the main points of the selection. Any of these tasks can be completed from your original notes and underlining. Each will give you a slightly more thorough understanding of what you have read.

Finally, read the questions and assignments following the essay to help focus your thinking for the second reading. Don't answer the questions at this time; just read them to make sure you are picking up the main ideas from the selection and thinking about relevant connections among those ideas.

R-2.3 REREADING A DOCUMENTED ESSAY

As you reread the following documented essay, take some time to think about the difference between fact and opinion, to weigh and evaluate the evidence presented for the arguments, to consider the sources the writers use, to determine what information the writer omitted, and to confirm your own views on the issues at hand. During this stage, you will also need to examine the sources to determine whether or not their information is credible. All these skills demand the use of critical thinking strategies at their most sophisticated level.

Your second reading of the essay is a time to develop a deeper understanding of the author's main ideas and argument. Concentrate on reading "with the grain," as the rhetorician John Bean calls it, meaning you are essentially trying to adopt the author's reasoning in an attempt to learn how he or she thinks and came to certain conclusions. This reading will expand your reasoning capacity and stimulate new ideas.

Also during this reading, you should answer the questions at the bottom of the pages of the essay (the "bridge" questions). These questions are marked throughout the text both in the essay and at the bottom of the pages by numbers within diamonds. Then, you might ask some additional questions of your own. As always, you will get the most out of this process if you respond in writing. Keeping a journal to collect these responses is especially effective as you attempt to make this essay your own.

Then, during your third reading, you should consciously read "against the grain," actively doubting and challenging what the author is saying. Do some detective work and look closely at the assumptions on which the essay is based: For example, how does the writer move from idea to idea? What hidden assertions lie behind these ideas? Do you agree or disagree with these assertions? Your assessment of these unspoken assumptions will often play a major role in your critical response to an essay. In Ehrenreich's essay, do you accept the unspoken connection she makes between our natural inclinations and aggression? What parts of the essay depend on your acceptance of this connection? What other assumptions are fundamental to Ehrenreich's reasoning? If you accept her thinking along the way, you are more likely to agree with the general flow of Ehrenreich's essay. If you discover a flaw in her premises or assumptions, your acceptance of her argument will begin to break down.

Next, answer the questions that follow the essay. The "Understanding Details" questions will help you understand and remember what you have read on both the literal and the interpretive levels. Some of the questions ask you to restate various important points the author makes (literal understanding), while others help you see relationships among the different ideas presented (interpretive understanding). Also, be aware of your own thought processes as you sort facts from opinions. Know where you stand personally in relation to each side of the issues.

You need to approach this final stage of reading with an inquiring mind, asking questions and looking for answers as you read the essays. Be especially conscious of the appeals (logical, emotional, and ethical) at work in each essay (see the section "Reading and Writing Argument/Persuasion Essays" in Chapter 12), and take note of other rhetorical strategies that support the author's main argument.

Following is a list of guidelines that summarize the reading process for documented essays.

R-2.4 A CHECKLIST FOR READING DOCUMENTED ESSAYS

READING DOCUMENTED ESSAYS

Preparing to Read
√ What assumptions can I make from the essay's title?
√ Can I guess what the general mood of the essay is?
√ What is the essay's purpose and audience?
√ What does the synopsis tell me about the essay?
√ What can I learn from the author's biography?

Reading
√ What is the author's main assertion or thesis?
√ What are my personal associations with the essay?
√ What sources does the author cite to support the thesis?
√ What questions do I have about this topic?

Rereading
√ How does the author use facts and opinions in the essay?
√ Are the sources the writer cites valid and reliable?
√ Does the author interpret facts accurately?
√ What do I agree with in the essay?
√ What do I disagree with in the essay?
√ What are my own conclusions on this topic?

R-2.5 READING AN ANNOTATED ESSAY

BARBARA EHRENREICH   (1941–   )

The Ecstasy of War

Barbara Ehrenreich is a respected author, lecturer, and social commentator with opinions on a wide range of topics. After earning a B.A. from Reed College in Chemistry and Physics and a Ph.D. from Rockefeller University in Cell Biology, she turned almost immediately to freelance writing, producing a succession of books and pamphlets on a dazzling array of subjects. Early publications examined student uprisings, healthcare in America, nurses and midwives, poverty, welfare, economic justice for women, and the sexual politics of disease. Her most recent books include *Fear of Falling: The Inner Life of the Middle Class* (1989), *The Worst Years of Our Lives: Irreverent Notes from a Decade of Greed* (1990), *Blood Rites: Origins and History of the Passions of War* (1997), *Nickel and Dimed* (2001), *Bait and Switch: The (Futile) Pursuit of the American Dream* (2005), *Dancing in the Street: A History of Collective Joy* (2007), and *This Land Is Their Land: Reports from a Divided Nation* (2008). Ehrenreich is also well known as a frequent guest on television and radio programs, including *The Today Show, Good Morning America, Nightline,* and *Crossfire*. Her many articles and reviews have appeared in the *New York Times Magazine, Esquire,* the *Atlantic Monthly,* the *New Republic, Vogue, Harper's,* and the *Wall Street Journal.* She has been an essayist for *Time* since 1990. Ehrenreich, whose favorite hobby is "voracious reading," lives in Syosset, New York.

Preparing to Read

Taken from *Blood Rites: Origins and History of the Passions of War* (1997), the following essay analyzes the psychology of war. Its citations and bibliography illustrate proper MLA (Modern Language Association) documentation style.

Exploring Experience: As you prepare to read this article, take a few minutes to think about aggression in society today: Do you think aggression plays a significant role in American society? In other societies? What do you think is the origin of aggression? In your opinion, what role does aggression play in war? In everyday life? How do you react to aggressive behavior? How do people you associate with react to aggressive behavior?

Learning Online: Search the Internet for descriptions of current video games with a war theme. You might visit Web sites for Electronic Arts, Activision, or Take 2 Interactive to peruse their current game lists. Consider the techniques and intents of these games while reading Ehrenreich's essay.

Special Note: For the express purpose of learning how to read documented essays and then prepare to write one of your own, the following essay is carefully annotated. Use these side notes to capture the essence of Ehrenreich's essay as you also think about using her strategies in your own essay.

> *"So elemental is the human need to endow the shedding of blood with some great and even sublime significance that it renders the intellect almost entirely helpless."*
>
> *(Van Creveld 166).*

General information/ Discussion of war

Different wars have led to different theories of why men fight them. [1] The Napoleonic Wars, which bore along with them the rationalist spirit of the French Revolution, inspired the Prussian officer Carl von Clausewitz to propose that war itself is an entirely rational undertaking, unsullied by human emotion. War, in his famous aphorism, is merely a "continuation of policy ... by other means," with policy itself supposedly resulting from the same kind of clearheaded deliberation one might apply to a game of chess. Nation-states were the leading actors on the stage of history, and war was simply one of the many ways they advanced their interests against those of other nation-states. If you could accept the existence of this new super-person, the nation, a battle was no more disturbing and irrational than, say, a difficult trade negotiation— except perhaps to those who lay dying on the battlefield.

[Example]

Common knowledge

[Comparison/ Contrast]

World War I, coming a century after Napoleon's sweep through Europe and northern Africa, led to an opposite assessment of the human impulse to war. World War I was hard to construe as in any way "rational," especially to that generation of European intellectuals, including Sigmund Freud, who survived to ponder the unprecedented harvest of dead bodies. History textbooks tell us that the "Great War" grew out of the conflict between "competing imperialist states," but this Clausewitzian interpretation has little to do with the actual series of accidents, blunders, and miscommunications that impelled the nations of Europe to war in the summer of 1914.[1] At first swept

[Cause/ Effect]

Footnote

Thinking Critically

[1] Why do you think most wars are fought?

up in the excitement of the war, unable for weeks to work or think of anything else, Freud was eventually led to conclude that there is some dark flaw in the human psyche, a perverse desire to destroy, counter-ing Eros and the will to live (Stromberg 82).

In-text citation

So these are, in crude summary, the theories of war which modern wars have left us with: That war is a means, however risky, by which men seek to advance their collective interests and improve their lives. Or, al-ternatively, that war stems from sub-rational drives not unlike those that lead individuals to commit violent crimes. In our own time, most people seem to hold both views at once, avowing that war is a gainful en-terprise, intended to meet the material needs of the groups engaged in it, and, at the same time, that it ful-fills deep and "irrational" psychological needs. ❷ <u>There is no question about the first part of this proposition— that wars are designed, at least ostensibly, to secure nec-essaries like land or oil or "geopolitical advantage." The mystery lies in the peculiar psychological grip war exerts on us.</u>

3

Thesis statement

Background of first point

In the 1960s and '70s, the debate on the psychol-ogy of war centered on the notion of an "aggressive instinct," peculiar to all humans or only to human males. This is not the place to summarize that debate, with its endless examples of animal behavior and clashes over their applicability to human affairs. <u>Here I would simply point out that, whether or not there is an aggressive instinct, there are reasons to reject it as the major wellspring of war.</u>

4

Writer's first point

Although it is true that aggressive impulses, up to and including murderous rage, can easily take over in the heat of actual battle, even this statement must be qualified to take account of different weaponry and modes of fighting. Hand-to-hand combat may indeed call forth and even require the emotions of rage and aggression, if only to mobilize the body for bursts of muscular activity. In the case of action-at-a-distance weapons, however, like guns and bows and arrows,

5

Evidence for first point

Thinking Critically

❷ In what ways do you think war "fulfills deep and irrational psychological needs"?

emotionality of any sort can be a distinct disadvantage. [3] Coolness, and the ability to keep aiming and firing steadfastly in the face of enemy fire, prevails. Hence, according to the distinguished American military historian Robert L. O'Connell, the change in the ideal warrior personality wrought by the advent of guns in the fifteenth and sixteenth centuries, from "ferocious aggressiveness" to "passive disdain" (119). So *In-text citation* there is no personality type—"hot-tempered," "macho," or whatever—consistently and universally associated with warfare.

More evidence for first point Furthermore, fighting itself is only one component 6 of the enterprise we know as war. Wars are not barroom brawls writ large, or domestic violence that has been somehow extended to strangers. In war, fighting takes place within battles—along with much anxious waiting, of course—but wars do not begin with battles and are often not decided by them either. Most of war consists of *preparation* for battle—training, the organization of supplies, marching and other forms of transport—activities that are hard to account for by innate promptings of any kind. There is no plausible instinct, for example, that impels a man to leave his home, cut his hair short, and drill for hours in tight formation. As anthropologists Clifton B. Kroeber and *Introduction to quotation* Bernard L. Fontana point out, "It is a large step from *Quotation* what may be biologically innate leanings toward individual aggression to ritualized, socially sanctioned, *In-text citation* institutionalized group warfare" (166).

[Comparison/ Contrast]

War, in other words, is too complex and collective 7 an activity to be accounted for by a single warlike instinct lurking within the individual psyche. Instinct may, or may not, inspire a man to bayonet the first enemy he encounters in battle. But instinct does not mobilize supply lines, manufacture rifles, issue uniforms, or move an army of thousands from point A on the map to B. [4] These are "complicated, orchestrated, *Quotation*

Thinking Critically

[3] Do you agree with Ehrenreich that emotionality can be a disadvantage in war? Why or why not?

[4] According to the author, what is the role of instinct during wartime?

highly organized" activities, as social theorist Robin
Fox writes, undertaken not by individuals but by en-
tities on the scale of nations and dynasties (15). "The
hypothesis of a killer instinct," according to a commentator summarizing a recent conference on the anthropology of war, is "not so much wrong as irrelevant"
(Clark McCauley in Haas 2).

*In-text
citation*

*Conclusion
of first point*

*In-text
citation*

In fact, throughout history, individual men have
gone to near-suicidal lengths to avoid participating in
wars—a fact that proponents of a warlike instinct tend
to slight. Men have fled their homelands, served
lengthy prison terms, hacked off limbs, shot off feet or
index fingers, feigned illness or insanity, or, if they
could afford to, paid surrogates to fight in their stead.
"Some draw their teeth, some blind themselves, and
others maim themselves, on their way to us" (Mitchell
42), the governor of Egypt complained of his peasant
recruits in the early nineteenth century. So unreliable
was the rank and file of the eighteenth-century Prussian army that military manuals forbade camping near
a woods or forest: The troops would simply melt away
into the trees (Delbrück 303).

*Writer's
second
point*

8

*In-text
citation*

Paraphrase

*In-text
citation*

Proponents of a warlike instinct must also reckon
with the fact that even when men have been assembled, willingly or unwillingly, for the purpose of war,
fighting is not something that seems to come "naturally" to them. In fact, surprisingly, even in the thick
of battle, few men can bring themselves to shoot directly at individual enemies.[ii] The difference between
an ordinary man or boy and a reliable killer, as any
drill sergeant could attest, is profound. A transformation
is required: The man or boy leaves his former self behind and becomes something entirely different, perhaps even taking a new name. In small-scale, traditional
societies, the change was usually accomplished through
ritual drumming, dancing, fasting, and sexual absti-
nence—all of which serve to lift a man out of his
mundane existence and into a new, warriorlike mode
of being, denoted by special body paint, masks, and
headdresses.

*Continuation
of second
point*

9

Footnote

*Key
concept*

As if to emphasize the discontinuity between the
warrior and the ordinary human being, many cultures

10

require the would-be fighting man to leave his humanness behind and assume a new form as an animal.[iii] [5] The young Scandinavian had to become a bear before he could become an elite warrior, going "berserk" (the word means "dressed in a bear hide"), biting and chasing people. The Irish hero Cuchulain transformed himself into a monster in preparation for battle: "He became horrible, many-shaped, strange, and unrecognizable," with one eye sucked into his skull and the other popping out of the side of the face (Davidson 84). Apparently this transformation was a familiar and meaningful one, because similarly distorted faces turn up frequently in Celtic art.

Footnote

[Example]

[Example]

In-text citation

Writer's third point

Often the transformation is helped along with drugs or social pressure of various kinds. Tahitian warriors were browbeaten into fighting by functionaries called Rauti, or "exhorters," who ran around the battlefield urging their comrades to mimic "the devouring wild dog" (Keeley 146). The ancient Greek hoplites drank enough wine, apparently, to be quite tipsy when they went into battle (Hanson 126); Aztecs drank pulque; Chinese troops at the time of Sun Tzu got into the mood by drinking wine and watching "gyrating sword dancers" perform (Sun Tzu 37). Almost any drug or intoxicant has served, in one setting or another, to facilitate the transformation of man into warrior. [6] Yanomamo Indians of the Amazon ingest a hallucinogen before battle; the ancient Scythians smoked hemp, while a neighboring tribe drank something called "hauma," which is believed to have induced a frenzy of aggression (Rolle 94–95). So if there is a destructive instinct that impels men to war, it is a weak one and often requires a great deal of help.

11

[Examples]

In-text citation

In-text citation

In-text citation

In-text citation

In seventeenth-century Europe, the transformation of man into soldier took on a new form, more concerted and disciplined, and far less pleasant, than wine.

12

Thinking Critically

[5] Why do you think so many cultures have encouraged their warriors to become like animals in order to fight fiercely?

[6] What role have intoxicants played in warfare in past centuries?

New recruits and even seasoned veterans were end-
lessly drilled, hour after hour, until each man began to
feel himself part of a single, giant fighting machine.
The drill was only partially inspired by the technology of firearms. It's easy enough to teach a man to
shoot a gun; the problem is to make him willing to get
into situations where guns are being shot and to remain there long enough to do some shooting of his
own. So modern military training aims at a transformation parallel to that achieved by "primitives" with
war drums and paint: In the fanatical routines of boot
camp, a man leaves behind his former identity and is
reborn as a creature of the military—an automaton
and also, ideally, a willing killer of other men.

This is not to suggest that killing is foreign to   13
human nature or, more narrowly, to the male personality. Men (and women) have again and again proved
themselves capable of killing impulsively and with
gusto. But there is a huge difference between a war
and an ordinary fight. War not only departs from the
normal; it inverts all that is moral and right: ⑦ In war
one *should* kill, *should* steal, *should* burn cities and farms,
should perhaps even rape matrons and little girls.
Conclusion Whether or not such activities are "natural" or at some
of third level instinctual, most men undertake them only by
point entering what appears to be an "altered state"—induced by drugs or lengthy drilling, and denoted by
face paint or khakis.

The point of such transformative rituals is not only   14
to put men "in the mood." Returning warriors may
go through equally challenging rituals before they can
celebrate victory or reenter the community—cover-
ing their heads in apparent shame, for example; vom-   In-text
iting repeatedly; abstaining from sex (Keeley 144).   citation
[Example] Among the Maori, returning warriors could not participate in the victory celebration until they had gone
through a whaka-hoa ritual, designed to make them
"common" again: The hearts of slain enemies were
roasted, after which offerings were made to the war

Thinking Critically

⑦ How does war invert "all that is moral and right"?

god Tu, and the rest was eaten by priests, who shouted spells to remove "the blood curse" and enable warriors to reenter their ordinary lives (Sagan 18). Among the Taulipang Indians of South America, victorious warriors "sat on ants, flogged one another with whips, and passed a cord covered with poisonous ants, through their mouth and nose" (Métraux 397). Such painful and shocking postwar rites impress on the warrior that war is much more than a "continuation of policy . . . by other means." In war men enter an alternative realm of human experience, as far removed from daily life as those things which we call "sacred."

In-text citation

[Example]

In-text citation

Conclusion

Notes

Footnotes (correspond with raised numbers in essay)

i See, for example, Stoessinger, *Why Nations Go to War,* 14–20.

ii See Grossman, *On Killing.*

iii In the mythologies of the Indo-European tradition, Dumézil relates, thanks "either to a gift of metamorphosis, or to a monstrous heredity, the eminent warrior possesses a veritable animal nature" (Dumézil 140).

Works Cited

Sources actually referred to in the paper: MLA Style

Davidson, Hilda Ellis. *Myths and Symbols in Pagan Europe: Early Scandinavian and Celtic Religions.* Syracuse: Syracuse UP, 1988. Print.

Delbrück, Hans. *The Dawn of Modern Warfare.* Lincoln: U of Nebraska P, 1985. Print.

Dumézil, Georges. *Destiny of the Warrior.* Chicago: U of Chicago P, 1969. Print.

Fox, Robin. "Fatal Attraction: War and Human Nature." *National Interest* Winter 1992/93: 11–20. Print.

Grossman, Lt. Col. Dave. *On Killing: The Psychological Cost of Learning to Kill in War and Society.* Boston: Little, Brown, 1995. Print.

Haas, Jonathan, ed. *The Anthropology of War.* Cambridge: Cambridge UP, 1990. Print.

Hanson, Victor Davis. *The Western Way of War: Infantry Battle in Classical Greece.* New York: Knopf, 1989. Print.

Keeley, Lawrence H. *War Before Civilization: The Myth of the Peaceful Savage.* New York: Oxford UP, 1996. Print.

Kroeber, Clifton B., and Bernard L. Fontana. *Massacre on the Gila: An Account of the Last Major Battle Between American Indians, with Reflections on the Origin of War.* Tucson: U of Arizona P, 1986. Print.

Métraux, Alfred. "Warfare, Cannibalism, and Human Trophies." *Handbook of South American Indians.* Vol. 5. Ed. Julian H. Steward. New York: Cooper Square, 1963. Print.

Mitchell, Timothy. *Colonizing Egypt.* Berkeley: U of California P, 1991. Print.

O'Connell, Robert L. *Of Arms and Men: A History of War, Weapons, and Aggression.* New York: Oxford UP, 1989. Print.

Rolle, Renate. *The World of the Scythians.* Berkeley: U of California P, 1989. Print.

Sagan, Eli. *Cannibalism: Human Aggression and Cultural Form.* New York: Harper and Row, 1974. Print.

Stoessinger, John G. *Why Nations Go to War.* New York: St. Martin's, 1993. Print.

Stromberg, Roland. *Redemption by War: The Intellectuals and 1914.* Lawrence: U of Kansas P, 1982. Print.

Sun Tzu. *The Art of War.* Translated and with an introduction by Samuel B. Griffith. London: Oxford University Press, 1971. Print.

Van Creveld, Martin. *The Transformation of War.* New York: Free Press, 1991. Print.

UNDERSTANDING DETAILS

1. What do you think Ehrenreich's main purpose is in this essay?
2. According to the author, what is the difference between hand-to-hand combat and fighting at a distance?
3. What does Ehrenreich say are the various elements of what we call "war"?
4. In what ways do some cultures ritualize the transformation from regular citizen to warrior? Give three examples.

READING CRITICALLY

5. Do you believe that war can ever be emotionless and rational, like "a difficult trade negotiation" (paragraph 1)?

6. What do Kroeber and Fontana mean when they say, "It is a large step from what may be biologically innate leanings toward individual aggression to ritualized, socially sanctioned, institutionalized group warfare" (paragraph 6)?
7. Why is "the hypothesis of a killer instinct" "not so much wrong as irrelevant" to the "anthropology of war" (paragraph 7)?
8. Are you convinced by this essay that "in war men enter an alternative realm of human experience, as far removed from daily life as those things which we call 'sacred'" (paragraph 14)?

DISCOVERING RHETORICAL STRATEGIES

9. Who do you think is Ehrenreich's main audience? How did you come to this conclusion?
10. The author begins her discussion of war with different "theories of why men fight" (paragraph 1). Is this an effective beginning for what Ehrenreich is trying to accomplish? Explain your answer.
11. What information in this essay is most persuasive to you? What is least persuasive?
12. What tone does the author establish by citing frequent statistics and referring to other sources in her essay?

MAKING CONNECTIONS

13. Compare and contrast Ehrenreich's insights on the psychology of war with Alice Lesch Kelly's "Toughen Up!" and Stephen King's "Why We Crave Horror Movies." How do their ideas support one another? How do they contradict each other?
14. Compare Ehrenreich's use of examples with those of Joel Stein in "You Are Not My Friend." Which author uses them more skillfully? Why do you think this is true?
15. In a conversation among Ehrenreich, Brent Staples ("A Brother's Murder"), and/or Dave Grossman ("We Are Training Our Kids to Kill") about the "aggressive instinct" in people, on what principal points would these authors agree and disagree? Give examples.

IDEAS FOR DISCUSSION/WRITING

Preparing to Write

Write freely about aggression in general: Why do people fight? Why do countries go to war? What are some ways in which people take out their aggression? Have you ever noticed people fighting just for the sake of fighting? When is aggression acceptable? When is it unacceptable?

Choosing a Topic

1. *Learning Online:* Ehrenreich claims that no personality type has a "single war-like instinct" (paragraph 7). How do her theories apply to video game users? Revisit the video game Web sites you found before reading Ehrenreich's essay.

Then develop a documented essay in which you test Ehrenreich's theories by applying them to video game users. Be sure to use credible sources to support your claims.

2. Ehrenreich claims that "even when men have been assembled, willingly or unwillingly, for the purpose of war, fighting is not something that seems to come 'naturally' to them" (paragraph 9). Do you agree or disagree with this statement? Explain your reaction in a clearly reasoned argumentative essay. Cite Ehrenreich's selection whenever necessary.

3. In the last paragraph of her essay, Ehrenreich suggests that warriors often have to go through rituals to return to their own civilizations. Use Ehrenreich's article as one of your sources; then read further on such transformations. Next write a clear, well-documented argument expressing your opinion on a specific transformation. Organize your paper clearly, and present your suggestions logically, using proper documentation (citations and bibliography) to support your position.

4. Use additional sources to study the circumstances of a war you are familiar with. Then, referring to Ehrenreich's explanation of "the anthropology of war" (paragraph 7), write a well-documented argument explaining the causes and effects of the war by discussing or analyzing in depth the consequences you have discovered.

R-3 Preparing to Write Your Own Documented Essay

You might be choosing a subject from infinite possibilities or working with an assigned topic. As you consider various topics, you should ask one very important question before you begin planning your essay: Will you be able to find enough information to back up your thesis statement? To make sure you are able to locate enough material to use as persuasive evidence in the body paragraphs of your essay, you must do a good job of choosing a subject, narrowing that subject, and then writing a provocative and interesting thesis statement. You will then prove this thesis statement with the information you find when you search for sources on your topic.

R-3.1 CHOOSING A TOPIC

Just as with any writing assignment, you should begin the task of writing a documented essay by exploring and limiting your topic. In this case, however, you will draw on other sources to help with this process. You should seek out both primary and secondary sources related to your topic. **Primary sources** are works of literature, historical documents, letters, diaries, speeches, eyewitness accounts, and your own experiments, observations, and conclusions; **secondary sources** explain and analyze information from other sources. Any librarian can help you search for both types of sources related to your topic.

After you have found a few sources on your general topic, you should look over and evaluate what you have discovered so you can limit your topic further. Depending on the required length of your essay, you will want to find a topic broad enough to be researched, established enough to let you discover ample sources on it in the library, and significant enough to demonstrate your ability to grapple with important ideas and draw meaningful conclusions. The Preparing to Write questions can help you generate and focus your ideas.

Our student writer decided to write on topic #1 (under Choosing a Topic on page 577) after reading and rereading Ehrenreich's essay. She narrowed her subject in the following way:

General Subject: Video games

   More Specific: Video games and "warlike instincts"

      More Specific: How video war-games can awaken "warlike instincts" in adolescents

This limited topic would be perfect for a documented essay. Our student writer could search for books, catalogs, and periodicals on the relationships among video games, violence, and war. While she is looking, she should be thinking about how to narrow her subject even further.

R-3.2 WRITING A GOOD, CLEAR THESIS STATEMENT

Just as a thesis statement is the controlling idea of an essay, a thesis statement also provides the controlling idea for your argument in a documented essay. This statement will guide the writing of your entire paper. Your assignments throughout college will usually be broad topics. To compose a good documented essay, you need to narrow a broad topic to an idea that you can prove within a limited number of pages. A working thesis statement will provide the direction for your essay, and the evidence you collect in your research is what proves that thesis statement. But you should keep in mind that your thesis is likely to be revised several times as the range of your knowledge changes and your paper takes different turns while you research and write.

Just as in a standard essay, the thesis statement in your documented essay is a contract between you and your readers. The thesis statement tells your readers what the main idea of your essay will be and sets guidelines for the paragraphs in the body of your essay. If you don't deliver what your thesis statement promises, your readers will be disappointed. The thesis statement is usually the last sentence in the introduction. It outlines your purpose and position on the essay's general topic and gives your readers an idea of the type of resources you will use to develop your essay.

Our student wrote the following thesis statement for her essay after reading several sources:

In a community where violence is an integral part of entertainment, war-based video games normalize the "aggressive instinct" and create an illusion of war that becomes both desirable and natural.

Her entire essay responds to Ehrenreich's claim that a natural "warlike instinct" does not exist. Although our student writer agrees with this statement, she believes, as her thesis states, that video games increase the possibility of a natural desire for war and violence. The paragraphs following this thesis statement supply evidence that proves her claim.

R-4 Finding Sources

No matter what you are studying in college, you should know how to find sources and evaluate them. An enormous amount of information is available to help you generate paper topics, teach you new information, challenge your thinking, support and/or refute your opinions, and make you smile. In today's electronic world, learning how to assess and use the resources available through the library's services is a basic survival skill.

Many of the sources you will use for your documented essays are available on the World Wide Web, often through subscribed databases that your library manages. In addition to online journals, magazines, and books, you might locate relevant information from electronic newsletters, discussion groups, bulletin boards, or email inquiries. It is important to remember that not all sources are equally accurate and reliable. Based on your topic, you need to exercise your best judgment and get your instructor's help in assessing the most useful online sources for your purposes.

R-4.1 SOURCES THAT ARE RELEVANT, RELIABLE, AND RECENT

The evidence of a documented essay lies in the sources that you use to back up your thesis statement. The sources must always be <u>R</u>elevant, <u>R</u>eliable, and <u>R</u>ecent. This "3Rs" approach to supporting evidence in a documented essay will help you write a solid essay with convincing evidence.

Here are some questions that will help you evaluate your sources in this regard:

The 3Rs: Relevant, Reliable, Recent

Relevant

- Does the source focus on your subject?
- Does the source deal in depth with the topic?

Reliable

- What is the origin of the source?
- Is the author an expert in the field?
- Is the author biased?
- Does the source represent all sides of an issue?
- Are the author's claims well supported?

Recent

- Is the source current enough for your subject and your purpose?

Our student writer's thesis suggests that video games can affect people's attitudes toward war and violence. To convince her readers that her thesis is correct, she consulted books, scientific and online journals, and general circulation publications. Here are some of her sources:

- **Book:** *Violent Video Game Effects on Children and Adolescents: Theory, Research, and Public Policy*
- **Scientific journal:** *Journal of Experimental Social Psychology*
- **Online journal articles:** *Brandweek*
- **Online article:** *Psychological Science Agenda*
- **General circulation publications:** *Time Magazine, Saturday Evening Post*

In these sources, our student writer found sources that did a thorough job of supporting her thesis statement. Information from articles in these books, journals, and magazines speaks to the average citizen. Even though these are not highly technical scientific sources, the evidence in them fulfills our "3R" criteria: **R**elevant, **R**eliable, and **R**ecent.

R-4.2 CONSULTING INTERDISCIPLINARY DATABASES, SUBJECT-SPECIFIC INDEXES, AND ELECTRONIC JOURNAL COLLECTIONS

Most instructors agree that students should use scholarly academic databases—such as Wilson Web, EBSCOhost, Proquest's ABI/INFORM, and LexisNexis—that you can access through your library. These databases contain articles, conference papers, and reports from a variety of sources, many of which are academic journals that have undergone peer review. Regardless of where you obtain your information, you should watch for bias and inaccuracy. Articles that have been academically peer reviewed or subjected to reputable editorial scrutiny are more reliable than those that have not.

The best places to begin searching for sources are interdisciplinary databases, subject-specific indexes, and electronic journal collections. You should have access to these services from home through your library's homepage or from a computer in your library. We will discuss each one separately. You may need a reference librarian to help you find these for the first time.

Interdisciplinary Databases

Online databases allow access to information on most topics. Some, such as Wilson's Omnifile or EBSCO's Academic Search, are general databases that provide access to full texts in a variety of subject areas. They could be described as "interdisciplinary databases." These databases direct you to a large number of books and journals on a wide range of subjects. The following are some online indexes provided by the Wilson company. Some are subject specific, and others are multidisciplinary.

Index	Primary Use
Biological and Agriculture Index	*Agriculture and Biology*
Business Full Text	*Business and Finance*
Education Full Text	*Education*
General Science Full Text	*Astronomy, Biology, Botany, Chemistry, Geology, Genetics, Mathematics, Medicine, Nutrition, Oceanography, Physics, Physiology, and Zoology*
Humanities Full Text	*Archeology, Art, Communications, Dance, Film, Folklore, Gender Studies, History, Journalism, Linguistics, Music, Performing Arts, Philosophy, Religion, and Theology*
Library Literature & Information Science Full Text	*Library and Information Sciences*
OmniFile Full Text Mega	*Multidisciplinary database that includes indexing, abstracts, and full text from the Wilson Education, General Science, Humanities, Readers' Guide, Social Sciences, and Business databases. It also includes the full-text articles from the Wilson Applied Science and Technology, Art, Biological and Agricultural, Legal, and Library Literature and Information Science databases.*
Readers' Guide Full Text	*Indexing and abstracting of the most popular general-interest periodicals published in the United States and Canada*
Social Sciences Full Text	*Addiction Studies, Anthropology, Community Health, Criminal Justice, Economics, Environmental Studies, Ethics, Family Studies, Gender Studies, Geography, Gerontology, International Relations, Law, Minority Studies, Public Administration, Political Science, Psychiatry, Psychology, Public Welfare, Social Work, Sociology, and Urban Studies*

- Indexing for Omni starts in 1982
- Abstracting generally starts in 1984 (Omni), 1993, or 1994 depending on the database.
- Full text coverage generally starts in January 1994, 1995, or 1996

Subject–Specific Indexes

Many databases index and abstract materials for specific subject disciplines, such as psychology or law. Others may index news articles.

Index*	Primary Use
Proquest ABI/Inform	News and business
Factiva	News and business
EBSCOhost	Many subject areas
HRAF	Ethnographies
Lexis-Nexis	News, business, and law
WilsonWeb	Popular magazines and newspapers, social science, humanities, business, general science, and education journals
PsycInfo	Psychology

Electronic Journal Collections

Electronic journal collections are online databases where you can obtain complete journal articles directly from your computer. The following collections might help you find information about the topic you have chosen.

Collection	Primary Use
American Chemical Society's Web Editions	American Chemical Society's 26 scientific journals
American Mathematical Journals	American Mathematical Society's proceedings and transactions
JSTOR	Back issues of core journals in the humanities, social sciences, and sciences
Project Muse	Humanities, social sciences, and math

Once you access an online database, index, or collection, you can easily find articles and books on your topic. Most databases have a "default search" that lets you explore multiple fields at once. You can also narrow searches by author, title, or subject. When you are searching for a title by subject, you should be aware of *Boolean connectors* or *operators*, which will allow you to narrow your search.

---

* Not all articles that are indexed in databases are available in full text. But it is common now for academic libraries to have cross database systems that makes accessing full text easier, regardless of the database you are searching.

Using Boolean Connectors or Operators

The Boolean connectors or operators used in a search are *AND, OR,* and *NOT.* By using these words, you can limit the search and find information directly related to your topic. Most databases no longer require that you type in the Boolean operators manually. They provide multiple search boxes, normally separated by a default AND. You would type each term (for example, *violence* in the first box and *video games* in the second. Then, you should separate your terms with the Boolean connector "AND" (for example, *violence AND video games*). This asks the computer to find all the records in which these two terms are combined. If you put "OR" between the key words (*violence OR video games*), you are separating the words and asking the computer to find articles and books for either one of them. If you add "NOT" (*video games NOT television*), you limit the search by excluding certain terms from the search.

Accessing Sources

Once you type your topic into the search function of a database, index, or journal collection, the computer will display the number of articles and books it has found in a "results list." Following are some examples of articles that our student writer finds on the topic of *video games AND violence* in an online database.

From an Interdisciplinary Database

6 of 692 in Academic Search Elite in EBSCOhost

Title: ***Video Games*** and Civic Engagement.

Authors: Perkins-Gough, Deborah *dperkins@ascd.org*

Source: Educational Leadership; Mar2009, Vol. 66 Issue 6, p94–94, 1p

Document Type: Article

Subject Terms:
* VIDEO games & teenagers
* TEENAGERS
* RESEARCH
* VIDEO games
* CONDUCT of life
* CITIZENSHIP
* COMMUNITY involvement
* SOCIAL aspects

Abstract: The article presents discussion on the connections between ***video game*** use in adolescents and civic involvement. Details are given outlining the "Teens, ***Video Games,*** and Civics" study conducted by the Pew Internet

Project and citing its findings that no correlation could be found between *game* usage and community life. It is suggested that *video games* are not necessarily isolating or *violent,* but that they should be steered towards more positive social themes.

Full Text Word Count: 471

ISSN: 00131784

Accession Number: 36666637

Persistent link to this record (Permalink):

http://web.ebscohost.com.falcon.lib.csub.edu/ehost/detail?vid=3&hid=101&sid=265ada4c-88b0-4c2b-b4aa-5a7592e2ee86%40sessionmgr109&bdata=JmxvZ2lucGFnZT1sb2dpbi5hc3Amc2l0ZT1laG9zdC1saXZl#db=afh&AN=36666637

Database: Academic Search Elite

From a Subject–Specific Index

ERIC

Title: Media and Children's Aggression, Fear, and Altruism

Personal Author: Wilson, Barbara J.

Journal Name: *Future of Children*

Source: *Future of Children* v. 18 no. 1 (Spring 2008) p. 87–118

Publisher Information: Woodrow Wilson School of Public and International Affairs at Princeton University and The Brookings Institution. 267 Wallace Hall, Princeton University, Princeton, NJ 08544. Tel: 609-258-6979; e-mail: FOC@princeton.edu; Web site: http://www.brookings.org/index/publications.htm

Publication Year: 2008

Abstract: Noting that the social and emotional experiences of American children today often heavily involve electronic media, Barbara Wilson takes a close look at how exposure to screen media affects children's well being and development. She concludes that media influence on children depends more on the type of content that children find attractive than on the sheer amount of time they spend in front of the screen. Wilson begins by reviewing evidence on the link between media and children's emotions. She points out that children can learn about the nature and causes of different emotions from watching the emotional experiences of media characters and that they often experience empathy with those characters. Although research on the long-term effects of media exposure on children's emotional skill development is limited, a good deal of evidence shows that media exposure can contribute to children's fears and anxieties.

Both fictional and news programming can cause lasting emotional upset, though the themes that upset children differ according to a child's age. Wilson also explores how media exposure affects children's social development. Strong evidence shows that violent television programming contributes to children's aggressive behavior. And a growing body of work indicates that playing violent video games can have the same harmful effect. Yet if children spend time with educational programs and situation comedies targeted to youth, media exposure can have more prosocial effects by increasing children's altruism, cooperation, and even tolerance for others. Wilson also shows that children's susceptibility to media influence can vary according to their gender, their age, how realistic they perceive the media to be, and how much they identify with characters and people on the screen. She concludes with guidelines to help parents enhance the positive effects of the media while minimizing the risks associated with certain types of content. (Contains 1 table, 1 figure and 133 endnotes.)

(Author)Descriptor/Subject: Environmental College students/Nutrition; Obesity/Nutritional aspects;

Descriptor/Subject: Mass Media Effects; Emotional Response; Child Behavior; Anxiety; Emotional Development; Aggression; Empathy; Gender Differences; Age Differences; Video Games; Violence; Altruism; Parent Role; Fear; Programming (Broadcast); Parents; Social Development

ISSN: 1054-8289

Language of Document: English

Document Type: Journal Articles; Reports—Evaluative

Date Entered: 20080101

Database: ERIC

ERIC Number: EJ795855

Accession Number: 150010795855000

Persistent URL: http://vnweb.hwwilsonweb.com.falcon.lib.csub.edu/ hww/results/getResults.jhtml?_DARGS=/hww/advancedsearch/advanced_ search.jhtml.3#curPg=31%7C40%7C10%7Cfull%7C0%7C31

From an Electronic Journal Collection

Entry 31 of 1607 (from JSTOR)

Title: Media and Risky Behaviors

Author(s): Soledad Liliana Escobar-Chaves and Craig A. Anderson

Source: *The Future of Children,* Vol. 18, No. 1, Children and Electronic Media (Spring, 2008), pp. 147–180

Published by: Princeton University

Stable URL: http://www.jstor.org/stable/20053123

Abstract: Liliana Escobar-Chaves and Craig Anderson investigate two important trends among American youth and examine the extent to which the two trends might be related. First, the authors note that U.S. youth are spending increasing amounts of time using electronic media, with the average American youngster now spending one-third of each day with some form of electronic media. Second, the authors demonstrate that American adolescents are engaging in a number of unhealthful behaviors that impose huge societal costs. Escobar-Chaves and Anderson detail the extent of five critical types of adolescent health risk behaviors identified by the Centers for Disease Control and Prevention—obesity, smoking, drinking, sexual risk taking, and violence. Obesity, the authors note, has become an epidemic among America's young people. Cigarette smoking among adolescents is one of the ten leading health indicators of greatest government concern. Alcohol abuse and alcohol dependence are widespread problems among the nation's youth and are the source of the three leading causes of death among youth. More than 20 percent of American high school students have sexual intercourse for the first time before they reach the age of fourteen. And twelve- to twenty-year-olds perpetrated 28 percent of the single-offender and 41 percent of multiple-offender violent crimes in the United States in 2005. Escobar-Chaves and Anderson present and evaluate research findings on the influence of electronic media on these five risk behaviors among adolescents. Researchers, they say, have found modest evidence that media consumption contributes to the problem of obesity, modest to strong evidence that it contributes to drinking and smoking, and strong evidence that it contributes to violence. Research has been insufficient to find links between heavy media exposure and early sexual initiation. The authors note the need for more large-scale longitudinal studies that specifically examine the cumulative effects of electronic media on risky health behavior.

Notice that these examples contain all the information you need for citing those works in the text and at the end of your paper. So make sure you keep lists like this when you print them so that you can cite your sources correctly.

R-4.3 SEARCHING FOR WEB SITES

To find a Web site related to your topic, you should go to the Internet through whichever browser you have (for example, Firefox or Microsoft Internet Explorer, etc.). When you access a search engine, such as Google or Yahoo, you will search millions of Web sites. Using the advanced search option in Google will allow you to narrow or expand your search. Most search engines will then begin helping you narrow your search and will provide a list of other possible topics. Here are some variations that our student writer explored while conducting her research.

Topic	Other Possible Topics
Video games and violence	*War in video games*
	Effects of media violence
	Media violence and adolescents
	Psychology of violence and war
	Aggression and military views

When the search is complete, your search engine will list the different Web sites in the order of most to least probable relevance to you. It will also briefly describe each Web site. After the description, you will usually find the Web site address (URL).

Evaluating Web Sites

Since anyone can put material on the Internet, you need to make sure you are not using biased or unreliable information in your academic papers. To use Web sites intelligently, follow these four guidelines.

1. *Understand the URL addresses you consult.* As you search for reliable Web sources, you should know that the endings of the URLs refer to different sources: *.com* stands for "commercial," *.edu* for "education," *.gov* for "government," and *.org* for "organization." As you consult these sources, you should first determine if the sites are maintained and current.

2. *Pay attention to the argument a site makes.* Who is the author, and what is his or her purpose for entering information on the site? If you log on to a Martin Luther King Jr. site and are inundated with racial slurs, chances are you've found a site that was created by a faction of the Ku Klux Klan. If the information does not fit the site or if the author has an obvious agenda, avoid the site altogether.

3. *Make sure the site is providing fact and not opinion.* For academic purposes, facts and statistics are generally more useful than opinions. If you are looking for a site that deals with gun control, you'll want to avoid the site that tells you story after story about innocent children dying or praises American liberties but fails to give you any specific information. Instead, you'll want to find a site that gives you examples that can be verified and supported with statistics.

4. *Check that the site provides information about the other sides of the argument.* If a site provides you with details only about its own viewpoint, you should wonder why it is omitting information. If you find a site on prayer in school and only see opinions about the reasons prayer should not be allowed in schools, you should be curious about why they don't present the argument on the other sides. The best sites provide all sides of an

argument so they can, in turn, show why one side is more valid than the others. If you find a Web site that does not offer balanced information, consider it biased, and avoid it altogether.

These four guidelines will help you determine whether or not you should use information you find on the Web. If you want to be certain the information you are using will be acceptable for your instructor, you should rely principally on academic sources, such as published literature in the library databases, for the bulk of your research. There are, however, a number of "open source" academic Web sites, where you can access articles that have been peer reviewed or refereed. This means the authors of the essays send them to the publication and the editors of the publication send the essays anonymously to readers for review. If the readers accept the pieces for publication, they consider the essays to be well researched and worth reading. If you can, you should use only these sources. Please note, however, that you still need to evaluate your peer-reviewed sources to make sure their arguments are sound.

Sample "Hits"

The following are three "hits" or Web sites from www.google.com for the topic *video games and violence*.

Violent Video Games Can Increase Aggression

After 40+ years of research, one might think that debate about media violence effects would be over. An historical examination of the research reveals that debate concerning whether such exposure is a significant risk factor for aggressive and violent behavior should have been over years ago.
www.apa.org/releases/videogames.html - 21k - Cached - Similar pages

PBS—"The Video Game Revolution: Eight Myths About Video Games Debunked"

A large gap exists between the public's perception of video games and what the research actually shows. The following is an attempt to separate fact from fiction.
www.pbs.org/kcts/videogamerevolution/impact/myths.html - Cached - Similar pages

Violent Video Games—Psychologists Help Protect Children from Harmful Effects

Psychological reseach confirms that violent video games can increase children's aggression, but that parents moderate the negative effects.
www.psychologymatters.org/videogames.html - Cached - Similar pages

R-4.4 USING THE LIBRARY

Once you have compiled a list of books and journals from databases and indexes or from Web sites, you should use your library to check out books or copy journal articles that were not available online. Usually, academic publishers make their current content available online. Older articles may need to be located in the library's periodical collection and copied.

First, you need to access your library's online catalog to see if your library has the book. If you have difficulty locating a book using the catalog, ask a librarian for help. You might also inquire whether this information is available online. You can search for authors and subjects through your library's catalog in much the same way that you would search online databases or program search engines. But since you have already done the preliminary research, all you have to do is search for the books and journals you need. Find the "title" section of the catalog, and type in the title of the book or journal you need.

If you are searching for a chapter or an essay contained in a book, be sure to type in the main book title. For example, if you were to search for "The Ecstasy of War" (by Barbara Ehrenreich), your library computer would tell you that the library does not carry it. You must type in the title of the book it came from, *Blood Rites: Origins and History of the Passions of War,* to find the essay. Once you have located the titles of your books or journals in the library's catalog, you should write down the call numbers so you can find the sources in your library. Then it's just a matter of finding the book itself in the stacks. If you need help, don't hesitate to ask a librarian.

R-5 Avoiding Plagiarism

Plagiarism is using someone else's words or ideas as if they were your own. It comes from a Latin word meaning "kidnapper." Because it is dishonest, plagiarism is a serious offense in college and beyond. Among student writers, plagiarism usually takes one of three forms: (1) using words from another source without quotation marks; (2) using someone else's ideas in the form of a summary or paraphrase without citing your source; and (3) using someone else's essay as your own. When you work with outside sources, you must give credit to the authors who wrote them. In other words, if you quote, paraphrase, or summarize from another source, you must provide your reader with information about that source, such as the author's name, the title of the book or article, and specifics about when it was written. Whenever you use other people's words or ideas without giving them credit, you are plagiarizing.

If you don't cite your sources properly, your readers will think the words and ideas are yours when they actually came from someone else. When you steal material in this way in college, you can be dismissed from school. When you commit the same offense in the professional world, you can get fired or end up in court. So make sure you understand what plagiarism is as you move through this chapter.

R-5.1 TYPES OF MATERIAL

A documented paper usually blends three types of material:

1. *Common knowledge, such as the places and dates of events (even if you have to look them up).* If you are referring to information such as historical events, dates of presidents' terms, and other well-known facts, like the effects of ultraviolet rays or smoking, you do not have to cite a source. This material is called *common knowledge* because it can be found in a number of different sources. You can use this information freely because you are not borrowing anyone's original words or ideas.

   Example: Although they were around for decades before, video games reached blockbuster popularity during the 1980s with classics such as the *Legend of Zelda* and *Super Mario Brothers,* and they have been gaining in popularity ever since.

2. *Someone else's thoughts and observations.* If, however, you want to use someone's original words or ideas, you must give that person credit by revealing where you found this information. This process is called *citing* or *documenting* your sources, and it involves noting in your paper where you found the idea. Since documented essays are developed around sources that support your position, citations are an essential ingredient in any documented essay.

   Example: President Ronald Reagan once said about video games, "Many young people have developed incredible hand, eye, and brain coordination in playing these games. The Air Force believes these kids will be our outstanding pilots should they fly our jets."

3. *Your own thoughts and observations.* These are conclusions that you draw from the sources you are reading.

   Example: While video games can be used for educational purposes, they often present glamorized pictures of violence and aggression to children, making these games a risky form of entertainment.

Of these three types of information, you must document or cite your exact source only for the second type. Negligence in citing your sources, whether purposeful or accidental, is *plagiarism.*

R-5.2 ACKNOWLEDGING YOUR SOURCES

Avoiding plagiarism is quite simple: You just need to make sure you acknowledge the sources of ideas or language that you are using to support your own contentions. Acknowledging your sources also gives you credit for the reading you have done and for the ability you have developed to synthesize and use sources to support your observations and conclusions. To

R-5

give credit to your sources, you must acknowledge them in two ways: (1) in-text citations that provide your reader with the author, page or paragraph numbers, and sometimes dates for each summary, paraphrase, or direct quotation you use and (2) a list of sources at the end of your paper that provides complete publication information on all the sources you have used in your essay. These two types of documentation work together to provide your readers with all the information they need to understand the exact details of the sources you read.

Two specific forms of documentation can sometimes cause students unexpected problems. But if you heed the following warnings, you will avoid these stumbling blocks. First, when you paraphrase (or put another writer's ideas in your own words), you cannot use the author's words or sentence structure. You must also cite your source at the end of a paraphrase. Second, when you put an author's words in quotation marks, you must print the words you want to use exactly as they are in the original source.

In our student writer's paper, every source she uses is acknowledged at least twice: (1) in the paper directly after a quotation or idea and (2) at the end of the paper in a list. The first type of citation is known as an *in-text citation*, and the second is a list of *works cited* in the paper. At the note-taking stage, you should make sure that you have all the information on your sources you will need later to acknowledge them in proper form in your paper. Having to track down missing details when you prepare your lists of works cited can be frustrating and time consuming.

R-5.3 DIRECT QUOTATION, PARAPHRASE, AND SUMMARY

As you read your sources and take notes for your paper, your notes will probably fall into one of four categories: (1) *direct quotations from sources;* (2) *paraphrase*—a restatement in your own words of someone else's ideas or observations; (3) *summary*—a condensed statement of someone else's thoughts or observations; or (4) *a combination of these forms.* Be sure to make a distinction in your notes between actual quotes and paraphrases or summaries. Also, record the sources (including page and/or paragraph numbers) of all your notes—especially of quoted, summarized, and paraphrased material—which you may need to cite in your essay.

This section explains these three options to you. We will begin with an original source and show you how to acknowledge material from this source in different ways.

The following quotation is from "Violent Video Games: Myths, Facts, and Unanswered Questions" by Dr. Craig A. Anderson. It was published in the scientific journal *Psychological Science Agenda* in October 2003.

Original Source

"Cartoonish and fantasy violence is often perceived (incorrectly) by parents and public policy makers as safe even for children. However, experimental studies with college students have consistently found increased aggression after exposure to clearly unrealistic and fantasy violent video games. Indeed, at least one recent study found significant increases in aggression by college students after playing E-rated (suitable for everyone) violent video games" (Anderson, par. 11).

Direct Quotation

If you use a direct quotation from another source, you must put the exact material you want to use in quotation marks:

Dr. Craig A. Anderson, in his article "Violent Video Games: Myths, Facts, and Unanswered Questions," responds to people who dismiss the threat of violence in children's video games: "Cartoonish and fantasy violence is often perceived (incorrectly) by parents and public policy makers as safe even for children. However, experimental studies with college students have consistently found increased aggression after exposure to clearly unrealistic and fantasy violent video games."

Direct Quotation with Some Words Omitted

If you want to leave something out of the quotation, use three dots (with spaces before and after each dot). Omitting words like this is known as *ellipsis*. Also, make sure that you place brackets [ ] around any words that you alter in the quotation.

Dr. Craig A. Anderson, in his article "Violent Video Games: Myths, Facts, and Unanswered Questions," states, "Cartoonish and fantasy violence . . . [causes] increased aggression."

Paraphrase

When you paraphrase, you are restating the main ideas of a quotation **in your own words.** *Paraphrase* literally means "similar phrasing," so it is usually about the same length as the original. Paraphrasing is one of the most difficult skills to master in college, but one trick you can use is to read the material, put it aside, and write a sentence or two from memory. Then compare what you wrote with the original to make sure they are similar but not exactly the same. If you look at the source while you are trying to paraphrase it, you might inadvertently take a word or phrase from the original, which would make you guilty of plagiarism.

Even though this information is in your own words, you still need to let your readers know where you found it. A paraphrase of our original source might look like this:

Dr. Craig A. Anderson, in his article "Violent Video Games: Myths, Facts, and Unanswered Questions," addresses the common misperception that video games intended for children do not contain violent or aggressive behavior. He cites scientific studies that show college students respond similarly to realistic and unrealistic violence in video games, leading researchers to believe that make-believe violence poses just as much threat as lifelike violence in the media.

Summary

To summarize, state the author's main idea in your own words. A summary is much briefer than the original or a paraphrase. As with a paraphrase, you need to furnish the details of your original source. Here is a summary of our original source:

In his article "Violent Video Games: Myths, Facts, and Unanswered Questions," Dr. Craig A. Anderson asserts that fantastical violence can be as harmful as realistic violence in video games.

R-6 Staying Organized

As you gather information, you should consider keeping a "research journal" where you can record your own opinions, interpretations, and analyses in response to your reading. This journal should be separate from your notes on sources and is the place where you can make your own discoveries in relation to your topic by jotting down thoughts and relationships among ideas you are exposed to, by keeping a record of sources you read and others you want to look at, by tracking and developing your own ideas and theories, and by clarifying your thinking on an issue.

R-6.1 TAKING NOTES ON SOURCES

As you read your sources, you should consider whether you might want to directly quote, paraphrase, or summarize the material. A general rule to follow is that you never want to have more than 10 percent of directly quoted information in your paper, which means 90 percent of the outside information you use in your essay should be paraphrased or summarized. The best way to determine whether you should use a direct quotation is by asking yourself if this is the best possible way to relay this information. If you can't phrase it any better than the original or if the author of the quotation is famous enough to give your argument credibility, then you should use a direct quotation. In most cases, however, you should try to put your research into your own words. Only occasionally should you use the author's exact words in your paper. So when you are reading and taking notes on your sources, you should keep this in mind.

As you take notes, notecards are an excellent tool because you can move them around as your paper takes shape. Writing down ideas and quotations on notecards allows you to reorganize your cards and put thoughts into different paragraphs. When you rearrange cards, you can work with them until you think the order will support your thesis. This note card method actually saves time in the long run.

Put only one idea on each note card. Taking notes this way will save you a lot of time in the future because you won't be scrambling around looking for the information on the source you just quoted. Taking notes electronically is another option. Whatever your choice, if you cannot find the original source for information you used in your paper and, therefore, cannot tell your reader where you found the quotation, then you cannot use the material.

The best time to start keeping track of the information for the citations in your paper is when you are taking notes. Listed here is all the information you will need later to cite a source in your paper.

For a book:
- Book title
- Author or authors
- Editor or editors (if applicable)
- City where published
- Publisher
- Year of publication

For an article:
- Article title
- Author or authors
- Title of the magazine or journal
- Date of issue (for a magazine)
- Year and volume number (for a journal)
- Pages on which the article appeared

If you put all this information on one card, you can record just the author's last name on all other cards from that same source. If you are using more than one book or article by the same author, add the source's date to the card. For both books and articles, you should also record the page where you found the information. That way you can easily find it again or cite it in your paper.

The format in which this information should be presented will depend on the field of study. A good handbook will help you with the formats of the various documentation styles, which include Modern Language Association (MLA) style for the humanities, American Psychological Association (APA) style for the social sciences, and Chicago Manual of Style (CMS) style for mathematics and science. Make sure you understand which documentation style your instructor wants you to use, because they are all slightly different. These styles are all explained in detail in section R-8, Documenting.

Our student writer used the Modern Language Association citation style. The Anderson essay in the MLA format would look like this:

Anderson, Craig. "Violent Video Games: Myths, Facts, and Unanswered Questions." *Psychological Science Agenda* 16.5 (2003): n. pag. Web. 28 May 2009.

When our student writer had to read and take notes on all the sources she found, she first made a set of bibliography cards with a notecard for every source she found. For the books, she recorded the book title, author or editor, city where published, publisher, and year of publication on each card; for the articles, she wrote down the article title, author, title of the magazine or journal, date of issue or volume and issue numbers, and page numbers on each card. Then she began to read her sources. She wrote only one idea or quotation per notecard, and she remembered to record on each notecard the author's name and the number of the page on which she found the information. She also made sure, as she took notes, to restate information in her own words or else put the author's exact words in quotation marks.

R-6.2 MAKING A WORKING OUTLINE

Before you begin your first draft, you might want to write an informal working outline for your own information. Such an exercise can help you check the range of your coverage and the order and development of your ideas. With an outline, you can readily see where you need more information, less information, or more reliable sources. Try to be flexible, however. This outline may change dramatically as your essay develops.

If you are using notecards, you can simply rearrange the notecards you have made to create a working outline. Start by putting all your notecards into small stacks of related ideas. Which ideas might work well together? Which should you put in the introduction? Which do you want to save for your conclusion? When you get all your notecards in stacks, label each group of cards according to its topic. These labels will then become the topics of your paper. You are now ready to start your working outline.

A good way to begin an outline is to write your tentative thesis statement at the top of a page and then list under that thesis the topics you have
developed. These topics should be arranged in some logical order that is easy
to follow and will help you prove your main point. Each topic should also
directly support your thesis statement. Leave room in your outline to add
subtopics and details throughout the paper. This outline then becomes a
guide for your writing. It will change and grow with every paragraph that
you add to your paper.

Our student writer started developing her paper by putting related notecards into stacks. Next, she labeled her stacks of notecards and then organized
these topics in different ways until they started making sense to her. Her list
of topics, with her thesis statement at the top, became her working outline.
She eventually turned these topics into topic sentences for her body paragraphs. The stack of cards for each topic became the content of her body
paragraphs.

R-7 Writing a Documented Essay

Writing the first draft of a documented essay is your chance to discover
new insights and to find important connections among ideas that you may
not have been aware of previously. This draft is your opportunity to demonstrate that you understand your topic and your sources on three increasingly
difficult levels—literal, interpretive, and analytical; that you can organize your
material effectively; that you can integrate your sources (in the form of summaries, paraphrases, or quotations) with your opinions; and that you can document (that is, cite) your sources.

To begin this process, look again at your thesis statement and your working outline, and adjust them to represent any new discoveries you have made
as you read your sources and wrote in your research journal. Then, organize
your research notes in some logical fashion.

When you begin to draft your paper, write the sections of the essay that
you feel most comfortable with first. Throughout the essay, feature your own
point of view by integrating your own analysis into the summaries, paraphrases, and quotations from other sources. Each point you make should be
a section of your paper consisting of your sources (in the form of facts, examples, summaries, paraphrases, and quotations) and your own conclusions.
Remember that the primary reason for doing such an assignment is to let
you demonstrate your ability to synthesize material, draw your own conclusions, and analyze your sources and your own reasoning.

R-7.1 WRITING THE INTRODUCTION

Construct an introduction that leads to your thesis statement. The introduction to a research paper is your chance to make a great first impression. Just like a firm handshake and a warm smile in a job interview, an essay's introduction should capture your readers' interest, set the tone for your essay, and state your specific purpose. Introductions often have a funnel effect. They typically begin with general information and then narrow the focus to your position on a particular issue. Regardless of your method, your introduction should "hook" your readers by grabbing their attention and letting them know what you are going to attempt to prove in your essay.

To lead up to the thesis statement, your introductory paragraph should stimulate your readers' interest. Some effective ways of capturing your audience's attention and giving necessary background information are to (1) use a quotation; (2) tell a story that relates to your topic; (3) provide a revealing fact, statistic, or definition; (4) offer an interesting comparison; or (5) ask an intriguing question. Be sure your introduction gives readers all the information they will need to follow your logic through the rest of your paper.

Our student writer's introduction starts out with a statement about the relationship of games and war. The paragraph then refers to the Ehrenreich essay and its claim about the "aggressive instinct." The last sentence of the first paragraph contains our student writer's thesis statement and ends the introduction.

R-7.2 WRITING THE SUPPORTING PARAGRAPHS

Develop as many supporting paragraphs or body paragraphs as you think are necessary to explain your thesis statement. Following the introductory paragraph, a research paper includes several body paragraphs that support and explain the essay's thesis statement. Each body paragraph covers a topic that is directly related to the thesis statement.

Supporting paragraphs, or body paragraphs, usually include a topic sentence, which is a general statement of the paragraph's contents, and examples or details that support the topic sentence.

To write your supporting paragraphs, you should first organize your notecards within each of your stacks. Next, add these details to your working outline. Finally, write your supporting paragraphs by following your working outline and your notecards. Make adjustments in your outline as you write so you can keep track of your ideas and make sure you are developing them in a logical fashion. The body of the paper and your outline should change and develop together with each sentence you draft.

After you write your body paragraphs, look at your thesis statement again to confirm that it introduces what you say in the rest of your paper. Your thesis statement should refer to all your topics, even if only indirectly, in the order you discuss them. It should also prepare your readers for the conclusions you are going to draw.

Our student writer's paper contains four body paragraphs, each making a separate point that is directly related to her thesis:

Paragraph	Point
2	*Although studies exist on either side of the controversy, most research shows that violent video games cause physiological changes, and these changes alter a player's attitude toward war and violence.*
3	*Authenticity in the realm of virtual warfare is highly sought after, contributing to the glamorized view many people have of war.*
4	*Video games remove the need for "transformation," enabling ordinary men and women to act upon their "aggressive instinct."*
5	*Many have criticized reports connecting video games and aggression [offering opposing viewpoints].*

Like the foundation of a solid building, these paragraphs provide support for the position our student writer takes in her thesis statement. The stronger the supporting paragraphs are, the stronger the final paper will be.

In addition to including strong topic sentences, you should also use concluding sentences in your body paragraphs to help reinforce your thesis statement or build a transition to the next paragraph. Concluding sentences bring a paragraph to a close just like a conclusion brings an essay to a close, and well-crafted concluding sentences also focus your readers on the highlights of your argument.

R-7.3 USING YOUR SOURCES

Make sure you use your sources as evidence for your argument. Although your argument will evolve as you read your sources, you should decide on your general position before you begin to take notes. Be sure to find appropriate sources that help you develop your argument. The best way to do this is to tell your reader the significance of the direct quotations, paraphrases, or summaries that you use. Look, for example, at an excerpt from one of our student writer's paragraphs:

> *Siobhan Morrissey cites trained law enforcement professionals when she says, "Officers raiding methamphetamine labs and gang hangouts often find violent video games left behind" (par. 9). Game players feel the adrenaline rush associated with violence and war in the comfort of their living rooms. As a result, "more young people have no compunction about opening fire on a man or woman in uniform" (Morrissey, par. 8). In this situation, we see that war and violence are localized and normalized.*

Notice how our student writer does not stop with her source's remarks. Instead, she includes a point about the significance of what the source says. She reminds her readers that game players are becoming comfortable with their relationship to violence and to war.

If you simply provide a series of quotations and let them argue for you, you are not demonstrating your understanding of the quotations or showing how they fit into your argument. Make sure to use the quotations as support for your argument, not let them serve as the argument itself.

R-7.4 WRITING YOUR CONCLUSION

Write a concluding paragraph.   The concluding paragraph is the final paragraph of an essay. In its most basic form, it should summarize the main points of the essay and remind readers of the thesis statement.

The best conclusions expand on these two basic requirements and bring the essay to a close with one of these creative strategies: (1) ask a question that provokes thought on the part of the reader, (2) predict the future, (3) offer a solution to a problem, or (4) call the reader to action. Each of these options sends a specific message and creates a slightly different effect at the end of the paper. The most important responsibility of the last paragraph is to bring the essay to an effective close. It is the last information that readers see before they form their own opinions or take action.

Our student writer's conclusion opens with a restatement of the problem:

War-based video games will not send you into war; they will, however, normalize the idea of war and amplify the instincts that propel men and women into combat.

At the end of her conclusion, she gives a solution and calls the reader to action:

We must respond to this problem by recreating some distance between the average game-player and the actual battlefield. By concentrating less on authenticity and more on entertainment, players would have an easier time separating their fantasy from the dim reality of war. Also, continued research should work to identify degrees of aggressive behavior in all levels of video games (from E—everyone to AO—adults only) in order to eliminate violence in games available to children and teens because they are the most eager to identify with the imaginary roles they play and the most susceptible to appropriating the "aggressive instinct."

Her concluding paragraph refocuses the reader's attention on the problem, offers a solution, and then calls the reader to action.

R-7.5 CREATING YOUR TITLE

Think of a catchy title.   Your title is what readers see first in any paper. A title is a phrase, usually no more than a few words, placed at the beginning of your essay that suggests or sums up the subject, purpose, or focus of the essay. Some titles are very imaginative, drawing on different sources for their meaning. Others are straightforward, like the title of this chapter—"Writing a Documented Essay." Besides suggesting an essay's purpose, a good title should immediately catch an audience's attention and make them want to read your paper. Our student writer's title, "War-Based Video Games and Real-Life Violence," will catch most readers' attention because of its relevant subject matter and the rhythm of its words.

Following is a checklist to guide you through the process of writing a documented essay:

R-7.6 A CHECKLIST FOR WRITING DOCUMENTED ESSAYS

WRITING DOCUMENTED ESSAYS

Preparing to Write
√ What is my purpose?
√ Who is my audience?

Writing
√ Do I have a thesis statement?
√ Have I organized my material effectively?
√ Have I avoided plagiarism and cited my sources correctly?
√ Do I use the appropriate documentation style?

Rewriting
√ Are the essay's assertions clear? Are they adequately supported?
√ Are other points of view recognized and examined?
√ Does the organization of my paper further my argument?
√ Are my summaries, paraphrases, or quotations presented accurately?
√ Do I introduce the sources in my paper when appropriate?
√ Are my sources in the proper format (MLA, APA, or another)?
√ Have I followed my instructor's guidelines for my title page, margins, page numbers, tables, and abstracts?
√ Do I have an alphabetical list of sources for the end of my paper?

R-8 Documenting

As you have already learned in this part of the text, you must document each source you use in your research paper with two types of citations that support each other: an in-text citation and an end-of-paper citation. Both kinds of citations are important, and both follow very strict guidelines based on the documentation style you use.

R-8.1 INTRODUCING YOUR SOURCES

Once you evaluate your sources and figure out which ones will help establish your argument, you then need to learn how to seamlessly integrate them into your paper. In other words, you should introduce them effectively while showing readers they are credible and provide valuable evidence to back up your argument. Integrating your sources into your argument will help your readers understand the kind of information you are using. You also must show them you are using evidence based in fact and taken from credible sources.

When you use a source for the first time, always (1) introduce the author(s) using the full name(s), (2) give the title of the source (use quotes for works inside larger works and italics or underlining for books), and (3) quote or paraphrase the information you need to build your argument. Here are some examples of good introductions of Daphnee Rentfrow's "S(t)imulating War: From Early Films to Military Games."

(1) Daphnee Rentfrow, in "S(t)imulating War: From Early Films to Military Games," explains that reenacting war on-screen can possibly lead to actual war.

(2) One problem, asserts Daphnee Rentfrow in "S(t)imulating War: From Early Films to Military Games," is that reenacting war on-screen can possibly lead to actual war.

(3) According to Daphnee Rentfrow in "S(t)imulating War: From Early Films to Military Games," reenacting war on-screen can possibly lead to actual war.

(4) Reenacting war on-screen can possibly lead to actual war, explains Daphnee Rentfrow in "S(t)imulating War: From Early Films to Military Games."

These model sentences are only a few options for introducing Rentfrow's ideas; you can probably think of many more. The main words in the titles are capitalized; commas and periods as end punctuation go inside the quotation marks. In addition, note that the verbs in these examples each express a slightly different meaning. Finally, you should refer to the author by last name only—"according to Rentfrow"—each subsequent time you use the source and mention the author.

R-8.2 DOCUMENTATION FORMAT

As you document your sources, you should know that documentation styles vary from discipline to discipline. Ask your instructor about the particular documentation style he or she wants you to follow. Three of the major documentation styles are Modern Language Association (MLA), used in humanities courses; American Psychological Association (APA), used in social science courses; and Chicago Manual of Style (CMS), used in history, mathematics, and science classes. Even though documentation styles vary somewhat from one field to another, the basic concept behind documentation is the same in all disciplines: You must give proper credit to other writers by acknowledging the sources of the summaries, paraphrases, and quotations that you use to support the ideas in your documented essay. Remember that you have two goals in any citation: (1) to acknowledge the author and (2) to help the reader locate the material. Once you grasp this basic concept and accept it, you will have no trouble avoiding plagiarism.

Because you may have to write different papers using all these documentation styles, you should have a basic understanding of their differences.

In-Text Citations

The major difference among in-text citations for MLA, APA, and CMS is that MLA and APA use parenthetical references, while CMS uses a footnote or endnote system. Look at the differences in the following sentences:

MLA: According to Dr. Nicholas L. Carnagey, Dr. Craig A. Anderson, and Dr. Brad J. Bushman, psychologists, "[P]laying a violent video game . . . can cause people to become less physiologically aroused by real violence" (494).

APA: According to Dr. Nicholas L. Carnagey, Dr. Craig A. Anderson, and Dr. Brad J. Bushman, psychologists, "[P]laying a violent video game . . . can cause people to become less physiologically aroused by real violence" (2007, p. 494).

CMS: According to Dr. Nicholas L. Carnagey, Dr. Craig A. Anderson, and Dr. Brad J. Bushman, psychologists, "[P]laying a violent video game . . . can cause people to become less physiologically aroused by real violence."[1]

Although the information is slightly varied, MLA and APA furnish the page number for the source (APA with a "p." and MLA without a "p."). APA also includes the year the article was written. For CMS, a reader would find the publication information (including the page number of the source) in the footnote/endnote.

On the other hand, certain in-text features are similar in all three documentation styles:

- You should include citation information directly after every quotation.
- You should include citation information after you have finished paraphrasing a source. (This could extend to more than one sentence.)

R-8

- Punctuation follows the parenthetical citation, not the quotation.
- Longer quotes are indented in block form to "1" and do not require quotation marks.
- Blocked quotes are double spaced in the same size font as the paper.

End-of-Paper Citations

One of the most obvious differences among MLA, APA, and CMS is how they list their sources at the end of the paper: MLA includes a "Works Cited" page; APA lists "References"; and CMS has a "Bibliography." Some other differences also exist among these three lists of sources. Works Cited and References pages list only those sources cited in the paper. These sources are listed alphabetically. Your in-text citations will work with your References page in that the in-text citations tell the reader the name and page number of the source you are using, and the Works Cited/References pages provide readers with the full bibliographic information.

A Bibliography lists every source you looked at while researching your paper. Documentation styles that include a Bibliography use a separate page for notes to show which of the sources on the Bibliography you actually cited in your paper. Pages for notes use a numbering system that corresponds to a number in the body of the paper. Writers using a Bibliography have the advantage of showing their readers all the sources they read for the paper, even if they took no material directly from a source.

Regardless of which documentation style you use, the source lists at the end of the paper share some common formatting features:

- The title is centered, and the title is in regular font. In other words, the title is not bolded, underlined, put in quotation marks, or italicized (unless you include another title within your own title).
- The page numbers are continuous from the body of the paper.
- The entries are all double-spaced.
- The entries all use a hanging indent (which can be accessed in Microsoft Word either through the "Paragraph" feature under "Format" or by manipulating the hourglass on the ruler). Note: Some documentation styles prefer paragraph indenting.
- The entries are all alphabetized. Note: You do not rearrange authors' names in a single entry so that they appear alphabetical. Leave the order as it appears in your source.

Regardless of the documentation style, the in-text citations, end-of-paper sources, and footnotes or endnotes (if applicable) all work together to help readers have access to all the bibliographic information about the source you are using.

R-8.3 MLA VERSUS APA

Because MLA and APA are the most popular documentation styles, you should know the major differences between the two. The logic behind both documentation styles is very similar, but subtle differences exist in each format.

In-Text Citations

MLA	APA
• *Author's full names are used.*	• *Author's last name and first initial are used.*
• *Dates don't necessarily have to be mentioned.*	• *Dates must follow either the author's name in the sentence or in the parentheses following the sentence.*
• *A parenthetical citation includes author's last name and a page number: (Turner 49).*	• *A parenthetical citation includes author's last name, date, and a page number: (Turner, 2005, p. 49).*

Works Cited/References Page

Notice the differences in the citation below. MLA and APA both require the same information but in a different order.

MLA   Carnagey, Nicholas L., Craig A. Anderson, and Brad J. Bushman. "The Effect of Video Game Violence on Physiological Desensitization to Real-Life Violence." *Journal of Experimental Social Psychology* 43 (2007): 489–496. *EBSCO.* Web. 25 May 2009.

APA   Carnagey, N., Anderson, C., & Bushman, B. (2007). The effect of video game violence on physiological desensitization to real-life violence. *Journal of Experimental Social Psychology, 43,* 489–496.

For more on the differences between MLA and APA (as well as the other documentation styles), consult a research handbook.

R-8.4 USING A HANDBOOK

In order to learn how to cite sources properly, you need to know how to navigate a research handbook. Handbooks provide information on both in-text and end-of-paper citations. After writing a few research papers, you'll become quite adept at introducing your sources and using in-text citations, but you will never remember how to cite all the different types of sources. Therefore, knowing how to navigate a handbook is important to being able to document your sources properly. Once you understand the logic of citing, you should be able to use the handbook quite easily.

R-8

Look at the following entry for a Works Cited list:

Carnagey, Nicholas L., Craig A. Anderson, and Brad J. Bushman. "The Effect of Video Game Violence on Physiological Desensitization to Real-Life Violence." *Journal of Experimental Social Psychology* 43 (2007): 489–496. *EBSCO.* Web. 25 May 2009.

In order to put this entry together, you need to look up two different source examples in the MLA guide: (1) "How to Cite Two or More Authors" and (2) "How to Cite an Article in a Scholarly Journal from an Online Database." If this source were found online, you would also need to include the retrieval date or date you found the article. Sometimes, you'll need to look at three or four different source examples in order to piece together one entry on your Works Cited or other reference page; you can't expect to find an example for every source you have. So when you use a handbook and cannot figure out how to do something, chances are the answer is there somewhere; you just have to find it and piece together a citation using the logic of other entries. Once you understand how to use the documentation styles sections of a handbook, you'll always be able to figure out how to properly cite sources.

If you have difficulty understanding the logic of your handbook or cannot figure out how to cite a specific source, you might want to consider a trip to your campus's tutoring center so they can show you how it works. And, of course, you can always ask your instructor.

R-8.5 SOME FINAL TIPS

et al.

If you use a source that has four or more authors (MLA) or three or more authors (APA), you are allowed to shorten the citation. Let's say you are using MLA and have a source with the following authors: Jennifer Smith, Shannon Taylor, Lauren Woods, and Sarah Jones. The first time you mention these authors, you must provide all their names, but instead of repeating throughout your paper, "Smith, Taylor, Woods, and Jones assert that . . . ," you can shorten your citation by saying, "Smith et al. assert that . . ." The "et al." means "and others." A trap many students fall into is thinking the "al." is singular, when it actually means "others," so be sure to treat this as a plural noun when you use it.

.pdf versus *html*

Given the opportunity, always download electronic research as a .pdf file. A .pdf file is like a snapshot of the original printed version, so it retains any formatting, including pictures. More importantly, though, a .pdf file retains original page numbers. If you have the original page numbers, you can cite your source using those page numbers. If you don't have page numbers, you have to use paragraph numbers in your citations.

R-8.6 SAMPLE STUDENT REFERENCES

Our student writer uses the MLA format on her paper, which she wrote for an English class. English instructors usually have their students use MLA. Our student writer includes a variety of sources in her paper, which we can use to illustrate the two types of citations. Listed here are some sample in-text citations, with the corresponding entries at the end of our student's paper.

Book—name of author, title of book, city of publication, name of publisher, year, medium of publication

In-Text Citation: *(Anderson, Gentile, and Buckley, 66)*

Works Cited: *Anderson, Craig A., Douglas A. Gentile, and Katherine E. Buckley.* Violent Video Game Effects on Children and Adolescents: Theory, Research, and Public Policy. *New York: Oxford University Press (2007). Print.*

Journal—name of author, title of article, name of journal, volume number, year, page number

In-Text Citation: *(Konijn, Bujvank, and Bushman, 1038)*

Works Cited: *Konijn, Elly A., Marije Nije Bujvank, and Brad J. Bushman. "I Wish I Were a Warrior: The Role of Wishful Identification in the Effects of Violent Video Games on Aggression in Adolescent Boys."* Developmental Psychology *43.4 (2007): 1038–1044. Print.*

Online Database—name of author, title of article, name of journal, volume number, date of publication, database, medium of publication, date you accessed the material

In-Text Citation: *(494)*

Works Cited: *Carnagey, Nicholas L., Craig A. Anderson, and Brad J. Bushman. "The Effect of Video Game Violence on Physiological Desensitization to Real-Life Violence."* Journal of Experimental Social Psychology *43 (2007): 489–496. EBSCO. Web. 25 May 2009.*

Note: In her essay, our student writer introduces the authors before quoting them, so she doesn't have to repeat their names in the in-text citation.

General-Circulation Magazine—name of author, title of article, name of magazine, volume number, date of publication, page numbers, medium of publication

In-Text Citation: *(Grossman 66)*

Works Cited: *Grossman, Lt. Col. Dave. "We Are Training Our Kids to Kill."* Saturday Evening Post *271.4 (1999): 64–72. Print.*

R-8

Note: Volume numbers are only necessary if the publication uses them; some magazines do not provide volume numbers.

These examples from our student writer's essay are just a few of the various types of citations that you will probably use in your own documented essays. Every source is cited in a slightly different way, depending on the type of source and the documentation style. Not even the best writers know the correct format for every source they use. So when you have chosen your sources and determined that they are relevant, reliable, and recent (Remember the "3Rs" from R-4.1?), your last step is to consult an appropriate, current manual or Web site to make sure you cite each source correctly.

R-9 Revising and Editing a Documented Essay

Part of the process of writing any paper, including a documented essay, is revising and editing your work.

R-9.1 REVISING

To revise a research paper, you should play the role of your readers and impartially evaluate your argument and the sources you have used as evidence in that argument. To begin with, revise your thesis to represent all the discoveries you made as you wrote your first draft. Then, look for problems in logic throughout the essay; you might even revise your working outline at this point to help evaluate your reasoning:

- Are the essay's assertions clear? Are they adequately supported?
- Are other points of view recognized and examined?
- Does the organization of your paper further your argument?

Next, check your documentation style:

- Are your summaries, paraphrases, and quotations presented accurately?
- Do you introduce the sources in your paper when appropriate?
- Are your sources in the proper format (MLA, APA, or another)?

Logic

Look at the following excerpt from our student writer's first draft:

(1) Whether or not people act on new thoughts of war, violence, and aggression is debatable; however, scientific evidence shows that physiological and

psychological changes do occur—when people participate in violent, interactive games, their "aggressive instinct" surfaces. (2) War-based video games are also controversial because of their lifelike quality. (3) Authenticity in the realm of virtual warfare is highly sought after, contributing to the glamorized view many people have of war.

On close inspection, our student writer found that this paragraph required revision. In this excerpt, she concludes her first point (sentence 1) and introduces her second point (sentences 2 and 3) in the same paragraph. Look at our student writer's revised text:

(1) Whether or not people act on new thoughts of war, violence, and aggression is debatable; however, scientific evidence shows that physiological and psychological changes do occur—when people participate in violent, interactive games, their "aggressive instinct" surfaces.

(2) War-based video games are also controversial because of their lifelike quality. (3) Authenticity in the realm of virtual warfare is highly sought after, contributing to the glamorized view many people have of war.

By starting a new paragraph with sentence 2, our student writer makes the paragraphs better organized and clearer for the reader.

Synthesis

When writers use more than one source in an essay, they are *synthesizing* their sources. In other words, they are taking pieces of information from different sources and weaving them into their own argument. If you've written any type of paper using more than one outside source, you were synthesizing material. As you write a documented essay, your own argument establishes the order of your ideas. Then your sources provide evidence or proof for your argument.

Look at how our student writer uses sources. Here is a paragraph from her first draft:

(1) Ehrenreich acknowledges that even without the "aggressive instinct," men and women have shown their ability to murder in cold blood in a multitude of environments. (2) History shows, though, that they are only able to act on these impulses after undergoing a transformation. (3) Video games remove the need for "transformation," enabling ordinary men and women to act upon their "aggressive instinct." (4) Ehrenreich states, "There is a huge difference between a war and an ordinary fight. War not only departs from the normal, it inverts all that is moral and right" (13). (5) She goes on to qualify this statement, explaining that individuals will only participate in this behavior "by

entering what appears to be an 'altered state'—induced by drugs or lengthy drilling, and denoted by face paint or khakis" (13). (6) Siobhan Morrissey cites trained law enforcement professionals: when she says, "Officers raiding methamphetamine labs and gang hangouts often find violent video games left behind" (par. 9). (7) Game players feel the adrenaline rush associated with war in the comfort of their living rooms. (8) As a result, "more young people have no compunction about opening fire on a man or woman in uniform" (Morrissey, par. 8). (9) In this situation, we see that war and violence are localized and normalized.

As our student writer was revising this paragraph, she realized she was forcing the reader to make connections between her sources and her argument because she was not providing explanations that made those connections. So she revised her paragraph, connecting her sources to her own ideas and making her argument clearer. Her changes are underlined:

(1) Ehrenreich acknowledges that even without the "aggressive instinct," men and women have shown their ability to murder in cold blood in a multitude of environments. (2) History shows, though, that they are only able to act on these impulses after *undergoing a transformation. (3) Video games remove the need for "transformation," enabling ordinary men and women to act upon their "aggressive instinct." (4) Ehrenreich states, "There is a huge difference between a war and an ordinary fight. War not only departs from the normal, it inverts all that is moral and right" (13). (5) She goes on to qualify this statement, explaining that individuals will only participate in this behavior "by entering what appears to be an 'altered state'—induced by drugs or lengthy drilling, and denoted by face paint or khakis" (13). (6) Game players lack this "transformation" that apparently turns mere men into killing machines; they can act out violence in their natural state of being—sitting on their couch at home. (7) Siobhan Morrissey cites trained law enforcement professionals when she says, "Officers raiding methamphetamine labs and gang hangouts often find violent video games left behind" (par. 9). (8) Game players feel the adrenaline rush associated with war in the comfort of their living rooms. (9) As a result, "more young people have no compunction about opening fire on a man or woman in uniform" (Morrissey, par. 8). (10) In this situation, we see that war and violence are localized and normalized. (11) When adolescents play video games, they do not undergo months of training and drilling; their survival instincts are not tested; they do not wear ritual garments; and they do not depend on drugs or alcohol to transform them into trained warriors. (12) Video games do away with the transformation and preparation that usually accompanies war, changing the "aggressive instinct" from innately unnatural, as Ehrenreich claims, to an ordinary impulse.*

By adding sentence (6), our student writer connects Ehrenreich's idea about transformation of ordinary men to warriors and her own thought that video games lack a similar transformation. She shows that she understands the quote as she incorporates it into her argument. Similarly, our student writer adds sentences (11) and (12) to the end of this paragraph to further her argument and to conclude her paragraph. The first sentence gives examples of how men have transformed into warriors in the past, which emphasizes our student writer's point that war-game players do not go through any of these transformations. The last sentence, which also acts as the paragraph's concluding sentence, brings readers back to our student writer's thesis: war-based video games bring out the "aggressive instinct" in players, distorting their perception of war and violence.

To better understand how our student writer's paragraph works as a combination of her ideas and sources, look at the following breakdown of her paragraph:

(1–2)   **Our student writer's** *introductory sentence*
(3)   **Our student writer's** *topic sentence*
(4–5)   **Quotation** *of Source A*
(6)   **Our student writer's** *statement about Source A, elaborating on the issue*
(7–9)   **Quotation/Paraphrase** *from Source B*
(10–11)   **Our student writer's** *commentary, elaborating on Source B*
(12)   **Our student writer's** *statement that pulls together and shows the danger of war-based video games*

This skeleton outline of our student writer's paragraph should help you see how she balances her opinions/observations and her sources so they work as one unit that supports her main argument. If you get stuck writing your own paragraphs, referring back to this outline might help you see where you need to add information.

R-9.2 EDITING

Now you must proofread carefully.

- Have you found and corrected all your grammar, usage, and syntax errors?
- Have you followed your instructor's guidelines for your title page, margins, page numbers, tables, and abstracts?
- Do you have an alphabetical list of your sources at the end of your paper?

After our student writer's revisions were complete, she edited her essay by correcting several grammar, usage, and syntax errors. Look at the following passage from our student writer's first draft:

(1) War becomes a game in a completely interactive way, players' instincts and impulses are significantly altered. (2) Games may cultivate or encourage violence or drug abuse, it could possibly foster the "war gene" that Ehrenreich dismisses in her essay.

As you can see, our student writer wrote comma splices in sentences (1) and (2), and the pronoun *it* does not agree with the antecedent *games* in sentence (2). After making corrections, our student writer's final draft looks like this:

(1) War becomes a game in a completely interactive way, and players' instincts and impulses are significantly altered. (2) Just as games may cultivate or encourage violence or drug abuse, they could possibly foster the "war gene" that Ehrenreich dismisses in her essay.

Any additional guidance you may need as you revise and edit your documented essays is furnished on the inside front cover of this book.

R-9.3 STUDENT ESSAY: DOCUMENTATION AT WORK

The following student documented essay uses sources to support its observations and conclusions about the connection between video games and aggressive behavior. First, the writer discusses the dilemma surrounding war-based video games. Then she goes on to show how video games can desensitize players and distort their perception of war. After recognizing and refuting some opposing views, this student writer ends her paper by asserting that changes need to be made to the current status of violent video games. Throughout the essay, the student writer carefully supports her main points with summaries, paraphrases, and quotations from other sources. Notice that she uses the MLA documentation style and closes the paper with an alphabetical list of "Works Cited." Look also for her uses of different rhetorical modes, which are identified in the margins in brackets ([ ]).

Focused title	**War-Based Video Games and Real-Life Violence**
Background/ general information	Games and war have a longstanding relationship. Consider examples of popular board games such as Battleship and Chess, which emphasize strategy and [Examples] elimination, or action figures such as G.I. Joe, who

Academic use of cartoon

provide rugged representations of armed forces. While these forms of entertainment may hint at some aspect of combat, none can compare to the accurate and thrilling portrayal of war found in contemporary video games. In her essay "The Ecstasy of War," Barbara Ehrenreich discusses the history and the psychology surrounding war. Ehrenreich's main point is that the human "aggressive instinct" is not the primary force behind "the major wellspring of war" (8). She argues that while aggression may be a natural impulse of human beings, there are several reasons why it cannot be held responsible for the world's extensive history of warfare. But war-based video games seem to directly activate this natural, aggressive impulse. In a community where violence is an integral part of entertainment, war-based video games normalize the "aggressive instinct" and create an illusion of war that becomes both desirable and natural.

Summary

Thesis statement

Common knowledge

[Cause/ Effect]

Over the last forty years, media violence has become a highly debated issue. Although studies exist on either side of the controversy, most research shows that violent video games cause physiological changes, and these changes alter a player's attitude toward war and violence. In their study "The Effect of Video Game Violence on Physiological Desensitization to Real-Life Violence," experts Carnagey, Craig Anderson,

Writer's first point

[Cause/Effect]

and Brad Bushman find that, "playing a violent video game, even for just 20 min, can cause people to become less physiologically aroused by real violence" (494). If playing violent games can affect our perception of violence, then participating in games based on war can adjust our opinions—and instincts—surrounding war. Another study by Konijn, Bujvank, and

Quotation

In-text citation

[Cause/Effect]

Bushman finds that "media-related aggression" is related to "identification with violent characters" (1038). Researchers also assert, "Adolescents are especially likely to look for role models to identify with because they are in the process of developing their own identities" (Konijn, Bujvank, and Bushman, 1038). War-based video games portray soldiers as killing machines: individuals on a murderous spree under the guise of national service. While this couldn't be farther from the reality of war, the games perpetuate this image, and as a result children and adolescents will choose to identify with the war-game version of soldiers. Some researchers have proven that violence, so prevalent in war-based video games, is problematic especially for adolescents. Whether or not people *act* on new thoughts of war, violence, and aggression is debatable; however, scientific evidence shows that physiological and psychological changes do occur—when people participate in violent, interactive games, their "aggressive instinct" surfaces.

In-text citation

In-text citation

[Cause/Effect]

Writer's second point

War-based video games are also controversial because of their lifelike quality. Authenticity in the realm of virtual warfare is highly sought after, contributing to the glamorized view many people have of war. One of the most accurate war-based video games is

[Example]

America's Army, a "government-sponsored video game" whose "primary mission is to recruit" (L. Grossman, par. 2). Lev Grossman, in an article for *Time* entitled "The Army's Killer App," reports that between 2002

In-text citation (Web-based source)

In-text citation (Web-based source)

and 2005, "*America's Army* . . . signed up 4.6 million registered players, and it adds 100,000 new ones every month" (par. 3). Ironically, this ultra-realistic game does not depict death. In her article "S(t)imulating War: From Early Films to Military Games," Daphnee Rentfrow comments, "Whereas films [and other games] have staged death in war in an attempt to make themselves realistic . . . *America's Army* refuses this same representation in order to highlight the game's status *as a game"* (95). By emphasizing the fantastical nature of the game, *America's Army* provides a sharp contrast to other games that willingly and grotesquely depict death on the battlefield and glorify war. The *Call of Duty* series, for example, boasts an "uncensored edge to combat" on the Treyarch Games website. For Carnagey et al. the consequences for players of these war-based games are clear: "Individuals who play violent video games habituate or 'get used to' all the violence and eventually become physiologically numb to it" (495). While a natural "aggressive instinct" is not enough to compel individuals to destroy others on its own, participation in violent, war-based games has the ability to motivate this milder impulse to more hostile thoughts and behavior. Lieutenant Colonel Dave Grossman would agree with their assessment. In his article "We Are Training Our Kids to Kill," Grossman says plainly, "Children don't naturally kill. It is a learned skill. And they learn it . . . most pervasively, from violence as entertainment in television, the movies, and interactive video games" (65). Whether this behavior is learned in a militaristic setting or in front of a television, it is still *learned.* He also points out that soldiers exercise caution and control by shooting only when absolutely necessary, as opposed to a game where the objective is to shoot (successfully) and to kill (72). Basically, the response of a trained professional and the response of an amateur gamer will differ greatly. While the games might seem authentic, and therefore desirable, they are not teaching the responsibility that is required by the roles players assume on the virtual battlefield. The seeming authenticity of war-based video games, coupled with the thrill and excitement associated with killing for amusement, fuels players' natural instincts for aggression and war.

Ehrenreich acknowledges that even without the "aggressive instinct," men and women have shown their ability to murder in cold blood in a multitude of environments. History shows, though, that they are

Margin annotations: In-text citation · [Comparison/Contrast] · [Example] · [Cause/Effect] · In-text citation · [Cause/Effect] · In-text citation · [Comparison/Contrast] · In-text citation

R-9

only able to act on these impulses *after* undergoing a

Writer's third point transformation. Video games remove the need for "transformation," enabling ordinary men and women to act upon their "aggressive instinct." Ehrenreich states, "There is a huge difference between a war and [Comparison/Contrast]

In-text citation an ordinary fight. War not only departs from the normal; it inverts all that is moral and right" (12). She goes on to qualify this statement, stating that individuals will only participate in this behavior "by entering what appears to be an 'altered state'—induced by drugs or

In-text citation lengthy drilling, and denoted by face paint or khakis" (12). Game players lack this "transformation" that apparently turns mere men into killing machines; they can act out violence in their natural state of being, sitting on their couch at home. Siobhan Morrissey cites trained law enforcement professionals when she says, "Officers raiding methamphetamine labs and gang [In-text citation (Web-based source)] hangouts often find violent video games left behind" (par. 9). Game players feel the adrenaline rush associated with war in the comfort of their living rooms. As

In-text citation (Web-based source) a result, "more young people have no compunction about opening fire on a man or woman in uniform" (Morrissey, par. 8). In this situation, we see that war and violence are localized and normalized. When adolescents play video games, they do not undergo months of training and drilling; their survival instincts are not tested; they do not wear ritual garments; and they do not depend on drugs or alcohol to transform them into trained warriors. Video games do away with the transformation and preparation that usually accompanies war, changing the "aggressive instinct" from innately unnatural, as Ehrenreich claims, to an ordinary impulse.

Acknowledging opposite side Many have criticized reports connecting video games and aggression. They believe that most people can separate the fantasy from reality, and they choose to embrace the few scientific studies that minimize this correlation. Expert Craig Anderson addresses this in his article "Violent Video Games: Myths, Facts, and Unanswered Questions":

Some studies have yielded nonsignificant [Indented quotation] video game effects, just as some smoking studies failed to find a significant link to lung cancer. But when one combines all relevant empirical studies using meta-analytic techniques, five separate effects emerge with considerable consistency. Violent video games are significantly associated with increased aggressive behavior, thoughts, and affect; increased physiological arousal; and decreased prosocial (helping) behavior. (par. 4)

In-text citation (Web-based source)

Others cite the Entertainment Software Review Board (ESRB), which rates games in a similar system as movies, as a successful remedy to the issue. Anderson, this time with colleagues Doug Gentile and Katherine Buckley, addresses the ineffectual nature of ratings in their book *Violent Video Game Effects on Children and Adolescents: Theory, Research, and Public Policy.* They expected to find that "participants who played one of the violent video games chose to punish their opponents with louder noise blasts than those who played the nonviolent video games" (Anderson, Gentile, and Buckley, 66). The fact that, "even cartoonish violent video games" had a similar effect, however, was surprising. "People tend to believe that T-rated [teen] games are *more* violent than E-rated [everyone] games, but what seems to matter is whether the game includes aggression" on any level (66). Those desensitized to violence from video games will certainly respond similarly to war. War becomes a game in a completely interactive way, and players' instincts and impulses are significantly altered. Just as games may cultivate or encourage violence or drug abuse, they could also foster the "war gene" that Ehrenreich dismisses in her essay.

In-text citation

In-text citation

[Comparison/ Contrast]

Conclusion

War-based video games will not send people into war; they will, however, normalize the idea of war and amplify the instincts that propel men and women into combat. The physiological and psychological changes inspired by war-based games, their authenticity, and their presence in everyday, normal lives help to make "war" accessible and even desirable. We must respond to this problem by recreating some distance between the average game-player and the actual battlefield. By concentrating less on authenticity and more on entertainment, players would have an easier time separating

[Cause/ Effect]

Summary

their fantasy from the dim reality of war. Also, continued research should work to identify degrees of aggressive behavior in *all* levels of video games (from E–everyone to AO–adults only) in order to eliminate [Cause/Effect] violence in games available to children and teens because they are the most eager to identify with the imaginary roles they play and the most susceptible to appropriating the "aggressive instinct."

List of sources used in paper: MLA Style

Works Cited

Anderson, Craig. "Violent Video Games: Myths, Facts, and Unanswered Questions." *Psychological Science Agenda* 16.5 (2003): n. pag. Web. 28 May 2009.   Alphabetical order

Anderson, Craig A., Douglas A. Gentile, and Katherine E. Buckley. *Violent Video Game Effects on Children and Adolescents: Theory, Research, and Public Policy.* Oxford University Press (2007). Print.

Carnagey, Nicholas L., Craig A. Anderson, and Brad J. Bushman. "The Effect of Video Game Violence on Physiological Desensitization to Real-Life Violence." *Journal of Experimental Social Psychology* 43 (2007): 489–496. EBSCO. Web. 25 May 2009.

Ehrenreich, Barbara. "The Ecstasy of War." *Blood Rites: Origins and History of the Passions of War.* New York: Henry Holt and Company, LLC (1997): 7–12. Print.

Grossman, Lt. Col. Dave. "We Are Training Our Kids to Kill." *Saturday Evening Post* 271.4 (1999): 64–72. Print.

Grossman, Lev. "The Army's Killer App." *Time Magazine.* Time. 21 Feb. 2005. Web. 26 May 2009.

Konijn, Elly A., Marije Nije Bujvank, and Brad J. Bushman. "I Wish I Were a Warrior: The Role of Wishful Identification in the Effects of Violent Video Games on Aggression in Adolescent Boys." *Developmental Psychology* 43.4 (2007): 1038–1044. Print.

Morrissey, Siobhan. "A Surge in Cop Killings." *Time Magazine.* Time. 28 Sept. 2007. Web. 25 May 2009.

Rentfrow, Daphnee. "S(t)imulating War: From Early Films to Military Games." *Computer Games as a Sociocultural Phenomenon: Games Without Frontiers, War Without Tears.* Ed. Andreas Jahn-Sudmann and Ralf Stockmann. New York: Palgrave Macmillan (2008): 87–96. Print.

Sutton, Ward. "Honey, did you see this silly article on
  video games." *The Onion.* The Onion. 43.13 (2007).
  Web. 25 May 2009.
Treyarch Games. Treyarch. 2008. Web. 31 May 2009.

Student Writer's Comments

From the moment this essay was assigned, I knew my topic would be violence and war-based video games because I felt the key to a convincing
argument was to select a subject I was interested in. Since I've been in college, I have been exposed to a whole new "video game culture," so it is a topic
I can discuss passionately. I wanted to bring together the ideas about war
and video games in a way that I thought would be new, and once I read
Ehrenreich's essay on the psychology of war, I knew I had an angle to attack:
I could talk about how war-based video games can make people think and
feel differently about war and violence. This seemed especially important
during a time when our country is so connected to modern warfare. I wanted
to be honest as I appealed to the emotions, concerns, and ethics of my audience. I don't dislike video games, and I think that they can be educational
and entertaining; however, I do think that games—especially war-based
games—have the power to increase aggression in the individuals who play
them. Video games are definitely a part of our media-saturated society, and
they always will be. Because of this, I felt like I needed to research and write
about the relationship between imaginary war and true war.

I began the process of writing this paper by getting on the computer
every chance I had (between classes, during lunch, and at night before I went
home) and collecting information about the war-based video games and
violence. I found plenty of material, but I also uncovered some counter-
arguments that I really didn't expect to find. I was fascinated by the information—both facts and opinions—that I discovered. But the material wasn't
taking any shape at all yet; so far, the only common denominators were the
general topic and my interest level.

I was taking notes on notecards, so I had filled quite a stack of cards when
I stopped to reread all my material to see if I could put it into any coherent
categories. Happily, my notes fell quite naturally into three divisions: (1) the
physical effects of video games (2) the authenticity of war-based games, and
(3) the accessibility of games. I could see right away that I had enough material from reputable sources on my topic. My notes on video games would
also be sufficient with a few more research sessions. I had some stray notes that
didn't fit any of these categories, but I decided to worry about those later. I
tried my hand at a thesis statement, which I think had been floating around
in my head for days. Then I wrote the paper topic by topic over a period of
several days. I didn't attempt the introduction and the conclusion until I began

to rewrite. As I composed the essay, I was especially aware of the types of material I had on each of my topics. I had a good distribution of summaries, paraphrases, and quotations and had remembered to keep careful notes on my sources, so I put my source and page numbers (or paragraph numbers) into my first draft. I also had several examples for each of my topics and a good blend of facts and opinions.

When I rewrote my essay, I kept in mind that I would be successful in arguing my case only if my words caused the readers to make a change, however small, in their own behavior. I reworked my research paper several times as I played different readers with various biases, paying special attention to word choice and sentence structure.

Overall, writing this paper gave me a great deal of pleasure. I feel even stronger in my determination that the content of video games needs to be evaluated and continued research should help game designers produce games that provide excitement without aggression.

GLOSSARY OF USEFUL TERMS

Numbers in parentheses indicate pages in the text where the term is defined and/or examples are given. Italicized terms within definitions are also defined in this glossary.

Abstract (158–159) nouns, such as *truth* or *beauty,* are words that are neither specific nor definite in meaning; they refer to general concepts, qualities, and conditions that summarize an entire category of experience. Conversely, *concrete* terms, such as *apple, crabgrass, computer,* and *French horn,* make precise appeals to our senses. The word *abstract* refers to the logical process of abstraction, through which our minds are able to group together and describe similar objects, ideas, or attitudes. Most good writers use *abstract* terms sparingly in their *essays,* preferring instead the vividness and clarity of *concrete* words and phrases.

Allusion is a reference to a well-known person, place, or event from life or literature. In "Summer Rituals," for example, Ray Bradbury alludes to Herman Melville's great novel *Moby Dick* when he describes an old man who walks on his front porch "like Ahab surveying the mild day" (66).

Analogy (319) is an extended *comparison* of two dissimilar objects or ideas.

Analysis (4–5, 31, 33, 201–202, 562–563) is examining and evaluating a topic by separating it into its basic parts and elements and studying it systematically.

Anecdote (110) is a brief account of a single incident.

Argumentation (468–482) is an appeal predominantly to *logic* and reason. It deals with complex issues that can be debated.

Attitude (113, 116) describes the narrator's personal feelings about a particular subject. In "You Are Not My Friend," Joel Stein shows his contempt for the insincere familiarity of "friend-based websites" like Facebook and MySpace.

Audience (40, 52, 57–59, 206–207, 472–473, 475–478) refers to the person or group of people for whom an *essay* is written. The primary audience of Jay Walljasper's "Our Schedules, Our Selves," for example, is people who feel enslaved by their frantic daily routines.

Cause and effect (421–433) is a form of *analysis* that examines the causes and consequences of events and ideas.

Characterization (117) is the creation of imaginary yet realistic persons in fiction, drama, and *narrative* poetry.

Chronological order (41, 112, 116, 164, 206) is a sequence of events arranged in the order in which they occurred. Brent Staples follows this natural time sequence in his *example* essay entitled "A Brother's Murder."

Classification (259–269) is the analytical process of grouping together similar subjects into a single category or class; *division* works in the opposite fashion, breaking down a subject into many different subgroups. In "The Ways We Lie," Stephanie Ericsson classifies lies into ten distinct categories.

Clichés are words or expressions that have lost their freshness and originality through continual use. For example, "busy as a bee," "pretty as a picture," and "hotter than hell" have become trite and dull because of overuse. Good writers avoid clichés through vivid and original phrasing.

621

Climactic order (164) refers to the *organization* of ideas from one extreme to another—for example, from least important to most important, from most destructive to least destructive, or from least promising to most promising.

Cognitive skills (4–5) are mental abilities that help us send and receive verbal messages.

Coherence (163) is the manner in which an essay "holds together" its main ideas. A coherent *theme* will demonstrate such a clear relationship between its *thesis* and its logical structure that readers can easily follow the argument.

Comparison (318–331) is an *expository* writing technique that examines the similarities between objects or ideas, whereas *contrast* focuses on differences.

Conclusions (48, 475) bring *essays* to a natural close by summarizing the argument, restating the *thesis,* calling for some specific action, or explaining the significance of the topic just discussed. If the *introduction* states your thesis in the form of a question to be answered or a problem to be solved, then your *conclusion* will be the final "answer" or "solution" provided in your paper. The *conclusion* should be approximately the same length as your *introduction* and should leave your reader satisfied that you have actually "concluded" your discussion rather than simply run out of ideas to discuss.

Concrete: See *Abstract.*

Conflict is the struggle resulting from the opposition of two strong forces in the plot of a play, novel, or short story.

Connotation and Denotation (477) are two principal methods of describing the meanings of words. *Connotation* refers to the wide array of positive and negative associations that most words naturally carry with them, whereas *denotation* is the precise, literal *definition* of a word that might be found in a dictionary. See, for example, Amy Tan's description of the terms "broken" or "fractured" English in "Mother Tongue" (299).

Content and Form (43, 48) are the two main components of an *essay. Content* refers to the subject matter of an *essay,* whereas its *form* consists of the graphic symbols that communicate the subject matter (word choice, spelling, punctuation, paragraphing, etc.).

Contrast: See *Comparison.*

Deduction (475) is a form of logical reasoning that begins with a *general* assertion and then presents specific details and *examples* in support of that *generalization. Induction* works in reverse by offering a number of *examples* and then concluding with a *general* truth or principle.

Definition (374–384) is a process whereby the meaning of a term is explained. Formal *definitions* require two distinct operations: (1) finding the *general* class to which the object belongs and (2) isolating the object within that class by describing how it differs from other elements in the same category. In "Beliefs about Families," Mary Pipher defines a family as "a collection of people who pool resources and help each other over the long haul" (407).

Denotation: See *Connotation.*

Description (51–64) is a mode of writing or speaking that relates the sights, sounds, tastes, smells, or feelings of a particular experience to its readers or listeners. Good descriptive writers, such as those featured in Chapter 4, are particularly adept at receiving, selecting, and expressing sensory details from the world around them. Along with *persuasion, exposition,* and *narration, description* is one of the four dominant types of writing. See, for example, Linda Hogan's "Dwellings," in which the author describes the "dwelling places" of several different animals.

Development (41–42) concerns the manner in which a *paragraph* of an essay expands on its topic.

Dialect is a speech pattern typical of a certain regional location, race, or social group that exhibits itself through unique word choice, pronunciation, and/or grammatical *usage.* See, for example, John McPhee's "The Pines," in which Fred and Bill, two residents of a wilderness area in southern New Jersey, speak in a discernible *dialect* or Amy Tan's description of her mother's "fractured" English in "Mother Tongue."

Dialogue is a conversation between two or more people, particularly within a novel, play, poem, short story, or other literary work. See, for example, the dialogue between the author and Ricardo in Jessica Blau's "Red-Headed."

Diction (40, 477) is word choice. If a vocabulary is a list of words available for use, then good *diction* is the careful selection of those words to communicate a particular subject to a specific *audience*. Different types of *diction* include *formal* (scholarly books and articles), *informal* (essays in popular magazines), *colloquial* (conversations between friends, including newly coined words and expressions), *slang* (language shared by certain social groups), *dialect* (language typical of a certain region, race, or social group), *technical* (words that make up the basic vocabulary of a specific area of study, such as medicine or law), and *obsolete* (words no longer in use).

Division: See *Classification.*

Documentation (601–608) refers to the process of acknowledging sources in a *documented essay* through in-text citations and end-of-paper citations.

Documented essay (562–563) is a research or term paper that integrates *paraphrases, summaries,* and *quotations* from secondary sources with the writer's own insights and conclusions. Such *essays* normally include bibliographic references within the paper and, at the end, a list of the books and articles cited. See Part III of this book: "Reference: Reading and Writing from Sources."

Dominant impression (54, 56, 58) in *descriptive* writing is the principal effect the author wishes to create for the *audience.*

Editing (42, 43–44, 48) is an important part of the *rewriting* process of an *essay* that requires writers to make certain their work observes the conventions of standard written English.

Effect: See *Cause and effect.*

Emphasis (111, 474) is the stress given to certain words, phrases, sentences, and/or *paragraphs* within an *essay* by such methods as repeating important ideas; positioning thesis and *topic sentences* effectively; supplying additional details or *examples;* allocating more space to certain sections of an *essay;* choosing words carefully; selecting and arranging details judiciously; and using certain mechanical devices, such as italics, underlining, capitalization, and different colors of ink.

Essay is a relatively short prose composition on a limited topic. Most *essays* are five hundred to one thousand words long and focus on a clearly definable question to be answered or problem to be solved. *Formal essays,* such as Claudia Wallis and Sonja Steptoe's "How to Bring Our Schools Out of the 20th Century," are generally characterized by seriousness of *purpose,* logical organization, and dignity of language; *informal essays,* such as Firoozeh Dumas' "Leffingwell Elementary School," are generally brief, humorous, and more loosely structured. *Essays* in this textbook have been divided into nine traditional *rhetorical* types, each of which is discussed at length in its chapter introduction.

Etymology (379) is the study of the origin and development of words.

Evidence (469, 472, 475–476) is any material used to help support an *argument,* including details, facts, *examples,* opinions, and expert testimony. Just as a lawyer's case is won or lost in a court of law because of the strength of the *evidence* presented, so, too, does the effectiveness of a writer's essay depend on the evidence offered in support of its *thesis statement.*

Example (158–169) is an illustration of a *general* principle or *thesis statement.* Harold Krents's "Darkness at Noon," for instance, gives several different examples of prejudice against handicapped people.

Exposition is one of the four main *rhetorical* categories of writing (the others are *persuasion, narration,* and *description*). The principal purpose of expository prose is to "expose" ideas to your readers, to explain, define, and interpret information through one or more of the following modes of exposition: *example, process analysis, division/classification, comparison/contrast, definition,* and *cause/effect.*

Figurative language (58, 477) is writing or speaking that purposefully departs from the literal meanings of words to achieve a particularly vivid, expressive, and/or imaginative image. When, for example, Scott Russell Sanders in "Homeplace" says that a tornado "peeled off the roof, splintered the garage, and rustled two cows" (339), he is using *figurative language.* Other principal figures of speech include *metaphor, simile, hyperbole, allusion,* and *personification.*

Flashback (116) is a technique used mainly in *narrative* writing that enables the author to present scenes or conversations that took place prior to the beginning of the story. See, for example, Ray Bradbury's "Summer Rituals," in which the author chronicles several nostalgic events from his youth.

Focus (39–40) is the concentration of a *topic* on one central point or issue.

Form: See *Content.*

Formal essay: See *Essay.*

Free association (37) is a process of generating ideas for writing through which one thought leads randomly to another.

General words (158–159) are those that employ expansive categories, such as *animals, sports, occupations,* and *clothing; specific* words are more limiting and restrictive, such as *koala, lacrosse, computer programmer,* and *bow tie.* Whether a word is *general* or *specific* depends at least somewhat on its context: *Bow tie* is more specific than *clothing,* yet less *specific* than "the pink and green striped bow tie Aunt Martha gave me last Christmas." See also *Abstract.*

Generalization (158–159, 160, 475–476) is a broad statement or belief based on a limited number of facts, *examples,* or statistics. A product of inductive reasoning, generalizations should be used carefully and sparingly in *essays.*

Hyperbole, the opposite of *understatement,* is a type of *figurative language* that uses deliberate exaggeration for the sake of emphasis or comic effect (e.g., "hungry enough to eat 20 chocolate eclairs").

Hypothesis (426, 562) is a tentative theory that can be proved or disproved through further investigation and analysis.

Idiom refers to a grammatical construction unique to a certain people, region, or class that cannot be translated literally into another language.

Illustration (158–159) is the use of *examples* to support an idea or *generalization.*

Imagery (57–59) is *description* that appeals to one or more of our five senses. See, for example, Malcolm Cowley's description in "The View from 80" of one of the pleasures of old age: "simply sitting still, like a snake on a sun-warmed stone, with a delicious feeling of indolence that was seldom attained in earlier years" (95–96). Imagery is used to help bring clarity and vividness to descriptive writing.

Induction: See *Deduction.*

Inference (475) is a *deduction* or *conclusion* derived from *specific* information.

Informal essay: See *Essay.*

Introduction (41) refers to the beginning of an *essay.* It should identify the subject to be discussed, set the limits of that discussion, and clearly state the *thesis* or general *purpose* of the paper. In a brief (five-*paragraph*) *essay,* your *introduction* should be only one *paragraph;* for longer papers, you may want to provide longer introductory sections. A good *introduction* will generally catch the audience's attention by beginning with a quotation, a provocative statement, a personal *anecdote,* or a stimulating question that somehow involves its readers in the topic under consideration. See also *Conclusion.*

Irony (173) is a figure of speech in which the literal, *denotative* meaning is the opposite of what is stated.

Jargon is the special language of a certain group or profession, such as psychological *jargon,* legal *jargon,* or medical *jargon.* When *jargon* is excerpted from its proper subject area, it generally becomes confusing or humorous, as in "I have a latency problem with my backhand" or "I hope we can interface tomorrow night after the dance."

Levels of thought (3–4) is a phrase that describes the three sequential stages at which people think, read, and write: literal, interpretive, and analytical.

Logic (469, 475) is the science of correct reasoning. Based principally on *inductive* or *deductive* processes, *logic* establishes a method by which we can examine *premises* and *conclusions,* construct *syllogisms,* and avoid faulty reasoning.

Logical fallacy (422–424, 475–476) is an incorrect conclusion derived from faulty reasoning. See also *Post hoc, ergo propter hoc,* and *Non sequitur.*

Metaphor (59, 477) is an implied *comparison* that brings together two dissimilar objects, persons, or ideas. Unlike a *simile,* which uses the words *like* or *as,* a *metaphor* directly identifies an obscure or difficult subject with another that is easier to understand. For example, when Ray Bradbury describes a piano as "yellow-toothed" (66), he is using a metaphor to explain how the piano keys are like stained human teeth.

Mood (116, 477) refers to the atmosphere or *tone* created in a piece of writing. The mood of Jessica Mitford's "Behind the Formaldehyde Curtain" is sarcastic and derisive, and of Marc Gellman's "Worry. Don't Be Happy," good-humored and sensible.

Narration (110–122) is storytelling: the recounting of a series of events, arranged in a particular order and delivered by a narrator to a specific *audience* with a clear *purpose* in mind. Along with *persuasion, exposition,* and *description,* it is one of the four principal types of writing.

Non sequitur, from a Latin phrase meaning "it does not follow," refers to a *conclusion* that does not logically derive from its *premises.*

Objective (52, 56) writing is detached, impersonal, and factual; *subjective* writing reveals the author's personal feelings and attitudes. Judith Wallerstein and Sandra Blakeslee's "Second Chances for Children of Divorce" is an *example* of *objective* prose, whereas Amy Tan's "Mother Tongue" is essentially *subjective* in nature. Most good college-level *essays* are a careful mix of both approaches, with lab reports and technical writing toward the *objective* end of the scale and personal *essays* in composition courses at the *subjective* end.

Organization (41, 43, 110, 116–117, 163–164, 206–207, 474–475, 478) refers to the order in which a writer chooses to present his or her ideas to the reader. Five main types of *organization* may be used to develop *paragraphs* or *essays:* (1) *deductive* (moving from general to specific), (2) *inductive* (from specific to general), (3) *chronological* (according to time sequence), (4) *spatial* (according to physical relationship in space), and (5) *climactic* (from one extreme to another, such as least important to most important).

Paradox is a seemingly self-contradictory statement that contains an element of truth. In "The View from 80," Malcolm Cowley paradoxically declares that the Ojibwa Indians were "kind to their old people" by killing them when they became decrepit (91).

Paragraphs are groups of interrelated sentences that develop a central topic. Generally governed by a *topic sentence,* a *paragraph* has its own *unity* and *coherence* and is an integral part of the logical *development* of an *essay.*

Parallelism is a structural arrangement within sentences, *paragraphs,* or entire *essays* through which two or more separate elements are similarly phrased and developed. Look, for example, at the following sentences from Sherman Alexie's "The Joy of Reading and Writing: Superman and Me": "I began to think of everything in terms of paragraphs. Our reservation was a small paragraph within the United States. My family's house was a paragraph, distinct from the other paragraphs of the LeBrets to the north, the Fords to our south, and the Tribal School to the west. Inside our house, each family member existed as a separate paragraph but still had genetics and common experiences to link us" (446–447).

Paraphrase (590, 592, 592–594) is a restatement in your own words of someone else's ideas or observations.

Parody is making fun of a person, an event, or a work of literature through exaggerated imitation.

Person (58–59, 116) is a grammatical distinction identifying the speaker or writer in a particular context: first person (I or we), second person (you), and third person (he, she, it, or they). The *person* of an *essay* refers to the voice of the narrator. See also *Point of view.*

Personification is *figurative language* that ascribes human characteristics to an abstraction, animal, idea, or inanimate object. Consider, for example, Robert Ramirez's description in "The Barrio" of the bakery that "sends its sweet messenger aroma down the dimly lit street, announcing the arrival of fresh, hot, sugary *pan dulce*" (391).

Persuasion (468–482) is one of the four chief forms of *rhetoric.* Its main purpose is to convince a reader (or listener) to think, act, or feel a certain way. It involves appealing to reason, to emotion, and/or to a sense of ethics. The other three main *rhetorical* categories are *exposition, narration,* and *description.*

Plagiarism (590–594) is using someone else's ideas as if they were your own. Students can protect themselves from plagiarism by carefully documenting their *sources.* See *Documentation.*

Point of view (58–59, 116) is the perspective from which a writer tells a story, including *person, vantage point,* and *attitude.* Principal *narrative* voices are first-person, in which the writer relates the story from his or her own vantage point ("I've often wondered if I would have been a different person had I not been physically handicapped" [369], from "You're Short, Besides!" by Sucheng Chan); omniscient, a third-person technique in which the narrator knows everything and can even see into the minds of the various characters; and concealed, a third-person method in which the narrator can see and hear events but cannot look into the minds of the other characters.

Post hoc, ergo propter hoc (423), a Latin phrase meaning "after this, therefore because of this," is a *logical fallacy* confusing *cause and effect* with *chronology.* Just because Cheryl wakes up every morning before the sun rises doesn't mean that the sun rises *because* Cheryl wakes up.

Premise (476) is a proposition or statement that forms the foundation of an *argument* and helps support a *conclusion.* See also *Logic* and *Syllogism.*

Prereading (23–25, 47) is thoughtful concentration on a topic before reading an *essay.* Just as athletes warm up their physical muscles before competition, so, too, should students activate their "mental muscles" before reading or writing *essays.*

Prewriting (36–41, 48), which is similar to *prereading,* is the initial stage in the composing process during which writers consider their topics, generate ideas, narrow and refine their *thesis statements,* organize their ideas, pursue any necessary research, and identify their *audiences.* Although prewriting occurs principally, as the name suggests, "before" an essay is started, writers usually return to this "invention" stage again and again during the course of the writing process.

Process analysis (201–212), one of the seven primary modes of *exposition,* either gives directions about how to do something (directive) or provides information on how something happened (informative).

Proofreading (42, 44, 48), an essential part of *rewriting,* is a thorough, careful review of the final draft of an *essay* to ensure that all errors have been eliminated.

Purpose (40, 54–55, 56, 472–473, 478) in an *essay* refers to its overall aim or intention: to entertain, inform, or persuade a particular *audience* with reference to a specific topic (to persuade an audience, for example, that violence on television and in video games is psychologically damaging our children in Dave Grossman's "We Are Training Our Kids to Kill"). See also *Dominant impression.*

Refutation is the process of discrediting the *arguments* that run counter to your *thesis statement.*

Revision (42–44, 48), meaning "to see again," takes place during the entire writing process as you change words, rewrite sentences, and shift *paragraphs* from one location to another in your *essay.* It plays an especially vital role in the *rewriting* stage of the composing process.

Rewriting (42–44, 48) is a stage of the composing process that includes *revision, editing,* and *proofreading.*

Rhetoric is the art of using language effectively.

Rhetorical questions are intended to provoke thought rather than bring forth a specific answer. See, for example, the following question by Barrett Seaman in "How Bingeing Became the New College Sport": "What would happen if the drinking age was rolled back to 18 or 19?" (492)

Rhetorical strategy or mode is the plan or method whereby an *essay* is organized. Most writers choose from methods discussed in this book, such as *narration, example, comparison/contrast, definition,* and *cause/effect.*

Sarcasm is a form of *irony* that attacks a person or belief through harsh and bitter remarks that often mean the opposite of what they say. See, for example, Jessica Mitford's sarcastic praise of the funeral director in "Behind the Formaldehyde Curtain": "He has relieved the family of every detail, he has revamped the corpse to look like a living doll, he has arranged for it to nap for a few days in a slumber room, he has put on a well-oiled performance in which the concept of *death* has played no part whatsoever. . . . He has done everything in his power to make the funeral a real pleasure for everybody concerned" (228). See also *Satire.*

Satire is a literary technique that attacks foolishness by making fun of it. Most good satires work through a "fiction" that is clearly transparent. Bill Cosby, for example, feigns amazement that anyone would ever want to have children in "The Baffling Question," yet he clearly loves kids and believes the opposite.

Setting refers to the immediate environment of a *narrative* or *descriptive* piece of writing: the place, time, and background established by the author.

Simile (59, 477) is a *comparison* between two dissimilar objects that uses the words *like* or *as.* See, for example, Ray Bradbury's description of the women in "Summer Rituals," who appear "like ghosts hovering momentarily behind the door screen" (67). See also *Metaphor.*

Slang is casual conversation among friends; as such, it is inappropriate for use in formal and informal writing, unless it is placed in quotation marks and introduced for a specific rhetorical purpose: "Hey dude, what's up?" See, for example, the use of slang throughout Jessica Blau's "Red-Headed."

Sources (580–590) are books, articles, magazines, Web sites, interviews, blogs, discussion boards, emails, newsletters, and similar resources from which writers gather material for documented papers.

Spatial order (111, 164) is a method of *description* that begins at one geographical point and moves onward in an orderly fashion. See, for example, the opening of John McPhee's "The Pines," which first describes the front yard of Fred Brown's house, then moves through the vestibule and into the kitchen, and finally settles on Fred himself, who is seated behind a porcelain-topped table in a room just beyond the kitchen (102).

Specific: See *general* words.

Style is the unique, individual way in which each author expresses his or her ideas. Often referred to as the "personality" of an *essay*, *style* is dependent on a writer's manipulation of *diction*, sentence structure, *figurative language, point of view, characterization, emphasis, mood, purpose, rhetorical strategy*, and all the other variables that govern written material.

Subjective: See *Objective*.

Summary (590, 592, 592–594) is a condensed statement of someone else's thoughts or observations.

Syllogism (476) refers to a three-step *deductive argument* that moves logically from a major and a minor *premise* to a *conclusion*. A traditional example is "All men are mortal. Socrates is a man. Therefore, Socrates is mortal."

Symbol refers to an object or action in literature that metaphorically represents something more important than itself. In Malcolm X's "Learning to Read," books are a symbol of freedom for the imprisoned man.

Synonyms are terms with similar or identical *denotative* meanings, such as *aged, elderly, older person*, and *senior citizen*.

Syntax describes the order in which words are arranged in a sentence and the effect that this arrangement has on the creation of meaning.

Thesis statement or thesis (40–41) is the principal *focus* of an *essay*. It is usually phrased in the form of a question to be answered, a problem to be solved, or an assertion to be argued. The word *thesis* derives from a Greek term meaning "something set down," and most good writers find that "setting down" their thesis in writing helps them tremendously in defining and clarifying their topic before they begin to write an outline or a rough draft.

Tone (116, 477) is a writer's *attitude* or *point of view* toward his or her subject. See also *Mood*.

Topic sentence is the central idea around which a *paragraph* develops. A *topic sentence* controls a *paragraph* in the same way a *thesis statement* unifies and governs an entire essay. See also *Induction* and *Deduction*.

Transition (116) is the linking together of sequential ideas in sentences, paragraphs, and essays. This linking is accomplished primarily through word repetition, pronouns, parallel constructions, and such transitional words and phrases as *therefore, as a result, consequently, moreover*, and *similarly*.

Understatement, the opposite of *hyperbole,* is a deliberate weakening of the truth for comic or emphatic purpose. Commenting, for example, on the great care funeral directors take to make corpses look lifelike for their funerals, Jessica Mitford explains in "Behind the Formaldehyde Curtain," "This is a rather large order, since few people die in the full bloom of health" (224).

Unity (164) exists in an *essay* when all ideas originate from and help support a central *thesis statement*.

Usage (43–44, 48) refers to the customary rules that govern written and spoken language.

Vantage point (58–59, 116) is the frame of reference of the narrator in a story: close to the action, far from the action, looking back on the past, or reporting on the present. See also *Person* and *Point of view*.

CREDITS

INDEX OF AUTHORS AND TITLES